THE

NEW BEDSIDE PLAYBOY

INTRODUCTION BY HUGH M. HEFNER
PREFACE BY RICHARD STERN

D0168292

PLAYBOY PRESS

HANOVER, NEW HAMPSHIRE/NEW YORK, NEW YORK

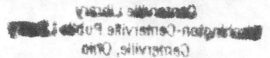

For information about permission to reproduce selections from this book, write to: Playboy Press / Steerforth Press, 25 Lebanon Street, Hanover, New Hampshire 03755

PRINTED IN THE UNITED STATES OF AMERICA

This volume has been catalogued by the Library of Congress.

FIRST EDITION

J. G. Ballard, "The Drowned Giant" from The Terminal Beach. Originally published in PLAYBOY May 1965. © 1965 by J. G. Ballard. Reprinted with the permission of Margaret Hanbury, Literary Agent. Jorge Luis Borges: First published in PLAYBOY May 1977 © 1977 by Jorge Luis Borges, permission of the Wylie Agency. Ray Bradbury: Reprinted by permission of Don Congdon Associates, Inc. © 1952 by Crowell Collier Publishing, renewed 1980 by Ray Bradbury. Arthur C. Clarke: Reprinted by permission of the author and the author's agents, Scovil Chichak Galen Literary Agency, Inc. Ian Fleming: "The Hildebrand Rarity" from PLAYBOY March 1960. © 1960 by Ian Fleming. Reprinted with the permission of Ian Fleming Publications Ltd. www.ianflemingcentre.com. Ian Fleming's James Bond books are available in the US from Penguin Group (USA) Inc., www.penguinputnam.com and outside the US from Penguin Group (UK) Ltd., www.penguin.co.uk. Grover Lewis: From SPLENDOR IN THE SHORT GRASS: THE GROVER LEWIS READER, edited by Jan Reid and W.K. Stratton, © 2005 by permission of the University of Texas Press. Vladimir Nabokov: By arrangement with the Estate of Vladimir Nabokov. All rights reserved. Walter Tevis: © 1956 Playboy. © renewed 1984 and assigned to Walter Tevis Copyright Trust. Reprinted by arrangement with the author and Susan Schulman, A Literary Agency, New York. P.G. Wodehouse: P.G. Wodehouse, "The Courting of the Muse" from PLAYBOY January 1962. © 1962 by P.G. Wodehouse. Permission granted by InkWell Management on behalf of the Trustees of the Wodehouse Estate.

Acknowledgments: Jason Broccardo, Paul Chan, Frederick Courtright, Kevin Craig, Fuzzy Gerdes, Kyle Kolbe, Malina Lee, Mark Lee, Bradley Lincoln, Maria Mandis, Jessica Riddle, Jennifer Thiele, Debra Tillou, Michelle Urry, Len Willis

Contents

HUMOR

RIBALD CLASSICS

CORRESPONDENCE

SPECIAL FEATURES

SPECIAL PICTORIALS

CARTOONS

Barsotti (359), *Clive Collins* (375), *Eldon Dedini* (49), *Alden Erikson* (472), *Finkstrom* (245), *Jerry King* (100), *B. Kliban* (145), *Don Madden* (171), *Charles E. Martin* (342), *Marty Murphy* (288, 450), *Roy Ramonde* (267), *Shel Silverstein* (19, 179), *Francis Smilby* (378), *Richard Taylor* (420), *Frank Thorne* (315, 403), *Mike Williams* (60), *Gahan Wilson* (219), *Rowland Wilson* (272)

COLOR INSERT

Olivia De Berardinis, Gahan Wilson, Doug Sneyd, B. Kliban, De Berardinis, Buck Brown, Eldon Dedini, De Berardinis

"Without you, I'd be the publisher
of a literary magazine."

—HUGH M. HEFNER AT A PLAYMATE REUNION
AT PLAYBOY MANSION WEST, 1970

Introduction

by HUGH M. HEFNER

I f, as an anonymous sage once observed, most of man's great pleasures can be found between a book's covers and beneath a bed's
coverlet, then *The New Bedside Playboy* combines the best of all possible
worlds. A sprightly compendium, chosen with care from six decades of
superlative offerings from America's most sophisticated magazine, it is
designed to provide the at-ease reader with divertissement from the
day's occupations, to relax taut muscles, to tone up tired gray matter
and buoy up flagging spirits. More than 40 years after the first *Bedside*
anthology appeared, we return with a new compilation designed to delight and dazzle. I needn't remind the astute reader of the changes that
have occurred since 1963. Yet, as is evident in this volume, art endures.

There are visual tonics by Olivia De Berardinis and a host of emi-
nent PLAYBOY cartoonists. Herein are science-fiction *déjà vus* and both
light fantastics and *danses macabres* by such esteemed probers of the
limits of imaginations as Ray Bradbury and Gabriel García Márquez.
There's nostalgic frolicking in the snows of yesteryear by Scott Turow
and Norman Mailer; observations—sometimes acerbic, sometimes in-
dulgent—on contemporary society's stratagems, follies and foibles by
David Mamet and William F. Buckley Jr.

There is, contained within, that special brand of PLAYBOY fiction
marked by a proper respect for plotline, an abiding interest in character
delineation, a subtle approach to making a point and tenacious determination to grip the reader from opening capital to closing period. Among
the master practitioners of this singular art of storytelling included here
are Vladimir Nabokov, Nadine Gordimer—one of four Nobel Prize–
winners in this volume—John Updike and Ian Fleming. The fiction
alone represents a formidable part of 20th century literary history.

For satire and copious quantities of wit in a variety of veins, we also
have a vintage crop of top authors. On tap to pique your risibilities are
Woody Allen, P.G. Wodehouse and Dave Barry.

INTRODUCTION

A stellar complement of additional attractions round out *The New Bedside Playboy*—a telling interview with Saul Bellow; our own caustic commentary on bachelor parties; a selection of PLAYBOY's antic Party Jokes and light-blue Ribald Classics; and much, much more.

All in all, with nearly a quarter-million well-couched words for the well-couched reader, *The New Bedside Playboy* is a cornucopian verbal and visual packet that might seem to preclude marathon perusing. And so it may, in most cases. In fact, the sapient nocturnal reader will sample it in canapé-sized tidbits, savoring its eclectic offerings as one would savor a postprandial liqueur. The astute Bedsideman will thus avoid overindulgence and assure himself many evenings of unalloyed entertainment, increasing in number those pleasurable occasions when *The New Bedside Playboy* may be plucked from the night table with anticipatory delight.

—Hugh M. Hefner,
Editor-in-Chief
PLAYBOY Magazine

Preface

by RICHARD STERN

H ugh Marston Hefner is 80. "Hef," the debonair wit invented by the girl-rejected Steinmetz High School sophomore, is 64. PLAYBOY, the magazine the 27-year-old employee of *Esquire* launched with $8,000 on the beautiful, airbrushed body of Marilyn Monroe, is 53.

Back then, in 1953, the proud Methodist descendant of the Puritan leader William Bradford was living across the Midway from the gray towers of the University of Chicago. Hef had been in the Army, graduated from the University of Illinois at Champaign–Urbana, written a paper on the Kinsey Report for a graduate sociology class at Northwestern and was now making sketches for a magazine that would rival *Esquire*, which had just refused to give him a $5 raise. Occasionally he'd play poker with Chicago students, one of whom, a European-trained intellectual named George Steiner, was convinced that among the brilliant people he'd met in Chicago, the only authentic genius was the ambitious cartoonist and sketcher. What I think enchanted Steiner was encountering in Hef the American Protestant empire builder—a Joseph Smith, a J.P. Morgan, a William Rainey Harper, a Woodrow Wilson, a Billy Graham, a Bill Gates, a Jeff Bezos. Hef's turn of this Protestant screw was founding his empire on the reversal of the sexual and sensual repression of his upbringing.

Ten years to the month after the first issue of PLAYBOY sold 51,100 copies, this writer sat in a Chicago courtroom as one of two witnesses testifying to the literary quality of the sensationally successful monthly. Spurred by one of the periodic seizures of sanctimony which every few American decades erupts into the desire to control other people's erotic taste and behavior, the city of Chicago wanted to declare PLAYBOY—at least its June 1963 spread on Jayne Mansfield—"obscene" and thus deny it the mailing privileges of the U.S. Post Office. The other literary witness was the grizzled old Chicago columnist Ben Hecht, co-author of the Chicago newspaper play *The Front Page*, novelist, screenwriter and the idol of the reporters who clustered around him at the back of the courtroom. While he and I testified—Hecht delightfully, fluently, knowledgeably (he even knew Jayne Mansfield)—PLAYBOY's bespectacled founder, editor and publisher sat in the back taking notes on a yellow pad, looking like a visiting professor from Mars (or rather, Venus). PLAYBOY's attorney, Bob Ming, then set me up as a learned professor, novelist and sage assessor of contemporary literature and morality. The city attorney didn't buy this. He put me in my small place, doubting that so ivory-towered an individual, who only skimmed the magazine, could be considered an expert witness. He finally asked if what I had read of the June 1963 PLAYBOY issue violated "community standards." I responded that in view of what I knew about such standards, "almost nothing would violate them."

Before this unhelpful response, I'd supplied a rather snotty assessment of the magazine as literature: "I feel that much of the material here is of some interest, that the literary quality is...lower middlebrow."

I had refused the $25 expert-witness fee I'd been offered, thinking that I wanted no one to think that such expertise as mine could be bought (at least for that sum). Three weeks later, Christmas morning, a station wagon pulled up in front of our Hyde Park house. The driver carried to our door an enormous wicker basket packed with a dozen wild-looking bottles of wonderful liqueurs and a card from Hef and PLAYBOY wishing me a merry Christmas. This was my first taste of the high life PLAYBOY promoted during these early years of the Cold War. A playboy was not only to enjoy lusty romance with the beauties concealed under every other skirt, he himself was decked out in the finest threads, he drank and ate like an exiled king in beautiful resorts and then, in well-earned repose, read in PLAYBOY the thoughts and stories of the best new writers. After all, *Esquire*, PLAYBOY's rival and model, had become itself by publishing the best new fiction and first-rate investigative, speculative or voyeuristic nonfiction. PLAYBOY hired fiction editors such as Robie Macauley, a one-novel novelist who'd helped revive the fame of his Olivet College teacher Ford Madox Ford and had written for such literary magazines as the *Kenyon Review*. Macauley, like the other fiction editors, spread the word that PLAYBOY paid well, and soon writers and their agents poured in their stories. It was clear that the stories PLAYBOY printed had either an erotic core or stimulating sexual elements. When Macauley invited me to become assistant fiction editor, one of the factors in my refusal was the monotonous character this requirement imposed on stories by writers whose other work was very different.

Forty years later, I've been asked to write this brief foreword to the anthology of writing that comes not from 10 but from over 50 years of PLAYBOY. The confidence of experience and success has clearly broadened the requirements of PLAYBOY writing. Its interviews with stars of all sorts, athletes, politicians, writers and actors are famously challenging and revealing. The one with Jimmy Carter ("I've committed lust in my heart") became an issue in his presidential campaign. The interview with Saul Bellow reprinted here is rich with the writer's exceptional personal brilliance. The stories are by some of the country's most interesting new writers—Thom Jones, Michael Chabon, Jonathan Safran Foer, T.C. Boyle—by their distinguished predecessors Updike, Coover and Oates and by such fine foreign writers as Borges, Nabokov, Garcìa Márquez and Gordimer. In the digital cornucopia of 2006, the lower middlebrow of 1963 is now at least middlebrow, and that means something.

Although it's long lost its carnal shock value (that happened when it refused to descend into the netherworld of *Penthouse* and *Hustler*) and its original mission is superfluous, if not almost touchingly old hat, PLAYBOY keeps publishing. Hefner is the world's liveliest octogenarian, and his magazine, at 53, remains on top of its somewhat smaller world. Yes, it bears the shadow of historic as well as current interest, but it is better to read than read about, still part of today's pleasures and today's concerns. As for the anthology, it augments delight in its contents with the perfume of nostalgia.

Richard Stern's 21st book, Almonds to Zhoof: Collected Stories, *appeared in 2005.*

How I Invented Playboy

humor by BUCK HENRY

L ate one night in Greenwich Village, early in the Fifties, there was a scratching at my door. When I opened it, a bedraggled, sodden man fell into my apartment, babbling incoherently about needing money for a magazine. I thought, of course, that he wanted to buy *Time* or *Newsweek* to catch up on the news. Since that seemed like a nice thing for a man who was so down and out to want to do, I gave him 50 cents for a magazine. Apparently, it was that 50 cents that started what became this extraordinary empire.

You can see why it's difficult for me to discuss PLAYBOY objectively. It's not so much what PLAYBOY has meant in my life as the part I've played in *its* life. I think if Hef—or "Ner," as he is known to his closest friends—were to list the ten or 12 people who were most fundamental to the building of his empire, I'd be up there in the top two or three. He's had a lot of free—or at least cheap—advice from many people, but I've been the one who tried to give him a Zen sense of what to do in every area. He was always calling, asking for advice. I'd be in Paris at a gala party filled with movie stars, and I'd get an emergency call from you-know-who, saying, "I'm stuck. What's my next move?" Often, one or two words, such as "Ace bandage" or "Reddi-wip," were all that he needed. Sometimes, it took hours of soothing advice.

The Rabbit Head logo was not a suggestion I expected him to take seriously. It was a kind of joke. I had said something like, "If you're going to produce a fantasy for boys and girls to make them behave like rabbits, you may as well print it on lettuce." Clearly, he was in a non-metaphorical mood and took me literally.

As for the Centerfold, I didn't say, "Look, why don't you put a fold-out picture of a naked lady in the middle of the magazine?" What I

1

did say—kiddingly, of course—was, "If you want to sell the magazine, deliver it to the reader's door. And have a naked lady jump out." It was a whimsy; but, as usual, he took the idea seriously and ran with it.

I've also given him advice of a more personal nature. About 25 years ago, he was having trouble finding clothes that fit. He has a very odd build for a man and needs extra freedom to move his arms and smoke his pipe. I said, "Hef, you know what the Chinese do?" He didn't know. He didn't know about China. I said, "They wear pajamas. They don't bother with all that stuff." Need I say more? I've probably saved him $60,000 in clothing bills.

I remember dark, rainy evenings talking with Hef. I'd rattle off names. "Are you familiar with Jorge Luis Borges?" He didn't know who that was, so I'd tell him. "Do you know about Malcolm X? Have you heard of Lord Bertrand Russell? Jean-Paul Sartre? Timothy Leary?" I tried to give him a sense of what people were looking for in literature, politics and philosophy.

I hope you understand that none of this in the slightest degree means I think that PLAYBOY owes me anything materially, though I will say that people in similar situations have been well compensated. I read about a guy who invented a ratchet for Sears. He got a $1 million judgment and is going for more. A ratchet is just a tool. That's hardly the unique and incalculable measure of the given idea—a couple of cogent, well-meant phrases that become 100 bound editions of an eagerly collected magazine and the awards and riches that follow.

I've given Hef so much, in fact, that it would probably be difficult for him to know where to begin to repay me. For instance, there's the story I told him about something that had happened to me. I had come upon a bizarre accident in the middle of the road late one night. A truck driver had crashed into a limousine, and the results were devastating—parts of the truck driver ended up in the backseat of the limousine with parts of what we later found out was the captain of an industrial empire. You couldn't tell one part from the other—they were just mangled men. If someone could find a way to bring the truck driver and the millionaire together in life, before death consigned them to that generalized country we will all visit someday, that person would be doing something truly meaningful.

Hef was always taken by that story, and I like to think he was slightly inspired by it. And that's why we now have the truck driver barreling along the road reading a story by Jorge Luis Borges and the multimillionaire in the back seat of his limo, looking at those Centerfolds and gently touching his pants.

The Other

fiction by JORGE LUIS BORGES

It was in Cambridge, back in February 1969, that the event took place. I made no attempt to record it at the time, because, fearing for my mind, my initial aim was to forget it. Now, some years later, I feel that if I commit it to paper others will read it as a story and, I hope, one day it will become a story for me as well. I know it was horrifying while it lasted—and even more so during the nights that followed—but this does not mean that an account of it will necessarily move anyone else.

It was about ten o'clock in the morning. I sat on a bench facing the Charles River. Some 500 yards distant, on my right, rose a tall building whose name I never knew. Ice floes were borne along on the gray water. Inevitably, the river made me think about time—Heraclitus' millennial image. I had slept well; my class on the previous afternoon had, I thought, managed to hold the interest of my students. Not a soul was in sight.

All at once, I had the impression (according to psychologists, it corresponds to a state of fatigue) of having lived that moment once before. Someone had sat down at the other end of the bench. I would have preferred to be alone, but not wishing to appear unsociable, I avoided getting up abruptly. The other man had begun to whistle. It was then that the first of the many disquieting things of that morning occurred. What he whistled, what he tried to whistle (I have no ear for music), was the tune of *La Tapéra*, an old *milonga* by Elias Regules. The melody took me back to a certain Buenos Aires patio, which has long since disappeared, and to the memory of my cousin Alvaro Melían Lafinur, who has been dead for so many years. Then came the words. They were those of the opening line. It was not Alvaro's voice but an imitation of it. Recognizing this, I was taken aback.

"Sir," I said, turning to the other man, "are you a Uruguayan or an Argentine?"

"Argentine, but I've lived in Geneva since 1914," he replied.

THE OTHER

There was a long silence. "At number 17 Malagnou—across from the Orthodox church?" I asked.

He answered in the affirmative.

"In that case," I said straight out, "your name is Jorge Luis Borges. I, too, am Jorge Luis Borges. This is 1969, and we are in the city of Cambridge."

"No," he said in a voice that was mine but a bit removed. He paused, then became insistent. "I'm here in Geneva, on a bench, a few steps from the Rhône. The strange thing is that we resemble each other, but you're much older and your hair is gray."

"I can prove I'm not lying," I said. "I'm going to tell you things a stranger couldn't possibly know. At home we have a silver maté cup with a base in the form of entwined serpents. Our great-grandfather brought it from Peru. There's also a silver washbasin that hung from his saddle. In the wardrobe of your room are two rows of books: the three volumes of Lane's *Arabian Nights*, with wood engravings and with notes in small type at the end of each chapter; Quicherat's Latin dictionary; Tacitus' *Germania* in Latin and also in Gordon's English translation; a *Don Quixote* published by Garnier; Rivera Indarte's *Tablas de Sangre*, inscribed by the author; Carlyle's *Sartor Resartus*; a biography of Amiel; and, hidden behind the other volumes, a book in paper covers about sexual customs in the Balkans. Nor have I forgotten one evening on a certain second floor of the Place Dubourg."

"Dufour," he corrected.

"Very well—Dufour. Is this enough, now?"

"No," he said. "These proofs prove nothing. If I am dreaming you, it's natural that you know what I know. Your catalog, for all its length, is completely worthless."

His objection was to the point. I said, "If this morning and this meeting are dreams, each of us has to believe that he is the dreamer. Perhaps we have stopped dreaming, perhaps not. Our obvious duty, meanwhile, is to accept the dream just as we accept the world and being born and seeing and breathing."

"And if the dream should go on?" he said anxiously.

To calm him and to calm myself, I feigned an air of assurance that I certainly did not feel. "My dream has lasted 70 years now," I said. "After all, there isn't a person alive who, on waking, does not find himself with himself. It's what is happening to us now—except that we are two. Don't you want to know something of my past, which is the future awaiting you?"

He assented without a word. I went on, a bit lost. "Mother is healthy and well in her house on Charcas and Maipú, in Buenos Aires, but Father died some 30 years ago. He died of heart trouble. Hemiplegia finished him; his left hand, placed on his right, was like the hand of a child on a giant's. He died impatient for death but without complaint. Our grandmother had died in the same house. A few days before the end, she called us all together and said, 'I'm an old woman who is dying very, very slowly. Don't anyone become upset about such a common, everyday thing.' Your sister Norah married and has two sons. By the way, how is everyone at home?"

"Quite well. Father makes his same antireligious jokes. Last night he said that Jesus was like the Gauchos, who don't like to commit themselves, and that's why he preached in parables." He hesitated and then said, "And you?"

"I don't know the number of books you'll write, but I know they'll be too many. You'll write poems that will give you a pleasure that others won't share and stories of a somewhat fantastic nature. Like your father and so many others of our family, you will teach."

It pleased me that he did not ask about the success or failure of his books. I changed my tone and went on. "As for history, there was another war, almost among the same antagonists. France was not long in caving in; England and America fought against a German dictator named Hitler—the cyclical battle of Waterloo. Around 1946, Buenos Aires gave birth to another Rosas, who bore a fair resemblance to our kinsman. In 1955, the province of Córdoba came to our rescue, as Entre Ríos had in the last century. Now things are going badly. Russia is taking over the world; America, hampered by the superstition of democracy, can't make up its mind to become an empire. With every day that passes, our country becomes more provincial. More provincial and more pretentious—as if its eyes were closed. It wouldn't surprise me if the teaching of Latin in our schools were replaced by Guarani."

I could tell that he was barely paying attention. The elemental fear of what is impossible and yet what is so dismayed him. I, who have never been a father, felt for that poor boy—more intimate to me even than a son of my flesh—a surge of love. Seeing that he clutched a book in his hands, I asked what it was.

"*The Possessed*, or, as I believe, *The Devils*, by Fyodor Dostoyevsky," he answered, not without vanity.

"It has faded in my memory. What's it like?" As soon as I said this, I felt that the question was a blasphemy.

THE OTHER

"The Russian master," he pronounced, "has seen better than anyone else into the labyrinth of the Slavic soul."

This attempt at rhetoric seemed to me proof that he had regained his composure. I asked what other volumes of the master he had read. He mentioned two or three, among them *The Double*. I then asked him if on reading them he could clearly distinguish the characters, as you could in Joseph Conrad, and if he thought of going on in his study of Dostoyevsky's work.

"Not really," he said with a certain surprise.

I asked what he was writing and he told me he was putting together a book of poems that would be called *Red Hymns*. He said he had also considered calling it *Red Rhythms*.

"And why not?" I said. "You can cite good antecedents. Rubén Darío's blue verse and Verlaine's gray song."

Ignoring this, he explained that his book would celebrate the brotherhood of man. The poet of our time could not turn his back on his own age, he went on to say. I thought for a while and asked if he truly felt himself a brother to everyone—to all funeral directors, for example, to all postmen, to all deep-sea divers, to all those who lived on the even-numbered side of the street, to all those who were aphonic, etc. He answered that his book referred to the great mass of the oppressed and alienated.

"Your mass of oppressed and alienated is no more than an abstraction," I said. "Only individuals exist—if it can be said that anyone exists. 'The man of yesterday is not the man of today,' some Greek remarked. We two, seated on this bench in Geneva or Cambridge, are perhaps proof of this."

Except in the strict pages of history, memorable events stand in no need of memorable phrases. At the point of death, a man tries to recall an engraving glimpsed in childhood; about to enter battle, soldiers speak of the mud or of their sergeant. Our situation was unique and, frankly, we were unprepared for it. As fate would have it, we talked about literature; I fear I said no more than the things I usually say to journalists. My alter ego believed in the invention or discovery of new metaphors; I, in those metaphors that correspond to intimate and obvious affinities and that our imagination has already accepted. Old age and sunset, dreams and life, the flow of time and water. I put forward this opinion, which years later he would put forward in a book. He barely listened to me. Suddenly, he said, "If you have been me, how do you explain the fact that you have forgotten your meeting with an elderly gentleman who in 1918 told you that he, too, was Borges?"

6

I had not considered this difficulty. "Maybe the event was so strange I chose to forget it," I answered without much conviction.

Venturing a question, he said shyly, "What's your memory like?"

I realized that to a boy not yet 20, a man of over 70 was almost in the grave. "It often approaches forgetfulness," I said, "but it still finds what it's asked to find. I study Old English, and I am not at the bottom of the class."

Our conversation had already lasted too long to be that of a dream. A sudden idea came to me. "I can prove at once that you are not dreaming me," I said. "Listen carefully to this line, which, as far as I know, you've never read."

Slowly I entoned the famous verse, "*L'hydre-univers tordant son corps écaille d'astres.*" I felt his almost fearful awe. He repeated the line, low-voiced, savoring each resplendent word.

"It's true," he faltered. "I'll never be able to write a line like that."

Victor Hugo had brought us together.

Before this, I now recall, he had fervently recited that short piece of Whitman's in which the poet remembers a night shared beside the sea when he was really happy.

"If Whitman celebrated that night," I remarked, "it's because he desired it and it did not happen. The poem gains if we look on it as the expression of a longing, not the account of an actual happening."

He stared at me, openmouthed. "You don't know him!" he exclaimed. "Whitman is incapable of telling a lie."

Half a century does not pass in vain. Beneath our conversation about people and random reading and our different tastes, I realized that we were unable to understand each other. We were too similar and too unalike. We were unable to take each other in, which makes conversation difficult. Each of us was a caricature copy of the other. The situation was too abnormal to last much longer. Either to offer advice or to argue was pointless, since, unavoidably, it was his fate to become the person I am.

All at once, I remembered one of Coleridge's fantasies. Somebody dreams that on a journey through paradise, he is given a flower. On waking, he finds the flower. A similar trick occurred to me. "Listen," I said. "Have you any money?" "Yes," he replied. "I have about twenty francs. I've invited Simon Jichlinski to dinner at the Crocodile tonight."

"Tell Simon that he will practice medicine in Carouge and that he will do much good. Now, give me one of your coins."

He drew out three large silver pieces and some small change. Without understanding, he offered me a five-franc coin. I handed him one of those not very sensible American bills that, regardless of their value, are all the same size. He examined it avidly.

"It can't be," he said, his voice raised. "It bears the date 1964. All this is a miracle," he managed to say, "and the miraculous is terrifying. Witnesses to the resurrection of Lazarus must have been horrified."

We have not changed in the least, I thought to myself. Ever the bookish reference. He tore up the bill and put his coins away. I decided to throw mine into the river. The arc of the big silver disk losing itself in the silver river would have conferred on my story a vivid image, but luck would not have it so. I told him that the supernatural, if it occurs twice, ceases to be terrifying. I suggested that we plan to see each other the next day, on that same bench, which existed in two times and in two places. He agreed at once and, without looking at his watch, said that he was late. Both of us were lying and we each knew it of the other. I told him that someone was coming for me.

"Coming for you?" he said.

"Yes. When you get to my age, you will have lost your eyesight almost completely. You'll still make out the color yellow and lights and shadows. Don't worry. Gradual blindness is not a tragedy. It's like a slow summer dusk."

We said goodbye without having once touched each other. The next day, I did not show up. Neither would he.

I have brooded a great deal over that meeting, which until now I have related to no one. I believe I have discovered the key. The meeting was real, but the other man was dreaming when he conversed with me, and this explains how he was able to forget me; I conversed with him while awake, and the memory of it still disturbs me.

The other man dreamed me, but he did not dream me exactly. He dreamed, I now realize, the date on the dollar bill.

—*Translated from the Spanish by Norman Thomas di Giovanni*

Emptiness

memoir by **JONATHAN SAFRAN FOER**

THE FIRST EMPTY PAGE

I started collecting empty paper soon after I finished my first novel, about two years ago. A family friend had been helping to archive Isaac Bashevis Singer's belongings for the university where his papers and artifacts were to be kept. Among the many items to be disposed of was a stack of Singer's unused typewriter paper. (Understandably it had been deemed to have no archival value.) My friend sent the top page to me— the next sheet on which Singer would have written—suspecting that I might take some pleasure in the remnant of the great writer's life.

Once white, the paper had started to yellow, and, at the corners, to brown. There was a slight wrinkle across the bottom (or was it the top?), and scattered about were specks of dust that were resistant to my gentle brushes, apparently having been ground into the paper's fibers. (I've read that 90 percent of household dust is actually composed of human epidermal matter. So I like to think of the page as holding the face that once looked over it—the wrinkle corresponds to Singer's pinched forehead.) But to the casual glance, it's a clean, perfectly ordinary sheet of typing paper.

For weeks, I kept it in the envelope in which it was sent. Only occasionally did I take it out to look at or to show to a visiting friend when the conversation slowed. I thought it was an interesting oddity and nothing more.

But I was wrong about the empty page. Or I was wrong about myself. A relationship developed. I found myself thinking about the piece of paper, being moved by it, taking it out of its envelope several times a day, wanting to see it. I had the page framed and put it on my living room wall. Many of the breaks I took from looking at my own empty paper were spent looking at Singer's.

Looking at what?

EMPTINESS

There were so many things to look at. There were the phantom words that Singer hadn't written and would never write, the arrangements of ink that would have turned the most common of all objects—the empty page—into the most valuable: a great work of art. The blank sheet of paper was at once empty and infinite. It contained no words and every word Singer hadn't yet written. The page was perhaps the best portrait of Singer—not only because it held his skin (or so I liked to think) but because it was free to echo and change. His books could be interpreted and reinterpreted, but they would never gain or lose words; his image was always bound to the moment of its creation. But the blank page contained everything Singer could have written and everyone he could have become.

And it was also a mirror. As a young writer—I was then contemplating how to move forward after my first effort—I felt so enthusiastically and agonizingly aware of the blank pages in front of me. How could I fill them? Did I even want to fill them? Was I becoming a writer because I wanted to become a writer or because I was becoming a writer? I stared into empty pages day after day, looking, like Narcissus, for myself.

MORE EMPTINESS

I decided to expand my collection. Singer's paper was not enough, just as Singer's books would not be enough in a library, even if they were your favorites. I wanted to see how other pieces of paper would speak to Singer's and to one another, how the physical differences among them would echo differences among the writers. I wanted to see if the accumulation of emptiness would be greater than the sum of its parts. So I began writing letters to authors—all of whom I admired, only one or two of whom I had ever corresponded with—asking for the next sheet of paper that he or she would have written on.

Richard Powers was the first to respond. "The favor is indeed strange," he wrote, "but wonderful. The more I think about it, the more resonance it gets: a museum of pure potential, the unfilled page!" He sent along the next sheet from the yellow legal pad on which he writes. When I held it to my face, I could see the indentations from the writing on the page that was once above it. Within a week the indentations had disappeared—the ghost words were gone—and the page was again perfectly flat.

I received a piece of paper from Susan Sontag. It was slightly smaller than the standard 8½″ x 11″, and her name was printed across the top—for archival purposes, I imagined. John Barth sent me an empty page. It was classic three-hole style with light-blue horizontal lines and

10

a red stripe up the margin. (How strange, I thought, that America's most famous metafictionist should compose on the most traditional, childlike paper.) His note: "Yours takes the prize for odd requests and quite intrigues me." A sheet of empty graph paper from Paul Auster, which evoked his style. An absolutely gorgeous mathematician's log from Helen DeWitt, accompanied by advice to the young writer about getting to know one's typesetter. A page ripped from David Grossman's notebook—small, worn even in its newness, somehow strong. He sent along a beautiful letter filled with observations, opinions, regrets, hopes and no mention of blank paper. A clean white page from Arthur Miller, no accompanying note. Paper from Zadie Smith, Victor Pelevin, David Foster Wallace ("You are a weird bird, JSF"), Peter Carey, John Updike.... Jonathan Franzen sent his page back in an envelope with no return address. Attached to the sheet was a note that read simply, "Guess whose?" (The postmark betrayed him.) A lengthwise-folded sheet of paper from Joyce Carol Oates. She explained that she likes to write on narrow pages so that she can view all of the text at once and complete pages twice as quickly. At the end of the three-page letter in which she carefully described her process of composition she wrote, "Truly, I believe...what we write is what we are."

I received an empty page from Don DeLillo. The paper itself was relatively ordinary: a uniform field of yellow, 8½" x 11". The accompanying note was typed onto a thin white sheet of typing paper (or was it tracing paper?), folded three times and fit into a 9"x 12" envelope:

Dear Jonathan,

A hundred years ago I used yellow paper every day in my job writing advertising copy, and when I quit the job to become a grown-up first and then a writer, I took (I guess) a fairly large quantity of this copy paper with me. The first draft of my first novel was typed on this paper, and through the years I have used it again, sparingly and then more sparingly, and now there are only five sheets left.

Back in those days I was the Kid, and the friends I made on the job are either older than I am or dead (two days ago I wrote and delivered a eulogy for one of them), and so this yellow paper carries a certain weight of friendship and memory. That's why I thought I'd entrust a sheet to your collection.
Best,
Don DeLillo

EMPTY FREUD

My most recent addition to the Empty Page Project came this past fall when I was paying a visit to the Freud Museum in London. (For those who haven't been there, it's the house in which Freud spent the last year of his life after having fled Nazi-occupied Austria. The books are left as he left them. His figurines haven't been moved. The famous couch draped in Persian carpets seems to hold the indentation of his final patient.) It was a beautiful Sunday afternoon, and with the help of a friend I was able to arrange for a private tour. The director led a memorable walk through the house, filling my head as we went with touching, funny anecdotes. At the end as we were about to part ways, I explained my collection to her. "I'm sure you can't help," I said, "but I'd hate myself if I left without asking."

She gave it a thought, which in itself was more than I ever would have anticipated, and then smiled wryly. I don't remember us speaking any more words to each other. She led me back to Freud's office, a room filled well beyond its capacity with busts, vases, books, ashtrays, rugs, prints, ancient artifacts, magnifying glasses, pieces of glass...things—the things one can't help but think of as expressing the man who collected them. One at a time and slowly, she moved aside the velvet ropes that marked off the protected area. (You know your heart is beating heavily when you become aware of the spaces between the beats.) She led me to Freud's desk, which hadn't been moved since his death, and opened the center drawer. It was filled with such beautiful...things: a velvet pouch, which held a lock of his wife's hair; appointment cards for his patients; the pieces of a broken statuette; and a stack of his blank paper. Across the top of each page read:

Prof. Sigm. Freud
20 Maresfield Gardens
London, N.W3.
Tel: Hampstead 2002

Carefully she slid off the top sheet and handed it to me.

IDEAL EMPTINESS

What would be the ideal sheet of empty paper? I know which ones I'd like. Kafka's would be wonderful. As would one of Beckett's. I'd love an empty page of Bruno Schulz's. That would mean the world to me. Nietzsche. Rilke. Why not Shakespeare while we're at it? Or Newton? More realistically, a sheet from W.G. Sebald would be great. (Would it have been as great, though, if he hadn't died, too young, in a car crash? And if not, what does that say about the collection?)

The ideal sheet would not necessarily be that of the greatest writer but that which held the most potential.

Through a lot of difficult research I was able to find out that Anne Frank's diary was not completely filled. (The family was betrayed and arrested; her writing ended abruptly.) There are empty pages, waiting there for the touch of a pen that will never come.

I read the diary as a child and have reread it several times since. But it wasn't until last year that I first visited the Anne Frank House. I was in Amsterdam to give a lecture for the release of my novel's Dutch translation. In one afternoon I saw the foreign edition of my book and the Anne Frank diary itself. Each experience moved me strongly, in what I now realize were opposite ways.

In the case of my book, I had become so accustomed to its familiar physical presence that to witness it as an idea—which it necessarily was for me, as I couldn't understand the Dutch—was jarring. I saw the ripples that emanated from the words I threw in the lake. The book—the ink that I had applied to the paper—had taken on a life in the world. It had grown in directions not under my control, or even in my view. It was becoming an abstraction.

And in the case of the diary, I was so accustomed to thinking of it as an idea, a sadness that resonated across languages and generations, that to see the physical referent, the actual book, was not only moving but shocking. I couldn't believe that the thing we had been thinking and talking about all of that time was actually a thing.

NAKED PAGES

I'm writing this essay for a magazine that, for all of its other attributes, is distinguished by its unclothed women. What about an unclothed page? Is that the page's "natural" state? And is there something equally taboo about it? Equally erotic? Does it make it more exciting to know that the advertising space in this issue runs somewhere in the neighborhood of $100,000 a page? And if so, why?

If I insert one blank page, when the magazine is printed it will become more than 3 million blank pages. Stacked, these blank pages would form an empty column the height of the Empire State Building. Laid end-to-end they could cover a path from Boston to Washington, D.C. And more than that, as PLAYBOY has a readership (as opposed to a circulation) of close to 10 million, the mental space that these empty pages would occupy is breathtaking. One blank page, created with the ease of a single hard return, will contain the potential of each of the 10 million people who look at it. What might they draw on it? What might

13

they write? What thoughts might it inspire in them? What image would they see in its depths? What image do you see?

THE LAST EMPTINESS

My little brother is going to be a senior in college this year. He's already started to worry about what to do with his life. (My telling him that he can be anything he wants doesn't help him at all. It hurts him.) He has some interest in documentary filmmaking, although he's done nothing to prepare himself for such a path; architecture seems interesting, but he's afraid of designing kitchens for the rest of his life; writing would be a consideration, except that both of his older brothers do it.

When he was a baby, I would carry him up and down the stairs even though my parents told me not to hold him unless they were watching. I knew even as a seven-year-old that I was putting him in danger. But I had to put him in danger so I could protect him from danger.

He's envious of me, and I'm envious of him. He wants direction in his life. He wants to have words to apply to his interests, recognizable ways to describe himself. (It isn't acceptable simply being someone who experiences the world deeply.) He wants an unchanging mailing address. He wants to accomplish things, to put empty paper behind him—whatever form that empty paper should take. I remember what it was like to be so uncertain, so scared. And I remember the joy of not knowing, of everything seeming possible and possibly wonderful. Or horrible. Or mediocre.

Every day I better know what to expect, and so the days grow shorter and fit tighter, and if it isn't like dying, it's like disappointment. But I can remember, as if it were yesterday, turning on my laptop, knowing that I was about to start my first novel—the moment before life wrote on me.

In his story "Gimpel the Fool," Singer writes of a "once-removed" world, a better world in which the foolish are redeemed and everyone gets what he deserves. In that world we never say all of the things we wish we hadn't said. And we say all of the things we wish we had. It's easy and impossible to imagine. We are graceful, in that world, and patient, the full expressions of what we know ourselves to be. It's nice to think about.

The Courting
of the Muse

humor by P.G. WODEHOUSE

W hen people come up to me—and I have witnesses to testify that this has happened—and say, "Tell me, Mr. Wodehouse, what are your literary methods?" I generally give one of my light, musical laughs and reply, "Oh, I just sit down at the typewriter and curse a bit." But actually the thing goes deeper than that, and if posterity is to get straight on this very important point, I shall have to add a few details.

I would like to say, as I have known other authors to say, that I spring from my bed, take a cold shower and am at my desk at nine A.M. sharp, but something tells me I could never get away with it. The reader is shrewd enough to know that no one is ever at his desk at nine. I do get to my desk, however, around about 10, and everything depends then on whether or not I put my feet up on it. If I do, I instantly fall into a reverie or coma, musing on ships and shoes and sealing wax and cabbages and kings. This goes on for some time. Many of my deepest thoughts have come to me when I have had my feet up on the desk, but I have never been able to fit one of them into any novel I have been writing.

If I avoid this snare, I pull chair up to typewriter, adjust the dachshund which is lying on my lap, chirrup to the boxer, throw a passing pleasantry to the cat and pitch in.

All the animal members of the household take a great interest in my literary work, and it is rare for me to begin the proceedings without a quorum. I sometimes think I could concentrate better in solitude, and I wish particularly that the cat would give me a word of warning before jumping on the back of my neck as I sit trying to find the *mot juste*, but I remind myself that conditions might be worse. I might be dictating my stuff.

15

THE COURTING OF THE MUSE

How anybody can compose a story by word of mouth, face to face with a bored-looking secretary with a notebook, is more than I can imagine. Yet many authors think nothing of saying, "Ready, Miss Spelvin? Take dictation. Quote No comma Lord Jasper Murgatroyd comma close quote said no better make it hissed Evangeline comma quote I would not marry you if you were the last man on earth period close quote Quote Well comma I'm not comma so the point does not arise comma close quote replied Lord Jasper comma twirling his mustache cynically period And so the long day wore on period End of chapter."

If I had to do that sort of thing I should be feeling all the time that the girl was saying to herself as she took it down, "Well comma this beats me period How comma with homes for the feeble-minded touting for customers on every side comma has a man like this Wodehouse succeeded in remaining at large all these years mark of interrogation."

Nor would I be more at my ease with one of those machines where you talk into a mouthpiece and have your observations recorded on wax. I bought one of them once and started *Thank You, Jeeves*, on it. *Thank You, Jeeves,* in case you don't know, begins as follows:

> *I was a shade perturbed. Nothing to signify, really, but still just a spot concerned. You couldn't have said that the brow was actually furrowed, and yet, on the other hand, you couldn't have stated absolutely that it wasn't. Perhaps the word "pensive" about covers it.*

And when I got as far as that I thought I would turn back and play the thing over to hear how it sounded.

It sounded too bloody awful for human consumption. Until that moment I had never realized that I had a voice like that of a very pompous schoolmaster addressing the young scholars in his charge from the pulpit in the school chapel, but if this contraption was to be relied on, that was the sort of voice I had. There was a kind of foggy dreariness about it that chilled the spirits. It stunned me. I had been hoping, if all went well, to make *Thank You, Jeeves* an amusing book—gay, if you see what I mean, rollicking, if you still follow me, and debonair—and it was plain to me that a man with a voice like that could never come within several million light years of being gay and debonair. With him at the controls, the thing would develop into one of those dim tragedies of peasant life in the Arkansas mountains which we return to the library after a quick glance at page one. I sold the machine the next day and felt like the Ancient Mariner when he got rid of the albatross.

My writing, if and when I get down to it, is a combination of longhand and typing. I generally rough out a paragraph or a piece of dialog in pencil on pad and then type an improved version. This always answers well unless while using the pad I put my feet up on the desk, for then comes the reverie of which I was speaking and the mind drifts off to other things.

I am fortunate as a writer in not being dependent on my surroundings. Some authors, I understand, can give of their jest only if there is a vase of roses of the right shade on the right spot of their desk, and away from their desk are unable to function. I have written quite happily on ocean liners during gales, with the typewriter falling into my lap at intervals, in hotel bedrooms, on trains, in woodsheds, in punts on lakes and in the Inspecteur's room at the Palais de Justice in Paris at the time when the French Republic suspected me of being a danger to it. (Actually, I was very fond of the French Republic and wouldn't have laid a finger on it if you had brought it to me asleep on a chair, but they did not know this.)

Writing my stories—or at any rate rewriting them—I enjoy. It is the thinking them out that puts those dark circles under my eyes. You can't think out plots like mine without getting a suspicion from time to time that something has gone seriously wrong with the brain's two hemispheres and the broad band of transversely running fibers known as the corpus callosum. It is my practice to make about 400 pages of notes before I start a novel, and during this process there always comes a moment when I pause and say to myself. "Oh, what a noble mind is here o'erthrown." If any good mental specialist could have read the notes I made for my last one—*The Ice in the Bedroom*—he would have been on the telephone urging men in white coats to drop everything and come and slap the straitjacket on me before he was halfway through.

The odd thing is that, just as I am feeling that I must get a proposer and seconder and have myself put up for the loony bin, something always clicks and after that all is joy and jollity. I shall have to rewrite every line in the book half a dozen times, but once I get my scenario set I know it is simply a matter of plugging away at it.

To me a detailed scenario is, as they say, of the essence. Some writers will tell you that they just sit down and take pen in hand and let their characters carry on as they see fit. Not for me any procedure like that. I wouldn't trust my characters an inch. They have to do just what the scenario tells them to, and no funny business. It has always seemed to me that planning a story out and writing it are two distinct and separate things. If I were going to run a train, I would feel that the square thing to do was to provide the customers with railroad lines and see that the switches were in working order. Otherwise—or so I think—I would have my public shouting, as did the lady in the old English music-hall song:

> Oh, Mister porter,
>   What shall I do?
> I want to go to Birmingham
>   And they're taking me on to Crewe.

Anyone who reads a novel of mine can be assured that it will be as coherent as I can make it—which, I readily agree, is not saying much, and that, though he may not enjoy the journey, he will get to Birmingham all right.

"I've written a sensational exposé of the publishing game...but no one will publish it!"

The Signal

ribald classic by GUY DE MAUPASSANT

The lovely Marquise de Rennedon was still asleep in her dark and perfumed bedroom.

In her soft, low bed between sheets of delicate cambric, fine as lace and caressing as a kiss, she was sleeping, alone and tranquil, the happy and profound sleep of a divorced woman.

She was awakened by loud voices in the drawing room and she recognized her dear friend, the Baroness de Grangerie, who was disputing with the lady's maid because the latter would not allow her to go into the marquise's room. So the marquise got up, opened the door, drew back the door hangings and showed her head, nothing but her fair head, hidden under a cloud of hair.

"What is the matter with you that you have come so early?" she asked. "It is not nine o'clock yet."

The pretty baroness, who was very pale, nervous and feverish, replied: "I must speak to you. Something horrible has happened to me."

"Come in, my dear."

She went in; and the marquise got back into her bed, while the lady's maid opened the windows to let in light and air. Then, when she had left the room, the marquise went on: "Well, tell me what it is."

Baroness de Grangerie began to cry, shedding those pretty bright tears which make women more charming. She sobbed out without wiping her eyes, so as not to make them red: "Oh, my dear, what has happened to me is abominable, abominable. I have not slept all night, not a minute, do you hear? Not a minute. Here, just feel how my heart is beating."

And, taking her friend's hand, she put it on her breast, on that firm, round covering of women's hearts which often suffices men and prevents them from seeking beneath. Her heart was beating violently.

She continued: "It happened to me yesterday during the day at about four o'clock—or half-past four; I cannot say exactly. You know my

20

apartments, and you know that my little drawing room, where I always sit, looks on to the Rue Saint-Lazare and that I have a mania for sitting at the window to look at the people passing. The neighborhood of the railway station is very gay, so full of motion and so lively—just what I like! Well, yesterday I was sitting in the low chair which I have placed in my window recess; the window was open and I was not thinking of anything, simply breathing the fresh air. You remember how fine it was yesterday!

"Suddenly I noticed a woman sitting at the window opposite—a woman in red. I was in mauve, you know, my pretty mauve costume. I did not know the woman (a new lodger, who had been there a month, and as it has been raining for a month, I had not yet seen her), but I saw immediately that she was a bad girl. At first I was very much shocked and disgusted that she should be at the window just as I was, and then by degrees it amused me to watch her. She was resting her elbows on the window ledge and looking at the men, and the men looked at her also, all or nearly all. One might have said that they knew of her presence by some means as they got near the house, that they sensed her presence by instinct, for they suddenly raised their heads and exchanged a swift look with her, a sort of secret signal. Her signal said: 'Will you?' Theirs replied: 'I have no time,' or else: 'Another day,' or else: 'I have no money,' or else: 'How dare you!'

"You cannot imagine how funny it was to see her carrying on such a piece of work, though after all it is her regular business.

"Occasionally she shut the window suddenly, and I saw a gentleman go in. She had caught him like a fisherman hooks a fish. Then I looked at my watch and I found that they never stopped longer than from twelve to twenty minutes. The whole procedure fascinated me!

"I asked myself: 'How does she manage to make herself understood so quickly, so well and so completely? Does she add a nod of the head or a motion of the hands to her looks? And I took my opera glasses to watch her proceedings. They were very simple: first of all a glance, then a smile, then a slight backward nod of the head which meant: 'Are you coming up?' But it was so slight, so vague, so discreet, that it required a great deal of knack to succeed as she did. And I asked myself: 'I wonder if I could do it as nicely as she?'

"I went and tried it before the looking glass and, my dear, I did it better than she, a great deal better! I was enchanted and resumed my place at the window.

"She caught nobody more then, poor girl, nobody. She certainly had no luck. It must really be very terrible to earn one's bread in that way, terrible and amusing occasionally, for really some of these men one meets in the street are rather nice.

"After that they all came on my side of the road and none on hers; the sun had turned. Then came one after the other, young, old, dark, fair, gray, white. I saw some who looked very nice, really very nice, my dear, far better than my husband or than yours—I mean than your last husband, as you have got your divorce.

"I said to myself: 'If I give them the signal, will they understand me? I, a respectable woman?' And I was seized with a mad longing to signal them. A terrible longing; you know, one of those longings which one cannot resist! I have some like that occasionally. How silly such things are, don't you think so? I believe that we women have the souls of monkeys. I have been told (and it was a physician who told me) that the brain of a monkey is very like ours. Of course we must imitate someone or other. We imitate our husbands when we love them during the first months after our marriage, and then our lovers, our female friends, our confessors when they are nice. We assume their ways of thought, their manners of speech, their words, their gestures, everything. It is very foolish."

"Yes, yes," the marquise said impatiently, "but what happened? Surely you did not yield to this temptation?"

"My dear, when I am tempted to do a thing I always do it. And so I said to myself: 'I will try it once, on one man only, just to see. What can happen to me? Nothing whatever! We shall exchange a smile and that will be all, and I shall deny it most certainly.'

"So I began to make my choice. I wanted someone nice, very nice, and suddenly I saw a tall, fair, very good-looking fellow coming along. I like fair men, as you know. I looked at him; he looked at me. I smiled; he smiled. I made the signal, oh, so faintly; he replied 'yes' with his head, and there he was, my dear! He came in at the large door of the house.

"You cannot imagine what passed through my mind then! I thought I should go mad. Oh, how frightened I was! Just think, he will speak to the servants! To Joseph, who is devoted to my husband! Joseph would certainly think that I had known that gentleman for a long time.

"What could I do? He would ring in a moment. I thought I would go and meet him and tell him he had made a mistake and beg him to go away. He would have pity on a woman, on a poor woman. So I rushed to the door and opened it just at the moment when he was going to ring the bell, and I stammered out quite stupidly: 'Go away, monsieur, go away; you have made a mistake, a terrible mistake. I took you for one of my friends whom you resemble. Have pity on me, monsieur.'

"But he only began to laugh, my dear, and replied: 'Good morning, my dear; I know all about your little story, you may be sure. You are married and so you want forty francs instead of twenty, and you shall have it, so just show me in, if you please?'

"And he pushed me inside, closed the door, and as I remained standing before him, horror-struck, he kissed me, put his arm round my waist and made me go back into the drawing room, the door of which had remained open. Then he began to look at everything, like an auctioneer, and continued: 'By Jove, it is very nice in your rooms, very nice. You must be very down on your luck just now to do the window business!'

"Then I began to beg him again. 'Oh, monsieur, go away, please go away! My husband will be coming in soon. I swear that you have made a mistake!' But he answered quite coolly: 'Come, my beauty, I have had enough of this nonsense, and if your husband comes in I will give him five francs to go and have a drink at the cafe across the street.' And then, seeing Raoul's photograph on the chimney piece, he asked me: 'Is that your husband?'

"'Yes, that is he.'

"'He looks like a nice, disagreeable sort of fellow. And who is this? One of your friends?'

"It was *your* photograph, my dear, you know, in that gown with the daring décolletage. I did not know any longer what I was saying, and I stammered: 'Yes, it is one of my friends.'

"'She is very nice,' he said. 'You shall introduce me to her.'

"Just then the clock struck five, and Raoul comes home every day at half-past! Suppose he were to come home before the other had gone; just think what would have happened! Then—then I completely lost my head—altogether. I thought—I thought—that—that the best thing would be—to get rid of—of this man—as quickly as possible. The sooner it was over—you understand."

The Marquise de Rennedon began to laugh, to laugh madly, with her head buried in her pillow, so that the whole bed shook, and when she was a little calmer she asked:

"And—and—was he good-looking?"

"Yes."

"And yet you complain?"

"But—but—don't you see, my dear, he said—he said—he should come again tomorrow—at the same time—and I—I am terribly frightened. You have no idea how persuasive he is and how obstinate. What can I do—tell me—what can I do?"

THE SIGNAL

The marquise sat up in bed to reflect, and then she suddenly said: "Have him arrested!"

The baroness looked stupefied and stammered out: "What do you mean? What are you thinking of? Have him arrested? Under what pretext?"

"That is very simple. Go to the commissary of police and say that a gentleman has been following you about for three months, that he had the insolence to go up to your apartment yesterday, that he has threatened you with another visit tomorrow and that you demand the protection of the law."

"But, my dear, suppose he tells them that—"

"They will not believe him, you silly thing, but they *will* believe you, who are an irreproachable woman, and in society."

"Oh! I shall never dare to do it."

"You must dare, my dear, or you are lost."

"But think how he will insult me if he is arrested!"

"Good! You will have witnesses to his insults, and he will surely be sentenced."

"Sentenced to what?"

"To pay damages. In such cases one must be pitiless!"

"Ah! Speaking of damages—there is one thing that worries me very much—very much indeed. He left forty francs on the mantelpiece."

"Forty francs?"

"Yes."

"No more?"

"No."

"That is very little. It would have humiliated me. Well?"

"Well? What am I to do with that money?"

The marquise hesitated for a few seconds, and then she replied in a serious voice:

"My dear, there is only one honorable thing to do with the money. You must make your husband a little present of it. That will be only fair!"

The Crazy One

memoir by **NORMAN MAILER**

I n Mexico, the hour before the bullfight is always the best hour of the
week. It would be memorable not to sound like Hemingway, but in
fact you would get happy the night before just thinking of that hour
next day. Outside the Plaza Mexico, cheap cafes open only on Sunday, and huge as beer gardens, filled with the public (us tourists, hood-
lums, pimps, pickpurses and molls, Mexican variety—which is to say
the whores had headdresses and hindquarters not to be seen elsewhere
on earth, for their hair rose vertically 12 inches from the head, and
their posteriors projected horizontally 12 inches back into that space
the rest of the whore had just marched through). The mariachis were
out with their romantic haunting caterwauling of guitar, violin, song
of carnival and trumpet, their song told of hearts which were true and
hearts which were broken, and the wail of the broken heart went right
into the trumpet until there were times, when drunk the right way on
tequila or Mexican rum, it was perhaps the best sound heard this side
of Miles Davis.

You see, my friends, the wild hour was approaching. The horrors of
the week in Mexico were coming to term. Indeed, no week in Mexico is
without its horrors for every last Mexican alive—it is a city and a country where the bones of the dead seem to give the smell of their char to
every desert wind and auto exhaust and frying tortilla. The mournful-
ness of unrequited injustice hangs a shroud across the centuries. Every
Mexican is gloomy until the instant he becomes happy, and then he is a
maniac. He howls, he whistles, smoke of murder passes off his pores, he
bullies, he beseeches friendship, he is a clown, a brigand, a tragic figure
suddenly merry. The intellectuals and the technicians of Mexico abomi-
nate their national character because it is always in the way. It puts the
cracks in the plaster of new buildings, it forgets to cement the tiles, it
leaves rags in the new pipes of new office buildings and forgets to put
the gas cap back on the tank. So the intellectuals and the technicians

hate the bullfight as well. You cannot meet a socialist in Mexico who approves of the running of the bulls. They are trying to turn Mexico into a modern country, and thus the same war goes on there that goes on in three quarters of the world—the battlefront is the new highways to the suburbs, and the corporation's office buildings, the walls of hospital white and the myopic sheets of glass. In Mexico, like everywhere else, it is getting harder and harder to breathe in a mood through the pores of the city because more and more of the city is being covered with corporation architecture, with surgical dressing. To the vampires and banshees and dried blood on the cactus in the desert is added the horror of the new technology in an old murder-ridden land. And four o'clock on Sunday is the beginning of release for some of the horrors of the week. If many come close to feeling the truth only by telling a lie, so Mexicans come close to love by watching the flow of blood on an animal's flanks and the certain death of the bull before the bravery and/or humiliation of the bullfighter.

I could never have understood it if someone tried to explain ahead of time, and in fact, I came to love the bullfight long before I comprehended the first thing about why I did. That was very much to the good. There are not too many experiences a radical American intellectual could encounter in those days (when the youngest generation was called the silent generation) which invaded his sure sense of his own intellectual categories. I did not like the first bullfights I saw, the formality of the ritual bored me, the fights appeared poor (indeed they were) and the human content of the spectacle came out atrocious. Narcissistic matadors, vain when they made a move, pouting like a girl stood up on Saturday night when the crowd turned on them, clumsy at killing, and the crowd, brutal to a man. In the Plaza Mexico, the Indians in the cheap seats buy a paper cup of beer, and when they are done drinking, the walk to the w.c. is miles away, and besides they are usually feeling sullen, so they urinate in their paper cup and hurl it down in a cascade of harvest gold Indian piss. If you are an American escorting an American girl who has blonde hair, and you have tickets in *sol*, you buy your girl a cheap sombrero at the gate, for otherwise she will be a prime target of attention. Indeed, you do well not to sit near an American escorting a blonde whose head is uncovered, for the aim of a drunken Indian is no better than you when your aim is drunk. So no surprise if one's early detestation of the bullfight was fortified in kidney brew, Azteca.

Members of a minority group are always ready to take punishment, however, and I was damned if I was going to be excluded from still another cult. So I persisted in going to bullfights, and they were a series of lousy bullfights, and then the third or fourth time I got religion. It was a windy afternoon, with threats of rain, and now and then again ten minutes of rain, poisonous black clouds overhead, the chill gloom of a black sky on Sundays in Mexico, and the particular torero (whose name I could not recall for anything) was a clod. He had a nasty build. Little spindly legs, too big a chest, a butt which was broad and stolid, real peasant ass, and a vulgar worried face with a gold tooth. He was engaged with an ugly bull who kept chopping at the muleta with his horns, and occasionally the bull would catch the muleta and fling it in the air and trample it and wonder why the object was either dead or not dead, the bull smelling a hint of his own blood (or the blood of some cousin) on the blood of the muleta, and the crowd would hoot, and the torero would go over to his sword handler at the *barrera*, and shake his head and come out with a new muleta, and the bull would chop, and the wind would zig the muleta out of control, and then the matador would drop it and scamper back to the *barrera*, and the crowd would jeer and the piss would fly in yellow arcs through the rain all the way down from the cheap seats, and the whores would make farting sounds with their spoiled knowledgeable mouths, while the aficionados would roll their eyes, and the sound of Mexican laughter, that operative definition of the echo of total disgust, would shake along like jelly-gasoline through the crowd.

I got a look at the bullfighter who was the center of all this. He was not a man I could feel something for. He had a cheap pimp's face and a dull thoroughgoing vanity. His face, however, was now in despair. There was something going on for him more humiliating than humiliation—as if his life was going to take a turn into something more dreadful than anything it had encountered until now. He was in trouble. The dead dull fight he was giving was going to be death for certain hopes in his psyche. Somehow it was going to be more final than the average dead dull fight to which he was obviously all too accustomed. I was watching the despair of a profoundly mediocre man.

Well, he finally gave up any attempt to pass the bull, and he worked the animal forward with jerks of his muleta to left and right, a competent rather than a beautiful technique at best, and even to my untutored eye he was a mechanic at this, and more whistles, and then desperation all over that vain incompetent pimp's face, he profiled with his sword, and got it halfway in, and the animal took a few steps to one side and the other and fell over quickly.

The art of killing is the last skill you learn to judge in bullfighting, and the kill on this rainy afternoon left me less impressed than the crowd. Their jeers were replaced by applause (later I learned the crowd would always applaud a kill in the lung—all audiences are Broadway audiences) and the approbation continued sufficiently for the torero to take a tour of the ring. He got no ears, he certainly didn't deserve them, but he had his tour and he was happy, and in his happiness I found there was something likable about him. So this bad bullfight in the rain had given a drop of humanity to a very dry area of my heart, and now I knew a little more and had something to think about which was no longer altogether in category.

We have presented the origin of an addiction. For a drug's first appeal is always existential—our sense of life (once it is made alert by the sensation of its absence) is thereupon so full of need as the desire for a breath of air. The sense of life comes alive in the happy days when the addict first encounters his drug. But all histories of addiction are the same—particularly in the beginning. They fall into the larger category of the history of a passion. So I will spare each and every one of us the titles of the books I read on the running of the bulls, and I will not reminisce about the great bullfighters I saw, of the majesties of Arruza and the machismo of Procuna, the liquidities of Silverio and the solemnity of César Girón; no, we will not micturate the last of such memory. The fact is that I do not dwell on Arruza and Procuna and Silverio and Girón, because I did not see them that often and in fact most of them I saw but once. I was always in Mexico in the summer, you see, and the summer is the *temporada de novillos*, which is to say it is the time when the *novilladas* are held, which is to say it is the time of the novices.

Now the fellow who is pushing up this article for you is a great lover of the bullfight—make on it no mistake. For a great bullfight he would give up just about any other athletic or religious spectacle—the World Series in a minute, a pro football championship, a Mass at the Vatican, perhaps even a great heavyweight championship—which, kids, is really saying it. No love like the love for four in the afternoon at the Plaza Mexico. Yet all the great matadors he saw were seen only at special festivals when they fought very small bulls for charity. The *novillada* is, after all, the time of the *novilleros*, and a *novillero* is a bullfighter approximately equal in rank to a Golden Gloves fighter. A very good *novillero* is like a very good Golden Gloves finalist. The Sugar Ray Robinsons and the Rocky Marcianos of the bullfighting world were glimpsed by me only when they came out of retirement long enough to give the equivalent of a snappy two-round exhibition. My love of bullfighting and my experience of it as a spectator was founded then by watching *novilleros* week after week over two separate summers in Mexico City.

After a while I got good at seeing the flaws and virtues in *novilleros*, and in fact I began to see so much of their character in their style, and began to learn so much about style by comprehending their character (for nearly everything good or bad about a novice bullfighter is revealed at a great rate) that I began to take the same furious interest and partisanship in the triumph of one style over another that is usually reserved for literary matters (is Philip Roth better than John Updike?—you know) or that indeed average Americans and some not so average might take over political figures. To watch a bullfighter have an undeserved triumph on Sunday afternoon when you detest his style is not the worst preparation for listening to Everett Dirksen nominate Barry Goldwater or hearing Lyndon Johnson give a lecture on TV about American commitments to the free universe. Everything bad and god-awful about the style of life got into the style of bullfighters, as well as everything light, delightful, honorable and good.

About the time I knew a lot about bullfighting, or as much as you could know watching nothing but *novilleros* week after week, I fell in love with a bullfighter. I never even met this bullfighter, I rush to tell you. I would not have wanted to meet him. Meeting him could only have spoiled the perfection of my love, so pure was my affection. And his name—not one in a thousand of you out there, dear general readers, can have heard of him—his name was El Loco. El Loco, the Crazy One. It is not a term of endearment in Mexico, where half the populace is crazy. To amplify the power of nomenclature, El Loco came from the provinces, he was God's own hick, and his real name was Amado Ramírez, which is like being a boy from Hicksville, Georgia, with a name like Beloved Remington. Yet there was a time when I thought Beloved Remington, which is to say Amado Ramírez, would become the greatest bullfighter in the whole world, and there were critics in Mexico City hoary with *afición* who held the same opinion (if not always in print). He came up one summer like a rocket, but a rocket with one tube hot and one tube wet and he spun in circles all over the bullfighting world of Mexico City all through the summer and fall.

But we must tell more of what it is like to watch *novilleros*. You see, novice bullfighters fight bulls who are called *novillos*, and these bulls are a year younger and 200 to 400 pounds lighter than the big fighting bulls up around 1,000 pounds which matadors must face. So they are less dangerous. They can still kill a man, but not often does that happen—they are more likely to pound and stomp and wound and bruise a *novillero* than to catch him and play him in the air and stab him up high on the horns the way a terrible full-grown fighting bull can do. In consequence, the analogy to the Golden Gloves is imperfect, for a talented *novillero* can at his best look as exciting, or more exciting, than a talented matador—the novice's beast is smaller and less dangerous, so his lack of experience is compensated for by his relative comfort—he is in less danger of getting killed. (Indeed, to watch a consummate matador like Carlos Arruza work with a new young bull is like watching Norman Mailer box with his three-year-old son—absolute mastery is in the air.)

Novilleros possess another virtue. Nobody can contest their *afición*. For every *novillero* who has a manager, and a rich man to house and feed him, and influential critics to bring him along on the sweet of a bribe or two, there are a hundred devoted all but unknown *novilleros* who hitch from *poblado* to *poblado* on back dirt roads for the hint of a chance to fight at some *fiesta* so small the results are not even phoned to Mexico City. Some of these kids spend years in the provinces living on nothing, half-starved in the desire to spend a life fighting bulls, and they will fight anything—bulls who are overweight, calves who are under the legal limit, beasts who have fought before and, so, are sophisticated and dangerous. These provincial *novilleros* get hurt badly by wounds which show no blood, deep bruises in the liver and kidney from the flat of a horn, deep internal bleedings in the gut, something lively taken off the groin. A number of them die years later from malnutrition and chronic malfunctions of some number of those organs; their deaths get into no statistics on the fatalities of the bullfight.

A few of these provincial *novilleros* get enough fights and enough experience and develop enough talent, however, to pick up a reputation of sorts. If they are very lucky and likable, or have connections, or hump themselves—as some will—to rich homosexuals in the capital, then they get their shot. Listen to this. At the beginning of the *novillada*, six new bullfighters are brought in every Sunday to fight one bull each in the Plaza Mexico. For six or eight weeks this goes on. Perhaps 50 fighters never seen before in Mexico have their chance. Maybe ten will be seen again. The tension is enormous for each *novillero*. If he fails to have a triumph or attract outstanding attention, then his years in the provinces went for nothing. Back again he will go to the provinces as a punishment for failing to be superb. Perhaps he will never fight again in the Plaza Mexico. His entire life depends on this one fight. And even this fight depends on luck. For any *novillero* can catch a poor bull, a dull mediocre cowardly bull. When the animal does not charge, the bullfighter, unless possessed of genius, cannot look good.

Once a *novillero* came into the Plaza on such an occasion, was hit by the bull while making his first pass, a *verónica*, and the boy and the cape sailed into the air and came down together in such a way that when the boy rolled over, the cape wrapped around him like a tortilla, and one wit sitting in *sol*, full of the harsh wine of Mexico's harsh grapes, yelled out, "*Suerte des enchiladas.*" The young bullfighter was named the Pass of the Enchiladas. His career could never be the same. He went on to fight that bull, did a decent honorable job—the crowd never stopped laughing. El Suerte des Enchiladas. He was branded. He walked off in disgrace. The one thing you cannot be in any land where Spanish is spoken is a clown. I laughed with the rest. The bullfight is nine tenths cruelty. The bullfight brews one's cruelty out of one's pores—it makes an elixir of cruelty. But it does something else. It reflects the proportions of life in Latin lands. For in Mexico it does not seem unreasonable that a man spend years learning a dangerous trade, be rapped once by a bull and end up ruined, a Suerte des Enchiladas. It is unfair, but then life is monstrously unfair, one knows that, one of the few gleams in the muck of all this dubious Mexican majesty called existence is that one can on occasion laugh bitterly with the gods. In the Spanish-Indian blood, the substance of one's dignity is found in sharing the cruel vision of the gods. In fact, dignity can be found nowhere else. For courage is seen as the servant of the gods' cruel vision.

On to Beloved Remington. He arrived in Mexico City at the end of the beginning of the *novillada* several years back. He was there, I think, on the next to last of the early Sundays when six bulls were there for six *novilleros*. (In the full season of the *novillada*, when the best new young men have been chosen, there are six bulls for only three *toreros*—each kid then has two bulls, two chances.) I was not yet in Mexico for Amado Ramírez' first Sunday, but I heard nothing else from my bullfighting friends from the day I got in. He had appeared as the last of six *novilleros*. It had been a terrible day. All of the *novilleros* had been bad. He apparently had been the last and the worst, and had looked so clumsy that the crowd in derision had begun to applaud him. There is no sign of displeasure greater among the Mexican bullfighting public than to turn their ovations upside down. But Ramírez had taken bows. Serious solemn bows. He had bowed so much he hardly fought the bull. The Plaza Mexico rang with merriment. It took him forever to kill the beast—he received a tumultuous ovation. He gave a turn of the ring. A wit shouted "*Olé*, El Loco." He was named. When they cheer incompetence, they are ready to set fire to the stadium.

El Loco was the sensation of the week. A clown had fought a bull in the Plaza Mexico and gotten out alive. The promoters put him on the following week as a seventh bullfighter, an extra added attraction. He was not considered worth the dignity of appearing on the regular card. For the first time that season, the Plaza was sold out.

Six young *novilleros* fought six mediocre bulls that day and gave six mediocre fights. The crowd grew more sullen. When there is no good bullfight, there is no catharsis. One's money has been spent, the drinks are wearing down, and there has been no illumination, no moment to burn away all that spiritual sewer gas from the horrors of the week. Dull violence breeds, and with it, contempt for all bullfighters.

Out came the clown, El Loco. The special seventh bullfighter. He was an apparition. He had a skinny body and a funny ugly face with little eyes set close together, a big nose and a little mouth. He had very black Indian hair and a tuft in the rear of his head stood up like the spike of an antenna. He had very skinny legs and they were bent at the knee so that he gave the impression of trudging along with a lunch box in his hand. He had a ludicrous butt. It went straight back like a duck's tail feathers. His suit fit poorly. He was some sort of grafting between Ray Bolger and Charlie Chaplin. And he had the sense of self-importance to come out before the bull, he was indeed given a turn of the ring before he even saw the bull. An honor granted him for his appearance the week before. He was altogether solemn. It did not seem comic to him. He had the kind of somber extravagant ceremoniousness of a village mayor in a mountain town come out to greet the highest officials of the government. His knees stuck out in front and his buttocks in back. The Plaza rocked and rocked. Much applause followed by circulating zephyrs of laughter. And under it all, like a croaking of frogs, the beginnings of the biggest thickest Bronx raspberry anybody ever heard.

Amado Ramírez went out to receive the bull. His first pass was a yard away from the animal, his second was six feet. He looked like a 55-year-old peon ready to retire. The third pass caught his cape, and as it flew away on the horns, El Loco loped over to the *barrera* with a gait like a kangaroo. A thunderstorm of boos was on its way! He held out his arm horizontally, an injunction to the crowd, fingers spread, palm down, a mild deprecatory pleasant gesture, as if to say, "Wait, you have seen nothing yet." The lip-farters began to smack. Amado went back out. He botched one pass, looked poor on a basic *verónica*. Boos, laughter, even the cops in every aisle were laughing. *¡Que payaso!*

Then, it happened. His next pass had a name, but few even of the *afición* knew it, for it was an old-fashioned pass of great intricacy which spoke of the era of Belmonte and El Gallo and Joselito. It was a pass of considerable danger, plus much formal content (for a flash it looked like he was inclining to kiss a lady's hand, his cape draped over his back, while the bull went roaring by his unprotected ass). If I remember, it was called a *Gallecina*, and no one had seen it in five years. It consisted of whirling in a reverse *serpentina* counterclockwise into the bull so that the cape was wrapped around your body just like the Suerte des Enchiladas, except you were vertical, but the timing was such that the bull went by at the moment your back was to him and you could not see his horns. Then the whirling continued, and the cape flared out again. Amado was clumsy in his approach and stepped on his cape when he was done, but there was one moment of lightning in the middle when you saw clear sky after days of fog and smelled the ozone, there was an instant of heaven—finest thing I had yet seen in the bullfight—and in a sob of torture and release, *"¡Ole!"* came in a panic of disbelief from one parched Mexican throat near to me. El Loco did the same pass one more time and then again. On the second pass, a thousand cried *¡Ole!* And on the third, the Plaza exploded and 50,000 men and women gave up the word at the same time. Something merry and corny as a gypsy violin flowed out of his cape.

After that, nothing but comedy again. He tried a dozen fancy passes, none worked well. They were all wild, solemn, courtly, and he was there with his peasant bump of an ass and his knobby knees. The crowd laughed with tears in their eyes. With the muleta he looked absurd, a man about to miss a train and so running with his suitcase. It took him forever to kill and he stood out like an old lady talking to a barking dog, but he could do no wrong now for this crowd—they laughed, they applauded, they gave him a tour of the ring. For something had happened in those three passes which no one could comprehend. It was as if someone like me had gotten in the ring with Cassius Clay and for 20 seconds had clearly outboxed him. The only explanation was divine intervention. So El Loco was back to fight two bulls next week.

He did little with either bull, and killed the second one just before the third *aviso*. In a good season, his career would have been over. But it was a dreadful season. A couple of weeks of uneventful bullfights and El Loco was invited back. He looked awful in his first fight, green of face, timid, unbelievably awkward with the cape, morose and abominably prudent with the muleta. He killed badly. So badly in fact that he was still killing the bull when the third *aviso* sounded. The bull was let out alive. A dull sullen silence riddled with Mexican whistles. The crowd had had a bellyful of laughs with him. They were now getting very bored with the joke.

But the second bull he liked. Those crazy formal courtly passes, the *Gallecinas*, whirled out again, and the horns went by his back six inches away. *¡Ole!* He went to put the *banderillas* in himself and botched the job, had to run very fast on the last pair to escape the bull and looked like a chicken as he ran. The catcalls tuned up again. The crowd was like a bored lion uncertain whether to eat entrails or lick a face. Then he came out with the muleta and did a fine series of *derechazos*, the best seen in several weeks, and to everyone's amazement, he killed on the first *estocada*. They gave him an ear. He was the *triunfador* of the day.

This was the afternoon which confirmed the beginning of a career. After that, most of the fights are mixed in memory because he had so many, and they were never without incident. All through that summer, he fought just about every week, and every week something happened which shattered the comprehension of the most veteran bullfighting critic. They decided after this first triumph that he was a mediocre *novillero* with nothing particular to recommend him except a mysterious flair for the *Gallecina*, and a competence with the *derechazo*. Otherwise, he was uninspired with the cape and weak with the muleta. So the following week he gave an exhibition with the muleta. He did four *pases de pecho* so close and luminous (a pass is luminous when your body seems to lift with breath as it goes by) that the horns flirted with his heart. He did *derechazos* better than the week before, and finished with *manoletinas*. Again he killed well. They gave him two ears. Then his second bull went out alive. A *fracaso*.

Now the critics said he was promising with the muleta but weak with the cape. He could not do a *verónica* of any value. So in one of the following weeks he gave five of the slowest, most luminous, most soaring *verónicas* anyone had ever seen.

Yet, for three weeks in a row, if he had cut ears on one bull, he let the other go out alive. A bullfighter is not supposed to let his animal outlive three *avisos*. Indeed, if the animal is not killed before the first *aviso*, the *torero* is in disgrace already. Two *avisos* is like the sound of the knell of the bell in the poorhouse, and a bullfighter who hears the third *aviso* and has to let his bull go out alive is properly ready to commit a Mexican variety of hara-kiri. No sight, you see, is worse. It takes something like three to five minutes from the first *aviso* to the last, and in that time, the kill becomes a pigsticking. Because the *torero* has tried two, three, four, five times, even more, to go in over the horns, and he has hit bone, and he has left the sword half in but in some abominable place like the middle of the back or the flank, or he has had a perfect thrust and the bull does not die and minutes go by waiting for it to die and the peons run up with their capes and try to flick the sword out by swirling cloth around the pommel guard and giving a crude Latin yank—nothing is cruder than a peon in a sweat for his boss. Sometimes they kick the bull in the nuts in the hope it will go down, and the crowd hoots. Sometimes the bull sinks to its knees and the *puntillero* comes in to sever its neck with a thrust of his dagger, but the stab is off-center, the spinal cord is not severed. Instead, it is stimulated by the shock, and the dying bull gets up and wanders all over the ring looking for its *querencia* while blood drains and drips from its wounds and the bullfighter, looking ready to cry, trots along like a farmer accompanying his mule down the road. And the next *aviso* blows. Such scenes are a nightmare for the torero. The average torero can afford less than one occasion a year when three *avisos* are heard. El Loco was allowing an average of one bull a week to go out unkilled.

For a period, criticism of El Loco solidified. He had brilliant details, he was able on occasion to kill with inspiration, he had huge talent, but he lacked the indispensable ingredient of the bullfighter, he did not know how to get a good performance out of a bad bull. He lacked tenacity. So Ramírez created the most bizarre *faena* in anyone's memory, a fight which came near to shattering the rules of bullfighting. For on a given Sunday, he fought a very bad bull and worked with him in all the dull, technical, unaesthetic ways a bullfighter has to work with an unpromising beast, and chopped him to left and to right, and kept going into the bull's *querencia* and coaxing him out, and this went on for minutes, while the public demonstrated its displeasure. And El Loco paid no attention and kept working with the bull, and then finally got the bull to charge and he made a few fine passes. But then the first *aviso* sounded and everyone groaned. Because finally the bull was going good, and yet Amado would have to kill him now. But Amado had his bull in shape and he was not going to give him up yet, and so with everyone on the scent of the loss of each second, he made *derechazos* and the pass with the *muleta* which looks like the *gaonera* with the cape, and he did a deliberate *adorno* or two and the second *aviso* sounded and he made an effort to kill and failed, but stayed very cool and built up the crowd again by taking the bull through a series of *naturales*, and with 20 seconds left before the third *aviso* and the Plaza in pandemonium he went in to kill and had a perfect *estocada* and the bull moved around softly and with dignity and died about ten seconds after the third *aviso*, but no one could hear the trumpet for the crowd was in a delirium of thunder, and every white handkerchief in the place was out. And Amado was smiling, which is why you could love him, because his pinched ugly little peasant face was full of a kid's decent happiness when he smiled. And a minute later there was almost a riot against the judges, for they were not going to give him the tail or two ears or even an ear—how could they if the bull had died after the third *aviso*? And yet the tension of fighting the bull on the very edge of his time had given a quality to this fight which had more than a hint of the historic, for new emotions had been felt.

Amado was simply unlike any bullfighter who had ever come along. When he had a great fight, or even a great pass, it was unlike the passes of other fine *novilleros*—the passes of El Loco were better than anything you had ever seen. It was as if you were looking at the sky and suddenly a bird materialized in the air. And a moment later disappeared again. His work was frightening. It was simple, lyrical, light, illumined, but it came from nowhere and then was gone. When El Loco was bad, he was not mediocre or dull, he was simply the worst, most inept and most comical bullfighter anyone had ever seen. He seemed to have no technique to fall back on. He would hold his cape like a shroud, his legs would bend at the knees, his sad ass seemed to have an eye for the exit, his expression was morose as Fernandel and his feet kept tripping. And when he was afraid, he had a nerveless incapacity to kill which was so hopeless that the moment he stepped out to face his animal you knew he could not go near this particular bull. Yet when he was good, the comic body suddenly straightened, the back took on the camber of the best back any Spanish aristocrat ever chose to display, the buttocks retired into themselves like a masterpiece of poise, and the cape and the muleta moved slowly as full sails, or whirled like the wing of that mysterious bird. It was as if El Loco came to be every comic Mexican who ever breathed the finest Spanish grace into his pores. For five-odd minutes he was as completely transformed as Charlie Chaplin's tramp doing a consummate impersonation of the one and only Valentino, the long-lost Rudolph.

Let me tell then of Amado's best fight. It came past the middle of that fine summer when he had an adventure every week in the Plaza and we had adventures watching him, for he had fights so mysterious that the gods of the bulls and the ghosts of dead matadors must have come with the mothers and the witches of the centuries, homage to Lorca!, to see the miracles he performed. Listen! One day he had a sweet little bull with nice horns, regular, pleasantly curved, and the bull ran with gaiety, even abandon. Now we have to stop off here for an imperative explanation: It is essential to discuss the attitude of *afición* to the *natural*. To them the *natural* is the equivalent of the full parallel turn in skiing or a scrambling T-formation quarterback or a hook off a jab—it cannot be done well by all athletes, no matter how good they are in other ways, and the *natural* is a dangerous pass, perhaps the most dangerous there is. The cloth of the muleta has no sword to extend its width. Now the cloth is held in the left hand, the sword in the right, and so the target of the *muleta* which is presented for the bull's attraction is half as large as it was before and the bullfighter's body is thus so much bigger and so much more worthy of curiosity to the beast—besides the bull is wiser now, he may be ready to suspect it is the man who torments him and not the swirling sinister chaos of the cloth in which he would bury his head. Moreover—and here is the mystique of the *natural*—the bullfighter has a psychic communion with the bull. People who are not psychic do not conceive of fighting bulls. So the torero fights the bull from his psyche first. And with the muleta he fights him usually with his right hand from a position of authority. Switching the cloth to the left hand exposes his psyche as well as his body. He feels less authority—in compensation his instinct plays closer to the bull. But he is so vulnerable! So a *natural* inspires a bullfighting public to hold their breath, for danger and beauty come closest to meeting right here.

It was *naturales* Amado chose to perform with this bull. He had not done many this season. The last refuge of his detractors was that he could not do *naturales* well. So here on this day he gave his demonstration. Watch if you can.

He began his *faena* by making no exploratory pass, no *pase de la muerte*, no *derechazos*, he never chopped, no, he went up to this sweet bull and started his *faena* with a series of *naturales*, with a series of five *naturales* which were all linked and all beautiful and had the Plaza in pandemonium because where could he go from there—how does Jack E. Leonard top himself?—and Amado came up sweetly to the bull, and did five more *naturales* as good as the first five, and then did five more without moving from his spot—they were superb—and then furled his *muleta* until it was the size of this page, and he passed the bull five more times in the same way, the horns going around his left wrist. The man and the bull looked in love with each other. And then after these 20 *naturales*, Amado did five more with almost no *muleta* at all, five series of five *naturales* had he performed. It is not much easier than making love 25 times in a row, and then he knelt and kissed the bull on the forehead he was so happy, and got up delicately, and went to the *barrera* for his sword, came back, profiled to get ready for the kill. Everyone was waiting on a fuse. If he managed to kill on the first *estocada* this could well be the best *faena* anyone had ever seen a *novillero* perform, who knew, it was all near to unbelievable, and then just as he profiled, the bull charged prematurely, and Amado, determined to get the kill, did not skip away but held ground, received the charge, stood there with the sword, turned the bull's head with the *muleta*, and the bull impaled himself on the point of the *torero*'s blade which went right into the proper space between the shoulders, and the bull ran right up on it into his death, took several steps to the side, gave a toss of his head at heaven, and fell. Amado had killed *recibiendo*. He had killed standing still, receiving the bull while the bull charged. No one had seen that in years. So they gave him everything that day, ears, tail, *vueltas* without limit—they were ready to give him the bull.

He concluded the summer in a burst of honors. He had great fights. Afterward they gave him a day where he fought six bulls all by himself, and he went on to take his *alternativa* and become a full-fledged matador. But he was a Mexican down to the bones. The honors all turned damp for him. I was not there the day he fought six bulls, I had had to go back to America and never saw him fight again. I heard about him only in letters and in bullfighting newspapers. But the day he took on the six bulls, I was told, he did not have a single good fight, and the day he took his *alternativa* to become a matador, both his bulls went out alive, a disgrace too great even for Amado. He fought a seventh bull. Gypsy magic might save him again. But the bull was big and dull and El Loco had no luck and no magic and just succeeded in killing him in a bad difficult dull fight. It was obvious he was afraid of the big bulls. So he relinquished his *alternativa* and went back to the provinces to try to regain his reputation and his nerve. And no one ever heard much of him again. Or at least I never did, but then I have not been back to Mexico. Now I suspect I'm one of the very few who remember the happiness of seeing him fight. He was so bad when he was bad that he gave the impression you could fight a bull yourself and do no worse. So when he was good, you felt as if you were good, too, and that was something no other torero ever gave me, for when they were good they looked impenetrable, they were like gods, but when Beloved Remington was good, the whole human race was good—he spoke of the great distance a man can go from the worst in himself to the best, and that finally is what the bullfight could be all about, for in dark bloody tropical lands possessed of poverty and desert and swamp, filth and treachery, slovenliness, and the fat lizards of all the worst lust, the excretory lust to shove one's own poison into others, the one thing which can keep the sweet nerve of life alive, is the knowledge that a man cannot be judged by what he is every day, but only in his greatest moment, for that is the moment when he shows what he was intended to be. It is a romantic self-pitying impractical approach to the 20th century's demand for predictable ethics, high production, dependability of function and categorization of impulse, but it is the Latin approach. Their allegiance is to the genius of the blood. So they judge a man by what he is at his best. By that logic, I will always have love for El Loco because he taught me how to love the bullfight, which is to say he taught me something about the mystery of form. And where is a writer or a lover without a knowledge of what goes on behind that cloth where shapes are born? *Olé*, Amado!

The Fisherman and the Jinn

fiction by ROBERT COOVER

The old fisherman has had another shitty day, hauling up the dead detritus of the sea. He's already cast his net three times; four's his limit. Why? He doesn't remember, but that's it, one to go. He tucks up his shirttails, wades in waist-deep, casts again for the thousand-thousandth time, give or take a throw or two. He waits for the net to sink. He can feel fish swimming between his legs, tickling his cods. Praise God, the bountiful sea. But this time his net snags on the bottom. It's not fair. He works his scrawny old ass to the bone, and what does he have to show for it? Wet rags and an empty belly. Even if he caught a fish, what would he do with it? He'd sell it to a rich man, go hungry and cast his net again. His existence is a ceaseless punishment. He throws off his clothes and dives under. The net's about all he's got in the world; he has to rescue it.

This time it has caught a brass jar with a lead stopper. Looks old, maybe he can sell it in the copper market. It's heavy, not easy to drag it out of there; he nearly drowns trying, and the net gets shredded. Maybe there's a jinn inside, he thinks. If he doesn't kill me, maybe I can wish for enough money to be free from these stupid labors, eat other people's fish. Or get my youth back, the old dangler functioning again. New teeth. The apple of Samarkand to cure my crotch itch. A young, beautiful wife who talks less. A rich princess maybe. Rule a kingdom. Ride horses. Kill a few people. Sure enough, the lead seal has been stamped with an ancient seal ring. For once in his life he's in luck. He gets out his knife but then has second thoughts. If there's a jinn bottled up inside, squashed in there for centuries, he could be in a pretty explosive mood. Life's shit, sure, but does he really want to end it and no doubt in some horrible way only jinns can imagine? But what other way does it ever end? Even now he can feel things in his bones that suggest bad times coming. Best to take a chance. He scrapes away at the lead stopper until he pries it loose.

What comes out might be smoke, it might be dust, smells like death. Maybe just somebody's ashes. But the muck continues to curl out of the neck of the jar, slowly rising into the sky over him and spreading out over the sea, more and more of it, until that's all he can see. The sun's blotted out, the sea's brighter than the sky, it's as if the world is turning upside down. Then the dark mist gathers and takes shape, and suddenly, with a great clap of thunder that sets his knees knocking, there's a monstrous jinn standing there, feet planted in the shallow waters at the shore, head in the clouds, eyes blazing like there's a fire in its head, its teeth big as gravestones, gnashing. Sparks fly. If the old fisherman had any boots, he'd be quaking in them. As it is, naked still from his dive, he's trembling all over like a thin, pale jellyfish. The jinn, in a pent-up rage, kicks the brass jar far out to sea. There goes his ticket to the copper market. The jinn might be talking to him, but he can't hear a thing. He's pissing himself with terror, his ears are popping, his tongue is dry, his jaws are locked as if hammered together. "What? What?" he croaks at last. "I said," says the jinn, his voice like the wind on a violent day, "make a wish, Master! Choose carefully, for I've time for only one!"

Master? Ah, it's true then, the old stories, it's really happening. He's just been making a list; he can't remember it. Wealth, yes, heaps of it. But of what use is wealth if he dies before he can spend it? Likewise bedding down with princesses. Marrying a princess without youth would be like fishing with a torn net. But wishing for youth without a princess would be like casting his net on the desert. Can he wish for more wishes?

"You cannot, Master, as I will not be here to fulfill them! Make haste while there's time!"

"Oh, I don't know! I can't think! I wasn't ready for this!"

The jinn is bigger and scarier than ever. He has long snaky hair and claws where his fingernails should be. But he's harder to see. It's as if his edges are dissolving. There's less of him even as there's more of him. Come on, think, think! The end of all disease? World peace? No, fuck the world! It's his turn! How about healthy and alert and virile for at least 200 years: Is that one wish or several? And what would happen when the 200 years were up, how could he face that? What about simply a long life, get it going, what the hell, see what happens? He knows what happens. Just prolonging the misery. Some sort of toy? A flying carpet? An invisible cloak? A bottomless beer jug?

"Hurry, Master! Before it's too late!"

"I'm too old to hurry, damn it!"

The jinn is huge now. Almost as big as the cloud from which he was formed. But you can see the sun shining through him, and the fire in his eyes has dimmed to a flicker. His voice has become thin and echoey, his face is losing its features, his extensions are growing vague, bits and pieces blowing away when the wind blows. Which may be only his own heavy breathing.

"I know! Power! I want power! No! I want endless joy!"

"What...?"

"Endless joy! I want——!"

"I can't *he-ea-ar you-u-u-u*...!"

"Wait! Stay where you are! Joy! Just make me happy!"

Nothing left of the jinn now but a few beardy wisps floating in the breeze, and then they too fade away.

"Please! Come back, damn it!" he cries. "At least mend my net!"

But the jinn is gone. Not a trace. It's too late. Praise God, fucked again. The old fisherman hauls on his shirt with its wet tails, rolls up the rotten shreds of his net. On the sand, he spies part of the stamped lead seal. Ah. So he got something out of the encounter after all. A story. You see this lead seal? Let me tell you what happened. Trouble is, he's told too many stories like it before, none of them true, so no one will believe him now. Why would they? He wouldn't believe himself. They might even put him away. Lock him up as an old loony. He is an old loony; he wouldn't have an argument. And even if they did believe him, they'd want to know what he did with the jar. They'd think he stole it and would cut off his hands for thieving. Fuck that. He pitches the lead seal into the sea. He'll repair his net and have another go tomorrow. Maybe he'll catch a mermaid.

The Handsomest Drowned Man in the World

fiction by GABRIEL GARCÍA MÁRQUEZ

The first children who saw the dark and slinky bulge approaching through the sea let themselves think it was an enemy ship. Then they saw it had no flags nor masts and they thought it was a whale. But when it washed up on the beach, they removed the clumps of seaweed, the jellyfish tentacles and the remains of fish and flotsam and only then did they see that it was a drowned man. And so they made a toy of him.

They had been playing with him all afternoon, burying him in the sand and digging him up again, when someone chanced to see them and spread the alarm in the village. The men who carried him to the nearest house noticed that he weighed more than any dead man they had ever known, almost as much as a horse, and they said to each other that maybe he'd been floating too long and the water had got into his bones. When they laid him on the floor, they said he'd been taller than all other men, because there was barely enough room for him in the house, but they thought that maybe the ability to keep on growing after death was part of the nature of certain drowned men. He had the smell of the sea about him and only his shape gave one to suppose that it was the corpse of a human being, because the skin was covered with a crust of mud and scales.

They did not have to clean off his face to know that the dead man was a stranger. The village was made up of only 20-odd wooden houses that had stone courtyards with no flowers and that were spread about on the end of a desertlike cape. There was so little land that mothers always

43

went about with the fear that the wind would carry off their children and the few dead that the years had caused among them had to be thrown off the cliffs. But the sea was calm and bountiful and all the men fit into seven boats. So when they found the drowned man, they simply had to look at one another to see that they were all there.

That night they did not go out to work at sea. While the men went to find out if anyone was missing in neighboring villages, the women stayed behind to care for the drowned man. They took the mud off with grass swabs, they removed the underwater stones entangled in his hair and they scraped the crust off with tools used for scaling fish. As they were doing that, they noticed that the vegetation on him came from faraway oceans and deep water and that his clothes were in tatters, as if he had sailed through labyrinths of coral. They noticed, too, that he bore his death with pride, for he did not have the lonely look of other drowned men who came out of the sea nor that haggard, needy look of men who drowned in rivers. But only when they finished cleaning him off did they become aware of the kind of man he was, and it left them breathless. Not only was he the tallest, strongest, most virile and best-built man they had ever seen but, even though they were looking at him, there was no room for him in their imagination.

They could not find a bed in the village large enough to lay him on nor was there a table solid enough to use for his wake. The tallest men's holiday pants would not fit him nor the fattest ones' Sunday shirts nor the shoes of the one with the biggest feet. Fascinated by his huge size and his beauty, the women then decided to make him some pants from a large piece of sail and a shirt from some bridal Brabant linen, so that he could continue through his death with dignity. As they sewed, sitting in a circle and gazing at the corpse between stitches, it seemed to them that the wind had never been so steady nor the sea so restless as on that night and they supposed that the change had something to do with the dead man. They thought that if that magnificent man had lived in the village, his house would have had the widest doors, the highest ceiling and the strongest floor, his bedstead would have been made from a midship frame held together by iron bolts and his wife would have been the happiest woman. They thought that he would have had so much authority that he could have drawn fish out of the sea simply by calling their names and that he would have put so much work into his land that springs would have burst forth from among the rocks, so that he would have been able to plant flowers on the cliffs. They secretly compared him with their own men, thinking that for all their lives, theirs were incapable of doing what he could do in one night, and they ended up dismissing them deep in their hearts as the weakest, meanest and most useless creatures on earth. They were wandering through that maze of fantasy when the oldest woman, who as the oldest had looked upon the drowned man with more compassion than passion, sighed:

"He has the face of someone called Esteban."

It was true. Most of them had only to take another look at him to see that he could not have any other name. The more stubborn among them, who were the youngest, still lived for a few hours with the illusion that when they put his clothes on and he lay among the flowers, his name might be Lautaro. But it was a vain illusion. There had not been enough canvas, the poorly cut and worse-sewn pants were too tight and the hidden strength of his heart popped the buttons on his shirt. After midnight, the whistling of the wind died down and the sea fell into its Wednesday drowsiness. The silence put an end to any last doubts: He was Esteban. The women who had dressed him, who had combed his hair, had cut his nails and shaved him were unable to hold back a shudder of pity when they had to resign themselves to his being dragged along the ground. It was then that they understood how unhappy he must have been with that huge body, since it bothered him even after death. They could see him in life, condemned to going through doors sideways, cracking his head on crossbeams, remaining on his feet during visits, not knowing what to do with his soft, pink, sea-lion hands while the lady of the house looked for her most resistant chair and begged him, frightened to death, sit here, Esteban, please, and he, leaning against the wall, smiling, don't bother ma'am, I'm fine where I am, his heels raw and his back roasted from having done the same thing so many times whenever he paid a visit, don't bother, ma'am, I'm fine where I am, just to avoid the embarrassment of breaking up the chair and never knowing, perhaps, that the ones who said, don't go, Esteban, at least wait till the coffee's ready, were the ones who later on would whisper, the big boob finally left, how nice, the handsome fool has gone. That was what the women were thinking beside the body a little before dawn. Later when they covered his face with a handkerchief so that the light would not bother him, he looked so forever dead, so defenseless, so much like their men that the first furrows of tears opened in their hearts. It was one of the younger ones who began the weeping. The others, coming to, went from sighs to wails, and the more they sobbed, the more they felt like weeping, because the drowned man was becoming all the more Esteban for them, and so they wept so much, for he was the most destitute, most peaceful and most obliging man on earth, poor Esteban. So when the men returned with the news that the drowned man was not from the neighboring villages either, the women felt an emptiness of jubilation in the midst of their tears.

"Praise the Lord," they sighed, "he's ours!"

The men thought the fuss was only womanish frivolity. Fatigued because of the difficult nighttime inquiries, all they wanted was to get rid of the bother of the newcomer once and for all, before the sun grew strong on that arid, windless day. They improvised a litter with the remains of foremasts and gaffs, tying it together with rigging so that it would bear the weight of the body until they reached the cliffs. They wanted to tie the anchor from a cargo ship to him, so that he would sink easily into the deepest waves, where fish are blind and divers die of nostalgia, and bad currents would not bring him back to shore, as had happened with other bodies. But the more they hurried, the more the women thought of ways to waste time. They walked about like startled hens, pecking with the sea charms on their breasts, some interfering on one side to put a scapular of the good wind on the drowned man, some on the other side to put a wrist compass on him, and after a great deal of get away from there, woman, stay out of the way, look, you almost made me fall on top of the dead man, the men began to feel mistrust in their livers and started grumbling about why so many main-altar decorations for a stranger, because no matter how many nails and holy-water jars he had on him, the sharks would chew him all the same, but the women kept piling on their junk relics, running back and forth, stumbling, while they released in sighs what they did not in tears, so that the men finally exploded with since when has there ever been such a fuss over a drifting corpse, a drowned nobody, a piece of cold meat. One of the women, mortified by so much lack of care, then removed the handkerchief from the dead man's face and the men were left breathless, too.

He was Esteban. It was not necessary to repeat it for them to recognize him. If they had been told Sir Walter Raleigh, even they might have been impressed with his gringo accent, the macaw on his shoulder, his cannibal-killing blunderbuss, but there could be only one Esteban in the world and there he was, stretched out like a sperm whale, shoeless, wearing the pants of an undersized child and with those stony nails that had to be cut with a knife. They had only to take the handkerchief off his face to see that he was ashamed, that it was not his fault that he was so big or so heavy or so handsome, and if he had known that this was going to happen, he would have looked for a more discreet place to drown in, seriously, I even would have tied the anchor from a galleon around my neck and staggered off a cliff like someone who doesn't like things, in order not to be upsetting people now with this Wednesday dead body, as you people say, in order not to be bothering anyone with this filthy piece of cold meat that doesn't have anything to do with me. There was so much truth in his manner that even the most mistrustful men, the ones who felt the bitterness of endless nights at sea fearing that their women would tire of dreaming about them and begin to dream of drowned men, even they and others who were harder still shuddered in the marrow of their bones at Esteban's sincerity.

That was how they came to hold the most splendid funeral they could conceive of for an abandoned drowned man. Some women who had gone to get flowers in the neighboring villages returned with other women, who could not believe what they had been told, and those women went back for more flowers when they saw the dead man, and they brought more and more, until there were so many flowers and so many people that it was hard to walk about. At the final moment, it pained them to return him to the waters as an orphan and they chose a father and mother from among the best people, and aunts and uncles and cousins, so that through him all the inhabitants of the village became kinsmen. Some sailors who heard the weeping from a distance went off course and people heard of one who had himself tied to the mainmast, remembering ancient fables about sirens. While they fought for the privilege of carrying him on their shoulders along the steep escarpment by the cliffs, men and women became aware for the first time of the desolation of their streets, the dryness of their courtyards, the narrowness of their dreams as they faced the splendor and the beauty of their drowned man. They let him go without an anchor, in order that he might come back if he wished and whenever he wished, and they all held their breath for the fraction of centuries the body took to fall into the abyss. They did not need to look at one another to realize that they were no longer all present, that they would never be. But they also knew that everything would be different from then on, that their houses would have wider doors, higher ceilings and stronger floors, so that Esteban's memory could go everywhere without bumping into the beams and so that no one in the future would dare whisper the big boob finally died, too bad, the handsome fool has finally died, because they were going to paint their house fronts gay colors to make Esteban's memory eternal and they were going to break their backs digging for springs among the stones and planting flowers on the cliffs. In future years, at dawn the passengers on great liners would awaken, suffocated by the smell of gardens on the high seas, and the captain would have to come down from the bridge in his dress uniform, with his astrolabe, his polestar and his row of war medals and, pointing to the promontory of roses on the horizon, he would say in 14 languages, look there, where the wind is so peaceful now that it's gone to sleep beneath the beds, over there, where the sun's so bright that the sunflowers don't know which way to turn, yes, over there, that's Esteban's village.

—*Translated from the Spanish by Gregory Rabassa*

"I assume you'll be wanting a double?"

Souvenir

fiction by J.G. BALLARD

O n the morning after the storm the body of a drowned giant was washed ashore on the beach five miles to the northwest of the city. The first news of its arrival was brought by a nearby farmer and subsequently confirmed by the local newspaper reporters and the police. Despite this the majority of people, myself among them, remained skeptical, but the return of more and more eyewitnesses attesting to the vast size of the giant was finally too much for our curiosity. The library where my colleagues and I were carrying out our research was almost deserted when we set off for the coast shortly after two o'clock, and throughout the day people continued to leave their offices and shops as accounts of the giant circulated around the city.

By the time we reached the dunes above the beach a substantial crowd had gathered, and we could see the body lying in the shallow water 200 yards away. At first the estimates of its size seemed greatly exaggerated. It was then at low tide, and almost all the giant's body was exposed, but he appeared to be little larger than a basking shark. He lay on his back with his arms at his sides, in an attitude of repose, as if asleep on the mirror of wet sand, the reflection of his blanched skin fading as the water receded. In the clear sunlight his body glistened like the white plumage of a sea bird.

Puzzled by this spectacle, and dissatisfied with the matter-of-fact explanations of the crowd, my friends and I stepped down from the dunes onto the shingle. Everyone seemed reluctant to approach the giant, but half an hour later two fishermen in wading boots walked out across the sand. As their diminutive figures neared the recumbent body a sudden hubbub of conversation broke out among the spectators. The two men were completely dwarfed by the giant. Although his heels were partly submerged in the sand, the feet rose to at least twice the fishermen's height, and we immediately realized that this drowned leviathan had the mass and dimensions of the largest sperm whale.

50

Three fishing smacks had arrived on the scene and with keels raised remained a quarter of a mile offshore, the crews watching from the bows. Their discretion deterred the spectators on the shore from wading out across the sand. Impatiently everyone stepped down from the dunes and waited on the shingle slopes, eager for a closer view. Around the margins of the figure the sand had been washed away, forming a hollow, as if the giant had fallen out of the sky. The two fishermen were standing between the immense plinths of the feet, waving to us like tourists among the columns of some water-lapped temple on the Nile. For a moment I feared that the giant was merely asleep and might suddenly stir and clap his heels together, but his glazed eyes stared skyward, unaware of the minuscule replicas of himself between his feet.

The fishermen then began a circuit of the corpse, strolling past the long white flanks of the legs. After a pause to examine the fingers of the supine hand, they disappeared from sight between the arm and chest, then re-emerged to survey the head, shielding their eyes as they gazed up at its Grecian profile. The shallow forehead, straight high-bridged nose and curling lips reminded me of a Roman copy of Praxiteles, and the elegantly formed cartouches of the nostrils emphasized the resemblance to sculpture.

Abruptly there was a shout from the crowd, and a hundred arms pointed toward the sea. With a start I saw that one of the fishermen had climbed onto the giant's chest and was now strolling about and signaling to the shore. There was a roar of surprise and triumph from the crowd, lost in a rushing avalanche of shingle as everyone surged forward across the sand.

As we approached the recumbent figure, which was lying in a pool of water the size of a field, our excited chatter fell away again, subdued by the huge physical dimensions of this dead colossus. He was stretched out at a slight angle to the shore, his legs carried nearer the beach, and this foreshortening had disguised his true length. Despite the two fishermen standing on his abdomen, the crowd formed itself into a wide circle, groups of people tentatively advancing toward the hands and feet.

My companions and I walked around the seaward side of the giant, whose hips and thorax towered above us like the hull of a stranded ship. His pearl-colored skin, distended by immersion in salt water, masked the contours of the enormous muscles and tendons. We passed below the left knee, which was flexed slightly, threads of damp seaweed clinging to its sides. Draped loosely across the midriff, and preserving a tenuous propriety, was a shawl of heavy open-weave material, bleached to a pale yellow by the water. A strong odor of brine came from the garment as it steamed in the sun, mingled with the sweet, potent scent of the giant's skin.

We stopped by his shoulder and gazed up at the motionless profile. The lips were parted slightly, the open eye cloudy and occluded, as if injected with some blue milky liquid, but the delicate arches of the nostrils and eyebrows invested the face with an ornate charm that belied the brutish power of the chest and shoulders.

The ear was suspended in midair over our heads like a sculptured doorway. As I raised my hand to touch the pendulous lobe, someone appeared over the edge of the forehead and shouted down at me. Startled by this apparition, I stepped back, and then saw that a group of youths had climbed up onto the face and were jostling each other in and out of the orbits.

People were now clambering all over the giant, whose reclining arms provided a double stairway. From the palms they walked along the forearms to the elbows and then crawled over the distended belly of the biceps to the flat promenade of the pectoral muscles which covered the upper half of the smooth, hairless chest. From here they climbed up onto the face, hand over hand along the lips and nose, or forayed down the abdomen to meet others who had straddled the ankles and were patrolling the twin columns of the thighs.

We continued our circuit through the crowd and stopped to examine the outstretched right hand. A small pool of water lay in the palm, like the residue of another world, now being kicked away by the people ascending the arm. I tried to read the palmlines that grooved the skin, searching for some clue to the giant's character, but the distention of the tissues had almost obliterated them, carrying away all trace of the giant's identity and his last, tragic predicament. The huge muscles and wristbones of the hand seemed to deny any sensitivity to their owner, but the delicate flexion of the fingers and the well-tended nails, each cut symmetrically to within six inches of the quick, argued a certain refinement of temperament, illustrated in the Grecian features of the face, on which the townsfolk were now sitting like flies.

One youth was even standing, arms wavering at his sides, on the very tip of the nose, shouting down at his companions, but the face of the giant still retained its massive composure.

Returning to the shore, we sat down on the shingle and watched the continuous stream of people arriving from the city. Some six or seven fishing boats had collected offshore, and their crews waded in through the shallow water for a closer look at this enormous storm catch. Later a party of police appeared and made a halfhearted attempt to cordon off the beach, but after walking up to the recumbent figure, any such thoughts left their minds, and they went off together with bemused backward glances.

An hour later there were a thousand people present on the beach, at least 200 of them standing or sitting on the giant, crowded along his arms and legs or circulating in a ceaseless melee across his chest and stomach. A large gang of youths occupied the head, toppling each other off the cheeks and sliding down the smooth planes of the jaw. Two or three straddled the nose, and another crawled into one of the nostrils, from which he emitted barking noises like a demented dog.

That afternoon the police returned and cleared a way through the crowd for a party of scientific experts—authorities on gross anatomy and marine biology—from the university. The gang of youths and most of the people on the giant climbed down, leaving behind a few hardy spirits perched on the tips of the toes and on the forehead. The experts strode around the giant, heads nodding in vigorous consultation, preceded by the policemen who pushed back the press of spectators. When they reached the outstretched hand, the senior officer offered to assist them up onto the palm, but the experts hastily demurred.

After they returned to the shore, the crowd once more climbed onto the giant, and was in full possession when we left at five o'clock, covering the arms and legs like a dense flock of gulls sitting on the corpse of a large fish.

• • •

I next visited the beach three days later. My friends at the library had returned to their work and delegated to me the task of keeping the giant under observation and preparing a report. Perhaps they sensed my particular interest in the case, and it was certainly true that I was eager to return to the beach. There was nothing necrophilic about this, for to all intents the giant was still alive for me, indeed more alive than many of the people watching him. What I found so fascinating was partly his immense scale, the huge volumes of space occupied by his arms and legs, which seemed to confirm the identity of my own miniature limbs, but above all, the mere categorical fact of his existence. Whatever else in our lives might be open to doubt, the giant, dead or alive, existed in an absolute sense, providing a glimpse into a world of similar absolutes of which we spectators on the beach were such imperfect and puny copies.

When I arrived at the beach the crowd was considerably smaller, and some 200 or 300 people sat on the shingle, picnicking and watching the

SOUVENIR

groups of visitors who walked out across the sand. The successive tides
had carried the giant nearer the shore, swinging his head and shoulders
toward the beach, so that he seemed doubly to gain in size, his huge body
dwarfing the fishing boats beached beside his feet. The uneven contours
of the beach had pushed his spine into a slight arch, expanding his chest
and tilting back the head, forcing him into a more expressly heroic posture. The combined effects of sea water and the tumefaction of the tissues
had given the face a sleeker and less youthful look. Although the vast
proportions of the features made it impossible to assess the age and
character of the giant, on my previous visit his classically modeled
mouth and nose suggested that he had been a young man of discreet
and modest temper. Now, however, he appeared to be at least in early
middle age. The puffy cheeks, thicker nose and temples and narrowing eyes gave him a look of well-fed maturity that even now hinted at a
growing corruption to come.

This accelerated postmortem development of the giant's character,
as if the latent elements of his personality had gained sufficient momentum during his life to discharge themselves in a brief final resume,
continued to fascinate me. It marked the beginning of the giant's sur-
render to that all-demanding system of time in which the rest of humanity finds itself, and of which, like the million twisted ripples of a
fragmented whirlpool, our finite lives are the concluding products. I
took up my position on the shingle directly opposite the giant's head,
from where I could see the new arrivals and the children clambering
over the legs and arms.

Among the morning's visitors were a number of men in leather jackets and cloth caps, who peered up critically at the giant with a professional eye, pacing out his dimensions and making rough calculations in
the sand with spars of driftwood. I assumed them to be from the public
works department and other municipal bodies, no doubt wondering
how to dispose of this monster.

Several rather more smartly attired individuals, circus proprietors
and the like, also appeared on the scene and strolled slowly around
the giant, hands deeep in the pockets of their long overcoats, saying
nothing to one another. Evidently its bulk was too great even for their
matchless enterprise. After they had gone the children continued to
run up and down the arms and legs, and the youths wrestled with each
other over the supine face, the damp sand from their feet covering the
white skin.

• • •

54

The following day I deliberately postponed my visit until the late afternoon, and when I arrived there were fewer than 50 or 60 people sitting on the shingle. The giant had been carried still closer to the shore, and was now little more than 75 yards away, his feet crushing the palisade of a rotting breakwater. The slope of the firmer sand tilted his body toward the sea, the bruised swollen face averted in an almost conscious gesture. I sat down on a large metal winch which had been shackled to a concrete caisson above the shingle, and looked down at the recumbent figure.

His blanched skin had now lost its pearly translucence and was spattered with dirty sand which replaced that washed away by the night tide. Clumps of seaweed filled the intervals between the fingers, and a collection of litter and cuttlebones lay in the crevices below the hips and knees. But despite this, and the continuous thickening of his features, the giant still retained his magnificent Homeric stature. The enormous breadth of the shoulders, and the huge columns of the arms and legs, still carried the figure into another dimension, and the giant seemed a more authentic image of one of the drowned Argonauts or heroes of the *Odyssey* than the conventional portrait previously in my mind.

I stepped down onto the sand and walked between the pools of water toward the giant. Two small boys were sitting in the well of the ear, and at the far end a solitary youth stood perched high on one of the toes, surveying me as I approached. As I had hoped when delaying my visit, no one else paid any attention to me, and the people on the shore remained huddled beneath their coats.

The giant's supine right hand was covered with broken shells and sand, in which a score of footprints were visible. The rounded bulk of the hip towered above me, cutting off all sight of the sea. The sweetly acrid odor I had noticed before was now more pungent, and through the opaque skin I could see the serpentine coils of congealed blood vessels. However repellent it seemed, this ceaseless metamorphosis, a macabre life-in-death, alone permitted me to set foot on the corpse.

Using the jutting thumb as a stair rail, I climbed up onto the palm and began my ascent. The skin was harder than I expected, barely yielding to my weight. Quickly I walked up the sloping forearm and the bulging balloon of the biceps. The face of the drowned giant loomed to my right, the cavernous nostrils and huge flanks of the cheeks like the cone of some freakish volcano.

Safely rounding the shoulder, I stepped out onto the broad promenade of the chest, across which the bony ridges of the rib cage lay like huge rafters. The white skin was dappled by the darkening bruises of countless footprints, in which the patterns of individual heel marks were clearly visible. Someone had built a small sand castle on the center of the sternum, and I climbed onto this partly demolished structure to get a better view of the face.

The two children had now scaled the ear and were pulling themselves into the right orbit, whose blue globe, completely occluded by some milk-colored fluid, gazed sightlessly past their miniature forms. Seen obliquely from below, the face was devoid of all grace and repose, the drawn mouth and raised chin propped up by gigantic slings of muscles resembling the torn prow of a colossal wreck. For the first time I became aware of the extremity of this last physical agony of the giant, no less painful for his unawareness of the collapsing musculature and tissues. The absolute isolation of the ruined figure, cast like an abandoned ship upon the empty shore, almost out of sound of the waves, transformed his face into a mask of exhaustion and helplessness.

As I stepped forward, my foot sank into a trough of soft tissue, and a gust of fetid gas blew through an aperture between the ribs. Retreating from the fouled air, which hung like a cloud over my head, I turned toward the sea to clear my lungs. To my surprise I saw that the giant's left hand had been amputated.

I stared with shocked bewilderment at the blackening stump, while the solitary youth reclining on his aerial perch a hundred feet away surveyed me with a sanguinary eye.

● ● ●

This was only the first of a sequence of depredations. I spent the following two days in the library, for some reason reluctant to visit the shore, aware that I had probably witnessed the approaching end of a magnificent illusion. When I next crossed the dunes and set foot on the shingle, the giant was little more than 20 yards away, and with this close proximity to the rough pebbles all traces had vanished of the magic which once surrounded his distant wave-washed form. Despite the giant's immense size, the bruises and dirt that covered his body made him appear merely human in scale, his vast dimensions only increasing his vulnerability.

His right hand and foot had been removed, dragged up the slope and trundled away by cart. After questioning the small group of people huddled by the breakwater, I gathered that a fertilizer company and a cattle-food manufacturer were responsible.

The giant's remaining foot rose into the air, a steel hawser fixed to the large toe, evidently in preparation for the following day. The surrounding beach had been disturbed by a score of workmen, and deep ruts marked the ground where the hands and foot had been hauled away. A dark brackish fluid leaked from the stumps, and stained the sand and the white cones of the cuttlefish. As I walked down the shingle I noticed that a number of jocular slogans, swastikas and other signs had been cut into the gray skin, as if the mutilation of this motionless colossus had released a sudden flood of repressed spite. The lobe of one of the ears was pierced by a spear of timber, and a small fire had burned out in the center of the chest, blackening the surrounding skin. The fine wood ash was still being scattered by the wind.

A foul smell enveloped the cadaver, the undisguisable signature of putrefaction, which had at last driven away the usual gathering of youths. I returned to the shingle and climbed up onto the winch. The giant's swollen cheeks had now almost closed his eyes, drawing the lips back in a monumental gape. The once-straight Grecian nose had been twisted and flattened, stamped into the ballooning face by the force of countless heels.

When I visited the beach the following day I found, almost with relief, that the head had been removed.

● ● ●

Some weeks elapsed before I made my next journey to the beach, and by then the human likeness I had noticed earlier had vanished again. On close inspection the recumbent thorax and abdomen were unmistakably manlike, but as each of the limbs was chopped off, first at the knee and elbow, and then at shoulder and thigh, the carcass resembled that of any headless sea animal—whale or whale shark. With this loss of identity, and the few traces of personality that had clung tenuously to the figure, the interest of the spectators expired, and the foreshore was deserted except for an elderly beachcomber and the watchman sitting in the doorway of the contractor's hut.

A loose wooden scaffolding had been erected around the carcass, from which a dozen ladders swung in the wind, and the surrounding sand was littered with coils of rope, long metal-handled knives and grappling irons, the pebbles oily with blood and pieces of bone and skin.

I nodded to the watchman, who regarded me dourly over his brazier of burning coke. The whole area was pervaded by the pungent smell of huge squares of blubber being simmered in a vat behind the hut.

Both the thighbones had been removed, with the assistance of a small crane draped in the gauzelike fabric which had once covered the waist of the giant, and the open sockets gaped like barn doors. The upper arms, collarbones and pudenda had likewise been dispatched. What remained of the skin over the thorax and abdomen had been marked out in parallel strips with a tarbrush, and the first five or six sections had been pared away from the midriff, revealing the great arch of the rib cage.

As I left, a flock of gulls wheeled down from the sky and alighted on the beach, picking at the stained sand with ferocious cries.

● ● ●

Several months later, when the news of his arrival had been generally forgotten, various pieces of the body of the dismembered giant began to reappear all over the city. Most of these were bones, which the fertilizer manufacturers had found too difficult to crush, and their massive size, and the huge tendons and discs of cartilage attached to their joints, immediately identified them. For some reason, these disembodied fragments seemed better to convey the essence of the giant's original magnificence than the bloated appendages that had been subsequently amputated. As I looked across the road at the premises of the largest wholesale merchants in the meat market, I recognized the two enormous thighbones on either side of the doorway. They towered over the porters' heads like the threatening megaliths of some primitive druidical religion, and I had a sudden vision of the giant climbing to his knees upon these bare bones and striding away through the streets of the city, picking up the scattered fragments of himself on his return journey to the sea.

A few days later I saw the left humerus lying in the entrance to one of the shipyards. In the same week the mummified right hand was exhibited on a carnival float during the annual pageant of the guilds.

The lower jaw, typically, found its way to the museum of natural history. The remainder of the skull has disappeared, but is probably still lurking in the waste grounds or private gardens of the city—quite recently, while sailing down the river, I noticed two ribs of the giant forming a decorative arch in a waterside garden, possibly confused with the jawbones of a whale. A large square of tanned and tattooed skin, the size of an Indian blanket, forms a back cloth to the dolls and masks in a novelty shop near the amusement park, and I have no doubt that elsewhere in the city, in the hotels or golf clubs, the mummified nose or ears of the giant hang from the wall above a fireplace. As for the immense pizzle, this ends its days in the freak museum of a circus which travels up and down the northwest. This monumental apparatus, stunning in its proportions and sometime potency, occupies a complete booth to itself. The irony is that it is wrongly identified as that of a whale, and indeed most people, even those who first saw him cast up on the shore after the storm, now remember the giant, if at all, as a large sea beast.

The remainder of the skeleton, stripped of all flesh, still rests on the seashore, the clutter of bleached ribs like the timbers of a derelict ship. The contractor's hut, the crane and scaffolding have been removed, and the sand being driven into the bay along the coast has buried the pelvis and backbone. In the winter the high curved bones are deserted, battered by the breaking waves, but in the summer they provide an excellent perch for the sea-wearying gulls.

"Oh, damn! It's another bloody penguin!"

Saul Bellow

If we judge our artists by the awards they receive, then Saul Bellow must be America's best living writer. He's won three National Book Awards (for *The Adventures of Augie March* in 1953, *Herzog* in 1964 and *Mr. Sammler's Planet* in 1970), the Pulitzer Prize (*Humboldt's Gift*, 1975), the Gold Medal for the Novel (1977), the National Institute of Arts and Letters Award (1952), the Friends of Literature Fiction Award, the James L. Dow, the Prix International, the Fomentor Award (for *Herzog*), the Croix de Chevalier (1968) and the 1976 Nobel Prize for Literature. He's received a Guggenheim Fellowship and a Ford Foundation grant and, in 1983, he was made a commander of the French Legion of Honor.

While Bellow has said that writers seldom wish other writers well, writers have come around to acknowledge his preeminent position. Philip Roth calls him "the grand old man of American Jewish writers" as well as "the country's most accomplished working novelist." John Updike thinks he's "the best portraitist writing American fiction." Irving Howe dubbed him "the best living American novelist." Joyce Carol Oates considers him a genius and places him "off the scale of even Truman Capote, Thomas Pynchon or Thomas Wolfe."

While Bellow could read Hebrew before he entered kindergarten (his mother hoped he would be a Talmudic scholar), his writing talent wasn't truly recognized until he was in his mid-20s, when *Partisan Review* first published some of his stories. His parents were Russian immigrants who moved in 1913 with their two sons and a daughter to Lachine, a suburb of Montreal. Their third son, Saul, was born there on June 10, 1915. At the age of eight he was diagnosed with a respiratory infection and had to be hospitalized for six months. Not long after his recovery the family moved to Chicago. His father, Abraham, worked in a bakery, sold wood scraps for fuel and did some bootlegging. Saul's mother, Liza, died when Saul was 17, before he entered the University of Chicago. After two years there he transferred to Northwestern University, where he majored in anthropology and sociology. In 1937 he married Anita Goshkin and got a job writing literary biographies for the federally funded WPA Writer's Project. During World War Two he was classified 2A because of a hernia and, after surgery, he joined the merchant marine. He sold a novel called *The Very Dark Trees*, but when the publisher delayed it because of the war, Bellow decided it wasn't good enough and destroyed it. He then wrote *Dangling Man*, about a young man waiting to be drafted, which earned him a $200 advance in 1944, the year his first son, Gregory, was born.

In 1947 Bellow wrote *The Victim*, which *Time* described as a novel "about a solemn and touchy Jew accused by a fanatic Gentile of having ruined him" and said it "has troubling depths of meaning which make it unusual among new novels." But the book sold only 2,257 copies, and it would be six years before Bellow's next novel appeared.

The Fifties were the dawn of a new golden age of the American novel. In the space of a few years came J.D. Salinger's *Catcher in the Rye*, Ralph Ellison's *Invisible Man*, J.P. Donleavy's *The Ginger Man*, Vladimir Nabokov's *Lolita*, William Gaddis's *The Recognitions* and Jack Kerouac's *On the Road*. Bellow contributed *The Adventures of Augie March* in 1953. It is the story of an optimistic, naive young man from Chicago who goes into the world seeking adventures and finds that "you do all you can to humanize and familiarize the world, and suddenly it becomes more strange than ever." With its bold gush of language, it remains a popular seller today. "Search no further," writer Martin Amis declared in *The Atlantic Monthly* in 1995. "The great American novel was a chimera; this mythical beast was a pig with wings. Miraculously, however, and uncovenantedly, Saul Bellow brought the animal home."

At the time it was published not all critics hailed it so enthusiastically. Norman Podhoretz considered the novel a failure; Anthony West wrote that Bellow's writing was wooden and dead. Norman Mailer called it "absurd, unconvincing, overcooked, overstuffed, unfelt heaps of literary bull-bull." What seemed to upset critics was that Bellow had so radically departed from his first two finely drawn and more confined novels, which Bellow now calls his M.A. and Ph.D. *Augie March* broke new ground.

His next novel, *Seize the Day* (1956), about a day in the anxiety-ridden life of a man named Tommy Wilhelm, was called "one of the finest short novels in the language" by *The Guardian*. In 1956 Bellow married his second wife, Alexandra Tsachacbasov, and a year later his second son, Adam, was born. That marriage lasted only three years and ended around the time Bellow's picaresque novel *Henderson the Rain King* appeared in 1959. This comical one-man journey into the heart of a mythical Africa was compared to the *Odyssey* and *Don Quixote* by *Newsweek*.

As had been the case with each of his novels, the raves were balanced by the pans. Elizabeth Hardwick condemned *Henderson* in the *Partisan Review*, charging that Bellow was trying too hard to be "an important American novelist." Dwight Macdonald came to Bellow's defense and condemned the magazine for publishing Hardwick's misguided review. Bellow's response to such controversy? "Oh well, I just write stories."

He married his third wife, Susan Glassman, in 1961, and their son, Daniel, was born in 1962. Bellow continued writing. His next novel, *Herzog*, about a sometimes suicidal intellectual who writes but never sends letters to world figures, hit number one on the *New York Times* best-seller list and remained there for 29 weeks. In 1970 came *Mr. Sammler's Planet*, about another cynical intellectual, which prompted the *Sunday Times* of London to proclaim Bellow "the most important writer in English in the second half of the 20th century."

A 1965 *Book Week* poll of novelists and critics found Bellow to have written the "most distinguished fiction of the 1945–1965 period." That poll found Bellow to have written three of the six best novels of the postwar years.

By this time Bellow had accepted a position at the University of Chicago as a professor on the Committee on Social Thought and had begun writing *Humboldt's Gift*, about a failed dead poet and a successful writer hounded by a gangster, a thinly veiled story about his relationship with the poet Delmore Schwartz. The London *Times* pronounced Bellow to be "one of the most gifted chroniclers of the Western world" and the Swedish Academy agreed, awarding Bellow the Nobel Prize for Literature in 1976. The academy felt his body of work represented an emancipation of American writing from the "hard-boiled" style that had become routine in Thirties literature, and was deserving for its mix of "exuberant ideas, flashing irony, hilarious comedy and burning compassion."

Bellow's next book, *To Jerusalem and Back*, was his first nonfictional work. Two novels (*The Dean's December* and *More Die of Heartbreak*), another book of stories (*Him With His Foot in His Mouth and Other Stories*), two novellas (*A Theft* and *The Bellarosa Connection*), a fiction collection (*Something to Remember Me By*) and a book of essays (*It All Adds Up*) were published in the last 14 years. His latest novella, *The Actual*, about a man who has become "a first-class noticer" in his later years, has just been published.

Bellow married his fourth wife, Alexandra Ionescu Tulcea, a mathematics professor, in 1975, and it was her mother's illness and their trip to visit her in Romania that Bellow dramatized in his 1982 novel *The Dean's December*.

More than 20 years ago, a 1975 *Newsweek* profile noted, "He has not succumbed to any of the classic fates America seems to reserve for most of its major writers. He did not crack up, like Fitzgerald; he was not consumed by his own myth, like Hemingway; he did not suffer from long-delayed recognition, like Faulkner. Nor is Bellow a specimen of that other American phenomenon, the writer as showbiz personality or sudden superstar." Indeed, despite a fifth wife, Janis Freedman, and their moves to Boston and Vermont, Bellow remains sane and has a remarkably clear vision of himself and literature.

No saint by any means, Bellow can be cranky and cantankerous and admits to being aggressive. He bristles when critics label him a Jewish writer. "People who make labels should be in the gumming business," he has said.

On the eve of Bellow's 18th book, we sent Contributing Editor Lawrence Grobel (who has interviewed James Michener and Joyce Carol Oates) to Boston. His report:

"When I first tried to contact Bellow for an interview, I heard from his secretary, who told me he had suffered an illness, was convalescing and couldn't talk with me. 'He's also trying to complete a novel he's been working on for nearly ten years,' she said. 'Frankly, I don't think he'll ever finish it.'

"Six months later I tried again. This time he responded, saying he was inclined to talk. Half a year later I flew to Boston, where we met at his office on the sixth floor of Boston University's Department of Theology. His solid brown desk was old, the windows behind it somewhat grimy. There were no couches to sink into, no paintings on the walls, just two flimsily framed pieces of paper: one his National Book Award for *Herzog*, the other the Harold Washington Literary Award. There were three black filing cabinets, one wall of books and four cardboard boxes on the worn purple carpet. It felt like the office of a cheap detective. We sat at a round table and spoke until dusk."

PLAYBOY: How sick have you been, and how are you now?

BELLOW: I've been very sick. I went down to St. Martin in the Caribbean with my wife to finish a book about two years ago and ate some fish that was toxic. The toxin is very dangerous and often fatal. It attacks the nervous system. I wasn't aware of this at all at first. Then I began to feel rather odd. I couldn't work and passed out one night in the bathroom. My wife sent for an ambulance but I wouldn't get into it, so she got me back to Boston somehow and over to the Boston University hospital just in time, because they told me I would have died that night. They thought I was going to die anyhow. I was in intensive care for five weeks and they didn't diagnose this strange ciguatera until I was out of intensive care. They thought it was Legionnaires' disease or dengue. First I had heart failure and then double pneumonia. And in between I also had a gallbladder operation, which set me back. Any one of these things at my age could have been fatal, but I survived, though I've had a hard time pulling myself together again.

PLAYBOY: After you recovered from this fish poisoning, were you able to write?

BELLOW: When I got out of the hospital I couldn't even sign my name. I couldn't manage my hand, I couldn't feed myself. They gave me a bowl of soup and a tablespoon and it was like beating a tom-tom on the side of the dish. It's taken a little more than a year to recover.

PLAYBOY: How has this affected the big novel you've been working on for the past decade, the one your former secretary believes you will never complete?

BELLOW: That's not accurate. Which is all I want to say about that for now.

PLAYBOY: What kinds of demands does Boston University place on your time?

BELLOW: I have a special arrangement with Boston University. I teach literature one term, the spring term. I don't teach writing classes.

PLAYBOY: Is it American, English or world literature?

BELLOW: It's whatever I like. I just finished teaching freshmen about ambitious young men in the 19th century. We read Balzac's *Pere Goriot*, Stendhal's *Red and the Black*, Dickens' *Great Expectations* and Dostoyevsky's *Crime and Punishment*.

PLAYBOY: You mean you don't teach graduate students?

BELLOW: No, I like to teach the younger students because I think I should try to instill some feeling for literature.

PLAYBOY: If you were entering college today, what would you study?

BELLOW: I would study history and literature. But it would be hard to find anybody teaching literature anymore because the profession has decided that we're better off without literature. The name of that trend is deconstructionism.

PLAYBOY: You've said that the teaching of literature has been a disaster. Why?

BELLOW: People now teach literature to expose the authors, no matter how ancient, as racists, colonialists, imperialists, chauvinists, misogynists, exploiters, parasites, etc. Sure, you can do this to Shakespeare—but why should you?

PLAYBOY: Are you encouraged or discouraged by the students you see today, as compared with other generations?

BELLOW: If they've gone to reasonably decent schools they've been assigned good books. But those books are now in competition with the media and films. The challenge of a film is to reveal the inner lives of the people in it without really entering into their inner lives. The difference between a work of fiction and a movie is that the work of fiction is not just an account of actions, it's not just external, it's internal. And it's that internal life you're missing in movies.

PLAYBOY: Plenty of people would say movies are the art form of our time.

BELLOW: That's like mixing up the sign over a hock shop with bowling balls. Just because the things are round and look as if they might roll doesn't mean they are what they seem to be, OK? Commercially there's no contest between the movies and the novel because people feel there's something pretentious about high art. The novel as high art has been demoted by the movie as high art, and the movie people are promoting this view.

PLAYBOY: Do you go to many movies?

BELLOW: I go to movies quite a lot. I have a wife who's a great movie fan, and she drags me off to see them.

PLAYBOY: Do the movies you see satisfy you or leave you empty?

BELLOW: I may be skeptical, but I can be captivated. These emotions are and should be childlike. I was highly suspicious of *Schindler's List*, but I was moved by it just the same. I couldn't deny that at the end I was carried away by some of the terrible things that had never been shown on film before, like the young woman presuming to offer advice, shot and killed right before your eyes. You can't help but be moved by that. Violently moved.

PLAYBOY: What did you think of Robin Williams' portrayal of Tommy Wilhelm in the PBS film of your novel *Seize the Day*?

BELLOW: I didn't like it much. I thought that Robin had succumbed to the temptation to make Tommy Wilhelm a very schmaltzy, Jewish hysterical character.

PLAYBOY: You once observed: "Give an actor a sentence with a subordinate clause and it kills him. He gets a hernia trying to heave it across the lights." Are there any actors you've seen who could make such a heave?

BELLOW: I like Jack Nicholson quite a lot, he's a very intelligent actor—that is to say, for an actor he's quite intelligent. He was interested in directing, not acting in, *Henderson the Rain King*. He had it under option for some years.

PLAYBOY: Did you meet with him?

BELLOW: Yeah, I enjoyed meeting him. I was impressed by the fact that he didn't throw the roaches of his marijuana away but kept them in a little silver case.

PLAYBOY: Must have been expensive dope.

BELLOW: Or they might have been auctioned as relics. Those guys are about as close to holy men as we get this removed from India.

PLAYBOY: Did you share a joint with Nicholson?

BELLOW: No, he didn't offer me any.

PLAYBOY: Actors obviously amuse you. Have you known any intimately?

BELLOW: The only actress I ever knew well was Marilyn Monroe, whom I knew quite well in the days when she was married to Arthur Miller. She was like somebody who had picked up a high-voltage wire and then couldn't get rid of it. You often felt that she was supercharged. There were moments of wistfulness when you could see how willingly she would have cut off the charge if she'd been able to do it, but she couldn't. I don't even think she was aware of the superexcited state she was in. She was very charming and too beautiful to be real. She had a kind of curious incandescence under the skin, which is rare.

PLAYBOY: MGM expressed interest in you after *Dangling Man* was published—but it wasn't to option the book, was it?

BELLOW: No. It was a guy named Goldwyn, not from the famous Goldwyns, who came to Chicago and called me up. I went downtown hoping he wanted to buy the book. Instead he told me that he'd seen pictures of me and thought that I would do well as an actor.

PLAYBOY: Did you give that suggestion any consideration?

BELLOW: I was outraged. [*Laughs*] I was wrong, I should have done it. In those days I was very proud of being a writer.

PLAYBOY: And you weren't thinking of making your fortune on the big screen?

BELLOW: I was never interested in being rich. Not in the slightest.

PLAYBOY: Years later you had your chance to appear, as yourself, in Woody Allen's *Zelig*. How'd he talk you into it?

BELLOW: That was a piece of foolishness. If I'd known what it was about I would never have done it. But Woody Allen made a great secret out of this. He wouldn't say what the film was about. All he said was that he was chatting up a certain number of intellectuals on an ill-defined subject. I knew some others who were doing it, including Bruno Bettelheim, whom I call the Bettelheim of the Republic, so I thought it might be a gas. He sent me some pages of dialogue. The circumstances were very amusing. It was being filmed in an old apartment on Central Park West. I went there and walked around and ran into a solitary young man drifting from room to room. He told me that he had inherited the apartment from his parents but couldn't maintain it, so he rented it out to movie companies. I said, "What do you do?" He said, "I'm a novelist."

PLAYBOY: Did this guy have any idea who you were?

BELLOW: I don't think so.

PLAYBOY: Perhaps that's a fitting image of the writer: one who wanders aimlessly among the rented empty rooms of an apartment he cannot afford to maintain.

BELLOW: Nowadays when a young man thinks of becoming a writer, first he thinks of his hairstyle and then what clothes he should wear and then what whiskey he's going to endorse.

PLAYBOY: What did you think of when you first thought of becoming a writer?

BELLOW: It wasn't that I was going to be a glamorous person who would impress people. I had no idea what being a writer meant, really.

PLAYBOY: Did you know in grade school that you wanted to be a writer?

BELLOW: Oh yes, I definitely knew.

PLAYBOY: Did your parents try to discourage you?

BELLOW: My mother didn't interfere with me. Of course, she died when I was 17. She was concerned, as I later learned—she would talk to the neighbors and to her friends and to her dressmaker. But my parents came from St. Petersburg and were fairly sophisticated people. They were readers. In principle they wouldn't have had any objection to my being a writer. They just doubted that a child could be serious about this and whether he had the stuff for it. How were they supposed to know that?

PLAYBOY: When did you become aware of the power of the written word?

BELLOW: When I found myself in the children's ward of a hospital when I was eight.

PLAYBOY: Was that when you came down with tuberculosis?

BELLOW: It wasn't tuberculosis. It was something called empyema, an infection of the respiratory system that fills the lung cavity with fluid. I had to be tapped and I ran a fever every afternoon.

PLAYBOY: How long did that last?

BELLOW: Nearly a year.

PLAYBOY: It must have been quite a formative year in your life.

BELLOW: Oh, yes, it was indeed, because I was away from home for the first time. It was a few years after World War One, and it was a very restricted, old-fashioned place.

PLAYBOY: Were there kids a lot sicker than you? Did you witness any children dying?

BELLOW: Yeah, it was quite upsetting. You'd see activity during the night, the nurses were running, a light would go on, a screen would be set up along somebody's bed, and in the morning it was an empty bed. And you knew the kid had died.

PLAYBOY: Did you think that you might die?

BELLOW: Yes.

PLAYBOY: Did it make you more determined to live, or were you resigned to possibly not making it?

BELLOW: Resigned? No, I would hunker down in my bed and make myself as small as possible.

PLAYBOY: So death couldn't find you?

BELLOW: Something like that. I met the world at the age of eight there in the hospital, and I had never known it on those terms before.

PLAYBOY: And how did you spend your time there?

BELLOW: Reading, though reading matter was very limited. There were the funny papers, which were very important then, with characters that don't exist anymore, like Happy Hooligan, Slim Jim, Mutt and Jeff, Boob McNutt.

PLAYBOY: That wasn't what introduced you to the power of the word, was it?

BELLOW: No. A lady brought me a copy of the New Testament. She was solemn, grim, middle-aged, dressed with many layers of clothing, long skirts, laced boots, a big hat. She was connected with some missionary society. First she tested me to see if I could read well enough. I learned to read the Old Testament when I was four—I was reading Genesis in Hebrew, which was a very powerful influence. The New Testament made a big hit with me. I was terribly moved by the Gospels. The rest was off-putting, but I read about the life and death of Jesus and realized he was a Jew. I began to feel a responsibility for the crucifixion. I loved Jesus. I realized I could not talk to my family when I got home about this. They would have been shocked and angry with me. So I kept it to myself. There were all kinds of things I had to keep to myself. And that was what I learned in the hospital.

PLAYBOY: How did the Depression affect your family?

BELLOW: It was harder to make a living. During the Depression my father was in a business selling wood for fuel to Jewish bakers. In those days they used scrap wood in their ovens, which he used to get from northern Wisconsin. I used to go around with him quite a lot, so I knew most of the Jewish bakers of Chicago. We were never hungry, we just didn't have any money.

PLAYBOY: Those who remember the Depression often consider it the most defining time of their lives.

BELLOW: It was defining in a curious way. Instead of breeding crime and antagonism it bred compassion and solidarity between people. They were much less harsh or severe than in times of prosperity. Sometimes I thought that the greatest blow of the Depression was not lack of money—it was damage to the pride of honest working people who felt the Depression was somehow a punishment.

PLAYBOY: Did you feel something like that when your mother died when you were 17?

BELLOW: That was a terrible shock. It was a long, drawn-out cancer death. I could not even imagine my mother being dead. It was the greatest challenge to my imagination when she died because I couldn't imagine existence without her. We were really a very close family, my two brothers, my sister, my parents.

PLAYBOY: How did her death affect your father?

BELLOW: He was devastated. He felt the sexual privation of her long illness and he didn't do anything while she was alive, I know, but she hadn't been dead very long before he began to see ladies in the neighborhood. He remarried within two years.

PLAYBOY: Did you like your stepmother?

BELLOW: I liked her, but I liked her like a good joke. She was a funny lady. I couldn't take her seriously, though.

PLAYBOY: You've said your father was violent, strong and authoritarian.

BELLOW: He was. He'd beat all of us.

PLAYBOY: With a strap or with his hand?

BELLOW: Whatever came first.

PLAYBOY: Have you experienced much violence in your life?

BELLOW: Quite a bit. I have seen a lot of it—enough to make me feel fright at being in a state of nature again, of having nothing but my naked self to depend upon.

PLAYBOY: Have you ever physically been a victim, other than from the hands of your father?

BELLOW: I was abused when I was a child by a stranger in an alley.

PLAYBOY: Sexually?

BELLOW: Yeah.

PLAYBOY: How old were you?

BELLOW: Seven, six.

PLAYBOY: Did he make you cry?

BELLOW: He threatened me.

PLAYBOY: How far did it go?

BELLOW: It went pretty far. I don't want to go into detail on that. [*Pauses*] I'm amused when I read about child abuse today because it is exaggerated and an unsavory falling back on one's legal status. It's also fashionable to hate your parents. It's a nasty little vice encouraged by society. It's a sign that people are unable to shed their childhood. It's a way of remaining childish, of explaining your own defects, that you were unjustly punished or abused as a child. I've never found it to be much more than a racket. I've been in courtrooms enough to know that there is such a thing as genuine child abuse, but when the middle class began to horn in on this, I said, uh-uh.

PLAYBOY: Did you follow the Lyle and Erik Menendez trial?

BELLOW: Yes, I did. The first trial was disgraceful. The court shouldn't have accepted the testimony about how their parents did them sexual harm. That the jury would take their word for it stank to high heaven.

PLAYBOY: Well, it was tried in California.

BELLOW: Yeah. California is like an artificial limb the rest of the country doesn't really need. You can quote me.

PLAYBOY: What did you think of the O.J. Simpson criminal trial?

BELLOW: Trial by jury is in trouble everywhere, but in California the whole justice system is in deep trouble. It's no longer reliable. Everything is immediately transformed into a big TV show or spectacle. They are so narcotized by entertainment that they tend to transform everything from real life into entertainment terms. The whole thing's unreal.

PLAYBOY: We take it then that you were shocked by the Simpson verdict?

BELLOW: Yes, I was shocked. I've never seen two murder victims so quickly forgotten. I could remember from my own childhood what an enormity a murder was. It was taken really very seriously. Now it's nothing to take a human life. It's like watching a comedy cartoon in which the hero falls in front of a steamroller and is rolled flat, then he's picked up and propped against a wall and in the next frame he's running again. So it had no reality.

PLAYBOY: More than half a century ago, in 1940, you were in Mexico when one of your heroes, Leon Trotsky, was killed by an assassin. Was that murder made more real when you saw Trotsky in his coffin?

BELLOW: Not in his coffin, just on a table in the hospital.

PLAYBOY: How did you manage that? Trotsky was an international figure—wasn't there security?

BELLOW: No. In those times, everybody went everywhere. I said I was an American journalist, so they let me in. Trotsky was wearing massive bloody bandages, his face and beard were smeared with blood.

PLAYBOY: Trotsky became labeled and wound up in exile. Is being labeled a Jewish writer as annoying to you as labels are to Joyce Carol Oates, who complains that she's categorized as a woman's writer?

BELLOW: If you'll excuse me, anti-Semitism is not in the same class as what people might call misogyny or antifeminism. It's very different.

PLAYBOY: Would you rather not be called a Jew?

BELLOW: I don't mind being called a Jew. I am a Jew.

PLAYBOY: Yet you do think that you've been a disappointment to those Jews who, as you've noted, "expect Jewish writers to do good work for them and propagandize for them."

BELLOW: Do they really care very much about what writers say? They don't. At the moment the push-button reaction to me is that I'm a conservative. But that's just foolish labeling—they don't know whether I am a conservative or not, they've just heard that. Everything is rumor, all opinion is rumor. People simply react to rumor by repeating it as though it were true. There's nothing I can do about that.

PLAYBOY: Do you consider *conservative* to be a negative word?

BELLOW: In some quarters it is, in some it's a positive word. At *Commentary* magazine it's a positive word. But *Commentary* doesn't review my books, and if I'm a conservative, why are my books not reviewed at *Commentary*?

PLAYBOY: *Commentary* did review *Henderson the Rain King*, and raised a point that might be said of many of your works: "What is so far chiefly missing in Bellow's writing is an account of what his heroes want to be free from." Is that a fair thing to expect from you?

BELLOW: There's an old Yiddish saying that translates: A fool throws a stone into a pond, ten sages go into the pond looking for it and can't find it. In other words, it takes almost nothing except a thoughtless tossing of a stone to motivate foolish people. Why should I answer that question? A dyspeptic book reviewer says something, and now I have to answer him at this moment? I don't have to answer him.

PLAYBOY: Philip Roth said that, unlike Elie Wiesel or Isaac Bashevis Singer, you are a figure of more importance to other Jewish writers than you are to the Jewish cultural audience. Is he right?

BELLOW: When *Herzog* went on the bestseller list, Hannah Arendt said it was because of the Jewish public. She was quite sensitive to that sort of thing. She had an interest in keeping me in the kike class. Philip Roth has no such interest, he's just wrong.

PLAYBOY: Seymour Krim wrote that he was "literally made, shaped, whetted and given a world with a purpose by the American realistic novel of the mid to late Thirties." Was it like that for you as well?

BELLOW: I think so. We all read Dreiser, Sinclair Lewis, Louis Bromfield and their English counterparts such as Archibald Cronin, Arnold Bennett and H.G. Wells.

PLAYBOY: Was there any novel that got to you emotionally?

BELLOW: I found Dreiser's *An American Tragedy* hard to read because it was so extremely painful, almost unbearable. One of those books I didn't finish reading until much later.

PLAYBOY: What made it so painful?

BELLOW: Just the horror of having taken a pregnant woman out in a boat and murdering her.

PLAYBOY: Your own first novel, *The Very Dark Trees*, dealt with a white man who turned black. What happened to that?

BELLOW: It was accepted by a publisher in San Francisco, Colt Press, which had published Henry Miller's *The Colossus of Maroussi*, so I was impressed by that. I was only 26 or 27, and after I reread it I decided to destroy it.

PLAYBOY: Why?

BELLOW: I was ashamed to be associated with it. I threw it down the incinerator drop in the building where I lived.

PLAYBOY: How many manuscripts have you done that with over the years?

BELLOW: A few.

PLAYBOY: In 1959 Norman Mailer wrote: "If I have one ambition above all others, it is to write a novel which Dostoyevsky and Marx, Joyce and Freud, Stendhal, Tolstoy, Proust and Spengler, Faulkner, and even old moldering Hemingway might come to read, for it would carry what they had to tell another part of the way." Did you have similar ambitions?

BELLOW: He deserved to fail with a fantasy like that. He wasn't thinking about writing a marvelous book, he was thinking of placing himself in a tradition. I never had such notions. And I doubt that many of those people had such notions. Mailer is an extraordinary writer of vigorous prose, but he doesn't have the kind of mind that goes with the kind of writing he chose to do. He does have historical ideas about himself, but they are foolish ideas.

PLAYBOY: What writers among your peers do you feel had the talent to pull off their ideas successfully?

BELLOW: Among my contemporaries I very much like John Cheever. I admired and loved Faulkner. I like Wright Morris and J.F. Powers a lot. They're all people with much more modest aims, which doesn't mean their novels are not good. They're first-rate.

PLAYBOY: What about the novels of Nabokov, Jack Kerouac, William Gaddis, Gabriel García Márquez?

BELLOW: Nabokov was a very accomplished writer, but he was also a cold narcissist who invited the reader to join him. Kerouac belonged to a movement—the Beat spirit of the country—and was sort of a cult writer. I never had much to do with that. Gaddis is an excellent writer, I like him a lot. He's an original, a great user of the language. I liked García Márquez' *One Hundred Years of Solitude*, but all the others are just reruns of that. As you grow older you don't like to involve yourself in reckless reading of a great number of books; you want to limit yourself to the best that your generation has to offer.

PLAYBOY: What was your impression of Samuel Beckett, whom you met in Paris?

BELLOW: He was a very great person. You had a feeling about him that he was humanly significant, physically even, when he strolled across the boulevard to meet you and sat down at a cafe table near the Pont Royal Hotel. It gave me marvelous comfort to see and talk with him, often about James Joyce. Beckett was so sane, so balanced, so quiet, so unpretentious.

PLAYBOY: Have you ever read Joyce's *Finnegans Wake*?

BELLOW: No. I'm waiting for the nursing home to read it.

PLAYBOY: Do you measure yourself against other writers?

BELLOW: Well, one does, you know? Recently I reread *Crime and Punishment*, and I said to myself, If only you could do this kind of thing, wouldn't it be great?

PLAYBOY: We know your strengths as a writer, but what would you consider your weaknesses?

BELLOW: One of my weaknesses as a writer is that I was far too modest in my choice of subjects. If I were going to invest my talent more profitably I should have had more ambitious themes than I allowed myself to have.

PLAYBOY: Can you be more specific? How could you have been more ambitious?

BELLOW: Well, *Augie March* was a very ambitious book, but it was ambitious in a different way. It was ambitious in language because I wanted to invent a more energized language that would allow me to move much more freely than I had hitherto been able to move. I wanted to be able to do American society in a way in which it had never been done before, and in part I succeeded in that book. But I failed because in the end I could not govern my discovery. I couldn't control it.

PLAYBOY: Cynthia Ozick considered *Augie* the second American prose revolution, after Hemingway. Did you have a sense of that?

BELLOW: I wanted to do it for myself; I had no idea of establishing a benchmark. I'm beginning to see that my ambitions were rather strangely limited. Not that I was modest. I've never been modest. But I set myself bounds, and I had to liberate myself from those bounds. *Augie March* starts out as a naive person and I don't let him get too sophisticated—that's a limitation in the book.

PLAYBOY: *Augie March* also set off a storm of critical side-taking. There were those, among them Dwight Macdonald, who highly praised it, and others, such as Elizabeth Hardwick and Norman Podhoretz, who didn't like it at all. How do you deal with such mixed reviews?

BELLOW: You have to have a thick skin. I began to understand what I had done with *Augie March* that had upset so many people. I had unintentionally turned over a good many WASP applecarts. I had introduced a note into American fiction that was dangerous. It was undisciplined, it was awkward, it was jazzy and it reflected immigrant—and particularly Jewish—points of view that were unwelcome to the WASP establishment. It had never occurred to me before that I might be treading on the toes of the Brahmins or the heirs of the Brahmins with an interest in controlling their undisciplined and disciplined unfortunate Jews who had not been sent to Harvard. *Augie March* was too unbuttoned, too red-skinned even for the redskins.

PLAYBOY: Do you feel that you succeeded in liberating the language and creating a truly original character with Augie?

BELLOW: Yes, I did. I felt that I had liberated the American novel from what was left of the English mandarin influence. And even from the Hemingway influence, because we did need liberation from that. Hemingway was a very marvelous and beautiful writer who was constricting. He produced novels with a highly polished surface. You didn't want to mar the surface of his beautifully constructed and polished stories or novels. But then it was too narrowing, because there were all kinds of experience which would never fit into that. Hemingway's personal attitudes intending to redefine American manhood were too constricting and too exclusive. But you could see what the social effects of Hemingway's books were.

PLAYBOY: Are writers defining the American character as much today?

BELLOW: This role has been taken over by journalism. Magazines such as PLAYBOY and *Esquire* instruct young men in the way to be acceptably and successfully American: how to date, how to dress, how to buy a car, how to order a meal, how to prepare a salad dressing, how to take a holiday.

PLAYBOY: Not long ago writers such as Tom Wolfe and other New Journalists were shouting that the novel had fallen and that journalists had wiped out the novel as literature's main event.

BELLOW: And here is Tom Wolfe making his fortune out of the novel some years later. Seems prophetically inconsistent.

PLAYBOY: Wolfe addresses you personally in his opening to *The New Journalism* by saying it started the first new direction in American literature in half a century. "Bellow, Barth, Updike, Roth—the novelists are all out there right now ransacking the literary histories and sweating it out, wondering where they stand. Damn it all, Saul, the Huns have arrived."

BELLOW: Yes, and the Huns were taught to read English and then they bought *Bonfire of the Vanities*, which was a whole series of the most stunning billboards along the highway that I ever saw. Let me tell you something: I'm a Jew, and when Jews hear the language of the Holocaust, because that's what it is—the world will be *Novelrein*, just as Hitler wanted to make Germany *Judenrein*, OK?—I say to myself, it's all meshuga. I am used to hearing this eliminationist talk.

PLAYBOY: Are you also used to hearing the kind of assessment a writer like Joyce Carol Oates has given of you, when she called you a genius in these pages and said you are "off the scale of even Truman Capote, Thomas Pynchon or Thomas Wolfe"?

BELLOW: I don't think Truman Capote gets near the tail of the comet. Pynchon I like, but he is sort of an endless virtuoso. It's like listening to 20 hours of Paganini. One would be plenty. I loved Thomas Wolfe when I was young. I stayed up all night reading *Look Homeward, Angel* when I was 19, and I remember in the morning how devastated I was to have no more Thomas Wolfe to read.

PLAYBOY: Getting back to Oates' remark: Modesty aside, do you have that sense about yourself and your work?

BELLOW: I don't think in those terms. I tend to agree with her, but Lenin said, when describing what happened in Russia in 1917, "The power was lying in the street, I just picked it up." [*Laughs*] I do have the feeling that, yes, I did do something. Not that anybody cares much about such things nowadays. The country has changed so that what I do no longer signifies anything, as it did when I was young. There was such a thing as a literary life in this country and there were people who lived as writers. All that changed in my lifetime. Of course, this is such an enormous country that sometimes I think that if only one tenth of one percent of the population were reading seriously, it would still mean a quarter of a million readers.

PLAYBOY: How relevant is the novelist today? Do we need novelists?

BELLOW: Do we need them? Yes. Do we know it? No. Although, as I say, you will still find a quarter of a million supporters somehow or other around the country. These are people who have preserved themselves secretly, like members of a lodge who are not allowed to give away the secret of the handshake.

PLAYBOY: If you had your own crystal ball, what might you see for the future of the novel?

BELLOW: It's a bad time for the novel. What's going to happen to the novel is what's going to happen culturally to this country. The number of readers is diminishing. Family life today is not creating more readers. Partly because of TV, partly because of schooling, partly because of books prepared for schoolchildren that pretend to be stories and that are so ill constructed and flat and corny that the kids have no regard for them. The experience of literature is missing from the lives of the younger generation of readers, and that's a bad deal. I don't think the classics are being read anymore. I know the Bible isn't being read much anymore, and the Bible is a great oceanic source for literature. When the Bible diminishes in stature, literature diminishes with it.

PLAYBOY: Having married five times, what do you make of the institution of marriage, and what have you learned about it that you can pass on to your grandchildren?

BELLOW: You should have asked me this serious question at first, when I was full of piss and vinegar. I learned that the sexual revolution is a very bloody affair, like most revolutions.

PLAYBOY: Divorces can be costly—to the soul and to the pocket. Are the divorce laws fair?

BELLOW: I had one big lawsuit relating to a divorce. Let me put it this way: I never yet saw a judge on the bench whom I would trust to condemn a man to death. That's one of my arguments against capital punishment. I don't think these people are often humanly qualified to decide these legal questions or to interpret the law.

PLAYBOY: You have three sons from three of your marriages. Has it been difficult for them?

BELLOW: Undoubtedly.

PLAYBOY: Any resentment in them, having you as their father?

BELLOW: Yeah, I guess so. However, let's get on with this.

PLAYBOY: Have you ever been in therapy?

BELLOW: I was lucky the writer in me survived all the therapy I had.

PLAYBOY: And have you been through analysis?

BELLOW: At the insistence of one of my wives, I went to a psychoanalyst for a while. I enjoyed talking with him, but I was never analyzed.

PLAYBOY: What about Reichian therapy? It's been said that your experiences with it freed you to write *Augie March*.

BELLOW: That's an incorrect theory, because I started writing *Augie March* in Paris two years before I ever heard of Wilhelm Reich.

PLAYBOY: So you're saying that Reichian sexual therapy wasn't responsible for changing your style of writing?

BELLOW: It would have been a disaster if it had. I protected my writing from the therapy, which I would call biological holistic therapy.

PLAYBOY: Reich wrote a book about orgasms and his orgone box. Did you ever use the box?

BELLOW: I would sit in it from time to time. I don't know what effect it had on me. It would heat me up quite a lot. It was agreeable to be in the box, because it shut off all kinds of outside influences and gave you a meditative hour, which never does any harm. But I never went beyond Reichian therapy—that was enough.

PLAYBOY: Why did you stop doing it?

BELLOW: Because it released violent feelings that I then couldn't govern. I'd lose my temper horrendously.

PLAYBOY: You had never lost your temper like that before?

BELLOW: Not to the point of getting into fights.

PLAYBOY: Physical fights? With strangers?

BELLOW: Yeah. I'd be insulted on the subway, I'd be ready to fight.

PLAYBOY: Ever get your nose broken or eye blackened?

BELLOW: No, luckily I'd be dragged away. [*Laughs*]

PLAYBOY: Were you a good fighter?

BELLOW: Not that good. I had exaggerated ideas about my powers. I think most men do.

PLAYBOY: Joyce Carol Oates said that she couldn't think of many of her male colleagues who've written compellingly or convincingly about women. She cited you, Faulkner and Melville as great writers who never created any female characters of great depth. What writers have best captured the way a woman thinks and feels?

BELLOW: It's a question you should address to a lady, since evidently I'm down here not as a misogynist but as somebody who's missed the boat on the other sex. Is this for your lady readers—a sort of sop to throw them another victim? Somebody else to hate? It's one thing to write about women in a time when women are happy to read about themselves. It's another thing in an ideological age when women read you in order to see whether you measure up ideologically to their standards.

PLAYBOY: John Gardner once called you a male chauvinist pig. Are you?

BELLOW: What should I say, that I'm not a pig? There's an old Irish gag from Chicago that goes: "Mike said you wasn't fit to live with pigs. But I stood up for you, I said you was." Why should I defend myself against charges by John Gardner or anybody else? They may well have been wrong. I never asked them to stand up to my charges.

Why do interviewers ask people questions that they wouldn't ask their neighbor for fear of being punched in the nose? Like, "Why are your bowel movements such a strange color?" Or, "Why do you piss through your ears?" I'm not responsible for what so-and-so said about me. I don't mind obliging you, I just don't like being put through the shredder.

PLAYBOY: We have confidence in your ability to retort. What do you make of the AIDS epidemic?

BELLOW: If I believed in God I would say that this is God's way of restoring the seriousness to sexual connections. Because AIDS is a phenomenon that comes from promiscuity, which is wider among homosexuals than among heterosexuals.

PLAYBOY: Some people think it's God's way of thinning the population, as wars did in the past.

BELLOW: If he wanted to thin the population, why did he start with homosexuals? They're the ones who are least likely to reproduce.

PLAYBOY: You don't believe in God?

BELLOW: I don't really know what to think. I know what I thought about him when I was a child—I had an image of God that over the years turned out to be the image of my big brother. He parted his hair in the middle and he had a round, moony sort of face, and he wasn't really benevolent.

PLAYBOY: Have you thought about an afterlife, immortality?

BELLOW: I think about those things all the time. There is nothing in death that science can tell you about with certainty. I find pretty good support in Plato because Socrates said it clearly in the *Dialogues*: Either there is a life after death or there is none. If there is none, then you go back to the state you were in before you were born, oblivion. So it's either oblivion or immortality.

PLAYBOY: What's your intuition: oblivion or immortality?

BELLOW: My intuition is immortality. No argument can be made for it, but it's just as likely as oblivion.

PLAYBOY: If you could come back as something else, what would it be?

BELLOW: I haven't the slightest idea. I think of life as a course of instruction and education and I think of the soul as a student coming back time after time. So life is just a graduate study program. [*Laughs*]

PLAYBOY: In *Mr. Sammler's Planet*, Sammler categorizes people who threaten him into various animals. If you were to describe yourself as an animal, what would it be?

BELLOW: Some sort of monkey. I like the idea of being an arboreal animal, hanging by my tail, eating a banana. Reminds me of a limerick:

There was a young man from Dundee
Who buggered an ape in a tree;
The results were most horrid,
All ass and no forehead,
Blue balls and a purple goatee.

PLAYBOY: Do you remember your short poem about a Polish girl that Mark Harris mentioned in his book about you, *Drumlin Woodchuck*, but never quoted?

BELLOW: That's the one John Berryman fell in love with:

You can biff me, you can bang me,
But get it you'll never.
Think because I'm a Polish girl
*   I fuck?*
Kiss my ass, that's what you are.

PLAYBOY: What has money meant to you?

BELLOW: I haven't got all that much money. I was married too many times to have much money.

PLAYBOY: Capote once observed that what makes the rich different is that they eat tiny fresh vegetables and meats that are nearly unborn.

BELLOW: Truman hated me.

PLAYBOY: Why?

BELLOW: I don't know enough about homosexual psychology to be able to explain it. When I first knew Truman Capote he was a charming little boy whom I met in Richard Wright's Paris apartment. He didn't have any ax to grind then, though he monopolized the conversation by talking about his society friends and his closeness to the House of Windsor and so on. But later on, he looked like a shrunken Sydney Greenstreet, and he was vicious about me.

PLAYBOY: He didn't think you deserved the Nobel Prize.

BELLOW: Maybe I didn't deserve the Nobel Prize, but it's a cinch he didn't even deserve the Pulitzer. I can't see what Truman deserved at all, except a kick in the ass.

PLAYBOY: He felt he created something new, the nonfiction novel, with *In Cold Blood*.

BELLOW: I wasn't bowled over. And his early books are just Southern faded fabrics, that's all.

PLAYBOY: Some of the stories he published certainly created a stir.

BELLOW: There was one story in which he said Jews ought to be stuffed and put in museums. [*Laughs*] That's where it is: That's where the little fairies like that really belong, in Auschwitz on the general's staff, in the Auschwitz barracks with a swagger stick.

PLAYBOY: Capote thought that *Answered Prayers* would kill any chance he had of winning any great literary prize. Did the Nobel Prize mean a great deal to you?

BELLOW: I didn't give a hoot about it one way or the other. I don't exist for that sort of thing, and I was very careful to see that it didn't affect my life too much.

PLAYBOY: How can it not?

BELLOW: It's just a prize, like any other. Proust didn't get it, nor Tolstoy nor Joyce. So it isn't as though you were in the royal line and you went to Stockholm for the coronation.

PLAYBOY: Is there a downside to having won the prize?

BELLOW: Yes, people feel that you are a public functionary, that you have to produce a certain amount of cultural shrubbery on God's little acre. [*Laughs*]

PLAYBOY: So it didn't affect the way you write?

BELLOW: Not at all.

PLAYBOY: Norman Mailer has been campaigning for the Nobel Prize for years. Do you think he should get it?

BELLOW: Well, I'd give it to him—if he had anything to trade. [*Laughs*]

PLAYBOY: You're already on record for saying that writers seldom wish other writers well. Did winning the Nobel Prize widen the gulf between you and your peers?

BELLOW: I suppose that was Truman's problem. Maybe even Gore Vidal's problem. Gore never mentions me without treating my head like an ashtray, nicking his cigarette on it.

PLAYBOY: Hold on. Vidal said in *Palimpsest* that, with the exception of you, his "celebrated contemporaries all seem to have stopped learning in their 20s."

BELLOW: Well, that's true. But I looked up some of the references in that book and they were not as kind as all that. He can't resist putting me down.

PLAYBOY: Is Vidal a better nonfiction or fiction writer?

BELLOW: His novels lack originality. His essays are much more interesting. Gore Vidal is a good writer, he's just not as good as he thinks he is. I often thought of Gore as a patrician who got trapped among plebeians, and somehow he was condemned by his sexual preferences to live a level or two beneath the station to which he's entitled. He's always resented it a great deal: He doesn't see why homosexuals should not also be aristocrats. Well, he's right about that.

PLAYBOY: Do you read any newer writers, such as David Foster Wallace, William Vollmann, T.C. Boyle?

BELLOW: I have read a little of Boyle. I rather like him. There's this terrific, meshuga young American writer named Denis Johnson, who wrote *Resuscitation of a Hanged Man*.

PLAYBOY: How about Don DeLillo, Cormac McCarthy, Joyce Carol Oates—are they Nobel-worthy?

BELLOW: I like Don DeLillo, he's often very amusing and penetrating. And I like Cormac McCarthy very much, grim as all get out—though I didn't like *All the Pretty Horses* so well because it was a little more conventional. Joyce Carol Oates offends people by being so prolific, which is the wrong reason to be offended. On the whole, I'm for her, she's a very good writer. I read James Dickey's *Deliverance* again recently and was knocked over by it. It's one of the finest books of that generation of writers.

PLAYBOY: Did you ever see the movie?

BELLOW: No, I avoid movies based on novels that I like a lot, because I don't like them to be damaged. I don't know how many times I've seen films of *Anna Karenina*, and they grow worse with every decade. The fact that *Anna Karenina* has survived all these movies and is still infinitely greater than any of them gives me hope.

PLAYBOY: Back to the future Nobel laureates: What about John Updike or Philip Roth?

BELLOW: I could see Roth; he's a little buggy now and then, but a very gifted writer.

PLAYBOY: And someone eight years your senior, James Michener?

BELLOW: I would rather see him get it than Toni Morrison, but I don't want to get into that. I'm not here to give prizes.

PLAYBOY: Geoffrey Wolff has written about how many writers drink and how many are drunks and alcoholics, listing Fitzgerald, London, Crane, Thomas Wolfe, Hammett, Capote, Berryman, Lardner, Parker, O'Hara, Kerouac, Poe, Thurber, etc. He also pointed out that five American Nobel Prize winners had the problem: O'Neill, Faulkner, Steinbeck, Hemingway and Sinclair Lewis. How did you escape it?

BELLOW: When we were in Canada my old man was a bootlegger. He had a still and we used to go out there. I was just a little kid. He'd get inside and pour some of the booze into a dish and set it afire. If it didn't all burn out and there was fluid left in the bottom that wasn't fit to sell, he'd make me taste it. I don't know, I just got my intoxication out of reading poetry. I found *Macbeth* intoxicating.

PLAYBOY: Whose ideas in this century have intoxicated you? You've said, "There are only a few big ideas. I can think of only a very small handful of people in the 20th century who were truly original." Who are they?

BELLOW: I think Kafka was truly original. Proust. Joyce. Probably Heidegger, though I don't care for him. Certain of our scientists, like Richard Feynman, who must have been a genuine original. Picasso was a real original. Matisse also. Hemingway. John Berryman. Eugene O'Neill.

PLAYBOY: And what about Tennessee Williams?

BELLOW: No, I don't think so. He was cut from a cloth that you see quite a lot of.

PLAYBOY: Arthur Miller?

BELLOW: No.

PLAYBOY: Sigmund Freud?

BELLOW: I'm quite puzzled by Freud. I don't really think all that much of him. First of all, his literary influence isn't clear to me; he is derivative, in a way. Second, Freud needed a theory of dreams, so he dreamed all the dreams himself. He went into business using himself as stock. He was a Jewish businessman. Whatever he needed, he made at home. He was a home industry. He was extremely ingenious, obviously a man of great gifts. But then he narrowed down everything to his own explanations, with the erotic as the root. It's not erotic in the great sense in which Plato and Socrates had an Eros. Freud's Eros is much narrower and it's biologically determined. It's instinctual with us to have the Oedipus complex. You have it whether you wish it or not; so, in a way, you're sentenced and Freud sentences you from the bench to manifest these deep, vital motives that are all sexual in character. You can't get away from that. I don't like to be boxed in like that. It's chutzpah on his part.

PLAYBOY: Do any 20th century musicians or composers move you?

BELLOW: Dmitry Shostakovich. Igor Stravinsky sometimes.

PLAYBOY: Not the Beatles, or Elvis or Barbra Streisand?

BELLOW: That's pop stuff. It's good, charming, but pop is pop.

PLAYBOY: Can a pop master such as Andy Warhol ever reach the status of a Matisse?

BELLOW: Well, Warhol is no longer here to sign tin cans. I don't know—I haven't seen all the tin cans assembled yet.

PLAYBOY: What did you think of Marlon Brando's comment that the Jews run Hollywood and that they never allow the image of the "kike" to reach the screen?

BELLOW: Well, I never thought he was a great thinker or a first-class philosophical character. I was a little surprised he could be so foolish. Most people are much better at concealing their anti-Semitism than Marlon Brando is. Anti-Semitism is extremely common. If you're still being shocked at the age of 80 by the random expressions of anti-Semitic views, there's something wrong with you. In a century where we experienced the Holocaust and two world wars, shock is a little more difficult to find. I don't expect much from a person like Brando. Why would I be shocked? Because he appeared in *On the Waterfront*? He had a script.

PLAYBOY: Were you shocked about the Oklahoma City bombing and the incarceration of Timothy McVeigh and Terry Nichols?

BELLOW: They're macho types, imaginary pioneers, militants, fighters in the cause of freedom. But, really, their minds have been poisoned by all kinds of ideological marijuana. There have always been these know-nothing movements in this country. I'm reading about the life of Lincoln now, and he obviously had to deal with it then.

PLAYBOY: You've written about all sorts of victims. Have you ever felt yourself to be one?

BELLOW: No, I don't feel myself to be a victim at all. I feel myself to be a winner, I always did. I was interested in victims as a subject.

PLAYBOY: Are you glad to have lived at this time, or would you have preferred another time in history?

BELLOW: You have to take what you can get, not make demands. That's what's so striking about Mailer. He sprang from his mother's womb with two fists filled with demands and requirements for what life was going to be.

PLAYBOY: What were the demands made of you back in 1970 when you were shouted off the stage at San Francisco State College?

BELLOW: There was one Mexican guy who had written a book, and he stood up and denounced me. He said, "What do you want to listen to this old man for? His balls are dried up, he can't come, he's absolutely of no interest." I didn't know what to say, except, "I didn't thrust myself upon you, I came here because I was invited to speak to you." They booed me.

PLAYBOY: Your silence was their loss.

BELLOW: There's one thing I do know: When I'm tempted to say something and I don't say it, I feel all the better for it. I feel I've gotten stronger.

PLAYBOY: J.D. Salinger must feel like Superman—he's kept quiet for three decades. Roth has called Salinger the writer of the age, because he didn't turn his back on the times. Do you have any insight into why he turned silent?

BELLOW: I don't know Salinger. I always liked his books; he's a very good writer. I don't know why he became so embittered as to turn into a hermit. I can understand it. I can even somewhat sympathize with it. It's better not to be doing what you and I are doing here. From my point of view.

PLAYBOY: But from our point of view, however——

BELLOW: Right. I'm a public commodity. I'm listed on the Amex.

PLAYBOY: Commodities are what sell. What did you think of Sotheby's auction of Jackie Onassis' estate?

BELLOW: That was a travesty.

PLAYBOY: You mean you wouldn't pay $770,000 for Kennedy's golf clubs?

BELLOW: I'm afraid not. I was not impressed by Kennedy. He was a charming man, very intelligent, but he was no president. Besides, his father bought the office for him. And I don't see why, in a country as sensitive about plutocrats as this one, they should have cheered when he became president.

PLAYBOY: Bill Clinton is a great admirer of JFK's.

BELLOW: I don't think Clinton is anything like a president of this country. He is a yuppie, a playboy. He's basically unserious. I don't even know why he wants to be there.

PLAYBOY: Let's turn to literary politics. Is there a literary establishment today?

BELLOW: No. There are poor shreds of it at *The New York Review of Each Other's Books*.

PLAYBOY: What did you think about Iran's fatwa on Salman Rushdie?

BELLOW: I thought it was horrendous, of course. But I also thought that Rushdie had so Westernized himself that he seems to have convinced himself, as so many writers do and have done since the Twenties— since the time of *Ulysses*—that anything can be said in a novel and be accepted. If Joyce could treat the Catholic Church slightingly, Rushdie thought, then he could do the same with Islam. He felt that he was going to do with Islam what Joyce had done with Catholicism. He was wrong. Which means he had lost touch with Islam and had become so thoroughly Westernized he didn't recognize that this was apt or likely to happen. Maybe it was inevitable.

PLAYBOY: In 1995 Nigerian writer Ken Saro-Wiwa was executed. Rushdie observed in his PLAYBOY interview that "all over the world, writers are being thrown in jail. They mysteriously die in police custody. It is open season on writers and it must stop." Will it ever be dangerous to be a writer in the U.S.?

BELLOW: No. They may knock us to the ropes once in a while and give us a rabbit punch to the kidneys, but nobody takes us seriously enough to kill us.

City Girls

commentary by AMY SOHN

T he three women who met me at Lot 61 to dish about their sex lives were so gorgeous and illustrious I had trouble keeping my head above the table during the meal. Though we all got along, we didn't agree on much of anything having to do with sex (except that we all love it). We are all in our 20s and 30s, we all live south of 14th Street and we all have swanky job titles such as fashion executive or comedy writer. In the interest of privacy, we decided to choose pseudonyms from the golden age of feminist TV, the Seventies. The names we selected were Barbara Cooper, Gloria Bunker Stivic, Pepper Anderson and Flo Jean Castleberry. (You'll have to guess who I am.) We began with the age-old controversial question, "Which is more intimate—a blow job or sex?"

BARBARA: For some reason during the last few years, having something to do with AIDS and wanting to have safe sex without sucking on a condom——

PEPPER: Who's ever used a condom for a blow job?

FLO: They do in these pornographic books I read. I'm not kidding. They give head with condoms on. She rolls the condom down and gives the best blow job. She sucks that head, whatever.

GLORIA: That's ridiculous.

FLO: It's absurd.

BARBARA: I'm not saying I've ever done that. I'm just talking about the issue of safe sex.

GLORIA: You would be more inclined to have sex using a condom than to give head without protection.

BARBARA: But beyond the safety thing, I actually feel more comfortable having sex with someone I don't know well than giving head to someone I don't know well.

FLO: I'm just the opposite. I will give head left and right, but I won't let them fuck me.

BARBARA: It would seem like that's the normal thing. But there's something about it I just don't enjoy.

GLORIA: I love it!

FLO: But do you finish?

GLORIA: Yes.

FLO: I would never swallow, ever, in my life.

PEPPER: Why not?

FLO: Because it makes me sick.

GLORIA: Have you ever swallowed?

FLO: I have, and I threw up Taco Bell on his stomach. I'm not kidding.

BARBARA: The big burrito special.

FLO: It was the worst. At least he was my boyfriend.

GLORIA: Is that the only time you've ever swallowed?

FLO: No. I've swallowed in the past, but it just makes me gag. It's so foul, so disgusting.

PEPPER: See, I'm aware of what it tastes like because I'm a vegetarian. I can taste the meat, their food, their fish. I'm like, "OK, this person had chicken." I can taste that. I swear to God I can.

BARBARA: You have to be kidding. You are so crunchy. To me it all tastes exactly the same, every single guy I've ever swallowed.

PEPPER: Well, you guys are all meat-eaters.

FLO: Aren't you grossed out by it?

BARBARA: Pretty much, but not enough that I won't do it.

FLO: I don't like a guy going down on me either. Do you?

BARBARA: Not that much.

FLO: Do you ever get off from it?

BARBARA: No. Like once in my life.

FLO: [*Shrieking with joy*] Me neither! Like once or something! I'm so glad to hear you say that! Because all the girls I know are like, "Oh, I love it, it's fabulous."

BARBARA: They're like, "Yes! Yes! It's the only way!" But in years of sex and comfortable relationships, long-term lovers, I have never been able to train a guy to make me come. The times I have come have been totally random, and I've been fantasizing like nobody's business or grinding myself into them. I especially don't like it early on. I'm just like [*whistles and pretends to be filing her nails*].

FLO: I'm the same way. I'm like, "Hurry up and get up here so we can fuck."

BARBARA: I give them the little tap and beckon. A rap on the shoulder, then a "come here" with my finger.

FLO: That's what I do, too. I do the leg move and then tell them to come on up.

GLORIA: And they want to keep going because they're loving it.

BARBARA: And they don't want to deal with the fact that they're not doing it right and I'm not going to come. It's also an ego thing, you getting them up there. Some little part of them knows it's because you're not going to come.

GLORIA: Do you explain that it just doesn't do it for you, so they don't take it personally?

FLO: Never, because then they think something's wrong. The general male population thinks women love head.

BARBARA: The only guys I've ever explained it to are the guys who made me come, which was like two. I said, "Oh my God. That was unbelievable. That never happens. You are indeed a true genius." But to the others I'll say, "It's tough to make me come that way. Don't worry about it."

FLO: It's foreplay for me.

PEPPER: I love it—as long as he's clean. I have to feel like he's brushed his teeth.

FLO: I won't let him go down there if I haven't bathed like two minutes before.

PEPPER: I'm so nervous about them smelling it.

FLO: Sometimes you can't stop a guy from going down on you even though you're not fresh and clean. And then he kisses you and you smell your pee, your pussy, on his face.

PEPPER: The sexiest guy who ever went down on me smelled like baby powder. His whole genital area. It was so clean.

GLORIA: You don't like the smell of sweat? It turns me on so much.

FLO: [To Gloria] You're kind of earthy. I can tell.

GLORIA: What do you mean? I shave my pits.

FLO: No, I know that. Still.

GLORIA: But there are so many hot smells during sex. The dick smell and pussy smell and sweat smell and come smell.

PEPPER: I don't want to smell anything. I want it to feel good and not smell.

FLO: What happens if you go down to give him a blow job and you smell that been-working-all-day kind of smell between the balls? Do you give him a blow job?

GLORIA: I love that smell!

FLO: I hate that smell! But I go ahead and do it anyway. I bite my tongue and I do it.

PEPPER: First of all, I've never been with a man who has that working-all-day smell.

FLO: Oh, come on! What is she talking about?

PEPPER: I'm not with construction workers.

GLORIA: It's not just construction workers. I love smelling the balls. It's kind of dirty, but that's exactly why it turns me on.

PEPPER: It's not like I'm saying, "I won't go down on him if he smells." If I'm attracted to someone, I can get past the smell because I know in the future I'll be able to edify him. It took me a long time to learn to like getting head. It was difficult at first because the face is very public and the vagina is very private. It was like public meets private, private meets public. It was very confusing. There was a real disparity and I had to reconcile it. Then I got used to it. [*To Barbara and Flo*] I can understand why it would make you uncomfortable.

BARBARA: It doesn't make me uncomfortable. It just doesn't hit the right spot for me.

PEPPER: My theory is that you're not relaxed. If you could relax, you might not be uptight about it.

BARBARA: I can get pretty relaxed, sweetie.

GLORIA: Have you ever had a guy go down sideways—give you a lip job?

FLO: What do you mean, sideways?

GLORIA: [*Demonstrates with her fingers a guy lying perpendicular to the woman, crouched over her pussy from the side*] I was the same as you until I met a guy who did it sideways, so his lips ran parallel to my pussy and his tongue moved against the grain of my clit. When the guy goes perpendicular the friction is much better. The other way, he's lifting the hood and then the hood's going down and sometimes it's too intense and sometimes it's not intense enough. But this way he's on top of it the whole time. He's also got a finger in there at the same time, which is a huge turn-on.

PEPPER: Wait a second. That's like a whole other ball of wax. I don't like double duty.

BARBARA: Me neither.

FLO: Me neither.

PEPPER: I like one or the other. Tongue or finger. I get overwhelmed when both are down there.

FLO: The rhythm is not right. There's no way you're going to get the tongue and the finger working in the same way. They're competing against each other.

GLORIA: I'm not talking coordination, just general finger action. The rhythm is all in the tongue.

BARBARA: General finger action I always get rid of immediately. I yank it right out.

PEPPER: I didn't understand how good oral sex could feel until I was with someone who did it really well. Now it's so much easier for me to have oral sex than it is to have intercourse. With intercourse, I'm being penetrated and it makes me so much more vulnerable. With oral sex it can just be about the orgasm, whereas with sex I get much more attached. When someone's inside me and they withdraw, I start to cry and get very emotional. Oral sex both ways, giving and getting, is much more detached.

FLO: I have to disagree with that. Giving head is detached. But I won't let them give me head until after we've had sex and they've gotten to know me. That's so personal for me. But giving head——

GLORIA: You give it just like that [*snaps fingers*].

FLO: I do.

BARBARA: I'm just the opposite. I'll take it whenever, but I certainly don't enjoy it.

FLO: You are such a martyr about that. "I'll take it—but I won't enjoy it, goddamn it!"

BARBARA: I enjoy that they're doing it and I enjoy that they're into it.

FLO: I have a problem with a guy who doesn't want to do it. He should almost beg to do it.

PEPPER: But what if he just doesn't like it? Then what do you do? I said lightheartedly to someone once, "So, how do you feel about oral sex?" As in, "Hint, hint." And he responded, "Not good."

GLORIA: That's really fucked up.

PEPPER: How come guys can't have the option not to feel good about it, but women can? Why isn't it acceptable the other way around?

GLORIA: Because there's this whole history of men claiming that going down is nasty. And I feel like we can't control the fact that our genitalia are inside. That we have holes and not sticks.

PEPPER: If you go over to someone's house and they make you dinner, you offer to do the dishes. If a guy doesn't offer to give you oral sex, it's like he's come to your house and won't do the dishes. You want him to at least be interested in helping out.

BARBARA: I'm with you. I appreciate the effort.

PEPPER: It's the effort. Most guys don't understand that their interest in it is the thing. "You wash, I'll dry."

GLORIA: What about getting a finger up the ass? Do you like that?

PEPPER: That is an exit, not an entrance.

GLORIA: I love doggy with a finger in the ass.

FLO: I love it too. It puts me over the edge.

PEPPER: OK. That, to me, is not right.

GLORIA: And, Flo, I'm not talking deep, are you?

FLO: No. I'm talking first joint, just circling the anus range.

BARBARA: I like doing that to them.

FLO: Guys love it.

BARBARA: When I discovered it for the first time it was like hitting the magic button.

FLO: They get so hard. It's because the prostate is up there.

PEPPER: I don't want to give him a prostate exam.

GLORIA: I'm much more willing to take it than give it. I get grossed out about sticking it in——

FLO: Doo-doo.

BARBARA: For some reason it doesn't bother me.

GLORIA: When a guy sticks a finger up my ass, I keep my eye on that finger for the rest of the night and make sure that baby goes nowhere near my you-know-what. [*To Flo*] Are you good about separating that finger? Once you do it to him are you conscious of where that finger is going?

FLO: Hell yes!

GLORIA: [*to Barbara*] Are you?

BARBARA: No. I stick it in his mouth.

[*Flo and Pepper simultaneously squeal, clap their hands over their mouths, and slide their seats two feet away from the table.*]

BARBARA: [*Laughing*] I'm just kidding.

PEPPER: I don't like this conversation.

BARBARA: That was a joke!

FLO: I thought you were serious!

BARBARA: I don't generally put my fingers in my own mouth, let alone his.

GLORIA: [*To Flo and Barbara*] Have you ever had a guy lick your ass, then try to kiss you?

FLO: I have.

GLORIA: What did you say?

FLO: "Don't kiss me."

GLORIA: But you don't want to come off as being mean.

PEPPER: The guy's going to give you a hundred diseases!

BARBARA: Why is that different from him going down on you and then kissing you?

GLORIA: There's not as much bacteria in your vagina as in your ass.

PEPPER: I don't let faces go anywhere near my ass. That's not happening. I barely let faces go near my face.

GLORIA: Once I was having sex with a guy doggy style, and he had a finger in my ass. I said, "That feels really good." He said, "Do you like it when I play with your butthole?" and the word *butthole* made me crack up. He said no other girl he'd been with had ever found that word funny.

FLO: Ass is better.

GLORIA: You say ass, though you're talking about the anus.

FLO: Do not call it the goddamn anus and expect me to have an orgasm.

PEPPER: Once you say the word *anus*, it's a very long way back to sexy. You can't say that word and expect me to get wet.

FLO: What about anal sex? Have you ever had that?

PEPPER: I have, as a favor on his birthday. Once. It was not good. It was *really* not good. It was painful and it was also——

FLO: Did he complete the act?

PEPPER: No.

GLORIA: How deep did he go?

PEPPER: I didn't measure.

GLORIA: I've had a guy go in two inches but I've never had a guy go in all the way. I would fucking freak!

FLO: I have.

GLORIA: Did you like it?

FLO: No. It takes a long time for them to open you up so that it's not painful.

GLORIA: Have you done it too?

[*Barbara nods.*]

GLORIA: To the point of him coming?

BARBARA: I made him take it out.

GLORIA: How can you relax enough?

FLO: You just do. You can. And you open up. It's amazing. I don't mean that in a good way, but you really open up.

GLORIA: Does it feel good?

PEPPER: It didn't feel good to me.

FLO: It can if he's stimulating your clitoris at the same time. Or if your hand is reaching down there. Or you have a vibrator on your clitoris.

PEPPER: If you have all that other stuff going on while he's in your ass, why does he need to be in your ass?

FLO: It's tighter.

PEPPER: For him.

FLO: It's a giving thing. And also the mentality of doing something so atrocious and dirty and forbidden.

BARBARA: That's the appeal for me too: "Fuck me up the ass."

GLORIA: I like that forbidden dirt thing. And guys like it too. That's why they get so turned on when you're having your period.

PEPPER: The guys I've been with are generally so squeamish that if I have my period they don't even want to go near my vagina.

BARBARA: Does that upset you?

PEPPER: I totally understand it. I don't want to go near my vagina when I have my period.

FLO: I like sex when I'm on the rag. I'm in the mood then.

BARBARA: I just put down a towel.

PEPPER: I don't know about that.

GLORIA: I've never had it right in the middle. Usually it's at the beginning or the end. I put down the towel, but nothing comes out onto it.

BARBARA: I've had it really bloody. Like the shower scene in *Carrie*.

FLO: Holy shit. That's a lot of blood.

BARBARA: I like it. As long as I don't have cramps.

GLORIA: Orgasms relieve cramps.

PEPPER: They also relieve migraines.

BARBARA: They're really good for back pain, too.

FLO: I'm sure they cure cancer. I'm sure of it. I just have to prove it.

Negotiations

 SIT DOWN, BERNARD— WHAT I'M GOING TO SAY MAY HURT YOU TERRIBLY—

YOU'RE GOING TO BREAK UP WITH ME, AREN'T YOU, ELOISE?

 YOU SUSPECTED? OH, MY POOR BERNARD!

IT'S THE STRANGEST THING—BECAUSE I JUST CAME OVER TO BREAK OFF WITH **YOU**!

 OH, MY POOR DARLING, I UNDERSTAND THAT YOU HAVE TO PROTECT YOURSELF—BUT IT'S **I** WHO AM BREAKING OFF WITH **YOU**!

NO, HONESTLY, **I** BROUGHT IT UP **FIRST**. I BROKE OFF WITH YOU BEFORE YOU HAD A **CHANCE** TO BREAK OFF WITH ME.

 THAT IS SIMPLY NOT **TRUE**! DIDN'T I **DISTINCTLY** SAY— "SIT DOWN, BERNARD. WHAT I'M GOING TO SAY MAY HURT YOU TERRIBLY"?

YES, BUT WHO FIRST USED THE ACTUAL WORDS "BREAK UP"? ADMIT IT! WHO?

 I DON'T CARE **HOW** DEFENSIVE YOU MUST GET TO HIDE FROM THE TRUTH—THE FACT REMAINS **I BROKE OFF FIRST**

YOU DID **NOT**! I DID! I DID! I DID!

 DON'T YOU THINK WE'RE BEING A LITTLE FOOLISH? WHY DON'T WE DISCUSS THIS AGAIN TOMORROW WHEN WE'RE BOTH A LITTLE MORE RATIONAL.

I'LL SEE YOU AT NINE.

 I WON'T BE HERE WHEN HE COMES. **I'LL** SHOW HIM WHO DOES THE BREAKING OFF AROUND HERE.

 I'M NOT COMING.

Forever Marilyn

commentary by SCOTT TUROW

M arilyn Monroe smiles at me every day. She is there on my living-room wall, in one of the zillions of silk-screened portraits of her that Andy Warhol began producing in the early Sixties, shortly after Marilyn's substance-induced death. Rendered in pastel hues of optic intensity, MM looks down heavy-lidded, with the wrinkle of a grin, wised-up and happily alluring.

Marilyn no doubt commands a shrine in thousands, perhaps millions, of homes around the world. As we approach what would have been her 75th birthday, she has emerged as the aboriginal pop culture heroine. But what's odd in my case is that, while she was around, I did not think Marilyn Monroe was much—conventional firepower, when some other women were thermonuclear.

With her pudgy nose, Marilyn really set no standard for classic female winsomeness. And her form, fully revealed to the nation in December 1953 when Marilyn was this magazine's first Sweetheart of the Month, was no better than fetching. For sheer flag-raising pulchritude, I always preferred MM's nearest competitor in the swelling ranks of blonde boobshells, Jayne Mansfield. Even PLAYBOY conceded in the text that ran with the now-renowned photo of Marilyn lounging against red plush, "Her curves really aren't that spectacular."

I'd grown up in one of those urban, ethnic enclaves where the beauties I knew—and for whom I had my first yens—were dark. Sophia Loren, sensual and passionate, was ideal. More to the point, Marilyn's blondeness came straight from the bottle. Whether she was Norma Jean Baker or Norma Jeane Mortenson at birth, a fact still disputed, she was, in the photos I've seen, nigh on to a brunette when she first married at 16. Thus, there was an element of the fake about her, a trait that persisted in the girl-off-the-farm routine for which she was best known. The ingenue who cooed as the subway draft fluttered her skirt to her waist in *The Seven Year Itch* was a sexual creature who men could have found fully bewitching only in a patriarchal and puritan era, a woman too naive and too slow on the uptake to recognize—and thus to control—the phenomenal power she exerted.

The real Marilyn, the one who seemed to be there behind the burlesque posturing, was too neurotic to command more than sympathy and too insubstantial to require much respect. Jayne Mansfield, at least, went to SMU and supposedly had an IQ over 160. Marilyn was famously temperamental. "I've been on a calendar," she admitted, "but never on time." Drunk and druggy, she had no apparent gratitude for what luck and good PR men had created for her. Billy Wilder, who directed my favorite of her films, *Some Like It Hot*, called Marilyn "the meanest woman I have ever known in this town." What could you say about somebody who married both Joe DiMaggio and Arthur Miller, except that she did not have a clue what she wanted?

Yet in the nearly 40 years since her death, one of us has changed. These days, the image I see in the print on my living room wall is of a unique figure who encompassed many of the dominating—and contradictory—impulses of the second half of the American century just concluded.

With Marilyn, sex seemed to be the heart of the matter. Her initial appearance on these pages embodied, in all senses, the first truly open communication in America about sexuality. Hef bought the photo rights from a calendar company, which had engaged in only limited distribution of the photo for fear that McCarthy-era morality would have led to prosecution for mailing obscene material. Hef, with little to lose, put Marilyn in the post, and with her image, essentially said to America, "Gather round."

The fact that she did not quail in that role was part of Marilyn's power. In 1933, Hedy Lamarr had appeared in her fabled nude swimming scene in *Ecstasy* and the resulting uproar initiated an era of censorship. The Motion Picture Producers and Distributors of America's Hays Code, effective in 1934, was so brainlessly restrictive that even characters who were supposed to be husband and wife could not be depicted in the same bed. Marilyn's appearance here was an announcement that at least one starlet was not about to succumb to shame—or modesty. She had it and flaunted it. She never pretended to have been caught unaware or exploited by the photos PLAYBOY presented. Indeed, she was back on these pages again, naked as God had made her, near the time of her death, when she was at the apex of her career. She was nude because she wanted to be.

The inherent feminine power wielded by the tease always underlaid Marilyn's on-screen persona. What I was too young to understand when I watched her playing the archetype disparaged in blonde jokes was that it was essential for her to be unconvincing. She-knew-that-we-knew-it was all a little too much. Marilyn was perhaps our first post-modern figure who addressed us in subtexts. Always traveling beneath the surface, as she lamely feigned innocence, was that canny frankness about the dominating nature of sexuality. We look back at her slithery rendition of *Happy Birthday to You* for JFK, wearing a dress for the ages, and feel ready to blush or to laugh out loud at an era so restrained by proprieties that it was decades before Americans could openly acknowledge the forthrightness of her come-ons.

Unlike any of her peers or predecessors, Marilyn added one further element: an undertone of regret. Yes, she was willing; but there was a tenderness about it, a sadness that she could not be that farm girl and thus relieved of the burden of the reactions she inspired. Because she made that bow toward the acceptable, Marilyn blurred the former distinctions between high art and low, between good taste and bad, between whore and Madonna. Her PLAYBOY pose seemed to be pasted to the wall in the dingy recesses of the backroom of every hardware store I visited in childhood, a lurid testimonial to the baseness of men. Yet Marilyn, somehow, was never confined to the shadows; her apparent vulnerability saved her. She also was welcomed—and probably schtupped—at the White House.

Looking backward, we now see the America that emerged from the Second World War as one where imagery and commerce were increasingly intertwined, where our national identity was rooted more and more in certain images marketed coast to coast. The endlessly photographed Monroe was probably the most famous face on earth—and as a self-conscious sex symbol, she made herself a virtual commodity. It is no accident that Warhol began turning out his serial portraits of her around the same time he was painting pictures of Brillo boxes and soup cans.

It was the eagerness with which she gave herself to that role that really distinguished Marilyn. She somehow suggested the degree to which *we* created her. She succumbed to us more powerfully, more willingly than any woman before, beaming back our callow, but widely shared, fantasies. Her celebrated allure was inherently democratic. She belonged to everybody—indeed, in retrospect, that is one of the clear messages of the fact she could attract both our best ballplayer and our preeminent playwright.

Nevertheless, it was death that ultimately made Marilyn Monroe larger than life—and spared her the excess that has overwhelmed the likes of Elizabeth Taylor. It is hard to imagine who Marilyn would be, approaching her dotage. Dietrich's legs still gathered raves when she was well into her 60s, but by 75, even Marilyn's sexual candlepower was bound to have dimmed. Instead, she remains in memory fully possessed of all her carnal appeal, like athletes who retire at the height of their powers.

The poignancy of her story lies in the fact that her end taught us to distrust so much of what she seemingly stood for. She may not have been the first celebrity destroyed by celebrity—that honor may belong to Socrates—but she was certainly the first one who was essentially photographed as she danced over the brink. Hollywood is a place that teaches over and over again the Greek gods' lessons about hubris. Marilyn stands—with Elvis and dozens of others—as the object lesson that fame is worth little in the end. That the most glamorous woman on earth died in desperation cements the message that "real life" is the only place to find a life.

As important, Marilyn was raised from the dead a feminist icon. It turned out that being craved by most of the men in America capable of an erection did not make a woman happy. Quite the opposite. Like her third husband's most famous hero, Willy Loman, Marilyn seemingly died because she had the wrong dreams. Her destruction inspired women to resist being similarly reduced to symbol or package.

It is far too romantic to believe Marilyn understood all of this. In fact, it is the essence of her legend that she fully surrendered herself to what everyone else wanted to make of her. But at 75, she seems certain to be remembered as the first emblem of the omnivorous nature of our developing pop culture, and of the ability of certain figures to become a River Ganges of national passions, into which all of them poured in— until they washed her away.

"I've got a lot of things to do, so I'd like to cut out the foreplay and go straight to the orgasm. So I won't be needing you today."

Mom Descending
a Staircase

fiction by NEIL LaBUTE

I hardly remember the reason for coming up here now, I mean, in the first place. Isn't that weird? Sometimes things happen, the smallest little thing during a day or a lifetime, and everything else that preceded it—even big, major events—becomes so insignificant or minor in comparison that it just doesn't seem to matter. Or register, even. It doesn't even register with you, not really.

I came up to the attic—it's barely that, actually, more of a crawl space above the back bedroom, which my brother and I had shared all while growing up—to make a routine check, see if there was any water damage or mouse droppings, that type of thing. Find out if it needed to be sprayed or fumigated or whatever. I didn't expect to find anything. I probably should have, though, been prepared, I'm saying, because my mom was a bit of a pack rat all of her life, a serious collector of things—and I'm talking about crap here, not like antiques or fur coats or stuff like that. She used to have just mounds and mounds of magazines and pocketbooks (that's what they used to call paperbacks when I was growing up; they'd call them pocketbooks, which was always confusing because that was also another name for a woman's purse—English is a weird language, when you get right down to it), all kinds of shit that she collected, mostly in the bedroom and heaped in that little alleyway created by her side of the mattress and the wall of the room, which would eventually be carted out by my dad to the garage, where he would either dump it all in the trash (if he was pissed on that particular day) or put it in a box and shove it in the closet so that she could sort through it later (if he was feeling benevolent). That's the way it worked in our house; it was a little like living on the coast of some tropical island. One day sunny and mild, the next day Hurricane Dad. When he was in one of his "moods"—which was usually only when he was awake—it was better just to put the plywood sheets up over the windows and evacuate. Mom put up with a lot in her day—her "day" having lasted some 63 years, until Thursday of last week when her heart gave out in the grocery store, near the (where else?) magazine rack. She died before they could get her to the emergency room, a copy of the *Enquirer* still clutched in one fist—and my wife and I are getting the house ready for sale. My brother, who now lives in Kansas doing God-knows-what for some software company, couldn't stay on after the funeral because he was saving vacation time for a family trip to Disney World and his company allows only three days off for episodes of grief—he actually called it that all while he was here, an "episode of grief," which finally made me pull him aside and say something during the little get-together we had after the funeral. People were starting to look at him funny, so what else could I do? Anyway, that's how we ended up here, Millie and I (that's my wife, Mildred, but I call her Millie), going through the house I grew up in and getting it ready to be put on the market.

Millie is in charge of the general sprucing up—she loves doing that, spring-cleaning or big projects like putting in a new flower bed—so I've found that it's better just to get out of the way and let her get things done. It's a pretty good excuse, anyway, for not having to pitch in and help out. I hate housework, lawn jobs, that sort of stuff. Always have. I'm a pretty good worker overall, but domestic chores are not my forte. Not at all. Because of that, and the fact that Millie has one of those take-charge personalities (she really does, even she would say so), I found it more useful to stake a claim on the perimeter of all this activity—call the real estate woman, place an ad in the paper for an estate sale, go through Mom's papers (including several bank accounts and a safety-deposit box) and assorted tasks like that. Basically, keep clear of the Windex. And that's how I find myself up in the attic above "the boys' room," lying on my stomach and searching around with a key-chain flashlight. I'm sure my dad would be doing this if he were here, but he's not. They got a divorce, my parents did, about 20 years ago—they thoughtfully stayed together all while we were growing up so that we could cower in fear and watch them engage in their daily shouting matches, but after I went off to college they decided the time had finally come, and my old man moved out, leaving Mom the house and all the worries that come with owning a property. And besides, he died in a car accident seven years ago last spring. Too bad for him; he should've been watching the road.

I've pretty much made my way to the end of the dwelling now by pulling myself along the length of two boards, laid out side by side, that run across the alternating pattern of rafters and insulation. An insect or two scurries away into the shadows, but the place seems pretty okay other than that. No watermarks on the wood, no pinpricks of daylight shining through above my head. I'm about to start down, crawling back the way I came, when (as I'm turning) my light plays across a shape tucked into one corner of the eaves. Off to my left. Curious, I turn the feeble blue beam of my Chet's Auto Supply light to one side and shine it across the mound. It turns out to be three boxes, all sporting the old U-Haul insignia across them, jammed into an area no bigger than a bread box (it's actually much bigger than that, but the bread box is the standard increment of measurement in our house) and sitting one on top of the other in a squat little stack. A thick layer of what might politely be called dust settled over the whole thing.

"Is everything okay?" rises up from below me like the cry of a phoenix as it claws its way out of the ashes. I drop my flashlight and cringe, totally caught off guard. Millie must be taking a break and has suddenly realized I'm not directly underfoot.

"I'm up here!" I shout back, knowing that this is vague and meaningless, but it should be enough to satisfy her. I employ a tone that means "I'm doing something useful," and that usually works. It seems to in this case, at least, because I hear no more out of her. I can tell she's moved into one of the bathrooms now, as the furious squeak of sponge on porcelain reaches my ears, even up here. I'm telling you, she's hell on wheels, Millie is, when she starts cleaning something.

"What're these?" I say, but barely loud enough for even myself to hear. I scuttle over to them and pull the top one toward me. A second or two later I have the flaps open and find a stack of old clothing staring up at me. I know, I know, clothing can't actually look at you, but I'm just saying that's what's in the box. Clothes. Our old scout uniforms—my brother's and mine—all carefully folded and placed in two rows, with a few little awards and ribbons arranged on top. It doesn't make me sad to see them—I mean, not really—but it's a definite surprise. My brother'll get a kick out of going through it all—see, he did the whole thing, Eagle Scout or whatever, so it was kind of a big deal. I smile at the memories that flood back as I pull the second box over toward me and snap open the lid. Books this time, which I had no idea my parents ever owned. I mean, we had maybe one set of encyclopedias when I was growing up, and that was about it. A *Good News Bible* that was kept in a drawer in the living room, where my dad could get at it to use when killing a spider, but we weren't exactly a literary family. At all. Well, my mom would read those cheap romances and stuff, which I already mentioned—the pocketbooks—but some kids I knew, families I had visited or had sleepovers with, had mountains of books. Walls and walls full of them, even separate rooms that they called dens or, this one friend of mine, a library. So this was a bit of a shock, to find a bunch of good-quality hardbacks tucked away at our place, even if they were technically hidden up in the attic. And these are nice ones, too, like Hemingway and Steinbeck and those guys, Fitzgerald. It's really hard to believe—my mom must've joined some club or something, Book-of-the-Month or that type of deal. At least until my old man found out; these had probably been banished up here for her daring to defy him (or spending "good money" on something other than Pabst Blue Ribbon). Smiling, I snatch one off the top, Samuel Butler's *The Way of All Flesh*—which I've never even heard of—and flip it open to the title page. And there she is. Staring up at me through a piece of tissue paper, but I can tell that it's her, very clearly, having seen other pictures from around that time. Right about when they got married, a year or two after that. It's my mother, her hair still that vibrant red that it was in her youth, looking straight into the camera. What I have here are three photos—old Polaroids, actually—that have been placed inside this one novel and tucked away. Shut up for however many years. Now of course I remember my father and his stupid Polaroid Land camera—I've got about a hundred photos of me as a kid from the 1970s, which are all faded and curled up on the edges—but this is a new one to me. Three pristine color snaps of my mother, sitting on the stairs that are almost directly beneath me, completely and utterly naked. I mean, not a stitch on. Well, except for a pair of pumps. Wow. How can this be?

"You want lunch?" comes Millie's voice up through the opening back behind me. Questioning. "I'm getting kind of hungry."

"*Ummm*, well, I'm up here now, so I should probably...." I don't really know what to say next, but she saves me by jumping in and taking over, just as she always does.

"I'll run down to Wendy's or something, it's fine. What do you want?"

"Spicy Chicken's good. The meal, okay, but Biggie Size it? And a Diet." This cryptic fast-food language is instantly processed and accepted by my wife in the ensuing silence.

"You want a Frosty?"

"Yeah, that sounds nice. Small."

"All right, see you in a minute." And then, "Is there anything up there?"

"*Ahhhhh*, no, not really. Just some…I'm checking for leaks and that sort of thing. I don't want some contract falling through because of a rainstorm or whatever, right?"

"I guess."

"I'll be down by the time you get back. Promise," I say, not really meaning it but knowing that it sometimes makes the difference—women love it when men set deadlines or express certainty. It's supposedly sexy or something. Don't ask me.

"Great. See you!" she calls out.

"Yeah, drive safe, okay? And don't forget that Barber is a one-way."

"I remember. God, what do you think I am, retarded?"

"*Ummm*, I prefer to think of you as 'special….'" I can hear her laughing from way up here, so that's good. Sometimes Millie takes my humor the wrong way.

"That's me, your 'special' girl. See you, sweetie!" The sound of the door closing a second later. I have to say, when that woman gets hungry, nothing stands in the way of her getting her next meal. No way.

"So, Dad, what is the story here?" I whisper, turning the pictures over, almost expecting an apology (or at least an explanation) to be penciled in on the back of each one. But nothing. Not one word. I flip the top one back over, leaning in with the light to study it. In two of the three, my mother—I guess if we're talking about her being all nude and everything you might as well know her name, which is Carolyn—she's leaning back against one stair, holding herself upright with her elbows. Both of these are shot from the waist up, so basically they show her breasts and face. Not close-ups, exactly, but what filmmakers might call medium shots. I guess you could almost say that they're artfully composed, what with the carpet from the stairs and the color of her hair complementing each other and the pale of her skin working as a kind of relief. Flaming scarlet lips that would be beautiful on anyone else but make my stomach flutter a bit as I catch myself thinking it. I don't know if I feel up to describing her bosom, but I'll give it a go—if it was a completely impartial assessment I was making, of some lady in a magazine or with a friend from college or something, then I'd say, without hesitation, that they are great. Almost perfectly shaped—too perfect, really—as if they were drawn by that dude who made *Fritz the Cat* or whatever. Just really, really lovely. I mean, I don't think I'm saying anything new when I report that women's tits can so easily turn out to be mediocre, or worse even, once you actually get a look at them, so it's still surprising—even at my age—when I see a knockout pair. And I mean especially that, a pair. Often you'll find some that are exquisite, and then, on closer inspection, you'll notice a flaw or imperfection on one or its partner. A leaning to the side or a sort of drooping, a discoloration in the nipple. A birthmark or a mole, even, lots of things that can keep the two from being magnificent when studied together. But here in my hand, sported by my own mom some 40 years ago, is an almost flawless set of mams. Two gorgeous examples of womanly flesh and captured forever in a snapshot. I mean, these are knockout boobs that my mom has, and until this very moment in my life I had no idea that she was built like that. I can only ever remember her in a kind of shapeless floral housedress all while I was growing up, so this newly discovered fact is equal parts disturbing and titillating. Well, maybe it errs a touch on the disturbing side, but still.

As I said, the second photo is almost a carbon copy of the first, so I skip past it and move on to the third, which is the one that really takes the cake. Again, this is a low-quality print I'm looking at, but the woman springs out of the composition, so gorgeous is she at that moment in her life. It's a full-body shot, this one is—and, yes, now I know for certain that she didn't dye her hair—but it's her positioning that's so startling, and not just because she's my mother, either, but from what little I know about that era itself. The Sixties, I mean. I realize there were magazines you could buy back then, pornography and that sort of stuff, but everything I've ever seen or heard of from that period is pretty chaste—at least the first part of the decade, and these pictures are from probably no later than 1963, or 1964 at the latest. Most shots from those times are these "girl next door" types sitting all coy and covered on a blanket, with their tops exposed but that's about it. And here's this woman who used to fix me my Cap'n Crunch every morning with her legs all spread and her fire-engine-red fingernails playing with one nipple, pinching at the tip. Lips puckered up. I really am taken aback by this now, the idea that my mother could've ever done this, even with the help of my father (although I'd bet good money on the fact that he had a lot to do with it; I just know that he did—he always seemed like that kind of man). Now, I realize that all parents have a life, a secret sort of life that exists before we ever get to know them; of course I understand that, but this is still pretty startling to find out about someone you both love desperately and take entirely for granted. The woman I call Mother had the makings of a pinup and a body that would've made Bettie Page weep into her broth. Life is just so damn silly, isn't it? I mean, when you really think about it.

The reason for all this naughtiness reveals itself when I finally put the photos aside and lift the piece of tissue paper they were wrapped in from inside the novel. Beneath it, folded into thirds, is a simple and direct response from the offices of PLAYBOY magazine in Chicago, Illinois—it's not signed by Hugh Hefner himself, unfortunately, or I'd probably sell the thing on eBay—that thanks my father for his submission, mentions how beautiful his wife is and goes on to say that, while she is certainly a worthwhile female specimen, they are sorry to inform him that they will not be pursuing her as a possible Centerfold at this time. What? And then suddenly it all makes sense; the entire enterprise makes itself clear to me as I'm lying there in the dark: Dad wanted to get Mom into PLAYBOY as a model. I mean, I've heard of this notion, that many men's magazines accept amateur photos and that type of thing, but I'm stunned by this new curve in what I already imagined to be a serpentine relationship between my two parents. How could he have done this? And how could *she*? It really is baffling. Even if they did love each other at one point—and I suppose they had to, I must begrudgingly admit, plus it's a medical fact that they had sex a few times, at least in the early days—this behavior is still so off the charts from what I know about them as a couple that I can feel myself drifting into a kind of shock. Just staring at the company logo at the top of the rejection notice, which is beginning to go slowly out of focus.

"I'm back! Honey?" comes roaring up from downstairs with such force that I nearly slip off the 2-by-12s I'm lying on. I sit up quickly and bang my head on the hard edge of a slanting truss. Shit.

"Coming!" I scream and fold the letter quickly into a little square, which I jam into that tiny coin pocket in the front of my jeans as I roll to one side. I steal one more glance at the wide shot of my mom, the third photograph—she seems to be calling out to me with her eyes, begging me to break with convention, the restrictive bonds of polite society, and spend a bit of quality time with her in the sack—then slip all three photos down inside my underwear. Don't ask me why, I'm not sure, but I hide them there and start crawling backward toward the lighted opening. I suppose I'm worried that I'll brush up against Millie during lunch and she'll feel something in my pocket, and I'm just not strong enough for that right now, I'm really not, this big explanation thing, so I figure I'll keep them in my undies and sort through this mess some other time. Back home in Seattle. Or maybe even on the plane after she falls asleep (Millie is usually out cold before we take off). Later.

As I'm inching back toward the top rung of the ladder, feeling for it with each foot as I go, a thought flashes through my head—a sudden awareness, as clear and pristine as if it were a vision sent down from on high—that I will (no doubt) never tell anyone about this discovery: the boxes, the photos, the note. None of it. Not Millie, not my brother. No one. I am also completely certain that I will spend a great deal of time alone with these Polaroids in the near future, sharing a hushed closeness with them unlike anything I ever enjoyed with my mother when she was alive and merely a phone call away.

PLAYBOY'S PARTY JOKES

A new sexual position has been invented. It's called the Rodeo. A woman gets on all fours, and a man enters her from behind. Then the man wraps his arms around her waist. He whispers, "You've got the fattest ass I've ever seen," and tries to hold on for eight seconds.

After getting tipsy during dinner, a wife told her husband, "Tonight you may do whatever you want to me."

The husband thought it over and dropped her off at her mother's house.

A chicken farmer walked into a bar and sat down next to a woman who was drinking champagne, and he ordered the same. He turned to her and said, "I'm drinking the good stuff because I'm celebrating."

The woman said, "Me too."

As they clinked glasses, the man asked, "What are you celebrating?"

She said, "For years my husband and I have been trying to have a baby. Today I found out I'm pregnant."

"What a coincidence," the man said. "I'm a farmer. For years all my chickens were infertile, but today they're finally pregnant."

"That's great," the woman said. "How did they become fertile?"

"I switched roosters," he replied.

"What a coincidence," the woman said. "So did I."

We just heard about the unlucky fellow who phoned his girlfriend to see if she was doing anything that evening. She said she wasn't, so he took her out. And sure enough, she wasn't.

Three married couples moved into town and wanted to join the local church. The minister told them that before they could be admitted, they had to abstain from sex for 30 days. One month later they returned. The minister asked them if they had fulfilled the requirement. The elderly couple said they had no trouble abstaining. The middle-aged couple said the first two weeks were difficult, but they managed to abstain. The third couple were newlyweds. The husband said, "We were doing okay until my wife dropped a can of paint."

The minister asked, "A can of paint?"

The husband said, "Yes. When she bent over to pick it up, I couldn't control myself and ravished her on the spot."

The minister said, "Well, I'm sorry. But given that fact, you won't be welcome in our church."

The husband said, "I understand. We're no longer welcome in Home Depot, either."

Why do mice have small balls? Not many of them know how to dance.

One afternoon, two women were sitting on a front porch. The first woman said, "Here comes my husband with a bunch of flowers. That means I'll be on my back with my legs in the air all weekend."

The other woman asked, "Why? Don't you have a vase?"

What's better than honor? Inner.

109

I Am Dying, Egypt, Dying

fiction by JOHN UPDIKE

C lem came from Buffalo and spoke in the neutral American accent that sends dictionary-makers there. His pronunciation was clear and colorless, his manners impeccable, his clothes freshly laundered and appropriate no matter where he was, however far from home. Rich and unmarried, he traveled a lot; he had been to Athens and Rio, Las Vegas and Hong Kong, Leningrad and Sydney and now Cairo. His posture was perfect, but he walked without swing; people at first liked him, because his apparent perfection reflected flatteringly upon them, and then distrusted him, because his perfection revealed no flaw. As he traveled, he studied the guidebooks conscientiously, picked up phrases of the local language, collected prints and artifacts. He was serious but not humorless; indeed, his smile, a creeping but finally complete revelation of utterly even and white front teeth, with a bit of tongue flirtatiously pinched between them, was one of the things that led people on, that led them to hope for the flaw, the entering crack. There were hopeful signs. At the bar he took one drink too many, the hurried last drink that robs the dinner wine of taste. Though he enjoyed human society, he couldn't dance. He had a fine fair square-shouldered body, surely masculine and yet somehow neutral, which he solicitously covered with oil against the sun that, as they moved up the Nile, grew sharper and more tropical. He fell asleep in deck chairs, beautifully immobile, glistening, as the two riverbanks at their safe distance glided by—date palms, taut green fields irrigated by rotating donkeys, pyramids of white round pots, trapezoidal houses of elephant-colored mud, mud-colored children silently waving, and the roseate desert cliffs beyond, massive parentheses. Glistening like a mirror, he slept in this gliding parenthesis with a godlike calm that possessed the landscape, transformed it into

110

a steady dreaming. Clem said of himself, awaking, apologizing and smiling with that bit of pinched tongue, that he slept badly at night, suffered from insomnia. This also was a hopeful sign. People wanted to love him.

There were not many on the boat. The war discouraged tourists. Indeed, at Nag Hammadi they did pass under a bridge in which Israeli commandos had blasted three neat but not very conclusive holes; a wooden ramp had been laid on top and the traffic of carts and rickety lorries continued. And at Aswan they saw anti-aircraft batteries defending the High Dam. But for the cruise between, the war figured only as a luxurious amount of space on deck and a pleasant disproportion between the 70 crewmen and the 20 paying passengers. These 20 were:

Three English couples, middle-aged but for one miniskirted wife, who was thought for days to be a daughter.

Two German boys who wore bathing trunks to the temples, yet seemed to know the gods by name and perhaps were future archaeologists.

A French couple in their 60s. The man had been tortured in World War Two: his spine had fused in a curve as he moved over the desert rubble and uneven stairways with tiny shuffling steps and studied the murals by means of a mirror hung around his neck. Yet he, too, knew the gods and would murmur worshipfully.

Three Egyptians, a man and two women, in their 30s, of a professional class, teachers or museum curators, cosmopolitan and handsome, given to laughter among themselves, even while the guide, a cherubic old Bedouin called Poppa Omar, was lecturing.

A fluffy and sweet, ample and perfumed American widow and her escort, a short bald native of New Jersey who for 20 years had run tours in Africa, armed with a fancy fly whisk and an impenetrable rudeness toward natives of Africa.

An amateur travelogist from Green Bay working his way south to Cape Town with 200 pounds of photographic equipment.

A stocky blond couple, 40ish, who kept to themselves, hired their own guides and were presumed to be Russian.

A young Scandinavian woman, beautiful, alone.

Clem.

Clem had joined the cruise at the last minute; he had been in Amsterdam and become oppressed by the low sky and tight-packed houses, the cold canal touring boats and the bad Indonesian food and the prostitutes illuminated in their windows like garish great candy. He had flown to Cairo and not liked it better. A cheeseburger in the Hilton offended him by being gamy. In the plaza outside, a man rustled up to him and asked if he had had any love last night. The city, with its incessant twinkle of car horns and furtive-eyed men in pajamas, seemed unusable, remote. The museum was full of sandbags. The heart of King Tut's treasure had been hidden in case of invasion; but his gold sarcophagus, feathered in lapis lazuli and carnelian, did touch Clem, with a whisper of death, of flight, of floating. A pamphlet in the Hilton advertised a six-day trip up the Nile, Luxor to Aswan, in a luxurious boat. It sounded passive and educational, which appealed to Clem; he had gone to college at the University of Rochester and felt a need to keep rounding off his education, to bring it up to Ivy League standards. Also, the tan would look great back in Buffalo.

Stepping from the plane at the Luxor airport, he was smitten by the beauty of the desert, roseate and motionless around him. His element, perhaps. What was his traveling, his bachelorhood, but a search for his element? He was 34 and still seemed to be merely visiting the world. Even in Buffalo, walking the straight shaded streets where he had played as a small boy, entering the homes and restaurants where he was greeted by name, sitting in the two-room office where he put in the few hours of telephoning that managed the parcel of securities and property fallen to him from his father's death, he felt somehow light, limited to 44 pounds of luggage, dressed with the unnatural correctitude people assume at the outset of a trip. A puff of air off Lake Erie and he would be gone, and the city, with its savage blustery winters, its deep-set granite mansions, its factories, its iron bison in the railroad terminal, would not have noticed. He would leave only his name in gilt paint on a list of singles tennis champions above the bar of his country club. But he knew he had been a methodical joyless player to watch, too full of lessons to lose.

He knew a lot about himself: He knew that this lightness, the brittle unmarred something he carried, was his treasure, which his demon willed him to preserve. Stepping from the airplane at Luxor, he had greeted his demon in the air—air ideally clean, with the poise of a mirror. From the window of his cabin he sensed again, in the glittering width of the Nile, bluer than he had expected, and in the unflecked alkaline sky, and in the tapestry strip of labored green between them, that he would be happy for this trip. He liked sunning on the deck that first afternoon. Only the Scandinavian girl, in an orange bikini, kept him company. Both were silent. The boat was still tied up at the Luxor dock, a flight of stone steps; a few yards away, across a gulf of water and paved banking, a traffic of peddlers and cart drivers stared across. Clem liked that gulf and liked it when the boat cast loose and began gliding between the fields, the villages, the desert. He liked the first temples: gargantuan Karnak, its pillars upholding the bright blank sky; gentler Luxor, with its built-in mosque and its little naked queen touching her king's giant calf; Hollywoodish Dendera—its restored roofs had brought in darkness and dampness and bats that moved on the walls like intelligent black gloves.

Clem even, at first, liked the peddlers. Tourist-starved, they touched him in their hunger, thrusting scarabs and old coins and clay mummy dolls at him, moaning and grunting English: "How much? How much you give me? Very fine. Fifty. Both. Take both. Both for 35." Clem peeked down, caught his eye on a turquoise glint and wavered; his mother liked keepsakes and he had friends in Buffalo who would be amused. Into this flaw, this tentative crack of interest, they stuffed more things, strange sullied objects salvaged from the desert, alabaster vases, necklaces of mummy heads. Their brown hands probed and rubbed; their faces looked stunned, unblinking, as if, under the glaring sun, they were conducting business in the dark. Indeed, some did have eyes whitened by trachoma. Hoping to placate them with a purchase, Clem bargained for the smallest thing he could see, a lapis-lazuli bug the size of a fingernail. "Ten, then," the old peddler said, irritably making the "give me" gesture with his palm. Holding his wallet high, away from their hands, Clem leafed through the big notes for the absurdly small five-piaster bills, tattered and silky with use. The purchase, amounting to little more than a dime, excited the peddlers: ignoring the other tourists, they multiplied and crowded against him. Something warm and hard was inserted into his hand, his other sleeve was plucked, his pockets were patted and he wheeled, his tongue pinched between his teeth flirtatiously, trapped. It was a nightmare; the dream thought crossed his mind that he might be scratched.

He broke away and rejoined the other tourists in the sanctum of a temple courtyard. One of the Egyptian women came up to him and said, "I do not mean to remonstrate, but you are torturing them by letting them see all those 50s and 100s in your wallet."

"I'm sorry." He blushed like a scolded schoolboy. "I just didn't want to be rude."

"You must be. There is no question of hurt feelings. You are the man in the moon to them. They have no comprehension of your charm."

The strange phrasing of her last sentence, expressing not quite what she meant, restored his edge and dulled her rebuke. She was the shorter and the older of the two Egyptian women; her eyes were green and there was an earnest mischief, a slight pressure, in her upward glance.

Clem relaxed, almost slouching. "The sad part is, some of their things, I'd rather like to buy."

"Then do," she said, and walked away with her hips swinging. So a move had been made. He had expected it to come from the Scandinavian girl.

● ● ●

That evening the Egyptian trio invited him to their table in the bar. The green-eyed woman said, "I hope I was not scolding. I did not mean to remonstrate, merely to tell."

"Of course," Clem said. "Listen. I was being plucked to death. I needed rescuing."

"Those men," the Egyptian man said, "are in a bad way. They say that around the hotels the shoeshine boys are starving." His face was triangular, pockmarked, saturnine. A heavy weary courtesy slowed his speech.

"What did you buy?" the other woman asked. She was sallower than the other, and softer. Her English was the most British-accented.

Clem showed them. "Ah," the man said, "a scarab."

"The incarnation of Khepri," the green-eyed woman said. "The symbol of immortality. You will live forever." She smiled at everything she said; he remembered her smiling with the word "remonstrate."

"They're jolly things," the other woman pronounced, in her stately way. "Dung beetles. They roll a ball of dung along ahead of them, which appealed to the ancient Egyptians. Reminded them of themselves, I suppose."

"Life is that," the man said. "A ball of dung we push along."

The waiter came and Clem said, "Another whiskey sour. And another round of whatever they're having." Beer for the man, scotch for the taller lady, lemonade for his first friend.

Having bought, he felt, the right to some education, Clem asked, "Seriously. Has the"—he couldn't bring himself to call it a war, and he had noticed that in Egypt the word Israeli was never pronounced—"trouble cut down on tourism?"

"Oh, immensely," the taller lady said. "Before the war, one had to book for this boat months ahead. Now, my husband was granted two weeks and we were able to come at the last moment. It is pathetic."

"What do you do?" Clem asked.

The man made a self-deprecatory and evasive gesture, as a deity might have, asked for employment papers.

"My brother," the green-eyed woman stated, smiling, "works for the

114

government. In, what do you call it, planning?"

As if in apology for having been reticent, her brother abruptly said, "The shoeshine boys and the dragomen suffer for us all. In everyone in my country, you have now a deep distress."

"I noticed," Clem said, very carefully, "those holes in the bridge we passed under."

"They brought *jeeps* in, jeeps. By helicopter. The papers said bombs from a plane, but it was jeeps by helicopters from the Red Sea. They drove onto the bridge, set the charges and drove away. We are not warriors. We are farmers. For thousands of years now, we have had others do our fighting for us—Sudanese, Libyans, Arabs. We are not Arabs. We are Egyptians. The Syrians and Jordanians, they are Arabs. But we, we don't know who we are, except we are very old. The man who seeks to make warriors of us creates distress."

His wife put her hand on his to silence him while the waiter brought the drinks. His sister said to Clem, "Are you enjoying our temples?"

"Quite." But the temples within him, giant slices of limestone and sun, lay mute. "I also quite like," he went on, "our guide. I admire the way he says everything in English to some of us and then in French to the rest."

"Most Egyptians are trilingual," the wife stated. "Arabic, English, French."

"Which do you think in?" Clem was concerned, for he was conscious in himself of an absence of verbal thoughts: instead, there were merely glints and reflections.

The sister smiled. "In English, the thoughts are clearest. French is better for passion."

"And Arabic?"

"Also for passion. Is it not so, Amina?"

"What so, Leila?" She had been murmuring with her husband.

The question was restated in French.

"Oh, *c'est vrai, vrai*."

"How strange," Clem said. "English doesn't seem precise to me; quite the contrary. It's a mess of synonyms and lazy grammar."

"No," the wife said firmly—she never, he suddenly noticed, smiled— "English is clear and cold, but not *nuancé* in the emotions, as is French."

"And is Arabic *nuancé* in the same way?"

The green-eyed sister considered. "More *angoisse*."

Her brother said, "We have 99 words for camel dung. All different states of camel dung. Camel dung, we understand."

"Of course," Leila said to Clem, "Arabic here is nothing compared with the pure Arabic you would hear among the Saudis. The language of the Koran is so much more—can I say it?—gutsy. So guttural, nasal; strange, wonderful sounds. Amina, does it still affect you inwardly, to hear it chanted? The Koran."

Amina solemnly agreed, "It is terrible. It tears me all apart. It is too much passion."

Italian rock music had entered the bar via an unseen radio and one of the middle-aged English couples was trying to waltz to it. Noticing how intently Clern watched, the sister asked him, "Do you like to dance?"

He took it as an invitation; he blushed. "No, thanks, the fact is I can't."

"Can't dance? Not at all?"

"I've never been able to learn. My mother says I have Methodist feet."

"Your mother says that?" She laughed; a short shocking noise, the bark of a fox. She called to Amina, "*Sa mère dit que l'Américain a les pieds méthodistes!*"

"*Les pieds méthodiques?*"

"*Non, non, aucune méthode, la secte chrétienne—méthodisme!*"

Both barked, and the man grunted. Clem sat there rigidly, immaculate in his embarrassment. The girl's green eyes, curious, pressed on him like gems scratching glass. The three Egyptians became overanimated, beginning sentences in one language and ending in another, and Clem understood that he was being laughed at. Yet the sensation, like the blurred plucking of the scarab salesmen, was better than untouched emptiness. He had another drink before dinner, the drink that was one too many, and when he went in to his single table, everything—the tablecloths, the little red lamps, the wailing droves of waiters in blue, the black windows beyond which the Nile glided—looked triumphant and glazed.

● ● ●

He slept badly. There were bumps and scraping above him, footsteps in the hall, the rumble of the motors and, at four o'clock, the sounds of docking at another temple site. Once, he had found peace in hotel rooms, strange virgin corners where his mind could curl into itself, cut off from all nagging familiarities, and painlessly wink out. But he had known too many hotel rooms, so they had become themselves familiar, with their excessively crisp sheets and boastful plumbing and easy chairs one never sat in but used as clothes racks. Only the pillows varied—neck-cracking fat bolsters in Leningrad, in Amsterdam hard little wads the size of a lady's purse, and as lumpy. Here on the floating hotel *Osiris*, two bulky pillows were provided and, toward morning, Clem discovered it relaxed him to put his head on one and his arms around the other. Some other weight in the bed seemed to be the balance his agitated body, oscillating with hieroglyphs and sharp remonstrative glances, was craving. In his dream, the Egyptian woman promised him something marvelous and showed him two tall limestone columns with blue sky between them. He awoke unrefreshed but conscious of having dreamed. On his ceiling there was a dance of light, puzzling in its telegraphic rapidity, more like electronic art than anything natural. He analyzed it as sunlight bouncing off the tremulous Nile through the slats of his Venetian blinds. He pulled the blinds and there it was again, stunning in its clarity: the blue river, the green strip, the pink cliffs, the unflecked sky. Only the village had changed. The other tourists—the Frenchman being slowly steered, like a fragile cart, by an Arab boy— were already heading up a flight of wooden stairs toward a bus. Clem ran after them, into the broad day, without shaving.

Their guide, Poppa Omar, sat them down in the sun in a temple courtyard and told them the story of Queen Hatshepsut. "Remember it like this," he said, touching his head and rubbing his chest. "Hat— cheap—suit. She was wonderful woman here. Always building the temples, always winning the war and getting the nigger to be slaves. She marry her brother Tuthmosis and he grow tired here of jealous and insultation. He say to her, 'OK, you done a lot for Egypt, take it more easy now.' She say to him, 'No, I think I just keep rolling along.' What happen? Tuthmosis die. The new king also Tuthmosis, her niece. He is a little boy. Hatshepsut show herself in all big statues wearing false beard and all flatness here." He rubbed his chest. "Tuthmosis get bigger and go say to her now, 'Too much jealous and insultation. Take it easy for Egypt now.' She say, 'No.' Then she die, and all over Egypt here, he take all her statue and smash, hit, hit, so not one face of Hatshepsut left and everywhere her name in all the walls here, become Tuthmosis!" Clem looked around, and the statues had, indeed, been mutilated, thousands of years ago. He touched his own face and the whiskers scratched.

On the way back in the bus, the Green Bay travelogist asked them to stop so he could photograph a water wheel. A tiny child met them, weeping, on the path, holding one arm as if crippled. "Baksheesh, baksheesh," he said. "Musha, musha." One of the British men flicked at him with a whisk. The bald American announced aloud that the child was faking. Clem reached into his pocket for a piaster coin, but then remembered himself as torturer. Seeing his gesture, the child, and six others, chased after him. First they shouted, then they tossed pebbles at his heels. From within the haven of the bus, the tourists could all see the child's arm unbend. But the weeping continued and was evidently real. The travelogist was still doing the water wheel and the peddlers began to pry open the window and thrust in scarabs, dolls, alabaster vases not without beauty. The window beside Clem's face slid back and a brown hand insinuated an irregular parcel about six inches long, wrapped in brown cloth. "Feesh mummy," a disembodied voice said, and to Clem it seemed hysterically funny. He couldn't stop laughing; the tip of his tongue began to hurt from being bitten. The Scandinavian girl, across the aisle, glanced at him hopefully. Perhaps the crack in his glaze was appearing.

Back on the *Osiris*, they basked in deck chairs. The white boat had detached itself from the brown land and men in blue brought them lemonade, daiquiris, salty peanuts called *soudani*. Though Clem, luminous with suntan oil, appeared to be asleep, his lips moved in answer to Ingrid beside him. Her bikini was chartreuse today. "In my country," she said, "the summers are so short, naturally we take off our clothes. But it is absurd, this myth other countries have of our paganism, our happy sex. We are a harsh people. My father, he was like a man in the Bergman films. I was forbidden everything growing up—to play cards, lipstick, to dance."

"I never did learn to dance," Clem said, slightly shifting.

"Yes," she said, "I saw in you, too, a stern childhood. In a place of harsh winters."

"We had two yards of snow the other year," Clem told her. "In one storm. Two *yards*."

"And yet," Ingrid said, "I think the thaw, when at last it comes in such places, is so dramatic, so intense." She glanced toward him hopefully.

Clem appeared oblivious within his gleaming placenta of suntan oil.

The German boy who spoke a little English was on the other side of him. By now, the third day, the sunbathers had declared themselves: Clem, Ingrid, the two young Germans, the bald-headed American, the young English wife, whose skirted bathing suits were more demure than her ordinary dresses. The rest of the British sat on the deck in the shade of the canopy and drank; the three Egyptians sat in the lounge and talked; the supposed Russians kept out of sight altogether. The travelogist was talking to the purser about the immense chain of tickets and reservations that would get him to Cape Town; the widow was in her cabin with Egyptian stomach and a burning passion to play bridge;

the French couple sat by the rail, in the sun but fully dressed, reading guidebooks, his chair tipped back precariously so he could see the gliding landscape.

The German boy asked Clem, "Haff you bot a caftan?"

He had been nearly asleep, beneath a light, transparent headache. He said, "*Bitte?*"

"*Ein* caftan. You shoot. In Luxor; go back tonight. He will measure you and haff it by morning ven ve go. Sey are good—wery cheap."

Hatcheapsuit, Clem thought, but granted that he might do it. His frozen poise contended within him with something promiscuous and American, that must go forth and test, and purchase. He felt, having spurned so many scarabs and alabaster vases, he owed Egypt some of the large-leafed money that fattened his wallet uncomfortably.

"It vood be wery handsome on you."

"Ravishing," the young English wife said behind them. She had been listening. Clem sometimes felt like a mirror that everyone glanced into before moving on.

"You're all kidding me," he announced. "But I confess, I'm a sucker for costumes."

"Again," Ingrid said, "like a Bergman film." And languorously she shifted her long arms and legs; the impression of flesh in the side of his vision disturbingly merged, in his sleepless state, with a floating sensation of hollowness, of being in parentheses.

That afternoon they toured the necropolis in the Valley of the Kings. King Tut's small two-chambered tomb; how had they crammed so much treasure in? The immense tunnels of Ramses III; or was it Ramses IV? Passageways hollowed from the limestone chip by chip, lit by systems of tilted mirrors, painted with festive stiff figures banqueting, fishing, carrying offerings of fruit forward, which was always slightly down, down past pits dug to entrap grave robbers, past vast false chambers, toward the real and final one, a square room that would have made a nice night club. Its murals had been left unfinished, sketched in gray ink but uncolored. The tremors of the artist's hand, his nervous strokes, were still there. Abdul, the Egyptian planner, murmured to him, "Always they left something unfinished; it is a part of their religion no one understands. It is thought perhaps they dreaded finishing, as closing in the dead, limiting the life beyond." They climbed up the long slanting passageway, threaded with electric lights, past hundreds of immaculate bodies carried without swing. "The dead, you see, are not dead. In their language, the word for death and the word for life are the same. The death they feared was the second one, the one that would come if the tomb lacked provisions for life. In the tombs of the nobles, more than here, the scenes of life are all about, like a musical—you say score?—that only the dead have the instrument to play. These hieroglyphs are all instructions to the dead man, how to behave, how to make the safe journey."

"Good planning," Clem said, short of breath,

Abdul was slow to see the joke, since it was on himself.

"I mean the dead are much better planned for than the living."

"No," Abdul said flatly, perhaps misunderstanding. "It is the same."

Back in Luxor, Clem left the safe boat and walked toward the clothing shop, following the German boy's directions. He seemed to walk a long way. The narrowing streets grew shadowy. Pedestrians drifted by him in a steady procession, carrying offerings forward. No peddlers approached him; perhaps they kept businessmen's hours, went home and totaled up the sold scarabs and fish mummies in impeccable lined ledgers. Radio Cairo blared and twanged from wooden balconies. Dusty intersections flooded with propaganda (or was it prayer?) and faded behind him. The air was dark by the time he reached the shop. Within its little cavern of brightness, a young woman was helping a small child with homework, and a young man, the husband and father, lounged against some stacked bolts of cloth. All three persons were petite; Egyptian children, Clem had noticed before, are proportioned like miniature adults, with somber, staring dolls' heads. He felt oversize in this shop, whose reduced scale was here and there betrayed by a coarse object from the real world—a steam press, the inflated pastel of Nasser on the wall. Clem's voice, asking if they could make a caftan for him by morning, seemed to boom; as he tuned it down, it cracked and trembled. Measuring him, the small man touched him all over; and touches that at first had been excused as accidental declared themselves as purposeful, determined.

"Hey," Clem said, blushing.

Shielded from his wife by the rectangular bulk of Clem's body, the young man, undoing his own fly with a swift light tailor's gesture, exhibited himself. "I can make you very happy," he muttered.

"I'm leaving," Clem said.

He was at the doorway instantly, but the tailor had time to call, "Sir, when will you come back tomorrow?" Clem turned; the little man was zipped, the woman and child had their heads bent together over the homework. Nasser, a lurid ocher, scowled toward the future. Clem had intended to abandon the caftan but pictured himself back in Buffalo, wearing it to New Year's Eve at the club, with sunglasses and sandals. The tailor looked frightened. His little mustache twitched uncertainly and his brown eyes had been worn soft by worry and needlework.

Clem said he would be back no later than nine. The boat sailed south after breakfast. Outside, the dry air had chilled. From the tingling at the tip of his tongue, he realized he had been smiling hard.

• • •

Ingrid was sitting at the bar in a backwards silver dress, high in the front and buckled at the back. She invited herself to sit at his table during dinner; her white arms, pinched pink by the sun, shared in the triumphant glaze of the tablecloth, the glowing red lamp. They discussed religion. Clem had been raised as a Presbyterian, she as a Lutheran. In her father's house, north of Stockholm, there had been a guest room held ready against the arrival of Jesus Christ. Not quite seriously, it had been a custom, and yet...she supposed religion had bred into her a certain *expectancy*. Into him, he thought, groping, peering with difficulty into that glittering blank area, which in other people, he imagined, was the cave of life, religion had bred a *dislike of litter*. It was a disappointing answer, even after he had explained the word litter. He advanced in its place the theory that he was a royal tomb, once crammed with treasure, that had been robbed. Her white hand moved an inch toward him on the tablecloth, intelligent as a bat, and he began to cry. The tears felt genuine to him, but she said, "Stop acting."

He told her that a distressing thing had just happened to him.

She said, "That is your flaw; you are too self-conscious. You are always in costume, acting. You must always be beautiful." She was so intent on delivering this sermon that only as an afterthought did she ask him what had been the distressing thing.

He found he couldn't tell her; it was too intimate, and his own part in provoking it had been, he felt, unspeakably shameful. The tailor's homosexual advance had been, like the child's feigning a crippled arm, evoked by his money, his torturing innocence. He said, "Nothing. I have been sleeping badly and don't make sense. Ingrid: Have some more wine." His palms were sweating from the effort of pronouncing her name.

After dinner, though fatigue was making his entire body shudder and itch, she asked him to take her into the lounge, where a three-piece band from Alexandria was playing dance music. The English couples waltzed and Gwenn, the young wife, frugged with one of the German boys. The green-eyed Egyptian woman danced with the purser. Egon, the German boy who knew some English, came and, with a curt bow and a curious hard stare at Clem, invited Ingrid. She danced, Clem observed, very close, in the manner of one who, puritanically raised, thinks of it only as a substitute for intercourse. After many numbers, she was returned to him unmarred, still silver, cool and faintly admonitory. Downstairs, in the corridor where their cabin doors were a few steps apart, she asked him, her expression watchful and stern, if he would sleep better tonight. Compared with her large eyes and long nose, her mouth was small; she pursed her lips in a thoughtful pout, holding as if in readiness a small slot of dark space between them.

He realized that her face was stern because he was a mirror in which she was gauging her beauty, her power. His smile sought to reassure her. "Yes," he said, "I'm sure I will, I'm dead."

And he did fall asleep quickly, but woke in the dark, to escape a dream in which the hieroglyphs and Pharaonic cartouches had left the incised walls and inverted and become stamps, sharp-edged stamps trying to indent themselves upon him. Awake, he identified the dream blows with the thumping of feet and furniture overhead. But he could not sink back into sleep; there was a scuttling, an occasional whispering in the corridor that he felt was coming toward him, toward his door. But once, when he opened his door, there was nothing in the corridor but bright light and several pairs of shoes. The problem of the morning prevented him from sinking back. If he went to pick up his caftan, it would seem to the tailor a submission. He would be misunderstood and vulnerable. Also, there was the danger of missing the boat. Yet the caftan would be lovely to have, a shimmering striped polished cotton, with a cartouche containing Clem's monogram in silver thread. In his agitation, his desire not to make a mistake, he could not achieve peace with his pillows; and then the telegraphic staccato of sunlight appeared on his ceiling and Egypt, that green thread through the desert, was taut and bright beyond his blinds. Leaving breakfast, lightheaded, he impulsively approached the bald American on the stairs. "I beg your pardon; this is rather silly, but could you do me an immense favor?"

"Like what?"

"Just walk with me up to this shop where something I ordered should be waiting. Uh...it's embarrassing to explain."

"The boat's pulling out in half an hour."

"I know. It wouldn't leave if two of us were missing."

The man sized Clem up—his clean shirt, his square shoulders, his open hopeful face—and grunted, "OK. I left my whisk in the cabin, I'll see you outside."

"Gee, I'm very grateful, uh——"

"Walt's the name."

Ingrid, coming up the stairs late to breakfast, had overheard. "May I come, too, on this expedition that is so dangerous?"

"No, it's stupid." Clem told her. "Please eat your breakfast. I'll see you on the deck afterward."

Her face attempted last night's sternness, but she was puffy beneath her eyes from sleep, and he revised upward his estimate of her age. Like him, she was over 30. How many men had she passed through to get here, alone; how many self-forgetful nights, traumatic mornings of separation, hung-over heartbroken afternoons? It was epic to imagine, her history of love; she loomed immense in his mind, a monumental statue, forbidding and foreign, even while under his nose she blinked, puckered her lips and went into breakfast, rejected.

On the walk to the shop, Clem tried to explain what had happened the evening before. Walt impatiently interrupted. "They're scum," he said. "They'll sell their mother for 20 piasters." His accent still had nasal Newark in it. A boy ran shyly beside them, offering them *soudani* from a bowl. "Amscray," Walt said, brandishing his whisk.

"Is very good," the boy said.

"You make me puke," Walt told him.

The woman and the boy doing homework were gone from the shop. Unlit, it looked dingy; Nasser's glass was cracked. The tailor sprang up when they entered, pleased and relieved. "I work all night," he said.

"Like hell you did," Walt said.

"Try on?" the tailor asked Clem.

In the flecked dim mirror, Clem saw himself gowned; a shock, because the effect was not incongruous. He looked like a husky woman, a big-boned square-faced woman, quick to blush and giggle, the kind of naïve healthy woman, with money and without many secrets, that he tended to be attracted to. He had once loved such a girl, and she had snubbed him to marry a Harvard man. "It feels tight under the armpits," he said.

The tailor rapidly caressed and patted his sides. "That is its cut," he said.

"And the cartouche was supposed to be in silver thread."

"You said gold."

"I said silver."

"Don't take it," Walt advised.

"I work all night," the tailor said.

"And here," Clem said. "This isn't a pocket, it's just a slit."

"No, no, no pocket. Supposed to let the hand through. Here, I show." He put his hand in the slit and touched Clem until Clem protested, "Hey."

"I can make you very happy," the tailor murmured.

"Throw it back in his face," Walt said. "Tell him it's a god-awful mess."

"No," Clem said. "I'll take it. The fabric is lovely. If it turns out to be too tight, I can give it to my mother." He was sweating so hard that the garment became stuck as he tried to pull it over his head, and the tailor, assisting him, was an enveloping blur of caresses.

From within the darkness of cloth, Clem heard a slap and Walt's voice snarl, "Hands off, sonny." The subdued tailor swiftly wrapped the caftan in brown paper. As Clem paid, Walt said, "I wouldn't buy that rag. Throw it back in his face." Outside, as they hurried back toward the boat, through crowded streets where women clad in black mantles stepped aside, guarding their faces as if from evil eyes—a cloud of faces in which one or two hung with a startled, unpainted beauty—Walt said, "The little queer."

"I don't think it meant anything, it was just a nervous habit. But it scared me. Thanks a lot for coming along."

Walt asked him, "Ever try it with a man?"

"No. Good heavens."

Walt said, "It's not bad." He nudged Clem in walking and Clem shifted his parcel to that side, as a shield. All the way to the boat, Walt's conversation was anecdotal and obscene, describing a night he had had in Alexandria and another in Khartoum. Twice Clem had to halt and shift to Walt's other side, to keep from being nudged off the sidewalk. "It's not bad," Walt insisted. "It'd pleasantly surprise you." Back on the *Osiris*, Clem locked the cabin door while changing into his bathing suit. The engines shivered; the boat glided away from the Luxor quay. On deck, Ingrid asked him if his dangerous expedition had been successful. She had reverted to the orange bikini.

"I got the silly thing, yes. I don't know if I'll ever wear it."

"You must model it tonight; we are having Egyptian Night."

Her intonation saying this was firm with reserve. Her air of pique cruelly pressed upon him in his sleepless, sensitive, brittle state. Ingrid's lower lip jutted in profile; her pale eyes bulged beneath the spears of her lashes. He tried to placate her by describing the tailor shop—its enchanted smallness, the woman and child bent over schoolwork.

"It is a farce," Ingrid said, with a bruising positiveness, "their schooling. They teach the poor children the language of the Koran, which is difficult and useless. The literacy statistics are nonsense."

Swirls of Arabic, dipping like bird flight from knot to knot, wound through Clem's brain and gently tugged him downward into a softness where Ingrid's tan body stretching beside him merged with the tawny strip of desert gliding beyond the ship's railing. Lemonade was being served to kings around him. On the ceiling of one temple chamber that he had seen, the goddess Nut was swallowing the sun in one corner and giving birth to it in another, all out of the same body. A body was above him and words were crashing into him like stones. He opened his eyes; it was the American widow, a broad cloud of cloth eclipsing the sun, a perfumed mass of sweet-voiced anxiety resurrected from her cabin, crying out to him, "Young man, you *look* like a bridge player. We're desperate for a fourth!"

● ● ●

The caftan pinched him under the arms; and then, later in Egyptian Night, after the meal, Ingrid danced with Egon and disappeared. To these discomforts the American widow and Walt added that of their company. Though Clem had declined her bridge invitation, his protective film had been broken and they had plunked themselves down around the little table where Clem and Ingrid were eating the buffet of *foule* and pilaf and *qualeema* and falafel and maamoule. To Clem's surprise, the food was to his taste—nutty, bland, dry. Then Ingrid was invited to dance and failed to return to the table, and the English couples, who had befriended the widow, descended in a cloud of conversation.

"This place was a hell of a lot more fun under Farouk," said one old man with a scoured red face.

"At least the poor *fellah*," a woman perhaps his wife agreed, "had a little glamor and excitement to look up to."

"Now what does the poor devil have? A war he can't fight and Soviet slogans."

"They *hate* the Russians, of course. The average Egyptian, he loves a show of style, and the Russians don't have any. Not a crumb."

"The poor dears."

And they passed on to ponder the inability, mysterious but a thousand times proven, of Asiatics and Africans—excepting, of course, the Israelis and the Japanese—to govern themselves or, for that matter, to conduct the simplest business operation efficiently. Clem was too tired to talk and too preoccupied with the pressure chafing his armpits, but they all glanced into his face and found their opinions reflected there. In a sense, they deferred to him, for he was prosperous and young and as an American the inheritor of their colonial wisdom.

All had made attempts at native costume. Walt wore his pajamas, and the widow, in bed sheet and sunglasses and *kútfiyah*, did suggest a fat sheik, and Gwenn's husband had blacked his face with an ingenious paste of Bain de Soleil and instant coffee. Gwenn asked Clem to dance. Blushing, he declined, but she insisted. "There's nothing to it—you simply bash yourself about a bit," she said, and demonstrated.

She was dressed as a harem girl. For her top, she had torn the sleeves off one of her husband's shirts and left it unbuttoned, so that a strip of skin from the base of her throat to her navel was bare; she was not wearing a bra. Her pantaloons were less successful: yellow St.-Tropez slacks pinned in loosely below the knees. A blue-gauze scarf across her nose—setting her hectic English cheeks and Twiggy eyes oddly afloat— and gold chains around her ankles completed the costume. The band played *Delilah*. As Clem watched Gwenn's feet, their shuffle, and the glitter of gold circlets, and the ten silver toenails, seemed to be rapidly writing something indecipherable. There was a quick half step she seemed unaware of, in counterpoint with her swaying head and snaking arms. "Why—oh—whyyy, De-liii-lah," the young Egyptian sang in a Liverpool whine. Clem braced his body, hoping the pumping music would take it. His feet felt sculpturally one with the floor; it was like what stuttering must be for the tongue. The sweat of incapacity fanned outward from the pain under his arms, but Gwenn obliviously rolled on, her pantaloons coming unpinned, her shirt loosening so that as she swung from side to side, one shadowy breast, and now the other, was exposed. She had shut her eyes, and in the haven of her blindness Clem did manage to dance a little, to shift his weight and jerk his arms, though he was able to do it only by forgetting the music. The band changed songs and rhythms without his noticing; he was conscious mostly of the skirt of his caftan swinging around him, of Gwenn's red cheeks turning and turning below sealed slashes of mascara, and of her husband's face. He had come onto the dance floor with the American widow; as the Bain de Soleil had sunk into his skin, the instant coffee had powdered his *gallabíyah*. At last the band took a break. Gwenn's husband claimed her, and the green-eyed Egyptian woman, as Clem passed her table, said remonstratingly, "You can dance."

"He is a dervish," Amina stated.

"All Americans are dervishes," Abdul sighed. "Their energy menaces the world."

"I am the world's worst dancer; I'm hopeless," Clem said.

"Then you should sit," Leila said. All three Egyptians were dressed, with disdainful chic, in Western dress. Clem ordered a renewal of their drinks and a brandy for himself.

"Tell me," he begged Abdul. "Do you think the Russians have no style?"

"It is true," Abdul said. "They are a very ugly people. Their clothes are very baggy. They are like us, Asiatic. They are not yet convinced that this world absolutely matters."

"*Mon mari veut être un mystique*," Amina said to Clem.

Clem persisted. Fatigue made him desperate and dogged. "But," he said, "I was surprised, in Cairo, even now, with our ambassador kicked out, how many Americans were standing around the lobby of the Hilton. And all the American movies."

"For a time," Amina said, "they tried films only from the Soviet Union and China, about farming progressively. The theater managers handed their keys in to the government and said, 'Here, you run them.' No one would come. So the Westerns came back."

"And this music," Clem said, "and your clothes."

"Oh, we love you." Abdul said, "but with our brains. You are like the stars, like the language of the Koran. We know we cannot be like that. There is a sullen place"—he moved his hand from his head to his stomach—"where the Russians make themselves at home. I speak in hope. There must be some compensation."

The waiter brought the tray of drinks and Amina said "Shh" to her husband.

Leila said to Clem, "You have changed girlfriends tonight. You have many girlfriends."

He blushed. "None."

Leila said. "The big Swede, she danced very close with the German boy. Now they have both gone off."

"Into the Nile?" Amina asked. "The desert? How jolly romantic."

Abdul said slowly, as if bestowing comfort, "They are both Nordic. They are at home within each other. Like us and the Russians."

Leila seemed angry. Her green eyes burned and Clem feared they would seek to scratch his face. Instead, her ankle touched his beneath the table; he flinched. "They are both," she said, "ice—ize—? They hang down in winter."

"Icicles?" Clem offered.

She curtly nodded, annoyed at needing rescue. "I have never seen one," she said in self-defense.

"Your friends the British," Abdul said, indicating the noisy table where they were finger-painting on Gwenn's husband's face, "understood us in their fashion. They had read Shakespeare. It is very good, that play. How we turned our sails and ran. Our cleverness and courage are all female."

"I'm sure that's not so," Clem said, to rescue him.

Leila snapped, "Why should it not be so? All countries are women, except horrid Uncle Sam." And though he sat at their table another hour, her ankle did not touch his again.

Floating on three brandies, Clem at last left the lounge, his robe of polished cotton swinging around him. The Frenchman was tipped back precariously in a corner, watching the dancers. He lifted his mirror in salute as Clem passed. Though even the Frenchman's wife was dancing, Ingrid had not returned, and this added to Clem's lightness, his freedom from litter. Surely he would sleep. But when he lay down on his bed, it was trembling and jerking. His cabin adjoined that of the unsociable plump couple thought to be Russian. Clem's bed and one of theirs were separated by a thin partition. His shuddered as theirs heaved with a playful, erratic violence; there was a bump, a giggle, a hoarse male sibilance. Then the agitation settled toward silence and a distinct rhythm, a steady, mounting beat that put a pulsing into the bed taut under Clem. Two or three minutes of this. "Oh": the woman's exclamation was middle-pitched, totally curved, languageless; a man's guttural grunt came right on top of it. Clem's bed, in its abrupt stillness, seemed to float and spin under him. Then from beyond the partition some murmurs, a sprinkling of laughter and a resonant heave as one body left the bed. Soon, faint snoring. Clem had been robbed of the gift of sleep.

After shapeless hours of pillow wrestling, he went to the window and viewed the Nile gliding by, the constellations of village lights, the desert stars, smaller than he had expected. He wanted to open the window to smell the river and the desert, but it was sealed shut, in deference to the air conditioning. Clem remembered Ingrid and a cold silver rage, dense as an ingot, upright as an obelisk, filled his body. "You bitch," he said aloud and, by repeating those two words, over and over, leaving his mind no space to entertain any other images, he managed to wedge himself into a few hours' sleep, despite the tempting, problematical scuttle of presences in the hall, who now and then brushed his door with their fingernails. *You bitch, you bitch, you....* He remembered nothing about his dreams, except that they all took place back in Buffalo, amid people he had thought he had forgotten.

• • •

Temples. Dour dirty heavy Isna sunk in its great pit beside a city market where Clem, pestered by flies and peddlers, nearly vomited at the sight of ox palates, complete with arcs of teeth, hung up for sale. Vast sun-struck Idfu, an endless square spiral climb up steps worn into troughs toward a dizzying view, the amateur travelogist calmly grinding away on the unparapeted edge. Cheery little Kom Ombo, right by the Nile, whiter and later than the others. In one of them, dead Osiris was resurrected by a hawk alighting on his phallus: in another, Nut the sky god flowed above them nude, swimming amid gilt stars. A god was having a baby, baby Horus, Poppa Omar bent over and tenderly patted the limestone relief pitted and defaced by Coptic Christians. "See now here," he said, "the lady squat, and the other ladies hold her by the arms so, here, and the baby Horus, out he comes here. In villages all over Egypt now, the ladies there still have the babies in this manner, so we have too many the babies here." He looked up at them and smiled with ancient benevolence. His eyes, surprisingly, were pale blue.

The man from Wisconsin was grinding away, the man from New Jersey was switching his whisk, the widow was fainting in the shade, beside a sphinx. Clem helped the Frenchman inch his feet across some age-worn steps; he was like one of those toys that walks down an inclined ramp but easily topples. The English and Egyptians were bored; too many temples, too much Ramses. Ingrid detached herself from the German boys and came to Clem. "How did you sleep?"

"Horribly. And you?"

"Well. I thought," she added, "you would be soothed by my no longer trying to rape you."

At noon, in the sun, as the Osiris glided toward Aswan, she took her accustomed chair beside Clem. When Egon left the chair on the other side of him and clamorously swam in the pool, Clem asked her, "How is he?"

"He is very nice," she said, holding her bronze face immobile in the sun. "Very earnest, very naive. He is a revolutionary."

"I'm glad," he said, "you've found someone congenial."

"Have I? He is very young. Perhaps I went with him to make another jealous." She added, expressionless, "Did it?"

"Yes."

"I am pleased to hear it."

In the evening, she was at the bar when he went up from an unsuccessful attempt at a nap. They had docked for the last time; the boat had ceased trembling. She had reverted to the silver dress that looked put on backward. He asked, "Where are the Germans?"

"They are with the Egyptians in the lounge. Shall we join them?"

"No," Clem said. Instead, they talked with the lanky man from Green Bay, who had ten months of advance tickets and reservations to Cape Town and back, including a homeward cabin on the *Queen Elizabeth II*. He spoke mostly to women's groups and high schools, and he detested the Packers. He said to Clem, "I take pride in being an eccentric, don't you?" and Clem was frightened to think that he appeared eccentric, he who had always been praised, even teased, by his mother as typically American, as even *too* normal and dependable. She sometimes implied that he had disappointed her by not defying her, by always returning from his trips.

After dinner, he and Ingrid walked in Aswan: a receding quay of benches, open shops burning a single light bulb, a swish of vehicles, mostly military. A true city, where the appetites did not beg. He had bought some postcards and let a boy shine his shoes. He paid the boy ten piasters, shielding his potent wallet with his body, like a grenade that might explode. They returned to the *Osiris* and sat in the lounge watching the others dance. A chaste circle around them forbade intrusion; or perhaps the others, having tried to enter Clem and failed, had turned away. Clem imagined them in the eyes of the others, both so composed and now so tan, two stately cool children of harsh winters. Apologizing, smiling, after three iced arracks, he bit his tongue and rose. "Forgive me, I'm dead. I must hit the hay. You stay and dance."

She shook her head, with a preoccupied stern gesture, gathered her dress tight about her hips and went with him. In the hall before his door, she stood and asked, "Don't you want me?"

A sudden numbness lifted from his stomach and made him feel unreally tall. "Yes," he said.

"Then why not take me?"

Clem looked within himself for the answer, saw only glints refracted and distorted by a deep fatigue. "I'm frightened to," he told her. "I have no faith in my right to take things."

Ingrid listened intently, as if his words were continuing, clarifying themselves; she looked at his face and nodded. Now that they had come so far together and were here, her gaze seemed soft, as soft and weary as the tailor's. "Go to your room," she said. "If you like, then, I will come to you."

"Please do." It was as simple as dancing—you simply bash yourself about a bit.

"Would you like me to?" She was stern now, and could afford to be guarded.

"Yes. *Please* do."

He left the latch off, undressed, washed, brushed his teeth, shaved the second time that day, left the bathroom light on. The bed seemed immensely clean and taut, like a sail. Strange stripes, nonsense patterns, crossed his mind. The sail held taut, permitting a gliding, but with a tipping. The light in the cabin changed. The door had been opened and shut. She was still wearing the silver dress; he had imagined she would change. She sat on his bed; her weight was the counterweight he had been missing. He curled tighter, as if around a pillow, and an irresistible peace descended, distinctly, from the four corners of space, along 45-degree angles marked in charcoal. He opened his eyes, discovering thereby that they had been shut, and the sight of her back—the belling solidity of her bottom, the buckle of the backward belt, the scoop of cloth exposing the nape of blonde neck and the strong crescent of shoulder waiting to be touched—covered his eyes with silver scales. On one of the temple walls, one of the earlier ones, Poppa Omar had read off the hieroglyphs that spelled WOMAN IS PARADISE. The ship and its fittings were still and, confident she would not move, he postponed the beginning for one more second.

He awoke feeling rich, full of sleep. At breakfast, he met Ingrid by the glass dining-room doors and apologetically smiled, blushing and biting his tongue. "God, I'm sorry," he said. He added in self-defense, "I told you I was dead."

"It was charming," she said. "You gave yourself to me that way."

"How long did you sit there?"

"Perhaps an hour. I tried to insert myself into your dreams. Did you dream of me?" She was a shade shy, asking.

He remembered no dreams but did not say so. Her eyes were permanently soft now toward him; they had become windows through which he could admire himself. It did not occur to him that he might admire her in the same fashion; in the morning light, he saw clearly the traces of age on her face and throat, the little scars left by time and a presumed promiscuity, for which he, though not heavily, did blame her. His defect was that, though accustomed to reflect love, he could not originate light within himself; he was as blind as the silver side of a mirror to the possibility that he, too, might impose a disproportionate glory upon the form of another. The world was his but slid through him.

In the morning, they went by felucca to Lord Kitchener's gardens, and the Aga Khan's tomb, where a single rose was fresh in a vase. The afternoon expedition, and their last, was to the Aswan High Dam. Cameras were forbidden. They saw the anti-aircraft batteries and the worried brown soldiers in their little wooden cartoon guardhouses. The desert became very ugly: no longer the rose shimmer that had surrounded him at the airport in Luxor, it was a merciless gray that had never entertained a hope of life, not even fine in texture but littered to the horizon with black flint. And the makeshift pitted roads were ugly, and the graceless Russian machinery clanking and sitting stalled, and the styleless, already squalid propaganda pavilion containing a model of the dam. The dam itself, after the straight, elegantly arched dam the British had built upriver, seemed a mere mountain of heaped rubble, hardly distinguishable from the inchoate desert itself. Yet at its heart, where the turbines had been set, a plume like a cloud of horses leaped upward in an inverted Niagara that dissolved, horse after horse, into mist before becoming the Nile again and flowing on. Startled greenery flourished on the gray cliffs that contained the giant plume. The stocky couple who had been impassive and furtive for six days now beamed and crowed aloud; the man roughly nudged Clem to wake him to the wonder of what they were seeing. Clem agreed; "*Khoro-sho*." He waited but was not nudged again. Gazing into the abyss of the trip that was over, he saw that—sparks struck and lost within a waterfall—he had been happy.

cc file

ISAAC B. SINGER
209 WEST 86TH STREET
NEW YORK, N. Y. 10024

A. C. SPECTORSKY

SEP 3 0 1969

Mr. A. C. Spectorsky
Editorial Director
Playboy

Sep 26 1969

Dear Mr. Spectorsky,

I just came back from a long trip and found your letter from July 31. Here is my answer:

For a man of my age an obituary is not something to joke about. It is a serious business to brood that a day comes when one will not be able to read a newspaper, listen to the radio, ~~visit a good~~ malign one's friend or just sit in a ~~cafeteria, and~~ eat rice pudding talk to the landsleit. However, the idea of living for ever is even more frithening. Just imagine an author ~~sitting and talking~~ boasting about his ~~billionth~~ novel! No matter how good he would be, he would have to repeat ~~itself~~ himself and the critics, ~~forever~~ alive and biting ~~who would also live and bite~~ forever, would tear pieces from him.

over

Also, no matter how many times a man would divorce and marry, he would have (sooner or later) to remarry his ancient wives, take back his veteran lovers, tell them the same primeval jokes, listen to their complaints. Nietzsche, who believed that the number of atoms in the universe is limited while time is boundless, spoke with despair about the Eternal Return. The thought that things must repeat themselves in the cosmos, drove him to insanity. Eternal life would certainly be impossible for a scribbler like myself. Where would I place an infinite number of reviews? I would need special planets for my archives. My favorite fantasy is to die and be reborn without remembering all the petty troubles and grudges of the past. This what happens in actuality. We have been here many time as humans, pigs, lice, skunks and frogs. Thank God that we don't remember these episodes and that we don't write and read memoires about them. Life, like a soap opera, must finally end. From a literary point of view death is sheer mercy. If Homer, Dante and Shakespear would still be living, a writer's life would be hell. By the way, they are still living...

The Conservationist

fiction by NADINE GORDIMER

Pale, freckled eggs. Swaying over the ruts to the gate of the third pasture, Sunday morning, the owner of the farm suddenly sees: a clutch of pale, freckled eggs set out before a half circle of children. Some are squatting; the one directly behind the eggs is cross-legged, like a vendor in a market. There is pride of ownership in that grin lifted shyly to the farmer's gaze. The eggs are arranged like marbles, the other children crowd round, but you can tell they are not allowed to touch unless the cross-legged one gives permission. The bare soles, the backsides of the children have flattened a nest in the long dead grass for both eggs and children. The emblem on the car's bonnet, itself made in the shape of a prismatic flash, scores his vision with a vertical-horizontal sword of dazzle. This is the place at which a child always appears, even if none has been in sight, racing across the field to open the gate for the car. But today the farmer puts on the brake, leaves the engine running and gets out. One very young boy, wearing a jersey made long ago for much longer arms but too short to cover a naked belly, runs to the gate and stands there. The others all smile proudly round the eggs. The cross-legged one (wearing a woman's dress, but it may be a boy) puts out his hands over the eggs and gently shuffles them a little closer together, letting a couple of the outer ones roll back into his palms. The eggs are a creamy buff, their glaze pored and lightly spotted, their shape more pointed than a hen's, and the palms of the small black hands are translucent-looking apricot pink. There is no sound but awed, snuffling breathing through snotty noses.

The farmer asks a question of the cross-legged one and there are giggles. He points down at the eggs but does not touch them, and asks again. The children don't understand the language. He goes on talking, with many gestures. The cross-legged child puts his head on one side, draws in his lower lip, smiling as if under the weight of praise, and cups one of the eggs from one hand to the other.

135

THE CONSERVATIONIST

Eleven pale, freckled eggs. A whole clutch of guinea-fowl eggs.

The baby at the gate is still waiting. The farmer goes back to the car, switches off the ignition and walks in the direction from which he has driven. He has left the road and struck out across the veld, leaping the dry donga to land with a springy crackle on dead cosmos and khaki weed that bordered it last summer. Over the hard ground his thick rubber soles scuff worn scrubbing brushes of closely grazed dead grass. He is making for the kraal; it is up beside the special paddock where the calves are kept at night. But the neat enclosure with oil drums cut in two to make feed troughs is empty; no one is about. From a line of rooms built of gray breeze blocks, the sound of radio music winds like audible smoke in the clean fine morning: It's Sunday. A woman appears from behind the lean-tos of wire and tin that obscure or are part of the habitations. When she sees him approach, she stands quite still, one of those figures with the sun in its eyes caught in a photograph. He asks where the chief herdsman is. Without moving, but grimacing as if she strains to understand, she makes an assenting noise and then answers. He repeats what she has said, to be sure, and she repeats the assenting noise, long and reassuring, like the grunting sigh of a satisfied sleeper. Her gaze steers his back in the direction she has indicated.

He is crossing a lucerne field. The last late cutting of autumn must have been made sometime that week; although the shriveled scraps (like bits of busted balloon) that remain have lost their clover shapes and faded to gray-green, underfoot they give out now and then a sweet sickish whiff of summer—breath from the mouth of a cow or the mouth of a warm sleepy woman turned to in the morning. Involuntarily he draws it deep into his lungs and it disappears into a keener pleasure, the dry, cool and perfect air of a high-veld autumn, which, shut up in the car that carried with it the shallow breath of the city, he has not yet taken. Not this morning, not for a week. As the air plunges in him, his gaze widens and sweeps: Down along the river the willows have gone blond, not yet at their palest, combed out into bare strands but still lightly spattered and delicately streaked with yellowed leaves. Around them is a slight smudgy ambiance, a mauvish-smoky blend between their outline and the bright air...extraordinary.

Eleven. A whole clutch of guinea-fowl eggs. Eleven. Soon there'll be nothing left. In the country. The continent. The oceans, the sky.

Suddenly he sees the figure of the black man, Jacobus, making for him. He must have come out of the mealies on the other side of the road beyond the lucerne and is lunging across the field with the particular stiff-hipped hobble of a man who would be running if he were younger.

But it's *he* who's looking for Jacobus; there's a mistake somewhere—how could the man already know that he is wanted? Some semaphore from the kraal? The farmer gives himself a little impatient, almost embarrassed snigger—and continues his own progress, measuredly, resisting the impulse to flag the man down with a wave of the hand, preparing in his mind what to say about the guinea fowl.

Although it is Sunday, Jacobus is wearing the blue overalls supplied him, and although there has been no rain and none can be expected for four months, he has on the rubber boots meant for wet weather. He's panting, naturally, but stops, as if there were a line drawn there, ten feet away from the farmer, and goes through the formalities of greeting, which include a hand movement as if he had a hat to remove. The farmer approaches unhurriedly. "Jacobus, I was coming to find you. How's everything?"

"No—everything it's all right. One calf he's borned Friday. But I try to phone you, yesterday night——"

"Good, that's from the red cow, eh?"

"No, the red cow she's not ready. This from that young one, that ones you buy last year from Pietersburg——"

Each is talking fast, in the manner of a man who has something he wants to get on to say. There is a moment's pause to avoid collision; but, of course, the right of way is the farmer's. "Look, Jacobus, I've just been down at the third pasture there——"

"I'm try, try to phone last night, master——"

But he has in his mind just exactly how to put it: "The children are taking guinea-fowl eggs to play with. They must've found a nest somewhere in the grass or the reeds and they've taken the eggs."

"There by the river...you were there?" The herdsman's lips are drawn back from his decayed horse teeth. He looks distressed, reluctant: Yes, he is responsible for the children, some are probably his, and anyway, he is responsible for good order among the dependents of the farm workers and already the farmer has had occasion to complain about the number of dogs they are harboring—a danger to the game birds.

"It's not as if they needed them for food. To eat, no, eh? You've got plenty of fowls. They're just pickanins and they don't know, but you must tell them, those eggs are not to play games with. If they find eggs in the veld, they are not to touch them, you understand? Mustn't touch or move them, ever." Of course, he understands perfectly well but wears that uncomprehending and pained look, to establish he's not to blame, he's burdened by the behavior of all those other people down at the kraal. Jacobus is not without sycophancy. "Master," he pleads.

"Master, it's very bad down there by the river. I'm try, try phone you yesterday night. What is happen there. The man is dead there. You see him." And his hand, with an imperious forefinger shaking it, stabs the air, through chest level of the farmer's body, to the line of willows away down behind him.

"A man?"

"*There—there*"—the herdsman draws back from his own hand as if to hold something at bay. His forehead is raised in three deep wrinkles.

"Somebody's died?"

The herdsman has the authority of dreadful knowledge. "Dead man. Solomon find it yesterday five o'clock."

"Has something happened to one of the boys? What man?"

"No. Yes, we don't know who is it. Or what. Where he come to be dead here on this farm."

"A strange man. Not one of our people?"

The herdsman's hands go out wide in exasperation. "Nobody can say who is that man." And he begins to tell the story again: Solomon ran, it was five o'clock, he was bringing the cows back. "Yesterday night, myself, I'm try sometime five time"—he holds up his spread fingers and thumb—"to phone you in town."

"So what have you done?"

"Now when I'm see the car come just now, I run from that side where the mealies are——"

"But with the body?"

This time the jutting chin as well as the forefinger indicate: "The man is there. You can see, still there, master, come I show you where is it."

The herdsman stumps past. There is nothing for the farmer to do but follow. Why should he go to look at a dead man near the river? He could just as well telephone the police and leave it to the proper channels that exist to deal with such matters. It is not one of the farm workers. It is not anyone one knows. It is a sight that has no claim on him.

But the dead man is on his property. Now that the farmer has arrived, the herdsman Jacobus has found the firmness and support of an interpretation of the event: His determined back in the blue overalls, collar standing away from slightly bent neck, is leading to the intruder. He is doing his duty and his employer has a duty to follow him.

They go back over the lucerne field and down the road. A beautiful morning, already coming into that calm fullness of peace and warmth that will last until the sun goes, without the summer's climax of rising heat. Ten o'clock as warm as midday will be, and midday will be no hotter than three in the afternoon. The pause between two seasons; days as complete and perfectly contained as an egg.

The children are gone; the place where they were might just as well have been made by a cow lying down in the grass.

The two men have passed the stationary car and almost reached the gate. A coyly persuasive voice blaring a commercial jingle comes out of the sky from the direction of the kraal.... YOUR GIANT FREE...SEND YOUR NAME AND ADDRESS TODAY TO.... The baby in the jersey bursts from nowhere but is disconcerted at the sight of the herdsman. Hanging from his plump pubis, his little dusty penis is the trunk of a toy elephant. He stands watching while Jacobus unwinds the loop of rusty wire that encloses the pole of the barbed fence and the pole of the gate, and the gate, which is just a freed section of the fence, falls flat.

The road has ruts and incised patterns from the rains of the season before last, petrified, more like striations made over millennia in rock than marks of wheels, boots and hooves in live earth. There was no rain this summer, but even in a drought year, the vlei provides some moisture on this farm and the third pasture has patches where a skin of greenish wet has glazed, dried, lifted, cracked, each irregular segment curling at the edges. The farmer's steps bite down on them with the crispness of biscuits between teeth. The river's too low to be seen or heard; as the slope quickens his pace through momentum, there is a whiff held in the dry air as the breath of clover was. A whiff—the laundry smell of soap scum. So the river's there, somewhere, all right.

And the dead man. They are jogging down to the willows and the stretch of reeds, broken, crisscrossed, tangled, collapsed against themselves, stockaded all the way to the other side—which is the rise of the ground again and someone else's land. Nobody goes there. When it is not a drought year, it is impossible to get across and the cows stand in midstream and gaze stupidly toward islands of hidden grass in there that they scent but cannot reach. The half-naked willows trail the tips of whips an inch or two above the threadbare picnic spot, faintly green, with its shallow cairn of stone filled with ashes among which the lettering on a fragment of beer carton may still be read by the eye that supplies the familiar missing letters. With the toe of his rubber sole, the farmer turns, as he goes, a glint where the bed of the river has dropped back; someone lost a ring here last summer. The blue overalls are leading through dead thistle, past occasional swirls of those swamp lilies with long ragged leaves arranged in a mandala, through a patch of tough reeds like the tails of some amphibians that keep their black-green flexibility all through winter. The two men plunge clumsy as cattle into the dry reeds, exploding a little swarm of minute birds, taking against their faces the spider-web sensation of floss, broken loose by their passage, from seeding bulrush heads. There lying on his face is the man.

The farmer almost ran onto him without seeing: He was close behind his herdsman and weltering along doggedly. The dead man.

Jacobus is walking around the sight. There is a well-trampled clearing about it—the whole kraal must have been down to have a look. "How is happen? What is happen here? Why he come down here on this farm? What is happen?" He talks on, making a kind of lament of indignation. The farmer is circling the sight, too, with his eyes.

The face is in the tacky mud; the tiny brown ears, the fine, felted hair, a fold or roll where it meets the back of the neck, because whoever he was, he wasn't thin. A brown pinstriped jacket, only the stubs of button shanks left on the sleeves, that must once have been part of some white man's business suit. Smart tight pants and a wide belt of fake snakeskin with fancy stitching. He might be a drunk, lying there, this city slicker. But his outdated "stylish" shoes are on dead, twisted feet, turned in brokenly as he was flung down into the reeds. Except for the face, which struck a small break or pocket between clumps, his body isn't actually on the earth at all but held slightly above it on an uneven nest of the reeds it has flattened, made for itself. From here, the only injury he shows is a long red scratch made by a sharp broken reed catching his neck.

The farmer bats at something clinging at his face. No mosquitoes now; bulrush gossamer. "He was dead when Solomon found him?"

"Dead, dead, finish." The herdsman walks over delicately toward the object and, bending toward it a little, turns his face back at his employer and says confidentially, rather as if he had been listening—"And now already is beginning to be little bit...." He wrinkles his nose, exposing the dirty horse teeth.

The farmer breathes quite normally; he does not take in the deep breaths of dry clear air that he did up on the lucerne field, but he does not reduce his intake, either. There is nothing, really nothing; whereas, up there, that sweetish whiff.

"You'd better not touch him. You're sure nobody here knows him? It's got nothing to do with any of you here?" He looks very deeply at his herdsman, lowering his head and hooding his eyebrows over his eyes.

Jacobus puts a hand dramatically on his own breast, where a stained vest shows through the unbuttoned overalls. He swings his head slowly from side to side: "Nobody can know this man. Nothing for this man. This is people from there—there"—he points that same accusing finger away in the direction of the farm's northern boundary.

The skin of the palm of a hand is too insensitive to detect the gossamer, but still it clings. The farmer projects his lower lip and blows sharply, upward over his face. And now he notices a single fly, one of the lingering, persistent kind, hovering above the neat brown ear down there. The fly is on the side to which the head is fractionally turned, although it is full-face in the mud, the side on which the mouth must be close to being exposed. The fly hovers and lands, unmolested.

"Just leave it as it is. The police must come."

"Ye-e-es, master," the herdsman says, long drawn out in sympathy for the responsibility that is no longer his. "Ye-e-es... is much better."

There is a moment's pause. The fly looks as if it ought to be buzzing but cannot be heard. There is the customary silence down here among the reeds, broken by the rifle crack (so it sounds, in contrast) of a dry stalk snapped by the movement of some unseen bird. The seething of the wind through the green reeds in late summer is seasonal.

They turn and thrash back the way they had come, leaving the man. Behind them, he is lying alone on his face.

The farmer takes the car to get up to the house and Jacobus comes with him, sitting carefully with feet planked flat on the carpeted floor and curled hands together on neat knees—he has the keys, so that he can always get into the house to telephone to town during the week, when the farmer is not a farmer but an industrialist, in pig iron. The house is closed up, because no one lives there all week. They enter through the kitchen door and the farmer goes straight to the telephone in the living room and turns the little crank on the box. The party line is busy and while he waits, he frees from the mud on his soles the slivers of dry reed stuck in it. He prizes one sole against the other and the mud wrinkles and blobs, like droppings, to the shiny linoleum patterned with orange-and-brown roses. The table is laid ready with hardware for a meal, under a net weighted at the hem with beads; an authoritative refrigerator, placed across the angle of a corner, hums to itself. The ring that he is waiting for makes him start. The line is free now and the exchange puts him through to the police station.

He always talks the white man's other language to officials and he is speaking in Afrikaans. "Look—Mehring here, from Vleibos, the Groendal Road. You must send someone. There's a dead man been found on my farm. Down in the vlei. Looks as if he'd been dumped there."

There is a blowing noise at the other end, air is expelled in good-natured exasperation. The voice addresses him as if he were an old friend: "Man...on Sunday...where'm I going to get someone? The van's out on patrol at the location. I'm alone here, myself. It's a Bantu, ay?"

"Yes. The body's lying in the reeds."

"Your boys have a fight or what?"

"It's a stranger. None of my boys knows who it is."

The voice laughs. "Yes, they're scared, they'll say they don't know. Was it a knife fight, I suppose?"

"I tell you, I've no idea. I don't want to mess about with the body and confuse your investigation. You must send someone."

"Hell, I don't know what I'm going to do about that. I'm only myself, here. The van's at the location.... I'll send tomorrow morning."

"But this body was found yesterday, it's been lying there 24 hours already."

"What can I do, sir? Man, I'm alone here!"

"Why can't you get hold of some other police station? Let them send someone."

"Can't do that. This's my district."

"Well, what am I to do about a dead body on my property? The man may have been murdered. It's obvious he's been knocked on the head or something and dumped. You can see from his shoes he didn't walk a step in that vlei."

"There's injuries on the head or where?"

"I've told you, that's your affair. I don't want my boys handling some- one who's been murdered. I don't want any trouble afterward about this business. You must get a man out here today, Sergeant."

"First thing in the morning. There won't be trouble for you, don't wor- ry. You're there by the vlei, near the location, ay? It comes from there all right, they're a terrible lot of Kaffirs there, we're used to that lot...."

The farmer replaces the receiver and says in English, "Christ Al- mighty"; and snorts a laugh, softly, so that Jacobus shall not hear.

The herdsman is waiting in the kitchen. "They'll come early tomorrow. I've told them everything. Just keep people away. And dogs. See that no dogs go down there." The herdsman doesn't react at all, although he has no doubt thought the farmer didn't know that the dogs that were supposed to be banished from the kraal have quietly reappeared again, not the same individual animals perhaps, but as a genus.

"Excuse, my master"—he indicates that he wants to pass before him into the living room and tramps, tiptoeing almost, across to a piece of furniture that must once have featured as the pride of a dining-room "suite" for the previous owner of the farm but is now used as a bar (a locked cupboard to which Jacobus has not got a key) and also reposi- tory (unlocked drawers) for farm documents, and pulling out one of the stiff drawers by its fancy gilt handle, feels surely under the feed bills tossed there. He has found what he apparently had hidden for safe-keeping: He brings in the bowl of his palms a huge, black-dialed watch with broad metal strap and a pair of sunglasses with a cracked right lens. He waits, indicating by the pause that his employer must put out his hand to receive, and formally gives over the property. "From him?" And the herdsman nods heavily.

"All right, Jacobus."

"All right, master."

"Send Alina up about one to make me lunch, eh?" he calls after him.

So they have touched the thing, lifted the face. Of course, the dark glasses might have been in a pocket. No money. Not surprising; these Friday payday murders are for money, what else? Jacobus took the objects (the Japanese-made steel watch is the kind black men offer surreptitiously for sale on street corners) into safekeeping to show that the people here've got nothing to do with the whole business.

Going to the drawer Jacobus has just shut, he finds a window envelope, already franked, that had carried some circular. The watch, with its flexible steel-mesh strap wrapped close, fits in easily, but the glasses prevent the flap from closing. He doubles a rubber band over his fingers and stretches it to secure envelope and contents. He writes on it, "Watch and Glasses, property of dead man." He adds, "For the Police," and places the envelope on the table, on top of the net, then moves it to the kitchen, putting it on the draining board of the sink, where it cannot fail to be in the line of vision as one walks into the house.

Outside the kitchen door, he distends his nostrils distastefully at the smell of duck shit and three or four pallid kittens whose fur is thin as the bits of duck down that roll softly about in invisible currents of air run from the threatening column of his body. "Psspsspss," he calls, but they cower and one even hisses. He strides away, past the barn, the paddock where the cows about to calve stand hugely in company and the tiny paddock where the bull, used less and less now, with the convenience of artificial insemination available, is always alone, and he continues by way of the mealie fields the long walk around the farm, on a perfect Sunday morning, he was about to begin when he stopped the car at the third pasture.

The matter of the guinea-fowl eggs has not been settled. He's conscious of this as he walks, because he knows it's no good allowing such things to pass. They must be dealt with. Eleven freckled eggs. It would have been useless to put them under the black Orpingtons; they must have been cold already. A red-legged partridge is taking a dust bath where it thinks it won't be spied, at the end of a row of mealies reaped and ready to be uprooted. But there are no guinea fowl feeding down in the far field where they usually come. Those bloody dogs; their dogs have probably been killing them off all summer. Eleven eggs, pointed, so different from hens' eggs made to lie in the standard depressions of plastic trays, in dozens, subject to seasonal price fluctuation. Soon there will be nothing left. (No good thinking about it; put a stop to it.) The hands of the child round the pale eggs were the color of the underside of an empty tortoise shell held up to the light. The mealies are nearly all reaped, the stalks stocked in pyramids with dry plumy apexes, the leaves peeling tattered. Distance comes back with these reaped fields, the plowed earth stretching away in fan-shaped ridges to its own horizon; the farm extends in size in winter, just as in summer as the mealies grow taller and thicker the horizon closes in, diminishes the farm until it is a series of corridors between walls of stiff green higher than his head. In a good year. If there is going to be a good year again. A cultivator has been left to rust on its side (no rain to rust it, but still, standing out here won't do it any good). Now is the time to clear the cankerweed that plagues this part of the field, near the eucalyptus trees, which have made a remarkable recovery—he can scarcely notice, for new branches, the stumps where they (up at the kraal) had chopped at them for firewood before he bought the place.

Although he had no sign of it when he set out this morning, a Saturday-night headache is now causing pressure on the bridge of his nose; closing his eyes against the light, he pinches the bone there between thumb and finger. He feels pleasantly, specifically thirsty for water. He makes for the windmill near an old stone outbuilding. The cement round the borehole installation is new and the blades of the windmill are still shiny. He puts his head sideways to the stiff tap and the water sizzles, neither warm nor cold, into his mouth. The windmill is not turning and he releases the chain and arm that brake it in order to set it going, but although it noses creakily, it does not begin to turn, because there is no wind today, the air is still, it is a perfect autumn day. He sets the brake again carefully.

A little after one, passing the room of the servant, Alina, beside the fowl run, on his way up to the house, he sees Jacobus talking there to her. He and the herdsman do not acknowledge each other, because they have seen each other before and no greeting is exchanged. He calls out, "You'd better take something—to put over"—his head jerks toward the river—"down there. An old tarpaulin. Or sacks."

In the Black Mill

fiction by MICHAEL CHABON

In the fall of 1948, when I arrived in Plunkettsburg to begin the fieldwork I hoped would lead to a doctorate in archaeology, there were still a good number of townspeople living there whose memories stretched back to the time, in the final decade of the previous century, when the soot-blackened hills that encircle the town fairly swarmed with savants and mad diggers. In 1892 the discovery, on a hilltop overlooking the Miskahannock River, of the burial complex of a hitherto-unknown tribe of Mound Builders had set off a frenzy of excavation and scholarly poking around that made several careers, among them that of the aged hero of my profession who was chairman of my dissertation committee. It was under his redoubtable influence that I had taken up the study of the awful, illustrious Miskahannocks, with their tombs and bone pits, a course that led me at last, one gray November afternoon, to turn my overladen fourth-hand Nash off the highway from Pittsburgh to Morgantown, and to navigate, tightly gripping the wheel, the pitted ghost of a roadbed that winds up through the Yuggogheny Hills, then down into the broad and gloomy valley of the Miskahannock.

As I negotiated that endless series of hairpin and blind curves, I was afforded an equally endless series of dispiriting partial views of the place where I would spend the next ten months of my life. Like many of its neighbors in that iron-veined country, Plunkettsburg was at first glance unprepossessing—a low, rusting little city, with tarnished onion domes and huddled houses, drab as an armful of dead leaves strewn along the ground. But as I left the last hill behind me and got my first unobstructed look, I immediately noted the one structure that, while it did nothing to elevate my opinion of my new home, altered the humdrum aspect of Plunkettsburg sufficiently to make it remarkable, and also sinister. It stood off to the east of town, in a zone of weeds and rust-colored earth, a vast, black box, bristling with spiky chimneys, extending over some five acres or more, dwarfing everything around it. This was, I knew at once, the famous Plunkettsburg Mill. Evening was coming on, and in the half-light its windows winked and flickered with inner fire, and its towering stacks vomited smoke into the autumn twilight. I shuddered, and then cried out. So intent had I been on the ghastly black apparition of the mill that I had nearly run my car off the road.

"'Here in this mighty fortress of industry,'" I quoted aloud in the tone of a newsreel narrator, reassuring myself with the ironic reverberation of my voice, "'turn the great cogs and thrust the relentless pistons that forge the pins and trusses of the American dream.'" I was recalling the words of a chamber of commerce brochure I had received last week from my hosts, the antiquities department of Plunkettsburg College, along with particulars of my lodging and library privileges. They were anxious to have me; it had been many years since the publication of my chairman's *Miskahannock Surveys* had effectively settled all answerable questions—save, I hoped, one—about the vanished tribe and consigned Plunkettsburg once again to the mists of academic oblivion and the thick black effluvia of its satanic mill.

• • •

"So, what is there left to say about that pointy-toothed crowd?" said Carlotta Brown-Jenkin, draining her glass of brandy. The chancellor of Plunkettsburg College and chairwoman of the antiquities department had offered to stand me to dinner on my first night in town. We were sitting in the Hawaiian-style dining room of a Chinese restaurant downtown. Brown-Jenkin was herself appropriately antique, a gaunt old girl in her late 70s, her nearly hairless scalp worn and yellowed, the glint of her eyes, deep within their cavernous sockets, like that of ancient coins discovered by torchlight. "I quite thought that your distinguished mentor had revealed all their bloody mysteries."

"Only the women filed their teeth," I reminded her, taking another swallow of Indian Ring beer, the local brew, which I found to possess a dark, not entirely pleasant savor of autumn leaves or damp earth. I gazed around the low room with its ersatz palm thatching and garlands of wax orchids. The only other people in the place were a man on wooden crutches with a pinned-up trouser leg and a man with a wooden hand, both of them drinking Indian Ring, and the bartender, an extremely fat woman in a thematically correct but hideous red muumuu. My hostess had assured me, without a great deal of enthusiasm, that we were about to eat the best-cooked meal in town.

"Yes, yes," she recalled, smiling tolerantly. Her particular field of study was great Carthage, and no doubt, I thought, she looked down on my unlettered band of savages. "They considered pointed teeth to be the essence of female beauty."

"That is, of course, the theory of my distinguished mentor," I said, studying the label on my beer bottle, on which there was printed Thelder's 1894 engraving of the Plunkettsburg Ring, which was also reproduced on the cover of *Miskahannock Surveys*.

"You do not concur?" said Brown-Jenkin.

"I think that there may in fact be other possibilities."

"Such as?"

At this moment the waiter arrived, bearing a tray laden with plates of unidentifiable meats and vegetables that glistened in garish sauces the colors of women's lipstick. The steaming dishes emitted an overpowering blast of vinegar, as if to cover some underlying stench. Feeling ill, I averted my eyes from the food and saw that the waiter, a thickset, powerful man with bland Slavic features, was missing two of the fingers on his left hand. My stomach revolted. I excused myself from the table and ran directly to the bathroom.

"Nerves," I explained to Brown-Jenkin when I returned, blushing, to the table. "I'm excited about starting my research."

"Of course," she said, examining me critically. With her napkin she wiped a thin red dribble of sauce from her chin. "I quite understand."

"There seem to be an awful lot of missing limbs in this room," I said, trying to lighten my mood. "Hope none of them ended up in the food."

The chancellor stared at me, aghast.

"A very bad joke," I said. "My apologies. My sense of humor was not, I'm afraid, widely admired back in Boston, either."

"No," she agreed, with a small, unamused smile. "Well." She patted the long, thin strands of yellow hair atop her head. "It's the *mill*, of course."

"Of course," I said, feeling a bit dense for not having puzzled this out myself. "Dangerous work they do there, I take it."

"The mill has taken a piece of half the men in Plunkettsburg," Brown-Jenkin said, sounding almost proud. "Yes, it's terribly dangerous work." There had crept into her voice a boosterish tone of admiration that could not fail to remind me of the chamber of commerce brochure. "Important work."

"Vitally important," I agreed, and to placate her I heaped my plate with colorful, luminous, indeterminate meat, a gesture for which I paid dearly through all the long night that followed.

• • •

I took up residence in Murrough House, just off the campus of Plunkettsburg College. It was a large, rambling structure, filled with hidden passages, queerly shaped rooms and staircases leading nowhere, built by the notorious lady magnate, "the Robber Baroness," Philippa Howard Murrough, founder of the college, noted spiritualist and author and dark genius of the Plunkettsburg Mill. She had spent the last four decades of her life, and a considerable part of her manufacturing fortune, adding to, demolishing and rebuilding her home. On her death the resultant warren, a chimera of brooding Second Empire gables, peaked Victorian turrets and baroque porticoes with a coat of glossy black ivy, passed into the hands of the private girls' college she had endowed, which converted it to a faculty club and lodgings for visiting scholars. I had a round turret room on the fourth and uppermost floor. There were no other visiting scholars in the house and, according to the porter, this had been the case for several years.

Old Halicek, the porter, was a bent, slow-moving fellow who lived with his daughter and grandson in a suite of rooms somewhere in the unreachable lower regions of the house. He too had lost a part of his body to the great mill in his youth—his left ear. It had been reduced, by a device that Halicek called a Dodson line extractor, to a small pink ridge nestled in the lee of his bushy white sideburns. His daughter, Mrs. Eibonas, oversaw a small staff of two maids and a waiter and did the cooking for the dozen or so faculty members who took their lunches at Murrough House every day. The waiter was Halicek's grandson, Dexter Eibonas, an earnest, good-looking, affable redhead of 17 who was a favorite among the college faculty. He was intelligent, curious, widely if erratically read. He was always pestering me to take him out to dig in the mounds, and while I would not have been averse to his pleasant company, the terms of my agreement with the board of the college, who were the trustees of the site, expressly forbade the recruiting of local workmen. Nevertheless I gave him books on archaeology and kept him abreast of my discoveries, such as they were. Several of the Plunkettsburg professors, I learned, had also taken an interest in the development of his mind.

"They sent me up to Pittsburgh last winter," he told me one evening about a month into my sojourn, as he brought me a bottle of Ring and a plate of Mrs. Eibonas' famous kielbasa with sauerkraut. Professor Brown-Jenkin had been much mistaken, in my opinion, about the best-laid table in town. During the most tedious, chilly and profitless stretches of my scratchings-about in the bleak, flinty Yuggoghenies, I was often sustained solely by thoughts of Mrs. Eibonas' homemade sausages and cakes. "I had an interview with the dean of engineering at Tech. Professor Collier even paid for a hotel for Mother and me."

"And how did it go?"

"Oh, it went fine, I guess," said Dexter. "I was accepted."

"Oh," I said, confused. The autumn semester at Carnegie Tech, I imagined, would have been ending that very week.

"Have you—have you deferred your admission?"

"Deferred it indefinitely, I guess. I told them no thanks." Dexter had, in an excess of nervous energy, been snapping a tea towel back and forth. He stopped. His normally bright eyes took on a glazed, I would almost have said a dreamy, expression. "I'm going to work in the mill."

"The *mill*?" I said, incredulous. I looked at him to see if he was teasing me, but at that moment he seemed to be entertaining only the pleasantest imaginings of his labors in that fiery black castle. I had a sudden vision of his pleasant face rendered earless, and looked away. "Forgive my asking, but why would you want to do that?"

"My father did it," said Dexter, his voice dull. "His father, too. I'm on the hiring list." The light came back into his eyes, and he resumed snapping the towel. "Soon as a place opens up, I'm going in."

He left me and went back into the kitchen, and I sat there shuddering. *I'm going in*. The phrase had a heroic, doomed ring to it, like the pronouncement of a fireman about to enter his last burning house. Over the course of the previous month I'd had ample opportunity to observe the mill and its effect on the male population of Plunkettsburg. Casual observation, in local markets and bars, in the lobby of the Orpheum on State Street, on the sidewalks, in Birch's general store out on Gray Road where I stopped for coffee and cigarettes every morning on my way up to the mound complex, had led me to estimate that in truth, fully half of the townsmen had lost some visible portion of their anatomies to Murrough Manufacturing, Inc. And yet all my attempts to ascertain how these often horribly grave accidents had befallen their bent, maimed or limping victims were met, invariably, with an explanation at once so detailed and so vague, so rich in mechanical jargon and yet so free of actual information, that I had never yet succeeded in producing in my mind an adequate picture of the incident in question, or, for that matter, of what kind of deadly labor was performed in the black mill.

What, precisely, was manufactured in that bastion of industrial democracy and fount of the Murrough millions? I heard the trains come sighing and moaning into town in the middle of the night, clanging as they were shunted into the mill sidings. I saw the black diesel trucks, emblazoned with the crimson initial M, lumbering through the streets of Plunkettsburg on their way to and from the loading docks. I had two dozen conversations, over endless mugs of Indian Ring, about shift schedules and union activities (invariably quashed) and company picnics, about ore and furnaces, metallurgy and turbines. I heard the resigned, good-natured explanations of men sliced open by Rawlings divagators, ground up by spline presses, mangled by steam sorters, half-decapitated by rolling Hurley plates. And yet after four months in Plunkettsburg I was no closer to understanding the terrible work to which the people of that town sacrificed, with such apparent goodwill, the bodies of their men.

● ● ●

I took to haunting the precincts of the mill in the early morning as the six o'clock shift was coming on and late at night as the graveyard men streamed through the iron gates, carrying their black lunch pails. The fence, an elaborate Victorian confection of wickedly tipped, thick iron pikes trailed with iron ivy, enclosed the mill yard at such a distance from the mountainous factory itself that it was impossible for me to get near enough to see anything but the glow of huge fires through the begrimed mesh windows. I applied at the company offices in town for admission, as a visitor, to the plant but was told by the receptionist, rather rudely, that the Plunkettsburg Mill was not a tourist facility. My fascination with the place grew so intense and distracting that I neglected my work; my wanderings through the abandoned purlieus of the savage Miskahannocks grew desultory and ruminative, my discoveries of artifacts, never frequent, dwindled to almost nothing, and I made fewer and fewer entries in my journal. Finally, one exhausted morning, after an entire night spent lying in my bed at Murrough House staring out the leaded window at a sky that was bright orange with the reflected fire of the mill, I decided I had had enough.

I dressed quickly, in plain tan trousers and a flannel work shirt. I went down to the closet in the front hall, where I found a drab old woolen coat and a watch cap that I pulled down over my head. Then I stepped outside. The terrible orange flashes had subsided, and the sky was filled with stars. I hurried across town to the east side, to Stan's Diner on Mill Street, where I knew I would find the day shift wolfing down ham and eggs and pancakes. I slipped between two large men at

151

the long counter and ordered coffee. When one of my neighbors got up to go to the toilet, I grabbed his lunch pail, threw down a handful of coins and hurried over to the gates of the mill, where I joined the crowd of men. They looked at me oddly, not recognizing me, and I could see them murmuring to one another in puzzlement. But the earliness of the morning or an inherent reserve kept them from saying anything. They figured, I suppose, that whoever I was, I was somebody else's problem. Only one man, tall, with thinning yellow hair, kept his gaze on me for more than a moment. His eyes, I was surprised to see, looked very sad.

"You shouldn't be here, buddy," he said, not unkindly.

I felt myself go numb. I had been caught.

"What? Oh, no, I—I——"

The whistle blew. The crowd of men, swelled now to more than a hundred, jerked to life and waited, nervous, on the balls of their feet, for the gates to open. The man with the yellow hair seemed to forget me. In the distance an equally large crowd of men emerged from the belly of the mill and headed toward us. There was a grinding of old machinery, the creak of stressed iron, and then the ornamental gates rolled away. The next instant I was caught up in the tide of men streaming toward the mill, borne along like a cork. Halfway there our group intersected with the graveyard shift and in the ensuing chaos of bodies and hellos I was sure my plan was going to work. I was going to see, at last, the inside of the mill.

I felt something, someone's fingers, brush the back of my neck, and then I was yanked backward by the collar of my coat. I lost my footing and fell to the ground. As the changing shifts of workers flowed around me I looked up and saw a huge man standing over me, his arms folded across his chest. He was wearing a black jacket emblazoned on the breast with a large M. I tried to stand, but he pushed me back down.

"You can just stay right there until the police come," he said.

"Listen," I said. My research, clearly, was at an end. My scholarly privileges would be revoked. I would creep back to Boston, where, of course, my committee and, above all, my chair would recommend that I quit the department. "You don't have to do that."

Once more I tried to stand, and this time the company guard threw me back to the ground so hard and so quickly that I couldn't break my fall with my hands. The back of my head slammed against the pavement. A passing worker stepped on my outstretched hand. I cried out.

"Hey," said a voice. "Come on, Moe. You don't need to treat him that way."

It was the sad-eyed man with the yellow hair. He interposed himself between me and my attacker.

"Don't do this, Ed," said the guard. "I'll have to write you up."

I rose shakily to my feet and started to stumble away, back toward the gates. The guard tried to reach around Ed, to grab hold of me. As he lunged forward, Ed stuck out his foot, and the guard went sprawling.

"Come on, professor," said Ed, putting his arm around me. "You better get out of here."

"Do I know you?" I said, leaning gratefully on him.

"No, but you know my nephew, Dexter. He pointed you out to me at the pictures one night."

"Thank you," I said, when we reached the gate. He brushed some dust from the back of my coat, handed me the knit stocking cap, then took a black bandana from the pocket of his dungarees. He touched a corner of it to my mouth, and it came away marked with a dark stain.

"Only a little blood," he said. "You'll be all right. You just make sure to stay clear of this place from now on." He brought his face close to mine, filling my nostrils with the sharp medicinal tang of his aftershave. He lowered his voice to a whisper. "And stay off the beer."

"What?"

"Just stay off it." He stood up straight and returned the bandanna to his back pocket. "I haven't taken a sip in two weeks." I nodded, confused. I had been drinking two, three, sometimes four bottles of Indian Ring every night, finding that it carried me effortlessly into profound and dreamless sleep.

"Just tell me one thing," I said.

"I can't say nothing else, professor."

"It's just—what is it you do, in there?"

"Me?" he said, pointing to his chest. "I operate a sprue extruder."

"Yes, yes," I said, "but what does a sprue extruder *do*? What is it *for*?"

He looked at me patiently but a little remotely, a distracted parent with an inquisitive child.

"It's for extruding sprues," he said. "What else?"

● ● ●

Thus repulsed, humiliated and given good reason to fear that my research was in imminent jeopardy of being brought to an end, I resolved to put the mystery of the mill out of my mind once and for all and get on with my real business in Plunkettsburg. I went out to the site of the mound complex and worked with my brush and little hand spade all through that day, until the light failed. When I got home, exhausted, Mrs. Eibonas brought me a bottle of Indian Ring and I gratefully drained it before I remembered Ed's strange warning. I handed the sweating bottle back to Mrs. Eibonas. She smiled.

"Can I bring you another, professor?" she said.

"No, thank you," I said. Her smile collapsed. She looked very disappointed. "All right," she said. For some reason the thought of disappointing her bothered me greatly, so I told her, "Maybe one more."

I retired early and dreamed dreams that were troubled by the scratching of iron on earth and by a clamoring tumult of men. The next morning I got up and went straight out to the site again.

For it was going to take work, a lot of work, if my theory was ever going to bear fruit. During much of my first several months in Plunkettsburg I had been hampered by snow and by the degree to which the site of the Plunkettsburg Mounds—a broad plateau on the eastern slope of Mount Orrert, on which there had been excavated, in the 1890s, 36 huge molars of packed earth, each the size of a two-story house—had been picked over and disturbed by that early generation of archaeologists. Their methods had not in every case been as fastidious as one could have hoped. There were numerous areas of old digging where the historical record had, through carelessness, been rendered illegible. Then again, I considered, as I gazed up at the ivy-covered flank of the ancient, artificial hillock my mentor had designated B-3, there was always the possibility that my theory was wrong.

Like all the productions of academe, I suppose, my theory was composed of equal parts of indebtedness and spite. I had formulated it in a kind of rebellion against that grand old man of the field, my chairman, the very person who had inculcated me with a respect for the deep, subtle savagery of the Miskahannock Indians. His view—the standard one—was that the culture of the builders of the Plunkettsburg Mounds, at its zenith, had expressed, to a degree unequaled in the Western hemisphere up to that time, the aestheticizing of the nihilist impulse. They had evolved all the elaborate social structures—texts, rituals, decorative arts, architecture—of any of the world's great religions: dazzling feats of abstract design represented by the thousands of baskets, jars, bowls, spears, tablets, knives, flails, axes, codices, robes and so on that were housed and displayed with such pride in the museum of my university, back in Boston. But the Miskahannocks, insofar as anyone had ever been able to determine (and many had tried), worshiped nothing, or, as my teacher would have it, Nothing. They acknowledged neither gods nor goddesses, conversed with no spirits or familiars. Their only purpose, the focus and the pinnacle of their artistic genius, was the killing of men. Nobody knew how many of the unfortunate males of the neighboring tribes had fallen victim to the Miskahannocks' delicate artistry of torture and dismemberment. In 1903 Professor William Waterman of Yale discovered 14 separate ossuary pits along the banks of the river, not far from the present site of the mill. These had contained enough bones to frame the bodies of 7,000 men and boys. And nobody knew why they had died. The few tattered, fragmentary blood-on-tanbark texts so far discovered concerned themselves chiefly with the recurring famines that plagued Miskahannock civilization and, it was generally theorized, had been responsible for its ultimate collapse. The texts said nothing about the sacred arts of killing and torture. There was, my teacher had argued, one reason for this. The deaths had been purposeless; their justification, the cosmic purposelessness of life itself.

Now, once I had settled myself on spiteful rebellion, as every good pupil eventually must, there were two possible paths available to me. The first would have been to attempt to prove beyond a doubt that the Miskahannocks had, in fact, worshiped some kind of god, some positive, purposive entity, however bloodthirsty. I chose the second path. I accepted the godlessness of the Miskahannocks. I rejected the refined, reasoning nihilism my mentor had postulated (and to which, as I among very few others knew, he himself privately subscribed). The Miskahannocks, I hoped to prove, had had another motive for their killing: They were hungry; according to the tattered scraps of the Plunkettsburg Codex, very hungry indeed. The filed teeth my professor subsumed to the larger aesthetic principles he elucidated thus had, in my view, a far simpler and more utilititarian purpose. Unfortunately, the widespread incidence of cannibalism among the women of a people vanished 4,000 years since was proving rather difficult to establish. So far, in fact, I had found no evidence of it at all.

I knelt to untie the canvas tarp I had stretched across my digging of the previous day. I was endeavoring to take an inclined section of B-3, cutting a passage five feet high and two feet wide at a 30 degree angle to the horizontal. This endeavor in itself was a kind of admission of defeat, since B-3 was one of two mounds, the other being its neighbor B-5, designated a "null mound" by those who had studied the site. It had been thoroughly pierced and penetrated and found to be utterly empty; reserved, it was felt, for the mortal remains of a dynasty that failed. But I had already made careful searches of the 34 other tombs of the Miskahannock queens. The null mounds were the only ones remaining. If, as I anticipated, I found no evidence of anthropophagy, I would have to give up on the mounds entirely and start looking else-where. There were persistent stories of other bone pits in the pleats and hollows of the Yuggoghenies. Perhaps I could find one, a fresh one, one not trampled and corrupted by the primitive methods of my professional forebears.

I peeled back the sheet of oiled canvas I had spread across my handi-work and received a shock. The passage, which over the course of the previous day I had managed to extend a full four feet into the side of the mound, had been completely filled in. Not merely filled in; the thick black soil had been tamped down and a makeshift screen of ivy had been drawn across it. I took a step back and looked around the site, certain all at once that I was being observed. There were only the crows in the treetops. In the distance I could hear the Murrough trucks on the tortuous highway, grinding gears as they climbed up out of the val-ley. I looked down at the ground by my feet and saw the faint imprint of a foot smaller than my own. A few feet from this, I found another. That was all.

I ought to have been afraid, I suppose, or at the least concerned, but at this point, I confess, I was only angry. The site was heavily fenced and posted with NO TRESPASSING signs, but apparently some local hood-lums had come up in the night and wasted all of the previous day's hard work. The motive for this vandalism eluded me, but I supposed that a lack of any discernible motive was in the nature of vandalism itself. I picked up my hand shovel and started in again on my doorway into the mound. The fifth bite I took with the little iron tooth brought out something strange. It was a black bandanna, twisted and soiled. I spread it out across my thigh and found the small, round trace of my own blood on one corner. I was bewildered, and again I looked around to see if someone were watching me. There were only the laughter and ragged fingers of the crows. What was Ed up to? Why would my rescuer want to come up onto the mountain and ruin my work? Did he think he was protecting me? I shrugged, stuffed the bandanna into a pocket and went back to my careful digging. I worked steadily throughout the day, extending the tunnel six inches nearer than I had come yesterday to the heart of the mound, then drove home to Murrough House, my shoulders aching, my fingers stiff. I had a long, hot soak in the big bath-tub down the hall from my room, smoked a pipe and read, for the 15th time at least, the section in *Miskahannock Surveys* dealing with B-3. Then at 6:30 I went downstairs to find Dexter Eibonas waiting to serve my dinner, his expression blank, his eyes bloodshot. I remember being sur-prised that he didn't immediately demand details of my day on the dig.

He just nodded, retreated into the kitchen and returned with a heated can of soup, half a loaf of white bread and a bottle of Ring. Naturally after my hard day I was disappointed by this fare, and I inquired as to the whereabouts of Mrs. Eibonas.

"She had some family business, professor," Dexter said, rolling up his hands in his tea towel, then unrolling them again. "Sad business."

"Did somebody—die?"

"My uncle Ed," said the boy, collapsing in a chair beside me and covering his twisted features with his hands. "He had an accident down at the mill, I guess. Fell headfirst into the impact mold."

"What?" I said, feeling my throat constrict. "My God, Dexter! Something has to be done! That mill ought to be shut down!"

Dexter took a step back, startled by my vehemence. I had thought at once, of course, of the black bandanna, and now I wondered if I were not somehow responsible for Ed Eibonas' death. Perhaps the incident in the mill yard the day before, his late-night digging in the dirt of B-3 in some kind of misguided effort to help me, had left him rattled, unable to concentrate on his work, prey to accidents.

"You just don't understand," said Dexter. "It's our way of life here. There isn't anything for us but the mill." He pushed the bottle of Indian Ring toward me. "Drink your beer, professor."

I reached for the glass and brought it to my lips but was swept by a sudden wave of revulsion like that which had overtaken me at the Chinese restaurant on my first night in town. I pushed back from the table and stood up, my violent start upsetting a pewter candelabra in which four tapers burned. Dexter lunged to keep it from falling over, then looked at me, surprised. I stared back, chest heaving, feeling defiant without being sure of what exactly I was defying. "I am not going to touch another drop of that beer!" I said, the words sounding petulant and absurd as they emerged from my mouth.

Dexter nodded. He looked worried.

"All right, professor," he said, obligingly, as if he thought I might have become unbalanced. "You just go on up to your room and lie down. I'll bring you your food a little later. How about that?"

● ● ●

The next day I lay in bed, aching, sore and suffering from that peculiar brand of spiritual depression born largely of suppressed fear. On the following morning I roused myself, shaved, dressed in my best clothes and went to the Church of St. Stephen, on Nolt Street, the heart of Plunkettsburg's Estonian neighborhood, for the funeral of Ed Eibonas. There was a sizable turnout, as was always the case, I was told, when there had been a death at the mill. Such deaths were reportedly uncommon; the mill was a cruel and dangerous but rarely fatal place. At Dexter's invitation I went to the dead man's house to pay my respects to the widow, and two hours later I found myself, along with most of the other male mourners, roaring drunk on some kind of fruit brandy brought out on special occasions. It may have been that the brandy burned away the jitters and anxiety of the past two days; in any case the next morning I went out to the mounds again, with a tent and a cookstove and several bags of groceries. I didn't leave for the next five days.

My hole had been filled in again, and this time there was no clue to the identity of the filler, but I was determined not to let this spook me, as the saying goes. I simply dug. Ordinarily I would have proceeded cautiously, carrying the dirt out by thimblefuls and sifting each one, but I felt my time on the site growing short. I often saw cars on the access road by day, and headlight beams by night, slowing down as if to observe me. Twice a day a couple of sheriff's deputies would pull up to the Ring and sit in their car, watching. At first whenever they appeared, I stopped working, lit a cigarette and waited for them to arrest me. But when after the first few times nothing of the sort occurred, I relaxed a little and kept on with my digging for the duration of their visit. I was resigned to being prevented from completing my research, but before this happened I wanted to get to the heart of B-3.

On the fourth day, when I was halfway to my goal, George Birch drove out from his general store, as I had requested, with cans of stew, bottles of soda pop and cigarettes. He was normally a dour man, but on this morning his face seemed longer than ever. I inquired if there were anything bothering him.

"Carlotta Brown-Jenkin died last night," he said. "Friend of my mother's. Tough old lady." He shook his head. "Influenza. Shame."

I remembered that awful, Technicolored meal so many months before, the steely glint of her eyes in their cavernous sockets. I did my best to look properly sympathetic.

"That is a shame," I said.

He set down the box of food and looked past me at the entrance to my tunnel. The sight of it seemed to disturb him.

"You sure you know what you're doing?" he said.

I assured him that I did, but he continued to look skeptical.

"I remember the last time you archaeologist fellows came to town, you know," he said. As a matter of fact I did know this, since he told me almost every time I saw him. "I was a boy. We had just got electricity in our house."

"Things must have changed a great deal since then," I said.

"Things haven't changed at all," he snapped. He was never a cheerful man, George Birch. He turned, hitching up his trousers, and limped on his wooden foot back to his truck.

That night I lay in my bedroll under the canvas roof of my tent, watching the tormented sky. The lantern hissed softly beside my head; I kept it burning low, all night long, advertising my presence to any who might seek to come and undo my work. It had been a warm, springlike afternoon, but now a cool breeze was blowing in from the north, stirring the branches of the trees over my head. After a while I drowsed a little; I fancied I could hear the distant fluting of the Miskahannock flowing over its rocky bed and, still more distant, the low, insistent drumming of the machine heart in the black mill. Suddenly I sat up: The music I had been hearing, of breeze and river and far-off machinery, seemed at once very close and not at all metaphoric. I scrambled out of my bedroll and tent and stood, taut, listening, at the edge of Plunkettsburg Ring. It *was* music I heard, strange music, and it seemed to be issuing, impossibly, from the other end of the tunnel I had been digging and redigging over the past two weeks—from within mound B-3, the null mound!

I have never, generally, been plagued by bouts of great courage, but I do suffer from another vice whose outward appearance is often indistinguishable from that of bravery: I am pathologically curious. I was not brave enough, in that eldritch moment, actually to approach B-3, to investigate the source of the music I was hearing; but though every primitive impulse urged me to flee, I stood there, listening, until the music stopped, an hour before dawn. I heard sorrow in the music, and mourning, and the beating of many small drums. And then in the full light of the last day of April, emboldened by bright sunshine and a cup of instant coffee, I made my way gingerly toward the mound. I picked up my shovel, lowered my foolish head into the tunnel and crept carefully into the bowels of the now-silent mound. Seven hours later I felt the shovel strike something hard, like stone or brick. Then the hardness gave way, and the shovel flew abruptly out of my hands. I had reached, at last, the heart of mound B-3.

And it was not empty; oh no, not at all. There were seven sealed tombs lining the domed walls, carved stone chambers of the usual Miskahannock type, and another ten that were empty, and one, as yet unsealed, that held the unmistakable, though withered, yellow, naked and eternally slumbering form of Carlotta Brown-Jenkin. And crouched on her motionless chest, as though prepared to devour her throat, sat a tiny stone idol, hideous, black, brandishing a set of wicked ivory fangs.

Now I gave in to those primitive impulses; I panicked. I tore out of the burial chamber as quickly as I could and ran for my car, not bothering to collect my gear. In 20 minutes I was back at Murrough House. I hurried up the front steps, intending only to go to my room, retrieve my clothes and books and papers and leave behind Plunkettsburg forever. But when I came into the foyer I found Dexter, carrying a tray of eaten lunches back from the dining room to the kitchen. He was whistling lightheartedly and when he saw me he grinned. Then his expression changed.

"What is it?" he said, while reaching out to me. "Has something happened?"

"Nothing," I said, stepping around him, avoiding his grasp. The streets of Plunkettsburg had been built on evil ground, and now I could only assume that every one of its citizens, even cheerful Dexter, had been altered by the years and centuries of habitation. "Everything's fine. I just have to leave town."

I started up the wide, carpeted steps as quickly as I could, mentally packing my bags and boxes with essentials, loading the car, twisting and backtracking up the steep road out of this cursed valley.

"My name came up," Dexter said. "I start tomorrow at the mill."

Why did I turn? Why did I not keep going down the long, crooked hallway and carry out my sensible, cowardly plan?

"You can't do that," I said. He started to smile, but there must have been something in my face. The smile fizzled out. "You'll be killed. You'll be mangled. That good-looking mug of yours will be hideously deformed."

"Maybe," he said, trying to sound calm, but I could see that my own agitation was infecting him. "Maybe not."

"It's the women. The queens. They're alive."

"The queens are alive? What are you talking about, professor? I think you've been out on the mountain too long."

"I have to go, Dexter," I said. "I'm sorry. I can't stay here anymore. But if you have any sense at all, you'll come with me. I'll drive you to Pittsburgh. You can start at Tech. They'll help you. They'll give you a job...." I could feel myself starting to babble.

Dexter shook his head. "Can't," he said. "My name came up! Shoot, I've been waiting for this all my life."

"Look," I said. "All right. Just come with me, out to the Ring." I looked at my watch. "We've got an hour until dark. Just let me show you something I found out there, and then if you still want to go to work in that infernal factory, I'll shake your hand and bid you farewell."

"You'll really take me out to the site?"

I nodded. He set the tray on a deal table and untied his apron.

"Let me get my jacket," he said.

• • •

I packed my things and we drove in silence to the necropolis. I was filled with regret for this course of action, with intimations of disaster. But I felt I couldn't simply leave town and let Dexter Eibonas walk willingly into that fiery eructation of the evil genius, the immemorial accursedness, of his drab Pennsylvania hometown. I couldn't leave that young, unmarked body to be broken and split on the horrid machines of the mill. As for why Dexter wasn't talking, I don't know; perhaps he sensed my mounting despair, or perhaps he was simply lost in youthful speculation on the unknown vistas that lay before him, subterranean sights forbidden and half-legendary to him since he had first come to consciousness of the world. As we turned off Gray Road onto the access road that led up to the site, he sat up straight and looked at me, his face grave with the consummate adolescent pleasure of violating rules.

"There," I said. I pointed out the window as we crested the rise. The Plunkettsburg Ring lay spread out before us, filled with jagged shadows, in the slanting, rust-red light of the setting sun. From this angle the dual circular plan of the site was not apparent, and the 36 mounds appeared to stretch from one end of the plateau to the other, like a line of uneven teeth studding an immense, devouring jawbone.

"Let's make this quick," I said, shuddering. I handed him a spare lantern from the trunk of the Nash, and then we walked to the edge of the aboriginal forest that ran upslope from the plateau to the wind-shattered precincts of Mount Orrert's sharp peak. It was here, in the lee of a large maple tree, that I had set up my makeshift camp. At the time the shelter of that homely tree had seemed quite inviting, but now it appeared to me that the forest was the source of all the lean shadows reaching their ravening fingers across the plateau. I ducked quickly into my tent to retrieve my lantern and then hurried back to rejoin Dexter. I thought he was looking a little uneasy now. His gait slowed as we approached B-3. When we trudged around to confront the raw earthen mouth of the passage I had dug, he came to a complete stop.

"We're not going inside there," he said in a monotone. I saw come into his eyes the dull, dreamy look that was there whenever he talked about going to work in the mill. "It isn't allowed."

"It's just for a minute, Dexter. That's all you'll need."

I put my hands on his shoulders and gave him a push, and we stumbled through the dank, close passage, the light from our lanterns veering wildly around us. Then we were in the crypt.

"No," Dexter said. The effect on him of the sight of the time-ravaged naked body of Carlotta Brown-Jenkin, of the empty tombs, the hideous idol, the outlandish ideograms that covered the walls, was everything I could have hoped for. His jaw dropped, his hands clenched and unclenched, he took a step backward. "She just died!"

"Yesterday," I agreed, trying to allay my own anxiety with a show of ironic detachment.

"But what…what's she doing out here?" He shook his head quickly, as though trying to clear it of smoke or spiderwebs.

"Don't you know?" I asked him, for I still was not completely certain of his or any townsman's uninvolvement in the evil, at once ancient and machine-age, that was evidently the chief business of Plunkettsburg.

"No! God, no!" He pointed to the queer, fanged idol that crouched with a hungry leer on the late chancellor's hollow bosom. "God, what is that thing?"

I went over to the tomb and cautiously, as if the figure with its enormous, obscene tusks might come to life and rip off a mouthful of my hand, picked up the idol. It was as black and cold as space, and so heavy that it bent my hand back at the wrist as I hefted it. With both hands I got a firm grip on it and turned it over. On its pedestal were incised three symbols in the spiky, complex script of the Miskahannocks, unrelated to any other known human language or alphabet. As with all of the tribe's inscriptions, the characters had both a phonetic and a symbolic sense. Often these were quite independent of one another.

"Yu…yug…gog," I read, sounding it out carefully. "Yuggog."

"What does that mean?"

"It doesn't mean anything, as far as I know. But it can be read another way. It's trickier. Here's tooth…gut—that's hunger—and this one——" I held up the idol toward him. He shied away. His face had gone completely pale, and there was a look of fear in his eyes, of awareness of evil, that I found, God forgive me, strangely gratifying. "This is a kind of general intensive, I believe. Making this read, loosely rendered, hunger…itself. How odd."

"Yuggog," Dexter said softly, a thin strand of spittle joining his lips.

"Here," I said cruelly, tossing the heavy thing toward him. Let him go into the black mill now, I thought, after he's seen *this*. Dexter batted at the thing, knocking it to the ground. There was a sharp, tearing sound

like matchwood splitting. For an instant Dexter looked utterly, cosmi-
cally startled. Then he, and the idol of Yuggog, disappeared. There
was a loud thud, and a clatter, and I heard him groan. I picked up
the splintered halves of the carved wooden trapdoor Dexter had fallen
through and gazed down into a fairly deep, smooth-sided hole. He lay
crumpled at the bottom, about eight feet beneath me, in the light of his
overturned lantern.

"My God! I'm sorry! Are you all right?"

"I think I sprained my ankle," he said. He sat up and raised his lantern. His eyes got very wide. "Professor, you have to see this."

I lowered myself carefully into the hole and stared with Dexter into a
great round tunnel, taller than either of us, paved with crazed human
bones, stretching far beyond the pale of our lanterns.

"A tunnel," he said. "I wonder where it goes."

"I can only guess," I said. "And that's never good enough for me."

"Professor! You aren't——"

But I had already started into the tunnel, a decision that I attributed
not to courage, of course, but to my far greater vice. I did not see that
as I took those first steps into the tunnel I was in fact being bitten off,
chewed and swallowed, as it were, by the very mouth of the Plunkettsburg evil. I took small, queasy steps along the horrible floor, avoiding
insofar as I could stepping on the outraged miens of human skulls,
searching the smoothed, plastered walls of the tunnel for ideograms or
other hints of the builders of this amazing structure. The tunnel, or at
least this version of it, was well built, buttressed regularly by sturdy iron
piers and lintels, and of chillingly recent vintage. Only great wealth, I
thought, could have managed such a feat of engineering. A few minutes
later I heard a tread behind me and saw the faint glow of a lantern.
Dexter joined me, favoring his right ankle, his lantern swinging as he
walked.

"We're headed northwest," I said. "We must be under the river by
now."

"Under the river?" he said. "Could Indians have built a tunnel like
this?"

"No, Dexter, they could not."

He didn't say anything for a moment as he took this information in.

"Professor, we're headed for the mill, aren't we?"

"I'm afraid we must be," I said.

We walked for three quarters of an hour, until the sound of pounding machinery became audible, grew gradually unbearable and finally
exploded directly over our heads. The tunnel had run out. I looked up

at the trapdoor above us. Then I heard a muffled scream. To this day I don't know if the screamer was one of the men up on the floor of the factory, or Dexter Eibonas, a massive hand clapped brutally over his mouth, because the next instant, at the back of my head, a supernova bloomed and flared brightly.

● ● ●

I wake in an immense room, to the idiot pounding of a machine. The walls are sheets of fire flowing upward like inverted cataracts; the ceiling is lost in shadow from which, when the flames flare brightly, there emerges the vague impression of a steely web of girders among which dark things ceaselessly creep. Thick coils of rope bind my arms to my sides, and my legs are lashed at the ankles to those of the plain pine chair in which I have been propped.

It is one of two dozen chairs in a row that is one of a hundred, in a room filled with men, the slumped, crew-cut, big-shouldered ordinary men of Plunkettsburg and its neighboring towns. We are all waiting, and watching, as the women of Plunkettsburg, the servants of Yuggog, pass noiselessly among us in their soft, horrible cloaks stitched from the hides of dead men, tapping on the shoulder of now one fellow, now another. None of my neighbors, however, appears to have required the use of strong rope to conjoin him to his fate. Without a word the designated men, their blood thick with the dark earthen brew of the Ring witches, rise and follow the skins of miscreant fathers and grandfathers down to the ceremonial altar at the heart of the mill, where the priestesses of Yuggog throw oracular bones and, given the result, take hold of the man's ear, his foot, his fingers. A yellow snake, its venom presumably anesthetic, is applied to the fated extremity. Then the long knife is brought to bear, and the vast, immemorial hunger of the god of the Miskahannocks is assuaged for another brief instant. In the past three hours on this Walpurgis Night, nine men have been so treated; tomorrow, people in this bewitched town, that in a reasonable age, has learned to eat its men a little at a time, will speak, I am sure, of a series of horrible accidents at the mill. The women came to take away Dexter Eibonas an hour ago. I looked away as he went under the knife, but I believe he lost the better part of his left arm to the god. I can only assume that very soon now I will feel the tap on my left shoulder of the fingers of the town librarian, the grocer's wife, of Mrs. Eibonas herself. I am guiltier by far of trespass than Ed Eibonas and do not suppose I will survive the procedure.

Strange how calm I feel in the face of all this; perhaps there remain traces of the beer in my veins, or perhaps in this hellish place there are other enchantments at work. In any case, I will at least have the satisfaction of seeing my theory confirmed, or partly confirmed, before I die, and the concomitant satisfaction, so integral to my profession, of seeing my teacher's theory cast in the dustbin. For, as I held, the Miskahannocks hungered; and hunger, black, primordial, unstaunchable hunger itself, was their god. It was indeed the misguided scrambling and digging of my teacher and his colleagues, I imagine, that awakened great Yuggog from its 4,000-year slumber. As for the black mill that fascinated me for so many months, it is a sham. The single great machine to my left takes in no raw materials and emits no ingots or sheets. It is simply an immense piston, endlessly screaming and pounding, like the skin of an immense drum, the ground that since the days of the Miskahannocks has been the sacred precinct of the god. The flames that flash through the windows and the smoke that proceeds from the chimneys are bits of trickery, mechanical contrivances devised, I suppose, by Philippa Howard Murrough herself, in the days when the revived spirit of Yuggog first whispered to her of its awful, eternal appetite for the flesh of men. The sole industry of Plunkettsburg is carnage, scarred and mangled bodies the only product.

One thought disturbs the perfect, poison calm with which I am suffused—the trucks that grind their way in and out of the valley, the freight trains that come clanging in the night. What cargo, I wonder, is unloaded every morning at the docks of the Plunkettsburg Mill? What burden do those trains bear away?

PLAYBOY'S PARTY JOKES

PLAYBOY CLASSIC: Two nuns were rehabbing a room in the convent. They didn't want to get paint on their habits, so they locked the door, took off their clothes and started painting. There was a knock on the door and a man's voice said, "Blind Man."

The two nuns conferred and decided that, since a blind man couldn't see, there was no need to get dressed before letting him inside. They opened the door. The man said, "Nice tits. Now where do you want me to hang these blinds?"

The expectant mother was in her seventh month when she decided to break the news to her small son.

"Darling," she said, "If you could have your choice, which would you like to have—a little brother or a little sister?"

"Well," said the child, "if it's not too much to ask, I would really prefer a pony."

An old retired sailor put on his uniform and went down to the waterfront once more for old times' sake. He found a prostitute and went up to her room with her, draping his sailor suit across the bed. He was going at it as best he could for a guy his age and asked, "How am I doing?"

The prostitute said, "Well, sailor, you're doing about three knots."

"How's that?" he asked.

She said, "You're not hard, you're not in, and you're not getting your money back."

The lanky Texas ranch hand was still a virgin at 21, so, on his first trip to the big city, he decided to visit a brothel and find out what he'd been missing. Upon securing the address of a rather exclusive establishment, he soon found himself lying in a bed with an attractive partner. Sensing the lad was somewhat inexperienced, the professional gently took his hand and placed it on the source of her income. "Is this what you're looking for?" she whispered seductively.

"Well, I don't rightly know, ma'am," the cowboy murmured shyly. "I'm a stranger to these parts."

During a job interview the employer said to the applicant, "For a man with no experience, you are certainly asking for a high salary."

The man said, "Well, work is much harder when you don't know what you are doing."

What do you get when you breed a donkey with an onion?

Most of the time just an onion with long ears, but now and then, a piece of ass that will make your eyes water.

Two secretaries were discussing their boss. One said, "He dresses so well."

The other replied, "And quickly, too."

A man walked into church on crutches. He stopped in front of the holy water, splashed some of it on his legs and then tossed aside his crutches. An altar boy witnessed the event and ran to tell the priest what he'd seen. The priest said, "Son, you've just witnessed a miracle. Tell me, where is this man?"

The altar boy replied, "Lying on the floor next to the holy water."

How to Tell if You're a Grown-up

humor by DAVE BARRY

I was born in 1947. I have a wife, a child, a mortgage, two dogs and gum disease. People who are years younger than I am routinely get elected lieutenant governor. So you would probably describe me as a grown-up. Which just goes to show how much you know.

Several years back, I began to suspect that, despite my age, I wasn't a grown-up at all, and neither was my wife. What tipped me off was furniture. I noticed that over the years, all our friends had gradually, somehow, acquired furniture that not only went together in terms of color but also looked as though nobody had ever spilled margaritas mixed with bean dip on it and then allowed it to harden for several days on account of being too hungover to attempt cleaning procedures. I wondered, How did our friends manage this? *Our* furniture looks as though a random collection of large, unattractive animals wandered into our living room and died. It always will.

I know this because recently, I came into possession of some unexpected money, and I decided, by God, that I was going to buy a new sofa. I was very determined about this. I took some measurements. I even started looking at sofas in furniture stores. So you can imagine my surprise when what I in fact brought home was a Gibson Les Paul electric guitar and an amplifier loud enough to bring down enemy aircraft. This was when I realized that, in terms of becoming a grown-up, I was heading in the wrong direction.

This is also true of people even older than I am. Ed, for example. Ed is, technically, a 48-year-old automobile mechanic. He has everything a mechanic should have: a building surrounded by broken cars, a uniform covered with stains containing enough petrochemicals to meet the energy needs of Utah for a year, a sign stating that if you try to pay with a personal check, he will kill you with a wrench, etc. But what Ed actually does with his time, as opposed to working on cars, is set off fireworks. This is the truth. You go into his shop and all you can see is this dense cloud of smoke, and suddenly, a rocket will go whizzing past your ear, or maybe a little fireworks tank will come scuttling toward your feet, sparking and shooting. In the background, through the smoke, you can hear Ed cackling. You are thinking, But surely, he doesn't set off fireworks *all* the time. True. He spends a lot of time ordering them over the phone. Lately, he has even started *making* them. It has become difficult to get him to even talk about, say, your brakes. So he is not the ideal mechanic if your criterion is whether your car actually gets fixed. But that's a very grown-up criterion. I think Ed's a great mechanic.

Perhaps you're wondering where you stand in regard to growing up. Perhaps you have seen subtle signs of maturity in yourself, such as you no longer own a working Pez dispenser, and you wonder, Does this mean I'm a grown-up now? Well, I've been doing a lot of serious thinking about this issue (not really, of course; I've been playing Nintendo), and I've come up with some ways to decide where you stand. One of the most important, of course, is

WHAT YOU DO WHEN "TWIST AND SHOUT,"
BY THE ISLEY BROTHERS, COMES ON THE CAR RADIO

If you're not a grown-up yet, you turn the radio all the way up and sing and dance in your seat and gradually increase your speed so that when they reach the part that goes, "Ah, ah, *ah*, *ah*, ahhhhhhhhhhhhhhhh. Well, shake it up, *baby*, now..." you're going—even if you're in a driveway—a minimum of 60 miles per hour faster than the highest speed you ever attained in driver-education class.

If you're a grown-up, you never hear "Twist and Shout," because you're tuned to one of those easy-listening stations that are always playing "Tie a Yellow Ribbon Round the Old Oak Tree," by the Dental Office Singers. Or, worse, you're listening to talk radio and finding out what average Americans think about issues (they think, Am I on? I *am*?! Let me go turn my radio down!). Or, worst of all, if you have reached a level of maturity verging on brain death, you're listening to somebody talk about what happened on the stock market and whether trading was active.

Which leads us to another important area:

HOW YOU DEAL WITH FINANCIAL MATTERS

Grown-ups know where all their insurance policies are, what their cash values are and exactly what they've insured. Nongrown-ups have a cardboard box somewhere containing various formal-looking documents that could be insurance policies but also could have something to do with bowling. There is no way to tell except to look at them, which nongrown-ups do not do.

Grown-ups reconcile their checking accounts and maintain minimum balances to avoid service charges. Nongrown-ups like automatic-banking tellers, because they can use them to find out if they have any money.

Grown-ups have Individual Retirement Accounts and long-term plans for financial security. The nongrown-up's retirement strategy is based on the assumption that he will die at the age of 55 in a motorboat accident.

Speaking of money, we need to discuss

BEHAVIOR IN THE WORKPLACE

Grown-ups have mapped out career paths for themselves and know who is on the fast track and who is not. Nongrown-ups maintain elaborate charts showing who is leading in the ongoing lunchtime Frisbee tournament.

Grown-ups have certificates on their office walls stating that they have successfully completed training programs in:

Administrative Motivation for Managers,

Managing and Administrating Motivators,

Motivating Administratively in Regard to Management,

Admonishing and Masturbating Administrators.

And so on. Grown-ups are always writing memoranda about what they have received and what they are enclosing, as in: "I have received your memorandum of the 14th and am enclosing a copy of my memorandum of the...." Nongrown-ups, as a precautionary measure, throw all incoming correspondence away unopened unless it looks like it might be a check or it comes from an active participant in the ongoing lunchtime Frisbee tournament. Grown-ups refer to the vice president for marketing as "Mr. Bivensworth." Nongrown-ups refer to him as "the asshole."

Which brings us to

SOCIAL BEHAVIOR

When grown-ups meet you at semiformal parties, they look you square in the eye and shake your hand firmly and remember your name. Nongrown-ups don't meet you at all, because they're in the host's bedroom watching the Celtics–76ers game and spilling beer on the bedspread in response to important dunks.

HOW TO TELL IF YOU'RE A GROWN-UP

Speaking of alcohol consumption, grown-ups know their limits. Nongrown-ups know where there's a liquor store open.

Which often leads to

SEX

Grown-ups view it as part of a deeper relationship that involves commitment, concern, honesty and sharing. Nongrown-ups view it exactly the same way until maybe ten seconds after it's over, at which time they start to wonder if the Celtics–76ers game is still on.

SOME EXAMPLES OF FAMOUS GROWN-UPS AND NONGROWN-UPS

GROWN-UPS

The Supreme Court
Mrs. Dan Quayle
Doonesbury
England

NONGROWN-UPS

The House of Representatives
Mr. Dan Quayle
Calvin and Hobbes
Italy

Of course, this is meant to give you only general, cursory guidelines for deciding whether you're a grown-up. To really *know* where you stand, you have to conduct a thorough self-examination of your values, your philosophy of life—your conceptualization of what the world is, where it's going and what it all means. My guess is, you'd rather shoot some baskets.

"For my talent sequence, I will require a volunteer from the audience."

Fighting Words

commentary by DAVID MAMET

I am a member of both the American Civil Liberties Union and the National Rifle Association.

Privileged to sit in these two mutually abhorrent camps, I have been struck by the similarity of their fundamentalist stance on two disparate issues: the First (ACLU) and Second (NRA) amendments to the Constitution.

The First Amendment states that there shall be no law limiting freedom of speech (the only exception being the advocacy of violent overthrow of the Government).

The ACLU and enlightened liberal thought have long held that the First Amendment could not be plainer and is open to no interpretation; that interpretation or emendation in the least degree must inevitably bring about destruction of the amendment's protective meaning.

The members of the ACLU do not, in the main, I am sure, derive pleasure from lurid pornography, but they are sufficiently concerned about the tenuousness of freedom of speech that they are prepared to submit to the dissemination of pornography rather than open the First Amendment to that interpretation they feel will lead to its emasculation.

The leadership of the ACLU is sufficiently devoted to the purity of the notion of freedom of speech that it came to the defense of American Nazis, a group whose very existence they must have found loathsome, when the Nazis were debarred from marching in Skokie, Illinois, a predominantly Jewish community and home to many survivors of the Nazi death camps. Many viewers on the right (as well as some on the left) must have looked on in wonder at this arguably Pyrrhic display. As must viewers of the left look on when the NRA opposes limitation of firearms whose only possible employment is in mayhem.

Well, the left says, yes, keep your guns for home defense and for sporting purposes, but why must you have your semiautomatic assault rifles? What possible purpose can they serve? To which an enlightened member of the NRA might answer in a twofold way: (1) A semiautomatic assault rifle is, the inflammatory modifiers removed, simply a *rifle*. The semiautomatic of the name refers to the action used to make the piece ready to fire again, semiautomatic being one of many possible actions, among them pump, lever and bolt. The "assault" of the name means that the rifle *is made to resemble,* and may even be made *by the manufacturers of* assault rifles, which are the modern evolution of the machine gun and are *fully* automatic; i.e., they fire more than one round with each pull of the trigger. The members of the NRA might be asked why they would think it necessary either to possess or to espouse the possession of such articles designed to resemble weapons of war, to which the response might be (and this is the second portion of the answer): (2) "None of your business—the Second Amendment to the Constitution states that the right of the people to keep and bear arms shall not be infringed. This statement is not open to interpretation."

"Yes, but," the interlocutor might state, "don't you see that your mindless pursuit of this idea leads to murder?"

To which the response might be, "No, I do *not* see that, any more than you see that pornography leads to rape; but I *do* see that *any* attempt to interpret the Second Amendment must inevitably lead to destruction of this freedom to bear arms, and I feel that this freedom is sufficiently important that I am willing to tolerate abuses in the name of its preservation."

Well, then. We are not too far removed from the viciousness that follows curtailing freedom of the press; e.g., the Red scare of the Fifties and its attempts at rebirth. Neither are we too far removed from the terror that can visit itself on a disarmed populace: the Czechs of Prague Spring, the Jews of Europe under the Third Reich.

Is this, then, a possible point of similarity between these organizations: the dedication to a nonreducible, noninterpretative reading of an aspect of American law?

Yes. And, further, both defend their particular amendment and hold to it as the epitome of the definition of a free individual. (1) A free individual is one possessed of the unalterable right to assert or protect his or her individuality (which is to say, his or her integrity) by means of free speech. (2) A free individual is one who is possessed of the unassailable right to protect and support his or her individuality (integrity) by force of arms.

A good case could be made (historically) for either or both of these assertions, and, in fact, in a more reflective, less troubled time, we might simply refer to the Constitution's first two amendments and say: Yes, what a good idea.

And we would see that unbridled freedom of expression *is*, in fact, a good idea when *your* authors are barred, when the writers expressing *your* views are imprisoned; and that the right to keep and bear arms is a rather good idea when the police/army is imprisoning/torturing/persecuting *your* people, that it can and *does happen here* (whatever "it" is, and wherever "here" is). It can and does and *will most probably* happen here, and that is what the ACLU and the NRA are concerned about. And they are sufficiently concerned that they are ready to abide abuses and censure and, indeed, the ridicule of their opponents.

The debate itself is good, and the purpose of law is to allow people of differing and heated feelings to settle their disputes fairly and amicably—if not always without compromise.

The retreat to fundamentalist positions is, of course, natural in times of great social upheaval and uncertainty—unsure of our future, of our place, of the integrity of the institutions we have created to protect us, we retrench behind that which we feel to be the most powerful and protective of our prerogatives: *We lighten our pack down to that which we cannot do without—free speech/the right to keep and bear arms.*

Now, what about abortion?

Like most fundamentalist arguments, it is symbolic. (This is, perhaps, the nature of most arguments of any persuasion: As in the more formal legal proceeding, each side elects what it feels is a representative issue or assertion, feeling, "If I can sustain this [finally arbitrary] position, I will be content that I have vanquished my opponent and am entitled to the prize.")

Can one say that abortion, the most heated of debates, is, in fact, an arbitrary and jurisprudential fiction, a mutually chosen battleground for the trial by ordeal of two opposing cultures?

The right says that life begins with fertilization, and it fights under the banner of Right to Life. Is this a banner of convenience? I would ask this question: *Is* the leadership of the Right to Life movement speaking for itself and on behalf of its constituents, embracing, in effect, the Eastern doctrine of ahimsa; i.e., absolute nonviolence toward all living things? Is this movement equally prepared to oppose capital punishment *absolutely as vehemently* as it opposes abortion on demand? Is it equally prepared to espouse complete submissive pacifism and unilateral disarmament? If not, then the argument of the sanctity of life's beginning at the moment of conception falters, and the movement limits

its protection to "that life which we, the movement, choose to specify."

The Right to Life movement, so-called, in the manner of the Catholic Church of the Inquisition, relaxes its protection of the sacred individual at birth; and, arguably, the movement masses *not* behind the right of the embryo to be born but behind the right of the movement to compel an unwilling pregnant mother to have a baby. And Right to Life is a flag of convenience.

What of the other side? Well, I find myself *with* the other side on this issue. I have been a young man myself, and have been with young women, and I am the father of two daughters, and political leanings to me are not the point. In this issue, the point, to me, is intellectual honesty, and, in my soul, I cannot say that I can support the notion that my daughters should be compelled by law to give birth to unwanted children. I have seen that abortion can be, in many ways and in many degrees, traumatic, and as to whether or not it is finally "wrong," it depends on the standards that you apply and the faith that you have; but, if it were my daughters, I would and will support their decision not to bear unwanted children, and I would not suffer them to be treated like outlaws for so deciding, and I would not vote to force them to flee the state or the country for adequate medical care should they so decide. That is what I find in my heart, and that is how I have to vote, and it's no more complex than that.

Are there people who feel differently? Yes. Am I appalled by the violence of some of those in the opposition to this view? Yes. I am. The bombing of abortion clinics, in my view, is despicable in the extreme: It is, I feel, shameful behavior to prosecute a dispute through violence, and it is behavior that is particularly reprehensible in a group that calls itself Right to Life. It is also behavior that I endorsed when, in the Sixties, it was practiced by and for the supposed furtherance of the views of the antiwar movement—itself fighting, one might say, under the banner of Right to Life.

And so what is the issue that moves one to traduce the very tenets one is supposedly trying to defend? What is the issue behind the vehemence of abortion debates?

The issue of this small war for which Choice and Life are the names of the flags is this: *We are the good people. There are only so many good people in the world, and they are found on our side. Lacking the convenience of racial or geographic distinctions to separate the good from the bad people, we will employ the irrefutable litmus test of an issue: "How do you stand on abortion?"*

(Now, do I feel that the above is, in this instance, truer of the right than of the left? Yes, I do; I'm sorry, but I do, as, being human, I do tend to ascribe just a *tad* more humanity to the people with whom I agree. [See above.] I also think that in the Sixties, the above was truer of the left.)

Why can there be only a limited number of good people?

Because we are frightened. Abortion on demand and criminalization of abortion, NRA and ACLU see real visions of social anarchy, and that is why they each hold to their weapons. The right and the left see anarchy around the corner, too; and the decision of the Supreme Court is both craven and effective: By weakening but not destroying the freedoms of *Roe v. Wade*, it effectively recognizes that prerogative, but not abortion, is the issue, and says to both sides: *You* fight it out; you people on the left know that the rich and the mobile and the aware will always be able to have abortions, and that with the ever-growing feminist consciousness in this country (think back to 1973), fewer and fewer women will feel constrained to abide by local laws that they feel intolerable and which they can evade through travel; you people on the right know that human nature is not going to change, that people will fornicate and that women will have unwanted pregnancies and that they will terminate them *as they see fit* (as they always have) but that, at least, government endorsement of practices you find morally abhorrent has been somewhat curtailed. The Court, in effect, ruled: "Take your fight out into the alley."

The end of all the show will be decided by time. The liberal presidents got to pack the Court with justices who would unalterably ruin the fabric of American life for quite a number of years; we are now in the era of the prerogative of the conservative presidents to pack the Court with justices who will unalterably ruin the fabric of American life.

Am I being too evenhanded? Possibly. Yes, it is not *my* ox being gored at this precise moment. And no one has yet tried to throw me in jail for the things I have written, or tried to kill me because of my race— though instances of each are happening to others every day, and have happened to others of my profession and race within my lifetime.

How will the abortion debate be settled? It will not be settled. It will pass. It is the Dreyfus affair of this century: a theater of the confusion of the times.

My War with the Machines

humor by WOODY ALLEN

Years ago I went to Hollywood looking for a job. Actually, I had seen an ad in *The New York Times* that said, "Boy wanted, part time, to direct *Cleopatra*." So I went out to the Coast and while I was there, I went to this big party. I took a producer's very unattractive daughter, but I was social climbing. She was a really bad-looking girl. Facially, she resembled Louis Armstrong's voice. And while I was at the party, I met a big Hollywood producer who spoke to me about a job. At that time, they wanted to make an elaborate Cinemascope musical comedy based on the Dewey decimal system, and they wanted me to punch it up. I had worked as a writer in New York. I had written a TV show called *Surprise Divorce*. We used to take a happily married couple out of the audience every week and divorce them on television. Anyhow, I got the job.

So I go out to the producer's office in Burbank, and I walk into his building, and I get into the elevator, and there's nobody in the elevator. No people. No buttons on the wall. No elevator operator. Nothing. And I hear a voice say, "Kindly call out your floors, please." And I look around, and there's nothing. And I hear it again. "Kindly call out your floors, please." Now, I'm a great panicker. In the event of any type of emergency, I lose control of the sphincter muscle. Anyway, I hear this voice, and I look on the wall and it's printed: "This elevator runs on a sonic principle. Please state your floor and the elevator will take you there."

So I said, "Three, please."

And the doors close. And the elevator starts going up to three. And on the way up, I felt very self-conscious, because I speak with a slight New York accent, and the elevator spoke quite well. And I get off, and as I'm walking down the hall, I thought I heard the elevator make a remark.

177

MY WAR WITH THE MACHINES

So I turn quickly, but the doors are shut and it's gone down. I didn't want to get involved with an elevator anyway—not in Hollywood.

But here's the paranoid part of the story. I have never had good relations with mechanical objects. Anything I can't reason with or kiss or fondle, I get into trouble with. I have a clock that runs counterclockwise, and my toaster shakes my toast from side to side and burns it, and I hate my shower. My shower hated me first, but then it got to be a thing of counterhostility. If I'm taking a shower and someone in America uses their water, that's it for me! I leap from the tub with a red streak down my back. I paid $150 for a tape recorder, and as I talk into it, it goes, "I know, I know!"

I have a suntan lamp. As I sit under it, it rains on me.

All right, one night some years ago, I was home alone. I called a meeting of my possessions. I got everything I owned. My toaster, my clock, my blender, into the living room. They had never been in the living room before. I spoke to them. I spoke to each appliance. I said, "I know what's going on, and cut it out!" I was brilliant. You would've loved me. I opened with a joke, and then I moved on and made each point.

I was very firm. Then I put them back where they belonged. And I felt good. Strong. Two days later, I'm watching my portable television set—Dr. Joyce Brothers—when suddenly the picture begins to jump up and down. All right, I always talk before I hit. I went up to the set and I said, "I thought we had discussed this." But the set kept going up and down, up and down, so I hit it! I felt good hitting it! And I beat the hell out of it! I kicked in the screen. I ripped off the knobs. I tore off the antenna. (That appeared in a dream three nights later.) And I felt fabulous. Very Hemingway. I destroyed the machine. Man triumphs.

Two days later, I go to my dentist. I had gone to my dentist, but I had a very deep cavity and he had sent me to a chiropodist, and I'm in a building in midtown Manhattan, and they have those sonic elevators. So I get in, and I hear a voice say, "Kindly call out your floors, please." And now I'm hip because I was to the Coast, and I say, "Sixteen, please." On the way up, it says to me, "Are you the guy that hit the television set!?"

Then it took me up and down fast between floors and it threw me out in the basement and it yelled out something that was anti-Semitic.

And the upshot of the whole story is, that day I call my parents, and my mother tells me my father was fired. My father, who worked 12 years for the same firm, was fired. He was replaced with a tiny gadget that does everything my father does only much better. The depressing thing is, my mother ran out and bought one.

"Oh, if you'd only listened to your old mother!
How I begged you...reasoned with you...pleaded with you—
'Have the getaway car overhauled!'—But no...."

Furry's Blues

memoir by STANLEY BOOTH

When we came into the alley, the children stopped playing. They stood poised, watching us. There were two-story brick buildings on both sides, with wooden stairways that shut out all but a thin blue strip of sky. Filthy rags and broken bottles lay on the concrete pavement. There were women sitting on the doorsteps, some of them together, talking, but most of them alone, sitting still, ignoring the heat and the buzzing flies.

"How are you?" Charley Brown spoke to one of them.

"I ain't doin' no good," she said. She did not look up. The children's gaze followed us as we walked on. The women talking would stop as we came near and then, as we went past, would start again.

Close by, a fat woman was holding a small brown-and-white dog to her bosom. "What you got there?" Charley asked her.

"Little spitz," she said. "Look how dirty he is. He pretty when he clean."

"Nice dog," he said. "Is Furry home?"

"Dey up deah. Dey ain't been long gone up."

We climbed the back stairs of the building on our left and went down a bare, dusty hall to a door with a metal number three over the cloth-patched screen. Charley started to knock, and then we heard the music and he waited. "'Got a new way of spellin','" a quiet, musing voice sang, "'Memphis, Tennessee.'" A run of guitar chords followed, skeptical, brief; "'Double M, double E, great God, A-Y-Z.'" Then two closing chords, like a low shout of laughter, and Charley knocked.

The door swung open. There, sitting next to a double bed, holding a guitar, was Furry Lewis. During the heyday of Beale Street, when the great Negro blues artists played and sang in the crowded, evil blocks between Fourth and Main, Furry, a protégé of W.C. Handy, was one of the most highly respected musicians. He was also one of the most popular, not only in the saloons and gambling dives of Memphis but in the medicine shows and on the riverboats all along the Mississippi. In Chicago, at the old Vocalion studios on Wabash Avenue, he made the first of many recordings he was to make, both for Vocalion and for RCA Victor's Bluebird label. But Beale Street's great era ended at the close of the 1920s; since then, Furry has had only one album of his own—a 1959 Folkways LP.

Nor, since the Depression, has he performed regularly, even in his hometown. He makes his living as a street sweeper. When he does play, it is usually at the Bitter Lemon, a coffeehouse that caters mainly to the affluent East Memphis teenaged set, but whose manager, Charley Brown, is a blues enthusiast and occasionally hires Furry between rock-and-roll groups.

Charley, a tall, blond young man, bent to shake hands with Furry. Furry did not stand. One leg of his green pajamas hung limp, empty below the knee.

The boy wearing gold-rimmed spectacles who had got up from a chair to let us in said, "I'm Jerry Finberg. Furry's been giving me a little guitar lesson." We shook his hand, then Charley introduced me to Furry and we all sat down. The room held a sizable amount of old, worn furniture: the bed, a studio couch, three stuffed chairs, a chiffo-robe and a dresser. Beside the bed, there was a table made from a small wooden crate.

"It's good to see you, Furry," Charley said.

"You, too," said Furry. "You hadn't been here in so long, I thought you had just about throwed me down."

Charley said that he could never do that and asked Furry if he would come out to the coffeehouse for a couple of nights in the coming week. Furry picked up a pair of glasses from the bedside table, put them on, then took them off again. He would like to, he said, but his guitar was at Nathan's. "This here one belongs to this boy, Jerry." He put the glasses back on the table. It held aspirin, cigarette papers and a Mason jar full of tobacco. Charley said not to worry, he'd get the guitar.

"Will you, sure enough?" Furry asked, looking at Charley with serious, businesslike gray eyes.

"I'll get it tomorrow. What's the ticket on it?"

"Sixteen dollars."

"I'll get it tomorrow."

"All right," Furry said, "and I'll come play for you." He reached out and shook hands solemnly with Charley.

"Could you play something now, or don't you feel like it?" Charley asked.

FURRY'S BLUES

Furry smiled. "I may be weak, but I'm willing," he said. He took a small metal cylinder from his pajama pocket and picked up the guitar. "I believe I'll take you to Brownsville." He slipped the cylinder over the little finger of his left hand and started to play, his short leg crossed over the longer one, his bare narrow foot patting softly the plain brown boards as he sang. "'Well, I'm goin' to Brownsville, I'm goin' take that right-hand road'"; the cylinder slid, whining, over the treble strings.

"I was in Brownsville, Tennessee," Furry said, "working on a doctor show, and I met a little girl I liked; but her parents wouldn't let me come around to see her, 'cause I was showfolks, and they was respectable. So I wrote this: 'And the woman I love's got great long curly hair.'" The guitar repeated the line, added a delicate, punctuating bass figure, and then, as if it were another voice, sang the next line with Furry, staying just behind or slightly ahead of the beat: "'But her mother and father do not allow me there.'"

As he played, I looked around the room. The brown-spotted wallpaper was covered with decorations: Over the bed were a few sprigs of artificial holly, an American flag, hanging with the stripes vertical and the stars at the bottom left, three brightly colored picture postcards and an ink sketch of Furry. On the wall behind the couch there was a child's crayon drawing in which Jesus, dressed in handsome red-and-blue robes, held out his arms to a enormous white rabbit. Furry's right hand swooped and glided over the guitar, striking notes and chords in what looked but did not sound like complete random. At times, he slapped the guitar box with two fingers or the heel of his hand as, in the same motion, he brushed the strings. "Call that 'spank the baby,'" he said. The guitar was both an echo of his voice and a source of complex and subtle accents. He sang, "'Don't you wish your woman was long and tall like mine?'" then repeated the line, leaving out, or letting the guitar speak, half the words. "'Well, she ain't good-lookin', but I 'clare, she takes her time.'" The bass figure followed, then one amused final chord. Furry laid the guitar down.

"You play beautiful guitar," Charley said.

"Yes, it is," Furry said, holding up the instrument. "Believe I'll be buried in this one."

"Was that Spanish tuning?" asked Jerry, who had been leaning forward, elbows on his knees, listening intently.

"They some beer in the icebox," Furry said.

Jerry sighed and stood up. "Come on," he said to me. "Help bring the glasses." We went into the kitchen. It was almost as large as the front room, with a stove, a refrigerator, a good-sized table and, in one

182

corner, another double bed. A cabinet held gallon jars of flour, sugar, lima beans and an assortment of canned goods: Pride of Illinois white sweet corn, School Day June peas. Showboat pork and beans, Lyke's beef tripe, Pride of Virginia herring, Bush's Best black-eyed peas and turnip greens.

Jerry took a quart of Pfeiffer's beer out of the refrigerator. I found four glasses on a newspaper-lined shelf, rinsed them at the square metal sink ("They clean," Furry called, "but no tellin' what's been runnin' over 'em") and we went back into the other room. We had just finished pouring when there was a knock at the door.

"That's my wife," Furry said, sliding the latch open. "Come in, Versie." She came in, a compact, handsome woman. I introduced myself and the others said hello. Versie, in a pleasantly hoarse voice, told us that only that morning, she had been asking Furry what he had done to make his boyfriends stay away so long.

"They all throwed me down," Furry said, then laughed and told Versie he was going out to play at the Bitter Lemon. She smiled and asked if she could get us anything to eat. We all said no, thank you, and she sat down.

"My wife loves to see after folks," Furry said. "Do anything in the world for people. Feed 'em, give 'em something to drink; if they get too drunk to go home, got a bed in there to put you to sleep on. And I'm the same way. But you know, there's one old boy, I see him every day at work, and every time I see him, he bum a cigarette from me. Now, it ain't much, but it come so *regular*. So the other day, I told him, 'Boy, ain't but one difference 'tween you and a blind man.' And he said, 'What's that?' And I told him, 'Blind man beg from everybody he hear, you beg from everybody you see.'"

"Well," Versie said, from her chair on the other side of the room, "it's a pleasure to do things for people who are so nice to us. We tried and tried to find out Furry's age, so he could get this Medicare, and Jerry went out to Furry's old school and made them look through the records and find out when he was born. He spent several days, just to help us."

"Found out I was born 1893," Furry said. "March the sixth, in Greenwood, Mississippi. But I moved to Memphis, with my mother and two sisters, when I was six. My mother and father were sharecroppers and they separated before I was born. I never saw my father, never even knew what he looked like." He took a drink of beer.

"Where did you live when you came here?" I asked.

"My mother had a sister lived on Brinkley Avenue," he said. "Call it

Decatur now. We stayed with her. They a housing project there now, but I could still show you the spot." He took another drink, looked at the glass, then emptied it. "I was raised right there and walked a few blocks to the Carnes Avenue School. Went to the fifth and that's as far as I got. Started going about, place to place, catching the freights. That's how I lost my leg. Goin' down a grade outside Du Quoin, Illinois, I caught my foot in a coupling. They took me to a hospital in Carbondale. I could look right out my window and see the ice-cream factory."

He took a cigarette from a pack of Pall Malls on the bedside table. "That was 1916," he said. "I had two or three hundred dollars in my pocket when that happened, too; I had just caught a freight 'cause I didn't feel like spending the money for a ticket." He struck a match, but the breeze from the window fan blew it out. Charley took the cigarette, lit it and handed it back. "Love you," Furry said. "Goin' put you in the Bible."

He stuck the cigarette in the corner of his mouth, picked up the guitar and played a succession of slow, blues-drenched chords that seemed to fill the room. "I'm doing all right," he said. "What you want to hear?"

"Do you remember *Stagolee*?" I asked.

"What song?"

"One you recorded a long time ago, called *Stagolee*."

"Long time ago—I wasn't born then, was I?" He quickly changed tunings and started to sing the song. He did one chorus, but it went off after the second, which began, "'When you lose your money, learn to lose.'"

"What was that last?" Charley asked.

Furry repeated the line. "That means, don't be no *hard* loser. That's what this song is about." He began again, but after a few bars, he lost the tune. He was tired.

Charley stood up. "We've got to go, Furry."

"No," Furry said. "You just got here."

"Got to go to work. I'll pick you up Tuesday night."

"I'm so glad you came by," Versie told Charley, in the hall. "Sometimes Furry thinks everybody has forgotten him."

It had rained while we were inside and the air in the alley smelled almost fresh. The women were gone now and only a few of the children were still out. It was nearly dark. We walked back to the car and drove down Beale Street, past the faded blocks of pawnshops, liquor stores and poolrooms. The lights were coming on for the evening.

● ● ●

The Beale Street that Furry Lewis knew as a boy had its beginnings when, after the Battle of Memphis in 1862, the Federal Army made its headquarters in the area. The Negro population of the city consisted mainly of former slaves, who felt they had good reason to fear the local citizenry and, therefore, stayed as close to Federal headquarters as possible. After the War, many Negroes came in from the country, trying to find their families. There were only about 4,000 Negroes in Memphis in 1860, but by 1870, there were 15,000. Beale Street drew them, it has been said, "like a lodestone."

The music the country Negroes brought, with its thumping rhythms, unorthodox harmonies and earthy lyrics, combined with the city musicians' more polished techniques and regular forms to produce, as all the world knows, the Beale Street blues. Furry cannot remember when he first heard the blues, nor is he certain when he started trying to play them.

"I was eight or nine, I believe," he said, "when I got the idea I wanted to have me a guitar." We were at the Bitter Lemon now, Furry, Versie, Charley and I, waiting for the crowd to arrive. The waitresses, pretty girls with long, straight hair, were lighting candles on the small round tables. We sat in the shadows, drinking bourbon brought from the liquor store on the corner, listening to Furry talk about the old days.

He was coatless, wearing a white shirt with a dark-blue tie, and he was smoking a wood-tipped cigar. "I taken a cigar box, cut a hole in the top and nailed a piece of two-by-four on there for a neck. Then I got some screen wire for the strings and I tacked them to the box and twisted them around some bent nails on the end of the two-by-four. I could turn the nails and tune the strings like that, you see. I fooled around with it, got so I could make notes, but just on one string. Couldn't make no chords. The first real guitar I had, Mr. Cham Fields, who owned a roadhouse, gambling house, and W.C. Handy gave it to me. They brought it out to my mother's and I was so proud to get it, I cried for a week. Them days, children wasn't like they are now." His cigar had gone out; he relit it from the candle on our table, puffing great gray clouds of smoke. "It was a Martin and I kept it twenty years."

"What happened to it?" Charley asked.

"It died."

Furry put the candle down and leaned back in his chair. "When I was eighteen, nineteen years old," he said, "I was good. And when I was twenty, I had my own band, and we could all play. Had a boy named Ham, played jug. Willie Polk played the fiddle and another boy, call him Shoefus, played the guitar, like I did. All of us North Memphis

185

boys. We'd meet at my house and walk down Brinkley to Poplar and go up Poplar to Dunlap or maybe all the way down to Main. People would stop us on the street and say, 'Do you know so-and-so?' And we'd play it and they'd give us a little something. Sometimes we'd pick up fifteen or twenty dollars before we got to Beale. Wouldn't take no streetcar. Long as you walked, you's making money; but if you took the streetcar, you didn't make nothing and you'd be out the nickel for the ride."

"That was Furry's wild days," Versie said. "Drinking, staying out all night. He'd still do that way, if I let him."

Furry smiled. "We used to leave maybe noon Saturday and not get back home till Monday night. All the places we played—Pee Wee's, Big Grundy's, Cham Fields's, B.B. Anderson's—when they opened up, they took the keys and tied them to a rabbit's neck, told him to run off to the woods, 'cause they never meant to close."

I asked Furry whether he had done much traveling.

"A right smart," he said. "But that was later on, when I was working with Gus Cannon, the banjo player, and Will Shade. Beale Street was commencing to change then. Had to go looking for work." He rolled his cigar's ash off against the side of an ashtray. "In the good times, though, you could find anything you could name on Beale. Gambling, girls; you could buy a pint of moonshine for a dime, store-bought whiskey for a quarter. We'd go from place to place, making music, and everywhere we'd go, they'd be glad to see us. We'd play awhile and then somebody would pass the hat. We didn't make too much, but we didn't need much back then. In them days, you could get two loaves of bread for a nickel. And some nights, when the people from down on the river came up, we'd make a batch of money. The roustabouts from the steamboats, the *Kate Adams*, the *Idlewild*, the *Viney Swing*—I've taken trips on all them boats, played up the river to St. Louis, down to New Orleans—white and colored, they'd all come to Beale. Got along fine, too, just like we doing now. 'Course, folks had they squabbles, like they will, you know. I saw two or three get killed."

There were enough squabbles to make Memphis the murder capital of the country. In the first decade of the century, 556 homicides occurred, most of them involving Negroes. Appeals for reform were taken seriously only by those who made them. When E.H. Crump ran for mayor on a reform ticket, W.C. Handy recorded the Beale Streeters' reaction: "We don't care what Mr. Crump don't allow, we goin' barrel-house anyhow."

But as the righteous Crump machine gained power, the street slowly began to change. Each year, the red-light district grew smaller; each year, there were fewer gambling houses, fewer saloons, fewer places for musicians to play.

Then came the Depression. Local newspapers carried accounts of starving Negroes swarming over garbage dumps, even eating the clay from the river bluffs. Many people left town, but Furry stayed. "Nothing else to do," he said. "The Depression wasn't just in Memphis, it was all over the country. A lot of my friends left, didn't know what they was goin' to. The boy we called Ham, from our band, he left, and nobody ever knew what became of him. I did have a little job with the city and I stuck with that. I had been working with them off and on when there wasn't anyplace to play. They didn't even have no trucks at that time. Just had mules to pull the garbage carts. Didn't have no incinerator; used to take the garbage down to the end of High Street, across the railroad tracks, and burn it."

Before Beale Street could recover from the Depression, World War Two brought hundreds of boys in uniform into Memphis; and, for their protection, Boss Crump closed the last of the saloons and whorehouses. It was the final blow.

Furry sat staring at the end of his cigar. "Beale Street really went down," he said after a moment. "You know, old folks say, it's a long lane don't have no end and a bad wind don't never change. But one day, back when Hoover was President, I was driving my cart down Beale Street and I seen a rat, sitting on top of a garbage can, eating a onion, crying."

● ● ●

Furry has been working for the city of Memphis sanitation department since 1923. Shortly after two o'clock each weekday morning, he gets out of bed, straps on his artificial leg, dresses and makes a fresh pot of coffee, which he drinks while reading the *Memphis Press-Scimitar*. The newspaper arrives in the afternoon, but Furry does not open it until morning. Versie is still asleep and the paper is company for him as he sits in the kitchen under the harsh light of the ceiling bulb, drinking the hot, sweet coffee. He does not eat breakfast; when the coffee is gone, he leaves for work.

The sky is black. The alley is quiet, the apartments dark. A morning-glory vine hanging from a guy wire stirs, like a heavy curtain, in the cool morning breeze. Cars in the cross alley are covered with a silver glaze of dew. A cat flashes between shadows.

Linden Avenue is bright and empty in the blue glare of the street lamps. Down the street, St. Patrick's looms, a sign, 100 YEARS WITH CHRIST, over its wide red doors. Furry, turning right, walks past the faded, green-glowing bay windows of an apartment house to the corner. A moving van rolls past. There is no other traffic. When the light changes, Furry crosses, heading down Hernando. The clock at Carodine's Fruit Stand and Auto Service reads 2:49.

The cafes, taverns, laundries, shoe-repair shops and liquor stores are all closed. The houses, under shading trees, seem drawn into themselves. At the Clayborn Temple African Methodist Episcopal Church, the stained-glass windows gleam, jewellike against the mass of blackened stone. A woman wearing a maid's uniform passes on the other side of the street. Furry says good morning and she says good morning, their voices patiently weary. Beside the Scola Brothers Grocery is a sycamore, its branches silhouetted against the white wall. Furry walks slowly, hunched forward, as if sleep were a weight on his shoulders. Handprinted posters at the Vance Avenue Market: CHICKEN BACKS, ½¢ LB.; HOG MAWS, 15¢; RUMPS 19¢.

Behind Bertha's Beauty Nook, under a large, pale-leafed elm, there are 12 garbage cans and two carts. Furry lifts one of the cans onto a cart, rolls the cart out into the street and, taking the wide broom from its slot, begins to sweep the gutter. A large woman with her head tied in a kerchief, wearing a purple wrapper and gold house slippers, passes by on the sidewalk. Furry tells her good morning and she nods hello.

When he has swept back to Vance, Furry leaves the trash in a pile at the corner and pushes the cart, with its empty can, to Beale Street. The sky is gray. The stiff brass figure of W.C. Handy stands, one foot slightly forward, the bell of his horn pointing down, under the manicured trees of his deserted park. The gutter is thick with debris: empty wine bottles, torn racing forms from the West Memphis dog track, flattened cigarette packs, scraps of paper and one small die, white with black spots, which Furry puts into his pocket. An old bus, on the back of which is written, in yellow paint, LET NOT YOUR HEART BE TROUBLED, rumbles past; it is full of cotton choppers: Their dark, solemn faces peer out the grimy windows. The bottles clink at the end of Furry's broom. In a room above the Club Handy, two men are standing at an open window, looking down at the street. One of them is smoking; the glowing end of his cigarette can be seen in the darkness. On the door to the club, there is a handbill: BLUES SPECTACULAR, CITY AUDITORIUM: JIMMY REED, JOHN LEE HOOKER, HOWLIN' WOLF.

Furry pushes the garbage onto a flat scoop at the front of the cart, then goes to the rear and pulls a jointed metal handle, causing the scoop to rise and dump its contents into the can. The scoop is heavy; when he lets it down, it sends a shock from his right arm through his body, raising his left leg, the artificial one, off the ground. Across the street, in a chinaberry tree, a gang of sparrows are making a racket. Furry sweeps past two night clubs and then a restaurant, where, through the front window, large brown rats can be seen scurrying across the kitchen floor. A red dog stands at the corner of Beale and Hernando, sniffing the air. A soldier runs past, heading toward Main. The street lamps go off.

When Furry has cleaned the rest of the block, the garbage can is full and he goes back to Bertha's for another. The other cart is gone and there is a black Buick parked at the curb. Furry wheels to the corner and picks up the mound of trash he left there. A city bus rolls past; the driver gives a greeting honk and Furry waves. He crosses the street and begins sweeping in front of the Sanitary Bedding Company. A woman's high-heeled shoe is lying on the sidewalk. Furry throws it into the can. "First one-legged woman I see, I'll give her that," he says and, for the first time that day, he smiles.

At Butler, the next cross street, there is a row of large, old-fashioned houses, set behind picket fences and broad, thickly leafed trees. The sky is pale-blue now, with pink-edged clouds, and old men and women have come out to sit on the porches. Some speak to Furry, some do not. Cars are becoming more frequent along the street. Furry readies out quickly with his broom to catch a windblown scrap of paper. When he gets to Calhoun, he swaps cans again and walks a block—past Tina's Beauty Shop, a tavern called the Section Playhouse and another named Soul Heaven—to Fourth Street. He places his cart at the corner and starts pushing the trash toward it.

From a second-story window of a rooming house covered with red brick-patterned tarpaper comes the sound of a blues harmonica. Two old men are sitting on the steps in front of the open door. Furry tells them good morning. "When you goin' make another record?" one of them asks.

"Record?" the other man, in a straw hat, says.

"That's right," says the first one. "He makes them big-time records. Used to."

Furry dumps a load into the cart, then leans against it, wiping his face and the back of his neck with a blue bandanna handkerchief.

Down the stairs and through the door (the old men on the steps leaning out of his way, for he does not slow down) comes the harmonica player. He stands in the middle of the sidewalk, eyes closed, head tilted to one side, the harmonica cupped in his hands. A man wearing dark glasses and carrying a white cane before him like a divining rod turns the corner, aims at the music, says cheerfully, "Get out the way! Get off the sidewalk!" and bumps into the harmonica player, who spins away, like a good quarterback, and goes on playing.

Furry puts the bandanna in his pocket and moves on, walking behind the cart. Past Mrs. Kelly's Homemade Hot Tamales stand, the air is filled with a strong odor. Over a shop door, a sign reads: FRESH FISH DAILY.

Now the sky is a hot, empty blue, and cars line the curb from Butler to Vance. Furry sweeps around them. Across the street, at the housing project, children are playing outside the great blocks of apartments. One little girl is lying face down on the grass, quite still. Furry watches her. She has not moved. Two dogs are barking nearby. One of them, a small black cocker spaniel, trots up to the little girl and sniffs at her head; she grabs its forelegs and together they roll over and over. Furry starts sweeping and does not stop or look up again until he has reached the corner. He piles the trash into the can and stands in the gutter, waiting for the light to change.

For the morning, his work is done. He rolls the cart down Fourth, across Pontotoc and Linden, to his own block, where he parks it at the curb, between two cars. Then he heads across the street toward Rothschild's grocery, to try to get some beer on credit.

● ● ●

While we were talking, people were coming in, and now the tables were nearly filled. Charley looked at his watch, then at Furry. "Feel like playing?" he asked.

Furry nodded abruptly, the way Indians do in movies. "I always feel like playing," he said. He drank the last of the bourbon in his glass. "Yes, sir. *Always* feel like that."

"I'll announce you," Charley said. He carried a chair onto the stage, sat down and repeated the lecture he uses whenever he hires an old-time musician. It begins, "Without the tradition of American Negro music, there would be no rock music." The lecture's purpose is to inspire the rock generation with love and respect for the blues. However, this audience, none of whom looks older than 20, seems more interested in each other than in anything else.

When the speech ended, with "I am proud to present..." Furry, carrying his battered Epiphone guitar, limped onto the stage. The applause was polite. Furry smiled and waved. "Ladies and gentlemen," he began, "I'm very pleased to be here tonight to play for you all. I've been around Memphis, playing and singing, for many years. My wife is with me tonight; we've been married many years. When we got married, I only had fifteen cents and she had a quarter." I looked at Charley. He avoided my eyes.

"And then one day," Furry went on, his tone altering slightly, "she upped and quit me, said I had married her for her money."

Furry laughed, Versie laughed, the crowd laughed, and Charley and I looked at each other and laughed and laughed, shaking our heads. "I love him, the old bastard," Charley said. "Sorry, Versie."

But Versie, watching Furry proudly, had not heard.

He had begun to play a slow, sad blues, one that none of us had ever heard, a song without a name: "'My mother's dead,'" he sang, the guitar softly following, "'my father just as well's to be. Ain't got nobody to say one kind word for me.'"

The room, which had been filled with noise, was now quiet. "'People holler mercy,'" Furry sang, "'don't know what mercy mean. People...'"—and the guitar finished the line. "'Well, if it mean any good, Lord, have mercy on me.'"

When, after nearly an hour, Furry left the stage, the applause was considerably more than polite. But I knew that it was only the third time Furry had heard public applause during the year and that in this year, as in most of the years of his life, his music would probably bring him less than $100. Soon, we would take him home and he would change clothes and go out to sweep the streets. I wondered, as Charley and Versie were congratulating him and pouring fresh drinks, how he had managed to last, to retain his skill.

Furry was sitting back in his chair, holding a drink in one hand and a new cigar in the other, smiling slightly, his eyes nearly closed. I asked him if he had ever been tempted to give up, to stop playing. "Give out but don't give up," he said. He tasted his drink and sat straighter in the chair. "No," he said, "all these years, I kept working for the city, thinking things might change, Beale Street might go back like it was. But it never did."

"But you went on playing."

"Oh, yes, I played at home. Sometimes, nothing to do, no place to play, I'd hock the guitar and get me something to drink. And then I'd wish I had it, so I could play, even just for myself. I never quit playing, but I didn't play out enough for people to know who I was. Sometimes I'd see a man, a beggar, you know, playing guitar on the sidewalk, and I'd drop something in his cup, and he wouldn't even know who I was. He'd think I was just a street sweeper."

SYMBOLIC SEX

a sprightly probing of the signs of our times
humor By DON ADDIS

FOR CRYIN' OUT LOUD, DOESN'T ANYBODY JUST **BALL** ANYMORE?!

HE'S OK, AS FAR AS HE GOES

GONNA PLAY HARD TO GET, EH?

I DON'T KNOW MUCH ABOUT ART, BUT I KNOW WHAT I LIKE

GUESS WHO!

OTHER THAN THAT, HOW DO YOU LIKE DOOR-TO-DOOR SALES WORK?

I KNOW YOU GUYS ARE DOING YOUR BEST, BUT **SOMEBODY** IS GETTING THROUGH TO THE HAREM

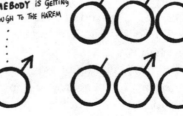

NOW THEN... YOUR PLACE OR MINE?

YOU MEN ARE ALL ALIKE!

PRETEND YOU DONT NOTICE HIM, SHIRLEY

I'VE JUST BEEN CHOSEN PLAYMATE OF THE MONTH!

GIRLS JUST CAN'T GET ENOUGH OF ME

I CAN'T STAND HER HOLIER-THAN-THOU ATTITUDE!

I GUESS IT'S YOUR AIR OF MYSTERY THAT FASCINATES ME

I FOUND HIM VERY DULL

A Sound of Thunder

fiction by RAY BRADBURY

T he sign on the wall seemed to quaver under a film of sliding warm
water. Eckels felt his eyelids blink over his stare, and the sign burned
in this momentary darkness:

TIME SAFARI, INC.

SAFARIS TO ANY YEAR IN THE PAST.

YOU NAME THE ANIMAL.

WE TAKE YOU THERE.

YOU SHOOT IT.

A warm phlegm gathered in Eckels' throat; he swallowed and pushed
it down. The muscles around his mouth formed a smile as he put
his hand slowly out upon the air, and in that hand waved a check for
$10,000 to the man behind the desk.

"Does this safari guarantee I come back alive?"

"We guarantee nothing," said the official, "except dinosaurs." He
turned. "This is Mr. Travis, your Safari Guide in the Past. He'll tell you
what and where to shoot. If he says no shooting, no shooting. If you
disobey instructions, there's a stiff penalty of another $10,000, plus pos-
sible government action, on your return."

Eckels glanced across the vast office at a mass and tangle, a snaking
and humming of wires and steel boxes, at an aurora that flickered now
orange, now silver, now blue. There was a sound like a gigantic bonfire
burning all of Time, all the years and all the parchment calendars, all
the hours piled high and set aflame.

A touch of the hand on this burning would, on the instant, beautifully
reverse itself. Eckels remembered the wording in the advertisements
to the letter. Out of chars and ashes, out of dust and coals, like golden
salamanders, the old years, the green years, might leap; roses sweeten
the air, white hair turn Irish-black, wrinkles vanish; all, everything fly
back to seed, flee death, rush down to their beginnings, suns rise in
western skies and set in glorious easts, moons eat themselves opposite

to the custom, all and everything cupping one in another like Chinese boxes, rabbits into hats, all and everything returning to the fresh death, the seed death, the green death, to the time before the beginning. A touch of a hand might do it, the merest touch of a hand.

"Hell and damn," Eckels breathed, the light of the Machine on his thin face. "A real Time Machine." He shook his head. "Makes you think. If the election had gone badly yesterday, I might be here now running away from the results. Thank God Keith won. He'll make a fine president of the United States."

"Yes," said the man behind the desk. "We're lucky. If Deutscher had gotten in, we'd have the worst kind of dictatorship. There's an anti-everything man for you, a militarist, anti-Christ, anti-human, anti-intellectual. People called us up, you know, joking but not joking. Said if Deutscher became president they wanted to go live in 1492. Of course it's not our business to conduct Escapes, but to form Safaris. Anyway, Keith's president now. All you got to worry about is———"

"Shooting my dinosaur," Eckels finished it for him.

"A *Tyrannosaurus rex*. The Thunder Lizard, the damnedest monster in history. Sign this release. Anything happens to you, we're not responsible. Those dinosaurs are hungry."

Eckels flushed angrily. "Trying to scare me!"

"Frankly, yes. We don't want anyone going who'll panic at the first shot. Six Safari leaders were killed last year, and a dozen hunters. We're here to give you the damnedest thrill a *real* hunter ever asked for. Traveling you back 60 million years to bag the biggest damned game in all Time. Your personal check's still there. Tear it up."

Mr. Eckels looked at the check for a long time. His fingers twitched.

"Good luck," said the man behind the desk. "Mr. Travis, now he's all yours."

They moved silently across the room, taking their guns with them, toward the Machine, toward the silver metal and the roaring light.

● ● ●

First a day and then a night and then a day and then a night, then it was day-night-day-night-day. A week, a month, a year, a decade! A.D. 2055. A.D. 2019. 1999! 1957! Gone! The Machine roared.

They put on their oxygen helmets and tested the intercoms.

Eckels swayed on the padded seat, his face pale, his jaw stiff. He felt the trembling in his arms and he looked down and found his hands tight on the new rifle. There were four other men in the Machine. Travis, the Safari Leader, his assistant, Lesperance, and two other hunters, Billings and Kramer. They sat looking at each other, and the years blazed around them.

"Can these guns get a dinosaur cold?" Eckels felt his mouth saying.

"If you hit them right," said Travis on the helmet radio. "Some dinosaurs have two brains, one in the head, another far down the spinal column. We stay away from those. That's stretching luck. Put your first two shots into the eyes, if you can, blind them, and go back into the brain."

The Machine howled. Time was a film run backward. Suns fled and 10 million moons fled after them. "Good God," said Eckels. "Every hunter that ever lived would envy us today. This makes Africa seem like Illinois."

The Machine slowed; its scream fell to a murmur. The Machine stopped.

The sun stopped in the sky.

The fog that had enveloped the Machine blew away and they were in an old time, a very old time indeed, three hunters and two Safari Heads with their blue metal guns across their knees.

"Christ isn't born yet," said Travis. "Moses has not gone to the mountain to talk with God. The Pyramids are still in the earth, waiting to be put up. *Remember* that. Alexander, Caesar, Napoleon, Hitler—none of them exists."

The men nodded.

"That"—Mr. Travis pointed—"is the jungle of 62,002,055 years before President Keith."

He indicated a metal path that struck off into green wilderness, over steaming swamp, among giant ferns and palms.

"And that," he said, "is the Path, laid by Time Safari for your use. It floats six inches above the earth. Doesn't touch so much as one grass blade, flower, or tree. It's an anti-gravity metal. Its purpose is to keep you from touching this world of the past in any way. Stay on the Path. Don't go off it. I repeat. *Don't go off.* For *any* reason! If you fall off, there's a penalty. And don't shoot any animal we don't okay."

"Why?" asked Eckels.

They sat in the ancient wilderness. Far birds' cries blew on a wind, and the smell of tar and an old salt sea, moist grasses and flowers the color of blood.

"We don't want to change the Future. We don't belong here in the Past. The government doesn't *like* us here. We have to pay big graft to keep our franchise. A Time Machine is damn finicky business. Not knowing it, we might kill an important animal, a small bird, a roach, a flower even, thus destroying an important link in a growing species."

"That's not clear," said Eckels.

"All right," Travis continued, "say we accidentally kill one mouse here. That means all the future families of this one particular mouse are destroyed, right?"

"Right."

"And all the families of the families of that one mouse! With a stamp of your foot, you annihilate first one, then a dozen, then a thousand, a million, a *billion* possible mice!"

"So they're dead," said Eckels. "So what?"

"So what?" Travis snorted quietly. "Well, what about the foxes that'll need those mice to survive? For want of ten mice, a fox dies. For want of ten foxes, a lion starves. For want of a lion, all manner of insects, vultures, infinite billions of life forms are thrown into chaos and destruction. Eventually it all boils down to this: 59 million years later, a caveman, one of a dozen in the *entire world*, goes hunting wild boar or saber-toothed tiger for food. But you, friend, have *stepped* on all the tigers in that region. By stepping on *one* single mouse. So the caveman starves. And the caveman, please note, is not just any expendable man, no! He is an *entire future nation*. From his loins would have sprung ten sons. From *their* loins 100 sons, and thus onward to a civilization. Destroy this one man, and you destroy a race, a people, an entire history of life. It is comparable to slaying some of Adam's grandchildren. The stomp of your foot, on one mouse, could start an earthquake, the effects of which could shake our earth and destinies down through Time to their very foundations. With the death of that one caveman, a billion others yet unborn are throttled in the womb. Perhaps Rome never rises on its seven hills. Perhaps Europe is forever a dark forest, and only Asia waxes healthy and teeming. Step on a mouse and you crush the Pyramids. Step on a mouse and you leave your print, like a Grand Canyon, across Eternity. Queen Elizabeth might never be born, Washington might not cross the Delaware, there might never be a United States at all. So be careful. Stay on the Path. *Never* step off!"

"I see," said Eckels. "Then it wouldn't pay for us even to touch the grass?"

"Correct. Crushing certain plants could add up infinitesimally. A little error here would multiply in 60 million years, all out of proportion. Of course maybe our theory is wrong. Maybe Time *can't* be changed by us. Or maybe it can be changed only in little subtle ways. A dead mouse here makes an insect imbalance there, a population disproportion later, a bad harvest further on, a depression, mass starvation, and, finally, a change in *social* temperament in far-flung countries. Something much more subtle, like that. Perhaps only a soft breath, a whisper, a hair, pollen on the air, such a slight, slight change that unless you looked close you wouldn't see it. Who knows? Who really can say he knows? We don't know. We're guessing. But until we do know for certain whether our messing around in Time *can* make a big roar or a little rustle in history, we're being damned careful. This Machine, this Path, your clothing and bodies, were sterilized, as you know, before the journey. We wear these oxygen helmets so we can't introduce our bacteria into an ancient atmosphere."

"How do we know which animals to shoot?"

"They're marked with red paint," said Travis. "Today, before our journey, we sent Lesperance here back with the Machine. He came to this particular era and followed certain animals."

"Studying them?"

"Right," said Lesperance. "I track them through their entire existence, noting which of them lives longest. Very few. How many times they mate. Not often. Life's short. When I find one that's going to die when a tree falls on him, or one that drowns in a tar pit, I note the exact hour, minute, and second. I shoot a paint bomb. It leaves a red patch on his hide. We can't miss it. Then I correlate our arrival in the Past so that we meet the Monster not more than two minutes before he would have died anyway. This way, we kill only animals with no future, that are never going to mate again. You see how *careful* we are?"

"But if you came back this morning in Time," said Eckels eagerly, "you must've bumped into *us*, our Safari! How did it turn out? Was it successful? Did all of us get through—alive?"

Travis and Lesperance gave each other a look.

"That'd be a paradox," said the latter. "Time doesn't permit that sort of mess—a man meeting himself. When such occasions threaten, Time steps aside. Like an airplane hitting an air pocket. You felt the Machine jump just before we stopped? That was us passing ourselves on the way back to the Future. We saw nothing. There's no way of telling *if* this expedition was a success, *if* we got our monster, or whether all of us—meaning *you*, Mr. Eckels—got out alive."

Eckels smiled palely.

"Cut that," said Travis sharply. "Everyone on his feet!"

They were ready to leave the Machine.

The jungle was high and the jungle was broad and the jungle was the entire world forever and forever. Sounds like music and sounds like flying tents filled the sky, and those were pterodactyls soaring with cavernous gray wings, gigantic bats out of a delirium and a night fever.

Eckels, balanced on the narrow Path, aimed his rifle playfully.

"Stop that!" said Travis. "Don't even aim for fun, damn it! If your gun should go off——"

Eckels flushed. "Where's our *Tyrannosaurus*?"

Lesperance checked his wristwatch. "Up ahead. We'll bisect his trail in 60 seconds. Look for the red paint, for Christ's sake. Don't shoot till we give the word. Stay on the Path. *Stay on the Path!*"

They moved forward in the wind of morning.

"Strange," murmured Eckels. "Up ahead, 60 million years, Election Day over. Keith made president. Everyone celebrating. And here we are, a million years lost, and they don't exist. The things we worried about for months, a lifetime, not even born or thought about yet."

"Safety catches off, everyone!" ordered Travis. "You, first shot, Eckels. Second, Billings. Third, Kramer."

"I've hunted tiger, wild boar, buffalo, elephant, but Jesus, this is *it*," said Eckels. "I'm shaking like a kid."

"Ah," said Travis.

Everyone stopped.

Travis raised his hand. "Ahead," he whispered. "In the mist. There he is. There's His Royal Majesty now."

• • •

The jungle was wide and full of twitterings, rustlings, murmurs and sighs.

Suddenly it all ceased, as if someone had shut a door.

Silence.

A sound of thunder.

Out of the mist, 100 yards away, came *Tyrannosaurus rex*.

"Jesus God," whispered Eckels.

"Sh!"

It came on great oiled, resilient, striding legs. It towered 30 feet above half of the trees, a great evil god, folding its delicate watchmaker's claws close to its oily reptilian chest. Each lower leg was a piston, 1,000 pounds of white bone, sunk in thick ropes of muscle, sheathed over in a gleam of pebbled skin like the mail of a terrible warrior. Each thigh was a ton of meat, ivory and steel mesh. And from the great breathing cage of the upper body those two delicate arms dangled out front, arms with hands which might pick up and examine men like toys, while the snake neck coiled. And the head itself, a ton of sculptured stone, lifted easily upon the sky. Its mouth gaped, exposing a fence of teeth like daggers. Its eyes rolled, ostrich eggs, empty of all expression save hunger. It closed its mouth in a death grin. It ran, its pelvic bones crushing aside trees and bushes, its taloned feet clawing damp earth, leaving prints six inches deep wherever it settled its weight. It ran with a gliding ballet step, far too poised and balanced for its ten tons. It moved into a sunlit arena warily, its beautifully reptile hands feeling the air.

"My God!" Eckels twitched his mouth. "It could reach up and grab the moon."

"Sh!" Travis jerked angrily, "He hasn't seen us yet."

"It can't be killed." Eckels pronounced this verdict quietly, as if there could be no argument. He had weighed the evidence and this was his considered opinion. The rifle in his hands seemed a cap gun. "We were fools to come. This is impossible."

"Shut up!" hissed Travis.

"Nightmare."

"Turn around," commanded Travis. "Walk quietly to the Machine. We'll remit one half your fee."

"I didn't realize it would be this *big*," said Eckels. "I miscalculated, that's all. And now I want out."

"It *sees* us!"

"There's the red paint on its chest!"

The Thunder Lizard raised itself. Its armored flesh glittered like a thousand green coins. The coins, crusted with slime, steamed. In the slime, tiny insects wriggled, so that the entire body seemed to twitch and undulate, even while the monster itself did not move. It exhaled. The stink of raw flesh blew down the wilderness.

"Get me out of here," said Eckels. "It was never like this before. I was always sure I'd come through alive. I had good guides, good safaris, and safety. This time, I figured wrong. I've met my match and admit it. This is too much for me to get hold of."

"Don't run," said Lesperance. "Turn around. Hide in the Machine."

"Yes." Eckels seemed to be numb. He looked at his feet as if trying to make them move. He gave a grunt of helplessness.

"Eckels!"

He took a few steps, blinking, shuffling.

"Not *that* way!"

The Monster, at the first motion, lunged forward with a terrible scream. It covered 100 yards in four seconds. The rifles jerked up and blazed fire. A windstorm from the beast's mouth engulfed them in the stench of slime and old blood. The Monster roared, teeth glittering with sun.

Eckels, not looking back, walked blindly to the edge of the Path, his gun limp in his arms, stepped off the Path, and walked, not knowing it, in the jungle. His feet sank into green moss. His legs moved him, and he felt alone and remote from the events behind.

The rifles cracked again. Their sound was lost in shriek and lizard thunder. The great lever of the reptile's tail swung up, lashed sideways. Trees exploded in clouds of leaf and branch. The Monster twitched its jeweler's hands down to fondle at the men, to twist them in half, to crush them like berries, to cram them into its teeth and its screaming throat. Its boulder-stone eyes leveled with the men. They saw themselves mirrored. They fired at the metallic eyelids and the blazing black iris.

Like a stone idol, like a mountain avalanche, *Tyrannosaurus* fell. Thundering, it clutched trees, pulled them with it. It wrenched and tore the metal Path. The men flung themselves back and away. The body hit, ten tons of cold flesh and stone. The guns fired. The Monster lashed its armored tail, twitched its snake jaws, and lay still. A fount of blood spurted from its throat. Somewhere inside, a sac of fluids burst. Sickening gushes drenched the hunters. They stood, red and glistening.

The thunder faded.

The jungle was silent. After the avalanche, a green peace. After the nightmare, morning.

Billings and Kramer sat on the pathway and threw up. Travis and Lesperance stood with smoking rifles, cursing steadily.

In the Time Machine, on his face, Eckels lay shivering. He had found his way back to the Path, climbed into the Machine.

Travis came walking, glanced at Eckels, took cotton gauze from a metal box, and returned to the others, who were sitting on the Path.

"Clean up."

They wiped the blood from their helmets. They began to curse too. The Monster lay, a hill of solid flesh. Within, you could hear the sighs and murmurs as the furthest chambers of it died, the organs malfunctioning, liquids running a final instant from pocket to sac to spleen, everything shutting off, closing up forever. It was like standing by a wrecked locomotive or a steam shovel at quitting time, all valves being released or levered tight. Bones cracked; the tonnage of its own flesh, off balance, dead weight, snapped the delicate forearms, caught underneath. The meat settled, quivering.

Another cracking sound. Overhead, a gigantic tree branch broke from its heavy mooring, fell. It crashed upon the dead beast with finality.

"There." Lesperance checked his watch. "Right on time. That's the giant tree that was scheduled to fall and kill this animal originally." He glanced at the two hunters. "You want the trophy picture?"

"What?"

"We can't take a trophy back to the Future. The body has to stay right here where it would have died originally, so the insects, birds, and bacteria can get at it, as they were intended to. Everything in balance. The body stays. But we *can* take a picture of you standing near it."

The two men tried to think, but gave up, shaking their heads.

They let themselves be led along the metal Path. They sank wearily into the Machine cushions. They gazed back at the ruined Monster, the stagnating mound, where already strange reptilian birds and golden insects were busy at the steaming armor.

A sound on the floor of the Time Machine stiffened them. Eckels sat there, shivering.

"I'm sorry," he said at last.

"Get up!" cried Travis.

Eckels got up.

"Go out on that Path alone," said Travis. He had his rifle pointed. "You're not coming back in the Machine. We're leaving you here!"

Lesperance seized Travis' arm. "Wait——"

"Stay out of this!" Travis shook his hand away. "This son of a bitch nearly killed us. But it isn't *that* so much. Hell, no. It's his *shoes*! Look at them! He ran off the Path. My God, that *ruins* us! Christ knows how much we'll forfeit! Tens of thousands of dollars of insurance! We guarantee no one leaves the Path. He left it. Oh, the damn fool! I'll have to report this to the government. They might revoke our license to travel. God knows *what* he's done to Time, to History!"

"Take it easy, all he did was kick up some dirt."

"How do we *know*?" cried Travis. "We don't know anything! It's all a damn mystery! Get out there, Eckels!"

Eckels fumbled his shirt. "I'll pay anything. I'll pay $100,000!"

Travis glared at Eckels' checkbook and spat. "Go out there. The Monster's next to the Path. Stick your arms up to your elbows in his mouth. Then you can come back with us."

"That's unreasonable!"

"The Monster's dead, you yellow bastard. The bullets! The bullets can't be left behind. They don't belong in the Past; they might change something. Here's my knife. Dig them out!"

The jungle was alive again, full of the old tremorings and bird cries. Eckels turned slowly to regard that primeval garbage dump, that hill of nightmares and terror. After a long time, like a sleepwalker, he shuffled out along the Path.

He returned, shuddering, five minutes later, his arms soaked and red to the elbows. He held out his hands. Each held a number of steel bullets. Then he fell. He lay there where he fell, not moving.

"You didn't have to make him do that," said Lesperance.

"Didn't I? It's too early to tell." Travis nudged the still body. "He'll live. Next time he won't go hunting game like this. Okay." He jerked his thumb wearily at Lesperance. "Switch on. Let's go home."

• • •

1492.   1776.   1812.

They cleaned their hands and faces. They changed their caking shirts and pants. Eckels was up and around again, not speaking. Travis glared at him for a full ten minutes.

"Don't look at me," cried Eckels. "I haven't done anything."

"Who can tell?"

"Just ran off the Path, that's all, a little mud on my shoes—what do you want me to do—get down and pray?"

"We might need it. I'm warning you, Eckels, I might kill you yet. I've got my gun ready."

"I'm innocent. I've done nothing!"

1999.   2000.   2055.

The Machine stopped.

"Get out," said Travis.

The room was there as they had left it. But not the same as they had left it. The same man sat behind the same desk. But the same man did not quite sit behind the same desk.

Travis looked around swiftly. "Everything okay here?" he snapped.

"Fine. Welcome home!"

Travis did not relax. He seemed to be looking at the very atoms of the air itself, at the way the sun poured through the one high window.

"Okay, Eckels, get out. Don't ever come back."

Eckels could not move.

"You heard me," said Travis. "What're you *staring* at?"

Eckels stood smelling of the air, and there was a thing to the air, a chemical taint so subtle, so slight, that only a faint cry of his subliminal senses warned him it was there. The colors, white, gray, blue, orange, in the wall, in the furniture, in the sky beyond the window, were...were... And there was a *feel*. His flesh twitched. His hands twitched. He stood drinking the oddness with the pores of his body. Somewhere, someone must have been screaming one of those whistles that only a dog can hear. His body screamed silence in return. Beyond this room, beyond this wall, beyond this man who was not quite the same man seated at this desk that was not quite the same desk…lay an entire world of streets and people. What sort of world it was now, there was no telling. He could feel them moving there, beyond the walls, almost, like so many chess pieces blown in a dry wind…

But the immediate thing was the sign painted on the office wall, the same sign he had read earlier today on first entering.

Somehow, the sign had changed:

TYME SEFARI INC.

SEFARIS TU ANY YEER EN THE PAST.

YU NAIM THE ANIMALL.

WEE TAEK YU THAIR.

YU SHOOT ITT.

Eckels felt himself fall into a chair. He fumbled crazily at the thick slime on his boots. He held up a clod of dirt, trembling. "No, it *can't* be. Not a *little* thing like that. No!"

Embedded in the mud, glistening green and gold and black, was a butterfly, very beautiful, and very dead.

"Not a little thing like *that*! Not a butterfly." cried Eckels.

It fell to the floor, an exquisite thing, a small thing that could upset balances and knock down a line of small dominoes and then big dominoes and then gigantic dominoes, all down the years across Time. Eckels' mind whirled. It *couldn't* change things. Killing one butterfly couldn't be *that* important! Could it?

His face was cold. His mouth trembled, asking: "Who—who won the presidential election yesterday?"

The man behind the desk laughed. "You joking? You know damn well. Deutscher, of course! Who else? Not that damn weakling Keith. We got an iron man now, a man with guts, by God!" The official stopped. "What's wrong?"

Eckels moaned. He dropped to his knees. He scrabbled at the golden butterfly with shaking fingers. "Can't we," he pleaded to the world, to himself, to the officials, to the Machine, "can't we take it *back*, can't we *make* it alive again? Can't we start over? Can't we——"

He did not move. Eyes shut, he waited, shivering. He heard Travis breathe loud in the room; he heard Travis shift his rifle, click the safety catch, and raise the weapon.

There was a sound of thunder.

A Midsummer Daydream

fiction by DONALD E. WESTLAKE

It having become advisable to leave New York City for an indefinite period, Dortmunder and Kelp found themselves in the countryside, in a barn, watching a lot of fairies dance. "I don't know about this," Dortmunder muttered.

"It's perfect cover," Kelp whispered. "Who'd look for us here?"

"*I* wouldn't, that's for sure."

The fairies all skipped off stage and some other people came on and went off, and then the audience stood up. "That's it?" Dortmunder asked. "We can go now?"

"First half," Kelp told him.

First half. Near the end of the first half, one of the players in bib overalls had gone out and come back in with a donkey's head on, which about summed up Dortmunder's attitude toward the whole thing. Oh, well; when in Rome, do as the Romans, and when in West Urbino, New York, go to the Saturday-afternoon summer theater. Why not? But he wouldn't come back Sunday.

Outside, the audience stood around in the sunshine and talked about everything except *A Midsummer Night's Dream*. The women discussed other women's clothing and the men brought one another up to date on sports and the prices of automobiles, all except Kelp's cousin, a stout man named Jesse Bohker, who smelled of fertilizer because that's what he sold for a living, and who talked about the size of the audience because he was the chief investor in this barn converted to an extremely barnlike summer theater, with splintery bleachers and nonunion actors up from New York. "Good gate," Bohker said, nodding at the crowd in satisfaction, showbiz jargon as comfortable as a hay stalk in his mouth. "Shakespeare brings 'em in every time. They don't want anybody to

205

think they don't have culture."

"Isn't that great," Kelp said, working on his enthusiasm because his cousin Bohker was putting them up until New York became a little less fraught. "Only 80 miles from the city, and you've got live theater."

"Cable kills us at night," cousin Bohker said, sharing more of his entertainment-world expertise, "but in the daytime, we do fine."

They rang a cowbell to announce the second half, and the audience obediently shuffled back in, as though they had bells round their own necks. All except Dortmunder, who said, "I don't think I can do it."

"Come on, John," Kelp said, not wanting to be rude to the cousin. "Don't you wanna know how it comes out?"

"I know how it comes out," Dortmunder said. "The guy with the donkey head turns into Pinocchio."

"That's OK, Andy," cousin Bohker said. He was a magnanimous host. "Some people just don't go for it," he went on, with the fat chuckle that served him so well in fertilizer sales. "Tell the truth, football season, I wouldn't go for it myself."

"I'll be out here," Dortmunder said. "In the air."

So everybody else shuffled back into the barn and Dortmunder stayed outside, like the last smoker in the world. He walked around a bit, looking at how dusty his shoes were getting, and thought about New York. It was just a little misunderstanding down there, that's all, a little question about the value of the contents of trucks that had been taken from Greenwich Street out to Long Island City one night when their regular drivers were asleep in bed. It would straighten itself out eventually, but a couple of the people involved were a little jumpy and emotional in their responses, and Dortmunder didn't want to be the cause of their having performed actions they would later regret. So it was better—more healthful, in fact—to spend a little time in the country, with the air and the trees and the sun and the fairies in the bottom of the barn.

Laughter inside the barn. Dortmunder wandered over to the main entrance, which now stood unguarded, the former ushers and cashier all away being fairies, and beyond the bleachers, he saw the guy in the donkey head and the girl dressed in curtains carrying on as before. No change. Dortmunder turned away and made a long, slow circuit of the barn, just for something to do.

This used to be a real farm a long time ago, but most of the land was sold off and a couple of outbuildings underwent insurance fires, so now the property was pretty much just the old white farmhouse, the red barn and the gravel parking lot in between. The summer-theater people were living in the farmhouse, which meant that out back, it had the most colorful clothesline in the county. Down the road thataway was West Urbino proper, where cousin Bohker's big house stood.

The second half took a long time, almost as long as if Dortmunder had been inside watching it. He walked around awhile, and then he chose a comfortable-looking car in the parking lot and sat in it—people didn't lock their cars or their houses or anything around here—and then he strolled around some more, and that's when the actor with the donkey's head and the bib overalls went by, maybe to make an entrance from the front of the theater. Dortmunder nodded his head at the guy, and the actor nodded his donkey head back.

Dortmunder strolled through the parked cars, wondering if there were time to take one for a little spin, and then Mr. Donkey came back again and they both did their head nod, and the donkey walked on, and that was it for excitement. Dortmunder figured he probably *didn't* have time to take a little drive around the countryside, particularly because, dollars to doughnuts, he'd get lost.

And it was a good thing he'd decided not to leave, because only about ten minutes later, a whole lot of applause sounded inside the barn and a couple of ex-fairies came trotting out to be traffic control in the parking lot. Dortmunder swam upstream through the sated culture lovers and found Kelp to one side of the flow, near the cashier's makeshift office, waiting for cousin Bohker to quit drooling over the take. "It was a lot of fun," Kelp said.

"Good."

"And it come out completely different from what you said."

Cousin Bohker emerged from the ticket office with a brand-new expression on his face, all pinched-in and pruny, as though he'd been eating his fertilizer. He said, "Andy, I guess your friend doesn't understand much about country hospitality."

This made very little sense at all; in fact, none. Kelp said, "Come again, cuz?"

"So you talk to him, Andy," cousin Bohker said. He wasn't looking at Dortmunder but his head seemed to incline slightly in Dortmunder's direction. He seemed like a man torn between anger and fear, anger forbidding him to show the fear, fear holding the anger in check; constipated, in other words. "You talk to your *friend*," cousin Bohker said in a strangled way, "you explain about hospitality in the country, and you tell him we'll forget——"

"If you mean John," Kelp said, "he's right here. This is him here."

"That's OK," the cousin said. "You just tell him we'll forget all about it this once, and all he has to do is give it back, and we'll never say another word about it."

Kelp shook his head. "I don't get what you mean," he said. "Give *what* back?"

"The receipts!" cousin Bohker yelled, waving madly at his ticket office. "Two hundred twenty-seven paid admissions, not counting freebies and house seats like *you* fellas had, at 12 bucks a head; that's $2,724, and I want it *back*!"

Kelp stared at his cousin. "The *box*-office receipts? You can't——" His stare, disbelieving, doubtful, wondering, turned toward Dortmunder. "John? You didn't!" Kelp's eyes looked like hubcaps. "Did you? You didn't! Naturally, you didn't. Did you?"

The experience of being unjustly accused was so novel and bewildering to Dortmunder that he was almost drunk from it. He had so little experience of innocence! How does an innocent person act, react, respond to the base accusation? He could barely stand up, he was concentrating so hard on this sudden inrush of guiltlessness. His knees were wobbling. He stared at Andy Kelp and couldn't think of one solitary thing to say.

"Who else was out here?" the cousin demanded. "All alone out here while everybody else was inside with the play. 'Couldn't stand Shakespeare,' was that it? Saw his opportunity, by God, and *took* it, and the hell with his host!"

Kelp was beginning to look desperate. "John," he said, like a lawyer leading a particularly stupid witness, "you weren't just playing a little *joke*, were you? Just having a little fun, didn't mean anything serious, was that it?"

Maybe innocent people are dignified, Dortmunder thought. He tried it: "I did not take the money," he said, as dignified as a turkey on Thanksgiving eve.

Kelp turned to his cousin: "Are you *sure* it's gone?"

"Andy," said the cousin, drawing himself up—or in—becoming even more dignified than Dortmunder, topping Dortmunder's king of dignity with his own ace, "this fellow is what he is, but you're my wife's blood relative."

"Aw, cuz," Kelp protested, "you don't think I was *in* it with him, do you?"

And that was the unkindest cut of all. Forgetting dignity, Dortmunder gazed on his former friend like a betrayed beagle. "You, too, Andy?"

"Gee whiz, John," Kelp said, twisting back and forth to show how conflicted all this made him, "what're we supposed to *think*? I mean, maybe it just happened accidental-like; you were bored, you know, walking around, you just picked up this cash without even thinking about it, you could...."

Wordlessly, Dortmunder frisked himself, patting his pockets and chest, then spreading his arms wide, offering himself for Kelp to search.

Which Kelp didn't want to do. "OK, John," he said, "the stuff isn't on you. But there wasn't anybody else *out* here, just you, and you know your own rep——"

"The donkey," Dortmunder said.

Kelp blinked at him. "The what?"

"The guy in the donkey head. He walked around from the back to the front, and then he walked around again from the front to the back. We nodded at each other."

Kelp turned his hopeful hubcaps in his cousin's direction.

"The guy with the donkey head, that's who you——"

"What, Kelly?" demanded the cousin. "Kelly's my junior partner in this operation! He's been in it with me from the beginning, he's the director, he takes character roles, he *loves* this theater!" Glowering at Dortmunder, exuding more fertilizer essence than ever, cousin Bohker said, "So is *that* your idea, Mr. Dortmunder?" Dortmunder had been "John" before this. "Is *that* your idea? Cover up your own crime by smearing an innocent man?"

"Maybe *he* did it for a joke," Dortmunder said vengefully. "Or maybe he's absentminded."

Kelp, it was clear, was prepared to believe absolutely anything, just so they could all get past this social pothole. "Cuz," he said, "maybe so, maybe that's it. Kelly's your partner; maybe he took the money legit, spare you the trouble, put it in the bank himself."

But Bohker wouldn't buy it. "Kelly *never* touches the money," he insisted. "*I'm* the businessman, he's the ar-tiste, he's——Kelly!" he shouted through the entranceway, toward the stage, and vigorously waved his fat arm.

Kelp and Dortmunder exchanged a glance. Kelp's look was filled with a wild surmise; Dortmunder's belonged under a halo.

Kelly came out to join them, wiping his neck with a paper towel, saying, "What's up?" He was a short and skinny man who could have been any age from nine to 14 or from 53 to 80, but nothing in between. The donkey head was gone, but that didn't make for much of an improvement. His real face wasn't so much lined as pleated, with deep crevices you could hide a nickel in. His eyes were eggy, with blue yolks, and his thin hair was unnaturally black, like work boots. Except for the head, he was still in the same dumb costume, the idea having been that the actors in bib overalls and black T-shirts were supposed to be some kind of workmen, like plumbers or whatever, and the actors dressed in curtains and beach towels were aristocrats. Kelly had been the leader of the bunch of workmen who were going to put on the play within the play—oh, it was grim, it was grim—so here he was, still in his overalls and T-shirt. And black work boots, so that he looked the same on the top and the bottom. "What's up?" he said.

"I'll tell you what's up," Bohker promised him and pointed at Kelp. "I introduced you to my wife's cousin from the city."

"Yeah, you did already." Kelly, an impatient man probably wanting to get out of his work clothes and into something a little more actorly, nodded briskly at Kelp and said, "How's it goin'?"

"Not so good," Kelp said.

"And *this*," Bohker went on, pointing without pleasure at Dortmunder, "is my wife's cousin's pal, also from the city, a fella with a reputation for being just a little light-fingered."

"Aw, well," Dortmunder said.

Kelly was still impatient: "And?"

"And he lifted the gate!"

This slice of jargon was just a bit too showbizzy for Kelly to grab on the fly like that; he looked around for a lifted gate, his facial pleats increasing so much he looked as though his nose might fall into one of the excavations. "He did *what*?"

Bohker, exasperated at having to use lay terminology, snapped, "He stole the money out of the box office."

"I did not," Dortmunder said.

Kelly looked at Dortmunder as though he'd never expected such treatment. "Gee, man," he said, "that's our eating money."

"I didn't take it," Dortmunder said. He was going for another run at dignity.

"He's got the gall, this fella," Bohker went on, braver about Dortmunder now that he had an ally with him, "to claim *you* took it!"

Kelly wrinkled up like a multicar collision: "*Me*?"

"All I said," Dortmunder told him, feeling his dignity begin to tatter, "was that you went around to the front of the theater."

"I did not," Kelly said. Being an actor, he had no trouble with dignity at all.

So he *did* do it, Dortmunder thought and pressed what he thought of as his advantage: "Sure, you did. We nodded to each other. You were wearing your donkey head. It was about ten minutes before the show was over."

"Pal," Kelly said, "ten minutes before the show was over, I was on stage, asleep in front of everybody, including your buddy here. And without my donkey head."

"That's true, John," Kelp said. "The fairies took the donkey head away just around then."

"In that case," Dortmunder said, immediately grasping the situation, "it had to be one of the other guys in bib overalls. *They* weren't all on stage then, were they?"

But Bohker already had his mind made up. "That's right," he said. "That's what *you* saw, the big-town sharpie, when you came out of this box office right here, with the cash receipts in your pocket, and looked through that door right there in at that stage way back there, and saw Kelly was the only rustic on stage, and the donkey prop was gone, and——"

"The what?" Dortmunder had missed something there.

"The donkey prop!" Bohker cried, getting angrier, pointing at his own head "The head! It's a prop!"

"Well, you know, Jesse," Kelly said thoughtfully, "in some union productions, you know, they'd call it a costume."

"Whatever it is," Bohker snapped, waving the gnats of showbiz cant away as though he hadn't summoned them up himself, then turning back to Dortmunder: "Whatever it is, you saw it, or didn't see it, when you looked right through there and saw Kelly asleep without his head, and none of the other rustics around, and right then you decided how you were gonna blame somebody else. And I'm here to tell you, it won't work!"

Well, innocence wasn't any help—overrated, as Dortmunder had long suspected—and dignity had proved to be a washout, so what was left? Dortmunder was considering violence, which usually tended at least to clear the air, when Kelp said, "Cuz, let me have a word in private with John, OK?"

"That's all I ever asked," Bohker said, with false reasonableness. "Just talk to your friend here, explain to him how we do things different in the country, how we don't take *advantage* of the kindness of people who take us in when we're on the *run*, how when we're away from the *city*, we behave like *decent, God-fearing*——"

"Right, cuz, right," Kelp said, taking Dortmunder by the elbow, drawing him away from the ongoing flow, nodding and nodding as though Bohker's claptrap made any sense at all, turning Dortmunder away, walking him back out toward the now nearly empty parking lot and across it to a big old tree standing there with leaves all over it, and Dortmunder promised himself, If Andy asks me even *once* did I do it, I'm gonna pop him.

Instead of which, once they'd reached the leafy privacy of the tree, Kelp turned and murmured, "John, we're in a bind here."

Dortmunder sighed, relieved and yet annoyed. "That's right."

"I dunno, the only thing I can think——How much did he say it was?"

"Two something. Something under three grand." And *that* got Dortmunder steamed in an entirely different way. "To think I'd stoop to grab such a measly amount of——"

"Sure you would, John, if the circumstances were different," Kelp said, cutting through the crap. "The question is, Can we cover it?"

"What do you mean, cover it?"

"Well, Jesse said if we give it back, he'll forget the whole thing, no questions asked."

Now Dortmunder was *really* outraged. "You mean, let the son of a bitch go on thinking I'm a thief?"

Kelp leaned closer, dropping his voice. "John, you *are* a thief."

"Not this time!"

"What does it matter, John? You're never gonna convince him, so forget it."

Dortmunder glared at the farmhouse, full now of actors, one of them with nearly three grand extra in his pocket. Probably looking out a window right now, grinning at him. "It's one of those guys," he said. "I can't let him get away with it."

"Why not? And what are you gonna do, play detective? John, we're not cops!"

"We watched cops work often enough."

"That isn't the same. John, how much money you got?"

"On me?" Dortmunder groused, reluctant even to discuss this idea, while out of the corner of his eye, he saw Kelly heading briskly toward the farmhouse. "Why *couldn't* it be him?" he demanded. "Partners steal from partners all the time."

"He was on stage, John. How much money you got?"

"On me, a couple hundred. In the suitcase, back at your goddamn cousin's house, maybe a grand."

"I could come up with eight, nine hundred," Kelp said. "Let's go see if we can cut a deal."

"I don't like this," Dortmunder said. "I don't go along with making restitution to begin with, and this is even worse."

Running out of patience, Kelp said, "What else are we gonna do, John?"

"Search that farmhouse there. Search the theater. You think some amateur can hide a stash so *we* can't find it?"

"They wouldn't let us search," Kelp pointed out. "We aren't cops, we don't have any authority, we can't throw any weight around. That's what cops do; they don't *detect*, you know that. They throw their weight around, and when you say 'Oof,' you get five to ten in Green Haven. Come on, John, swallow your pride."

"I'm not gonna say I did it," Dortmunder insisted. "You wanna pay him off, we'll pay him off. But I'm not gonna say I did it."

"Fine. Let's go talk to the man."

They walked back to where cousin Bohker waited in the narrow trapezoid of shade beside the barn. "Cuz," said Kelp, "we'd like to offer a deal."

"Admitting nothing," Dortmunder said.

"Two thousand, seven hundred twenty-four dollars," the cousin said. "That's the only deal I know."

"We can't quite come up with that much," Kelp said, "on accounta John here didn't actually take your money. But we know how things look and we know what John's reputation is——"

"Hey," Dortmunder said. "What about *you*?"

"OK, fine. The reputations we both have. So we feel we'll try to make good on what you lost as best we can, even though we didn't do it, and we could probably come up with $2,000. In or around $2,000."

"Two thousand, seven hundred twenty-four dollars," said the cousin, "or I call the troopers."

"Troopers?" Dortmunder stared at Kelp. "He's gonna call in the *Army*?"

"State troopers, he means," Kelp explained, and turned back to his cousin to say, "That wouldn't be a nice thing to do, cuz. Turn us over to the law and we're really in trouble. Can't you take the two——"

"Two thousand, seven hundred twenty-four dollars," said the cousin.

"Oh, the hell with this guy," Dortmunder abruptly said. "Why don't we just go take a hike?"

"I thought you might come up with that next," the cousin answered. He was smeared all over with smugness. "So that's why I sent Kelly for reinforcements."

Dortmunder turned, and there was Kelly back from the farmhouse, and with him were all the other rustics. Five of them, still in their bib overalls and T-shirts, standing there looking at Dortmunder and Kelp, getting a kick out of being the audience for a change.

It's one of them, Dortmunder thought. He's standing there and I'm standing here, and it's one of them. And I'm stuck.

Kelp said something, and then the cousin said something, and then Kelp said something else, and then Kelly said something; and Dortmunder tuned out. It's one of these five guys, he thought. One of these guys is a little scared to be out here, he doesn't know if he's gonna get away with it or not, he's looking at me and he doesn't know if he's in trouble or not.

Their eyes? No, they're all actors; the guy's gotta know enough to behave like everybody else. But it's one of them.

Well, not the fat one. You look at skinny Kelly there, and you see this fat one, and even with the donkey head on, you'd know it wasn't Kelly, having already seen Kelly in the first half, wearing the donkey head, and knowing what he looked like.

Hey, wait a minute. Same with the tall one. Kelly's maybe 5'5" or 5'6", and here's a drink of water must be 6'4", and he stands all stooped, so if *he* had the donkey head on, the donkey's lips would be on his belt buckle. Not him.

Son of a gun. Two down. Three to go.

Conversation went on, quite animated at times, and Dortmunder continued to study the rustics. That one with the beard, well, the beard wouldn't show inside the donkey head, but look how hairy he is anyway; lots of bushy black hair on his head and very hairy arms below the T-shirt sleeves, all that black hair with the pale skin showing through. With the donkey head on, he'd look maybe a little *too* realistic. Would I have noticed? Would I have said, "Wow, up close, that's some hairy donkey?" Maybe, maybe.

Shoes? Black work boots, black shoes; some differences, but not enough, not so you'd notice.

Wait a minute. That guy, the one with the very graceful neck, the one who would be kept in the special block for his own protection if he were ever given five to ten at Green Haven, the one who moves like a ballet dancer; his bib overalls have a *crease*. Not him. He could cover himself in an entire donkey and I'd know.

Number five. Guy in his mid-20s, average height, average weight, nothing in particular about him except the watch. He's the guy, during the first half, while I'm waiting for it to be over, trying to find something to think about, he's the guy with the pale mark around his wrist where he usually wears a watch, so it isn't tanned. And now he's wearing the watch. Did the guy who walked by me have a pale mark on his wrist? Would I have noticed?

"John? John!"

Dortmunder looked around, startled out of his reverie. "Yeah? What is it?"

"What *is* it?" Kelp was looking frantic and he clearly wanted to know why Dortmunder wasn't frantic as well. "Do you think she could or *not*?" he demanded.

"I'm sorry," Dortmunder said, "I didn't hear the question. Who could what? Or not?" And thinking, It's either the hairy arms or the watch; hairy arms or watch.

"May," Kelp said, elaborately patient. "Do you think if you phoned May, she could send us a grand to pay off my cousin?"

Hairy arms or watch. Nothing shows on either face, nothing in the eyes.

"John? What's the *matter* with you?"

"Well," Dortmunder said, and put a big smile on his face, and even forced a little laugh, or something similar to a laugh, "well, you got us, cuz."

Kelp stared. "*What?*"

"Yeah, we took the money," Dortmunder said, shrugging. "But it was just for a joke, you know; we never meant to keep it."

"Yeah, I'm sure," Bohker said with a sarcastic smirk, while Kelp stood as though turned to stone. Limestone. In acid rain.

Kelly, cold and brisk, said, "Where is it?"

"Well, I don't know exactly," Dortmunder said. "I gave it to my partner to hide."

Kelp squawked; it sounded exactly like those chickens that a neighbor of Bohker's kept in his backyard. He squawked, and then he cried, "John! You never did!"

"Not you," Dortmunder told him. "My other partner, the actor in the cast here that's an old pal of mine. I slipped him the money and he went and hid it in the house." Hairy arms or watch; hairy arms or watch. Dortmunder turned and grinned easily at the kid with the pale band under his watch. "Didn't I?" he said.

The kid blinked. "I don't get you," he said.

"Aw, come on; the gag's over," Dortmunder told him. "If Bohker here calls his state troopers, I'll just tell them I gave you the money to hide and they'll go look in the house there and find it, and everybody *knows*

I was never in that house, so it was you. So now the gag is over, right?"

The kid thought about it. Everybody standing there watched the kid thinking about it, and everybody knew what it meant that the kid had something to think about. The kid looked around and saw what it was that everybody knew, and then he laughed and clapped his hands and said, "Well, we sure had them going there for a while, didn't we?"

"We sure did," Dortmunder said. "Why don't you and me go in the house now and get the cousin his money back?"

Bohker, sounding tough, said, "Why don't we *all* go in and get the goddamn money?"

"Now, now," Dortmunder said, mild as could be, "why don't you let us have our little secrets? We'll go in and we'll come out with the money. You'll get your money back, cousin, don't worry."

Dortmunder and the kid walked across the parking lot and up the stoop and across the porch full of gaping actors and went into the house. The kid led the way upstairs and down the hall and into the third room on the left, which contained two narrow beds and two small dressers and two wooden chairs. "Hold it a second," Dortmunder said, and looked around, and saw the one dresser drawer open about three inches. "Taped it to the back of the dresser drawer," he said.

"OK, OK, you're Sherlock Holmes," the kid said, sounding bitter. He went over and pulled the drawer out and put it on the bed. Masking tape held a bulky white envelope to the back of the drawer. The kid peeled it off and handed it to Dortmunder, who saw that it had a printed return address on the upper left corner: BOHKER & BOHKER, FERTILIZER & FEED.

"How'd you figure it out?" the kid asked.

"Your shoes," Dortmunder said. Which was a variant on the old untied-shoelace gag, because when the kid looked down at his shoes, what he saw was Dortmunder's fist coming up.

Outside again, Dortmunder crossed to the waiting rustics and held the envelope out in front of himself, flap open, so everybody could see the money wadded inside. "OK?"

Kelly said, "Where's Chuck?"

"Resting."

Bohker reached for the envelope, but Dortmunder said, "Not yet, cuz," and tucked the envelope inside his shirt.

Bohker glowered. "Not yet? What are you playing at, fella?"

"You're gonna drive Andy and me to your house," Dortmunder told him, "and we're gonna pack, and then you're gonna drive us to the bus depot, and when the bus comes in, I'll hand you this envelope. Play around, I'll make it disappear again."

"I'm not a vengeful fella," Bohker said. "All I care about is I get my money back."

"Well, that's one difference between us," Dortmunder said, which Bohker maybe didn't listen to hard enough.

Bohker's station wagon was one of the few cars left in the parking lot. Bohker got behind the wheel, his cousin Kelp beside him, and Dortmunder got in back with the old newspapers and cardboard cartons and fertilizer brochures and all the junk, and they drove off toward town. Along the way, Bohker looked in the rearview mirror and said, "I been thinking about what happened back there. You didn't take the money at all, did you?"

"Like I said."

"It *was* Chuck."

"That's right."

Kelp twisted around to look over the back of the seat and say, "John, how did you figure out it was him? That was goddamn genius."

If Kelp wanted to think what had happened was genius, it would be better for Dortmunder to keep his thought processes to himself, so he said, "It just come to me."

Bohker said, "You had to mousetrap Chuck like you did or he'd have just denied it forever."

"Uh-huh."

"Well, I owe you an apology," Bohker said, being gruff and man-to-man about it.

"That's OK," Dortmunder told him.

"And there's no reason you fellas have to move out."

"Oh, I think we're ready to go, anyway," Dortmunder said. "Aren't we, Andy?"

"Yeah, I think so," Kelp said.

As Bohker turned the station wagon in to the driveway at his house, Dortmunder said, "Does that glove compartment lock?"

"Yeah, it does," Bohker said. "Why?"

"I tell you what we'll do," Dortmunder told him. "We'll lock this envelope in there for safekeeping, and you give me the key off the ring, and when we get on our bus, I'll give it back to you. On account of I know you don't trust me."

"Now, that's not fair," Bohker said defensively, parking beside his house. "I apologized, didn't I?"

"Still," Dortmunder said, "we'll both be happier if we do it this way. Which key is it?"

So Bohker took the little key off his key ring, and he and Kelp watched Dortmunder solemnly lock the envelope away in the crowded, messy glove compartment, and an hour and 45 minutes later, on the bus to Buffalo, Kelp turned in his seat and said, "You did, didn't you?"

"Sure, I did," Dortmunder agreed, taking Bohker's money out of his pants pockets. "Treat me like that, threaten me with *troopers*."

"What's cousin Bohker looking at in that envelope?"

"Fertilizer brochures."

Kelp sighed, probably thinking about family complications. "Still, John," he said, "you can't blame the guy for jumping to conclusions."

"I can if I want," Dortmunder said. "Besides, I figured I earned this, with what he put me through. That stuff, what's it? Anguish, you know the kind. Mental, that's it. Mental anguish, that's what I got," Dortmunder said, and stuffed the money back into his pockets.

"Gentlemen, third parties are ordinarily a long
shot—but not with clones of these guys!"

My Favorite Sleuths

commentary by **KINGSLEY AMIS**

I t is only in books that one finds the brilliant amateur detective X; real policemen are obstinate and hardheaded, are slow and literal-minded, are frequently mean and nearly always narrow: They have to be. They are part of the administrative machine, a tool of government control...."

So reflects Van der Valk, Nicolas Freeling's Amsterdam inspector, on his way to try to stop a beautiful female aristocrat and ex-ski champion from ambushing a Dutch businessman with a hunting rifle on a lonely road in southern France. With this latest adventure, *The King of the Rainy Country*, Van der Valk confirms his status as one of the most promising arrivals on the post-War crime-fiction scene. In his account of real policemen he is actually a little hard on himself. Obstinate and slow he may be, but these are only rude names for the Netherlander's inbred conscientiousness. As for literal-minded, he is given to reflecting self-accusingly that he is too much of a northerner, with his veins full of Ibsen, and is able without difficulty to work out the motivation of a suicide by pondering over the poem of Baudelaire's alluded to in the title. Besides all this, he is intelligent, thoughtful and good-natured—the last of these by no means a standard characteristic of fictional sleuths. (Even Sherlock Holmes has been known to come back at Watson with a quick impatient snarl or so when the chase is really on.) Van der Valk is an impressive man interestingly rendered. His only shortcoming as a hero, the only thing that robs him of the almost mythical and mystical glamor of a Holmes or a Nero Wolfe, is that he, unlike them, is very much a real policeman.

The point is even clearer with Simenon's celebrated Inspector Maigret. In *My Friend Maigret*, the inspector takes along a Scotland Yard detective called Pyke to investigate a murder on a French island. Pyke—incidentally, an amusing and sympathetic portrayal—is supposed to be studying French police methods. At the end of the book it is suggested that Pyke, apart from having thrown down a good deal of the local wine, has been wasting his time, because there just are no such methods. None, that is, but the universal ones of interrogation of witnesses, suspects, neighbors and the like, thumbing through records and dossiers, consulting London, Ostend, Zurich and the like, and more interrogation. None of those brilliant intuitions, those miraculous leaps in the dark, those questions about what seem to be insanely irrelevant matters, that are so firmly in the middle of the great detective tradition inaugurated by Poe's Auguste Dupin. And Maigret himself, apart from taking an occasional applejack too many, has virtually no characteristics beyond those required to solve his cases. We know all too well that he will never in a million years start playing the violin or suddenly insist on cultivating orchids. That sort of thing is the prerogative of the unreal policeman, or rather the unreal nonpoliceman: Van der Valk's brilliant amateur detective X, who exists only in books. All the sleuths we remember and reverence and take into our private pantheon of heroes are figures not of realism but of fantasy, great talkers, great eccentrics, men who use inspiration instead of hard work, men to whom Venetian old masters mean more than police files and a good bottle of burgundy more than fingerprints. (Scope here for a scholarly footnote on the parallel with spy fiction: James Bond will still be around long after all the spies who came in from the cold, Ipcress-file-mongers and similar "real" secret agents have been forgotten.)

Halfway between the policeman and the amateur comes the private investigator, of whom Dashiell Hammett's Sam Spade and Raymond Chandler's Philip Marlowe are typical, plus, in a rather different way, Mickey Spillane's Mike Hammer. Theirs is a fantasy world all right, that of the toughie whose sacred objects are the gun, the boot, the bottle of rye and (less so in Chandler than in the others) the male organ. It has often been objected against the tough school that their values are lopsided or nonexistent, that in regard to ethics, and pretty well everything else, the police and the D.A.'s men are no better than the crooks or the Commies and the private eye is at least as bad as all the others. This loss of moral focusing is felt to be unedifying, even dangerous. Maybe. My own view is that the immoral or amoral hero of this type is bound to forfeit some of the reader's esteem and, along with it, some of his desire to identify with the hero. The story thus goes rather cold. In crime or spy fantasies the interest is partly a fairy-tale one, good versus bad in a rather basic way; James Bond would not mean so much to us if we were unable to feel that he was on the right side and that his cause was just. The toughies have no decent cause. Self-interest is all.

This would probably matter less than it does if these writers wrote better. Spillane is the best of the three cited—an unpopular view, which I would defend hotly. Legitimate shock and horror at the beastliness of Hammer's universe should not be allowed to weigh against the technical brilliance with which the whole thing is stage-managed. Few novelists on any level can match Spillane's skill in getting his essential facts across palatably and without interrupting the action, in knowing what to leave out; and the impression received that the narrative is just tumbling out of the corner of Hammer's mouth at 200 words a minute is a tribute to real professional competence. With all this granted, what makes the stories finally stultifying is Hammer's total facelessness, or mindlessness. He is a mere network of gristle connecting mouth, fist, trigger finger and penis. A hero needs more substance than that.

Sam Spade perhaps has a little more. *The Maltese Falcon*, in the period just after its publication (1930), was certainly taken as having opened up an undiscovered area in popular fiction. No doubt the removal of conventional ethics caught the taste of a public who, in mid-Depression, must have been more than ready to believe that almost any cynical view of the world was likely to approximate the way things really were, and did not care to notice the story's manifold improbabilities. Looking back now, it seems hard to understand what the fuss was about. Spade, the blond satan with the yellow-gray eyes, grinning wolfishly on every other page and making growling animal noises in his throat nearly as often, the most committed cigarette smoker before our friend 007, turns out to be faintly funny. Where Hammett presents Spade's toughness as real and probable, as the way things are did we but know it, the result is unbelievable; where the toughness is offered as exceptionally cool, exceptionally tough, it just seems corny. And both sorts come down much of the time to mere rudeness and bad temper. All of it is ladled out in low-budget-TV-show dialog. The gloss and the glow, if they were ever there, have been rubbed out by time.

Raymond Chandler was undoubtedly the most ambitious writer of the tough-thriller school, and for some time was, in England at any rate still is, a toast of the intellectuals. W.H. Auden went on record with the view that "Chandler's powerful books should be read and judged not as escape literature but as works of art." This advice strikes me as hazardous in the extreme. The books have undoubtedly worn less badly than Hammett's, having had for one thing less time to do so, since they belong roughly to the period 1939–1959. Philip Marlowe is an improvement on Spade. Some of Marlowe's toughness does boil down to meanness, unreticent dislike of the rich and indeed of most other groups and individuals, rudeness to servants and to women. On the other hand, there are some things he will not do, he will protect his clients under great pressure, he can show compunction and even sensitivity. What disfigures him is, again, the way he is presented by his creator. The tough catchphrases—don't kid me, son; quit stalling; on your way, brother—died with, or before, Bogart. There is also a moral pretentiousness whereby Marlowe is now and again made the vehicle for criticizing the sordid lives of Hollywood's denizens: the perverted producers, the writers drowning in bourbon and self-hatred, the chicks who will do absolutely anything to get a part—all that. Most of this comes ill from a private eye, even a comparatively honest one. Bits of stylistic pretentiousness underline the effect. *The Big Sleep* has bubbles rising in a glass of liquor "like false hopes" and, after an intermission of four words, a girl's breath being "as delicate as the eyes of a fawn." Is this our tough Chandler (let alone a work of art), or has some heart-throbbing female dream-purveyor grabbed the pen?

Perry Mason provides a convenient stopover point. There would be a lot to be said for not noticing him at all, if it were not for the hideous frequency of his appearances in print and on television. I am afraid there can be very few people in our culture who would not know that, although Mason is not in the strict sense a detective, is a mere lawyer employing the Drake Detective Agency to do his legwork for him, he does investigate crimes, ending up ten times out of ten by winning one of those objection-overruled-objection-sustained rituals in concert with the D.A. and the judge. The TV films faithfully reflect the Erle Stanley Gardner novels in their portrayal of the inevitable three-stage progress from seeing-the-client through seeing-the-witnesses to going-to-court, with an expected unexpected revelation at the end. Mason has an impressive claim to being considered the most boring foe of criminality in our time, which is saying something if we make the effort to remember such cobwebbed figures as Inspector French (in the works of Freeman Wills Crofts) or Philo Vance (S.S. Van Dine). The nullity of Mason is nowhere better displayed than in his relations, or lack of any, with his assistant—I cannot bring myself to say girl Friday—Della Street. Della Street, whose name appears in full every time Gardner mentions her, answers the telephone and listens to Mason telling her that the law is not a rat race unless you run with the rats. Oh, and sometimes she worries because Mason looks so tired. Nothing more; whereas the vital role of the assistant in detective fiction is to encourage and provoke the great man to reveal his hidden inner nature, as we shall see.

I hope we shall see much more than that. The sleuths put up to question so far have admittedly been treated in a rather carping or, as we British say, *knocking* spirit. My admiration is reserved for the detective who detects, whose claim to fame is his mind rather than his way with a girl or a jury. Heroes of this type show a strong family resemblance. Such a man will show some physical impressiveness, along the lines of Holmes's tall, lean figure and piercing eyes, or Wolfe's vast poundage: 285 of them. If unimpressive, he will be spectacularly unimpressive, small and with an egg-shaped head like Poirot; small, round-faced and bespectacled like Father Brown. He is unmarried, or at least his wife is kept firmly off stage. A crucial point, this. Holmes hit the nail on the head for his group when he declared that he would never marry, lest he biased his judgment. But let Dr. Watson spell the point out:

> All emotions, and that one [i.e., love] particularly, were abhorrent to his cold, precise, but admirably balanced mind. He was, I take it, the most perfect reasoning and observing machine that the world has seen.... He never spoke of the softer passions, save with a gibe and a sneer.... For the trained observer to admit such intrusions into his own delicate and finely adjusted temperament was to introduce a distracting factor which might throw a doubt upon all his mental results.... (—*A Scandal in Bohemia*)

And no doubts must be thrown on any of those mental results. Quite right. But what are we to make of this avoidance of the fair sex, which in Wolfe's case rises, or sinks, to panic at the mere prospect of being alone with a woman? Could there be something a bit...you know...? Let us take a look at a famous incident in *The Three Garridebs*, wherein John Garrideb, alias Killer Evans, shoots Watson in the thigh. Holmes promptly disposes of Evans, and then...

> ...My friend's wiry arms were round me, and he was leading me to a chair.
> "You're not hurt, Watson? For God's sake, say that you are not hurt!"
> It was worth a wound—it was worth many wounds—to know the depth of loyalty and love which lay behind that cold mask. The clear, hard eyes were dimmed for a moment, and the firm lips were shaking. For the one and only time I caught a glimpse of a great heart as well as of a great brain. All my years of humble but single-minded service culminated in that moment of revelation.
> "It's nothing, Holmes. It's a mere scratch."

Is it without significance that, whereas the moment of revelation is dated by Watson in 1902, his account of it was held back from book publication until the more tolerant days of 25 years later? Answer: Yes. Utterly. Though it might be more fun to believe the opposite, Holmes is no fag. His lack of interest in women, made a positive characteristic to aid in the building up of his character, can be accounted for in at least two innocent ways. Just as the true Western fans in the moviehouse sigh and groan when Destry stops shooting and starts loving—and a large part of our feelings about Holmes are on this sort of level—so we should feel cheated and affronted if the great brain left Watson to get after the Man with the Twisted Lip for a spell and himself started taking Miss Violet de Merville off Baron Adelbert Gruner. Further, although Holmes would not have been difficult to turn into a lover, any adventure featuring him as such could not be a detective story but, as experience of other writers shows, some kind of thriller or pursuit story or psychological melodrama. The magnifying lens and the dozen red roses belong to different worlds.

Holmes is the memorable figure he is because Conan Doyle grasped the essential truth that the deductive solving of crimes cannot in itself throw much light on the character doing the solving, and therefore that character must be loaded up with quirks, hobbies, eccentricities. It is always these irrelevant qualities that define the figure of the great detective, not his mere powers of reasoning. One thinks of Lord Peter Wimsey's collections of Sevres vases and early editions of Dante (including the Aldine 8vo of 1502 and the Naples folio of 1477), Poirot's dandified clothes and tiny Russian cigarettes, Dupin's expertise about paving stones, grasses, astronomy, fungi and probably much more.

In Holmes's opinion, Dupin was "a very inferior fellow. That trick of his of breaking in on his friends' thoughts with an apropos remark after a quarter of an hour's silence is really very showy and superficial." I agree. Apart from his irritating mannerisms, all three of Dupin's cases are very shaky. He could never have got ahead of the police in *The Murders in the Rue Morgue* without their incredible ignorance; his deductions in *The Mystery of Marie Roget* are at least highly dubious at several key points; and in *The Purloined Letter* he not only again had stupid police to help him out but also a dementedly foolhardy criminal. However, something deeper than professional contempt or jealousy was at work to give Holmes so jaundiced a view of his—rightly or wrongly—famous French predecessor. Holmes was intelligent enough to see that Dupin was his predecessor in much more than just the chronological sense.

There are plenty of comparatively minor resemblances between the two detectives: the pipe-smoking, the love of long pedantic monologs (plus, in each case, the presence of a devoted associate who knows just what to break in with or at least stays awake), the hatred of company and intrusions on privacy. Holmes, we are told, "loathed every form of society with his whole bohemian soul"; Dupin went so far as to solve the Roget case without leaving his armchair, recalling to us a more recent and much fatter detective who makes a point of operating in the same way. More important among Dupin-Holmes resemblances is the possession of vast and variegated learning. Holmes improves on Dupin's astronomy and mycology to the extent of being able to hold forth, in the course of one dinner, about miracle plays, medieval pottery, Stradivarius violins and the Buddhism of Ceylon. As regards the modern world he is frighteningly well-informed. It seems that he has always card-indexed the whole of each day's press, "docketing all paragraphs concerning men and things," a testing task unassisted even for Holmes, "so that it was difficult to name a subject or a person on which he could not at once furnish information." Obviously. An occasionable pebble from this vast mountain of lore is of course immediately applicable to the case in hand. Just as stuff about grasses and fungi helped Dupin with Marie Roget, so Holmes would benefit from the research that went into that unforgettable monograph on the varieties of tobacco ash. But the real point of all this knowledge is much less what you do with it than the simple and memorable fact that you have it.

Knock Dupin as one may, his final and vital legacy to Holmes was what created the detective story as we have known it. However suspect Dupin's chains of inference may be at any particular link, what we are witnessing overall is a convinced demonstration of the power of the human mind to observe and to reason. This is what Holmes is constantly up to. He may, as the story unfolds, deny the reader vital clues and information—or Watson will do it for him, giving him the opportunity, in one of the two stories he narrates himself, to sneer at Watson's habit of contriving "meretricious finales" by the use of this kind of suppression. A bit hard on poor Watson, this, considering he could only put in as much as Holmes would tell him. Anyway: Holmes may also irk us, or give us the wrong kind of laugh, by overdoing the demonstration, as when he discovers everything that happened at the scene of a fairly complicated crime by working on the footmarks with his lens, or by deducing 17 separate facts, 11 of them nonphysical, about a man by examining his hat, one of the 11 being that his wife has ceased to love him. (Not all that difficult when you know how: The hat had not been brushed for a long time, and its age would have shown the man was too poor to afford a servant.) But many of the imaginative leaps are valid and thrilling: for instance, the moment when Holmes decides why an elderly pawnbroker has been induced to join a league of red-haired men after a glance at the trouser legs of the old boy's assistant. "Holmes, this is marvelous!" Watson is supposed to cry when this sort of thing happens, though my recollection is that he never quite does. But he would have been right. It is marvelous.

The deductive prodigies are strongly supported by Doyle's gifts for suspense, horror and action writing, all carried forward on an unfailing flow of ingenious ideas. Holmes founded a dynasty. One of its more unexpected recent members is the Martian detective Syalok, a birdlike creature who wears a *tirstokr* hat, smokes a pipe in which the tobacco is cut with permanganate of potash, and in Poul Anderson's story *The Martian Crown Jewels* recovers the theft of these diadems by a strict application of Holmesian principles—rather stricter, in fact, than the master often used himself. But Holmes has, in one sense, been even further afield than Mars. His exploits have been the subject of fierce controversy in Russia. I am indebted to G.F. McCleary for the information that some years ago the stories were issued there on a large scale, and that the librarians of the Red Army recommended Holmes to the troops as "the exterminator of crimes and evils, a model of magnificent strength of thought and great culture." This, McCleary continues, went down badly with a writer in the newspaper *Vechernaya Moskva*, who thought the tales offended socialist ideology by "poisoning the minds of readers with false morals concerning the strength of the foundations of private property, and diverting attention from the social contradictions of capitalist reality." Even Holmes himself might not have been able to deduce that much from the facts.

With few but shining exceptions, the heirs of Sherlock Holmes are an undistinguished lot. Lord Peter Wimsey has never quite survived, in my mind at least, the initial impression given by his righty-ho, dear-old-thing, don't-you-know, chin-chin style of dialog and his mauve dressing gown, primrose silk pajamas, monocle and the rest of the outfit. Here I should in fairness make it plain that Wimsey is no more of a fag than Holmes is: He merely looks and sounds like one, as a certain kind of English aristocrat does to virtually all American, and the vast majority of British, eyes and ears. As for Wimsey, one might also lead that the bally-fool persona is, at least in part, put on to fool criminals. But what lies beneath the mask, if it is a mask, is hardly more attractive and certainly less vivid. Lord Peter is just an old connoisseur and clubman who gets asked along to help out upper-crust families or trips over a stray corpse. In his later career the deductive faculty in him ran thin and he would fall back more on luck. He certainly got it, having once happened, for example, to have deposited a bag at a luggage counter where another bag that happened to be the twin of the first one happened also to have been deposited. The second bag happened to have somebody's head in it. In other adventures he got tied up with a ghostly female egghead, thus establishing to some extent his heterosexual *bona fides*, but at the same time forgetting about crime and talking to the female egghead instead, clear evidence for my rule that love and detection do not mix. Even in his heyday he often seemed to differ from the other people in the story by being merely slow on the uptake while they were moronic or crazed.

Hercule Poirot. Miss Marple, Ellery Queen, Inspector—later Assistant Commissioner Sir John—Appleby deserve, or at any rate will get, shorter shrift from me. I have never understood the fame of the two Agatha Christie characters, both of whom seem straight out of stock— Poirot the excitable but shrewd little foreigner, Marple the innocent, helpless-looking old lady with the keen blue eyes. And although some of the early Christies (*Why Didn't They Ask Evans?* for instance) had splendidly ingenious plots, the later Poirots and Marples have become thinned down, not surprising in a writer who has been hard at work for 45 years. Queen, who has been around just since 1929, has had his ingenuities, too, but he is too slight a figure to sustain more than a tiny corner of Holmes's mantle, acting mostly as a sounding board for the other characters, a camera for the story, and a mouthpiece when the author wants to chat things over with the reader. Ellery of the silver-colored eyes is seldom much more than an extension of the plot.

To label as a similar plot device so distinguished a personage as Michael Innes' Appleby may look a little rough, but here I am doing it, and if Appleby could know, he would do no more than shrug his well-tailored shoulders, murmur a quotation from Donne or Hardy and perhaps reach for another modest measure of that liqueur brandy of his that surpasses anything in the Duke of Horton's cellar. Appleby has become an establishment figure, moving in a world that would be anathema to Holmes's bohemian soul. The Appleby method of detection is to sit back and wait for the unconscious to come up with a solution, though the sitting back is purely mental: There can be plenty of physical rushing about in pursuit of stolen masterpieces, errant scientists with lethal secrets and such. Appleby is mostly the man to whom it all happens; most of it could happen to anybody, or nobody. The opposite is true of the novels of Edmund Crispin, who yet owes something to Innes. Crispin's detective, Gervase Fen, is an Oxford don, an eccentric after the fashion of Holmes or Wimsey, but funnier and in one sense grander than they, in that he seems to create his own kind of adventure. Nobody but Fen could find himself in a room whose occupant had unconsciously re-created the setting of Poe's *The Raven,* or in a situation to which the only clue depends on an intimate knowledge of Edward Lear's limericks. There is ingenuity here, too, including a nonelectronic method of eavesdropping on a conversation out of earshot of the eavesdropper.

So far I have tried to anatomize six American and five British detectives, plus a few doubtful cases emanating from the general northwestern-European area. This seems fair treatment of an Anglo-American literary form that has always had connections with France and thereabouts. Despite these connections, which go back at least as far as 1828, when the real-life detective François Eugene Vidocq began publishing his famous *Mémoires,* the detective story has flourished typically in the English language. A.E. Murch suggests in his detailed and fascinating work *The Development of the Detective Novel* that the law in France, among other places, is set up in such a way that the public tends to regard the police with some fear and suspicion, at any rate without the instinctive feelings of support common to Americans and British, who thus find it easy and natural to sympathize with a hero working on the side of the police. Possibly. But then all kinds of genre writing, offshoots from the main stem of literature, are largely confined to English: not just the Western novel, but science fiction, the ghost story, to some extent the cloak-and-dagger thriller. Something vague and basic to do with the language? Decide for yourself.

The three great successors of Sherlock Holmes are G.K. Chesterton's Father Brown, Rex Stout's Nero Wolfe and John Dickson Carr's Doctor Fell. The first one is British, the second American, the third British again but written about by an American, and so neatly preserving the balance.

Father Brown is not an eccentric in the superficial, violin-playing or orchid-rearing sense. But he is extraordinary enough, more so today than when Chesterton was writing, for Brown's extraordinariness is founded in his religion. Whether we like it or not, the little man's devotion, total courage, human insight and unshakable belief in reason are at any rate statistically uncommon. Some readers have found too much Roman Catholic propaganda in the stories. I feel that the Christian element, which is sometimes built into the plot, is never narrowly sectarian, and that part of it which overlaps with the advocacy of sheer common sense ought to be acceptable to everybody. It would be truer to say that what propaganda there is gets directed against atheism, complacent rationalism, occultism and superstition, all those shabby growths which the decline of Christian belief has fostered, and many, though perhaps not most, readers will sympathize here, too. My only real complaint is that this bias sometimes reveals the villain too early. We know at once that the prophet of a new sun cult is up to no good, and are not surprised that it is he who allows a blind girl to step to her death in an empty elevator shaft.

Like Gervase Fen, though on a more serious level, Brown is made for the situations he encounters and they for him. They embody his love of paradox and of turning things back to front, his gift for seeing what is too obvious for everyone else to notice, his eye for the mentally invisible man. Only Brown could have wandered into a house where the recently dead owner's diamonds lay in full view minus their settings, heaps of snuff were piled on shelves, candles littered the tables, and the name of God had been carefully cut out of the family Bible every single time it occurred. And when the owner is dug up and found to be minus his head, only Brown would have taken this as natural and inevitable, the final clue showing that no crime had been committed after all. (You will have to read "The Honor of Israel Gow" in *The Innocence of Father Brown* to find the answer.)

Rather too often, Brown runs into impersonations, twin brothers, secret passages, unlikely methods of murder: It would take a lot of good luck to succeed first try in dropping a noose round someone's neck from a dozen feet above him, and again to hit your man on the head with a hammer thrown from a church tower. But the good ideas are many and marvelous. The howling dog that gave away a murderer, the trail to an archcrook that began with somebody (guess who) swapping the contents of the sugar and salt containers in a restaurant, the man who seemed to have got into a garden without using the only entrance and the other man who got out of the same garden partly, but not completely—these are pretty standard occurrences in Father Brown's world. That world is vividly atmospheric, thanks to Chesterton's wonderful gift for depicting the effects of light on landscape, so that the stories glow as well as tease and mystify. They are works of art.

It is a goodish step from here to the old brownstone on West 35th Street where Nero Wolfe and Archie Goodwin chew the fat, eat their heads off, infuriate Inspector Cramer and incidentally catch crooks. The weakness of Stout's hugely readable stories is always the story. The idea of splitting the conventional detective into two—Wolfe to do the thinking, Archie the legwork—cuts both ways. It gives great scope for rounding out Wolfe's character, but it inevitably diminishes Archie in proportion. I find Archie faintly unsympathetic anyhow, a bit too effortlessly attractive to women, a bit too free with his fists, a bit too reminiscent of Sam Spade. Certainly, when he goes ferreting for Wolfe at Cramer's headquarters, or Lon Cohen's *Gazette* office, or wherever the crime may have taken place, the interest slackens. We want to be back with Wolfe. I can seldom be bothered with the details of the investigation, which usually proceeds by revelation and discovery rather than by actual deduction. What counts for most readers, I am sure, is the snappy dialog, Archie's equally snappy narrative style, his relations with Wolfe (he is always sympathetic here), and finally, massively, triumphantly, Wolfe himself.

Wolfe gets about as far as a human being can, much further than Sherlock Holmes, in his suspicion, fear, almost hatred of humanity. We all have such moods, and Wolfe is there to reassure us that these feelings are quite proper for an intelligent, learned, humane and humorous man. This is perhaps the secret of his attraction, for attractive he abundantly is. Along with this goes a marked formidable quality, such that one would, on meeting Wolfe in the flesh, feel grateful for his approval and daunted by his contempt. All really great detectives inspire this reaction, perhaps by acting as some version of a father figure. Brown does it to us, Dr. Fell does; even, granted the shift in general outlook since late-Victorian times, Holmes does. Any kind of real policeman does not, and anybody Mike Hammer took a liking to ought to feel a twinge of alarm.

Another part of Wolfe's appeal is his addiction to views and attitudes that seem both outdated and sensible, reactionary and right, the sort of thing you and I ought to think and feel, and probably would if we had Wolfe's leisure and obstinacy. Who has not wanted to insist on never going out, living to an unshakable routine, distrusting all machines more complicated than a wheelbarrow and having to be heavily pressured each time before getting into a car, allowing hardly anybody to use one's first name, keeping television out and reading all the time, reacting so little in conversation that an eighth-of-an-inch shake of the head becomes a frenzy of negation, using an inflexible formal courtesy such that proven murderers are still referred to as "Mr." and an 18th century style of speech that throws off stuff like "Afraid? I can dodge folly without backing into fear" and "Madam, I am neither a thaumaturge nor a dunce"? Wolfe is every man's Tory, a contemporary Dr. Johnson. The original Dr. Johnson was a moralist before everything else, and so at heart is Wolfe. This, I suppose, makes him even more of an antique.

Lastly, Dr. Gideon Fell. I must explain at once that, when writing under his pseudonym of Carter Dickson, John Dickson Carr uses a detective called Sir Henry Merrivale, or H.M., who according to me is an old bore. His adventures, however, are as fascinating as any of Fell's, and I should not want to put anybody off masterpieces like *The White Priory Murders*, *The Reader Is Warned* and *The Ten Teacups*. They are, of course, as are the best Carr novels, minor masterpieces. Perhaps no detective story can attain the pitch of literary excellence. Perhaps it can only offer ingenuity raised to the point of genius. In Carr-*cum*-Dickson it does, perhaps two dozen times in all, and this author is a first-rate artist. A neglected one, naturally, and likely to remain so while detective fiction remains undervalued, while most of those who should know better remain ignorant of the heights of craftsmanship and virtuosity it can reach. I will offer a small prize to any such person who can read the first chapter of Carr's *The Burning Court* and not in honesty have to go on. Neither Fell nor H.M. nor any great detective features here, only an adequate one. The book is a tour-de-force blending of detection and witchcraft: both ingredients genuine.

To return at length to Dr. Fell—it would have been useful in one way to come to him straight after Father Brown. The character of Fell has little to do with that of Brown, but a great deal, especially physically, with Chesterton himself. The huge girth, the bandit's mustache, the box-pleated cape and shovel hat, the enthusiasm for English pubs, beer and roast beef, all these are taken straight from that brilliant but so often unsatisfactory English writer who died 30 years ago. And more than this. Fell's world is that of Brown made more probable, the wilder flights of fancy brought under control, the holes in the plot conscientiously plastered over and made good. Like Brown, Fell constantly encounters the impossible murder, but Fell shows its possibility more convincingly. Most often, almost always, the victim is discovered in a locked room, last seen in good health, exits and entrances secured or watched or even guarded by responsible and provenly innocent outsiders. Carr boasts that he has devised over 80 different solutions to the locked-room puzzle, and in one of the novels Fell, a monologist with the best of them, delivers a fascinating lecture on the subject. This is *The Three Coffins*, to quote the inexcusable American retitling of the British edition *The Hollow Man*, which perfectly suggests the macabre menace of the story. That man must indeed have been hollow who, watched of course by a responsible and innocent witness, was seen to enter a room without other access in which, later, there is found the corpse of the room's occupant, but of course no hollow man. This is Chestertonian, or Brownian, though its explanation has a Carrian validity; and another novel, *The Crooked Hinge*, takes as the epigraph of its final section a quotation from a Father Brown story that begins: "There was one thing which Flambeau, with all his dexterity of disguise, could not cover, and that was his singular height." Fell is dealing with a chap who could have taught Flambeau a trick or two, and for once the chap gets away. Ingenuity deserves a prize now and again.

The light in Gideon Fell's study is burning low. He still works desultorily at his great chronicle of *The Drinking Customs of England from the Earliest Days*, still gives great rumbling sniffs and plies his red bandanna handkerchief. But without conviction. He makes rare and comparatively ineffectual public appearances now. His heyday came to an end somewhere about 1950, and there died with it the classical detective story, in which all the clues were scrupulously put before the reader, the kind of writing of which Fell's creator has been the greatest exponent.

Elsewhere the picture is the same. Recruitment to the ranks of potential great detectives has fallen to nothing. Real policemen are all the rage. Fell always got on well with them, had no hesitation about saving himself trouble by using their findings, but though they were smart and often nearly right, he was smarter and always right. He would view the activities of contemporary real policemen like Van der Valk with tolerance, even appreciation, but he would have little time for the character who has usurped his place in the sun: the secret agent, the international spy. I can hear him muttering under his bandit's mustache about the sad substitution of brawn for brain as the up-to-date hero's essential characteristic, of action for thought and glamor for decency. I would only go part of the way with him there. But I can sympathize.

PLAYBOY'S PARTY JOKES

While attending an engagement party given by his friends, the reformed player cast an eye over the assembled guests. "You know," he declared to his best man, "I've slept with every girl in this room except my sister and my fiancée."

"That's interesting," his friend responded dryly. "Between the two of us, we've had them all."

A couple had been married 50 years. The wife asked her husband what he wanted for their anniversary. He replied, "I'd like you to perform oral sex on me. In the 50 years we've been married, you've never given me a blow job."

She said, "It's just that I'm afraid you won't respect me afterward."

He replied, "Won't respect you afterward? We have been married for 50 years. Of course I'll respect you."

"Okay," she said. "Ill do it just this one time."

So she knelt down and gave him oral sex. An hour later the phone rang. The husband answered. "Here, cocksucker," he said. "It's for you."

PLAYBOY CLASSIC: Two women were bicycling along a cobblestone path through town. One woman said, "I've never come this way before,"

The other said, "It's the cobblestones."

After their wedding reception a newly married couple went to their hotel and asked for the honeymoon suite. "Do you have reservations?" the desk clerk asked.

"Only one," the groom replied. "She's not into anal sex."

A guy ran into an ex-girlfriend on the street and said, "You know, I was with another woman last night, but I was still thinking of you."

She said, "Why, because you miss me?"

He replied, "No, because it keeps me from coming too fast."

An elderly married couple scheduled their annual medical exams on the same day so they could travel together. After the examinations the doctor said to the elderly man, "You are in good health. Do you have any medical concerns you would like to ask me about?"

"In fact I do," the man said. "After I have sex with my wife the first time, I'm usually hot and sweaty. But after I have sex with her the second time, I'm cold and chilly."

After examining the elderly woman, the doctor said, "Everything appears to be fine. Do you have any medical concerns you would like to discuss with me?"

The lady replied that she had no questions or concerns. The doctor then said, "Your husband had an unusual concern. He said he is usually hot and sweaty after having sex with you the first time and then cold and chilly after the second time. Do you know why?"

"Oh, that crazy old son of a bitch!" she replied. "That's because the first time is usually in July and the second time is in December!"

An optimist is a man who looks forward to marriage. A pessimist is a married optimist.

Don't Pet the Donkey

commentary by CHRISTOPHER NAPOLITANO

They say the wilder the bachelor party, the better the marriage. Try telling that to your girlfriend. Will you learn something from having your forehead sandpapered smooth by the crotch of some minx in a G-string? Maybe, but you're sure to forget it by morning. As these tales from anonymous—and mostly untrustworthy—sources make clear, repeating the stories is your reward for surviving the parties intact. Naturally, all the names have been changed.

THAT THING CALLED LOVE: "Contrary to popular female opinion, the typical party doesn't necessarily involve sex. Once a friend's fiancée asked me, 'I just want to know one thing. Did they touch his thingie?' Happily for her, the answer was no. The girls were far more into each other. It was such a beautiful sight it left one guest in tears. 'I want a girl like that,' he sobbed. He was really messed up. 'I want a girl like that.' Her impact on him was so funny. We couldn't stop laughing."—Noel, 29, record promoter from San Francisco.
Cost: $150.
Emotional price: "A brief feeling of longing, but I washed it away at the bar."
Would you do it again? "Sure. You just have to be strong and not let their looks get to you."

A CAUTIONARY TALE ABOUT WHY YOU SHOULD MARRY A STRIPPER: "I like to say there's a difference between strippers who will and strippers who won't, and it's usually about 20 years. But what happens when a young one gets married? That's the story I'm going to live off of for the next 40 years. This guy I know was getting married—he's totally Joe Trader. Works on Wall Street, and he was marrying this sexy, sweet stripper. I wasn't surprised to see two strippers—friends of the bride's—at Joe's party. But, man, as soon as they got there they fucking kicked his chair

235

out from underneath him, knocked him to his back and took off all his clothes. Their clothes came off next. There was no seduction, no dancing. They just went at it. The fact that they were in a cold basement surrounded by 15 drunken, laughing friends made it hard for him to perform. That's when I realized this party wasn't about the groom.

"They were giving him head. They were trying to fuck him. It was just a shock. A live sex show erupted out of what was supposed to be a good-natured strip party. It soon became apparent that our friend could not consummate the act. So after 20 minutes these two girls got on a pool table—we were downstairs at a restaurant—and they started to perform on each other. Then some people at the party—I can assure you I was not one of them, I'll tell you right off the bat"—it's always the other guy—"some people started groping them. Then they started climbing up onto the pool table and kind of rolling through these two girls. There was a line of guys waiting to roll over and through them and writhe on the table with them for a few minutes. Like a breakdance circle. These girls were whacked out. They had a look of distant longing in their eyes. At a certain point a few guys stayed on the pool table for a long stretch. Then it became too bizarre to watch. That's when I hit my weirdness limit.

"Eventually these two girls and four guys ended up retiring to the bathroom for a 45-minute drug-and-sex orgy. I heard there were various double and triple penetrations happening. It was incredible. You walked out of there shocked. Guys were walking out unable to speak. Feeling dirty. You know how bachelor parties end drunk and happy? This one ended with everyone sobered by the experience. We walked out into a cold Manhattan street and got into cabs alone."—Ali, 27, software geek from San Francisco.

Cost: $150.

Emotional price: "It rattled me at the time, but now that I look back it's sort of excellent."

Would you do it again? "Nothing can shock me now."

BEST SUPPORTING FEMALE: "I've been a best man five times and I've planned five bachelor parties. The best one ever was for a guy who was my best and oldest friend. My favorite restaurant in the LA area is in Santa Monica. Not many people know that there are two private rooms above the main dining room. Brent's was the only bachelor party they ever had or will have. I got these amazing Cuban cigars. We had all this amazing booze. We had a big trade with the restaurant, so the food was, like, caviar, foie gras, lobster—the best of the best. It was the nines. Even with all the favors I cashed in, it cost me thousands of dollars. We had two poker tables set up—new chips, new cards. There was one caveat: Brent's friend Kristen insisted on attending. They'd known each other from college. So we played poker, we're well-fed and the entertainment arrives. The thing is, it's a bouncer and one girl. The other girl never shows. How are we going to have a lesbian show? I got one girl—that's not lesbo, that's masturbation. Anyway, we set up a circle. Music comes on, the girl starts doing a show—with lap dances all around. So. There's Kristen. When the stripper gets to Kristen, she starts undoing Kristen's blouse. Kristen doesn't do anything. Then she undoes her bra. Suddenly, she's topless in front of all these guys she's known for years. Being the trouper she is, she goes at it with the other girl. They are kissing each other, fondling and kissing each other's breasts. Kristen is a real-estate developer from Denver. This is not a bimbo. She turned to Brent and said, 'Is this what you want?' And she just went at it with this girl for a long time. The guys went nuts. Then the stripper turned to Brent. She stripped him to his underwear, covered him head to toe in whipped cream, licked it all off and blew him in front of everyone. We had our own bartender, so he's getting the busboys and chef and the owner—who didn't know this orgiastic stuff would happen. The owner sees Brent covered in whipped cream and come. There wasn't enough money in the world for this girl. Every guy got a serious lap dance—this is no Scores lap dance. This is dry hump. You could feel her pussy, her ass, her tits—she did anything. And Kristen was basically lounging around in nothing but her panties. These worldly LA guys—there was a well-known attorney and some other guys in their 40s and 50s—said to me, 'All these years we've gone to bachelor parties, this is the best ever.' I said you can't go wrong with lesbians, blow jobs, lap dances, poker, booze and cigars. When I threw my next bachelor party I called the manager to let me use the room again, but he said, 'Never, ever again. Not for you, not for anyone. Not for me.'"—Rich, 30, a Los Angeles cigar retailer.

Cost: "Must have cost me $3,500."

Emotional price: "It was a lift. A huge lift."

Would you do it again? "If I still had that kind of money, I would."

HIGHEST BODY COUNT: "These two girls did the strip thing. Then they did each other and it got dirtier and dirtier. It was at a house in the Hollywood Hills. They started doing guys in the bathroom and then they did the groom big-time. Somehow the bride found out. The party was a week before the wedding. Not only did she cancel the wedding, but one of the other guys at the party ended up getting a divorce over it. It was the bachelor party from hell. The sex show turned out to be so wild that guys started talking. They were just blabbing about it afterward: 'You won't believe what happened.' No one realized what was at stake."—Steve, 45, PR guy in Los Angeles.

Cost: "Can't remember."

Emotional price: "I don't want to remember."

Would you do it again? "Did it turn me off bachelor parties? No."

WHEN BAD THINGS GO GOOD: "A woman I knew who lived outside Boston had a horrible husband who had a friend who was going to get married. Though Michelle's marriage was falling apart, her husband insisted she hold a party for the bride and the girls while he held the bachelor party for his friend. The bride and her mom and family and friends show up at Michelle's house. They're critical. 'You don't have a dipper? What do you put your dip in?' Very unpleasant. They sit around and talk and the bride reveals she is more sexually accomplished than the groom. Things he couldn't or wouldn't do or had never done. Then the conversation turns to, 'I wish we knew where the guys were.' Michelle, who hates them all at this point, says, 'I know!' She gives them the address. She stays home to clean up. The procession of cars leaves. Minutes later, they return. Bride-to-be is crying. She needs help getting out of the car. Apparently they went to the place. There was noise coming out of the house. There was the smell of beer, loud music and it was dark. They walk in and *voilà!* On a table there's a hooker in an orange wig and the groom is fucking her as everyone else is clapping rhythmically! As the bride sees her sexually inexperienced groom fucking, their eyes meet and, *woosh!* The groom throws up. So the ladies packed it up and returned to Michelle's and the wedding took place the next day. If they hadn't pissed off Michelle, they would never have learned of the secret location. And if he hadn't thrown up, there probably wouldn't have been a wedding."—JB, 56, financier in New York.

Cost: "Free to me."

Emotional price: "Guilt all around."

Would you do it again? "The marriage ended in divorce after five years."

BEST OATER: "At the last party I attended, we went to the Russian baths and ended up in the back room of a Ukrainian restaurant in the East Village. The groom's buddy casually placed a camcorder on the table when the stripper arrived. We all thought it was hilarious when things got out of hand. She was a dominatrix. Put a saddle on the near-naked bachelor and rode him around the table, spanking him to go faster. She had him make noises like a donkey. He was crocked and didn't realize he was being taped. We watched the tape without him the next day and it was weird. Maybe a little eerie and disturbing, too. We all felt like shit for doing that to him. That was the first time I felt sorry for Pam Anderson and Tommy Lee."—Ed, 29, New York musician.

Cost: $50.

Emotional price: "Mild."

Would you do it again? "Never bring a camera. Never."

MOST SICKENING CASE OF PDA: "We were barhopping for a bachelor party and we came across some girls who were having a bachelorette party. They had the bride-to-be covered in candy or Life Savers or something—for a dollar you could bite one off with your teeth. So my friend Greg walks over with 100 bucks and says, 'Here. Now you have to hang with us.' The numbers were even and we had a great time—eventually pairing off. The bride and groom were like prom king and queen. I swear, about five of my friends hooked up that night."—Kevin, 27, bartender from New Jersey.

Cost: "That 100 bucks was worth it,"

Emotional price: "I got a phone number and I called the next day."

Would you do it again? "Yes. Whenever people complain about how hard it is to meet people, I think of that night."

MOST SICKENING CASE OF BEER: "Cards and beer, beer and cards. We made a pact we would rent a hotel room and spend 24 hours in it playing cards and drinking beer. We went through every fart joke known to man, with sound effects. Finally, we got so crazy—I mean the stupidest stuff was making us laugh, there was a flood in the bathroom—we started calling people to show up and bring us stuff. By the end we had a potted plant in there, these inflatable toys, even a dog. And this 80-year-old guy showed up. Cool guy. Heard us down the hall and decided, you know, 'I can't beat you so I have to join you.'"—Todd, 28, pool installer from Florida.

Cost: "I actually made money. Plus, the bottle returns totaled something like $47."

Emotional price: "The dog wasn't ours, so we felt bad when we returned it."

Would you do it again? "No way. Twenty-four hours is definitely a serious commitment."

DON'T PET THE DONKEY

WORST STORY TO READ IF YOU'RE THINKING OF INVITING YOUR FATHER-IN-LAW: "Seventeen years ago, when I was in college, I watched a guy from my summer job get blown while his best friend banged the woman from behind. And this was my first bachelor party. My boss, Jimmy, was an ex-motorcycle repairman, and the party crowd was full of beer-guzzling bikers. I was crocked by the time the entertainment arrived—a wonderful Asian chick who was accompanied by a man-mountain from the Hell's Angels. First, she did a 15-minute, tendon-popping floor show. I was in love. Until, for the finale, she sat Jimmy in a chair and ministered to him while the lucky groom brought up the rear. The real crazy thing was that the bride's father was there—and he was hooting and hollering with the rest of the guys. Whoa."—Bobby, 36, graphic designer in New York.

Cost: "I don't remember paying anything. I think Jimmy footed the bill. It might also have been the night his wraparound porch collapsed under everybody's weight, but I'm really not sure. If it was, then the party was more expensive than he planned."

Emotional cost: "None. Not for me, not for the groom. Not for the bride's dad, either, apparently."

Would you do it again? "Like I said, I didn't do anything."

BEST STORY TO READ IF YOU'RE THINKING OF INVITING YOUR FATHER-IN-LAW: "One guy I knew invited everyone, including the men from the family of the bride. During the course of this drunken evening, secrets were exchanged between father and groom—without the protective filter of the bride. The prospective groom was no Phi Beta Kappa. I think he was trying to explain how much he loved this guy's daughter because she knew how to do this and that sexually. It was probably the best party. It erupted into a fistfight between the father of the bride and the groom. The wedding was called off. There are two rules to follow about bachelor parties. One is: Don't pet the donkey. The other is: Never invite your father-in-law. Never! I went to another party after which a guy went home and told his girlfriend what the stripper had done to the groom. That wedding was canceled also."—Paul, 31, Chicago fireman.

Cost: "A wicked hangover."

Emotional price: "A steep price paid by the ex-groom."

Would you do it again? "I love that sort of thing."

WHY STUPID TO US IS EVIL TO HER: "I once found myself in the middle of my living room stuck between my friends Mark and Jennifer. Thanks to a gossipy girlfriend, Jennifer had caught sour wind of a bachelor

240

party that Mark had attended. Jennifer was crying and Mark was wilting under her hydraulic pressure. He had taken part in a stupid stripper stunt. Each guy at the party took turns lying on his back. The stripper then straddled his face, her third eye winking at him from a few inches up, and proceeded to pour beer onto her pussy and into his mouth. 'And you're going to be the father of my child?' Jennifer sobbed (did I mention that she was pregnant?). 'Phil would never do anything like that.' My omniscient wife turned to look at me, half-smiling. I just shrugged. I was more concerned with what the strippers called that drink in private. Pussy punch? Malt lick-her? Sour mash? A head of beer? If she didn't shave, then it would be billy goat brew. If she did, why, then it would be a mess."—Phil, 32, Chicago salesman.

Cost: "I think he spent $75."

Emotional price: "Heavy. Major."

Would he do it again? "Yeah. I got the sense he wasn't caving in because he didn't want to promise to never do it again."

LONGEST RUN OFF-BROADWAY: "In my hometown, you could go to a bachelor party every weekend. You didn't have to know the groom or anybody else. You could just buy a ticket from Ralph or Teddy or Jimmy. 'You know—the guy who's friends with Kenny. The guy who once fixed Stephanie's Camaro? He used to go out with Angie? His brother Vinny Goombatz is getting married. $30.' You show up at the basement of a family-style Italian restaurant and it's all you can eat and drink, with entertainment. One night a stripper, as they sometimes did, started giving $20 blow jobs in the bathroom. When she took the occasional cigarette break she sat next to my friend John. He could charm the shorts off a female golfer. So he was honored to accept her offer of a free fuck at the end of the evening. It was something he bragged about the next day until someone asked 'Did you use a condom?' John's face turned green. Thankfully, his dick never did. At least he didn't go down on her. I think."—Pete, 31, actor from LA.

Cost: "A hangover."

Emotional price: "He was nervous until he got tested."

Would you do it again? "Nah, those buy-a-ticket parties get boring."

NASTIEST SCRUM: "I'm a former semipro rugby player. I was living with my wife in a duplex in Louisville, Kentucky. A guy from another rugby team lived upstairs. He was throwing a bachelor party for his brother and he invited me. I couldn't go because it was on a Wednesday night. Well, at 2:30 in the morning the fucking music is blaring and I can't go to sleep. My wife says, 'You have to go upstairs and tell them to knock it off.' Shit. I trudge up the back stairs, walk through the open kitchen door and there are like eight guys, you know, in a circle. They all have their dicks out and this girl is sucking one off and getting it from behind from another. She's taking turns blowing everybody. I go, 'Oh, Jesus Christ.' Caleb looks at me and goes 'You want a piece of this?' I go, 'No man, I gotta get up early in the morning. I'll take a rain check.' He goes, 'The music's kind of loud, isn't it?' I go, 'Yeah. If you could just turn it down a bit.' All I remember is the girl was like a clock, doing one guy then rotating to the next. They're all sitting there with cherubic smiles on their faces. You know, it's a professional rugby team. What can I say? They share too much. No intimacy issues there. So I went back downstairs and tried to get to sleep. My wife said, 'What's going on up there?' And I said, 'Honey, you don't want to know.' Some things are just better left unsaid."—Bill, 33, TV production guy from Washington, D.C.

Cost: "Free, obviously."

Emotional price: "The loss of my innocence" [*laughs*].

Would you do it again? "I don't need to see that again."

BEST DUMB STUNT: "Two Tons of Fun was a woman who performed at a party in central Connecticut. This lady was big—real big. About 300-plus pounds. She stood behind me and wrapped her tits around my head. I couldn't see or breathe. She even did it to my friend Joe, who has a monster noggin. For her finale, she picked up the groom like an old-fashioned wrestler, put him on her shoulders and twirled him around. Set him down just in time for him to heave in the bathroom. I ended up passing out at my parents' house after going to a strip club. This cutie had pulled my glasses off my head and run them up and down—once in each direction—in her snatch. Popped them back on my head. I remember hearing everyone roaring. I couldn't see them laugh, though, because the lenses were fogged up. Next thing I know, my father is shaking me awake the next morning at six A.M. I was lying on my back in the den, white snow blaring on the TV, my belt undone and my hand wedged down my pants. He was going ballistic—I had fallen asleep with my mouth open and I stunk pretty bad. It wasn't until my dog walked over and stuck her tongue down to my tonsils that I could moisten my mouth enough to croak a response. I had to leave pronto if I wanted to make the wedding that morning. Did I mention that I had to pick up my boss and her son, who lived an hour away? My parents wanted to punish me for being in such crappy shape. They didn't want me to use their car, so I shocked them by dialing up cab service (remember, this is Connecticut) to take me to an Avis. My boss looked oddly at the Grand Am ('I thought your family drove Camrys') but didn't notice it was a rental. I was 24. I felt pretty satisfied with the whole thing until the church ceremony, when my boss's son asked me to explain a portion of the ceremony. I leaned over and told him. 'Man,' he said, loud enough to turn heads, 'your breath stinks!'"—Tom, 26, dot-com dude, Connecticut.

Cost: "Dunno. Money flew out of my pocket."

Emotional price: "Neutral. Tense moments with the parents, but it was a turning point."

Would you do it again? "I never do anything the day after a party like that."

SCARIEST MOMENT: "To be sure, guys are some fucked monkeys. Sometimes it's best not to know what makes your buddy tick. In the mustier recesses of my mind, there is a scene from a party my brother took me to. There wasn't much but drinking going on. On a TV in the corner of one room porn videos were playing in an endless loop. The novelty wore off early for the groom. Finally, most guys drifted away from the set until only one guy was left. There was talk of going to a strip club. In one of those odd, movie-style moments, the conversation ebbed just in time for the man in front of the tube—lost in his own world and forgotten in ours—to suddenly shout at the screen, 'Yeah, fuck her, fuck her, yeah. *Punch her in the cunt!*' Talk about a showstopper. Nobody said anything for a good 30 seconds."—Carl, 34, banker in Boston.

Cost: $30.

Emotional price: "The guy never lived it down."

Would you do it again? "Sure."

THE INSIDE WORD ON MEN'S CLUBS—AND WHY YOU WANT TO JOIN ONE: "Since I'm the manager at a men's club, I keep a card on file for the guys who want much more than the standard strip show. These two girls, Coco and Electra, are absolutely unbelievable. We're talking butt beads. One girl will stick them all the way up the other girl's butt and then have a guy pull them out for her with his mouth. They both have strap-ons, and they do each other in the pussy and the ass. I mean, it's incredible. Or they'll put a lollipop in the groom's mouth and they will pull it out with their vagina lips. It's just 45 minutes of hardcore lesbianism, dildos, everything. I've called them in three times for people who want to get really, really raunchy. Coco is Hispanic. Electra is absolutely gorgeous. She's the one who I guess you'd say fits the submissive role. She takes most of the stuff in her ass and all that other good stuff. Since we're a private club I can close it off. Nobody gets hurt or gets seen, and I don't say anything. They pay me to keep my mouth shut. Usually it starts at 10 or 11 o'clock. The groom will pass out, they'll just prop him up in a chair, you know, take his clothes off. You know, it's not about the groom. We have side rooms, too. Stuff happens behind closed doors, so I don't care. Just be sure that you're out of here when I tell you to go. Many times the party will pay for the girls to do stuff to us. Put some whipped cream on the tits and give one to the bartender or manager. Some of them have offered to pay for blow jobs and whatever, but, unfortunately, I'm wearing the world's smallest handcuff on my finger."—Duffy, 46, private club director in Philadelphia.

Cost: "I get paid to watch this stuff."

Emotional price: "Not for nothing, but you get sort of jaded after a while."

Would you do it again? "All in all, I get good reactions. I haven't heard any complaints."

"The bad news is, I was unable to remove the vibrator. The good news is, I was able to change the batteries."

Carny

memoir by HARRY CREWS

I woke up screaming and kicking, catching the ride boy in the ribs with the toe of my boot (which I had not bothered to take off), and when the toe of the boot struck him just below the armpit, he screamed, too, and that caused the lot lady he was rolled in the blanket with to scream—and there the three of us were, thrashing about in my Dodge van, driven stark raving mad on a crash from Biphetamine 20s (a wonderfully deadly little capsule that, taken in sufficient quantities, will make you bigger than anybody you know for at least 96 hours running) and driven mad, too, by the screaming siren that woke us up to start with. It was the middle of the night—or, more accurately, the middle of the morning, about four A.M.—and the electronic system set to catch burglars and tire thieves had tripped, but I—addled and nine tenths stunned from too long on the road with a gambler, chasing carnivals across half a dozen states—I didn't know it was my siren or that I was in my van or who I was with or why I was where I was.

But as soon as I opened the side door and saw the black Ferris wheel and the tents standing outlined against the sky, I calmed down enough to get the keys out of my jacket. I couldn't find the right key to turn off the alarm, though, and all the while the siren was screaming and the ride boy, who was about 50 years old, had come out of the van naked from the waist down with his lot lady, who looked like she might have been 15, hanging on his back.

"What the hell?" the ride boy kept shouting at me. "What the hell?"

"Alarm!" I kept shouting back. "Alarm." It was all I could get my mouth to say as I fought with the keys.

Lights were coming on in trailers all around us and out of the corner of my eye I saw the Fat Lady from the ten-in-one show standing beside the little wheeled box that her manager used to haul her from carnival to carnival behind his old Studebaker. She was so big that her back was

246

at least a foot deep in fat. By the time I got the key in the switch and turned the alarm off, the Midget had appeared, along with several men who had apparently been gambling in the G-top. Unfortunately, the sheriff's deputy, red-faced and pissed off, had arrived, too. He pushed his flat-brimmed hat back on his head and looked at the van and then at the freaks from the ten-in-one show and then at me.

"You want to take you driver's license out of you billfold and show it to me?" he said.

"My what?" I said.

"You want to get on back in there and put you britches on?" he said to the ride boy. The ride boy didn't move, but the lot lady, who was a local and in some danger, maybe, of being recognized by the cop, turned and got into the van.

He had a flashlight on my license now and without looking up, he said, "You want to tell me how come you got that sireen?"

"Look," I said, pointing. "There's a goddamn air jack." The sight of that jack slipped under the front end of my van made me mad enough to eat a rock.

But the deputy sheriff refused to look. He said, "Only you fire, law-enforcement and you rescue vehicles allowed to have a sireen."

The carny people had closed in around us now. The cop flashed his light once at them, but when the light fell upon the illustrated face of the Tattooed Man, he looked immediately back at the license.

"You want to——"

But I cut him off and said that two months earlier some malevolent son of a bitch had jacked up my van and taken the wheels. I'd come out of the house one morning and found it up on concrete blocks. So I had the doors and hood wired and had a mercury tilt switch rigged to the chassis. If anyone tried to jack it up, a siren went off. While I talked about the tilt switch and the rigged hood and doors, his face drew together on itself. He had never heard of such a thing and it obviously upset him.

"You want to come on down to the station with me?" he said.

"But what for?" I was getting a little hysterical now. "What about the jack? What about the fucking jack?"

He glanced briefly at Big Bertha where she loomed enormous in the slanting light from a trailer. "You want to watch you language in front of——"

"Hello, Jackson."

We all turned and there was Charlie Luck, sometimes called Chuck and sometimes Luck and sometimes Chuckaluck and sometimes many other things.

"This man here's got a sireen, Charlie. I think it might be illegal."

Charlie bit his lip and shook his head in disgust. "Has he still got that? I told you, boy, to git rid of that goddamn siren." He had, of course, told me no such thing.

Charlie was beautiful in a brown suit and soft brown cap and square-toed brown shoes. There was no flash to him at all. Everything he was wearing was very muted and very expensive. He came over and put his arm on the cop's shoulder. "Officer Jackson," he said in just about the most pleasant voice you've ever heard, "could I talk to you over here for a moment?"

They turned away from us and immediately Big Bertha was struggling up the steps into her little wheeled box. The ride boy got back into the van with his lot lady, mooning us all as he went. The trouble was over. Everybody knew everything was fine, now that Charlie Luck was here. I stood watching, admiring the earnest, head-to-head talk he was having with Officer Jackson, who was nodding now, agreeing for all he was worth with whatever Charlie Luck was saying.

My feeling for Charlie Luck went far beyond admiration. I loved him. He was a hero. Some people have only one or two heroes; I have hundreds. Sometimes I meet six or seven heroes in a single day. Charlie Luck was a great man who just happened to be a gambler, in the same way that Bear Bryant is a great man who just happens to be a football coach. Bryant could have stumbled into a brokerage house when he was 20 and owned Wall Street by now. Instead, he happened into football. Same with Charlie Luck. Somebody showed him a game when he was 16 and he never got over it. He became perfect of his kind. The perfect carny. The perfect hustler.

Charlie Luck has never registered for the draft. He's never paid any income tax. Officially, he does not exist. Or, said another way, he exists in so many different forms, with so many different faces, that there is no way to contain him. He knows a place in Mississippi where he can mail away for an automobile tag that is not registered. If somebody takes his number, it can't be traced. And even if it could be traced, it would be traced to an alias.

To my knowledge, Charlie Luck has six identities, complete with phony Social Security cards and driver's licenses, even passports. He has six and he's contemplating more. He's very imaginative with his life. With his past. Sometimes he's from Texas. Other days, from Maine. I sometimes wonder if he knows where he's from or who he is. He's probably forgotten.

The sheriff's deputy turned and, without looking at me once, walked to his car. Charlie Luck came over to where I was. He watched me for a moment, a little half-smile showing broken teeth.

"A siren?" he said. "Well, what do you know about that? I heard the thing over in the G-top. Thought it was a fire truck. Thought maybe something was burning up."

"What did you say to the cop?"

He shrugged. "One thing and another. I told him I'd shut you down, take your siren away."

"You wouldn't do that."

"Of course not." He pointed to the open door, where the ride boy was locked with the lot lady. His mouth suddenly looked like he tasted something rotten. "I told you about letting those things use your van."

"She came up and he didn't have anyplace. I couldn't think of a way to turn him down."

"You better start finding a way or you'll queer everything." He started to walk away but then stopped. "Hang on to that jack. We'll send it into town sometime and sell it."

I got back into the van and listened to the snores of the ride boy and the cotton-candy wind-breakings of the lot lady. Charlie Luck was disappointed in me for letting the ride boy sleep in my van, because the workers, the guys who up and down the rides and operate them, are at the very bottom of a well-defined carny social structure. A lot lady is a carnival groupie. She is given to indiscriminately balling the greasy wired men and boys who spend their lives half-buried in machinery. It was definitely uncool of me to associate with them. And inasmuch as I was traveling as Charlie Luck's brother it was even worse.

Charlie had been reluctant—very reluctant—to let me in with him to start with. But he owed me. Back in November, I had managed to persuade a cowboy down in a place near Yeehaw Junction, Florida, which is great cattle country and where they have one of the last great cowboy bars, not to clean out one of Charlie Luck's ears with the heel of his boot. Charlie had been grateful ever since. That day in Florida, he bought me a beer after the cowboy left and we went to a back booth, where he watched me drink it and I watched him bleed.

"Name's Floyd Titler," he said. "Friends—and you definitely a friend—friends call me Short Arm."

"Harry Crews is mine." We shook hands across the table.

"Son of a bitch nearly killed me," he said, dabbing at an eye that was rapidly closing with a handkerchief he'd just soaked in a draft.

"I never saw anybody do that," I said, pointing to the handkerchief.

"You just have to be careful none of the alcohol gets in your eyes. Otherwise it's great for the swelling."

I finally got around to asking what he was doing in Florida, because nobody is *from* Florida, and he said he wintered down there and worked games in a carnival up North in the summer.

"You work hanky-panks or alibis or flats?" I said.

He stopped with the handkerchief. "You with it?" he said.

"A sort of first-of-May," I said. "I ran with a carnival a little about 20 years ago."

To a carny, you are said to be "with it" if you have been on the road with a carnival for years and run your particular hustle well enough to be successful. They call anyone who's been with a carnival for only a short time a first-of-May. I wanted to talk to him about his game. He didn't want to talk. Not about that. But it was easy enough to find out that he ran a flat joint, also called flat store or sometimes a grind store or simply a flat.

"I've seen most of them," I said.

"Good," he said. "That's good." He went back to working on his eye.

The more I talked with him, the more I wanted to get back with a carnival. I thought if I did it right, I might get him to let me travel with him some the following summer. But I made the mistake of telling him I was a writer. I suppose I would have had to tell him sooner or later, anyway.

"That'd burn down my proposition," he said.

Nobody has a job in a carnival; he has a proposition.

"I've never blown anybody's cover. Never."

"It'd be dull, anyway," he said.

"No such thing as a dull subject. Only dull writers. Think about it, will you?"

"I'll think about it."

I figured I might as well remind him he owed me. That's the way I am. "You could still be over there on the floor with that cowboy walking around on your face."

It took a little doing, but he finally let me go with him for a while. I particularly wanted to see the gamblers one more time on the circuit and I knew I had to do it soon or they would be gone forever. Twenty years ago, practically every carnival had flat stores. But the flats are not welcome in very many carnivals today. Of the more than 800 carnivals that work this country, probably fewer than 50 still have flat joints. Ten years from now, I don't believe there will be any at all.

They are condemned because of the heat they generate. If a flat is allowed, as the carnies say, to work strong, there will be fistfights, stabbings and maybe even a shooting or two in a season, all direct results of the flat-store operation. Every carnival has a patch, who does just what the word says. He patches up things. He is the fixer, making right whatever beefs come down. Generally, flats keep the patch very busy.

Perhaps unique in the history of carnivals, Charlie Luck—a flattie himself—was also the patch. He was able to operate as the patch only because he usually did not actively run a joint. Rather, he had two agents who worked for him in flat stores he independently booked with the owner of the carnival. So far, I'd traveled 600 miles with him and I'd seen no real violence in his flats—some very pissed-off people but no violence. And now, this was to be the last weekend before I went back to Florida. We'd just made a circus jump—tearing down and moving and setting up in less than a single day. It took me a long time to get back to sleep, because the ride boy had dropped another capsule, strapped on the lot lady and was noisily working out at the other end of the van.

They did, however, finally rock me to sleep and I didn't wake up until late afternoon. The carnival Charlie Luck was with worked nothing but still dates, which is to say it never joined any fairs where they have contests for the best bull or the best cooking or the biggest pumpkin. Fair dates work all day. Still dates never have much business until late afternoon and night. I changed my clothes in the van and went out onto the midway.

The music on the Ferris wheel and at the Octopus had already cranked up. The smell of popcorn and cotton candy and caramel apples was heavy on the air. A few marks from the town had showed up with their kids. Several fat, clucking mothers were herding a group of retarded children down the midway like so many ducks. I didn't know where Charlie was. He had a trailer, but he usually slept in a motel. I walked over to get a corn dog and while I was waiting for it, I listened to two ride boys, both of them in their early 20s, talk about shooting up. They were as dirty as they could get and as they talked, their teeth showed broken and yellow in their mouths. All the workers on carnivals have European teeth. Anybody with all his teeth is suspect. Several locals were standing about eating corn dogs, but the two ride boys went right ahead discussing needles and the downers they had melted and shot up. They were speaking Carny, a language I can speak imperfectly if I do it very slowly. When I hear it spoken rapidly, I can understand it just well enough to know what the subject of discussion is without knowing exactly what is being said.

The marks stared at the two boys babbling on in this strange language full of Zs and Ss. God knows what the marks thought they were speaking. In Carny, the word beer becomes bee-a-zeer and the sentence Beer is good becomes Bee-a-zeer ee-a-zay gee-a-zood. It is not too difficult as long as you are speaking in monosyllables. But when you use a polysyllabic word, each syllable becomes a kind of word in itself. The word mention would be spoken mee-a-zen shee-a-zun.

It is a language unique to carnivals, with no roots anywhere else, so far as I know. And it does what it is supposed to do very effectively by creating a barrier between carnies and outsiders. Above everything else, the carny world is a self-contained society with its own social order and its own taboos and morality. At the heart of that morality is the imperative against telling outsiders the secrets of the carnival. Actually, it goes beyond that. There is an imperative against telling outsiders the truth about anything. That was what made being there with Charlie Luck as risky as it was. Either one of us could have been severely spoken to if what we were doing had got out.

I ate my corn dog as I walked down past the Octopus and the Zipper and the Sky Wheel and past the House of Mirrors. I was on my way for a quick look at the ten-in-one, which I had seen every day I'd traveled with Charlie Luck. Ten-in-one is the carny name for a freak show, possibly because there are often ten attractions under one tent. This was a good one but not a great one.

I was especially fond of the Fat Lady and her friends there under the tent. I think I know why, and I know I know when I started loving freaks.

Almost 20 years ago, when I had just gotten out of the Marine Corps, I woke up one day in an Airstream trailer in Atlanta, Georgia. The trailer was owned by a man and his wife. They were freaks. I was a caller for the show. My call was not particularly good, but it was good enough to get the job and to keep it. And that was all it was to me, a job, something to do. The second week I had the job, I was able to rent a place to sleep in the Airstream from the freak man and his freak wife. I woke up that morning in Atlanta looking at both of them where they stood at the other end of the trailer in the kitchen. They stood perfectly still in the dim, yellow light, their backs to each other. I could not see their faces, but I was close enough to hear them clearly when they spoke.

"What's for supper, darling?" he said.

"Franks and beans, with a nice little salad," she said.

"I'll try to be in early," he said.

And then they turned to each other under the yellow light. The lady had a beard not quite as thick as my own but three inches long and very black. The man's face had a harelip. His face, not his mouth. His face was divided so that the top of his nose forked. His eyes were positioned almost on the sides of his head and in the middle was a third eye that was not really an eye at all but a kind of false lid over a round indentation that saw nothing. It was enough, though, to make you taste bile in your throat and cause a cold fear to start in your heart.

They kissed. Their lips brushed briefly and I heard them murmur to each other and he was gone through the door. And I, lying at the back of the trailer, was never the same again.

I have never stopped remembering that, as wondrous and special as those two people were, they were only talking about and looking forward to and needing precisely what all of the rest of us talk about and look forward to and need. He might have been any husband going to any job anywhere. He just happened to have that divided face. That is not a very startling revelation, I know, but it is one most of us resist because we have that word *normal* and we can say we are normal because a psychological, sexual or even spiritual abnormality can—with a little luck—be safely hidden from the rest of the world. But if you are less than three feet tall, you have to deal with that fact every second of every day of your life. And everyone witnesses your effort. You go into a bar and you can't get up onto a stool. You whistle down a taxi and you can't open the door. If you're a lady with a beard, every face you meet is a mirror to give you back the disgust and horror and unreasonableness of your predicament. No matter which corner you turn on which street in which city of the world, you can expect to meet that mirror.

And I suppose I have never been able to forgive myself the grotesqueries and aberrations I am able to hide with such impunity in my own life.

Inside the tent, the Fat Lady was already up on her platform, ready for the day's business. She had a pasteboard box under her chair. The box was filled with cinnamon buns that her manager bought for her. She could get through about ten pounds of cinnamon buns a day. Her manager said he'd owned her—that was his phrase, owned her—for three years and in that time he had never seen her eat any meat. She stuck, he said, pretty much to pastries.

"How is it today, Bertha?"

CARNY

She nodded to me, put the last of a cinnamon bun into her mouth and reached for another one. Her little eyes deep in her face were very bright and quick as a bird's.

"You seen Charlie Luck?" I said. I wasn't really looking for him. I just wanted to talk a little to Bertha.

"He was here with one-eyed Petey," she said. "You want one of these?"

"Thanks, but I just had a corn dog."

"Luck's probably back in the G-top, cutting up jackpots."

"Probably," I said.

Cutting up jackpots is what carnies call it when they get together and tell one another about their experiences, mostly lies. The Tattooed Man came in with the Midget and the Midget's mother. The Midget's mother was nearly as tall as I was and very thin. She always looked inexpressibly sad. During the show, she wandered among the marks, selling postcards with a picture of her tiny son on them for a quarter apiece. The Tattooed Man had intricate designs in his ears. Little flowers grew on his nose and disappeared right up his nostrils. He was a miracle of color.

"I surely do admire your illustrations," I said.

"How come I got 'm," he said. He was from Mississippi and had a good grit voice.

"How many dollars' worth you reckon you got?"

"Wouldn't start to know. For years all I'd do was put ever nickel I could lay hand to for pictures."

He had eyelashes and an eyelid tattooed around his asshole. It looked just like a kind of bloodshot eye and he could make it wink. For $2 over and above the regular price of admission to the ten-in-one show, you could go behind a little curtain and he'd do it for you. Carnies have nothing but a deep, abiding contempt for marks and what they think of as the straight world, and nowhere is that contempt more vividly expressed than in the Tattooed Man's response when I asked him why he had the eye put in there.

"Making them bastards pay $2 to look up my asshole gives me more real pleasure than anything else I've ever done."

Charlie Luck came in looking for me and handed me $5. "I sent the jack into town. That's your half."

"Charlie, that was a $50 jack."

"The guy took it said he got $10."

"And you believed him?"

He took another $5 out of his pocket and handed it to me. "What the

254

hell, take it all. He was probably lying and, besides, it was your van. You oughtta have it all."

Charlie dearly loved a hustle, any hustle, on anybody. "Come on out here; I want to see you a minute."

As we were leaving, Bertha called around a mouthful of cinnamon bun, "That's a wonderful siren; I liked it a lot."

"Thank you. Bertha," I said. "That's sweet of you to say."

Out on the midway, Charlie Luck said, "You thought any more about what I asked you?"

"Charlie," I said, "I told you already."

"Look what I'm doing for you and you can't even do this little thing for me."

"It's not a little thing. I'm liable to get my head handed to me."

"You not working the show, you just traveling with me. You don't know anybody on this show. It'll be all right. Nobody's going to mind."

"You don't know that."

"I'm telling you I do know that. It'll be all right. You're leaving to-morrow, anyway. And I gotta know. I gotta have a firsthand, detailed report."

"Report, for Christ's sake!"

"I gotta know."

Charlie Luck's problem was this. He was nailing this lady named Rose who worked in the girlie show. Like the Tattooed Man, Rose had a specialty act that the marks could see by paying extra. Rose also had a husband. A large, mean, greasy husband who worked on the Ferris wheel. Charlie Luck wanted to know what she did in her specialty act. She wouldn't tell him. He couldn't go see for himself, because one of the strongest taboos in the carnival world is against carnies' going to the girlie show. Most of the girls have carnies for husbands and the feeling is that it is all right to show your wife to the marks but fundamentally wrong to show her to another carny, one of your own world.

"Hey, come in here and let me get my fortune told," I said.

We were passing a gypsy fortuneteller and I was reminded of the gypsies and their wagons passing through Georgia when I was a boy. But mostly I was just trying to get Charlie Luck to stop thinking about Rose and her specialty act.

"You let that raghead touch your hand and you never come on to my game again."

"I just wanted my fortune——"

"Ragheads can't tell time, much less fortunes."

CARNY

Carnies are not the most liberal people in the world. A few blacks are tolerated as laborers, and maybe an occasional gypsy to run a mitt camp, or fortune-telling booth, but not too long ago, it wasn't unusual to see advertisements in *Amusement Business*, the weekly newspaper devoted in part to carnivals, that said plainly NO RAGHEADS.

"Look," said Charlie Luck. "You think you seen my proposition. But you haven't seen me take any real money off anybody. Go bring this thing back for me and I'll run the game tonight. I'll run it strong."

"You don't have to run it strong," I said.

"I will, though, if you'll do this thing."

Charlie got bent bad over women. I found out later that the cowboy was on him in the bar in Yeehaw Junction over a woman, although I never found out precisely what it was about. But Charlie was, to use the kindest word, kinky when it came to ladies. Everybody I talked to said the same thing about him. I don't know why this was true, or how long it had been true of him, and I didn't try to find out. It wasn't any of my business, unless he wanted to tell me, and he didn't seem to. The girlie show had only joined us at the date preceding the circus jump. I was with Charlie Luck the first time he saw Rose in the G-top. He had known her now a total of four days, but he reminded me of the way I'd been when I fell totally and deeply in love the first time, at the age of 13. He'd honed for Rose from the first second he saw her and had managed to nail her two hours later in my van. He'd asked me for the van because he was afraid to take her to his trailer.

She came out of the van first and left. Then he came out—face radiant under his soft brown cap—and kept saying to me, "Did you see her? Did you?"

"I saw her, Charlie."

"Was she beautiful? God, I practically almost never seen anything like her in the world."

"Right," I said.

She looked about 48 years old, thick in thigh and hip, but had slender, almost skinny calves. The left calf was badly varicosed. Her face was a buttery mask of make-up. I couldn't figure what the hell she had done in there to him to string him out so bad. When I finally got into the van to drive to town, it smelled as though most of the salmon of the world had been slowly tortured to death all over my red-and-black carpeting.

"All right," I said finally, as we walked down the midway. "I'll catch Rose's bit for you, if you want me to. But I want you to remember one thing. Afterward, I don't want any conversation about it. You know, they used to cut off the heads of the guys who brought bad news to the king."

"Now, what the hell's that supposed to mean?"

"Nothing," I said. "It means nothing."

"I'll catch you after the eight-o'clock show." he said. "I gotta go settle a beef about a 50-cent piece of slum. The shit I put up with."

Slum is what carnies call the cheap merchandise they give out in the little booths that line the midway. For that reason, hanky-panks and alibis are also called slum joints. Hanky-panks are simple games of skill such as throwing darts at balloons. Alibis are games in which the agent is continually making alibis about why you did not win. Also, alibis—unlike hanky-panks—are liable to be gaffed, or rigged, and they are also liable to have a stick who is said to work the gaff. A stick is a guy who pretends to be a mark and by his presence induces the towns-people to play.

I strolled down the midway and watched it all come down. A stick who was working the gaff at a game called six cat was winning tons of slum. Six cat is an alibi in which the object is to knock down two cats at once with a ball. The stick quit playing as soon as he had attracted half a dozen marks. The agent was singing his song, alibiing his ass off:

"Hey, woweee! Look at that! That was just a little too high! A hair! No more 'n a hair an' you woulda won! Too much left. Bring it down, bring it down and win it for the lady."

I watched the mark finally get thrown a piece of plush, in this case a small, slightly soiled cloth giraffe. The poor bastard had paid only $12 for something he could have bought for $2.25 out in the city. The six cat was gaffed, or fixed, and the agent had done what's called cooling the mark by rewarding him with a prize after he had taken as much money as he thought he could get away with.

Eighty-five million people or thereabouts go to carnivals every year in this country and I do not want to leave the impression that all of them are cheated. Most of them are not. But the particular carnival Charlie Luck was running with is called a rag bag and it means that every-thing is pretty run-down, greasy and suspect. The man who books the dates and organizes the lot in such an operation will allow anything to come down he thinks the locals will stand for. Few people realize that one person or family almost never owns a carnival. One person will put together a tour—a combination of dates in specific locations—and then invite independent concessionaires to join him. If you look in the publication I mentioned earlier, *Amusement Business*, a sweet little paper you can subscribe to for $20 year, you will find such notices as these:

CARNY

"Now booking Bear Pitches, Traveling Duck, can also use Gorilla Show."
"Will book two nice Grind Shows. Must be flashy."

The independent concessionaires pay what is known as privilege to work these dates. The privilege is paid to the man responsible for lining up the dates, organizing and dispensing necessary graft and arranging for a patch. It is interesting to notice that the farther South a show goes, the rougher it becomes. There may not be a single girlie show or flat in Pennsylvania, but flatties and girlies both may be playing wide open and woolly in Georgia. Whether it is true or not, it is the consensus among carnies that you can get away with a hell of a lot more in the South than you can in the North.

Carnies can conveniently be divided into front-end people and back-end people. Front-enders are carnies who work games, food and other concessions. The back-enders are concerned with shows: freak shows, gorilla shows, walking-zombie shows and—where I was going now—girlie shows.

The guy out front was making his call, but it wasn't a very good call. His voice was more than tired, it was dead. He rarely looked at the marks who were crowding in front of the raised platform now, and once he stopped in midsentence and picked his nose.

"Come on in, folks. See it all for 50 cents, one half a dollar."

Four middle-aged ladies in spangled briefs and tasseled halters—all of it a little dirty—were working to a Fifties phonograph record about young love. The ladies were very active, jumping about in a sprightly fashion, their eyes glittering from Biphetamine 20s, the speeder far and away the favorite with carnies. From Thursday to Tuesday, whole carny families—men, women and children—ate them like jelly beans. Rose looked right at me but either didn't see me or didn't give a damn, for which I was grateful. I didn't want her paying any attention to me, because I kept thinking of her huge greasy husband out on the Ferris wheel right now splicing cable with his broken teeth.

I paid my half dollar, went inside feeling like a fool and saw the same ladies doing pretty much what they had been doing out front and doing it, if you can believe it, to the same goddamn phonograph record. But before they began, the semicomatose caller pointed out that there would be a second show right after this one to which no one who was female or under 18 would be admitted. Those who were admitted would have to pay $3 a head. That threw several good old boys into a fit of leg slapping and howling and Hot-damning. They were randy and ready and seemed to know something I did not know. Rose even permitted herself a small smile and a couple of winks to the boys who apparently

258

knew who she was, had maybe seen her show before and were digging hell out of the whole thing.

After the first show was over and they had made us lighter by $3, things happened quickly. Peeling the eggs took the longest. But first they added a drummer to the act. Really, a drummer. The ladies had retired behind a rat-colored curtain and out onto the little platform came an old man dressed in an ancient blue suit with a blue cap that at first I thought belonged to the Salvation Army. And it may have. Ligaments stood in his scrawny neck like wire. He sat on a chair and put his bass drum between his legs. The caller started the record we had already heard twice, which, incidentally, was by Frankie Valli, and the old man started pounding on his drum. His false teeth bulged in his old mouth every time he struck it. Never once during the performance did he look up. I know he did not see Rose. I was fascinated that he would not look at her when she came out onto the stage. She was naked except for a halter. I swear. She had her tits cinched up, but there was her old naked beaver and strong, over-the-hill ass. She was carrying six eggs in a little bowl. She carried it just the way a whore would have carried a bowl, except she had eggs in it instead of soap and water. She squatted in front of us—taking us all the way to pink—while she peeled the eggs. When they were peeled, she placed them one by one in her mouth, slobbered on them good and returned them to the dish. Then, still squatting, with Frankie Valli squealing for all he was worth and the old man single-mindedly beating his drum, and several of the good old boys hugging each other, she popped all of the eggs into her pussy and started dancing. She did six high kicks in her dance and each time she kicked, she fired an egg with considerable velocity out into the audience. On a bet with his buddies, a young apprentice madman caught and ate the last two.

I left the tent disappointed, though. I'd seen the act before. Once, many years ago, I knew a lady in New Orleans who could do a dozen. Not a dozen of your grade-A extra-large, to be sure. They were smalls, but a dozen nonetheless.

I found Charlie Luck down in the G-top. A G-top is a tent set up at the back of the lot exclusively for carnival people to socialize with one another. Marks are not allowed there and the carnies' socializing usually comes in the form of gambling games of one kind or another. It is not unusual for a carny to walk into the G-top at the end of the May-to-October season with $20,000 in his pocket and walk out the next morning wondering how he's going to get a dime to call his old mother for a ticket home on the Trailways. Some very heavy cheese changes hands in that tent, and I was amazed that the other carnies would sit down to a table with Charlie Luck. He had exceedingly quick hands and more than once he showed me his shortchange proposition. You could open your hand flat and he would count out 90 cents into it. You could watch him do it, but when he finished and you counted your change, you'd be a quarter short. He would press a nickel into your palm and at the same instant take out a quarter he'd just put down. He could count nine $1 bills or a five and four ones into your hand and inevitably he would take back over half of it. It's called, among other things, laying the note, and it's a scam usually run off in a department store or a supermarket.

"Down where I come from," I'd said to him once, "we don't sit down to seven card with folks who have fingers like you do."

He looked me dead in the eye and said, "These guys know I would never cheat in the G-top. When we do a little craps or cards back there, they know that's my leisure, my pleasure. Cheating is business. The only place, and I mean the *only* place I ever steal is when I'm working the joint right out there on the midway. I'd be ashamed of myself to do it anywhere else."

Charlie Luck saw me from across the G-top and immediately got up from the table and came to meet me. We walked back out onto the midway. It was dark now and the lot, laid out in a U shape, was jammed with men and women and their children, laughing and eating, their arms loaded with slum. Screaming shouts of pleasure and terror floated down out of the night from the high rides, glittering and spinning there above us.

"Did you see it?" he finally said after we'd walked for a while. "Did you see her do it?"

"Yeah, I saw her do it."

"The specialty act, too?"

"I told you I'd go."

"Then lay it out for me."

I laid it out.

"Eggs? Hard-boiled fucking eggs?"

"Right."

"And she'd kick and fire?" He took out two capsules. "You want one of these?"

"You know I'm a natural wire," I said. "What I need is a drink to calm me down. Let's go by the van before we go to the game."

He swallowed both capsules and made a face, but the face was not from the dope. "Goddamn eggs and goddamn drummer. I'd need a drink, too. I may even have one."

By the time we got to the van, he'd worked himself into a pretty good state over Rose and her specialty act.

"I don't put my dick where hard-boiled eggs've been," he kept saying. "Jesus, a pervert. I'm tainted."

"You ain't tainted, man," I said. "You just like you were before. I wish to God somebody could guarantee me my dick wouldn't go nowhere worse than a few boiled eggs. Besides, I don't know what you expected, taking her out of a girlie show."

"How was I to know? I never been in a girlie show once, not once," he said. "Over half my life I'm with a carnival. Never once did I go near a girlie show."

"Didn't you talk to her?" I said. "You should have asked if she ever put anything up in there."

Charlie Luck jerked his cap lower on his ears and stared straight ahead. "You don't ask a lady a thing like that," he said.

He poured a little straight vodka on top of the speed and we walked over to his proposition. The flat was near a punk ride between a glass pitch and a grab joint. The grab joint sold dogs and burgers and a fruit punch called flukum. Charlie Luck let the kid off for the rest of the night and we got behind the counter. Charlie banged things around, positioning his marbles and his board and muttering to himself. He finally quit and stared hatefully out at the passing crowd. He made no attempt to draw anybody in. Nobody so much as looked at us.

"You taking it in tomorrow?" he asked.

"I told you," I said. "I got to get back. There's only so much of this that'll do me any good, anyway."

"Maybe I'll go in, too," he said. "There's not but a little more than a week left on the season."

"I've enjoyed it," I said. "We'll cross again. Maybe we can sit in and have a beer with the cowboys."

He smiled. "Maybe." He sighed deeply. Then, "You don't gamble with cripples or ladies or children. I keep them out of my proposition. You beat one of them and you got heat, bad heat. Gamble with a fat guy who looks like he can afford it. The thing you like is if he's dressed up real good, too."

"One thing, Charlie," I said. "I been meaning to say this to you, but I didn't yet. Maybe I shouldn't now. But you don't gamble. You're not a gambler. No offense, Charlie, but you're a thief is what you are."

"Actually," he said. "I'm a gambler who doesn't lose. That's what I like to think I am. I just took the risk out of it."

"No risk, no gamble. No gamble, no gambler. You're a thief."

CARNY

"Well, sort of. The word doesn't bother me. I only do what they let me do."

The thing you have to know right off is you can't win from a carny gambler unless he wants you to. And he doesn't want you to. Of course, like any other hustler, he may give you a *little* something so he can take away a *lot* of something. But that's a long way from winning.

The carny's success in flat joints depends upon having a good call, an expert knowledge of just how far he can push a mark and the certainty that there is larceny in all of us. A good call simply means someone is passing on the midway and you are able to "call" him to you and get him involved with your hustle. A call itself is a hustle. The agent plays the mark off against the clothes he's wearing, or the woman he's with, or his youth, or his old age—in fact, anything that will make him rise to the challenge, which doesn't appear to be much of a challenge to start with. Many times an agent will walk out onto the midway, calling as he goes, and literally grab a mark, take hold of him and lead him over to the proposition. I've known agents who could consistently operate like that and get away with it. Others can't. The moment I touch a guy, he swings on me. He thinks he's being attacked.

Beside me in the store, Charlie Luck had dropped another Biphetamine 20. His eyes were wet as quicksilver and he was mumbling constantly about Rose. Finally, he said to me, "Lay it out for me again. How it was, what she did, the crowd. Six, you said, half a dozen, and none of 'm mashed when she fired 'm out at the marks?"

I laid it out for him again, just as straightforward and with as much detail as I could, even to the smells in the tent, saving nothing.

When I finished, he seemed to think about it for a moment. "All right," he said.

"Don't you think we ought to try to take a little money now, Charlie?"

"OK. Yeah." He turned to watch a middle-aged couple approaching down the midway. He looked back at me. "One thing. Don't call me Charlie Luck anymore."

"What should I call you?"

"Tuna," he said.

"Tuna?"

"Like in fish. Tommy Tuna. A name I always liked. Brings me good things."

"I got it," I said. "OK."

"You got to be careful with names." he said. "Names can be bad for you. Or names can be good for you. You know?"

I didn't know, so I didn't say anything.

"A name can get dirty. Start to rot. Bring you nothing but trouble." He sucked his teeth and sighed. The middle-aged couple had stopped and were looking at us. The lady carried two little pieces of slum, a ceramic duck and a small cloth snake. "I don't think I'll be Charlie Luck anymore."

"You mean for a little while."

"I mean ever."

I loved him for that. He just willed himself to be someone else, submerged as Charlie Luck and came up Tommy Tuna. I knew how easily I did the same thing. My fix is other people's lives. It always has been. As I stood there watching the well-dressed couple, secure in their middle age and permanent in their home, a fantasy started in me, a living thing. I felt my teeth go rotten and broken, my arms fill with badly done, homemade tattoos. I was from some remote place like Alpine, Texas, and I'd joined the carnival when I was 14 and ever since been rootless, no home except the back of a semi carrying a disassembled Octopus, and I lived off people—marks—those two there smiling at me. I suddenly smiled back. They had no way of knowing my secret and utter contempt.

"Tuna," I said quietly, "let me take this."

"Take what?"

"These two here. Let me do it."

"Do it."

"All right, here we go," I called. "Hey! Lookahere! *Your* game. Yeah! You. Come here. Come *here*. In here and let me show you the little game. I can tell by the look on your face, big fella. This is your game! A quarter. Nothing but 25 cents. Win the little lady this right here. Big panda. Come here! Come on!"

They smile uncertainly at each other.

The lady blushes. The guy looks away.

"*Hey*, you just married? I can see it, I can see how in love you are, how you want this right here for the little lady, right? *Come over here*."

They've turned now and they're mine. I had thought they might walk on and, in spite of the fact that I've never been a caller who could actually grab anybody, I was ready to vault the counter and take the guy by the arm. The rule is that the mark gets deeper into your hustle with every move he makes toward you. He looks at you. He moves a little nearer. He lets you explain your game. He bets. If you can get him to do that much and don't take everything he's got, or as much of it as you want, you ought to find another business.

CARNY

"See that bear? See that bear right here? You want it for the lady?" Tommy Tuna keeps his bear nice. An enormous panda under clear cellophane. The bear must be worth $20. "Look, she wants it! Look at her face! A quarter, it's yours for a quarter! OK? Can I show the game to you?"

The lady is blushing and squeezing the guy's arm and pressing into him. And he's already got his quarter out.

"Look, I got marbles and I got a board." I whip the board out and show it to him. The board has little indentations on it. On the bottom of each indentation is a number: a one or a two or a three on up through nine. There's a little chute that leads down to the board. "You need 100 points to win this game. Right? One hundred points to win that bear. Cost you a quarter. You roll the marbles down the chute, we add up the total. Each total gives a number toward the 100 points you need. Right?"

He's still got his quarter in his hand. Both of them are leaning over the board. He wants to give me the quarter so bad it's hurting him and he's not even heard the game. He just knows he's risking only 25 cents.

"Right? Each total gives a number toward the 100 points you need." I look him in the eye and smile. I take him by the wrist and pull him a little closer. "Here's the kicker. You keep rolling till you get the 100 points you need to win. *Without paying another penny.*" I pause again. He's smiling. She's smiling. I'm smiling. Tommy Tuna's smiling. "Unless...unless the total you roll is 30. If you roll a 30, the cost of the game doubles, but you *keep* the points you've earned toward the 100 and roll again."

The lady says, "Do it, honey. Oh, do it."

And here is where much of the carnies' contempt for the mark starts. The guy walks up to my game. He doesn't know the game, has never seen it. He sure as hell doesn't know me. He doesn't see or doesn't care that on the board there are not an equal number of ones, twos, threes, and so on. If he cared to check the board or think about it, he'd see the odds are overwhelming that he'll roll the losing number nearly every time. And each time you roll a 30, though you keep the points you already have, you don't get to count the 30.

He rolls the marbles. As soon as they stop in the slots, I'm taking them out again as fast as I can, palm partially obscuring the board, adding aloud in a stunned, unbelieving voice, "Two and nine, 11, and six is 17 and, wow, oh, golly! Nine and nine and nine...27 to the 17 and...that's

44 *big* points, almost half of what you need to win that bear for the little lady. This must be your lucky night!"

He had, of course, rolled a 30. He takes the marbles again and I quick-count him to 52. "Hey, this bear's gone tonight. It looks like your night." He's flushed. You'd think he had $5,000 on the line. He whips down the marbles, and guess what? He rolled that 30. But he's got 50 cents out almost before I can count the losing number for him. We go again and I take him up to 65. He rolls and loses. The bet's a dollar. Before he knows what's happened, he's looking at an $8 bet and he needs only 22 points to win.

I was just about to give him the marbles and made the mistake of looking at the lady. You'd have thought the guy was losing the mortgage on the house. She was nearly in tears. I hand him the marbles. He rolls a 30, but I count him into 105. Pandemonium. Squeals. Hurrahs. Down comes the bear and off they go. Tommy Tuna took me by the arm and led me to the back of the booth.

"You son of a bitch," he said.

"Yeah, I guess. But don't come down on me too hard. I'll pay you for the bear."

"Not the point. You had the gaff so deep into that fucker, you coulda made him bet his wife."

"It was the lady. Hadn't been for the lady, I could've done it."

"It's all right. You done good, anyway." He smiled toward the front of the booth, where four marks—all men, well fed, well dressed and apparently at the carnival together—were yelling to come on and play the game. They had been drawn to the booth by my loud counting and they'd stayed to see the man easily win the bear.

Tommy Tuna went over to the four marks. He shrugged, looked sadly at his board. "Maybe I'm crazy," he said, "but I feel like a little action." He leaned closer to the marks. "Fuck the bears. Let's bet some money." He went into his pocket and came out with the biggest roll of bills I've ever seen. He showed the roll to the marks. I saw nothing but $100s. "I'll play you no limit. Just like with the fucking bear, it takes 100 points to win. The first bet'll cost you a buck. The bets double after that. I'll pay ten to one. Did you get that? Ten to one I'm paying. If you're betting $100 when you reach the 100 points to win, I'll pay you $1,000."

He said it quickly, in a flat, unemotional voice. They were into it immediately and Tuna quick-counted them to 37 points. There seemed to be no way to lose. All four guys were pooling their money with the intention of splitting the take. But by the time they had accumulated 82 points, they'd lost $255. The next bet was gonna cost them $256. The whole thing had taken about five minutes, but Tuna pointed out they needed only 18 more points to win and, after all, he *was* giving ten-to-one odds.

"Sumpin' mighty goddamn funny goin' on here," said the biggest and meanest-looking of the four.

"Gee," said Tommy Tuna in a quiet, sad voice. "You fellas do seem to be having a real bad run of luck. I can hardly believe it myself."

They withdrew a few steps to consult and then came back and went for the bet. They rolled a 30. Tommy Tuna scooped up the money. All four of them howled simultaneously as if they'd been stung by wasps. They'd been cleaned out. The big, mean one moved to come over the counter when, as if by magic, Officer Jackson appeared on the midway, only a few feet away.

He came over and said, "You want to tell me why you hollering like this?"

The big one said, "This bastard's running a crooked game, that's why."

"You want to tell me what kind of game?"

He told Officer Jackson what kind of game. He also told him they'd been taken for over $500 in less than ten minutes.

"Gambling?" Officer Jackson could hardly believe it. "That's against the law. It's against the law for everybody here. If it's true, I'll have to lock you up. All of you." Then he turned to the four guys and actually said, "And if I do, and if it's true, he's got your money to bail himself out with." He paused and looked at each of the four in turn. "You want to tell me what you want to do?"

After the four guys had left, Officer Jackson and Tommy Tuna went over to the corner and had a short, earnest conversation, which I did not hear. Then Officer Jackson left.

Tommy watched the cop disappear down the midway and said in a wondering voice, "You know, I once took $12,000 off a oilman in Oklahoma. He never said a word about it. A real fine sport."

I said, "Some days chicken salad. Some days chickenshit."

"Actually, I just wondered if I could use your bathroom."

Marvin the Torch

humor by JIMMY BRESLIN

I deally, the American businessman should work hard, make money and seek to expand. Sometimes, however, the American businessman loses money. When this happens, the businessman seeks to cut back. There are a number of legal ways to do this. There also is an illegal way to do this. The businessman can do a very bad thing and call on the services of an outfit that is in the business of burning down places that are not making any money and have insurance.

This is known as arson, and the best in this field is the firm of Marvin the Torch and his partner, Benjamin, who also plays with matches. They hold the North American record for arson, one-story buildings, and arson, restaurants that are losing; and they are known wherever there is a man who is running a business not too well. They are not the finest of people, Marvin and Benjamin, and neither are their clients. But they are, like stealing, a part of life in this country.

Insurance companies, with their usual stiffness, do not like arson. In fact, Brendan P. Battle, director, New York Board of Underwriters, has been very mad at Marvin the Torch lately. Battle has been calling for a national campaign against Marvin the Torch. He claims that Marvin, and others who are trying to be like him, are responsible for millions of dollars in losses suffered by insurance companies. Brendan P. Battle is so mad over this that he wants the police to arrest Marvin the Torch. This attitude has, in turn, made Marvin the Torch very mad at Brendan P. Battle.

"I am going to burn down Brendan P. Battle's garage," Marvin the Torch says.

Battle calls Marvin's work "insurance fraud fires." This is a rather stuffy description. Marvin the Torch and Benjamin call it "belting the joint out" or "building an empty lot."

Battle also keeps asking for Marvin's address. "It is your duty as a citizen to inform us of his whereabouts so we can have him apprehended,"

Battle says. This is fine, law-abiding sentiment. But Marvin the Torch, while sort of friendly, does have a definite policy about a Public Speaker. Marvin takes him out fishing in the ocean. He then puts a rope around the Public Speaker's neck. The rope is attached to a big old jukebox. The big old jukebox then is thrown overboard. The Public Speaker invariably follows.

Marvin the Torch is the boss of the firm and he takes credit for some amazing jobs. Once he contracted to handle a restaurant in Florida located on an ocean inlet. With great artistry, Marvin blew one wall of the joint out into the inlet. "It takes off in one piece and when it hits the water it goes down just like the Titanic," Benjamin says proudly.

On many occasions Marvin has done what he calls an Apache Indian job on restaurants. This means that the next morning only the chimney is left, surrounded by smoking ruins. There are, however, times when Marvin gets mad at chimneys and he sticks something in them to make them go away, too.

As a rule, a stiff north wind can be Marvin's best friend, although once it got him into trouble. As a personal favor, he belted out a custard stand that was located just outside a big amusement park. Marvin, experimenting, loaded the custard stand up so much that it disappeared in one puff. But a stiff wind grabbed at the explosion and carried some of the wreckage into the amusement area. A $1 million six-alarmer took place. The fire was officially labeled arson, and as a result the town was so hot for Marvin that he had to give up several good clients in the area who needed work done. He spent the rest of the summer working as a guard at a bungalow colony in the Catskill Mountains. The owner made Marvin sit on a dock by the bungalow colony's lake. The owner claimed that people were stealing his water. At the end of the summer, when the owner looked at his books, he screamed for Marvin.

"You're a gangster, do something for me," he told Marvin. "Make my place go away."

Marvin said yes. Then he went to the dock and sat down to think. "How do you burn down a lake?" he asked himself. He thought about this for a few days. Then he gave up and the owner had to settle for a spectacular bungalow-colony fire.

Their greatest effort, the one Marvin the Torch and Benjamin are best known for, was a $1.5 million five-alarmer. It is particularly noteworthy because only Marvin and Benjamin worked the job. Usually, arson takes three men. One is called the "blanket man." He stands right outside the door with a car blanket in his hands in case somebody comes running out with the back of his pants on fire. The blanket man also keeps track of the empty gasoline cans. They must be carted away, because this Brendan P. Battle is awfully obstinate about sending insurance checks when one of his men finds gas cans in the ruins of your fire. Two pourers, working inside, complete the team. At light-up time, one of the pourers runs outside and becomes the car driver. The other pourer then steps up and, his cigarette lighter shaking in sheer joy, starts the proceedings.

The job came about when a group of eight shopkeepers formed a sort of association and brought in Marvin for consultation. Marvin asked for $7,500 and received a substantial down payment from a man who had the dry-goods store at the end of the block.

The dry-goods-store man was a worrier. "I got a fire wall in my store, what are you going to do about that?" he asked.

Marvin the Torch got mad at him. "What do you think I am, some little kid with matches?" he said. "I'm going to put enough in there to belt out the Chrysler Building."

Then Marvin and his partner went to work. Right away, you could see that Marvin was out to do something special. He set up a solid board against the wall in a corner of one of the stores. The fire starter, a small object containing gelled kerosene, was placed between the board and the wall. The board acts as a heat baffle. This confines the heat and radiates it, downward in this case, without obstructing the draft. This is great for making the floor go into the cellar.

"What's that other thing you do that I like so much?" Benjamin asked.

"The door in the corner," Marvin said. He found one in a novelty shop. The door, in a corner of the room, was opened slightly. This formed a triangular chimney with the corner. The fire starter, placed inside the triangular chimney, gets at the ceiling in a great hurry and produces decisive action.

"This is going to be beautiful," Benjamin said.

The two of them worked hard and put so much kerosene and so many bombs in the stores that Benjamin's back hurt from carrying empty cans to the car. Then, finally, Benjamin got in the car and fled and Marvin stood at the back door of one of the stores and flipped in a burning matchbook. There was an immediate result. The floor of the store caved into the cellar. It caved in because of all the bombs on it.

Marvin the Torch then went to an apartment a block away that overlooked the fire. The dry-goods man, still worried, was waiting for him in the apartment.

"What about my fire wall?" he said.

Marvin didn't listen to him. He was puffing a cigar and watching, with the glazed eyes of a true professional, while his fire developed. Every shop on the block was in flames quickly. Except the dry-goods store. This one wasn't even singed. This did not worry Marvin. But the dry-goods man was wailing.

"I'm going to be the only one left," he said. "I told you about the fire wall."

"I done a special thing to the wall," Marvin said. "You're in with artists and you're acting like a jerk."

"I'm a jerk with a store."

The dry-goods man kept wailing, and the entire block was in flames except for his store; and then all of a sudden something happened to the dry-goods store. The roof went straight up into the air. The front window blew out into the middle of the street. And the fire wall disappeared with a loud report and a cloud of smoke. It was an awesome sight.

Marvin held out his cigar and flicked ashes onto the floor. Then he turned and looked smugly at the dry-goods-store man.

"Nuclear," Marvin the Torch said.

"I guess a reservation __wasn't__ necessary."

The Wrong Bed

ribald classic by GIOVANNI BOCCACCIO

A poor man called Giulio once made his living by providing food and drink for travellers in the Mugnone Valley. His family consisted of a cat, a handsome wife, a small baby and a ravishingly beautiful daughter named Niccolosa.

Pinuccio, a hot-blooded buck from nearby Florence, often saw Niccolosa as he passed the house, and yearned to possess her. So great was his ardor that the girl could sense it, and she let him know that a meeting between them would not displease her.

Pinuccio therefore enlisted the aid of his good friend Adriano, and together they evolved a plan. They hired two horses and made their way to the Mugnone Valley just as night was falling. When they arrived at Giulio's house, they knocked on the door and asked for shelter.

"Gentlemen," said Giulio, "my house is small and I do not usually accommodate sleeping guests. But since night has overtaken you, I will put you up as best I can."

The house was indeed small. It had but one bedroom, in which they made up three beds: one for Giulio and his wife, one for the two travellers and one for the lovely Niccolosa. The small baby slept in a cradle at the foot of Giulio's bed. Since it was already late, the family and their guests lost no time in retiring.

When everyone seemed to be asleep, Pinuccio arose and crept to Niccolosa's bed. Somewhat frightened but nevertheless eager, the girl received him and they soon climbed to the peak of pleasure.

While they were thus refreshing themselves, the cat knocked over a vase and woke Giulio's wife. She got up and went to the place where she had heard the noise.

Meanwhile, Pinuccio's friend Adriano had also roused himself to answer a natural call. Finding the cradle blocking his path, he moved it from the foot of Giulio's bed to the foot of his own bed and went about his business. He did not trouble to replace the cradle when he returned.

273

THE WRONG BED

The wife, having swept up the broken vase and scolded the cat, began to feel her way to bed in the dark. Touching the cradle, she naturally assumed it was at her bed and promptly climbed in beside Adriano, thinking he was her husband. Adriano did not undeceive her. Instead, he took her in his arms and pleasured both himself and her.

Pinuccio then left the lovely Niccolosa's bed because he feared he might fall asleep there and be discovered in the morning. He, too, was led astray by the misplaced cradle and instead of getting into bed with his friend Adriano, climbed in beside Giulio, his host.

All might have been well had not Pinuccio seen fit to boast of his prowess. "Three times!" he whispered in his bed-partner's ear. "Ah, believe me, Niccolosa is the most luscious of creatures!"

"Wretch!" cried Giulio. "Is this how you repay me for my kindness?"

Giulio's wife, hearing the commotion in the other bed, said to her companion, "Oh, husband, listen to our guests quarreling!"

Adriano foolishly answered her: "They've had too much to drink."

Hearing his voice, the lady realized the situation and immediately arose without a word. Moving the cradle to Niccolosa's bed, she climbed in beside the girl and pretended to be awakened by Giulio's clamor. "What is amiss?" she asked.

"Amiss?" shouted her husband. "Everything! This rogue has lain with Niccolosa!"

"Nonsense," his wife replied. "I have been with her all night and surely would have known if Pinuccio had entered this bed. But what is he doing in your bed, Giulio?"

Adriano, seeing the clever way she was hiding her shame and that of her daughter, said, "Sleepwalking again, eh Pinuccio? And dreaming of amorous feats as usual! Come back to bed."

This ruse satisfied Giulio, who laughed as Pinuccio was escorted back to his rightful bed.

The next morning, two satisfied travellers rode out of the valley, leaving behind them a happy young girl and her even happier mother.

King Bee

fiction by T.C. BOYLE

I n the mail that morning, there were two solicitations for life insurance, a coupon from the local car wash promising a "100 Percent Brushless Wash," four bills, three fliers and a death threat from his ex-son, Anthony. Anthony had used green ink, the cyclonic scrawl of his longhand lifting off into the loops, lassos and curlicues of heavy weather aloft, and his message was the same as usual: *I eat the royal jelly. I sting and you die. Bzzzzzzzz. Pat, too, the bitch.* He hadn't bothered to sign it.

"Ken? What is it?"

Pat was right beside him now, peering over his elbow at the sheaf of ads and bills clutched in his hand. She'd been pruning the roses and she was still wearing her work gloves. They stood there out front, the mailbox rising up like a tombstone between them. "It's Anthony," she said, "isn't it?"

He handed her the letter.

"My God," she said, sucking in a whistle of breath like a wounded animal. "How'd he get the address?"

It was a good question. They'd known he was to be released from juvenile hall on his 18th birthday, and they'd taken precautions—like changing their phone number, their address, their places of employment and the city and state in which they lived. For a while, they'd even toyed with the idea of changing their name, but then Ken's father came for a visit from Wisconsin and sobbed over the family coat of arms till they gave it up. Over the years, they'd received dozens of Anthony's death threats—all of them bee-oriented; bees were his obsession—but nothing since they'd moved. This was bad. Worse than bad.

"You should call the police," he said, "and take Skippy to the kennel."

• • •

Nine years earlier, the Mallows had been childless. There was something wrong with Pat's fallopian tubes—some congenital defect that reduced her odds of conception to 222,000 to one—and to compound the problem, Ken's sperm count was inordinately low, though he ate plenty of red meat and worked out every other day on the racquetball court. Adoption had seemed the way to go, though Pat was distressed by the fact that so many of the babies were—well, she didn't like to say it, but they weren't white. There were Thai babies, Guianese babies, babies from Haiti, Kuala Lumpur and Kashmir, but Caucasian babies were at a premium. You could have a nonwhite baby in six days—for a price, of course—but there was an 11-year waiting list for white babies—12 for blonds, 14 for blue-eyed blonds—and neither Ken nor Pat was used to being denied. "How about an older child?" the man from the adoption agency had suggested.

They were in one of the plush, paneled conference rooms of Adopt-a-Child, and Mr. Denteen, a handsome, bold-faced man in a suit woven of some exotic material, leaned forward with a fatherly smile. He bore an uncanny resemblance to Robert Young of *Father Knows Best*, and on the wall behind him was a photomontage of plump and cooing babies. Pat was mesmerized. "What?" she said, as if she hadn't heard him.

"An older child," Denteen repeated, his voice rich with insinuation. It was the voice of a seducer, a shrink, a black marketeer.

"No," Ken said, "I don't think so."

"How old?" Pat said.

Denteen leaned forward on his leather elbow patches. "I just happen to have a child—a boy—whose file just came to us this morning. Little Anthony Cademartori. Tony. He's nine years old. Just. Actually, his birthday was only last week."

The photo Denteen handed them showed a sunny, smiling towheaded boy, a generic boy, archetypal, the sort of boy you envision when you close your eyes and think boy. If they'd looked closer, they would have seen that his eyes were like two poked holes and that there was something unstable about his smile and the set of his jaw, but they were in the grip of a conceit and they didn't look that closely. Ken asked if there was anything wrong with him. "Physically, I mean," he said.

Denteen let a good-humored little laugh escape him. "This is your average nine-year-old boy, Mr. Mallow," he said. "Average height, weight, build, average—or above average—intelligence. He's all boy, and he's one heck of a lot fitter than I am." Denteen cast a look to the heavens —or, rather, to the ceiling tiles. "To be nine years old again," he said, sighing.

"Does he behave?" Pat asked.

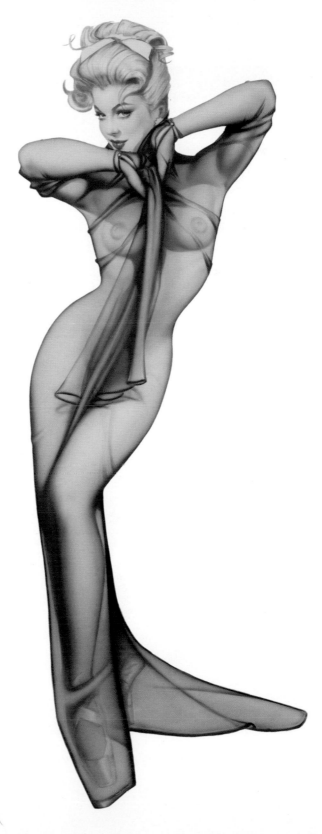

*"I'm sorry, but
I really have nothing
to wear..."*

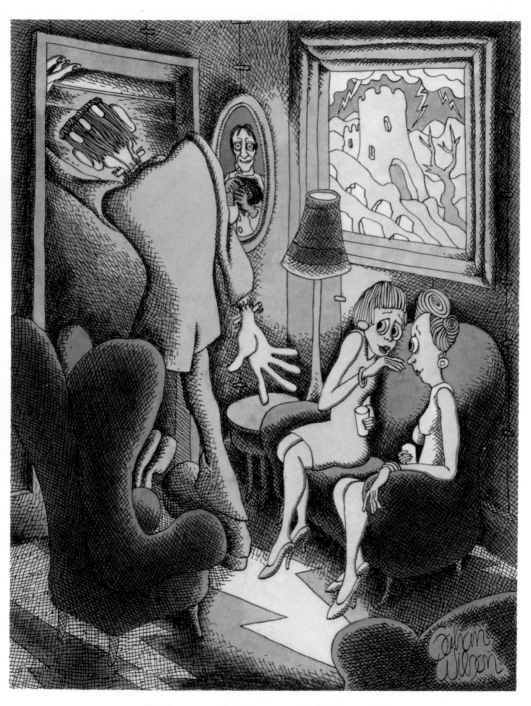

"Of course, he's into really kinky sex!"

*"If it weren't for the casual sex I have with you and Gwen,
I wouldn't have any meaningful relationships at all!"*

"*I know what you want, Howard…I can read you like a book!*"

"*A penny for your thoughts…!*"

"Good news, everyone! Granny is rallying!"

"This is Dr. Baumgarten, your sex therapist. How's it going over at your house tonight?"

"I think you have the wrong number...but come over anyway!"

"Does he behave?" Denteen echoed, and he looked offended, hurt almost. "Does the President live in the White House? Does the sun come up in the morning?" He straightened up, shot his cuffs, then leaned forward again—so far forward that his hands dangled over the edge of the conference table. "Look at him," he said, holding up the picture again. "Mr. and Mrs. Mallow—Ken, Pat—let me tell you that this child has seen more heartbreak than you and I'll know in a lifetime. His birth parents were killed at a railway crossing when he was two, and then, the irony of it, his adoptive parents—they were your age, by the way—just dropped dead one day while he was at school. One minute they're alive and well, and the next they're gone." His voice faltered. "And then poor little Tony...poor little Tony comes home...."

Pat looked stunned. Ken reached out to squeeze her hand.

"He needs love, Pat," Denteen said. "He has love to give. A lot of love."

Ken looked at Pat. Pat looked at Ken.

"So," Denteen said, "when would you like to meet him?"

• • •

They met him the following afternoon, and he seemed fine. A little shy, maybe, but fine. Superpolite, that's what Pat thought. May I this and may I that, please, thank you and it's a pleasure to meet you. He was adorable. Big for his age—that was a surprise. They'd expected a lovable little urchin, the kind of kid Norman Rockwell might have portrayed in the barber's chair atop a stack of phone books, but Anthony was big, already the size of a teenager—big-headed, big in the shoulders and big in the rear. Tall, too. At nine, he was already as tall as Pat and probably outweighed her. What won them over, though, was his smile. He turned his smile on them that first day in Denteen's office—a blooming, angelic smile that showed off his dimples and the perfection of his tiny white glistening teeth—and Pat felt something give way inside her. At the end of the meeting, she hugged him to her breast.

The smile was a regular feature of those first few months—the months of the trial period. Anthony smiled at breakfast, at dinner, smiled when he helped Ken rake the leaves from the gutters or tidy up the yard, smiled in his sleep. He stopped smiling when the trial period was over, as if he'd suddenly lost control of his facial muscles. It was uncanny. Almost to the day the adoption became formal—the day that he was theirs and they were his—Anthony's smile vanished. The change was abrupt and it came without warning.

"Scooter," Ken called to him one afternoon, "you want to help me take those old newspapers to the recycling center and then stop in at Baskin and Robbin's?"

Anthony was upstairs in his room, which they'd decorated with posters of ballplayers and airplanes. He didn't answer.

"Scooter?" Silence.

Puzzled, Ken ascended the stairs. As he reached the landing, he became aware of an odd sound emanating from Anthony's room—a low hum, as of an appliance kicking in. He paused to knock at the door and the sound began to take on resonance, to swell and shrink again, a thousand muted voices speaking in unison. "Anthony?" he called, pushing open the door.

Anthony was seated naked in the middle of his bed, wearing a set of headphones Ken had never seen before. They were attached to a tape player the size of a suitcase. Ken had never seen the tape player before, either. And the walls—gone were the dazzling sun-struck posters of Fernando Valenzuela, P-38s and Mitsubishi Zeros, replaced now by black-and-white photos of insects, torn, he saw, from library books that lay scattered across the floor, gutted, their spines broken.

For a long moment, Ken merely stood there in the doorway, the sizzling pulse of that many-voiced hum leaking out of Anthony's headphones to throb in his gut, his chest, his bones. It was as if he'd stumbled upon some ancient rite in the Australian outback, as if he'd stepped out of his real life in the real world and into some cheap horror movie about demonic possession and people whose eyes lighted up like Christmas-tree ornaments. Anthony was seated in the lotus position, his eyes tightly closed. He didn't seem to be aware of Ken. The buzzing was excruciating. After a moment, Ken backed out of the room and gently shut the door.

At dinner that evening, Anthony gave them their first taste of his why-don't-you-get-off-my-back look, a look that was to become habitual. His hair stood up jaggedly, drawn up into needlelike points—he must have greased it, Ken realized—and he slouched as if there were an invisible piano strapped to his shoulders. Ken didn't know where to begin—with the scowl, the nudity, the desecration of library books, the tape player and its mysterious origins (had he borrowed it—perhaps from school? A friend?)? Pat knew nothing. She served chicken croquettes, biscuits with honey and baked beans, Anthony's favorite meal. She was at the stove, her back to them, when Ken cleared his throat.

"Anthony," he said, "is there anything wrong? Anything you want to tell us?"

Anthony shot him a contemptuous look. He said nothing. Pat glanced over her shoulder.

"About the library books...."

"You were spying on me," Anthony snarled.

Pat turned away from the stove, spoon in hand. "What do you mean? Ken? What's this all about?"

"I wasn't spying, I——" Ken faltered. He felt the anger rising in him. "All right," he said, "where'd you get the tape player?"

Anthony wiped his mouth with the back of his hand, then looked past Ken to his adoptive mother. "I stole it," he said.

Suddenly, Ken was on his feet. "Stole it?'" he roared. "Don't you know what that means, library books and now stealing?"

Anthony was a statue, big-headed and serene. "Bzzzzzzzz," he said.

• • •

The scene at the library was humiliating. Clearly, the books had been willfully destroyed. Mrs. Tutwillow was outraged. And no matter how hard Ken squeezed his arm, Anthony remained poker-faced and unrepentant. "I won't say I'm sorry," he sneered, "because I'm not." Ken gave her a check for $112.32 to cover the cost of replacing the books, plus shipping and handling. At Steve's Stereo Shoppe, the man behind the counter—Steve, presumably—agreed not to press charges, but he had a real problem with offering the returned unit to the public as new goods, if Ken knew what he meant. Since he'd have to sell it used now, he wondered if Ken had the $87.50 it was going to cost him to mark it down. Of course, if Ken didn't want to cooperate, he'd have no recourse but to report the incident to the police. Ken cooperated.

At home, after he'd ripped the offending photos from the walls and sent Anthony to his room, he phoned Denteen. "Ken, listen, I know you're upset," Denteen crooned, his voice as soothing as a shot of whiskey, "but the kid's life has been real hell, believe me, and you've got to realize that he's going to need some time to adjust." He paused. "Why don't you get him a dog or something?"

"A dog?"

"Yeah. Something for him to be responsible for, for a change. He's been a ward—I mean, an adoptee—all this time, with people caring for him, and maybe it's that he feels like a burden or something. With a dog or a cat, he could do the giving."

A dog. The idea of it sprang to life and Ken was a boy himself again, roaming the hills and stubble fields of Wisconsin, Skippy at his side. A dog. Yes. Of course.

"And listen," Denteen was saying, "if you think you're going to need professional help with this, the man to go to is Maurice Barebaum. He's one of the top child psychologists in the state, if not the country." There was a hiss of shuffling papers, the flap of Rolodex cards. "I've got his number right here."

• • •

"I don't want a dog," Anthony insisted, and gave them a strained histrionic look. We're on stage, Ken was thinking, that's what it is. He looked at Pat, seated on the couch, her legs tucked under her, and then at his son, this stranger with the staved-in eyes and tallowy arms who'd somehow won the role.

"But it would be so nice," Pat said, drawing a picture in the air, "you'd have a little friend."

Anthony was wearing a black T-shirt emblazoned with red and blue letters that spelled out MEGADETH. On the reverse was a full-color representation of a stupendous bumblebee. "Oh, come off it, Pat," he sang, a keening edge to his voice. "That's so stupid. Dogs are so slobbery and shitty."

"Don't use that language," Ken said automatically.

"A little one, maybe," Pat said, "a cocker or a shelty."

"I don't want a dog. I want a hive. A beehive. That's what I want." He was balancing like a tightrope walker on the edge of the fireplace apron.

"Bees?" Ken demanded. "What kind of pet is that?" He was angry. It seemed he was always angry lately.

Pat forestalled him, her tone as soft as a caress. "Bees, darling?" she said. "Can you tell us what you like about them? Is it because they're so useful, because of the honey, I mean?"

Anthony was up on one foot. He tipped over twice before he answered. "Because they have no mercy."

"Mercy?" Pat repeated.

"Three weeks, that's how long a worker lasts in the summer," Anthony said. "They kick the drones out to die. The spent workers, too." He looked at Ken. "You fit in or you die."

"And what the hell is that supposed to mean?" Ken was shouting; he couldn't help himself.

Anthony's face crumpled up. His cheeks were corrugated, the spikes of his hair stood out like thorns. "You hate me," he whined. "You fuck, you dickhead—you hate me, don't you, don't you?"

"Ken!" Pat cried, but Ken already had him by the arm.

"Don't you ever——" he said.

"Ever what? Ever what? Say fuck? You do it, you do it, you do it!" Anthony was in a rage, jerking away, tears on his face, shouting. "Upstairs, at night. I hear you. Fucking. That's what you do. Grunting and fucking just like, like, like *dogs*!"

• • •

"I'll need to see him three days a week," Dr. Barebaum said. He was breathing heavily, as if he'd just climbed three flights of stairs.

Anthony was out in the car with Pat. He'd spent the past 45 minutes sequestered with Barebaum. "Is he—is he all right?" Ken asked. "I mean, is he normal?"

Barebaum leaned back in his chair and made a little pyramid of his fingers. "Adjustment problems," he breathed. "He's got a lot of hostility. He's had a difficult life."

Ken stared down at the carpet.

"He tells me"—Barebaum dredged up the words as if from some inner fortress—"he tells me he wants a dog."

Ken sat rigid in the chair. This must be what it feels like before they switch on the current at Sing Sing, he thought. "No, you've got it wrong. *We* wanted to get *him* a dog, but he said no. In fact, he went schizoid on us."

Barebaum's nose wrinkled up at the term *schizoid*. Ken regretted it instantly. "Yes," the doctor drawled, "hmmph. But the fact is, the boy quite distinctly told me the whole blowup was because he does, indeed, want a dog. You know, Mr., ah——"

"Mallow."

"Mallow, we often say exactly the opposite of what we mean; you are aware of that, aren't you?"

Ken said nothing. He studied the weave of the carpet.

After a moment, the doctor cleared his throat. "You do have health insurance?" he said.

• • •

In all, Anthony was with them just over three years. The dog—a shelty pup Ken called Skippy and Anthony referred to alternately as Ken and Turd—was a mistake, they could see that now. For the first few months or so, Anthony had ignored it, except to run squealing through the house, the puppy's warm excreta cupped in his palms, shouting, "It shit! It shit! The dog shit!" Ken, though, got to like the feel of the pup's wet nose on his wrist as he skimmed the morning paper or sat watching

TV in the evening. The pup was alive, it was high-spirited and joyful and it took him back to his own childhood in a way that Anthony, with his gloom and his sneer, never could have. "I want a hive," Anthony said, over and over again. "My very own hive."

Ken ignored him—bees were dangerous, after all, and this was a residential neighborhood—until the day Anthony finally did take an interest in Skippy. It was one of those rare days when Pat's car was at the garage, so Ken picked her up at work and they arrived home together. The house was quiet. Skippy, who usually greeted them at the door in a paroxysm of licking, rolling, leaping and tail thumping, was nowhere to be seen. And Anthony, judging from the low-threshold hum washing over the house, was up in his room listening to the bee tapes Pat had given him for Christmas. "Skippy," Ken called. "Here, boy!" No Skippy. Pat checked the yard, the basement, the back room. Finally, together, they mounted the stairs to Anthony's room.

Anthony was in the center of the bed, clad only in his underwear, reprising the ritual Ken had long since grown to accept (Barebaum claimed it was nothing to worry about—"It's his way of meditating, that's all, and if it calms him down, why fight it?"). Huge color photographs of bees obliterated the walls, but these were legitimate photos, clipped from the pages of *The Apiarian's Monthly*, another gift from Pat. Anthony looked bloated, fatter than ever, as pale and white as a grub. When he became aware of them, he slipped the headphones from his ears.

"Honey," Pat said, reaching down to ruffle his hair, "have you seen Skippy?"

It took him a moment to answer. He looked bewildered, as if she'd asked him to solve an equation or name the 20 biggest cities in Russia. "I put him in his cell," he said finally.

"Cell?" Ken echoed.

"In the hive," Anthony said. "The big hive."

It was Ken who noticed the broomstick wedged against the oven door, and it was Ken who buried Skippy's poor singed carcass and arranged to have the oven replaced—Pat wouldn't, couldn't cook in it, ever again. It was Ken, too, who lost control of himself that night and slapped Anthony's sick, pale, swollen face till Pat pulled him off. In the end, Anthony got his hive, 30,000 honeybees in a big white box with 15 frames inside, and Barebaum got to see Anthony two more days a week.

At first, the bees seemed to exert a soothing influence on the boy. He stopped muttering to himself, used his utensils at the table and didn't seem quite as vulnerable to mood swings as he had been. After school and his daily session with Barebaum, he'd spend hours tending the hive, watching the bees at their compulsive work, humming softly to himself as if in a trance. Ken was worried he'd be stung and bought him a gauze bonnet and gloves, but he rarely wore them. And when he was stung—daily, it seemed—he displayed the contusions proudly, as if they were battle scars. For Ken and Pat, it was a time of accommodation, and they were quietly optimistic. Gone was the smiling boy they'd taken into their home, but at least now he wasn't so—there was no other word for it—so *odd*, and he seemed less agitated, less ready to fly off the handle.

The suicide attempt took them by surprise.

Ken found him, at dusk, crouched beneath the hive and quietly bleeding from both wrists. Pat's X-Acto knife lay in the grass beside him, black with blood. In the hospital the next day, Anthony looked lost and vulnerable, looked like a little boy again. Barebaum was there with them. "It's a phase," he said, puffing for breath. "He's been very depressed lately."

"Why?" Pat asked, sweeping Anthony's hair back from his forehead, stroking his swollen hands. "Your bees," she choked. "What would your bees do without you?"

Anthony let his eyes fall shut. After a moment, he lifted his lids again. His voice was faint. "Bzzzzzzzz," he said.

They kept him at the Hart Mental Health Center for nine months, and then they let him come home again. Ken was against it. He'd contacted a lawyer about voiding the adoption papers—Anthony was just too much to handle; he was emotionally unstable, disturbed, dangerous; the psychiatric bills alone were killing them—but Pat overruled him. "He needs us," she said. "He has no one else to turn to." They were in the living room. She bent forward to light a cigarette. "Nobody said it would be easy," she said.

"Easy?" he retorted. "You talk like it's a war or something. I didn't adopt a kid to go to war—or to save the world, either."

"Why did you adopt him, then?"

The question took him by surprise. He looked past Pat to the kitchen, where one of Anthony's crayon drawings—of a lopsided bee—clung to the refrigerator door, and then past the refrigerator to the window and the lush, still yard beyond. He shrugged. "For love, I guess."

As it turned out, the question was moot—Anthony didn't last six months this time. When they picked him up at the hospital—"Hospital," Ken growled, "nut hatch is more like it"—they barely recognized him. He was taller and he'd put on weight. Pat couldn't call it baby fat anymore—this was true fat, adult fat, fat that sank his eyes and strained at the seams of his pants. And his hair—his rich, fine white-blond hair—was gone, shaved to a transparent stubble over a scalp the color of boiled ham. Pat chattered at him, but he got into the car without a word.

Halfway home, he spoke for the first time. "You know what they eat in there," he said, "in the hospital?"

Ken felt like the straight man in a comedy routine. "What do they eat?" he said, his eyes fixed on the road.

"Shit," Anthony said. "They eat shit. Their own shit. That's what they eat."

"Do you have to use that language?"

Anthony didn't bother to respond.

At home, they discovered that the bees had managed to survive on their own, a fact that somehow seemed to depress Anthony; and after shuffling halfheartedly through the frames and getting stung six or seven times, he went to bed.

The trouble—the final trouble, the trouble that was to take Anthony out of their hands for good—started at school. Anthony was almost 12 now, but because of his various problems, he was still in fifth grade. He was in a special program, of course, but he took lunch and recess with the other fifth graders. On the playground, he towered over them, plainly visible 100 yards away, like some great unmoving statue of the Buddha. The other children shied away from him instinctively, as if they knew he was beyond taunting, beyond simple joys and simple sorrows. But he was aware of them—aware in a new way—of the girls, especially. Something had happened inside him while he was away—"Puberty," Barebaum said. "He has urges like any other boy"—and he didn't know how to express it.

One afternoon, he and Oliver Monteiros, another boy from the special program, cornered a fifth-grade girl behind one of the temporary classrooms. There they "stretched" her, as Anthony later told it—Oliver had her hands, Anthony her feet—stretched her till something snapped in her shoulder and Anthony felt his pants go wet. He tried to tell the principal about it, about the wetness in his pants, but the principal wouldn't listen. Dr. Collins was a gray-bearded black man who believed in dispensing instant justice. He was angry, gesturing in their faces, his beard jabbing at them like a weapon. When Anthony unzipped his fly to show him what had happened, Collins suspended him on the spot.

Pat spoke with Anthony, and they both—she and Ken—went in to meet with Collins and the members of the school board. They took Barebaum with them. Together, they were able to overcome the principal's resistance, and Anthony, after a week's suspension, was readmit-ted. "One more incident," Collins said, his eyes aflame behind the discs of his wire-framed glasses, "and I don't care how small it is, and he's out. Is that understood?"

At least Anthony didn't keep them in suspense. On his first day back, he tracked down the girl he'd stretched, chased her into the girls' room and, as he told it, put his "stinger" in her. The girl's parents sued the school district, Anthony was taken into custody and remanded to juve-nile hall following another nine-month stay at Hart, and Ken and Pat finally threw in the towel. They were exhausted, physically and emo-tionally, and they were in debt to Barebaum for some $30,000 above what their insurance would cover. They felt cheated, bitter, worn down to nothing. Anthony was gone, adoption a sick joke. But they had each other and, after a while—and with the help of Skippy II—they began to pick up the pieces.

• • •

And now, six years later, Anthony had come back to haunt them. Ken was enraged. He, for one, wasn't about to be chased out of this house and this job—they'd moved once, and that was enough. If he'd found them, he'd found them—so much the worse. But this was America, and they had their rights, too. While Pat took Skippy to the kennel for safe-keeping, Ken phoned the police and explained the situation to an Of-ficer Ocksler, a man whose voice was so lacking in inflection, he might as well have been dead. Ken was describing the incident with Skippy I when Ocksler interrupted him. "I'm sorry," he said, and there was a faint animation to his voice now, as if he were fighting down a belch or passing gas, "but there's nothing we can do."

"Nothing you can do?" Ken couldn't help himself: He was practically yelping. "But he broiled a harmless puppy in the oven, raped a fifth-grade girl, sent us 32 death threats and tracked us down even though we quit our jobs, packed up and moved and left no forwarding address." He took a deep breath. "He thinks he's a bee, for Christ's sake."

Ocksler inserted his voice into the howling silence that succeeded this outburst. "He commits a crime," he said, the words stuck fast in his throat, "you call us."

The next day's mail brought the second threat. It came in the form of a picture postcard, addressed to Pat and postmarked locally. The pic-ture—a Japanese print—showed a pale, fleshy couple engaged in the act of love. The message, which took some deciphering, read:

KING BEE

Dear Mother Pat,
I'm a king bee,
Gonna buzz round your hive,
Together we can make honey,
Let me come inside.
                    Your son, Anthony

Ken tore it to pieces. He was red in the face, trembling. White babies, he thought bitterly. An older child. They would have been better off with a seven-foot Bantu, an Eskimo, anything. "I'll kill him," he said. "He comes here, I'll kill him."

It was early the next morning—Pat was in the kitchen, Ken upstairs shaving—when a face appeared in the kitchen window. It was a large and familiar face, transformed somewhat by the passage of the years and the accumulation of flesh, but unmistakable, nonetheless. Pat, who was leaning over the sink to rinse her coffee cup, gave a little gasp of recognition.

Anthony was smiling, beaming at her like the towheaded boy in the photograph she'd kept in her wallet all these years. He was smiling, and suddenly that was all that mattered to her. The sweetness of those first few months came back in a rush—he was her boy, her own, and the rest of it was nothing—and before she knew what she was doing, she had the back door open. It was a mistake. The moment the door swung open, she heard them. Bees. A swarm that blackened the side of the house, the angry hiss of their wings like grease in a fryer. They were right there, right beside the door. First one bee, then another, shot past her head. "Mom," Anthony said, stepping up onto the porch, "I'm home."

She was stunned. It wasn't just the bees, but Anthony. He was huge, six feet tall at least, and so heavy. His pants—they were pajamas, hospital issue—were as big as a tent, and it looked as if he'd rolled up a carpet beneath his shirt. She could barely make out his eyes, sunk in their pockets of flesh. She didn't know what to say.

He took hold of the door. "I want a hug," he said. "Give me a hug."

She backed away from him instinctively. "Ken!" she called, and the catch in her throat turned it into a mournful, drawn-out bleat. "Ken!"

Anthony was poised on the threshold. His smile faded. Then, like a magician, he reached out his hand and plunged it into the mass of bees. She saw him wince as he was stung, heard the harsh sizzle of the insects rise in crescendo, and then he drew back his hand, ever so slowly, and the bees came with him. They moved so fast—glutinous, like meringue clinging to a spoon—that she nearly missed it. There was something in his hand, a tiny box, some sort of mesh, and then his hand was gone, his arm, the right side of his body, his face and head and the left side, too. Suddenly he was alive with bees, wearing them, a humming, pulsating ball of them.

She felt a sharp pain on her ankle, another at her throat. She backed up a step.

"You sent me away," Anthony scolded, and the bees clung to his lips. "You never loved me. Nobody ever loved me."

She heard Ken behind her—"What is this?" he said, then a weak curse escaped him—but she couldn't turn. The hum of the bees mesmerized her. They clung to Anthony, one mind, 30,000 bodies.

And then the blazing ball of Anthony's hand separated itself from his body and his bee-thick fingers opened to reveal the briefest glimpse of the gauze-covered box. "The queen," Anthony said. "I throw her down and you're"—she could barely hear him, the bees raging, Ken shouting out her name—"you're history. Both of you."

For a long moment, Anthony stood there motionless, afloat in bees. Huge as he was, he seemed to hover over the linoleum, derealized in the mass of them. And then she knew what would happen, knew that she was barren then and now and forever and that it was meant to be, and that this, her only child, was beyond human help or understanding.

"Go away," Anthony said, the swarm thrilling louder. "Go...into the... next room...before, before——" and then Ken had her by the arm and they were moving. She thought she heard Anthony sigh, and as she darted a glance back over her shoulder, he crushed the box with a snap as loud as the crack of a limb. There was an answering roar from the bees, and in her last glimpse of him, he was falling, borne down by the terrible animate weight of them.

"I'll kill him," Ken spat, his shoulder pressed to the parlor door. Bees rattled against the panels like hailstones.

She couldn't catch her breath. She felt a sudden stab under her collar, and then another. Ken's words didn't make sense—Anthony was gone from them now, gone forever—didn't he understand that? She listened to the bees raging round her kitchen, stinging blindly, dying for their queen. And then she thought of Anthony, poor Anthony, in his foster homes, in the hospital, in prison, thought of his flesh scored 1,000, 10,000 times, wound in his cerement of bees.

Anthony was wrong, she thought, leaning into the door as if bracing herself against a storm—they do have mercy. They do.

"Oh, <u>here</u> you are, Gloria! I said we'd meet you under the big <u>clock</u>!"

Dunlup Crashes In

fiction by LARRY McMURTRY

R oyce Dunlup was lying in bed with a cold can of beer balanced on
his stomach. The phone by the bed began to ring and he reached
over and picked the receiver up without disturbing the can of beer. He
has a big stomach and it was no real trick to balance a can of beer on it,
but in this instance the can was sitting precisely over his navel and keeping it there while talking on the phone was at least a little bit of a trick.

Since leaving Rosie and taking up, more or less formally, with his
girlfriend Shirley Sawyer, Royce had learned a lot of new tricks. For
one thing, he had learned to have sex lying flat on his back, something
he had never done in all his conservative years with Rosie. Nobody
had ever tried to teach Royce anything like that before, and at first he
made a nervous pupil, but Shirl soon broke him in. While she was in the
process of breaking him in, she talked to him about something called
fantasy, a concept she had picked up in her one year of junior college in
Winklebury, Arizona. Fantasy, as Shirley explained it, meant thinking
about things you really couldn't do, and her own favorite fantasy involved having sex with a fountain. In particular, Shirley wanted to have
it with Houston's new Mecom fountain, a splendid gusher of water in
front of the equally splendid Warwick Hotel. At night, the Mecom fountain was lit up with orange lights, and Shirley insisted that she couldn't
think of anything better than seating herself right on top of a great
spurt of orange water, right there in front of the Warwick.

That wasn't possible, of course, so Shirley had to make do with the
next best, which was seating herself every night or two on what she
primly referred to as Royce's "old thing." About all that was required of
Royce at such times was to keep still while Shirley jiggled around and
made little spurting sounds, in imitation of the fountain she imagined
herself to be sitting on. Royce's only worry was that someday Shirley
might lose her balance and fall backward, in which case his old thing

289

was bound to suffer; but so far it hadn't happened and Royce had never been one to look too far ahead.

His own favorite fantasy was simpler; it involved setting the beer can on his navel. What Royce liked to pretend was that the beer can had a little hole in its bottom and his navel a secret hole in its top, so that when he put the can of beer over his navel, a nice stream of cold beer squirted right down into his stomach with no effort on his part at all. That way, the two pleasantest things in life, sex and beer drinking, could be accomplished without so much as lifting a hand.

Shirley evidently liked sitting on his old thing so much that she was willing to support him to keep it handy, so Royce had become a man of substantial leisure. His memory had never been very keen, and in three weeks he managed to forget Rosie and his seven children almost completely. Now and then, longings for his darling, Little Buster, would come over him, but before they got too strong, Shirley would come home and set a cold beer on his navel and the longings would subside. Shirley lived in a three-room house on Harrisburg, right next door to a used-tire center, and Royce spent much of his day staring happily out the window at a mountain of some 20,000 worn-out tires. For activity, he could walk two blocks down Harrisburg to a 7-Eleven and buy some more beer or, if he were especially energetic, walk another block and spend an afternoon happily playing shuffleboard at a bar called the Tired Out Lounge, the principal hangout of his old friend Mitch McDonald.

Mitch was a retired roustabout who had had a hand pinched off in an oilfield accident years before. It had been he, in fact, who had introduced Royce to Shirley. She had been Mitch's girlfriend for years, but they had had a falling out that started (Shirley later told Royce) because Mitch's old thing acquired the bad habit of falling out of Shirley just at the wrong time. Despite this, Mitch and Shirley had decided to stay friends, and in a moment of lethargy, Mitch had handed his friend Shirley over to his friend Royce. He himself regarded Royce as far too crude for Shirley, and he was very upset when they happened to hit it off. It was his own doing, however, and he managed to keep quiet about how wrong it all was, except to Hubbard Jr., the nervous little manager of the Tired Out Lounge. Mitch frequently pointed out to Hubbard Jr. that Royce and Shirley couldn't last, and Hubbard Jr., a very neat man who had the bad luck to own a bar that was only three blocks from a used-tire center, always agreed, as he did with everybody, no matter what they said.

Still, on the surface, Royce and Mitch stayed buddies, and it was no great surprise to Royce that it was Mitch who called him on the phone.

"What's up, good buddy?" Mitch asked when Royce said hello.

"Restin'," Royce said. "Havin' a few beers."

"You're gonna need something stronger than that when you hear what I got to say," Mitch said. "I'm over here at the J-Bar Korral."

"Aw, yeah?" Royce said, not much interested.

"It's this here East Tex hoedown," Mitch went on. "They have it ever Friday night, unescorted ladies free. The pussy that walks around loose over here ain't to be believed."

"Aw, yeah?" Royce repeated.

"Anyhow, guess who just come in?" Mitch said.

"John F. Kennedy," Royce guessed, feeling humorous. "Or is it old LBJ?"

"Nope," Mitch said. "Guess again."

Royce racked his brain. He could think of nobody they both knew who might be likely to turn up at the East Tex hoedown—in fact, in his relaxed state, he could not even think of anybody they both knew.

"Too tired to guess," Royce said.

"All right, I'll give you a hint," Mitch said. "Her name starts with an R."

Mitch expected that crucial initial to burst like a bombshell in Royce's consciousness, but once again, he had miscalculated.

"Don't know nobody whose name starts with an R," Royce said. "Nobody 'cept me, an' I ain't hardly even got out of bed today."

"Rosie, you dumb shit," Mitch said, exasperated by his friend's obtuseness. "Rosie, Rosie, Rosie."

"Rosie who?" Royce said automatically, all thought of his wife still far from his mind.

"Rosie Dunlup!" Mitch yelled. "Your wife, Rosie, ever hear of her?"

"Oh, Rosie," Royce said. "Ask her how Little Buster's doin', will you?"

Then the bombshell finally burst. Royce sat up abruptly, spilling the can of beer off his navel. He didn't notice it until the cold liquid began to leak underneath him—then, since when he sat up his stomach hid the can, he thought the sudden shock must have caused him to wet the bed.

"Rosie?" he said. "You don't mean Rosie?"

"Rosie," Mitch said quietly, savoring the moment.

"Go tell her I said to go home," Royce said. "What's she think she's doin' over there at a dance with all them sluts? She oughtn't to be out by herself," he added.

"She ain't out by herself," Mitch added. It was another moment to savor.

DUNLUP CRASHES IN

Royce stuck his finger in the puddle he was sitting in and then smelled the finger. It smelled like beer, rather than piss, so at least he was rid of one anxiety. Dim memories of his married life began to stir in him, but only vaguely, and when Mitch dropped his second bombshell, the room of Royce's memory went black.

"Whut?" he asked.

Mitch adopted a flat, informative tone and informed Royce that Rosie had arrived with two short men, one of whom wore a mustache. The other was a well-known oilman who drove a white Lincoln.

There was silence on the line while Royce absorbed the information. "Fuck a turkey," he said finally, running his fingers through his hair.

"Yeah, don't that beat all?" Mitch said. "I guess what they say is true: While the cat's away, the mouse will play."

"Why, what does she mean, goin' off an' leavin' the kids?" Royce said. A sense of indignation was rising in him. "She's a married woman," he added forcefully.

"She sure ain't actin' like one tonight," Mitch said. "Her an' that Cajun's dancin' up a storm."

"Don't tell me no more, you're just makin' it hard for me to think," Royce said. He was trying to keep in mind a paramount fact: Rosie was his wife and she was in the process of betraying him.

"You comin' over?" Mitch asked.

In his agitation, Royce hung up the phone before he answered. "You goddamn right I'm coming over," he said, to no one. Problems lay in his way, however. One of his shoes was lost. Shirley had a scroungy little mongrel named Barstow, after her hometown, and Barstow was always dragging Royce's shoes off into corners so he could nibble at the shoestrings. Royce found one shoe in the kitchen, but the other one was completely lost. While he was looking for it, though, he found a bottle of Scotch he had forgotten they had, a good deal of which he gulped down while he was looking for the shoe. The shoe refused to turn up and Royce, tormented by the thought of what his wife was getting away with, grew more and more frantic. He turned the bed upside down, thinking it might be under there—then he turned the couch upside down—then he stepped outside to kick the shit out of Barstow, who had vanished as neatly as the shoe.

As the minutes ticked by, Royce's desperation increased, and his fury with it. Finally, he decided the shoe was nonessential; he could do what he had to do with one shoe on. He rushed out into the street and jumped into his delivery truck, but unfortunately, thanks to a month of inactivity, the truck's battery was dead. Royce felt like turning the truck over, as he had the bed and the couch, but sanity prevailed. After trying vainly to flag down a couple of passing cars, he hobbled rapidly up to the Tired Out Lounge. Everybody got a good laugh at the sight of him with one shoe on and one shoe off, but Royce scarcely heard the uproar.

"Shirley's damn turd-hound stole it," he said, to silence speculation. "Got an emergency. I need somebody to come help me jump-start my truck."

Nothing wins friends in a bar like someone else's emergency, and in no time Royce was getting a jump start from a 1958 Mercury, his shoe problem forgotten. Five or six experts from the used-tire center stood around, idly kicking at the tires of Royce's truck while the jump-starting took place. Several of them tried not too subtly to find out what the emergency was; after all, they had left their drinking to participate in it and had done so with the expectation—always a reasonable one on Harrisburg—of gunshots, screaming women and flowing blood. A used potato-chip truck with a run-down battery was a poor substitute, and they let Royce know it.

"What the fuck, Dunlup?" one said. "Your old lady's house ain't even on fire."

Royce was not about to admit the humiliating truth: that his wife was out honky-tonking with other men. He silenced all queries by slamming his hood down and roaring away, although the hood popped up again before he had gone a block, mainly because, in his haste, he had neglected to remove the battery cables and had slammed it down on them.

The men who had helped him watched him go with a certain rancor. "The son of a bitch is too ignorant even to put on both shoes," one of them said. They were hoping maybe he'd have a car wreck before he got out of sight, but he didn't and they were left to straggle back to the bar without even a story to tell.

"Dumb bastard," another tire whanger said. "I wouldn't help him next time if a snappin' turtle had aholt of his cock."

• • •

Over at the J-Bar Korral, meanwhile, a colorful evening was in progress. A group called the Tyler Troubadours was flailing away at a medley of Hank Snow favorites and the customers had divided themselves roughly into three equivalent groups: those who had come to drink, those who had come to dance and those who hoped to accomplish a little of both. Brylcreem and Vitalis gleamed on the heads of those men who bothered to take their Stetsons off, and the women's hair was mostly upward coiffed, as if God had dressed it himself by standing over them with a comb in one omnipotent hand and a powerful vacuum cleaner in the other.

Everybody was happy and nearly everybody was drunk. One of the few exceptions to both categories was Vernon, who sat at a table, smiling uncomfortably. He was not sober on purpose, but then, neither was he unhappy on purpose. Both states appeared to belong to him, which was just as well, since as near as he could tell, nobody else wanted them.

Certainly, Rosie didn't. She had immediately flung herself into dancing, figuring that was the easiest way to keep her mind off the fact that she was out on a date with F.V. d'Arch. It was very clear to her that it was a date, since at the last minute she had let him pay for her ticket; beyond that, her imagination refused to take her. She had more or less forgotten why she had been so determined to drag poor Vernon along, but she was glad that she had, anyway, just in case problems arose with F.V.

Fortunately, though, F.V. had shown himself to be a model of comportment. He had flung himself into dancing just as eagerly as Rosie had, mostly to keep his mind off the fact that he couldn't think of anything to say to Rosie. For years, the two staples of their conversation had been Bossier City, Louisiana, and Packard engines, and neither seemed quite the right thing to talk about on their first date.

Also, looming in both their minds was the specter of Royce Dunlup. Despite the fact that he had not been heard from in weeks and might be in Canada, or even California, both Rosie and F.V. secretly assumed that somehow he would find them out and turn up at the dance. They also secretly assumed that by their being there together, they were guilty—probably in the eyes of God and certainly in the eyes of Royce—of something close to adultery, although they had as yet to exchange even a handshake. Both were sweaty before they had danced a step, from guilt and nervousness, and the dancing proved to be an enormous relief. At first, F.V. danced with great Cajun suavity, from the hips down, never moving his upper body at all, which struck Rosie as slightly absurd. She was used to lots of rocking and dipping and hugging when she danced, and while she didn't especially want F.V. to try any hugging, she did expect him at least to turn his head once in a while. Right away, she poked him in the ribs, to make her point.

"Loosen up there, F.V.," she said. "We ain't standin' in no boat, you know. You're gonna be a dead loss when they play one of them jitterbugs if you can't twist no better'n that."

294

Fortunately, a little practice and five or six beers and the fact that there was no sign of Royce did wonders for F.V.'s confidence, and Rosie had no more cause for complaint. F.V. had her on the floor for every dance and they were cut in on only twice, both times by the same massive drunk, who couldn't seem to get over the fact that Rosie was as short as she was. "Ma'am, you're plumb *tiny*," he said, several times.

"That's right, be careful you don't fall on me. I'd just be a smear on the floor if you was to," Rosie said, charitable in her happiness at finding out she could go about in the world and dance with various men without any lightning bolts striking her dead.

In her happiness, and because the inside of the J-Bar Korral was roughly the temperature of a bread oven, she began to drink beer rapidly during the intermissions. F.V. drank beer rapidly, too, and Vernon bought beer as rapidly as they drank it. The top of their table was a puddle from all the moisture that had dripped off the bottles, and Vernon amused himself while they danced by soaking up the puddle with napkins.

"F.V., we ort to of been doing this years ago," Rosie said, during one intermission. She was feeling more and more generous toward F.V.—the fact that he had gotten up the nerve to mumble "Wanta go?" that morning was the beginning of her liberation.

"We ort, we ort," F.V. said. "Wanta come next week?"

"Oh, well," Rosie said, fanning herself with a napkin.

"They have these dances ever week," F.V. said. He paused. "Ever week on the dot," he added, in case Rosie doubted it.

"That's sweet," Rosie said vaguely, looking around the room in such a way as to leave in question as much as possible. It was rather vulgar of F.V. to rush her so, she felt, and the thought of having to commit herself to something a whole week away was scary.

"It's the same band all the time," F.V. persisted.

"Vernon, you ort to try a dance or two," Rosie said, hoping to slip quietly off the spot she was on.

"I was raised Church of Christ," Vernon explained. "They ain't partial to dancing."

Vernon was not going to be of any help, Rosie saw. He was merely waiting politely for the evening to be over. Meanwhile, F.V.'s dark Cajun eyes were shining and he was waiting to find out if he had a date for next week.

"Well, if Little Buster ain't been kidnaped, or the sky don't fall..." Rosie said, and she let her sentence trail off.

That was enough for F.V. Anything less crushing than blank refusal had always been enough for F.V. He leaned back and drank beer, while Vernon ate pretzels.

Vernon felt as if the road of his life had just suddenly forked, giving him no time to turn. He had left the old, straight road of his life, probably forever, on the impulse of an instant, yet it did not surprise him very much that the fork had so quickly led him into the sand. He did not expect to get back on the old road, and to him the sweat and the roar of the J-Bar was just part of the sand. He watched and ate his pretzels rather disconnectedly, mild in his dullness, not thinking of much.

None of them knew that outside, in the far reaches of the J-Bar parking lot, a baby-blue delivery truck was revving up. Royce Dunlup had arrived and was preparing his vengeance.

He had not, however, parked his truck. On the way over, he had had the feeling that a few beers might clear his head, so he had stopped at an all-night grocery and bought two six-packs of Pearl. To his annoyance, everyone in the store had laughed at him because he had on only one shoe—it was beginning to seem to Royce that he must be the first person in the history of the world to have a shoe carried off by a girl-friend's dog. The cashier at the grocery store, no more than a pimply kid, had felt obliged to crack a joke about it.

"What happened, Hoss?" he asked. "Did you forget to put the other one on or forget to take this one off?"

Royce had taken his six-packs and limped to his truck, followed by the rude jeers of several onlookers. The incident set him to brooding. People seemed to assume that he was some kind of nut, a kind who liked to wear only one shoe. If he went limping into a big dance like the East Tex hoedown wearing only one shoe, hundreds of people would probably laugh at him—his whole position would be automatically undermined. For all he knew, Rosie could have him committed to an insane asylum if he showed up at a dance with only one shoe on.

It was a thorny problem, and Royce sat in his truck at the far end of the J-Bar parking lot and drank his way rapidly through a six-pack of beer. It occurred to him that if he waited patiently enough, some drunk was sure to stagger out and collapse somewhere in the parking lot, in which case it would be no trouble to steal a shoe—the only risky part about such a plan was that Rosie and her escorts might leave before he could find a collapsed drunk. In light of the seriousness of it all, the matter of the missing shoe was a terrible irritation, and Royce made up his mind to strangle Barstow the next time he came home, Shirley or no Shirley. He drank the second six-pack even more rapidly than the first—drinking helped keep him in a decisive mood. The J-Bar was only a cheap, prefabricated dance hall, and Royce could hear the music plainly through the open doors. The thought that his own wife of 27 years was in there dancing with a low-class Cajun put him in a stomping mood, but, unfortunately, he had nothing but a sock on his better stomping foot.

Then, just as he was finishing his 12th beer, a solution to the whole problem accidentally presented itself. Royce had about decided to wait in the truck and try to run over Rosie and F.V. when they came out. He killed his motor and prepared to lie in wait, and just as he did, the solution appeared in the form of two men and a woman, all of whom seemed to be very happy. When they stepped out of the door of the J-Bar, they had their arms around one another and were singing about crawfish pie; but by the time they had managed to stagger the length of the building, the party mood had soured. One of the men was large and the other small, and the first sign of animosity Royce noticed came when the big man picked up the little man by his belt and abruptly flung him at the rear wall of the J-Bar Korral.

"Keep your fuckin' slop-bucket mouth shut around my fiancée, you little turd, you," the big man said, just about the time the little man's head hit the wall of the J-Bar Korral. Royce couldn't tell if the little man heard the command or not—instead of answering, he began to writhe around on the asphalt, groaning out indistinct words.

The woman paused briefly to look down at the small writhing man. "Darrell, you never need to done that," she said calmly. "I've heard the word titty before, anyway. I got two of 'em, even if they ain't the biggest ones in the world."

The big man evidently didn't think her comment deserved an answer, because he grabbed her arm and stuffed her into a blue Pontiac without further ado. The two of them sat in the Pontiac for a while, watching the little man writhe; then, somewhat to Royce's surprise, the big man started the car and drove away, without bothering to run over the little man. The little man finally managed to get one foot under himself—the other foot evidently wouldn't go under him, because he hopped on one leg right past Royce's potato-chip truck and on into the darkness of the parking lot.

Royce scarcely gave him a glance. He had just had an inspiration. When the little man struck the building, it seemed to Royce that the building crunched. He distinctly heard a crunching sound—obviously, the building was flimsy; it was probably made of plywood and tar paper. There was no reason for him to wait half the night so as to run over Rosie and F.V. in the parking lot. A building that would crunch under the impact of a small dirty-mouthed man wouldn't stand a chance against a six-year-old potato-chip truck in excellent condition. He could drive right through the wall and run over Rosie and F.V. while they were actually dancing together.

Without further contemplation, Royce acted. He drove his truck up parallel to the rear wall and leaned out and punched the wall a time or two with his fist. It felt like plywood and tar paper to him, and that was all he needed. He chose as his point of entry a spot right in the center of the rear wall, backed up so as to give himself about a 20-yard run at it, revved his engine for all it was worth and, with blood in his eye, drove straight into the wall.

The J-Bar Korral was a big place, and at first only those customers who happened to lie drinking or dancing at the south end of the building noticed that a potato-chip truck was in the process of forcing its way into the dance. The first impact splintered the wall and made a hole big enough for the nose of the truck, but it was not big enough for all the truck and Royce was forced to back up and take another run at it. A couple from Conroe were celebrating their first wedding anniversary at a table only a few yards from where the nose of the truck broke through, and the young couple and their friends, while mildly surprised to see the wall cave in and the nose of a truck appear, took a very mature attitude toward the whole thing.

"Look at that," the husband said. "Some sorry son of a bitch missed his turn an' hit the wall."

Everybody turned and watched, curious to see whether the truck was going to break on through. "I hope it ain't a nigger," the young wife said. "I'd hate to see a nigger while we're celebratin', wouldn't you, Goose?" Goose was her pet name for her husband—he didn't like her to use it in company, but the sight of the truck caused her to forget that temporarily. Her first name was Beth-Morris and that's what everybody called her, including her husband's best friend, Big Tony, who happened to be sitting right next to her at the table, helping her celebrate her first anniversary.

No sooner had she uttered the forbidden nickname than Big Tony gave her a best-friendly hug and began to make goose talk right in her little white ear. "Shit, your husband's already too drunk to cut the mustard; let's you an' me sneak out to the car and play a little goosey-gander," Big Tony said.

Before Beth-Morris could take a firm stance, Royce and his truck burst right into the J-Bar Korral. Annoyed at being stopped the first time, Royce had backed halfway across the parking lot for his second run. Beth-Morris looked up just in time to see a potato-chip truck bearing right down on their table. She screamed like a banshee, spoiling everyone's anniversary mood. Big Tony instantly had all thought of goosey-gander driven from his mind—he had just time to fling his beer at Royce's windshield before the edge of the front bumper hit his chair and knocked him under the table.

For a brief moment, there was a lull. The people at the south end of the dance hall stared at Royce and his truck, unwilling to believe what they were seeing. Royce turned on his windshield wipers to get Big Tony's beer off his windshield, at which point people began to scream and push back their chairs. Royce knew he had no time to lose: Rosie and F.V. might escape him in the confusion. He let out his clutch and roared right out onto the dance floor, scattering tables like matchsticks.

Of the people Royce sought, F.V. was the first to see him. He and Rosie were dancing near the bandstand. They had both heard the first screams, but screams were not uncommon at a big dance, and they didn't immediately stop dancing. At the sound of gunfire they would have stopped dancing, but screams ordinarily just meant a fistfight, and fistfights were not worth stopping for.

Thus, it was a severe shock to F.V. to complete what he thought was a nicely executed step and look up to see Royce Dunlup's potato-chip truck driving straight toward the bandstand. If shocks really froze blood, his circulatory system would have achieved a state of immediate deep freeze. As it was, except for a couple of involuntary jerks, he managed to control himself rather well.

"Don't look now," he said to Rosie. "Royce is here. Don't look now."

Rosie felt instantly weak. It was not a surprise, though; the only thing surprising was that she seemed to hear the sound of a truck. It was bound to be her imagination, however, and F.V.'s tone had more or less convinced her that her life depended on keeping her head down, so she did. She assumed Royce was stalking through the dancers, probably with a gun in his hand; since she had nowhere else to put it, she reposed her trust in F.V. Perhaps he could steer them out the door, so they could make a run for it.

But F.V. had stopped dancing and stood stock-still, and the sound of a truck got louder; then the sound of screams got far too loud to be the result of a fistfight and the musicians suddenly lost the beat. "My Gawd," the vocalist said, and Rosie looked up just in time to see her husband driving past in his familiar baby-blue delivery truck.

For a moment, Rosie felt deeply happy. There was Royce in his delivery truck, driving with both hands on the wheel, just like he always did.

DUNLUP CRASHES IN

Probably all that had happened had been a dream. Probably she was not at a dance but home in bed; the dream would be over any minute and she would be back in the life she had always lived.

A happy relief swelled in her as she stood there, expecting to wake up. Then, instead of her waking up, Royce's truck hit the bandstand, flinging musicians left and right. The drummer's drums all fell on top of him and the vocalist was knocked completely off the platform, into the crowd. To make matters worse, Royce backed the truck up and went at the bandstand again. The drummer, who had just managed to get to his feet, was once again knocked sprawling into his drums. The second crash did something bad to the electrical system—it spluttered and flashed a very white light, and the electric guitar, which was lying off by itself in a corner, suddenly emitted a horrible scream, frightening everyone in the place so badly that all the women screamed, too. All the musicians who could move picked themselves up and fled—except one, the bull-fiddle player, a tall, gangly fellow from Port Arthur who preferred death to cowardice. He leaped over the fallen drummer and smashed at the potato-chip truck with his bull fiddle. "Son-of-a-bitch bastard!" he yelled, raising the fiddle on high.

Royce was mildly surprised at the stance the bull-fiddle player took, but he was far from daunted. He backed up a few feet and went at the bandstand a third time. The gallant from Port Arthur got in one tremendous swing before being flung backward into the drums and the drummer. The fight was not gone from him, though: He rose to his knees and flung a cymbal at the truck, cracking Royce's windshield.

"Security, security, where's the goddamn security?" the vocalist yelled from the midst of the crowd.

As to that, no one knew, least of all the two owners of the J-Bar, Bobby and John Dave, who had run out of their office to watch the destruction of their place of business. They were both middle-aged businessmen, long accustomed to dealing with rowdiness, but the spectacle that confronted them was more than they had bargained for.

"How'd that get in here, John Dave?" Bobby asked, astonished. "We never ordered no potato chips."

Before John Dave could answer, Royce was off again. He was largely satisfied with the destruction of the bandstand and whirled the truck around to face the crowd. He began a fast trip around the dance hall, honking as loudly as he could in order to scatter the many bunches of people. It worked, too: The people scattered, hopping around like grasshoppers over the many fallen chairs. In order to block the exit, Royce then began to use his truck like a bulldozer, pushing chairs and tables into the one door and then smashing them into a kind of mountain of nails and splinters.

Vernon, ever a cool head in an emergency, had rushed to Rosie's side as soon as he figured out what was happening, and the two of them were concentrating on trying to keep F.V. from panicking, which might give their position away. The fact that they were all short gave them some advantage, though it didn't seem so to F.V. "Good as dead, good as dead," he kept saying.

"Damn the luck," he added mournfully.

"It ain't luck, it's justice," Rosie said grimly. She was not especially calm, but she was a long way from panic—she had not lived with Royce 27 years without learning how to take care of herself when he was mad.

Vernon watched the little blue truck chug around the room, smashing what few tables it hadn't already smashed. The three of them had taken refuge behind the huge man who had danced with Rosie; fortunately, he was with his equally huge wife. The two of them seemed to be enjoying the spectacle enormously.

"That's a pretty little blue truck," the huge lady said. "Whyn't we get one of them to haul the kids in?"

At that very moment, the pretty little blue truck veered their way. "Here's what you do, you two run for the ladies' room," Vernon said. "Run, run!"

Rosie and F.V. broke for it and the moment they did, Royce spotted them. He braked, in order to get an angle on where they were going, and while he was slowed down, six drunks rushed out of the crowd and grabbed his rear bumper. The huge man decided to get in on the sport and ran right over Vernon, who had just moved in front of him to try to get into the truck. Royce jerked the truck into reverse and flung off all but two of the drunks; then he shot forward again and the last two let go. As the truck went by, the huge man threw a table at it, but the table only hit one of the drunks.

F.V. outran Rosie to the ladies' room, only to remember, at the last second, that he wasn't a lady. He stopped and Rosie ran into him.

"Ooops! Where's the men's room?" he asked.

Rosie looked around and saw that the crowd had parted and that Royce was bearing down on them. There was no time for commentary—she shoved F.V. through the swinging door and squeezed in behind him, about two seconds before the truck hit the wall.

The part of the J-Bar where the rest rooms were had once been the projection area when the J-Bar had been a drive-in theater, rather than a dance hall. It had cinder-block walls. Royce had expected to plow right through, into the ladies' john, but instead he was stopped cold. He even bumped his head on his own windshield.

His confusion at finding a wall he couldn't drive through was nothing, however, to the confusion inside the rest room. Most of the women who had been using it were blissfully ignorant of what was going on out on the dance floor. They had heard some screaming, but they had just assumed it was a bigger-than-usual fight and more or less resolved to stay where they were until it was over. Several were in the process of combing their hair upward, one or two were regluing false eyelashes and one, a large redhead named Gretchen, who had just finished getting laid out in the parking lot, had one leg propped up over a lavatory and was douching.

"Lord knows the trouble it saves." she remarked, to general agreement, and the conversation, such as it was, was largely concerned with the question of unwanted pregnancies. A woman who was sitting in one of the toilets was regaling everyone with a story about unwanted triplets when, with no warning at all, a small male Cajun popped through the door and right into their midst. The appearance of F.V. was so startling that no one noticed the small, frightened-looking redhead who was right on his heels; but the shock that followed when the truck hit the wall was nothing anyone could miss. Gretchen fell down beside the lavatory, and a blonde named Darlene opened her mouth to scream and dropped a false eyelash into it. F.V., off balance to begin with, had the bad fortune to fall right on top of Gretchen.

"It's a monster; get him away," Gretchen screamed—she assumed she was about to be raped and rolled onto her belly and kept screaming. A couple of women rolled out from under the doors of the toilet stalls. They assumed a tornado had struck, but when they saw F.V., they began to scream for the police. Rosie had her ear to the door and could hear the wheels of the truck spinning on the slick dance floor. When she looked around, she saw that F.V. was in real trouble. Five or six women had leaped onto him to keep him from raping Gretchen, and a particularly tough-looking young brunette was trying to strangle him with a tubular syringe.

"Naw, naw," Rosie said. "He ain't out to hurt nobody, he just run in here to hide. My husband tried to run over him in a truck."

"He dove at me," Gretchen said.

"You mean there's a truck loose in this dance?" the young brunette said. "That's the dumbest thing I ever heard of."

She hurried over and peeked out the door. "Aw," she said, "it's just a little truck. I thought you meant a cattle truck or something like that. Anyway, it's driving off."

Gretchen was still looking at F.V. with burning eyes—the news that a truck was loose in the dance hall seemed to mean nothing to her at all. "I still think he's an ole sex fiend," she said, looking at F.V. "A man that waits till he's right between my legs to fall down may fool you, honey, but he ain't fooling me."

F.V. decided Royce was the lesser of two evils—he ran out the door, with Rosie close behind him. On the dance floor, a scene of pandemonium reigned. Royce had a headache from bumping his windshield and had decided to go back to his original plan, which had been to run over the two sinners in the parking lot. To make that work, he had to get back to the parking lot, and it wasn't proving easy. The patrons of the J-Bar had had time to size up the situation and a number of the drunkest and most belligerent began to throw things at the truck—beer bottles, particularly. The outraged vocalist had managed to locate the two security policemen, both of whom had been taking lengthy craps when the trouble started. The two policemen rushed onto the dance floor with guns drawn, only to discover that the criminal was in retreat.

Royce ignored the rain of beer bottles and plowed on across the dance floor, honking from time to time. The two policemen, plus Bobby and John Dave and the vocalist, began to chase the truck. Neither of the policemen was the sort to enjoy having a crap interrupted, though, and they weren't running their best. When a small man jumped out at them and yelled "Stop!" they stopped.

"Don't stop," the vocalist yelled, very annoyed.

Rosie joined Vernon. "It's all right, it's all right," she assured the policemen. "It's my husband. He's crazed with jealousy, that's all."

"I knowed it, Billy," one of the policemen said. "Just another goddamn family fight. We could have stayed where we was."

"Family fight my Lord in heaven," John Dave said. "Lookit this dance hall! Hurricane Carla never done us this much damage."

"No problem, no problem," Vernon said quickly, pulling out his money clip. He peeled off several hundred dollars. "The man's my employee and I'll make good your damages," he assured them.

At that moment, there was the sound of a car wreck. Despite the bottles and an occasional chair, Royce had managed to drive more or less calmly down the length of the dance floor and out the hole he had made coming in. It was just after he got out that the wreck occurred. The large man in the blue Pontiac had thought it all over and decided to come back and throw the little man against the wall again, and he was driving along slowly, looking for him, when Royce drove through his hole. Darrell, the large man, was not expecting anyone to drive out of the wall of the dance hall and was caught cold. The impact threw Royce out the door of his truck and onto the asphalt of the parking lot.

The next thing Royce knew, he was looking up at a lot of people he didn't know, all of whom were looking down at him. The surprising thing was that there was one person in the crowd he did know; namely, his wife, Rosie. The events of the evening, particularly the unexpected car wreck, had confused Royce a good deal and he had for the moment completely forgotten why it was he had come to the J-Bar Korral in the first place.

"Royce, just keep still now," Rosie said. "Your ankle's broken."

"Aw," Royce said, looking at it curiously. It was the ankle belonging to the foot on which he had no shoe, and the sight of his sock, which wasn't even particularly clean, made him feel deeply embarrassed. "I never meant to come with just one shoe on, Rosie," he said, doing his best to meet his wife's eye. "The reason is Shirley's damn old dog carried the other one off."

"That's all right, Royce," Rosie said. She saw that Royce had forgotten her little indiscretion, for the moment; he just looked tired, drunk and befuddled, as he often did on Friday night, and squatting down beside him in the parking lot, with hundreds of excited people around, was, indeed, a little bit like waking up from a bad dream, since the man before her was so much like the same old Royce instead of the strange new hostile Royce she had been imagining for several weeks.

Royce, however, felt a little desperate. It seemed very important to him that Rosie understand that he had not deliberately set out to embarrass her. Long ago his own mother, a stickler for cleanliness, had assured him that if he didn't change his underwear at least twice a week, he was sure to be killed in a car wreck someday wearing dirty underwear, a fact that would lead inevitably to the disgrace of his whole family. A dirty sock and one shoe was maybe not so bad as dirty underwear, but Royce still felt that his mother's prophecy had finally been fulfilled, and he needed to do what he could to assure Rosie it hadn't really been his fault.

"Lookt everwhere for it," he said morosely, hoping that Rosie would understand.

Rosie was plain touched. "That's all right, Royce, quit worryin' about that shoe," she said. "Your ankle's broke an' you wouldn't be able to wear it, anyhow. We got to get you to a hospital."

304

Then, to Royce's great surprise, Rosie put her arm around him. "Little Buster askt about you, hon," she said softly.

"Aw, Little Buster," Royce said, before relief, embarrassment, fatigue and beer overwhelmed him. Soon, though, he was completely overwhelmed. He put his head on his wife's familiar slate-hard breastbone and began to sob.

In that, he was not alone for long. Many of the women and even a few of the men who had gathered around forgot that they had come out to tear Royce limb from limb. At the sight of such a fine and fitting reunion, the urge for vengeance died out in the crowd's collective breast—a number of women began to sob, too, wishing they could have some kind of reunion. Darrell, the owner of the ill-fated Pontiac, decided to forgive Royce instead of stomping him and went off with his fiancée to continue the argument they were having over whether titty was an OK word. Bobby and John Dave shook their heads and accepted ten of Vernon's $100 bills as collateral against whatever the damages might be. They realized that, once again, the East Tex hoedown had been a big success. The two policemen went back to their bowel movements, Vernon started an unsuccessful search for F.V., and Mitch McDonald, Royce's best buddy, immediately went to a phone booth to call Shirley and tell her Royce had gone back to his wife. He made it clear that he had nothing but forgiveness in his heart and hinted rather broadly that his own, very own old thing was aching to have Shirley come and sit on it again—to which Shirley, who was filling beer pitchers with her free hand at the time, said, "Sit on it yourself, you little tattletale, I got better things to do, if you don't mind."

Rosie knelt by her husband, gratefully receiving the warm sentiments of the crowd. Many a woman leaned down to tell her how happy she was that she and her husband had got it all straightened out. Royce had cried himself to sleep against her breast. Soon an ambulance with a siren and a revolving red light screamed up and took Royce and Rosie away, and then two big white wreckers came and got the Pontiac and the potato-chip truck. Some of the crowd straggled back through the hole in the wall to talk things over; others drifted off home; and many stayed where they were—all of them happy to have witnessed, for once, such passion and compassion. Then, when all was peaceful, a spongy raft of clouds blew in from the Gulf, hiding the high wet Houston moon, and the clouds began to drop a soft, lulling midnight drizzle onto the parking lot, the cars and the happy, placidly milling crowd.

PLAYBOY'S PARTY JOKES

A mother took her young daughter to an art museum. They came across a statue of a naked man. The daughter pointed to its penis and asked, "What's that?"

The mother said, "That's something boys have and girls don't."

Her daughter said, "But I want one."

Wanting to end the conversation as quickly as possible, the mother said, "Well, if you're a good girl you'll have one when you grow up."

Her daughter asked, "And what if I'm bad?"

A security guard who overheard the conversation mumbled, "Then you'll have lots of them."

What do a nearsighted gynecologist and a puppy have in common?

A wet nose.

A teacher asked her class if anyone could use the word "contagious" in a sentence. One girl raised her hand and said, "The mumps are contagious."

"Very good," the teacher said. "Would anyone else like to try?"

A boy raised his hand and said, "Our next door neighbor was painting her house by herself and my dad said it would take the contagious."

A naked woman walked into a bar and asked if she could get a drink. The bartender said, "No problem, but it doesn't look like you'll be able to pay for it."

The woman pointed to her pussy and said, "Will this do?"

The bartender took a look and said, "Got anything smaller?"

Two teenagers were arrested for possession of marijuana. At the police station the sergeant told them they were entitled to one phone call. An hour later a man entered the station and asked for the teenagers by name. The sergeant said, "I suppose you're their lawyer."

"Nope," the man replied, "I'm just here to deliver their pizza."

A pink elephant, a green kangaroo and two yellow snakes strolled up to the bar.

"You're a little early, boys," said the bartender. "He ain't here yet."

Two guys were hiking up a mountain when they came upon some people bungee jumping. One said to the other, "How about it?"

The other replied, "No way. I came into this world because of a broken rubber. I'm not leaving it the same way."

Young Quigly and his brother decided to attend a masquerade ball at the country club, dressed in a rented cow costume. However, after an hour, they grew tired of their tandem togetherness and he suggested that they slip outside for a breath of fresh air. Still in costume, the twosome was trotting across a nearby field when Quigly spotted a huge Hereford bull that was preparing to charge. "What are we going to do?" quavered his frightened sibling from the posterior position.

"I'm going to eat some grass," the lad croaked as the thundering hooves came closer. "But, ah, you might want to brace yourself."

Redefining Smart

commentary by WILLIAM F. BUCKLEY JR.

T his year, we subscribed to cable television, mostly because when cable television comes around, subscribe to it is one of the things that with-it households do, even as, 50 years ago, they would have subscribed eventually to larger encyclopedias, larger dictionaries; bought more magazines.

But suddenly I realized the subscribing—to encyclopedias, dictionaries, magazines, newspapers, newsletters, book clubs, catalogs, still other cable networks, etc.—had to stop. Go to a large newsstand. Do you know there are more than 400 magazines devoted to computing alone? More than 40,000 books published per year? More television played commercially in one year than movies produced since the industry began? And, through all this flood of information, occasionally you will want to take time to remind yourself that the sky is blue, the grass green, the waters pure (except for those Gary Hart talked about in a speech in which Ronald Reagan featured).

Which brings us to the question at hand: How is it possible to keep up in today's world?

The answer is that it *isn't* possible to "keep up," not even at a rudimentary level. To which dismaying observation one reasonably asks, "What do you mean by a rudimentary level?" To which I answer—why not?—*People* magazine. It is rudimentary, isn't it, to have a working knowledge of the stars and the starlets of the society we live in?

Well, hear this. Last Christmas, my wife and I sailed in the Caribbean with a couple with whom we have for many years shared the season. Richard Clurman is my best-informed friend in the entire world. When serving as chief of correspondents for *Time* and *Life*, he cultivated and developed those habits that required that he know everything about everything going on. So he arrived, as usual, with his heavy rucksack of books and magazines. Among the latter, I remember offhand *Scientific American, The Economist, The Atlantic, Harper's, The New Republic, The Na-*

tion, National Review, Esquire, Time, Newsweek, PLAYBOY, *Business Week, Foreign Affairs,* and I am certain to have forgotten a supplementary dozen. He reads at a rate that would leave the ordinary computer puffing to keep up. After a day or two, he had gone through the magazines and started in on the books.

One week later, in the Virgin Islands, I sauntered about an old colonial town in search of periodical matter, finding, at the drugstore, only *People*, for a copy of which I exchanged a dollar and a quarter.

It was the year-end issue, and thumbing through it in the cockpit that night, sipping a planter's punch, I came upon what is evidently a yearly feature enumerating 16 persons who had committed renowned gaffes of one type or other, 25 persons who had committed extraordinary feats of one kind or other. My eyes traveled down the list with progressive dismay in search of a name I recognized. I did discover one, finally, in each category, and paused for a moment, taking a deep draft of rum to console myself over my confirmed deracination from my own culture.

It struck me to recite the names I had just read to Richard Clurman. So I gave them out, one after another. He scored better than I did, recognizing three out of 41. (Neither one of us—this was December 1983—had ever heard the name Michael Jackson.) I am 59, Clurman a year older. Was this merely a generational gap? Is it that each of us develops habits of mind, perhaps needing to do so for self-protection, winnowing the flood of information that comes at us so that certain phenomena become, for all that they are ubiquitous, for all intents and purposes imperceptible?

Or was it sheer chance? Individual lacunae? But I told the story of going over the names of the featured galaxy of *People* to Henry Grunwald at a party a few months later, and he shrugged his shoulders. He is, after all, among other things the editor in chief of *People*, even as he is editor in chief of all the publications put out by Time, Inc. "I know what you mean," Grunwald said. "When they tell me who they have scheduled for the cover of the next issue of *People*, half the time I have never heard of him or her."

• • •

Someone once said that Erasmus (1466–1536) was the last man on earth about whom it could more or less safely be said that he knew everything there was to know. But even in the 16th century, "everything" was defined as everything common to Western culture. Erasmus could hardly have known very much about cultures whose existence neither he nor anyone else in the Western world had written about. What they meant to say was that Erasmus had probably read every book then existing in those Western languages in which books were then written. The library at the University of Salamanca, founded in the 13th century, still has, framed and hanging over the little arched doorway that leads into the room in which all of the books of one of the oldest universities in Europe were once housed, a papal bull of excommunication directed automatically at any scholar who left the room with one of those scarce, sacred volumes hidden in his vestments. Books copied out by hand can be very valuable. The tradition is not dead, thanks to the Russian *samizdat*, by which Soviet dissenters communicate with one another, even as early Christians communicated by passing about tablets in the catacombs. Knowledge in those days, in the early years of movable type, was difficult to come by. But then there was not so much of it as to overwhelm. In that relatively small room in Salamanca were housed all the books an Erasmus might be expected to read—granted that his mind was singular and his memory copious. So had been Thomas Aquinas', a man modest except when laying down certitudes, who admitted, sheepishly one must suppose, that he had never come across a single page he had not completely and instantly understood. If, *per impossibile*, Thomas was required to linger a few days in purgatory for committing the sin of pride, I am certain that the torturers stood over him demanding that he render the meaning of the typical "documentation" (that is what they call instructions) of a modern computer.

Never mind the exceptional intelligence. It is sufficient to meditate that in the 16th century it was acknowledged as humanly possible to be familiar with all the facts and theories then discovered or developed; to read all the literature and poetry then set down. To know the library of Western thought.

Move forward now 250 years and ask whether or not Benjamin Franklin could have been surprised by an eldritch scientific datum, an arcane mythological allusion, a recondite historical anecdote, an idiosyncratic philosophical proposition. Of course he could have been, even bearing in mind that Benjamin Franklin was a singular intelligence, eclectically educated, and that he was surrounded, at the convention in Philadelphia, by men most of whom moved sure-footedly in the disciplines then thought appropriate to the background of statesmen. The standards at Philadelphia were high; indeed, it has been opined that at no other deliberative assembly in history was there such a concentration of learning and talent.

But these are anomalies. We ask, and continue to do so, How much was there lying about to be learned? Two hundred and fifty years having passed since the last man died who "knew" everything, then by definition it follows that there were "things" Ben Franklin didn't know. Perhaps we are circling the target. "Things." What things?

• • •

It is said that twice as much "knowledge" was charted in 1980 as in 1970. How can one make an assertion of that kind? At a purely technical level, it isn't all that hard to conceive. Suppose, as an example, that every decade, the penetrating reach of a telescope doubles. In that case, you begin the decade knowing X about astronomic phenomena. At the end of the first decade, you know $2X$; at the end of the second decade, $4X$; and so on.

It is so (the epistemologists tell us) primarily because computer science advances us (we fall back on ancient metaphors) at an astronomic rate. It was somewhere reported that when George Bernard Shaw was advised that the speed of light was equal to 186,000 miles per second, he greeted that finding as a madcap effrontery—either that or a plain, bald lie.

Such sullen resistance to the advancement of physical knowledge is behind us; indeed, it has left us blasé rather than awed. When we pick up the telephone and lackadaisically dial Hong Kong, we simply submit—to a kind of magic we never presume to understand. The inquisitive minority among those who use such instruments for such purposes is mindful that something quite extraordinary is going on, triggered by rudimentary digital exertions by one finger of one hand, the result of which is to rouse a friend (he had better be a friend, considering that it's midnight in Hong Kong) by ringing his telephone 8,000 miles away: a process that combines a knowledge of "things"—things such as transistors, transmitters, radio beams, oscilloscopes, etc., etc., etc.—they will simply never understand and are unlikely to burden themselves with the challenge of attempting to understand.

So it is that the knowledge explosion, as we have come to refer to it, is acquiescently and routinely accepted by both the thoughtful and the thoughtless, the grateful and the insouciant. Every now and then one identifies a little cry of frustrated resentment. Ten years ago, I took to Bermuda a self-effacing boatwright in his mid-60s to give expert testimony in a lawsuit. He was asked by the defendant's lawyer how he could presume to qualify as an expert in all that had to do with the construction of a seagoing boat—woodwork, electricity, engine, rigging, plumbing, sail. William Muzzio answered diffidently that, in fact, he knew as much as any of the specialists who worked for him who had mastered only the expertise in their separate fields.

He then paused for a brief moment in the little, attentive courtroom....

He did not, he corrected himself, know—himself—how to fabricate transistors for ships' radio gear. Thus the sometime complete boatwright formally acknowledged the progressive relative finiteness even of his own very wide expert knowledge of all that used to be required to launch a seagoing yacht. Others acknowledge their progressive relative ignorance by the simpler expedient of paying no attention to it whatever.

• • •

Consider, in the light of our general concern about our increasing ignorance, the obsessive interest in the working habits of the president of the United States. It is widely acknowledged that Ronald Reagan devotes fewer hours to studying the data that flow into the Executive cockpit than his predecessor did. But two questions are begged by those who stress invidiously the comparison. The first is: Is this difference reflected in the quality of Reagan's performance as chief executive? And the second, How could his predecessor, Jimmy Carter, reasonably assume that he had mastered all the data conceivably relevant to the formulation of the most enlightened decision? How do we correlate—or do we?—knowledge and performance in nonscientific situations? Unflattering things have been said about Carter's handling of the presidency, but nobody ever accused him of dereliction at the homework level. And then again, five presidents back, John F. Kennedy was once overheard to say that the presidential workload was entirely tolerable. Notwithstanding this nonchalant evaluation of arguably the most taxing job in the world, Kennedy, as chief executive, had probably more full-time bards working to apotheosize him than any president since, oh, Abraham Lincoln.

What are we to make of all this confusion on the matter of time devoted to acquisition of knowledge?

• • •

So we move in on an intimation of the painless acclimation of our culture to an unspoken proposition: that every day, every way, man knows more and more, while every day, in every way, individual men know less and less. The question arises whether we give in, by our behavior to complacency, or acknowledge philosophically, even stoically,

311

force majeure much as we acknowledge biological aging and, eventually, death. There is, after all, nothing an epistemological reactionary can do to erase human knowledge. Buckminster Fuller remarked that it is impossible to learn less. Valiant efforts at Luddite nescience have been made, most notably by Pol Pot, who recently set out to kill everyone in Cambodia who was literate—save, presumably, those in his circle who needed to read his instructions to kill everyone else who could read his instructions. He was stopped, finally, after he had killed somewhere between one quarter and one third (the estimates vary) of all Cambodians. But poor Pol Pot, all he ultimately accomplished was the premature death of millions of people and a testimonial dinner in his honor by Communist China.

Given, then, that we cannot hope to read, however much time we give over to the effort, one hundredth of the books published in America alone every year, nor read one periodical out of every 100 published, and all of this to say nothing of catching up with those masterpieces written yesterday that silt up into public recognition, some of them 10, 20, even 50 years after first published, how can we hope to get about with any sense of—self-satisfaction isn't quite the right word, because self-satisfaction is not something we ought ever to strive after—rather, well: *Composure* is probably as good a word for it as comes readily to mind?

● ● ●

Nothing I have ventured until now is, I think, controversial. Is it controversial to bridge over to the final point; namely, that inhabitants of a common culture need to have a common vocabulary, the word vocabulary here used in the most formal sense as the instrument of intercommunication?

It is probably not a culturally disqualifying civic delinquency, or even civic abnegation, to come late, say six months or even a year late, to the recognition of Who is Michael Jackson? and What exactly is it that makes him, after two hours at a studio, create something the price of which Picasso would not have dared to ask after 20 hours' work at his easel? But I do think it hovers on civic disqualification not to know what is meant, even if the formulation is unfamiliar, when someone says, "Even Homer nodded."

Now, any time anybody comes up with something everybody ought to know on the refined side of, say, *The world is round, not flat*, or, *A day comprises 24 hours*, you will encounter an argument over whether knowledge of that particular datum is really necessary to integration as a member of a culture. So that what I just said about Homer's nodding

312

will be objected to by some as not intrinsic to a "common vocabulary" in the same way that, let us say, it is intrinsic to know the answer to the question What was Hitler's Holocaust? Subgroups within a culture will always feel that a knowledge of certain "things"—even of certain forms, certain recitations—is indispensable to a common knowledge and that without them, intercourse (social intercourse, I suppose I should specify, writing for PLAYBOY) is not possible. These "things" go by various names and are of varying degrees of contemporary interest. For instance, there is "consciousness enhancement" as regards, oh, black studies, or malnutrition, or Reagan's favoritism toward the rich. But these are, I think, faddist in any large historical perspective. Not so much more remote "things," such as Homer's nodding.

With the rise of democracy and the ascendancy of myth-breaking science, the need arose to acknowledge man's fallibility, preferably in a way that also acknowledged man's vanity. This was the period during which a belief in the divine right of kings began to wither on the overburdened wings of certitude. So that it became common in the 17th century, the lexicographers tell us, to reflect that if it—i.e., human fallibility—could strike out at Homer, the more so could it overtake us. Homer was the symbol for the poet universally regarded as unerring (the divine Homer); yet objectivity raises its obdurate voice to point to errors (mostly factual inconsistencies) committed by the presumptively unerring. Only just before the beginning of the Christian era, Horace had written that "even Homer sometimes nods." And as recently as 1900, Samuel Butler spotted a picture of a ship in the *Odyssey* with the rudder at the front.

And so an entire complexion of social understanding unfolds before us: so that by recalling that even Homer nodded, we are reminded of the vulnerable performance of lesser human beings—indeed, of *all* human beings. And if we acknowledge our weaknesses, then we inherit insight into such terms as "government by laws not by men"; of such propositions as that "nobody is above the law"; and of such derivative things as checks and balances; insights, even, into the dark side, and black potential, of human nature.

In the age of the knowledge explosion, the struggle, by this reckoning, should be not so much to increase our knowledge (though that is commendable even if we recognize, fatalistically, that we fall further behind every day) as to isolate those things that no data that have been discovered have ever persuasively challenged and—here we approach an act of faith—no data will ever plausibly challenge. These are known, sometimes, as the "eternal verities." A secular version of one of these verities is that no one has the right to deprive another man of his rights. Let the discussion proceed over exactly what the man's rights are but not over the question of whether or not he has rights. But in order to carry on that discussion intelligibly, we need to share that common vocabulary that reaches out and folds protectively into a common social bosom those common verities. If, next Monday, all Americans were to suffer an amnesic stroke, forgetting everything we had ever known, what is it that would be required before we reassembled—if ever—around such propositions as are asseverated in the Declaration of Independence and in Lincoln's Gettysburg Address?

Western culture is merely a beachhead in space, Whittaker Chambers reminds us. That insight is what distinguishes today the Renaissance man. He is not the man who, with aplomb, can fault the béarnaise sauce at Maxim's before attending a concert at which he detects a musical solecism, returning to write an imperishable sonnet before preparing a lecture on civics that the next day will enthrall an auditorium. No: The Renaissance man is, I think, someone who bows his head before the great unthreatened truths and, while admitting and even encouraging all advances in science, nevertheless knows enough to know that the computer does not now exist, nor ever shall, that has the power to repeal the basic formulas of civilization. "We know," Edmund Burke wrote, "that we have made no discoveries; and we think that no discoveries are to be made, in morality—nor many in the great principles of government, nor in the ideas of liberty, which were understood long before we were born, altogether as well as they will be after the grave has heaped its mold upon our presumption, and the silent tomb shall have imposed its law on our pert loquacity."

"Wow, Dad! Look at this great action figure!"

A Midnight Clear

fiction by THOM JONES

For days Mrs. Gordon beseeched her stepson, Freddy, to drive her up to the state hospital in Granite Falls. Every Christmas she put together a fruit basket for her third cousin Eustace. His principal relatives had carried out the annual deliveries over the years, but winter had struck early in northern Illinois, and struck with a vengeance, dumping one record snowstorm after another. The storms were followed by fierce winds and two weeks of bitter cold. Christmas spirit notwithstanding, no one in the Gordon family wanted to venture outside, especially for a fruit-basket mission to the mental hospital. So Mrs. Gordon worked on Freddy, who had been bragging recently about the virtues of his Swedish Saab, a car undaunted even by polar climes.

"If this car is as good as you say, 20 miles on a four-lane highway will be a cruise. Are you the right man for the job? Am I talking to the right fella?"

At last Freddy said, "The car is an ace. I'll do it."

Mrs. Gordon had never been to a state mental hospital. For her it conjured up images of gothic horror. In a small way, this was part of the visit's appeal. Also, reports of Eustace's recent stroke made his future seem pretty iffy. One more blood clot and he could be out. Mrs. Gordon knew she could not live with herself if she did not make a last-minute appeal for this poor soul's heavenly salvation. Because Freddy was a doctor, she figured he would know what to do if things got out of hand. As an emergency room physician, he wrangled with crazed drug addicts, autistics and demon-inspired assault-prone schizophrenics on a daily basis.

Freddy showed up at four in the afternoon, three hours late. Although he was dressed in a jacket and tie, he did not look presentable. The hair on the back of his head had rooster-tailed and he needed a shave. His eyes looked like two balls of fire. In spite of being late, Freddy demanded caffeine. Mrs. Gordon wanted to kill him. Instead she convinced him to clean up while she made a pot of Starbucks. Freddy was blowing his

316

nose when she barged into the bathroom with a plastic traveler's cup of coffee. "Let's get this show on the road," she said.

The sun sat low in the winter sky and they weren't even out of the driveway yet. Freddy complained that the coffee was too hot and got out of the car to break off a hunk of snow to cool it down. By now Mrs. Gordon was having second thoughts. She had spent most of the morning putting on makeup and getting dressed. Then she'd paced about the house like a madwoman, exhausting herself thinking of the barbarous scenes that might transpire at the hospital.

Freddy started the car and flipped on the soundtrack from the film *Crumb*. Concentrating on his coffee, he drove the Saab through the west side of town and then caught the highway to Granite Falls. *Crumb*'s syncopated ragtime rhythms were like theme music, by turns festive, exuberant and depressing. Except for roadwork vehicles and the intrepid Saab, very few cars were out. The road was ghostly.

Highway 31 ran parallel to the Fox River and when the Saab wasn't chugging through heavy snow, it faced winding curves slick with ice. Freddy braked for a van, the car spun and Mrs. Gordon slapped her hand against the dash. Freddy smiled. "You don't trust my driving skills."

"The road conditions are utterly *harrowing*, and you're driving one-handed. I got up at nine, I've been drinking coffee all day and I'm a nervous wreck," she said. "Absolutely shot."

Freddy laughed. "You said I look bad? You look worse. Haggard. A bag lady."

"I'm hagged," Mrs. Gordon said, letting out a sigh. She studied the old estates lining the river. Such scenes normally gave her pleasure, but now all she could think of was the upkeep and the heating bills. The owners would have to be millionaires, literally, with money to burn. She turned to Freddy and said, "What if someone attacks us? Crazy people have the strength of 30. They're like Samson. Even the little ones."

"That's why they lock them up," Freddy said. "Given enough time the mentally ill—an M.I.—will pull some crazy-ass shit. Most are tame, but murder and mayhem have a way of unfolding in their presence. We *could* be killed at the hands of some violent monster. More likely I'll roll the car and we'll drown in the river. I'm not Mario Andretti. I can't believe I agreed to do this in such shit weather, with a hangover yet."

"You're driving like a maniac!" Mrs. Gordon said. "I need...Dramamine or something. One more wild curve and I'll die. I can't take any more."

Freddy raised his voice over the music. "I can't take it either. I'm just trying to get this whole thing over with and get my ass back home and into bed. This was all your big idea. Eustace won't even remember us. He's not there, never was."

Mrs. Gordon bristled. "He's got an immortal soul," she said, "and this is Christmas."

Freddy shook his head with finality. "He won't be judged. He is defective."

"His dad took him to *whores!*" Mrs. Gordon said. "That's sin of the worst sort."

"What did you say?" Freddy cranked down the stereo. "He took him to a whorehouse? I thought they were big Christians."

Mrs. Gordon corrected her posture. Looking straight ahead she said, "When he came of age, Eustace sort of got out of control. His doctor had the name of some woman. It wasn't a whorehouse."

Freddy scratched the stubble on his neck. "Geez. I never figured that Eustace got laid. Just that he fell 95 feet off the water tower. Somehow I never imagined anything sexual happened with him."

"Once a week," Mrs. Gordon said, "something sexual happened."

Freddy turned off the stereo. "I have to fight to hear you. What did this woman look like?"

"She must have been a bird," Mrs. Gordon said. "To be able to put up with that. But, then, it was probably over quick——"

"And it calmed him? It did the trick?"

"As far as I know. But you just can't say he won't be judged."

The Saab hit a straightaway by the Campana factory and Freddy turned to his stepmother. "Eustace is an imbecile! You want to bring him to your house and take care of him in the true Christian spirit? Change diapers and stuff? No! I didn't think so. You think a fruit basket is going to help? The glue factory. That's where we're going. I'm not a Nazi. I'm just sayin'."

The Saab's radar detector began to blink as they approached the city limits of Granite Falls. The state hospital was situated on the east side of the highway, across from the river. It consisted of 22 Victorian-era buildings, only half of which were still operational. The hospital had been built on spacious grounds at a time when land and labor were cheap. It sat amid a grove of oak, elm and maple trees, their branches laden with dripping daggers of clear ice. Snow swirled in drifts over a deeper layer of packed snow, white, untrampled except for animal tracks. Mrs. Gordon clapped on a pair of sunglasses and studied the frigid landscape. A formidable wrought iron fence, interspersed with brick pillars, surrounded the grounds. There was no chain-link or razor wire, but the fence was tall and artistically deceptive. It was there for security. Freddy wheeled through the main gate and parked in the visitors' lot. "Here we are at last, my dear, the bughouse. The snake pit. Vermin and reptiles abounding."

Mrs. Gordon's throat was dry. "I really don't know if I can go through with it."

"Well, you simply must, dear heart. And let me say that this is yet another fine mess you've gotten us into!" Freddy grabbed the fruit basket from Mrs. Gordon's lap. "One more." As he opened the door, a bitter crosswind hit him like a slap in the face. He pulled up the collar on his overcoat and cursed himself for not wearing a hat. Mrs. Gordon put her head down against the wind and followed, vainly attempting to preserve her hairdo.

"Slow down," she said. "I'm wearing heels. I can't keep up with you."

"Flash frozen," Freddy said. "Antarctica. It's like liquid nitrogen."

A patient in a stocking cap and a Navy pea coat stopped Freddy to cadge a cigarette. Freddy shook off his gloves and pulled a pack of Kools from his pocket. He gave them to the man and said, "Keep them, buddy. I quit as of now. My New Year's resolution."

At this, a very short man wearing an overcoat and a dark homburg came around from the side of a beige Electra. His mustache was white with frost yet he seemed oblivious to the cold. The Buick had a flat and the two men were attempting to replace it with a mini spare. Now that he had been engaged, Freddy felt compelled to help them. He pulled on his gloves and replaced the lug nuts on the wheel. The man in the pea coat tightened them with the lug wrench while Mrs. Gordon held her ears and winced.

"Va-boom!" the short fellow said. His voice was deep and powerful. "Done. Ah-ho-yeah!" But as he let the jack down and the full weight of the car came to bear, the mini spare went flat. "Oh brother!" he said. "What's this country coming to? Why can't they give you a real tire for a spare? I *knew* this was going to happen. I'm calling a tow truck, Norman. This is intolerable!"

Freddy asked where Ward Six was located and the short man pointed at the hospital clock tower. "The gray building behind the clock tower," he said. "Jarrad Hall. There's a plaque on the door. If you get to the water tower, you've gone too far. Those two chimneys from the power plant beyond...see there? It's the last outpost of civilization. Chinese Turkistan, Outer Mongolia, man. You will never make it back alive."

Freddy nodded his head briskly at the two men. "Gotcha! Good day, gentlemen."

"Come on," Mrs. Gordon said as she plodded on ahead. "If we stand here another minute, I'll die."

"The guy is right, those little tires are ridiculous. I mean, who thought of that? It's not exactly what you call a grand inspiration."

"They were thinking in terms of space saving," Mrs. Gordon said. "Cargo space. If you want to transport dope, a dead body or something, there's more room."

"Yes, of course, but what stupid, fucking goddamn assholes they are just the same. The empire is in terminal decline."

"You have the foulest mouth of anyone alive," Mrs. Gordon said.

Freddy looked at her sharply. "I traverse hell on a daily basis. I'm known for my poignant effusions. To imagine that any human escapade could turn out well seems unthinkable to me, but this trip, Iona? Oh, do forgive me! You know I have a perception of things very few can endure. I will abstain from burrowing any further into my fourth dimension of despair except to say that this very planet has gangrene."

"The earth has gangrene," she said. "It's not paradise. Not by a long shot."

The pair followed the walkway around the clock tower and reached a gray building with locked doors. Freddy bolted ahead until he came upon the water tower. He turned around and ran back to his stepmother. "We're lost. I don't know what to do. I haven't even got a plan." He pulled off his coat and put it over his head like a blanket. They stood together shivering for a moment until a maintenance worker driving a snowplow stopped and gave them a lift back. He pulled a key ring from his belt, unlocked the door and let them inside.

The lobby was dark and empty, but it was warm. Freddy kicked off his loafers and began to rub his feet in a savage fashion. "Son of a bitch, it's cold!"

Mrs. Gordon blew on her hands and rubbed her face. "Oh God!" she said. "That was absolute hell!"

"Changing that tire. Shit! Goddamn motherfucker! Why was I born?"

"You were born because your dad screwed a bimbo," Mrs. Gordon said. "And now that you're here, you just have to make the best of it, like all the rest. Don't think of the philosophical implications."

Mrs. Gordon sat on a narrow bench next to Freddy and had begun to rub her own feet when a voice rattled over the intercom. "Please step forward and state your business."

Freddy spotted a small TV camera just above the intercom speaker.

He moved before it and said, "Dr. Frederick Blaine here to see Eustace Elliot Eckstrom."

Freddy heard someone giggling in the background. The same voice pitched an octave lower said, "Eckstrom, Eustace, joost von moment. Ees he yah patient, doc-taw?"

"He's my relative!"

Mrs. Gordon clutched her body under her coat. "I'm frozen down to the core level," she said. "How do penguins take it?"

"I don't know. They have antifreeze in their blood. Maybe they hate their lives." Freddy peered through the metal mesh gate that bisected the lobby. "I'm not kidding, if I could push a button and never have been born, I'd push. The deal is this: We are in hell. It's just that they call it earth. If they just called it hell, it would make more sense."

"People could take it better if the right information were put out," Mrs. Gordon said. "I agree with that. Calling it earth is propaganda. Chinese Communist bullshit."

The intercom crackled. "Dot's Ward Six, duke-tor. I wan' you an' the little lady to prozeed down zee 'all to elevator C and take her to d' t'oid floor. How's zat sound to y'all?"

"That's peachy, sir," Freddy said. "That's dandy! We're coming. We're on our way. So look out."

A buzzer sounded and the iron gate slid open. Assaulted by a variety of indefinable but powerful odors, they followed the buffed terrazzo hall to elevator C.

The entrance to Ward Six was an oversize steel door painted with shiny white enamel but covered with greasy handprints, dried blood, snot, scuff marks and indentations that made it look like a guardrail at the Indy 500. Freddy pointed them out. "Look at that! The Incredible Hulk. After his TV series bombed, they sent him here."

"He's in there with green skin and a bad temper," Mrs. Gordon said. "We were fools to come."

Freddy smiled. "Think *hell* and it will all approximate fun."

Mrs. Gordon checked her lipstick in a cosmetic mirror. "H-E double hockey sticks."

Freddy rang the buzzer, then cupped his hands to peer through the thick yellow Plexiglas window of the door. A lanky orderly in a white uniform was seated at the charge desk reading a paperback copy of *The Sea Wolf*, by Jack London. He had a short black beard and long hair and his reading glasses were attached around his neck by a lanyard. Freddy watched him take off his glasses, set the book down and remove a large brass key from his belt. The man wore a name tag that read STE-PHENS. He opened the door and said, "Evening visiting hours are over at 5:30."

Freddy flashed his hospital identification and Stephens waved the couple inside. Stephens went back to his desk and returned to his book. Freddy asked where Cousin Eustace could be located and, without looking up, Stephens adjusted his glasses and pointed to the back of the ward.

A group of patients watching TV turned toward the door to see what was going on. They did not look nearly as crazy as Mrs. Gordon had imagined. In fact, they looked pretty normal. In a moment they turned back to the television, where Christopher Walken was doing a song and dance routine with elves and a snowman. Suddenly the biggest woman Mrs. Gordon had ever seen got up from a large chair and began to bear down on her.

Orderly Stephens jumped up from the desk, pointing a finger at the woman. In an even tone he said, "Stop it right there, Marla! I'm in no mood for fucking bullshit today. So just cool your jets!" Stephens sat down and bent back the spine of his paperback, waiting for Marla to comply.

Mrs. Gordon smiled nervously, hiding behind Stephens and Freddy. Not only was Marla tall, everything about her was large. She had enor-mous shoulders, huge hands and big legs. She had coarse facial fea-tures. Her teeth were large, but they were regular. Her hair was black and cut at shoulder length. She wore a plain black dress that looked homemade, a pearl choker and black penny loafers. She waited behind a grizzly, middle-aged man in a blue-striped cotton robe and pajamas who was smoking a cigarette and playing a game of solitaire. When Stephens had beaten the spine of his book into submission, he made a flicking motion with his hand, as if he were shooing a fly. "Eckstrom's way back thataway."

The ward was hot, and the air heavy and stale. Freddy unbuttoned his coat and loosened his tie, looking around. He had never been to Granite Falls before, but he had been in more than a few psychiatric facilities. For a state hospital, Granite Falls was not a bad place. The dayroom was L-shaped with a high ceiling, a blond-stained oak floor and four large alcoves of leaded glass windows that were obscured by thick mesh screens. It was a capacious room, and though there was much evidence of hard wear, it retained a kind of bygone elegance. Apart from a set of old mahogany dining tables, the furniture in Ward Six was a hodgepodge of Salvation Army couches and lounge chairs. In the center of the room, next to the television, was a nine-foot Christmas tree that was festooned with tiny blinking lights, tinsel and at least a dozen paper angels. Pine wreaths, brightened with glossy red holly berries and more homemade angels, hung from the mesh window security screens.

As the pair continued to linger, Stephens beat his book cover against the edge of his desk and said, "Go on, get out of here. I'm sick of looking at you."

Freddy smiled, put on his I'm-in-hell-it-doesn't-matter voice and said, "Thank you for your patience and consideration, Mr. Stephens."

As Freddy pulled Mrs. Gordon away from the charge desk, a man wearing a crucifix and a black cloak sidled up to the visitors. He had thick curly red hair, bushy red eyebrows and a face full of freckles. His pale green eyes were ringed with gold flecks that made Freddy wonder if he suffered from Wilson's disease, a syndrome that is marked by the inability to metabolize copper. The man said, "Good afternoon. Mr. Eckstrom is in the back attending to matters of the highest importance. I'm Charlie White. Allow me to present my dear friend, Marla Hollingsbury."

"You look like Jacqueline Onassis," Marla said. She had a deep voice and a theatrical manner. "Are you her?" She reached out and took Mrs. Gordon's hand.

"Well, people tell me that," Mrs. Gordon said. "I think it's because of the way I do my hair. I mean, I don't try to cultivate the look." She tried to withdraw her hand but Marla continued to pump it vigorously.

Freddy was getting a kick out of this. He smiled at the man in black. "If your name is Charles White, how come you wear all that black? You wearin' a whole lotta black."

"I'm a man of Dostoyevskian complexity," Mr. White said.

"I thought maybe you were like Zorro or something," Freddy said.

Marla continued to pump Mrs. Gordon's hand with such vigor that Iona inadvertently stepped out of her left shoe. "Charlie has seizures," Marla said.

"That's true," White said. "But otherwise I'm in perfect health."

"Take it easy, Marla, you're hurting me," Mrs. Gordon said. "Let go of my hand!"

Marla began to laugh hysterically. "I'm really nervous."

Charles White grabbed Marla's wrist, which seemed as thick as a railroad tie, and loosened her grip. "Marla's excited. She doesn't meet many celebrities in this place."

"But I'm not a celebrity. My name is Iona Gordon."

"We know that you aren't the former first lady," Charlie told her. "She's been dead for some time now! Three years, seven months, four days and 21 hours, 16 minutes."

Marla continued to giggle. "Charlie and I are Jackie's Granite Falls fan club. I'm sorry, Iona. You're such a lovely woman. You do look like her. And your friend looks like John Cassavetes."

Mrs. Gordon was appalled at Marla's tongue. It was black and seemed to be a yard long. Freddy picked up his stepmother's shoe and began to usher her away. She stopped to slip it on. The back of the ward was dark and they moved in that direction with trepidation.

"What's with her tongue?" Mrs. Gordon whispered.

"Pepto-Bismol. The bismuth does that," Freddy said. "Stomach upsets. Either that or she's a chow dog."

Cousin Eustace was on his knees at the back of the dayroom, carefully laying a bead of ketchup along the oak baseboard. "Hey-ya," Freddy said. "What's going on, bro?"

Eustace Eckstrom was in his middle 50s, but he looked much older. He had gone entirely bald since Freddy had last seen him. The left side of his face was sagging. His mouth was set askew. His right eyelid twitched. Eustace wore a pair of loose khaki pants, shower shoes and a dingy cotton singlet. He had the sort of beard that made him look badly in need of a shave, even after a shave. This effect was accentuated by his skin's deathly pallor. Eustace's shoulders were slumped and his countenance was downcast. He took in the presence of his cousins and said, "Those motherfuckers are at it again—pumping gas in here."

"Oh yeah?" Freddy said.

"Yeah!" Eustace said. "I can hear them talking when I take my urine. I can't see them. Just hear tinkle voices."

"In your piss?" Freddy said.

"Yeah, my urine."

"That can happen," Freddy said with a mischievous smile. "I wouldn't worry about it. Hey, look who came here to see you."

Cousin Eustace worked the ketchup container like a caulking gun, edging the nozzle along the baseboard. "It's Aunt Iona," Cousin Eustace said. "I already saw her. She sends me the same thing every year and I never eat it. Trying to poison me and collect on insurance, that's all."

"You could do with some vitamin C, Eu," Freddy said.

"Soda crackers. That's all I eat. Saltines."

Mrs. Gordon said, "You're working awfully hard, Eustace. Would you like to have a little visit with us? Go out for a ride, maybe? I'll get you a present you really want. What do you say?"

Eustace got up and laid a bead of ketchup along the base of a window. "Smell the gas?"

Freddy shook his head and said, "Brother, it smells like you got a load in your pants."

"There's a war in heaven," Cousin Eustace said. "That's what the piss voices say. I'm on the punishment brigade. You better just leave me alone from now on."

Freddy wriggled a finger in his ear and said, "Aunt Iona brought some really boring family pictures she thought you might want to see."

"I'm busy here," Eustace said.

"OK," Freddy said. "I'd like to ask you a question. What's this I hear about you having sex on weekends back in the days of your youth?"

Eustace's features brightened. "Did you talk to Vera?"

"Is that her name? What did she look like?" Freddy said.

"Vera Simpson?" Mrs. Gordon said. "Ho, boy! I remember her."

"She sent me a Christmas card, Aunt Iona. From Oklahoma. Drive me there! OK?"

"To Oklahoma?" Mrs. Gordon said. "I don't know. That's pretty far."

Cousin Eustace thought this over for a moment and a dark look came over his face. He said, "You offered me a present and then you chink out! Go fuck!"

Mrs. Gordon followed Freddy back to Stephens' desk. It was obvious that everyone in the ward had listened to their conversation. Iona Gordon felt so conspicuous she hardly knew how to walk.

Eustace called after them. "I'm not a woman, Fred. I have an Adam's apple."

A patient in a knit hat looked up from the TV and cried out, "That's right! And you are one snoring-ass motherfucker. Know what else, asshole? Romeo and Juliet? If they don't commit suicide, they get sick of each other. Put them in a hotel room for six weeks! Six dick-fucking weeks and they'll be singing a whole different tune."

Stephens looked up from his book and yelled, "Can it, Edwall!"

At the charge desk Stephens told Freddy he would need an OK from a staff physician to review Cousin Eustace's records. "Today that would be Dr. Bangladesh," the orderly said, picking up the phone. "I'll page him. He might still be around."

Freddy looked at the patients watching the television. Others were sleeping on couches, even on the floor. Various isolatos sat or stood, preoccupied with their own thoughts and seemingly oblivious to their environment.

Charles White twisted the crucifix hanging from his neck. He said,

325

"We are held in lower regard than barnyard animals. This is a warehouse for the damned."

"I've been told there's a war raging in heaven," Freddy said.

Charlie fluffed his curly fringe of red hair and Freddy saw large yellow flecks of dandruff spring into the air. "More than war, it's a reckoning," White said. "From your flippant tone I can tell you aren't picking up on this. I'm here. I'm on the inside. Michael and his angels fought against the dragon; and the dragon fought, and his angels, and prevailed not. And the great dragon was cast out, that old serpent, called the devil, and Satan, which deceiveth the whole world. He was cast out into the earth, and his angels were cast out with him."

"So that's what's wrong with the world?" Freddy said. The tumbler on the steel door's lock rattled and the short man Freddy had encountered in the parking lot walked in. His black mustache had thawed and, while it was thick, joining his lip to his hawklike nose, it was no wider than a postage stamp. He wore a pair of half-frame glasses that were steamed from the weather. Freddy watched as he reached up and hung his homburg and overcoat on a wall hook in the meds station. Although his face was ruddy, he did not seem to have suffered especially from the cold. If anything, he seemed invigorated. He slipped on a white lab coat and clipped a beeper to his belt. When he spotted Freddy through the office window, his eyes twinkled and he walked back into the ward. "Va-boom!" he said. "Ah-ho-yeah! So we meet again. I'm Oscar Bangladesh. How can I help you?"

"I'm Freddy Blaine from the City Hospital. And this is my stepmother, Iona Gordon, wife of the late Dr. William Blaine. I wondered if I could take a look at Mr. Eckstrom's records. He's a relative. My cousin."

Dr. Bangladesh escorted the visitors back into the office and dropped the venetian blinds over the window. Freddy, who was 6'1", towered over the psychiatrist. "New shoes?" Freddy said. "Two-tones. Very snazzy."

The doctor wore a pair of white-and-brown Bostonian shoes with smooth toe caps. "Hah! Correct. Christmas present," Dr. Bangladesh said. "Special order from Massachusetts. It's expensive as hell being a little person."

"I never considered that," Mrs. Gordon said. "But it must be true. All the stuff in your house must be different. Your furniture, I mean."

"So true. I live in a gingerbread house," Dr. Bangladesh said. "It requires constant attention."

From the ward Charlie White called, "It gets green mold on it. Or he gets hungry and eats it."

"Isn't that amazing?" Dr. Bangladesh whispered. "The most incredible sense of hearing I've ever encountered. And he can calculate numbers like a wizard. Baseball stats are his thing."

"I am a genius," Charles said. "You are a house eater."

"Yes, Charles, periodically I become ravenous and devour an entire house. Of course! In fact, I could eat a skyscraper right now! The Empire State Building—an appetizer. Hah! Va-boom!"

Mrs. Gordon realized she was staring at the little man. Apart from his new shoes, Dr. Bangladesh wore a brown three-piece gabardine suit that was beginning to shine with age and a dirty yellow tie festooned with miniature golfers driving off from tees. He stood before Freddy and Mrs. Gordon with a square hand tucked into his vest, Napoleon style.

Freddy said, "Eustace doesn't look so hot. There's motor impairment on the whole left side of his body, slurred speech, his eye——"

Dr. Bangladesh smoothed his bushy eyebrows, then steepled his blunt fingers and took on an air of doctorly concern. "Yes, Mr. Eckstrom. A stroke, but there was all the previous physical impairment from a fall he suffered. He hasn't done well here. Twelve years now and nothing but trouble. Few have sufficient ego strength to withstand the rigors of long-term confinement. Have a seat, both of you, please."

"No, thanks. I'm going back out there," Mrs. Gordon said. "I can't breathe." She brushed past Freddy and stepped out into the ward.

Dr. Bangladesh snapped on a floor fan. "Does it really *smell* in here? People say it does. I've been here so long, I can't tell anymore." He pulled a manila-backed chart from a battered gray filing cabinet, glancing at it before passing it to Freddy. "Mr. Eckstrom suffered a series of small strokes, was sent to the City Hospital, and when he stabilized, he was returned to the ward. He's been on heparin and there's been bruising. We didn't know he had family. Is there anyone who might——"

"Take him in? I don't think so," Freddy said. "Not possible."

Dr. Bangladesh's hand clung to the top drawer of the filing cabinet. He hung his head and looked down at the floor. "Well, I'm afraid he can't last much longer."

Freddy poked his head out into the ward and took a look at the back of the room. Eustace was again on his knees with the ketchup container. "He told me someone is pumping gas into the ward."

"Someone *is* pumping gas in here," Charles White said from a dining table chair. Freddy watched him scratch his fringe of red hair.

Dr. Bangladesh stepped into the ward, hiking up his slacks. He placed his hands on his hips, large hips for such a small man. "I have already explained this to you, Charles. Our ventilation system is old. It's inadequate."

"Bullcrap! They've been making buildings for thousands of years." White slammed his fist on the table. "We've got windows! Why can't we open those windows? There's gas in this suckhole."

Dr. Bangladesh looked at the floor and shook his head wearily. "And what sort of gas would that be, Mr. White?"

A woman who was sitting alone in a dark corner crying wiped tears from her eyes with the sleeves of her pajamas and sat up defiantly. She had a British accent.

"It's vaguely...buttholish. We could do with some fresh air, Doctor. Everyone is turning yellow."

From the back of the ward a faraway voice cried, "This motherfucker smells like a ripe ass."

A thin man in his 70s pulled off his plaid snap-billed cap and slapped it against his thigh. "Smells like cat pee," he said.

Stephens clapped his hands and pointed a finger at the old man. "Hen Pierce, you calm down, mister! I'll have you in an isolation cell so fast you won't know what hit you."

"Are you talking to me?" Pierce said. "What I said was mild. People are throwing the F word around again."

Charles White turned to Freddy. "Zyklon B, Dr. Blaine. You're in it with him. They must have sent you over here from Germany with a new supply."

Freddy said, "You're a fraud, Mr. White. All I'm hearing from you is clichéd nuthouse ideation. I think they should give you a bottle of Dilantin and discharge you. Get a job! Hack it out there in the real world."

Dr. Bangladesh pulled a roll of wintergreen Life Savers from his pocket and peeled off the foil top. He put four of the candies in his mouth. "Think of it like this, Charles. If the staff were pumping gas in, would we not also be asphyxiating ourselves?"

"Selective infusions. You're never here for them, Oscar," Charles White said. "Once in a blue moon you pass through the joint and that's it. All you do is play golf."

"Don't attack me. Your argument just doesn't hold up and you know it. Who plays golf when it's 20 below?" Dr. Bangladesh removed his half frames and wiped them with his sleeve. There were beads of perspiration on his forehead. He looked at Freddy. "It's hot in here, I'll give him that."

Charles White said, "Two things: hot and no oxygen."

"Bring it up in group on Tuesday. In the meantime, kindly subdue yourself! I'm tired too."

"You are tired," Charlie said. "Very tired, Oscar. Not good at all."

Stephens set *The Sea Wolf* on the charge desk. "Knock it off, Charlie, or I'll come over there! Those isolation cells are ready, willing and able. I'm counting to three!"

Mr. White turned away and plopped down in a chair before the TV set. He draped his arms along the sides of the chair and sulked. Freddy watched him for a moment. His head and right hand twitched every few seconds. Suddenly he got up and changed channels. Another patient snapped out of a hypnotic daze to protest, and the two started arguing. They could barely be heard over the high volume of the TV.

Dr. Bangladesh waved Freddy back into the office and shut the door. He lowered his voice and said, "Being in the presence of a manic personality is exhausting for me. They suck up all the energy in the room and leave you drained. Every time I walk in the door, there he is, ready to assail me with the most unimaginable kind of stupid crap you could ever think of. A 45-minute rap over nothing."

Freddy studied the doctor's face. "He's right, though. You don't look very well. Your left pupil is a pinpoint and the right is dilated."

Dr. Bangladesh took a step back, alarmed. "Really? What does that mean, medically? I'm not a doctor, I'm a psychiatrist. Is that some cardinal signal?"

"Probably it means nothing," Freddy said. "Just tired, that's all."

"No, there's more," Dr. Bangladesh said. "I feel sicker than a dog. Everything is swirly. An attack of hypoglycemia?" Dr. Bangladesh braced himself against the wall. "Damn! I feel actively sick. I'm dizzy as shit. You don't think I might have an aneurysm or something, do you?"

"Get something to eat," Freddy said. "You haven't got an aneurysm. You're tired."

Dr. Bangladesh held his head in his hands. "Alas, the carcass makes itself known again; I can't think. Ugh! It has to be hypoglycemia. I have a very rapid metabolism. I need to eat. Feel free to sit in here. You will be more comfortable. Excuse me, I have to go eat a little bite and lie down for a minute in the staff lounge."

The doctor's two-tone shoes squeaked as he walked across the oak floor. Freddy watched him reach up to open the heavy steel door and then disappear. As the door slammed shut, Freddy shook his head. Either the job was getting to the man or he had never been quite right in the first place. He closed the door of the office, sat down and began to page through the Eustace Eckstrom chart. What was there was much as he had expected. Eustace had dangerously high blood pressure readings, but there were no recorded vascular studies or MRIs. He was being treated with beta-blockers and diuretics that were adequate but not exactly state of the art. He was receiving stupendous doses of the blood thinner heparin, also Haldol for auditory hallucinations, and large doses of a standard antidepressant drug—a tricyclic that was too much, really, for a person with a tricky circulatory system and funny heart rhythms. On top of that, they were giving Eustace valproate for seizures. Cousin Eustace had a stated IQ of 82. Freddy flipped his tie over his shoulder as a nurse with small breasts, a pitted face and a low-slung ass came into the office. "Are you Dr. Blaine?"

Freddy set the chart down and said, "Yes. What's wrong?"

"It's Dr. Bangladesh. Please, come with me," she said. "He's out."

Freddy and the nurse ran down two flights of stairs to the staff lounge, a small room with a table and chairs, a refrigerator, microwave oven and a coffeepot. Dr. Bangladesh was lying on a Naugahyde couch, bathed in sweat. One of his new shoes was lying on the floor.

"What's going on here?" Freddy said.

"I don't know," the nurse said. "He was all right one minute, and then he just started acting like he was...out of it. I couldn't make any sense out of him. He said something about being gassed."

Freddy laughed. "Gassed, huh?"

"Yes. He was sweating furiously and then he passed out."

Freddy unbuttoned the little man's jacket, vest and shirt. "Any known health problems? Heart disease? Diabetes?"

The nurse thought for a moment. "He guzzles water and goes to the bathroom constantly."

"Where's the house physician?" Freddy said as he removed the doctor's lab coat, jacket and tie. "I don't even work here."

The nurse lowered her voice and said, "The house doctor, Zarkov? We don't want him. He's a bungler."

Freddy took the nurse's stethoscope and began to listen to Oscar's heart. "Meningitis in this place?"

"No," the nurse said.

"Get me a glucose meter and a glucagon kit," Freddy said. He expertly moved the stethoscope about the doctor's chest and then began to poke his abdomen.

When the nurse returned, Freddy said, "I can hear a squeak in his lungs. His pulse is 170. His organs feel normal. Run a check on his sugar. Have they got tuberculosis?"

"No." The nurse pricked the doctor's finger with a spring-loaded lancet. She cocked the device and did it again, looking up at them in frustration. "I can't get any blood," she said. "His hands are freezing."

Freddy took the lancet from her, recocked it and popped Dr. Bangladesh in the earlobe. He squeezed a drop of blood onto the test strip. "Never fails," Freddy said. "Ready? Here we go: countdown!" The glucose meter flashed 45, and second by second the number began to run backward as pulses of red light flashed through the test strip. "How does one acquire a name like Oscar Bangladesh?" Freddy said.

"It's not his real name," the nurse said. "His parents are very high up in India, I think. Maharajas or something. Did he lay that 500-watt smile on you?"

"Yeah. 'Va-boom! Ah-ho-yeah!'"

The nurse laughed. "His parents were pissed that he didn't marry a traditional woman. What they don't know is that he's gay. At least that's the rumor. It must be true—he listens to Broadway show tunes. And here's the clincher—he has three Burmese cats!"

"Three? That cinches it. He's a flamer."

The glucose meter beeped and the nurse handed it to Freddy. "He's down to 28."

"That's pretty low. Saw a guy walk in with a seven once, and he was...walking! Look." He held up one of Dr. Bangladesh's tiny hands. "The tips of these three fingers look like pin cushions. That's why you couldn't get any blood—he's got calluses from self-testing. And look here," he said, pulling up the doctor's shirt. "See these bruises all over his abdomen? Injection sites. He's a diabetic, overweight." Freddy removed the syringe from the emergency kit and squirted the diluting solution into the bottle of powdered glucagon. He shook it for a second, drew the mixed solution back into the syringe and injected it into the doctor's thigh. "What's the date on the package?"

The nurse picked up the box and peered. "It's 15 months old. It expired three months ago."

Freddy said, "It should work fine. Essentially there's a thousand times more, or so, than he needs, and he's a little guy."

The nurse said, "You really are a pretty cool customer, Doctor. Where do you practice?"

"At City. Trauma surgery. In the eye of the storm. Only then am I calm. I cannot say why that is so."

The nurse preened her hair. "Would you like to go out for a drink sometime?"

"I'm pretty busy," Freddy said. "I work. It's about all I do. But thanks just the same."

"You aren't gay, are you?"

"I don't have any Burmese cats," Freddy said. He lifted up Oscar's bare foot, pointing at his little toe. "This little piggy has bunionettes," he said.

The nurse laughed. "You mean that he's too small to get actual bunions?"

"Bunionettes, a.k.a. tailor's bunions, commonly occur with bunions. He's going to end up with a hammertoe."

The nurse laughed. "A hammertoe!"

"Check out the proximal interphalangeal joint on his middle toe. It's swollen. He's got a corn on it. It's a hammertoe fucking waiting to happen."

"It's just bent a little," the nurse said.

"The hammertoe is the converse of the mallet toe, but his metatarsal phalangeal joint is contracted as well. Let me revise my opinion. I predict a claw toe, which is the super-whompo-jumbo combo—hammer and mallet. Bad shoes don't cause claw toes." He kicked the brown shoe on the floor. "No one knows really what does. It can be something systemic like diabetes. Probably just that. When I eyed his foot in the beginning, I was thinking in terms of Charcot's joint. A breakdown of the ligaments and tendons—joint dislocation. This is a very strange foot, nurse."

"Nancy. My name is Nancy. What's yours?"

"Frederick. See here, he has no hair on his foot or toes. He's got shit for peripheral circulation. The nails are thick with fungus. Fissures, dry skin. Ought to try some Sporanox for those nails. It works. The metatarsal head of the big toe is pushed medially and the phalanx is pointing toward the second toe, see?"

"Yes. So what?"

"It's no big deal," Freddy said, "in the cosmic sense. But take an interest in medicine. It's your job. Don't you like it? Aren't you fascinated by it?"

"I hate this place. And I'm beginning to hate you."

The color returned to Dr. Bangladesh's face and he opened his eyes. Freddy said, "Welcome back to the very strange world of rock and roll, Doctor."

Dr. Bangladesh looked at him without comprehension. "Where am I? What happened? It felt like I was drowning. Some horrible Godzilla-like reptilian monster was strangling me."

Freddy said, "You just had an insulin reaction, my friend."

"That's not possible!" Dr. Bangladesh sat up. "I vehemently deny that scabrous accusation. I have an extremely rapid metabolism. I eat 9,000 calories a day. I vaguely have hypoglycemia. I'm overworked. Hell, they

332

work me like a goddamn hound. Where are my glasses?"

The nurse picked up his glasses from the floor and handed them to him. As soon as he put them on he looked at Freddy. "The work of 40 Sabine slaves and 17 horses and never so much as a thank you!"

"It's not against the law to be a diabetic," Freddy said.

"I'm not!" Dr. Bangladesh said.

"Hey, brother, I'm just sayin', you know." Freddy reached over and picked up the doctor's shoe. A lace was broken.

Dr. Bangladesh snatched the shoe from Freddy's hand. "I demand confidentiality on this, from both of you."

Freddy said, "You had a severe insulin reaction. I just want to make sure you know what you are doing. Get a second opinion. You're just feeling rowdy from the incident. I'm not going to say fucking shit to anyone, but I'm right and you've been told."

The little doctor snarled, "Swear."

Freddy held his palm up and backed out of the room. "I don't know nothin'."

Freddy took the stairs back to Ward Six. In a moment the nurse, Nancy, caught up with him and pressed a card with her number on it into his hand. Her cheeks were flushed. She said, "Call me."

Freddy pocketed the card and said, "See that Dr. Bangladesh gets something to eat. Tell him if he doesn't educate himself about diabetes, he's a goner."

The nurse stood before Freddy with her hands on her hips. She said, "You won't call, will you? Well, you can just go to hell!"

Freddy buzzed back into the ward and waited for Stephens to open the office. As he was returning Cousin Eustace's file, he spotted a medical bag lying open on the floor. Inside it was a glucose meter and two portable insulin syringe cases. Also two bottles of Dexedrine. He wondered why Dr. Bangladesh would be taking speed. Probably for kicks. He closed the bag and stepped back out into the ward.

His stepmother was in the middle of the dayroom working Marla's hair over with a brush and a can of hair spray. An array of cosmetics had been laid out on a table. She shifted her weight back on one heel and studied Marla's face. After examining Dr. Bangladesh, Freddy found it hard to factor a giantess into his consciousness. Marla was huge. Mrs. Gordon was saying, "Your hair is very dark. I think we could go with some more rouge."

"We have recreation in the gym," Marla said. "The men let me play basketball with them. They always choose me. I'm good at softball too. You know, I was watching a rerun of *Cheers* the other day and the bartender, Sam—the one who was supposed to be a baseball player—came out from behind the bar and was walking around, bending over and stuff, and I was shocked to see how skinny his legs were. Toothpicks. I don't think it's realistic for the audience to believe that he used to be a professional ballplayer with those thin legs. From the top up, maybe. But not after you get a load of those legs. I used to enjoy the program until I made that observation. I can't get into it anymore. Sam should lift leg weights or something. That guy Woody has a pretty nice body, but too many of the characters on that show are bald. Count 'em. Count baldies next time you check it out. Plus, nobody can be as stupid as Woody. With a chick he would never get to first base."

"I think they're both cute," Mrs. Gordon said.

Marla said, "Frasier is a cue ball. Sam has cotton candy for hair, blow-drier hair. The post office guy is another baldy and he makes me depressed. The fat guy has hair but he's so fat! And it's that wiry kind of hair. Imagine a ton of that all over your pillows or in your bathroom sink. Ecchh! It springs! I can clog dance. I mean…I'm learning how."

Freddy plopped down in a chair next to Marla and said, "What's going on here, some kind of total makeover?" Without waiting for an answer he said, "Christ! I'm having a nicotine fit and I gave away my cigarettes."

Marla said, "Mr. Stephens smokes. Bum a coffin nail offa him."

"He's gone," Freddy said. "Where in fuck, I don't know."

Mrs. Gordon gave Freddy a reproving look. "Stop swearing so much. We're just having a little girl fun. Calm down and check this out. You're going to like it."

She placed her sunglasses on Marla's face. "Perfect, no?" She handed Marla a little hand mirror so she could see herself.

Marla said, "I want a man with a head full of hair, not some cue ball."

Mrs. Gordon snorted.

"Some damn cue ball with a hatchet face," Marla said. "It wrecks the entertainment value of the show, which sometimes has good lines."

Mrs. Gordon shuddered with laughter. Marla pounded her fist against her knee, threw back her head and roared.

"Christ, have you two been smoking a joint, or what?" Freddy said.

"We took a hit off a doobie, so what?" Mrs. Gordon said. "Don't be such a tightass."

"What, you can smoke dope here?"

"Not officially," Marla said.

There was a clamor in the hallway. In a moment the steel door swung open as Charlie White and Stephens struggled to push three aluminum food carts into the ward. Freddy gave them a hand setting up the carts as patients began to line up, selecting trays and utensils.

Once the carts were in place, Charlie White slipped on an apron. "Christmas dinner, folks! And not a bad one for a change. Hot turkey and dressing, the vegetable medley, spice cake with raisins. Mira, turn off the TV! You, Hen P, quit that grab-assing. There's plenty for every-one. And you two, over there laughing. Cut it out. I mean it."

Marla mimicked a scene from *Cheers.* "'Can I get you another beer, Norm?' 'Yeah, sure, sticklaig. 'Cause those ain't legs, them are laigs.'"

Before Charlie White began to ladle out food, he cleared his throat. "Dear Lord, thanks for the food, leftovers though they may be, and the roof over our heads. Thanks for the crappy weather since it canceled the VA Christmas entertainment. That was a blessing. Amen."

Marla and Mrs. Gordon joined the line, picking up serving trays while Freddy helped Stephens pull a case of milk out of the refrigerator and set it next to the serving table. When Stephens gave Freddy a cigarette and a light, Freddy said, "The devil has left the premises!"

Charlie White said, "He's gone. Through the power of dynamic prayer, I can make the sick well. Hemophiliacs, I can cure by the dozen. Or when inclined, I lay a spell on you."

"You better be careful there, Mr. White," Mrs. Gordon said, her eye-brows raised. "They call him Shootin' Bill."

Charlie looked at Freddy. "Who? Him?"

"That's right," Freddy said, taking a big drag on the cigarette. "I'm Shootin' Bill. And I'll shoot ya."

Charlie's face dissolved into a warm smile. "Oh yeah?"

"Take heed. I'm deadly," Freddy said. "So look out!"

"Or you'll be in big trouble, Charlie White," Marla said.

"It's true, I'm a malefactor," Freddy said. "Check it out. The Christ-mas program got canceled, but two mysterious strangers arrive on the scene. Angels? Possibly. Watch this." Freddy moved away from the serv-ing cart and went to the tables, performing a magic trick he often used to great effect with the children in the city hospital ER. "The disap-pearing hankie. Where did it go? Why, nobody knows."

"What else can you do?" Hen Pierce said. "Is that it?"

Freddy picked up four saltshakers and began to juggle, mugging to the audience. The slower patients responded with peals of laughter. "I can't always make the sick well, and I cannot turn water into wine," he said, enlarging the arc of the spinning saltshakers. He would pretend to let one fall, only to kick it back into the configuration with the side of his shoe. The patients waited for him to drop one, but Freddy was adept and well practiced. He edged over to a table and fed two pepper shakers into the arc. His cigarette was pursed in the middle of his mouth and he squinted his eyes against the smoke. "What I can do—I can patty-patty-bop-bop-wop-bop-a-shoo-bop."

Mrs. Gordon said, "You're getting salt all over everything."

Hen Pierce said, "He reminds me of that ice-skater, what's-his-face."

"Brian Boitano," Marla said.

"No," Hen Pierce said. "Scott or Kent or somebody. A fairy."

"Already told ya. They call me Shootin' Bill," Freddy said. "If I had my six-gun I would demonstrate my deadeye aim, but firearms are prohibited in this ward." He caught the saltshakers, set them on the table and dusted himself off.

"Shootin' bull is more like it," Hen Pierce said.

The steel door banged open and Dr. Bangladesh stepped into the ward. His eyes sparkled and his entire condition seemed much improved. "I'm as hungry as a bear," he said. His shoes squeaked as he walked over to the food carts.

Marla set down her food tray, fluffed out her dress and said, "I'm really feeling happy today. I will dance for you. Guys? C'mon!" Marla stepped away from the table and began to dance and sing, "Have a holly jolly Christmas, it's the best time of the year...." She danced like a marionette on strings. Her massive shoulders became liquid and she let her dangling elbows and wrists jackknife akimbo. Her shoe leather slapped against the hard oak floor.

Charlie White said, "All right then, enjoy yourself. Just remember, it all comes to nothing. Our trials and tribulations on this earth are lamentable."

"So does everything come to nothing," Dr. Bangladesh said, taking a bite of turkey. "Please, Charles, no more of your negativity. I've been through absolute hell today——"

"And you think I haven't?" Charlie White said. He handed Eustace a carton of milk and a green plastic bowl filled with cellophane packets of saltine crackers. "OK, Doc, though I've been grazed by every form of failure in the world, I'm not just your plain ordinary loser, and I resent the way you imply that I am."

Dr. Bangladesh set down his fork and picked up a carton of milk. "Have you been taking your meds, Charles?"

"Don't you give me your evil eye, Oscar, the one you learned in Gypsy camps in Afghanistan. I've been taking my meds—taking my meds, taking my meds! There! I've told you three times: Yes!"

336

"The man takes his meds," Freddy said. "For God's sake, Charlie, chill!" Stephens said.

Dr. Bangladesh looked over the top of his half frames. "We all like the highs, but the lows aren't so good, Charles. I'm going to have to review your chart. I really hope you don't start in with your multiple personality shenanigans. I will not tolerate it!"

An orderly from another ward buzzed to be let in. He said, "I've been looking all over for you, Dr. Bangladesh. There's a guy on his way in a tow truck. Who's on the damn phones, anyhow? I've called up here a million times."

"I'm serving dinner," Stephens said. "Marla, knock off with the dancing and sit down."

"Triple A? Is on its way?" Dr. Bangladesh said, walking rapidly to the window. "Send him up when he gets here. The Wienermobile has a flat." He raised up on his tiptoes and looked through the mesh wire. "I can't see anything. You can never get a cab to come out here, and I don't want to be stranded all night." Dr. Bangladesh removed an Allen wrench from his key ring, unlocked the protective mesh guard and cupped his hands on the steamy window. "I can't see anything! When in the hell is the last time anyone cleaned these windows?"

"Never," Charlie White said. "Since never."

The psychiatrist wiped his small hands on his white lab coat. "Yech! Nicotine," he said. "It's terrible. A rotten dirty mess. Somebody get me some window cleaner. Stephens! Call down for some window cleaner and some terrycloth towels. For crying out loud."

Stephens walked over to the call desk and picked up the phone. Dr. Bangladesh returned to his meal. Without bothering to sit down, he began shoving turkey and dressing into his mouth. He looked over at Freddy and said, "I make no apologies, I like to eat. What the hell. I won the pie-eating contest at the Fourth of July picnic. No one can outeat me. Ate a huckleberry pie, a raisin pie, apple, cherry, pumpkin, peach, apricot, blueberry. These were good pies. The secret to a good pie is the crust. And the secret to the crust is lard. When I was done, my little belly stuck out like a bowling ball. Mr. Stephens, what sort of scrumptious goodies do we have for dessert?"

"The spice cake," Charles White said. "Or we have chocolate-flavored tapioca."

"Give me three of each and call an ambulance," Dr. Bangladesh said. "Hah!"

"You can't get Freddy to eat anything," Mrs. Gordon said. "He's skinny beyond belief."

Dr. Bangladesh took off his half frames, wiping the lenses on his coat. "You are anorexic, Dr. Blaine."

"I got sick in Africa," Freddy said.

"Whereabouts? I spent seven years in Zaire," Dr. Bangladesh said. "Before the virus."

"I was there," Freddy said, "after the virus."

A staff custodian came into the ward with an armful of towels and three spray bottles. Dr. Bangladesh said, "Bring that stuff over here. I want to show you something. Come here. This ward is a mess. Look at the lights, for instance. Half the bulbs need to be replaced."

The custodian looked up at the ceiling. "Hey! This isn't my area. I don't even work in this building. I just brought up this stuff. They told me you wanted it. I'm supposed to be on my lunch break."

Dr. Bangladesh took a towel and a bottle of window cleaner and went over to the first alcove. He said, "Some people, professional cleaners, use squeegees and a bucket of ammonia water. Some use vinegar. That's fine if you're on a skyscraper 100 stories high, where every moment is a peril. Ah! What adventure! Well, for small jobs like this, nothing beats a commercial product like Windex or Glass Plus and a good absorbent towel." He squirted some glass cleaner on a section of the window, stopped to fine-tune the spray nozzle and began rubbing the window with a towel. "Start from the top and work down. I'm too short, actually, and there's no ladder. Fie!"

Marla got up and went over to the doctor. He handed her a spray bottle and a towel. "You fold the towel in quarters, Marla, spray the glass and work from the top down."

"I know what to do," Marla said. With her long arms, she was able to cover the entire top of the window in a few swaths. When she was through she looked at the towel. "It's filthy."

"Turn the towel to a clean surface and hit it again," the doctor said.

"This is the most rotten dirty window I've ever seen in my life," Marla said.

After the second try, Dr. Bangladesh handed her a clean towel. "Hit it again. Repeat the whole process."

Marla sprayed the window, and when she began to wipe it down the glass squeaked. "Hear that?" Dr. Bangladesh tucked his right hand in his vest and bounced on his toes. "It's squeaking. You're finally getting it clean. Ho-yeah!"

Marla said, "I need another towel. I haven't got it all off yet."

The patients at dinner fell silent and listened to the squeaking of the glass.

338

Charlie said, "He's never here. We never see him, and now he comes in like this just to show off, bossing everyone around."

"Look! Guys!" Marla said. "You can see the river. You can see the city lights. Cars going by. Cool!"

Cousin Eustace moved next to Marla and took in the view. He said, "Cars pass by the window."

"The nighttime is the right time to clean a window, any window," Dr. Bangladesh said. "The sun's glare will fool you. The nighttime is the right time! Heh-heh." Dr. Bangladesh polished a section of glass and then handed Cousin Eustace a towel. "Wipe down the mesh with this wet one. I don't think these windows have been cleaned in 50 years."

"I want to do another one," Marla said. "At last we can see."

Dr. Bangladesh unlocked the wire mesh guards on the next set of windows and Marla immediately set to work.

A few patients got up from their table and came over to look out the window. "Whoa!" Hen Pierce said. "There's icicles on them trees. *Staglatites!*"

"Stalactites," Charles White said. "Those are *stalactites*."

"There are so many of them," Pierce said.

At this, everyone got up and went to the windows.

"Don't just stand there gawking, all you lazybones," Dr. Bangladesh said. "Pick up a towel and get to work. I'll open the rest of the screens."

"This is great," Marla said.

"It's fun," Cousin Eustace said. "I like it. Goddamn it! Look at that! A shooting star! Right through the trees."

"I saw it," Marla said.

"Where?" Hen Pierce said.

"God! Look! There goes another one!" Marla said.

"Shit, yes," Hen said. "It lasted too."

Dr. Bangladesh said, "It was no hallucination." He handed Marla another towel. "Who did your hair, girl? You look, like, great."

"She looks terrific," Charlie said. "I've been saying that all along."

Mrs. Gordon removed her blazer and draped it on the back of her chair. "What are you doing?" Freddy said.

"I'm going to pitch in too," she said.

Freddy said, "Wait until tomorrow: the three-day pot hangover."

Mrs. Gordon said, "It's like Tom Sawyer whitewashing a fence. That thing. It's infectious."

"Little Oscar isn't doing diddle," Charlie said. "All he's doing is just handing out towels."

"Charlie!" Stephens said. "Quit your fucking goddamn bitching all the time!"

Mrs. Gordon began to clean the windowsills. "I wish I had windows like this," she said. "They have to be worth a fortune."

"I'd jump," Charlie said. "But it's not high enough for suicide."

"Make a note, Stephens," Dr. Bangladesh said. "Mr. White has been tonguing his meds. That's why he's so grumpy. Heh-heh. Come on, get with it, Charlie. We are all having a good time over here. It's very simple, you know. Human beings need to have purpose, we need meaning. It always comes down to just exactly that."

Charlie laughed. "You're the man who said it all comes to nothing, that you went through hell today."

"That was before I ate. All my troubles are gone. I feel great. Ah-ho-yeah! It's a beautiful night. The windows are clean. We've got a clear view. The majestic oaks and maples are covered with a profusion of genuine ice-crystal stalactites. It's a wonderful life. It's just going to get better and better and better, on and on, forever and forever. Come on, take a look, Mr. White. On a midnight clear, you can see forever."

"You're the one who needs lithium," White said. "What's with all this big-time cheer?"

"I feel good, man!" Dr. Bangladesh said. "Hey, Dr. Blaine, eat your cake—it will make you feel better."

"You say it with such conviction." Freddy looked at the cake before him. It looked dry and nasty.

"Trust me," Dr. Bangladesh said.

"He's right, Freddy," Iona said. "You have to eat. I don't know what you think you're doing."

Cousin Eustace said, "Go on, Fred. Eat something."

Freddy bent forward and took a whiff of the cake. It had been hard to single out any one particular odor since he walked into the hospital. All the odors seemed to meld. "A scrumptious goody," he said.

"Eat the goddamn thing before I stuff it down your throat," Stephens said.

Cousin Eustace snagged a piece of the cake with his thumb and shoved it in his mouth. "Look!"

"Now I'm really not going to eat it," Freddy said.

"Eustace ate cake," Charlie said. "He actually ate something new. Hurrah!"

Cousin Eustace said, "The war in heaven is over."

Stephens popped over to the table and set a fresh piece of cake before Freddy.

Marla said, "It's happy cake."

Freddy said, "I hate cake."

Cousin Eustace brought the fruit basket up from the back of the ward and peeled away the cellophane gift wrapping. Freddy selected a red apple and took a bite.

"Yeah." Cousin Eustace rubbed his hands together with enthusiasm. "Charlie told the old devil to get lost."

"Good going, Charlie. I knew you had it in you," Dr. Bangladesh said. "Tra-la-la! It came upon a midnight clear."

"It's about time I got a little credit," Charlie said petulantly. He reached into the fruit basket and selected a Bartlett pear. "Come on, everybody. There's fresh fruit."

The patients took fruit from the basket but then gravitated back to the windows, dragging their chairs with them so they could sit and look outside. Only the first alcove had been done properly. The second had been abandoned and dirty towels lay all about the floor. Hen Pierce bit into a peeled orange and had to jump back from the spray. "I hope there's more shooting stars. I like them long-lasting dudes."

Outside, headlights from the cars passing the state hospital reflected off the crystal daggers of ice hanging from the trees, causing them to shimmer. The night air was clear and the star show profuse. A hush fell over the patients of Ward Six until Charles White broke the silence. "It's a magnificent sight. A good omen portending the remission of evil. It's Christmas."

Freddy said, "The Christmas spirit has been eluding me this year."

Dr. Bangladesh said, "One of those stars belongs to you alone, Doctor."

Freddy shrugged. "If one of those stars belongs to me," he said, "I presume it to be a dim and unlucky one. A celestial dud. I will cling to it nonetheless and nevermore will I complain."

"Look! Another one," Oscar shouted. "A real shooter. Va-boom!"

Hen Pierce nudged closer to the windows, licking orange juice from his fingers. "Those are the biggest, the best and the most. Never in all my life have I seen such beautiful staglamites."

"Mr. Brown can't see you now. He's taking his coffee break."

Let There Be Light

fiction by ARTHUR C. CLARKE

E dgar and Mary Burton were a somewhat ill-assorted pair, and none of their friends could explain why they had married. Perhaps the cynical explanation was the correct one: Edgar (who was almost 20 years older than his wife) had made a quarter of a million on the stock exchange before retiring at an unusually early age to live the life of a country gentleman and to pursue his one absorbing hobby—astronomy.

For some reason, it seems to surprise many people that an interest in astronomy is compatible with business acumen or even with common sense. This is a complete delusion, but in Edgar's case, shrewdness did seem to have been combined with a vague impracticality in one and the same person; once he had made his money he took no further interest in it, or indeed in *anything* except the construction of progressively larger reflecting telescopes.

On his retirement, Edgar had purchased a fine old house high up on the Yorkshire Moors. It was not so bleak and Wuthering-Heightish as it may sound; there was a splendid view, and the Bentley would get you into town in 15 minutes. Even so, the change did not altogether suit Mary, and it is hard not to feel rather sorry for her. There was no work for her to do, as the servants ran the house and she had few intellectual resources to fall back on. She took up riding, joined all the book clubs, read *The Tatler* and *Country Life* from cover to cover, but still felt there was something missing.

It took her about four months to find what she wanted; and then she met it at an otherwise dismal village fete. It was a six-foot-three, ex-Coldstream Guard, with a family that looked on the Norman Conquest as a recent and regrettable piece of impertinence. It was called Aethelred Pendragon Tuncks (we'll forget about the other six Christian names) and it was regarded as the most eligible bachelor in the district.

Aethelred being a high-principled English gentleman, brought up in the best traditions of the aristocracy, it was two full weeks before

343

he succumbed to Mary's blandishments. His downfall was accelerated by the fact that his family was trying to arrange a match for him with the Honorable Felicity Fauntleroy, who was generally admitted to be no great beauty. Indeed, she looked so much like a horse that it was risky for her to go near her father's famous stables when the stallions were exercising.

Mary's boredom, and Aethelred's determination to have a last desperate fling, had the inevitable result. Edgar saw less and less of his wife, who found an amazing number of reasons for driving into town during the week. At first he was quite glad that the circle of her acquaintances was widening rapidly, and it was several months before he realized that it was doing nothing of the sort.

It is quite impossible to keep any liaison secret for long in a small country town like Stocksborough, though this is a fact which every generation has to learn afresh, usually the hard way. Edgar discovered the truth by accident, but some kind friend would have told him sooner or later. He had driven into town for a meeting of the local astronomical society—taking the Rolls since his wife had already gone with the Bentley—and was momentarily held up on the way home by the crowds emerging from the last performance at the local cinema. In the heart of the crowd was Mary, accompanied by a handsome young man whom Edgar had seen before but couldn't identify at the moment. He would have thought no more of the matter, but Mary had gone out of her way the next morning to mention that she'd been unable to get a seat in the cinema and had spent a quiet evening with one of her women friends.

Even Edgar, engrossed though he now was in the study of variable stars, began to put two and two together when he realized that his wife was gratuitously lying. He gave no hint of his vague suspicions, which ceased to be vague after the local Hunt Ball. Though he hated such functions (and this one, by bad luck, occurred just when U Orionis was going through its minimum and he had to miss some vital observations), it occurred to him that this would give him a chance to identify his wife's companion, since everyone in the district would be there.

It proved absurdly easy to locate Aethelred and to get into conversation with him. Although the young man seemed a little ill at ease, he was pleasant company and Edgar was surprised to find himself taking quite a fancy to him. If his wife had to have a lover, on the whole he approved of her choice.

And there matters rested for some months, largely because Edgar was too busy grinding and figuring a 15-inch mirror to do anything about it. Twice a week Mary drove into town, ostensibly to meet her friends or to go to the cinema, and arrived back at the lodge just before midnight. Edgar could see the lights of the car for miles away across the moor, the beams twisting and turning as his wife drove homewards with what always seemed to him excessive speed. That had been one of the reasons why they seldom went out together; Edgar was a sound but cautious driver, and his comfortable cruising speed was 10 miles an hour below Mary's.

About three miles from the house the lights of the car would disappear for several minutes as the road was hidden by a hill. There was a dangerous hairpin bend at this point; in a piece of highway construction more reminiscent of the Alps than of rural England, the road hugged the edge of a cliff and skirted an unpleasant 100-foot drop before it straightened out on the homeward stretch. As the car rounded this bend, its headlights would shine full on the house, and there were many evenings when Edgar was dazzled by the sudden glare as he sat at the eyepiece of his telescope. Luckily, this stretch of road was very little used at night; if it had been, observations would have been well-nigh impossible, since it took Edgar's eyes 10 or 20 minutes to recover fully from the direct blast of the headlights. This was no more than a minor annoyance, but when Mary started to stay out four or five evenings a week it became a confounded nuisance. Something, Edgar decided, would have to be done.

Throughout all this affair Edgar Burton's behavior was hardly that of a normal person. Indeed, anyone who could have switched his mode of life so completely from that of a busy London stockbroker to a near-recluse on the Yorkshire Moors must have been a little odd in the first place. One would hesitate, however, to say he was more than eccentric until the time when Mary's midnight arrivals started to interfere with the serious business of observation. And even thereafter, one must admit that there was a certain crazy logic in his actions.

He had ceased to love his wife, but he did object to her making a fool of him. And Aethelred Pendragon Tuncks seemed a pleasant young chap; it would be an act of kindness to rescue him. Well, there was a beautifully simple solution, which had come to Edgar in a blinding flash—literally, for it was while he was blinking in the glare of Mary's headlights that Edgar conceived his perfect murder.

It is strange how apparently irrelevant factors can determine a man's life; though it were churlish to say anything against the oldest and noblest of the sciences, it cannot be denied that if Edgar had never become an astronomer he would never have become a murderer. For his hobby provided part of the motive and a good deal of the means....

LET THERE BE LIGHT

He could have made the mirror he needed—he was quite an expert by this time—but astronomical accuracy was unnecessary in this case, and it was simpler to pick up a second-hand searchlight reflector at one of those war-surplus shops in Lisle Street. The mirror was about three feet across, and it was only a few hours' work to fix up a mounting for it and to arrange a crude but effective arc-light at its focus. Getting the beam lined up was equally straightforward, and no one took the slightest notice of his activities since his experimenting was now taken for granted by wife and servants alike.

He made the final brief test on a clear, dark night and settled down to await Mary's return. He did not waste the time, of course, but continued his routine observations of a group of selected stars. By midnight, there was still no sign of Mary, but Edgar did not mind as he was getting a nicely consistent series of magnitudes which were lying smoothly on his curves. Everything was going well, though he did stop to wonder just why Mary was so unusually late.

At last he saw the headlights of the car flickering on the horizon, and rather reluctantly broke off his observations. When the car had disappeared behind the hill, he was waiting with his hand on the switch. His timing was perfect: the instant the car came round the curve and the headlights shone on him, he closed the arc.

Meeting another car at night can be unpleasant enough even when you are prepared for it and are driving on a straight road. But if you are rounding a hairpin bend, and know there is no other car coming, yet suddenly find yourself staring into a beam 50 times as powerful as any headlight—well, the results are more than unpleasant.

They were exactly what Edgar had calculated. He switched off his beam almost at once, but the car's own lights showed him all he wanted to see. He watched them swing out over the valley and then curve down, ever more and more swiftly, until they disappeared below the crest of the hill. A red glow flared for a few seconds, but the explosion was barely audible, which was just as well, as Edgar did not want to disturb the servants.

He dismantled his little searchlight and returned to the telescope as he had not quite completed his observations. Then, satisfied that he had done a good night's work, he went to bed.

His sleep was sound but short, for about an hour later the telephone started to ring. No doubt someone had found the wreckage, but Edgar wished they could have left it until morning, for an astronomer needed all the sleep he could get. With some irritation he picked up the phone, and it was several seconds before he realized his wife was at the other end of the line. She was calling from Tuncks Place, and wanted to know what had happened to Aethelred.

It seemed they had decided to make a clean breast of the whole affair, and Aethelred (not unfortified by strong waters) had agreed to be a man and break the news to Edgar. He was going to call back as soon as he had done this and tell Mary how her husband had received it. She had waited with mounting impatience and alarm as long as she could, until at last anxiety had got the better of discretion.

It goes without saying that the shock to Edgar's already somewhat unbalanced nervous system was considerable.

In the long run, Mary came out of it rather well. Acthelred wasn't really very bright, and it would never have been a satisfactory match. As it was, when Edgar was duly certified and safely put out of harm's way, Mary received power of attorney for the estate and promptly moved to Dartmouth, where she took a charming flat near the Royal Naval College and seldom had to drive the new Bentley for herself.

OWL FARM

Thompson, Hunter

May 21,'69

David Butler
Playboy
919 N. Michigan ave
Chicago 60611

David....

       Here's the Killy expense tab. I feel a bit pre-
sumptuous sending it ahead of the piece, but my credit ~~card~~
card bills are starting to come in -- second notices, etc., so
I thought I should get this off. At one point my daily notebook
list showed $1000 plus, but I tore the list out and clipped it to
something I can't find, so I'll have to live with this failure.
Airfares are the bulk of it, and there's a weird lack of lodging
items -- particularly in Wv. Valley, where things got hopelessly
scrambled; you'll just have to take my word that those two days
cost me ~~#$5~~ at least $35. My check stubs show more like $75, but
not all of it is justifiable.... like $4.90 for for a six-pack of
beer, and that sort of thing. In all, I think this is a fairly
straight accounting.

        If anything bugs you, to hell with it. I'd rather
not argue. There's one item, for instance, that I can't understand at all: it's that $26.25 cash-paid ticket on Rocky Mtn.
airways, a flight I clearly remember taking from Denver to Aspen --
but it doesn't seem to fit, so I left it out.

       The piece itself is now in the chopping stages. I
suspect you'll like it, but I'm not at all sure it's a good bet
for print. We'll see.... and meanwhile, give my best to whomever
mid-wifed that piece on the Paramilitary Right (June). It was a
first class thing -- leaving me, as I finished reading it, to cast
a baleful eye on my Killy ms. And so much for that. My bundle
will be along shortly, for good or ill.

                                 Ciao,

                                 Hunter

Woody Creek, Colorado

OWL FARM

May 21, 1969

EXPENSE STATEMENT

Out-of-pocket expenses incurred by Hunter S. Thompson during
research on Jean-Claude Killy profile for Playboy.....

$198.45 ... Aspen-Chicago RT for Auto Show and 2 days for initial
            Killy contact -- air-fare.

  48.46 ... Calls to Killy and Bud Stanner (Head Ski) from Aspen
            to Sun Valley... and other calls, 3/10 -- 3/17

 220.50 ... RT airfare Aspen, Salt Lake, Chicago, Denver, Aspen
            for airborne interview with Killy, 3/13

  10.40 ... Holiday Inn lodging 3/13 (Denver)

   9.65 ... cabs to & from Denver airport & one meal, 3/14

  27.65 ... one nite Charter House, Cambridge Mass. 3/19

  66.36 ... car rental for 3-day Killy-ski scene at Waterville
            Valley, N.H. -- 328 miles

 268.80 ... RT airfare, Aspen-Boston-Aspen (Killy N.H. gig)

  15.50 ... cabs in Chi. -- 3 RT Stockyards trips

   9.90 ... two tape cartridges hmm

   4.50 ... meal for Killy & self, SLC airport

  30.00 ... Misc. expenses, figured at $5 per day for six days,
            including food & drink at Auto Show, all tips, etc.

  35.00 ... total expenses for 2 days at Waterville Valley N.H ski
            resort -- receipts not available.

$942.97 ... Total
-300.00 ... paid
$742.97 ... Due

Thanks,

Hunter S. Thompson

Woody Creek, Colorado

The Dashing Fellow

fiction by VLADIMIR NABOKOV

O ur suitcase is embellished with bright-colored stickers: Nürnberg, Stuttgart, Köln—and even Lido (but that one is fraudulent). We have a swarthy complexion, a network of purple-red veins, a black mustache, trimly clipped, and hairy nostrils. We breathe hard through our nose as we try to solve a crossword puzzle in an *émigré* paper. We are alone in a third-class compartment—alone and, therefore, bored.

Tonight we arrive in a voluptuous little town. Freedom of action! Fragrance of commercial travels! A golden hair on the sleeve of one's coat! Oh, woman, thy name is Goldie! That's how we called Mama and, later, our wife, Katya. Psychoanalytic fact: Every man is Oedipus. During the last trip, we were unfaithful to Katya three times, and that cost us 30 reichsmarks. Funny—they all look a fright in the place one lives in, but in a strange town they are as lovely as antique hetaerae. Even more delicious, however, might be the elegancies of a chance encounter: Your profile reminds me of the girl for whose sake years ago.... After one single night we shall part like ships.... Another possibility: She might turn out to be Russian. Allow me to introduce myself: Konstantin.... Better omit the family name—or maybe invent one? Obolenski. Yes, relatives.

We do not know any famous Turkish general and can guess neither the father of aviation nor an American rodent. It is also not very amusing to look at the view. Fields. A road. Birches-smirches. Cottage and cabbage patch. Country lass, not bad, young.

Katya is the very type of a good wife. Lacks any sort of passion, cooks beautifully, washes her arms as far as the shoulders every morning and is not overbright; therefore, not jealous. Given the sterling breadth of her pelvis, one is surprised that for the second time now, she has produced a stillborn babikins. Laborious years. Uphill all the way. *Absolute* marasmus in business. Sweating 20 times before persuading one customer. Then squeezing out the commission drop by drop. God, how one longs to tangle with a graceful gold-bright little devil in a fantastically lit hotel room! Mirrors, orgies, a couple of drinks. Another five hours of travel. Railroad riding, it is proclaimed, disposes one to this kind of thing. Am extremely disposed. After all, say what you will, but the mainspring of life is robust romance. Can't concentrate on business unless I take care first of my romantic interests. So here is the plan: starting point, the cafe that Lange told me about. Now, if I don't find anything there——

Crossing gate, warehouse, big station. Our traveler let down the window and leaned upon it, elbows wide apart. Beyond a platform, steam was issuing from under some sleeping cars. One could vaguely make out the pigeons changing perches under the lofty glass dome. Hot dogs cried out in treble, beer in baritone. A girl, her bust enclosed in white wool, stood talking to a man, now joining her bare arms behind her back, swaying slightly and beating her buttocks with her handbag, now folding her arms on her chest and stepping with one foot upon the other, or else, holding her handbag under her arm and with a small snapping sound thrusting nimble fingers under her glossy black belt; thus she stood, and laughed, and sometimes touched her companion in a valedictory gesture, only to resume at once her twisting and turning: a sun-tanned girl with a heaped-up hairdo that left her ears bare, and a quite ravishing scratch on her honey-hued upper arm. She does not look at us, but never mind, let us ogle her fixedly. In the beam of the gloating tense glance, she starts to shimmer and seems about to dissolve. In a moment, the background will show through her—a refuse bin, a poster, a bench; but here, unfortunately, our crystalline lens had to return to normality, for everything shifted; the man jumped into the next carriage, the train jerked into motion and the girl took a handkerchief out of her handbag. When, in the course of her receding glide, she came exactly in front of his window, Konstantin, Kostya, Kostenka thrice kissed with gusto the palm of his hand, but his salute passed unnoticed: With rhythmical waves of her handkerchief, she floated away.

He shut the window and, on turning around, saw with pleased surprise that during his mesmeric activities the compartment had managed to fill up: three men with their newspapers and, in the far corner, a brunette with a powdered face. Her shiny coat was of gelatin-like translucency—resisting rain, maybe, but not a man's gaze. Decorous humor and correct eye reach—that's our motto.

Ten minutes later, he was deep in conversation with the passenger in the opposite window seat, a neatly dressed old gentleman; the prefatory theme had sailed by in the guise of a factory chimney; certain statistics came to be mentioned and both men expressed themselves with melancholic irony regarding industrial trends; meanwhile, the white-faced woman dismissed a sickly bouquet of forget-me-nots to the baggage rack and, having produced a magazine from her traveling bag, became engrossed in the transparent process of reading: Through it comes our caressive voice, our commonsensical speech. The second male passenger joined in: He was engagingly fat, wore checked knickerbockers stuck into green stockings and talked about pig breeding. What a good sign—she adjusts every part you look at. The third man, an arrogant recluse, hid behind his paper. At the next stop, the industrialist and the expert on hogs got out, the recluse retired to the dining car and the lady moved to the window seat.

Let us appraise her point by point. Funereal expression of eyes, lascivious lips. First-rate legs, artificial silk. What is better—the experience of a sexy 30-year-old brunette or the silly young bloom of a bright-curled romp? Today the former is better, and tomorrow we shall see. Next point: Through the gelatin of her raincoat glimmers a beautiful nude, like a mermaid seen through the yellow waves of the Rhine. Spasmodically rising, she shed her coat but revealed only a beige dress with a piqué collaret. Arrange it. That's right.

"May weather," affably said Konstantin, "and yet the trains are still heated."

Her left eyebrow went up and she answered: "Yes, it *is* warm here, and I'm mortally tired. My contract is finished, I'm going home now. They all toasted me, the station buffet there is tops, I drank too much, but I never get tipsy, just a heaviness in my stomach. Life has grown hard, I receive more flowers than money and a month's rest will be most welcome; after that I have a new contract, but of course, it's impossible to lay anything by. The potbellied chap, who just left, behaved obscenely. How he stared at me! I feel as if I had been on this train for a long, long time, and I am so very anxious to return to my cozy little apartment far from all that flurry and claptrap and rot."

"Allow me to offer you," said Kostya, "something to palliate the offense."

He pulled from under his backside a square pneumatic cushion, its rubber covered in speckled satin: He always had it under him during his flat, hard hemorrhoidal trips.

"And what about yourself?" she inquired.

"We'll manage, we'll manage. I must ask you to rise a little. Excuse me. Now sit down. Soft, isn't it? That part is especially sensitive on the road."

"Thank you," she said. "Not all men are so considerate. I've lost quite a bit of flesh lately. Oh, how nice! Just like traveling second-class."

"*Galanterie, Gnädigste,*" said Kostenka, "is an innate property with us. Yes, I'm a foreigner. Russian. Here's an example: One day my father had gone for a walk on the grounds of his manor with an old pal, a well-known general. They happened to meet a peasant woman—a little old hag, you know, with a bundle of firewood on her back—and my father took off his hat. This surprised the general, and then my father said: 'Would your Excellency really want a simple peasant to be more courteous than a member of the gentry?'"

"I know a Russian—I'm sure you've heard his name, too—let me see, what was it? Baretski...Baratski.... From Warsaw. He now owns a drugstore in Chemnitz. Baratski...Baritski. I'm sure you know him?"

"I do not. Russia is a big country. Our family estate was about as large as your Saxony. And all has been lost, all has been burned down. The glow of the fire could be seen at a distance of 70 kilometers. My parents were butchered in my presence. I owe my life to a faithful retainer, a veteran of the Turkish campaign."

"How terrible," she said, "how very terrible!"

"Yes, but it inures one. I escaped, disguised as a country girl. In those days, I made a very cute little maiden. Soldiers pestered me. Especially one beastly fellow.... And thereby hangs a most comic tale."

He told his tale. "*Pfui!*" she uttered, smiling.

"Well, after that came the era of wanderings and a multitude of trades. At one time I even used to shine shoes—and would see in my dreams the precise spot in the garden where the old butler, by torchlight, had buried our ancestral jewels. There was, I remember, a sword, studded with diamonds——"

"I'll be back in a minute," said the lady.

The resilient cushion had not yet had time to cool when she again sat down upon it and with mellow grace recrossed her legs.

"And, moreover, two rubies, that big, then stocks in a golden casket, my father's epaulets, a string of black pearls——"

"Yes, many people are ruined at present," she remarked with a sigh, and continued, again raising that left eyebrow: "I, too, have experienced all sorts of hardships. I had a husband, it was a dreadful marriage, and I said to myself: Enough! I'm going to live my own way. For almost a year now, I'm not on speaking terms with my parents—old people, you know, don't understand the young—and it affects me deeply—sometimes I pass by their house and sort of dream of dropping in—and my second husband is now, thank goodness, in Argentina; he writes me absolutely marvelous letters, but I will never return to him. There was another man, the director of a factory, a very sedate gentleman; he adored me, wanted me to bear him a child, and his wife was also such a dear, so warmhearted—much older than he—oh, we three were such friends, went boating on the lake in summer, but then they moved to Frankfurt. Or take actors—such good, gay people—and affairs with them are so *kameradschaftlich*, there's no pouncing upon you, at once, at once, at once...."

In the meantime Kostya reflected: We know all those parents and directors. She's making up everything. Very attractive, though. Breasts like a pair of piggies, slim hips. Likes to tipple, apparently. Let's order some beer from the diner.

"Well, some time later, there was a lucky break, brought me heaps of money. I had four apartment houses in Berlin. But the man whom I trusted, my friend, my partner, deceived me.... Painful recollections. I lost a fortune but not my optimism; and now, again, thank God, despite the Depression.... Apropos, let me show you something, madam."

The suitcase with the swanky stickers contained (among other meretricious articles) samples of a highly fashionable kind of vanity-bag looking glass: little things neither round nor square, but *Phantasie*—shaped, say, like a daisy or a butterfly or a heart. Meanwhile came the beer. She examined the little mirrors and looked in them at herself; blinks of light shot across the compartment. She downed the beer like a trooper and with the back of her hand removed the foam from her orange-red lips. Kostenka fondly replaced the samples in the valise and put it back on the shelf. All right, let's begin.

"Do you know—I keep looking at you and imagining that we met once years ago. You resemble to an absurd degree a girl—she died of consumption—whom I loved so much that I almost shot myself. Yes, we Russians are sentimental eccentrics, but believe me, we can love with the passion of a Rasputin and the naivete of a child. You are lonely and I am lonely. You are free and I am free. Who, then, can forbid us to spend several pleasant hours in a sheltered love nest?"

Her silence was enticing. He left his seat and sat next to her. He leered, and rolled his eyes, and knocked his knees together, and rubbed his hands, as he gaped at her profile.

"What is your destination?" she asked.

Kostenka told her.

"And I am returning to——"

She named a city famous for its cheese production.

"All right, I'll accompany you and tomorrow continue my journey.

Though I dare not predict anything, madam. I have all grounds to believe that neither you nor I will regret it."

The smile, the eyebrow.

"You don't even know my name yet."

"Oh, who cares, who cares? Why should one have a name?"

"Here's mine," she said and produced a visiting card: Sonja Bergmann.

"And I'm just Kostya. Kostya and no nonsense. Call me Kostya, right?"

An enchanting woman! A nervous, supple, interesting woman! We'll be there in half an hour. Long live life, happiness, ruddy health! A long night of double-edged pleasures. See our complete collection of caresses! Amorous Hercules!

The person we nicknamed the recluse returned from the diner and flirtation had to be suspended. She took several snapshots out of her handbag and proceeded to show them: "This girl's just a friend. Here's a very sweet boy, his brother works for the radio station. In this one I came out appallingly. That's my leg. And here—do you recognize this person? I've put spectacles on and a bowler—cute, isn't it?"

We are on the point of arriving. The little cushion has been returned with many thanks. Kostya deflated it and slipped it into his valise. The train began braking.

"Well, so long," said the lady.

Energetically and gaily he carried out both suitcases—hers, a small fiber one, and his, of a nobler make. The glass-topped station was shot through by three beams of dusty sunlight. The sleepy recluse and the forgotten forget-me-nots rode away.

"You're completely mad," she said with a laugh.

Before checking his bag he extracted from it a pair of flat folding slippers. At the taxi stand there remained one cab.

"Where are we going?" she asked "To a restaurant?"

"We'll fix something to eat at your place," said terribly impatient Kostya. "That will be much cozier. Get in. It's a better idea. I suppose he'll be able change 50 marks? I've got only big bills. No, wait a sec, here's some small cash. Come on, come on, tell him where to go."

The inside of the cab smelled of kerosene. We must not spoil our fun with the small fry of osculatory contacts. Shall we get there soon? What a dreary town. Soon? Urge becoming intolerable. That firm I know. Ah, we've arrived.

The taxi pulled up in front of an old, coal-black house with green shutters. They climbed to the fourth landing and there she stopped and said: "And what if there's somebody else there? How do you know that I'll let you in? What's that on your lip?"

"A cold sore," said Kostya, "just a cold sore. Hurry up. Open. Let's dismiss the whole world and its troubles. Quick. Open."

They entered. A hallway with a large wardrobe, a kitchen and a small bedroom.

"No, please wait. I'm hungry. We shall first have supper. Give me that 50-mark note, I'll take the occasion to change it for you."

"All right, but for God's sake, hurry," said Kostya, rummaging in his wallet. "There's no need to change anything, here's a nice tenner."

"What would you like me to buy?"

"Oh, anything you want. I only beseech you to make haste."

She left. She locked him in, using both keys. Taking no chances. But what loot could one have found here? None. In the middle of the kitchen floor, a dead cockroach lay on its back, brown legs stretched out. The bedroom contained one chair and a lace-covered wooden bed. Above it, the photograph of a man with fat cheeks and waved hair was nailed to the spotty wall. Kostya sat down on the chair and in a twinkle substituted the morocco slippers for his mahogany-red street shoes. Then he shed his Norfolk jacket, unbuttoned his lilac braces and took off his starched collar. There was no toilet, so he quickly used the kitchen sink, then washed his hands and examined his lip. The doorbell rang.

He tiptoed fast to the door, placed his eye to the peephole but could see nothing. The person behind the door rang again and the ring was heard to knock. No matter—we can't let him in even if we wish to.

"Who's that?" asked Kostya insinuatingly through the door. A cracked voice inquired: "Please, is *Frau* Bergmann back?"

"Not yet," replied Kostya, "why?"

"Misfortune," the voice said and paused. Kostya waited.

The voice continued: "You don't know when she will be back in town? I was told she was expected to return today. You are *Herr* Seidler, I believe?"

"What's happened? I'll pass her the message."

A throat was cleared and the voice said, as if over the telephone:

"Franz Loschmidt speaking. She does not know me, but tell her, please...."

Another pause and an uncertain query: "Perhaps you can let me come in?"

"Never mind, never mind," said Kostya impatiently, "I will tell her everything."

"Her father is dying, he won't live through the night: He has had a stroke in the shop. Tell her to come over at once. When do you think she'll be back?"

"Soon," answered Kostya, "soon. I'll tell her. Goodbye."

After a series of receding creaks, the stairs became silent. Kostya made for the window. A gangling youth, death's apprentice, rain-cloaked, hatless, with a small close-cropped smoke-blue head, crossed the street and vanished around the corner. A few moments later from another direction appeared the lady with a well-filled net bag.

The door's upper lock clicked, then its lower one.

"Phew!" she said, entering. "What a load of things I bought!"

"Later, later," cried Kostya, "we'll sup later. Quick to the bedroom. Forget those parcels. I beseech you."

"I want to eat," she replied in a long-drawn voice.

She smacked his hand away and went into the kitchen. Kostya followed her.

"Roast beef," she said. "White bread. Butter. Our celebrated cheese. Coffee. A pint of cognac. Goodness me, can't you wait a little? Let me go, it's indecent."

Kostya, however, pressed her against the table, she started to giggle helplessly, his fingernails kept catching in the knit silk of her green undies and everything happened very ineffectually, uncomfortably and prematurely.

"*Pfui!*" she uttered, smiling.

No, it was not worth the trouble. Thank you kindly for the treat. Wasting my strength. I'm no longer in the bloom of youth. Rather disgusting. Her perspiring nose, her faded mug. Might have washed her hands before fingering eatables. "What's that on your lip?" Impudence! Still to be seen, you know, who catches what from whom. Well, nothing to be done.

"Bought that cigar for me?" he inquired.

She was busy taking knives and forks out of the cupboard and did not hear.

"What about that cigar?" he repeated.

"Oh, sorry, I didn't know you smoked. Shall I run down to get one?"

"Never mind, I'll go myself," he replied gruffly and passed into the bedroom, where he put on his shoes and coat. Through the open door he could see her moving gracelessly as she laid the table.

"The tobacconist's right on the corner," she sang out and, choosing a plate, arranged upon it with loving care the cool, rosy slices of roast beef, which she had not been able to afford for quite a time.

"Moreover, I'll get some pastry," Konstantin said and went out. Pastry, and whipped cream, and a chunk of pineapple, and chocolates with brandy filling, he added mentally.

Once in the street, he looked up, seeking out her window (the one with the cacti or the next?), then turned right, walked around the back of a furniture van, nearly got struck by the front wheel of a cyclist and showed him his fist. Farther on there was a small public garden and some kind of stone *Herzog*. He made another turn and saw at the very end of the street, outlined against a thundercloud and lit up by a gaudy sunset, the brick tower of the church, past which, he recalled, they had driven. From there it was but a step to the station. A convenient train could be had in a quarter of an hour: In this respect, at least, luck was on his side. Expenses: bag check, 30 pfennigs; taxi, 1.40; she, ten marks (five would have been enough). What else? Yes, the beer, 55 pfennigs, with tip. In all: 12 marks and 25 pfennigs. Idiotic. As to the bad news, she was sure to get it sooner or later. I spared her several sad minutes by a deathbed. Still, maybe I should send her a message from here? But I've forgotten the house number. No, I remember: 27. Anyway, one may assume I forgot it—nobody is obliged to have such a good memory. I can imagine what a rumpus there would have been if I had told her at once! The old bitch. No, we like only small blondes—remember that once and for all.

The train was crammed, the heat stifling. We feel out of sorts but do not quite know if we are hungry or drowsy. But when we have fed and slept, life will regain its looks and the American instruments will make music in the merry cafe described by our friend Lange. And then, sometime later, we die.

—Translated from the Russian by Dmitri Nabokov in collaboration with his father.

"I'm sorry, Priscilla, but I've met someone else."

Fahrvergnügen

fiction by JANE SMILEY

R amsey was an irritable man. It had cost him one wife, and it was going to cost him again, but irritability was something that it looked
like Ramsey couldn't give up. You could take, for example, his present circumstances, pacing the shoulder of a sun-blasted road in Kerhonkson, New York, just down from the Texaco station, where his car,
only 2,000 miles on its $46,000 engine, had stalled and jerked to an
unforgiving halt. He could just see its ivory flank if he looked back,
but he didn't dare look back; he knew he would feel that bright flare
of irritation ($92 a mile, so far, not counting gas or insurance) that had
already sparked him into sarcasm with the garage mechanic (Ramsey
believed his exact words had been, "There are still three good hours
in the working day, you know, even assuming you knock off at four"),
resulting, when he asked about a loaner to get home, in a stubborn
and you might say (he said) bovine idiocy on the mechanic's face,
and a shrug. "No taxi, I'll bet," said Ramsey, his voice sharpening,
his eyes rolling.

"Nope," said the mechanic, and Ramsey knew, and he knew that the
mechanic knew he knew, that there might or might not be a taxi, but
the mechanic would never tell him and, furthermore, the promised
repair of his expensive and self-indulgent vehicle would take days and
more days—long enough for the defective part to be manufactured by
hand and carried to Kerhonkson over earthen tracks by wagon train.

Ramsey's head was burning. Not having foreseen a breakdown, he
had forgotten his hat. He kept pressing his finger into his glabrous
crown. He couldn't see the mark he was making, but knowing that
ever-deepening redness was flowing into the white imprint of his finger,
a sure sign of sunburn, got him so irritated that he kept at it, poking
his head over and over until he could feel a moonscape of little craters
up there.

That, in a nutshell, was Ramsey's problem, and he understood it, though he hadn't ever quite been able to explain it to his wife, his daughter, his present mistress or her daughter, all of whom, he knew, found him more or less insufferable. The problem was his body, the way that it felt everything. He could smell the difference between a rare steak and a medium one, feel the difference between 40 percent polyester and 100 percent cotton, hear dissonance in tones that were harmonious to others. On top of that, as soon as he imagined something, he could feel that, too. He was extraordinarily careful never to read in the newspapers about accidents or injuries.

Ramsey stuck out his thumb. Just under the nail, there was a tiny red mark where a sliver had inserted itself two nights before. As Ramsey looked down the road to see if any cars were coming, the tip of his thumb seemed on fire again. It was strange and irritating, too, to look at it and see just a thumb. No cars came. He opened his shirt. The hair on his chest and back, he thought, had thickened in the past year and now dusted his shoulders, as well. He wouldn't have felt so hot five years, or even a year, before.

The garage mechanic could be seen at the cash register inside the station, smoking a cigarette. Ramsey advanced prudently down the road. There was no telling how he might be further spurred to vent his irritation on the man.

The road skirted a copse of maples, and Ramsey positioned himself in this shade, though the curve obstructed, for oncoming Jaguars, say, or Mercedeses, a good look at his respectability. He stood there. On a Friday afternoon, Kerhonkson was no vortex of activity. Since no one was around, he put both of his hands to his head and smoothed away the craters. He pretended he was rubbing in a nice aloe-vera gel.

Perhaps as a result of this concentration, he didn't see the VW bus until it had already stopped about ten yards beyond him. At first, he forgot that it had stopped for him, but then an arm arced out of the passenger's window and motioned him forward. In spite of its sausage-like, elderly style, not very safe or comfortable, its blue and white paint job shone in the sunlight so that Ramsey had to shade his eyes. And the rear bumper carried a sticker—WAR IS NOT HEALTHY FOR CHILDREN AND OTHER LIVING THINGS—its blue and yellow sunflower-crisp, unfaded. Ramsey felt a powerful surge. All through the Gulf War, he'd been uniquely irritated, even for him, the way those peace people who had come out of the woodwork hadn't had a single new idea, hadn't even had a single new haircut, in 20 years. He passed the right rear fender, tickticking the glistening paint job with his fingernail. Amazing the way someone had gotten just that VW color in this day and age. Annoying, too. The paint on his own car was guaranteed not to chip or blister in the worst Saharan or arctic conditions. He'd been congratulating himself on that moments before the breakdown. In Newburgh, Ramsey consoled himself, he could rent something he'd prefer—a Caddy if nothing else.

It wasn't so easy getting into these old buses. You had to pull the door in pretty hard, and then it took three tries to make the latch take hold. By the time Ramsey had seated himself on the edge of the homemade bed, he was huffing and puffing from the effort. He looked around. Things were worse than he'd realized. There were two dogs on the bed, staring right at him. There was a bead curtain in the back window. The bucket seat bolted to the floor behind the driver's seat was draped with a length of muslin decorated with peace signs. The copper-colored ponytail of the kid who was driving swayed against the back of his seat as he shifted and the bus strained for second gear. Only the woman's wide and welcoming smile reassured Ramsey. She had promising teeth, large and white. Ramsey preferred that in a woman, because women like that were usually too good-humored to take his moods seriously. She said, "Hey. Been out there long?"

"Long enough."

The man said, "Where you headed?"

One of the dogs turned its gaze away from Ramsey, but only to roll against his leg. The hairy radiator of the dog's body prickled through Ramsey's cotton slacks. He said, "Newburgh will be fine. It's not that far." He tried to sound polite, even though the pressure of the dog seemed to be throbbing in every direction from his leg, suffusing him in heat. The dog opened its mouth and its tongue lolled out, dripping. Ramsey said, "What's the dog's name?"

The woman said, "That's Shantih. The other one's Attila. Shantih had that name when we got her. Isn't that cool? That's exactly what we would have named her."

Ramsey said, "Shantih, down."

The woman said, "She always lies on the bed. That's her spot." And, indeed, it was. The paisley cotton bedspread looked swampy with grime. In the distance, the road climbed out of the broad valley they traveled in and curved into the treetops.

Ramsey introduced his hand between his thigh and the dog and pushed. The dog pushed back. Ramsey licked his lips. He could feel the ever-hot coals of his irritation begin to glow. Shantih bared her teeth. The woman said, "Oh, look. Shantih has a great smile. They don't smile among themselves, you know, just at people." Ramsey pushed again, harder. The dog growled. The woman exclaimed, "See? She's trying to talk, too. She's very people-oriented." She turned away, evidently satisfied with Ramsey and Shantih's interaction. Ramsey pushed again, this time fairly violently. Shantih growled with keener resolve. Ramsey looked into the dog's obsidian-black eyes, upside down beside his knee. They came to an understanding. Ramsey removed his hand and put it out of the way, behind himself.

In the front seat, the woman reached across and removed a slender, expertly rolled joint from between the man's lips and put it to her own. A frisson of fear penetrated Ramsey's irritation. Smoking marijuana and driving this unstable, high-center-of-gravity vehicle? No seat belts, either, and certainly only limited insurance coverage. Of course (Ramsey stretched to peer over the driver's shoulder), they were going only 43 miles per hour. The woman's hand, slender, long-fingered, her wrist and her forearm, the skin tan and the hair blonde from the sun, loomed in his face. She said, "Want a hit?"

Ramsey shook his head. She said, "My name's Sun. This is Blues. We named ourselves after our favorite things."

"When did you do that?"

"When time ceased to have meaning for us."

Ramsey said, "Oh, right."

Unfazed by his tone, the woman picked a marijuana seed off her tongue and placed it carefully in a cup on the dashboard, then said, "You in school around here?"

Ramsey thought about what this might mean. There were schools of all kinds in the Hudson Valley, and possibly this girl, in her vividly colored and considerably outdated ensemble, taught at one of them in some capacity. It was Ramsey's experience that academics did wear the same clothes year after year. They took a species of pride in resoling their shoes, patching the elbows of dull-looking tweed jackets and replacing their shirts with new shirts of the same color and style. It was a kind of monastic robe. Ramsey himself was a modish man, though without a modish figure, he had to admit. The only conservative clothes he liked to wear were those aged by others, such as Ralph Lauren. After a moment, he said to the woman, "No, I'm not."

She said, "That's cool. Blues, here, and I swore off that book trip, too. Blues was, like, four credits away from graduating. We just took off."

"When was that?"

"I told you. Time has no meaning for us. You hung up on time?"

Ramsey looked at his watch, an ultra-thin Concord that he'd bought himself for Christmas when it looked as if his mistress wasn't going to produce it in spite of his many hints. He said, "You could say that." It was a beautiful watch, and it considerably eased the pain of aging. Sun smiled indulgently at him. She looked maybe 27, and Blues younger than that, his ponytail glossy and thick, boy's hair. And his hairline curved robustly across his brow. Ramsey suspected that the missed graduation was a recent one, as recent as just this past June. In spite of their old clothes, both Blues and Sun had an apricot blush on their cheeks and a smooth, resilient creaminess to their skin that was not careful preservation but was youth itself.

Blues said, "I might be running from the draft by now. I didn't leave a forwarding address." He shrugged.

"There isn't a draft anymore."

Blues turned and looked at him, full face. He said, "There isn't? Cool!" Then he said to Sun, "There isn't a draft anymore." He sounded satisfied, vindicated more than anything else.

Sun smiled. "Well," she said, "we try not to read newspapers or watch TV anymore, either. It's a statement for life over death."

Ramsey had stopped listening. It was too irritating. He had to watch himself, not let the internal pressure rise too high, push him into betraying his self-interest. Now wasn't the time to burst their little bubble. He reached up and felt his head. Hot to the touch. He would have to remember to buy Lanacane in Newburgh. He thought for the first time in a few minutes of the car. What would these two have thought if he had picked them up in that? The oxblood-leather seats still exhaled that delicious, expensive animal smell. The nap on the carpeting sprang up fresh and grit-free—he'd vacuumed every day with the car vac he'd bought just for the purpose. Kids like these wouldn't know what to do in a car like that. Dogs in the back, on the floor, of course. If he had picked them up, which he wouldn't have. He hadn't picked up a hitchhiker in 20 years.

"What was your major?" Ramsey felt the prick of actual curiosity—his daughter Jeanine was about to apply to college. He had advised her to major in chemistry, but to little effect. According to her mother, comparative literature was in the wind. Just this morning, Ramsey had debated how far he could carry the threat not to pay her tuition before risking her enrollment at the state university. Ramsey himself was in insurance, business insurance. Insurance had been a lucrative career for him, but Jeanine, he thought, he hoped, had real talents. Blues turned fully around, looked squarely at him and drawled, "Chemistry." Beyond his glowing copper head, the road up the mountain jagged to the left. Beyond the guardrail, the mountainside dropped into dizzying violet space. Ramsey inhaled sharply, but the bus hugged the curve. Ramsey said, "Hey, watch your driving."

Blues gave him one of those self-satisfied smiles and said, "OK, man."

"That's a good major," said Ramsey.

"Too linear," said Blues. He turned to Ramsey again, this time beatifically. He said, "Made some great acid, though."

Sun said, "That's how we bought this van. It's practically new. Guy brought it over from West Germany and decided he didn't like it. It's only got 10,000 miles on it. Did you see the D?"

Blues said, "The D is cool." Then he grew loquacious. "The thing was, man, I took this course called Skiing and Being? And what it was was 12 of us at a ski lodge for the winter quarter, and we skied all day, then had philosophy seminars all night, till, like, three and four A.M. Changed my whole life."

"Your parents must have been thrilled. Where was this?"

Nowhere on Jeanine's application list, Ramsey hoped.

Blues didn't answer. Instead, he yawned, gaping sybaritically and closing his eyes for at least half a mile. The moment he opened them, the road switched back and Blues casually spun the wheel.

Ramsey tried again. "Where are you headed?"

Sun said, "Nirvana."

Ramsey sucked in his breath to stifle an exasperated snort. Such shallowness had always annoyed him, though possibly no more than anything else did.

Still, she looked happy to be headed there. When she turned her gaze from Ramsey to Blues, Ramsey saw on her face an unmistakable look of fondness. Love, even. Her thick curls caught between her back and the seat. She thrust her arm beneath them and lifted, revealing for the briefest instant the white of her neck. Ramsey coughed. He felt an unaccustomed expanding feeling, as if he were sorry for them, then realized that he *was* sorry for them, for all the mistakes they had made and were making. Kids like Jeanine and her friends would definitely ridicule these two, and yet they were friendly and kind in a way that Jeanine and her friends were not. He couldn't imagine Jeanine picking up a hitchhiker. It wasn't only that he and her mother had forbidden her ever to do so, it was also that she would disdain, and possibly fear, someone who had no car.

Sun said, "You been there? It's a macrobiotic kosher restaurant in New Paltz. We work there. Blues always thinks it's good karma to drive hitchhikers though. We took this one guy all the way to Albany." Blues turned his gaze from the road and they exchanged a long and, in Ramsey's view, complacent look.

Soon they were whispering. He tried not to notice. Attila the dog had moved closer and begun licking his hand. Ramsey put the hand in his lap. Suddenly, Attila set his paws on Ramsey's shoulder and began licking the back of his neck. The dog had a sticky, warm tongue, and the saliva trickling beneath the collar of his shirt seemed to erode a meaty, slimy rut down his spine. He jerked forward and yelled, "Ecch! Stop that! Yech." He gave an involuntary shiver of revulsion.

Blues said, "Down, Attila. He doesn't like you."

"I like him fine," said Ramsey, not wishing to offend a dog named Attila. "But down is fine, too. You know, it's a mistake to give up on something like a chemistry major right at the end like that. Starting salaries——"

Sun interrupted him. She said, "Wanna ball?"

Ramsey said, "A ball?"

Sun said, "Wanna *ball*? Wanna *make it*?"

Ramsey considered himself an experienced and manly man. In fact, for many years, he had excelled at the one-night stand, both at making the connection and at breaking it. He had grown more cautious in recent years, but most women were lamentably irritating over the long haul. Their little habits and quirks tended to accumulate; however, he liked them otherwise. With Jeanine's mother, he had made a concerted effort, but she'd driven him crazy after two years. He'd driven her crazy after six months. His present mistress, Eloise, was remarkably accommodating, but the tread was wearing thin. It grieved him, but the grief only swelled his irritation.

At the same time, Sun, here, was young, and Blues, who had removed his shirt just now by taking his hands entirely off the wheel and pulling it dangerously over his head, was obviously in his well-muscled prime. Gazing at the two of them, Ramsey knew himself: bald, sunburned, middle-aged, hirsute, paunchy, wrinkled around the knees and droopy around the jowls.

"Don't be nervous," she said. "Blues doesn't mind."

"Sun's her own person," said Blues. "That's why her name's Sun."

Sun said, "I'll come back there." She gestured at the bed.

Ramsey said, "What about the dogs?"

"They don't mind, either." She swung her foot over the hump of the engine well and torpedoed at him.

He said, "How far is it to Newburgh?"

"We've got plenty of time." Now she was beside him, and the fact was, her odor, compounded of sandalwood and a fresh citrusy scent that smelled like youth itself, drove away thoughts of safe sex. He took a deep breath, then another one. She slid her hand into his shirt and began to run her palm back and forth across his nipples, then down over the swell of his paunch. It seemed to be an affectionate gesture, and he had another of those unaccustomed feelings, this one of gratitude. His dick began to harden. Nevertheless, he wrapped his fingers around her wrist and removed her hand. She said, "Hey, don't worry. It's fun. There's this thing called tantric yoga? It's like this sex religion. That's what Blues and I believe in." She said this in a low, seductive but girlish voice that Ramsey found sadly appealing.

He said, "How long have you believed in it?"

"Why are you so uptight about time? It's not a very becoming quality."

She unbuckled the 18-kt.-gold band of his Concord. He watched as she put it into the little sink beside the bed, distantly aware that this could well be the point of his adventure. That watch was worth plenty. But he let it be taken. Then she unbuttoned his shirt, undid his woven Polo belt, pulled her own gauzy cotton blouse over her head. Her breasts, set wide apart, seemed to float. The nipples, with their dusky areolae, pointed forward like headlights. Ramsey very much wanted to touch them. He could feel that precise desire tingle in his fingertips, as well as in his dick, as well as in the center of his forehead, where a certain spot always burned when he was aroused.

Sun said, "Hmmmmm." Or "Ommm." Ramsey was beginning to feel a little dizzy. The back of Blues's head radiated a nimbus in the afternoon sun. How late was it, then? The bus puttered upward, the trees passing to either side like water.

But, to be honest, there was something else. Even while Ramsey began to nuzzle those breasts, and then the barely detectable pale down on the smooth curve of Sun's belly, he knew that the obstreperous dick in his pants that had never left him alone before this would certainly betray him now. She kneeled over him, for he was lying back, and he ran his fingertips down the sides of her neck, from her earlobes to her upper arms. The contours there were majestic and mysterious, way beyond anatomical. It would be better for him to stick to this—to deeply felt appreciation.

But then she was poking into his pants, finding the betrayer, believing its braggadocian promise.

Ramsey then began to pant a little, nothing embarrassing.

FAHRVERGNÜGEN

The dog Shantih flopped her head between them and looked him in the eye. Sun kissed the animal on top of the head.

The fact was, Ramsey would probably be able to perform well enough. Even after two years with Eloise, he didn't fail at that. He could get it hard, keep it hard and fuck as long as ever. It was himself who was betrayed, because there wasn't any pop anymore. No matter how grand the build-up, no matter how energetically Eloise performed her part just so, his orgasm ran out like water left in the garden hose, more pissing than coming, not much worth the effort and certainly not worth the maddening anticipation that suckered him almost every time. But being here, with Sun, so young and willing, reminded him forcibly that it all had once been very different, with orgasms that were, well, religious. He wanted to shout to the back of Blues's shining head that tantric yoga was the yoga that didn't last. The religion of chemistry would serve him better in the end.

Sun kissed him on the lips, suddenly hiding other considerations from his gaze with her mantle of dark hair. Kissing aroused him. It always did, and the Great Betrayer bucked out of his underwear and into the breeze like a chimp pounding its chest. Sun's thighs made a V above it, and it jumped toward her, full of beans and vainglory. Ramsey could feel the road unroll this way and that beneath his back, and it was the strangest, and maybe the most knitted-together, feeling he had ever had in a car.

Ramsey was beginning to relax, beginning to accept whatever might happen, when the trees opened out at the top of the mountain and Blues stopped for a stop sign, then turned right. The road sloped downward and away. Ramsey could feel the brakes catch and loosen and catch again—it broke the spell. He clasped Sun firmly by the shoulders and moved her to one side, then sat up.

She said, "Hey, man, what's wrong? I was just getting off on this."

Did she sound petulant? If so, Ramsey's own petulance rose to meet hers.

But then, in a slower, more honeyed tone, she said, "Hey. Are you still afraid?" She looked at him speculatively, then said, "OK. You know, I didn't ask you your name. That was pretty rude."

"It's Bill."

"I bet your friends call you Billy."

"Not many of them."

She smiled, apparently amused by this reply, then smoothed his cheek with her hand. "How old are you, Billy?"

Now, here was an irritating question for which Ramsey could think of myriad snappish replies. He said, "How old do you think?"

Sun shrugged. They were speeding along again, so to speak, dropping down the mountain, and she suddenly pushed him backward with a butt of her shoulder, then she started kissing him with soft ferocity, tongue lips tongue teeth. He felt her cool fingertips on the Great Betrayer, which had as yet shown no scruples, and suddenly he was inside her. She crooned, "I think you're trying to look 18, but my guess is you aren't 16 yet," and Ramsey came. He came so hard that in his gaze, Sun's face blacked out and disappeared. He came so hard that he forgot to wonder whether she had come, so hard that he might as well never have fucked anyone before in his life.

When Ramsey next knew himself, he saw they were on not the Newburgh bridge but the Tappan Zee, almost to Tarrytown. He did not remember sleeping but the bus had gotten magically far. Ramsey quickly transformed his exclamation into a cough. Sun was back in the front seat, taking her hair down and pinning it up again by twisting it around a knitting needle. He put his hand on the peace-sign-covered bucket seat and levered himself back onto the bed. Blues said, "Hey, man. You cool?"

"I guess so," said Ramsey. They crossed the bridge. Eloise lived off Sleepy Hollow Road, so there was no reason to stop and rent a car. Ramsey wiped the sweat off his face with his shirt, then buttoned same. Two buttons, genuine bone, imported from Switzerland, were missing. Another one was broken in half. He pushed it through the hole and put on his watch. Sun said, "You sure you want to look at that thing all the time?"

Ramsey said, "No."

Sun gave him her warm, amused smile. The bus turned down Eloise's road. He could see her mailbox 50 yards off, with its three decorative cattails. He said, "You can drop me there. Number 64." And then the sliding door creaked and banged, and then he was out, and Sun and Blues shouted for him to stay cool, Shantih and Attila barked an enthusiastic chorus, then the shining blue-and-white bus was 20 yards away, too far for him to make out the license plate. It was yellow, he could tell that. And then, as a single westering beam of sunlight struck it, burning it almost gold, while the dogs were still barking and Blues was still waving, the bus disappeared with a silent pop, like a soap bubble, leaving a glittering scatter of bright particles floating in the air.

There were some things, Ramsey decided after a bit, that it was fruitless to question. You just had to accept them.

Eloise's driveway was more of a lane, with feathery grass growing between the wheel ruts. It dipped and then swung upward, around an ancient clump of luxuriant and fiery tiger lilies. Ramsey felt his cheeks with the backs of his hands, checking for fever. Cool and damp. He quickly pulled out the front of his shirt and dipped his nose for a whiff. Not bad. He smelled his hands. Just him. No revealing traces of sandalwood and citrus. Ramsey realized he had been walking quickly, too quickly, at a pace that could bring him into Eloise's presence before he was ready. He stopped and leaned against the fragrant bark of a black-cherry tree.

All he had to do was claim it. That was all. That was all. That was all.

He claimed it. He turned his head and smelled the bark of the tree, its sweet velvet redolence. It swirled through his flesh like cream through coffee and soothed him. He monitored his extremities—pate, thumbs, feet. All was quiet. Ramsey felt himself smile.

Kay, Eloise's daughter, stood on the flagstone patio, watering a big pot of red-and-green coleus. When she caught sight of Ramsey, she dropped the hose and snatched it up again. Ramsey heard the distinct clink of the nozzle against the flagstones. Jeanine had once told him that Kay probably didn't like him because her parents had divorced when she was 11, a bad age. Now Kay was 13. Ramsey didn't know whether Kay liked him, but most of the time, she acted more or less politely. Until now, that had been plenty. As Ramsey approached, she gave him a formal smile, said, "Hi," then shouted, "Mo-o-om!" She shoved the nozzle of the hose into the next pot and mumbled in his direction, "I guess I've got some other chores. See ya."

"Kay?" he called out. He was still smiling. He wished he had a present for her; she was a cute girl.

Eloise stepped through the French doors, slowly wiping her hands on her shorts. She did smile at Ramsey, and he had to scratch behind his ear to keep himself from running toward her. He didn't want to run. He was too short and overweight to look good running. But Eloise looked great, distracted and pretty. "Hey," he said, "did I ever give Kay a present?"

"I don't think so," said Eloise. "What are you doing here? I thought you were going up to Oneonta."

"I want to give Kay a present. What does she want?"

Eloise shrugged, and Ramsey pressed himself toward her. She gave him a hug.

"It's almost dinnertime. Let's have some lobsters for dinner. I'll go down to the Grand Union."

She looked past him. "Where's your car?"

"Broke down in Kerhonkson. I'll get some of those French breads, too. The baguettes. We can dip——"

Eloise sniffed, always a sign of resistance. Ramsey could take that if he had to. She said, "We ate. We didn't expect you."

"Well, I'm starving. What time is it? It's only seven. Why did you eat already?"

"I'm going to take Kay to *Arachnophobia*."

"Do it tomorrow night." He knew as he said it that he should have made that a suggestion, or a request, but he was suddenly finding himself in an ordering mood.

"I promised. She invited Annie. We're just about to leave."

"Goddamn you." Apparently, the day's events hadn't changed him as much as he had thought.

Eloise's lips disappeared as if by magic, and white flecks appeared in her green eyes. She said, "I've had it, Ramsey. That's it for us."

"Wait a minute——"

She looked at her watch. "I've got to leave, or I'd stay to kick you out." She turned.

"I don't have a car!"

"Call a cab."

"I'm dirty, I——"

"All of that's your problem now. I'm so tired of you, I can't even remember how this got started." She charged through the French doors, calling, "Kay! Kay! Time to go!" Then she stopped and spun to face him. "I mean it."

Ramsey had heard her use that tone to Kay. He had liked it when she used it, because it was a tone that Kay never challenged, not even by rolling her eyes. Ramsey licked his lips, then turned and began to walk back down the lane. He stepped aside without looking when they passed him in Eloise's Camry wagon.

But when she was gone, Ramsey ran back up the driveway and scuttled into the house. Dried sweat covered him like a shell and he had to shower. He knew for a fact that there was a clean shirt of his in Eloise's closet. The pants he could stand. After that, he would leave. He swore to himself he would leave.

But he didn't. Instead, he put on Eloise's terrycloth bathrobe and sat on one of the big white-duckcloth sofas in her study, watching the darkness gather outside the French doors. Water from Kay's hose had spilled over the rim of the flowerpot and onto the stones of the patio.

FAHRVERGNÜGEN

A shimmering sheet ran into the grass. Ramsey was annoyed enough not to get up and turn off the outside faucet. But an undergrowth of conflicting feelings burgeoned as well.

There was envy for Blues, that poor sap, a fool with a body and a grace that Ramsey had never had, young or old. Ramsey thought Blues could, and certainly did, look at Sun with desire and will unmuddied by self-consciousness.

There was love for Sun, yes, at this safe remove, love, desire, longing, the sort of thing he'd felt in college at UCLA, on beaches, in parking lots, in cafes, something that always, for him, came before sex, but this one time came after, making him want to cry (what an embarrassment that was).

As separate from him, now, as they were, was a picture of his former self, the wrong sort for UCLA, for all of the West, where he had been born and raised, sweaty, dark, hairy, anxious, fast-talking, always divvying any group check down to the penny, following friends out to the street, even, saying, "You still owe me seven cents," or, maybe worse, pressing the seven cents he still owed on the unwilling recipient. Adult life had seen Ramsey's victory—the clothes, the accessories, the car, his move to the East, where he was recognized and welcomed. Guys like Blues were nobodies now, driving Ford Escorts these days, no longer attractive to women like Sun. Victory; defeat: Sitting in the dark in Eloise's study, where he wasn't supposed to be, it all hurt.

He heard the front door open and the noise of Kay hustling up to her room, two steps at a time. Water began to rush through the pipes. It took Eloise a long time to get to the study. In the interval, Ramsey changed his spot, so that the wedge of light from the door would fall immediately upon him, and his presence wouldn't surprise and frighten her.

The knob turned. The door creaked. Eloise stared, and then said, "What the hell——"

"I was so sweaty, I——"

"God, Ramsey, I don't think I ever want to hear about your body again. Just get something on. I'll call a cab."

"I wish you'd sit down."

"For what?"

"We can talk."

"All you ever talk about is complaints. Your complaints. I used to think you were letting me get close to you, but you just complain. I'm tired of it."

"I won't complain."

She paused in the doorway, then went in, striding quickly to the couch where Ramsey had been sitting.

Except that he couldn't really tell her about his day.

He thought of something. "Have you been to that restaurant in New Paltz? The Nirvana or something like that?"

"Not in a while." She pursed her lips. "It burned to the ground 18 or 20 years ago."

Ramsey felt his eyebrows climb. He lowered them. He would think about that part later.

They sat.

Eloise began to fidget. Her legs had been crossed, but suddenly she uncrossed them and her feet fell like brake shoes to the hardwood floor. She began to stand up. "Well——"

"Wait a minute."

"For what?"

Ramsey kneaded his brain for something to say that wasn't a complaint, wasn't about Sun.

Eloise sat up. "Just tell me one thing you've ever done with anyone else in mind. One thing. One good thing." She spoke rhetorically, already knowing there had been nothing.

As for Ramsey, he wasn't irritated. All the fires of irritation were quenched by a spout of panic. "OK," he said, "OK. There was this one time." And then there it was. The memory, released by the thoughts of those girls in college, expanded. "This time, I was in a guy's wedding, back in L.A. I was driving his new VW Squareback, and I was assigned to take all the bridesmaids to the wedding. It wasn't a hippie wedding, either. All these four girls had on yellow organdy with these rosebud bouquets, and there wasn't enough room. Their dresses poufed out everywhere, over the backs of the seats, in our faces. We had the windows down so the moving air would keep them fluffed up."

"You drove some girls to a wedding?" Eloise clearly wasn't impressed.

"But we got lost. We got lost on the freeway because I missed the exit, and then we got more lost, and we just missed the wedding altogether." Let's talk about sweat, he thought, let's talk about panic. "When we finally found the church, there was this note saying that the wedding had gone on and giving the address of the reception, so we jumped in the car again, and everyone was crying, all the girls, and their flowers were wilting, so the girl in the front threw hers out the window."

All crying. The sound, with all of them doing it, hadn't been scary, just girlish and choral, almost inspiring.

"But we didn't find the reception, either. It was a part of town I wasn't familiar with."

He'd said that over and over, a litany of excuse, "I don't know this part of town. I was raised in Pasadena."

"This is a cute story, Ramsey, but it doesn't qualify." Eloise sighed and rubbed her hand over her mouth. She would stand up, he could tell.

"It does, because I found them a wedding. A big wedding reception at a club in Malibu, outdoors with lights, under a tent. I pulled up, dropped off the car and took them inside. We didn't know anyone, and the bridesmaids for that wedding were wearing pink. The bride had left by that time, so she wasn't there to stop us. I didn't take no for an answer. Then I went around to all the best-looking guys and I found them partners, and they danced and ate wedding cake and drank champagne. I did it for them because I didn't want them to end the day with nothing."

That was something he could do. Just go up to people and ask them for something, offer them something. Those bridesmaids were the first thing he'd ever sold anybody on. Or, you could say, the one thing he'd given away. Not long afterward, he'd come East.

Eloise's laughter filled the dark room.

Ramsey said, "Eloise, don't kick me out." Now it was gone, irritability, panic, envy, longing. There was just waiting.

She said, "I want you to go home, Ramsey. But you can take my car and bring it back tomorrow. We can eat the lobsters then." Her voice still lilted with the afterglow of her laughter. Ramsey let out a deep, deep breath and smoothed the film off his upper lip. It had been a long day. His head hurt a little, more like a pinging, less like a throbbing. But he didn't mention it.

"Hi there. Would you like to come up here for an early moring dip?"

The High Cost of Fame

commentary by MARIO PUZO

Mario Puzo spent years as a scrambling, debt-ridden freelance writer before his novel about the Mafia, "The Godfather," sold 7 million copies and solved his financial problems—at least for the time being. He is presently trying to unclutter his life and begin a new novel. When asked what it's about, he replies, "Everything."

The paraphernalia, the logistics of being a success are the worst thing about it. There's fuckin' deals—you gotta see your agent, your lawyer. I told my lawyer, "I'll pay the fuckin' taxes rather than keep track of everything I spend. I don't want to mess around writing that stuff down at the end of the day." It's the worst, worst pain in the ass. You got a lot of money, you're supposed to invest. I don't want to be bothered. All the stocks go down, everybody's getting wiped out and meanwhile I'm blowing all my dough and I feel so virtuous I can't tell you. The old Italians don't believe in all those deals. Get the money in cash, bury it, spend it, buy a house. That's better.

The curious thing is that I'd always been a heavy gambler, but since I became successful, I don't enjoy gambling anymore. I don't understand why, but it's a shame, because it was one of my great fun things.

I've found that success, aside from the money, is not really that gratifying. I feel uncomfortable giving interviews. And I would never give lectures. I really think I became a success too late. It doesn't mean that much anymore. People want to come up to you and say how great the book is and that's nice, but you can do without it.

Success knocks the shit out of your writing. I know why I became a writer and that's to have as little contact with the world as possible. You feel more comfortable keeping the world at a distance. You get into your little cave, you write, you come out at times and those little times there's less danger. You're exposed for so little time to society and your friends. So when you have a success, you got a lot of time on your hands, so what do you do? You go out, you meet the world. Right? Therefore, you're more exposed to shock. You get insulted more. There's a lot of shocks to your nervous system in success. It's a shock to me to meet new people. I used to avoid parties. Nobody called and I didn't have the time to fool around. So now I go out. Right? And it's great. I'm a wheel. But now because I'm a success, I'm exposed and I get zapped.

Success corrupts your emotional processes. It makes you impatient with the ordinary aspects of your life, so without realizing it, you sometimes put your friends down and your family. The great thing about writing is that it washes that corruption away.

I'll tell you, I'm glad I'm successful. I did it and I'm glad. But the thing is, if you can't be young again, what the hell's the difference? And I don't like to own things. I never even bought a new car. I bought one suit. My agent took me out and made me buy a $400 suit. I hate that fuckin' suit.

"I tell you, by the time I've finished, Mount Rushmore will be forgotten."

The Braggart King

ribald classic by HERODOTUS

Candaules, King of Lydia, was a man of many faults, but supreme among them was this: He loved to brag.

He bragged of his riches, he bragged of his power, he bragged of his palace, he bragged of his horses and, worst of all, he bragged openly and continually, to everyone he met, sparing no details, of the beauty, fidelity, passion and prowess of his Queen.

Candaules had another fault, a fault not uncommon among kings: He distrusted people and imagined he was being laughed at, his boasts ridiculed and disbelieved. One day, in his typical style, he said to Gyges, the captain of his guard: "The Queen—she is a handsome woman, Gyges, is she not? But let me tell you, her real beauties you have never seen. The beauty of her belly, which is smooth and cool as an alabaster vase, the beauty of her breasts——"

"Indeed, sire," said Gyges, "these perfections you have been kind enough to catalogue for me before."

"And did you believe me?"

"Why——"

"Ah, I can see it in your face, dissembler! You believed not a word!"

"My lord——"

"Enough! I will *prove* to you that my Queen is all I say, and then in the future when I speak of her beauties and am met with incredulity, I will have only to turn to you and say, 'My good Gyges here can certify all my claims.'"

"But how——"

"Men's eyes believe what their ears do not. This night will you stand behind the door in the Queen's chamber. You will watch her disrobe, down to her silken skin, as she prepares herself for my couch. You will note the excellence of her charms; of *all* her charms, Gyges; of her belly, which is——"

"But sire," cried Gyges, "that would be most unseemly! It is not fit-

379

ting, nor is it even lawful, for me to look upon the naked flesh of another man's wife. And when that man is my *King*, it becomes an offense most high, a wicked thing, a crime tantamount to sacrilege!"

"What is seemly," said Candaules, "what is fitting, lawful, offensive, wicked, criminal or sacrilegious in this kingdom—I decide. Therefore tonight, doubting Gyges, you will see for yourself that Candaules has for wife the fairest woman in all Lydia."

That night Gyges hid in the Queen's chamber and, as she unveiled herself for bed, her beauties were revealed to the young captain, one by one. His sovereign, boastful though he was, had not spoken falsely. All went as Candaules had planned, with one regrettable exception: the Queen saw Gyges behind the door. Her first impulse—to cry out—she stifled, for knowing the integrity of the captain, she divined that he was there by her foolish husband's wishes. Therefore, she said nothing.

In the morning, however, she sent for Gyges. Sensing something was afoot, he went to her uneasily. When he arrived, she came to the point at once.

"Captain," she said severely, "you are a man of honor, and yet you hid in my chamber last night and watched me undress. I can only assume you did so at the King's command. Is this correct?"

Gyges was, indeed, a man of honor: He could not bring himself to lie. "It is correct, my lady," he replied.

"So." The Queen's beautiful eyes narrowed to slits. The full sensuality of her lips straightened to a hard, determined line of scarlet. "Captain Gyges," she said at last, "this was an onerous and unlawful thing you did last night."

"It was, madam," he agreed.

"A punishable thing."

"Yes, madam."

"Who, however, is to be punished? The master or the man? He who gave the order, or he who obeyed it? Who, handsome Gyges? Who must die?"

"*Die*, madam?"

"It was my word, Gyges. As a man of honor, a man of more honor than my braggart King, I will leave the decision to you. What is your answer?"

In the annals of Lydian history, the despotism of King Candaules is more than balanced by the just, wise, long and clement reign of King Gyges and his lovely Queen.

WORD PLAY By ROBERT CAROLA

*fun and games with the king's english in which
words become delightfully self-descriptive*

NONCON*F*ORMIST

SUICIDE

SN◯RE

REDUNDUNDANT

ALON   E

.

LOШCUT

eject

pregnant
O

knocЖneed

ERORR

balloon

RESTING

EXXTRA

HONEYMOON

ASTIGMATISM

drip

mispell

cockeyed

INCOMPLET

PRO$TITUTE

trivial

IMPORTANT

INDIꟻERENT

FRUGL

BⱯR
T
SⱢOOL

CL!MAX

CⱯRET

omıt

KANGAROO

KISꙄ

ᐁIRGIN

visït

O
PT
OME
TRIST

K
ICK

TUNNEL

forgetful

QUICKSAND

LITHP

._mpotent

mispalce

YOGA

REFLECTION

HICCUPS

LOS and FOUNDT

MIRROR

immature

Who's the Bull Goose Loony Here?

memoir by GROVER LEWIS

T he midmorning sky over the Oregon State Hospital in Salem looks liverish, quiverish, ready to collapse with torrential rain at any second. On the crew-cut lawn behind the main building, an orderly shoos his excursion troupe of exercising patients back to shelter past a charter bus disgorging a troupe of Hollywood film technicians.

The two lines of shuffling men pay scarce attention to each other, even when one of the patients—a spindly Latino in a Hawaiian shirt—suffers some sort of convulsive seizure and slams face first to the ground. The orderly quickly kneels beside the victim, clawing for his tongue, while the other patients stand around in a frieze of distracted inattention. "*Mama, mama, ayúdeme,*" the stricken man manages to cry in a wet strangle. "Crazy," one of the film technicians clucks, then cuts his eyes away uneasily.

A rush of wind blows a hole in the overcast. The squall begins.

● ● ●

A few minutes later, wearing $35 squeakless sneakers and somebody else's awning-sized windbreaker, Jack Nicholson comes barreling down the Oregon asylum's ground-floor corridor. His gait would be arresting anywhere—a speeded-up version of the moneymaker-shaking street strut he choreographed to near-squeakless perfection in *The Last Detail*. Nicholson walks like Martin Balsam sounds—solid, chunky, chock full of cod-liver oil.

Strolling along the drab-linoleumed institutional corridor in the opposite direction, Michael Douglas is escorting a visiting writer through the archaic, all-too-grossly authentic mad wards where Milos Forman is directing Fantasy Films' $3,000,000 production of *One Flew Over the*

WHO'S THE BULL GOOSE LOONY HERE?

Cuckoo's Nest. Douglas is Kirk's kid—the one who plays Inspector Steve Keller in the TV series *The Streets of San Francisco.* Michael Douglas is also the coproducer of *Cuckoo's Nest,* and right now, without all that much visible effort, he is being charming, courteous, even voluble when called upon. He has, in fact, just introduced into the conversation the pleasant fiction that he and the writer had met "years before...in San Francisco, wasn't it?" Michael Douglas is a smooth-rising young biscuit in all respects except that he wears hideously disfigured cowboy boots the writer figures he must have copped from some dying wino in Stockton.

The writer is trying his mightiest to stay attentive, but his mind is blipping into erratic wigwags and test patterns. He has a root-canal case of the fantods. His sphincter is fluttering, he is breaking out in a sour sweat, and he is wishing to hell he had an amyl or something harder to bite on.

What's queering the writer's internal wiring isn't Douglas' pleasant fiction nor Nicholson's abrupt, looming presence—which in itself registers about a 6.5 on the Richter scale. N-o-o-o, the germ of the trouble lies in this rotten, overwhelmingly oppressive and repulsive *place.* At long last, lunacy—the funny farm, the loony bin, Rubber Room Inn. For years, assorted editors and ex-wives have been predicting the writer will wind up in just such a cuckoo's nest and—well, he's been here now for half an hour and he's wondering queasily if he will be allowed to leave when it's time to go. He is also wondering about *his notebook.* Has he mislaid it somewhere? That notebook is too goddamned important to lose—it's an Efficiency Reporter's Note Book No. 176, and scribbled among its 200 leaves and 400 pages are the liver and lights for two unwritten stories, plus an itemized list of business expenses totaling over $1,300—*God have mercy, where is that slippery fucker?*

The notebook, of course, is securely glued to the viscous resin bubbling out of the writer's swampy palm. When he discovers this, the writer executes a jerky, agitated little flamenco of relief and gratitude.

Passing abreast of Douglas and his visiting charge by now, Nicholson instantly registers the dysfunction. The actor flashes Douglas a high-caloric hi sign in greeting, then swivels his gaze to zero in on the writer's sagging knee action. Unsmiling but not unsympathetic, he notices the man's small, panicky dance of distress and release, the jittering aftershock of wrenching visceral trauma. He files it all away for future reference. Nicholson notices things like that and no doubt uses them to flesh out his riveting film performances.

Without irony, the writer regards Nicholson as a national treasure. This literalist view of the actor will get in the way of the substantive story waiting to be perceived here, but not for long. Meanwhile, Nicholson whips past in his squeakless sneakers, vanishing soundlessly down the institutional corridor.

• • •

With the writer in tow, Douglas advances a kilometer or so into the bowels of the fortresslike asylum, pulling up short at a point in the corridor where the color of the walls abruptly changes from scabrous green to shit brindle. In his voluble register, Douglas is explaining—no, *proving*—that this is no gypo movie of the week they're engaged in here; nosirreebob, this is the quality goods, a AAA feature of the caliber that's rarely indulged in anymore for all your ersatz disaster operas and *Godfather* begats. Standing near the wire-mesh entrance to ward four, the film's principal set, Douglas ticks off *Cuckoo*'s championship qualities on his pale, pencil-thin fingers:

"Our daily nut is $35,000, see, so with that kind of dough at stake, we're not chintzing around about *anything*. When Saul and I decided to do the picture"—Saul Zaentz is the Main Man at Fantasy Records / Films in Berkeley and *Cuckoo*'s other producer—"we agreed first off that we'd only settle for the best. I mean, screw it, across the board, whatever the field of talent, whatever the cost. And we got it all, man—everybody and everything we wanted—bam, bam, bam! Nicholson was our first and only choice for McMurphy. Nicholson *is* the 'bull goose loony'—watch his stuff this afternoon and you'll understand what I mean."

Nicholson as McMurphy—a dead-solid ringer. Back in the Sixties, before the bliss ninnies began slouching toward Hesse and Tolkien, McMurphy was a kind of fictive national treasure in his own right. Everybody—everybody who could read, anyway—copped a hint of style and character from the hell-raising drifter who feigned insanity to escape a penal farm, who locked horns in the mental slammer with the tyrannical Big Nurse, who both won and lost the battle and in between gave life-to-life resuscitation to the Chronics and Acutes on his ward.

"And Milos," Douglas goes on, "he's just goddamn marvelous—one of the finest directors in the world. It's a wild thing to watch happen. We've got a great cast, down to the tiniest walk-on, and probably the best crew in the business. Jack Nitzsche is composing the score.... Bill Butler's our cinematographer—he just did *Jaws*. And, lessee—oh, yeah, the sound man, Larry Jost? He's up for an Oscar for *Chinatown*—just like Jack. But, come on, let's go take a run around the set. Brace yourself, though. I warn you, man, it's terrible—it's ghastly."

Yes, exactly. Ward four would gag a maggot. It is a cagelike enclosure

387

furnished in the brutal paraphernalia of shrink-tank pathology run absolutely amuck: cramped rows of hospital cots with rumpled gray sheets and matted blankets...obscenely stained bed tables littered with puke pans and hot-water bottles...a scattered fleet of decrepit, cane-backed wheelchairs...framed calendar portraits of dogs and wild geese hung uniformly awry...and perched above all this mess, on a high, centrally located shelf, a smeary-windowed TV set bearing the brand name of its manufacturer, one "Madman" Muntz.

An immaculate, glassed-in nurses' station controlling egress to the ward cage rounds out the picture. Big Nurse's Orders of the Day are posted there on slot cards in a wallboard. The slot cards read:

THE YEAR IS 1963

TO DAY IS WEDNESDAY

THE DATE IS DECEMBER 11

THENEXTHOLIDAY

CHRISTMAS

THE NEXT MEAL IS BREAKFAST

THE WEATHERIS CLOUDY

Ye gods, The Compleat Toilet—"Ol' Mother Ratched's Therapeutic Nursery," in Kesey's phrase. Which prompts the writer to clutch his sweat-slick notebook all the tighter and wonder aloud about Kesey's connection with the film.

Douglas takes on the expression of a man who's just been put on hold during a transoceanic call. He motions vaguely toward the ward's rain-blurred windows. "I can't say for sure," he mutters, "but I've heard he's out there in the hills somewhere muttering rip-off. We hired him—paid him over $10,000—to write a first-draft screenplay. We found out pretty quick that he couldn't write screenplays to suit our standards, and he couldn't get along with the people involved, and he couldn't or wouldn't show up for production meetings. From what I hear, he's been spreading the word that the movie version distorts his book. Well, fuck it—I just have to disagree, that's all. We've taken some liberties with the basic material, sure, but all of us expect the picture will come very close to the spirit, the wallop of the book. Milos thinks it will, and Nicholson thinks so, too, and so, in fact, do I."

Douglas dismisses the subject with a short shrug and points along the corridor, grinning. "See that place where the color of the walls changes? That's Milos for you—a stickler to the teeth. He made us repaint the whole ward—dirty beige, I guess you'd call it. I asked him, 'Why, Milos?' And he said, '*Vy*? Because ve cahn't chute an entire comedy against *green*, dot's vy.'"

By this time, members of the technical crew have started work around the nurses' station, hammering and sawing and wheeling around bulky film equipment on dollies. Wandering among the electricians and gaffers and grips are a dozen or so other men—odd-looking spooks dressed in ratty old hospital robes and felt slippers. These, presumably, are some of the actors who portray Kesey's Chronics and Acutes. Uh-huh...and where, uh, are the real patients, the certified dafts?

"Everywhere," Douglas crows with a gleeful sweep of his arms. "Well, no...let me qualify that. The patients committed here are quartered on the third floor. Oregon, you understand, like a lot of other states, is releasing a high percentage of its mental patients to so-called local responsibility.

"But, see, the director of this hospital—a terrific guy named Dean Brooks—has very advanced and, I believe, civilized ideas about what constitutes good therapy, and the distance from the third to the first floor is just two flights of stairs. In other words, there's an amazing crossover between the film troupe and the patients. Everybody visits back and forth, plays pool, plays cards, horses around together. A couple or three of the patients are even working for us in various small jobs—and you can actually see the effect on their spirit, their morale. After a while, they start to blend in, and—hell, at times there's no way to tell the patients from the crew. Look over there—see the little fellow with the broom? He's on the payroll—Ronnie the Patient—interesting guy, as I'm sure you'll discover. Two months ago, Ronnie was classified as a catatonic mute."

Douglas indicates a frail, stoop-shouldered boy-man, perhaps 25, who is abstractedly sweeping sawdust into a pile near the entrance to the nurses' station. He is wearing vague, Permaprest civvies and a vague, Permaprest smile that disappears into a brush mustache and no chin at all. He is clearly crazy at a glance, but just as clearly harmless.

The writer stares toward the nurses' station, scanning the individual faces of the workers and actors congregated there. Sure, he nods numbly. Crazy.

● ● ●

The lingering insane of Oregon—some of them the criminally insane—are upstairs on the third floor. Well, except for the ones fraternizing down here on the first floor. The writer considers this awhile and searches out a hidey-hole where he can repair unobserved. There, in crying need of repair himself, he hikes up his coattails and jams his Efficiency Reporter's Note Book No. 176 deep into the rear waistband of his trousers, snug between belt and bum. The writer feels immensely better for this, although he has somehow lost track of his Sony TC-126 tape recorder.

● ● ●

The hospital's Tub Room looks like a used-bathtub lot washed up the coast from the psychic environs of L.A.'s Pico and Western. A few minutes before noon, Forman is in there having a heart-to-heart with Scatman Crothers and Louisa Moritz. The two are about to play a seduction scene involving a drunken ward attendant and a fragged-out semi-pro whore. Roughly three dozen technicians and onlookers are shoe-boxed into the sweltering, seedy-tiled hydrotherapy facility where Oregon's crazies used to assemble faithfully for the purpose of undergoing water torture. The writer is huddled spine down in one of the enamel-peeling tubs, keeping an eye on as much of the elbow-to-ass action as he can follow. "Quiet, please—let's get it *very* quiet in here," one of the assistant directors bawls.

Forman concludes his huddle with Crothers and Ms. Moritz, nods curtly and strides off a few paces to fire up his pipe. A human path peels open for him wherever he chances to move. The Czech-born director is hairy on the head, arms and chest and built like a lunch box wrapped in a pair of old San Pedro–style dungarees. He is prone to yelling a lot when he gets excited.

Louisa Moritz, with the face of a zonked china doll, scratches a lank flank through her grungy pedal pushers and puts on what could be interpreted as a pensive look. In a glissando croak, she allows to Scatman that she doesn't much care for one of her lines. "Say anything you want to, honey," he urges, patting her hand comfortingly. "Don't worry about it, you hear what I'm tellin' you? Fuck it." "Oh, I know!" Louisa crows in inspiration. "I'll say—at the end?—I'll say, 'Oh, well, what the hell—any old fart in a storm.' Isn't that better?" Scatman cackles and claps his hands on his slick black pate in delight: "Yeah, yeah, crazy, that's fine, that's awright! Listen, I tell you what, girl—why'n't we just wing it? Hell, let's have us some *fun*! Shoo-be-doop! Jabba-dee-boom! Skee-doop! Zack!" Louisa giggles into her fingers and crosses to her toe mark.

"*Everybody quiet!*" another assistant thunders. Forman raises and lowers a hand in the hanging silence. "Roll, please," Bill Butler murmurs to his camera operators. Two grips with slapsticks spring before the massive Panavision cameras. "A and V 107, take one, A camera." "B camera."

The cameras begin to whir with a faint ta-pocketa-pocketa, and the scene flows like water. Scatman, playing an orderly named Turkle, entices Louisa, a dim-witted mattressback, into a deserted corner of the Tub Room, where he plies her for a taste of strange with Smirnoff, Tokay and generous doses of speedy sweet-talk. She responds by covering her head with a brown paper bag—that's her impression of a fish—and prattling off a long, disjointed story about a dead boyfriend who got that way by gobbling light bulbs. During this synapse-rattling recitative, Turkle is steadily stroking his way up her pedal pushers, but just as he is about to lay hands on her trade goods, a prearranged KAW-BLONG! offcamera propels him to his feet in petrified consternation. *What the fuck—those goddamn Chronics and Acutes—they're stagin' a midnight insurrection out yonder in ward four! Holy fuckin' doomsday—Big Nurse will mess her whites!*

Scatman and Louisa play the scene five times, five different ways. They play it fast and slow, sweet and sour, mournful and manic. They play it fey and lyric—every way but poorly or backward. For one take, Scatman improvises the line, "Let's get drunk and *be* somebody." For the next take, he rephrases it, "Let's get drunk and be somebody *else*." Louisa fields all of Scatman's wild tumbling and burns back a few swifties of her own. The two are natural foils, the Lunt and Fontanne of bull-goose loonydom.

Forman watches the good times roll with tooth-sucking detachment. His response to all but the final take is unvarying: "Cut, cut, cut, cut. Very good, very perfect. Ve vill chute it again, please."

● ● ●

As the crew begins to strike the set, Scatman and Louisa wink, embrace and take their leave of Bathtub City. Entranced, the writer flexes out of his porcelain squat and trails them to a makeshift dressing room furnished in rump-sprung rattan. Plopped down beside Louisa on a litter-strewn settee, Scatman airily waves the writer toward a chair positioned beneath a Lenny Bruce poster. "Set down, friend," Scatman croons, "you look like you come from about halfway decent stock."

Scatman produces a tenor guitar from somewhere, an age-burnished Martin, and begins whanging hell out of its four strings: "'Who's sorry now / Who's sorry now.'... Ain't that tasty, though? Listen, you ever watch *Chico and the Man*? I'm Louie the garbage man on that mutha— I'm the man who empties your can! Can you dig it? 'Cause never forget, you are what you throw out!"

Louisa has a guitar, too, a Japanese job, and she starts singing something that goes "Da-da-da-dee-da-da." The effect is singular—comparable, maybe, to the death rattle of a squeegee. Scatman tries his best to harmonize with her. "Ain't she pretty?" he beams. "I love this lady—I'm *crazy* 'bout her. She's the *real* Divine Miss M!"

Louisa segues into *Behind Closed Doors*, but she hits a clinker that makes her stamp her foot and hiss, "Oh, for the luvva shit!" She winks conspiratorially at the writer and asks, "Did you see our little scene just now?...Oh, I'm *so glad*. It was supposed to make you laugh. Did you see my Alka-Seltzer commercial last night? It was supposed to make you buy Alka-Seltzer....I do a lot of commercials, uh-huh, but I also do the Carson show, and I'm doing more movie roles lately. Some pulp men's magazine ran a story on me last month, but they didn't get my credits right for the last four years. *Truly.* I just did the second lead in a picture with David Carradine called *Death Race 2000*, and they didn't even mention it. I mean, you would think people would do their jobs or something."

"There's a man does his job—the head nigger of this joint!" Scatman cries, racing to the door and tugging Dean Brooks into the room by a tweed sleeve. An affable, gracefully graying man, the director of the hospital shakes hands all around and murmurs something sympathetic about Louisa's chord-strumming ability. "Oh, well, thank you," she chirrups, "I only started playing, lessee, oh, about three hours ago." "Dr. Brooks here is one *helluva* doctor," Scatman assures the writer, "one *helluva* shrink. And you know what? He plays that same part in the movie—a shrink. Ain't that weird? Wobba-dee-doo-bop! Pa-hoochas-matoo-chas! Merf!" "I've got one more scene to go," Brooks mock sighs, "but right now I'm on my way back up to the third floor, where it's safe."

Scatman follows the doctor away, seeking, as he says in a braying aside, "free medical advice—all I can get. Hell, babies. I'm 64." Louisa waves toodle-oo to the two and commits murder one on the intro to *Sounds of Silence*. She snuffs the rest of the song, too, chord by chord, line by line. "Isn't that pretty?" she asks at the end. She laughs at the writer's poleaxed expression and pokes a good-natured finger at his midsection: "Don't forget to put it in about *Death Race 2000*."

● ● ●

The commissary is another recycled mad ward, where the *Cuckoo* troupe assembles en masse at four P.M. daily to be served up mess (yes) by a local catering outfit. In the early afternoon, the place is virtually deserted. Saul Zaentz, the picture's coproducer, is in there noshing a fast bear claw.... The brawny kid with the purple birthmark who tends to the coffee urn is tending to the coffee urn.... An actor named Danny DeVito is escorting his kinky-haired ladyfriend fresh from da Bronx on a tour of the dingy dining area. *Kind of a neat-o place, once you get the drag of it. Tablecloths. Funny pictures and shtick on the walls. Almost like the old Village, sort of....* The lady has the drag of the place at a glance and she is rolling her eyes in speechless revulsion. She is scanning all visible surfaces for—who knows?—cockroaches, spirochetes.... *God, and she flew all the way across the country to break bread in this Dachau of the stomach?*

The writer enters the mess hall in search of anything wet and he tunes in a sound. *Rrr, rrr.* Low but distinct, the sound reminds him of—he can't immediately think what. Zaentz strolls across the tatty linoleum and pokes out a family-sized paw in greeting. "Good to see you again," the shmoo-shaped producer says with a benign show of teeth. "We met years ago, if I'm not mistaken—in Berkeley, wasn't it?"

That pleasant fiction again. The writer puzzles over it briefly, but it doesn't yield up much of a mystery. In plain-vanilla usage, it's a mode of status shorthand that is commonplace among film folk. It's Gollywood's way of saying: *I'm OK—you're OK. If you're here among the Somebodies, then you must be a Somebody, too. But I already know all the Somebodies, so we must have met somewhere before.... Sure, we met before...Berkeley...Barcelona...some fucking place....*

Rrr, rrr—that sound again—sinister.

"Been a lot of yelling around the set recently," Zaentz muses as he munches the heel of his bear claw, "but that's par for the course, a deal like this. I mean, this has been a goddamn long location. We got here the first week in January and we're halfway into what now—March? That's ten weeks—lots of long hours, tough setups. And we've got two, three more weeks to go, so naturally everybody's getting a little—edgy...you know how it goes. Hell, I'm a little edgy myself. But in my estimation, it's all been worth it. We've put together one classy picture—everybody connected swears it's a killer. Who'd stoop to shitting about a thing like that?"

"Lemme tell you about this picture," Danny DeVito chimes in. The actor stands about four feet nothing, and from the hairline down, he is built like a potbellied stove. He chooses his words with excruciating care. "This—picture—is—the—weirdest—experience—of—my—entire—existence—as—a—human—bean.

"Lemme explain, OK? I'm from New York City, see, so naturally I was figurin' on seein' the famous, gorgeous countryside around here—Oregon, you know, the Pacific Northwest, all that shit. Well, I end up workin' straight through for the first nine weeks I'm here, and then finally I get a couple of days off. Terrific, I think—fan-fuckin'-tastic!—and so I run downtown, I rent a car, I score some deli for a picnic and…I couldn't leave. I drove out here from the hotel for lunch. So help me, I came out here and peeked in the ward at my *bed*!"

The writer turns at a tiny tug on his sleeve. It is Ronnie the Patient—surprise, surprise—clutching that errant Sony TC-126. Without explanation, Ronnie shoves the tape machine forward and bolts off into the corridor. The *rrr, rrr* clicks off like a radio in a distant room.

• • •

An hour later, a Chautauqua of dementia is rampaging around the nurses' station. Every crazy in showbiz except Dub Taylor and Sam Peckinpah is queuing up on the set for A and V 108, take one. In ensemble, the actors who portray *Cuckoo*'s gallery of lames are shatteringly convincing. They hobble around on crutches, carom around in wheelchairs. They wander the ward in flapping hospital gowns, mismatched pajamas, piss-stained Jockey shorts. They belch, fart, scratch their scruffy asses. They call up visions of creatures out of Dante, or the crowd at Spec's in North Beach.

Nicholson doesn't look as bombed and strafed as the rest, nor is he supposed to, but he bounds around the set with demonic energy, all snap and *brio*. He whomps William Redfield on the shoulder, feints punches at Brad Dourif and Vincent Schiavelli. He tickles fingers with Sydney Lassick and Will Sampson, whispers something obscene to De-Vito, laughs aloud at the sight of Michael Berryman and Delos V. Smith Jr. Skidding to a halt, he waggles his fanny at Phil Roth and puts the arm on Scatman for a cigarette.

"C'mon B.S., a nail—*a nail*."

"Nothin' but tobacco in that, Jack. Need a light, too, do you?"

"Naw, I got this here little Cricket——"

"I could fan your ass, you need a little suction. Just say the word——"

"Not necessary at all B.S., but it's a real pleasure to see you here. Welcome to the stairway-to-heaven party."

Scatman squinches his eyes shut, flings his head back, croons. "We'll—build—a—freeway—to—the—stahs…."

"Ah, B.S., you're a rock to me—a rock to me. The Louis Armstrong of the tenor guitar."

"Say what?"

"And—I sometimes suspect this—the father of black comedy. Am I correct?"

"Yeah, that's correck, Jack. In both senses. Ah-hah, that was your

394

faithful Scatman in the original woodpile. Jobba-dee-wop! So-cony mo-beel! Zoop!'"

Nicholson and Scatman continue poppin' their chops until Forman stalks across the set and positions them firmly in front of the cameras. Both assistant directors bellow the babbling company to order. "Shot—shot!" "This'll be picture, people. Quiet—*shut up!*"

The scene shows Nicholson, aka the badass McMurphy, dispensing illicit pills and Jim Beam to his fellow Chronics and Acutes in a spontaneous-combustion midnight revel. Midway through the caper, Scatman/Turkle bursts in on the group, sputtering, outraged: *What the shit's goin' on here? McMurphy, you motherfucker, get outta here—alla you motherfuckers! G'wan, I don't wanna hear none of your crazy shit! Get your asses outta here! Pron-toe!*

The dramaturgy goes dit-dit-dit, but a light bank blows and Forman blows with it: "No, no, no, NO!" Two more scuttled takes and everybody is yelling—Nicholson, Scatman, Forman, the Chronics and Acutes, even a grip or two.

During the interminable delays, Scatman entertains the idlers on the sidelines: "Gentlemen, I'll show you a tough one. Ver-ry difficult, so watch closely. My impression...of a lighthouse in the middle of an ocean." Slowly, he pivots in a circle, flapping his mouth open and shut at ten-second intervals. When the cackles hit high C, Scatman mock scowls and snaps his fingers impatiently: "Aw-right, cut the shit and levity—who's got a cigafoo around here? I'm in need of a nail! I need a nail *bad*." Grinning, he accepts one of Nicholson's filter tips.

Nicholson starts hopping up and down on one leg. "Give us some kind of move over here, will ya?" he catcalls to Forman.

"HEY, MY-LOS!" Scatman brays. "You remember ol' King Solomon? Man said there's a time to dance and a time to grieve...a time to harvest...and a time to GET THIS MOTHERFUCKER ON THE ROAD."

"Yeah," Nicholson yowls, "*let's shoot this turkey!*"

"Wait a minute, though," Scatman mutters with a frown, "have I got time to go wet? I got to go wet."

Nicholson continues to hop in place, but he shifts to the other leg. "B.S.... Benjamin Sherman 'Scatman' Crothers. By God, you look like the real thing, B.S. What number is this for us?"

"Our third masterpiece together, Jack. The first was *The King of Marvin Gardens*, and then came *The Fortune*——"

"Hmm...number three it is. You got a great memory, B.S. You're a great American."

"That's right, FA-ROOK! ZA-GOOF!"

● ● ●

In the commissary, the writer is toying queasily with a serving of vulcanized chicken when Nicholson straddles a chair opposite him. "What's Hefner like?" the actor asks abruptly. The writer blinks a few times and confesses he's never had the pleasure. Nicholson seems disappointed at the reply, but he continues unloading his overfreighted lunch tray.

Two salads. Four buttered rolls. Three side orders of vegetables. Mashed potatoes and gravy. Half a chicken. A glass of iced tea. Two half pints of milk. A double wedge of fruit pie. When Nicholson has all this archipelago of nourishment arrayed in front of him, he sprinkles hot sauce over vast geographic portions of it. Scanning the faces at the surrounding tables, Nicholson spots Scatman. "Hey. B.S.," he calls out, "you want some *speed*?" Scatman fields the lobbed bottle of salsa in a chamois-colored palm.

Nicholson makes some amiable small talk, but food is what figures most precious in his life at the moment and he bends to it with wolfish gusto. "Jesus," he groans. "I haven't been this hungry"—gnawing relentlessly on a drumstick—"since breakfast." The writer laughs, feels at ease for the first time since—breakfast. Nicholson talks and eats and turns out to be exactly what he looks like: a personable black-Irishman from Pickup Truck America—a stand-up guy who played schoolboy sports in New Jersey, who got smart, who got out, who got to be a star. No, make that a national treasure. Any dumbass can be a star.

● ● ●

Forman resumes shouting and shooting after the dinner hour, but the writer retreats to the downtown hotel where most of the film troupe is quartered. Holed up with a slash of Scotch in handy reach, he studies his notes—fast-draw impressions of the asylum, the movie people, the eerily unsettling *rrr, rrr* phenomenon. He goes through the material three times and stares for a long while out a window at the rain sweeping the swimming pool.

Around midnight, the writer pulls on his boots and wanders down to the hotel bar to join B.S. Crothers and Will Sampson for some pro-am elbow calisthenics. Sampson is a butter-hearted lad, but he looks like the toughest, rottenest seven-foot Indian in the world, and he savors the part on and off the screen. "I'm mean as hell when I drank," he growls, "and I drank a little all the time." "Cheers," Scatman toasts, "and Roebuck."

The bar is a sort of color-coordinated bull pen, one of those places where people order things like salty dogs. A trash band plays moldy show tunes to scattered bursts of apathy from a table occupied by four or five of the film folk. The *Cuckoo* hands—a couple of actors, a couple of technicians—are nuzzling close to a round-robin of local belles, licking the ladies' ears and such. "Stunt fucking." Scatman explains succinctly. "All them cats are married, see—got families and mortgages back in Beverly Hills, but they been up here for three months now and...well, you know. Stunt fucking."

The band cranks for dear life: "'Life is a cab-o-ray, old chum, life is a cab-o-ray....'"

"You looked around Salem any?" Sampson asks. "Bah God, it's *weird*, I tell you. The city buses all got big signs on 'em that say CHEERIOT, and the suckers shut down runnin' for the night about seven. Yessir, *seven fuckin' o'clock*. And there's a joint down yonder just off Court Street? Got live midgets rasslin' in there, and people just streamin' in to see it. Christamighty, three and a half a head. I call that *flat-out purr-verted*."

Scatman gargles egregiously of the grape and pretty soon sinks face down in the sea of glasses on the tabletop. This doesn't inhibit some tub-butted dentist and his harpy wife from force-feeding their way into the booth beside him, gabbling like loons.

The harpy says she's a member of some civic committee that brings in chamber quartets and Henry Fonda as Clarence Darrow (a last-minute cancellation, that one, and God bless Pacemakers), and she enjoys celebrities just ever so much—they "tone up little old Salem." In light of his present assignment, she regards the writer, even, as a sort of crypto-Somebody, so she snaps her beringed fingers at the hot dog who's dispensing the busthead—*she's buying this round, by jingo, for the glory of Greater Salem!*

The writer shrinks away, trying to shun the frumious bandersnatch, but she can't or won't dry up. "Why do you use That Word?" she snaps at him sharply. "I would think it would be far beneath someone of your education." The writer explains. In some clinical detail. Calling on all his vast educational resources. The harpy grows pale and rises to depart in fairly steep dudgeon. The dentist trails along behind her like a strand of floating dental floss.

Scatman snores on, the band chugs on. Sampson removes a burning cigarette from Scat's fingers. He grins fondly. "I've drank many a merciful cup of Christian whiskey with this little gentleman," the big Indian reflects softly.

• • •

At the hospital early the next morning, the troupe from the bus troops to the nurses' station, but nobody exactly stampedes to work. The young honey of a blonde who serves as stand-in for the actresses takes up a sitting-Shiva position by a window, staring gloomily out at the gusting rain. "I feel crummy," she wails. "I woke up in the wrong crummy room."

Several of the technicians whip together a card game, others nurse on coffee mugs or take turns bashing a soggy punching bag. "Umm, umm," Scatman clucks, "if Brother Zaentz was up to see all this big-bucks talent fuckin' off out here, he'd weep like a limbless orphan."

Bill Butler, the cinematographer, arrives on the set seconds in advance of Forman, and the crew heaves to lustily. Butler is silent, bearded, monkish in appearance. He talks to nobody except his camera operators, and then in tones so low that no one can overhear. The workmen give him a wide berth.

Scatman is wearing dark glasses, and Michael Douglas cackles fiendishly at the sight. "Fell in the vinegar again, huh? How long you plan to wear the blinders, Scat?" "Till my eyes congeal, man."

The actors on call for the morning's routine pickup shots labor in ten-minute bursts, then dawdle for a couple of hours. They doze in chairs, bullshit one another outrageously, pass around the Hollywood trade papers. They gab endlessly about the stars ("Raquel got famous by inventing this zipper that wouldn't close, see") and in chorus they rattle off more household names than the Yellow Pages, but their gossip isn't meant to be smart or, in most cases, even unkind—it's just all they know, all they care about. It's like reading the trades. The damn things appear there in front of them—*they* didn't plan it that way.

"Bright little turn there, turkey. Take a load off."

"Make that *Mister* Turkey, if you please."

"And I told that broad and her mother both, I says, 'Don't let the door hit you where the dog bit you.' It got real quiet after that. You could've heard pissants walkin' on ice cream——"

"Shit, yeah, I done time in the Service, sonny. I worked for Standard Oil for ten years. Scobba-dee-zoot!"

"Ah, the Scatman cometh—never quiteth, in fact. I thought he was a dream of my youth, you know—like J.D. Salinger——"

"Would you believe I saw Roy Rogers on the box last night?"

"Sure, the singing cowboy's always with us. Look at Dennis Weaver."

"I wonder if Nixon ever ran off a print of *Save the Tiger*."

Somebody arrives with the news that Aristotle Onassis is dead.

"Christ, too bad, too bad…but that leaves Jackie in line for half a billion."

"BOO!"

"So what's to crab about, chum? That's just takin' poon and makin' it pay."

● ● ●

Ronnie the Patient sidles up to the writer in the corridor, offering to show some snapshots of his fiancée. The girl in the photos is sweet-faced, having fun on a picnic. Ronnie says she is a fellow patient over in the Women's Facility and he loved her the first instant he saw her.

● ● ●

Rain peppers the windows in the commissary. The writer is bent over his Efficiency Reporter's Note Book No. 176, recording some notes at one of the long tables. He block prints:

First met Kesey in '62, Menlo Park. Savored his book but put off by the Author. Figured him for a benign Manson, although didn't know the term back then. Neal Cassady also present that afternoon, chasing Stanford girls through the underbrush. Didn't catch any.

Reminded of this by brief encounter with Louise Fletcher, who plays Big Nurse. Inspired casting. Not a big-bazoomed hag but a young, petite hag, chillier than a blue norther. Had no impulse to linger with her beyond bare amenities.

Crazy factor here is strong enough to siphon gas. Take Delos V. Smith Jr. (Puh-leeze!) Smith was friends with Monroe at Actors Studio, intimates he has loads of skinny on her—tapes, letters, etc. Politely evasive about it, though. Maybe if I——

The dining hall is empty except for the writer and the coffee atten-dant—and here comes that *rrr, rrr* again, higher pitched than before, quantum scarier, too—a sound full of blood rage and murder foul. It clicks this time: It's Lawrence Talbot turning into the Wolfman… *rrr, rrr*…and here comes that brawny kid with the purple birthmark banzai-charging across the tatty linoleum with a wet mop raised high above his head like an ax, and *whop!*—he flails it down—slosh—on the writer's instep.

The writer glances up only long enough to see too much white in the kid's eyes, then resumes block printing. He block prints the word "help" 73 times. Man, flop a wet mop on your boot down where the wri-ter grew up, you generally jump on his bones. But this is different. This is the Oregon State Playpen for Bent Yo-Yos & Mauled Merchandise.

Five minutes later, the *rrr, rrr* has leveled off to a sullen drone and the kid has mopped his way to the far side of the room. The writer rises, measures his steps to the door. Out in the corridor, he takes a deep breath. Another.

• • •

Out of a mixed sense of protocol and craven dread of underachieving, the writer braves the commissary again an hour later. Nicholson is in the chow line, bellying up to the steam tables like a famished wolverine. The actor smacks his chops over the shit-and-shucks cuisine, orders a little of this, a whole lot of that, and pauses undecided before a vile-looking vat of boiled okra. The writer glides up behind him, coughs discreetly and says for openers:

Hiya, Jack.... Gee, listen, we're going to have to meet stopping like this.

Inexplicably, it comes out that way. Nicholson half-turns and cocks his head to one side, his expression hang gliding somewhere between disbelief and morbid curiosity. He picks up two dishes of the boiled okra and moves along. The writer trails Nicholson into the dining area and asks the actor if he might be available to sit and talk seriously sometime.

"Can't say, pal," Nicholson says around a quarter-pound chaw of Swiss steak. "Why don't you ask my agent about it?" He mentions a name and number in Beverly Hills.

• • •

The writer goes back to the hotel in the rain and experiences a mild epiphany in the bathtub. Up to his glottis in Mr. Bubble, he realizes he can't think of anything more he wants to know about Nicholson—nothing at all. It occurs to him that madness upstages all creatures great and small, and maybe in its wicked varieties of mystery, it, too, is a national treasure—purr-verted, of course. *Rrr, rrr....*

The writer dresses, shit-cans the Beverly Hills agent's phone number, makes reservations for a flight home and journeys down to the bar, where he immediately encounters the harpy. She is sans dentist tonight and all gussied up to party in a $300 pantsuit the color of kitty litter. "My *dear*," she exclaims, "how *marvelous* to see you again. How's your little story coming along? I've never read anything of yours, but I'll bet you're right up there with Miss Rona. Oh, I've always been a sucker for talent. A sucker, know what I mean?"

• • •

Her name is...should be...Bambi. Late in the evening, she is sitting in the hotel saloon with an actor escort, the writer and a roustabout from the film company. Bambi is a sleek sloop of a girl with an ozone-charged voice and an original face. The writer takes her for an actress or maybe a model.

Bambi's actor companion is drunk, has been for hours. Pretty soon, he can't see past his glasses. He wobbles away into the cab-o-ray darkness without explanation—none needed. Bambi shrugs and slides around next to the roustabout. "I'm Shelley Winters' daughter," she announces theatrically. "Well, not really. I mean, I don't believe that, but my mother does. What can I say?"

When the Mixmaster band unplugs for a break, Bambi is on her feet. "Come on," she urges, "I know a boîte just down the block." *A boîte?* "You, too," she says to the writer.

A boîte, you bet. A poured-concrete bunker with dime-store Modiglianis on the walls and a singer who knows all of Neil Young's gelatinous repertoire. "Far out," the roustabout whoops, hanging on every quavery verse during a millennium-long set. Facing away from the others, the writer noodles in his Efficiency Reporter's Note Book No. 176—fantasizes that he is on the verge of grasping something momentous about the lunatic tropisms of Hollywood, of America....

The Neil Young manqué takes his bows to the sound of two or three hands clapping and the house lights flash up. A waiter bends near and asks the roustabout and the writer to please remove their goddamned ladyfriend from the goddamned premises. Bambi, as it happens, is juiced to the tits—knee-walking blotto. She has been downing double gins on the sly for the past hour, the waiter says, and the tab comes to $23.80.

The roustabout and the writer steer Bambi out onto the rain-slick sidewalk and clumsily maneuver her toward a steakhouse where the roustabout says she works. "Yeah, she's a waitress, man," the roustabout grunts, sucking for breath. "I thought you knew her in front. Shit, what a deal."

Two blocks of towing a rudderless sloop through choppy weather and Bambi's boss spots the approaching convoy. He tears out of the steakhouse, his face changing colors, his arms flailing. "I'll take the cunt home," he snaps, "but don't bring her in the gah-dam ca-fay." The man drives away with Bambi unconscious beside him in a mud-spattered Datsun.

"Sonofabitch, I could've scored, too," the roustabout complains. He does a couple of quick knee bends to ease the kinks, then shrugs philosophically. "Well, that's stunt fucking for you. Always chancy."

• • •

The teamster who drives the writer to the airport the next morning chews tobacco and lives in mortal fear of the patients at the state hospital. "Lots of folks are fucked, you know, but especially your nuts. I mean, makin' a movie with all them basket cases hangin' around—what kind of nigger riggin' is that? Listen, my friend, I've personally known a bunch of them creepos out there since I was in first grade, and you can take my word for it, they ain't fit to be runnin' loose. You notice that beefy kid in the commissary, the one got the birthmark? Wonderful guy, swell guy—the mayor oughta give him a kiss and a medal. Fucker killed four people with his bare hands."

• • •

About 200 miles into the Rockies, the writer's fantods stop vibrating and over a healing beaker of brandy he monitors a cassette tape of B.S. Crothers spritzing, clowning, blowing the shit.

You ever smoke these things? Lord, we used to smoke this stuff back in '29— smoked it on the street and nobody ever bothered us. Ace leaf was common as dirt down yonder in Texas. We used to go into them fuckin' Mexican joints where they sold hot dogs and shit? They'd say, "You want some mmm-mmm?" I'd say, "Yeah, lemme have a quarter's worth." Guy'd give me a penny matchbox full, already manicured, and a few papers, and it would roll out to about ten things. For a quarter. Godamighty, man, it was good….

Ah, that Scatman! Another of your basic national treasures.

"The food sucks. . .and frankly, so do I!"

The Swimmers

fiction by JOYCE CAROL OATES

There are stories that go unaccountably wrong and become imper-
meable to the imagination. They lodge in the memory like an old
wound never entirely healed. This story of my father's younger brother
Clyde Farrell, my uncle, and a woman named Joan Lunt, with whom he
fell in love, years ago, in 1959, is one of those stories.

Some of it I was a part of, aged 13. But much of it I have to imagine.

• • •

It must have been a pale, wintry, unflattering light he first saw her in,
swimming laps in the early morning in the local YMCA pool, but that
initial sight of Joan Lunt—not her face, which was obscured from him,
but the movement of her strong, supple, creamy-pale body through
the water, and the sureness of her strokes—never faded from Clyde
Farrell's mind.

He'd been told of her; in fact, he'd come to the pool that morning
to observe her, but still you didn't expect to see such serious swimming, 7:45 A.M. of a weekday, in the antiquated white-tiled "Y" pool,
light slanting down from the wired glass skylight overhead, a sharp medicinal smell of chlorine and disinfectant pinching your nostrils. There
were a few other swimmers in the pool, ordinary swimmers, one of
them an acquaintance of Clyde's who waved at him, called out his name
when Clyde appeared in his swim trunks on the deck, climbed up onto
the diving board, then paused to watch Joan Lunt swimming toward
the far end of the pool...just stood watching her, not rudely but with a
frank, childlike interest, smiling with the spontaneous pleasure of seeing another person doing something well, with so little wasted motion.
Joan Lunt in her yellow bathing suit with the crossed straps in back and
her white rubber cap that gleamed and sparked in the miniature waves:
an attractive woman in her mid-30s, though she looked younger, with

an air of total absorption in the task at hand, swimming to the limit of her capacity, maintaining a pace and a rhythm Clyde Farrell would have been challenged to maintain himself, and Clyde was a good swimmer, known locally as a very good swimmer, a winner, years before, when he was in his teens, of county and state competitions. Joan Lunt wasn't aware of him standing on the diving board watching her, or so it appeared. Just swimming, counting laps. How many she'd done already he couldn't imagine. He saw that she knew to cup the water when she stroked back, not to let it thread through her fingers like most people do; she knew as if by instinct how to take advantage of the element she was in, propelling herself forward like an otter or a seal, power in her shoulder muscles and upper arms, and the swift scissors kick of her legs, feet flashing white through the chemical-turquoise glitter of the water. When Joan Lunt reached the end of the pool, she ducked immediately down into the water in a well-practiced maneuver, turned, used the tiled side to kick off from in a single graceful motion that took her a considerable distance, and Clyde Farrell's heart contracted when, emerging from the water, head and shoulders and flashing arms, the woman didn't miss a beat, just continued as if she hadn't been confronted with any limit or impediment, any boundary. It was just water, and her in it, water that might go on forever, and her in it, swimming, sealed off and invulnerable.

Clyde Farrell dived into the pool, and swam vigorously, keeping to his own lane, energetic and single-minded, too, and when, after some minutes, he glanced around for the woman in the yellow bathing suit, the woman I'd told him of meeting, Joan Lunt, he saw, to his disappointment, that she was gone.

His vanity was wounded. He thought, She never once looked at me.

• • •

My father and my uncle Clyde were farm boys who left the farm as soon as they were of age: joined the U.S. Navy out of high school, went away, came back and lived and worked in town, my father in a small sign shop and Clyde in a succession of jobs. He drove a truck for a gravel company, he was a foreman in a local tool factory, he managed a sporting-goods store; he owned property at Wolf's Head Lake, 20 miles to the north, and spoke with vague enthusiasm of developing it someday. He wasn't a practical man and he never saved money. He liked to gamble at cards and horses. In the Navy, he'd learned to box and for a while after being discharged, he considered a professional career as a welterweight, but that meant signing contracts, traveling around the country, taking orders from other men. Not Clyde Farrell's temperament.

He was good-looking, not tall, about 5′9″, compact and quick on his feet, a natural athlete, with well-defined shoulder and arm muscles, strong, sinewy legs. His hair was the color of damp sand, his eyes a warm liquid brown, all iris. There was a gap between his two front teeth that gave him a childlike look and was misleading.

No one ever expected Clyde Farrell to get married, or even to fall seriously in love. That capacity in him seemed missing, somehow: a small but self-proclaimed absence, like the gap between his teeth.

But Clyde was powerfully attracted to women, and after watching Joan Lunt swim that morning, he drifted by later in the day to Kress's, Yewville's largest department store, where he knew she'd recently started to work. Kress's was a store of some distinction, the merchandise was of high quality, the counters made of solid, burnished oak; the overhead lighting was muted and flattering to women customers. Behind the counter displaying gloves and leather handbags, Joan Lunt struck the eye as an ordinarily pretty woman, composed, intelligent, brunette, with a brunette's waxy-pale skin, carefully made up, even glamorous, but not a woman Clyde Farrell would have noticed, much. He was 32 years old, in many ways much younger. This woman was too mature for him, wasn't she? Probably married or divorced, likely with children. Clyde thought, In her clothes, she's just another one of them.

So Clyde walked out of Kress's, a store he didn't like anyway, and wasn't going to think about Joan Lunt, but one morning a few days later, there he was, unaccountably, back at the YMCA, 7:30 A.M. of a weekday in March 1959, and there, too, was Joan Lunt in her satiny-yellow bathing suit and gleaming white cap. Swimming laps, arm over strong, slender arm, stroke following stroke, oblivious of Clyde Farrell and of her surroundings, so Clyde was forced to see how her presence in the old, tacky, harshly chlorinated pool made of the place something extraordinary that lifted his heart.

That morning, Clyde swam in the pool for only about ten minutes, then left and hastily showered and dressed and was waiting for Joan Lunt out in the lobby. Clyde wasn't a shy man, but he could give that impression when it suited him. When Joan Lunt appeared, he stepped forward and smiled and introduced himself, saying, "Miss Lunt? I guess you know my niece Sylvie? She told me about meeting you." Joan Lunt hesitated, then shook hands with Clyde and said in that way of hers that suggested she was giving information meant to be clear and unequivocal, "My first name is Joan." She didn't smile but seemed prepared to smile.

Joan Lunt was a good-looking woman with shrewd dark eyes, straight dark eyebrows, an expertly reddened mouth. There was an inch-long white scar at the left corner of her mouth like a sliver of glass. Her thick, shoulder-length dark-brown hair was carefully waved, but the ends were damp; although her face was pale, it appeared heated, invigorated by exercise.

Joan Lunt and Clyde Farrell were nearly of a height, and comfortable together.

Leaving the YMCA, descending the old granite steps to Main Street that were worn smooth in the centers, nearly hollow with decades of feet, Clyde said to Joan, "You're a beautiful swimmer—I couldn't help admiring you in there," and Joan Lunt laughed and said, "And so are you—I was admiring you, too," and Clyde said, surprised, "Really? You saw me?" and Joan Lunt said, "Both times."

It was Friday. They arranged to meet for drinks that afternoon, and spent the next two days together.

In Yewville, no one knew who Joan Lunt was except as she presented herself: a woman in her mid-30s, solitary, very private, seemingly unattached, with no relatives or friends in the area. No one knew where exactly she'd come from, or why; why here of all places, Yewville, New York, a small city of fewer than 30,000 people, built on the banks of the Eden River, in the southwestern foothills of the Chautauqua Mountains. She had arrived in early February, in a dented rust-red 1956 Chevrolet with New York State license plates, the rear of the car piled with suitcases, cartons, clothes. She spent two nights in Yewville's single good hotel, the Mohawk, then moved into a tiny furnished apartment on Chambers Street. She spent several days interviewing for jobs downtown, all of which you might call jobs for women specifically, and was hired at Kress's, and started work promptly on the first Monday morning following her arrival. If it was sheerly good luck, the job at Kress's, the most prestigious store in town, Joan Lunt seemed to take it in stride, the way a person would who felt she deserved as much. Or better.

The other saleswomen at Kress's, other tenants in the Chambers Street building, men who approached her—no one could get to know her. It was impossible to get beyond the woman's quick, just slightly edgy smile, her resolute cheeriness, her purposefully vague manner. Asked where she was from, she would say, "Nowhere you'd know." Asked was she married, did she have a family, she would say, "Oh, I'm an independent woman, I'm well over 18." She'd laugh to suggest that this was a joke, of a kind, the thin scar beside her mouth white with anger.

It was observed that her fingers were entirely ringless.

But the nails were perfectly manicured, an enamel-hard red.

It was observed that, for a solitary woman, Joan Lunt had some curious habits.

For instance, swimming. Very few women swam in the YMCA pool in those days. Sometimes Joan Lunt swam in the early morning, and sometimes, Saturdays, in the late morning; she swam only once in the afternoon, after work, but the pool was disagreeably crowded, and too many people approached her. A well-intentioned woman asked, "Who taught you to swim like *that*?" and Joan Lunt said quietly, "I taught myself." She didn't smile and the conversation was not continued.

It was observed that, for a woman in her presumed circumstances, Joan Lunt was remarkably arrogant.

It seemed curious, too, that she went to the Methodist church Sunday mornings, sitting in a pew at the very rear, holding an opened hymnbook in her hand but not singing with the congregation; and that she slipped away afterward without speaking to anyone. Each time, she left a neatly folded dollar bill in the collection basket.

She wasn't explicitly unfriendly, but she wasn't friendly. At church, the minister and his wife tried to speak with her, tried to make her feel welcome, *did* make her feel welcome, but nothing came of it, she'd hurry off in her car, disappear. In time people began to murmur that there was something strange about that woman, something not right, yes, maybe even something wrong; for instance, wasn't she behaving suspiciously? Like a runaway wife, for instance? A bad mother. A sinner fleeing Christ?

Another of Joan Lunt's curious habits was to drink, alone, in the early evening, in the Yewville Bar & Grill, or the White Owl Tavern, or the restaurant-bar adjoining the Greyhound Bus Station. If possible, she sat in a booth at the very rear of these taverns where she could observe the front entrances without being seen herself. For an hour or more she'd drink bourbon and water, slowly, very slowly, with an elaborate slowness, her face perfectly composed but her eyes alert. In the Yewville Bar & Grill there was an enormous sectioned mirror stretching the length of the taproom, and in this mirror, muted by arabesques of frosted glass, Joan Lunt was reflected as beautiful and mysterious. Now and then men approached her to ask if she were alone. Did she want company? How's about another drink? But she responded coolly to them and never invited anyone to join her. Had my uncle Clyde approached her in such a fashion, she would very likely have been cool to him, too, but my uncle Clyde wasn't the kind of man to set himself up for any sort of public rejection.

One evening in March, before Joan Lunt met up with Clyde Farrell, patrons at the Yewville Bar & Grill, one of them my father, reported with amusement hearing a exchange between Joan Lunt and a local farmer who, mildly drunk, offered to sit with her and buy her a drink, which ended with Joan Lunt's saying, in a loud, sharp voice, "You don't want trouble, mister. Believe me, you don't."

Rumors spread, delicious and censorious, that Joan Lunt was a man-hater. That she carried a razor in her purse. Or an ice pick. Or a lady's-sized revolver.

● ● ●

It was at the YMCA pool that I became acquainted with Joan Lunt, on Saturday mornings. She saw that I was alone, that I was a good swimmer, might have mistaken me for younger than I was (I was 13), and befriended me, casually and cheerfully, the way an adult woman might befriend a young girl to whom she isn't related. Her remarks were often exclamations, called across the slapping little waves of the turquoise-tinted water, "*Isn't* it heavenly!"—meaning the pool, the prospect of swimming, the icy rain pelting the skylight overhead while we, in our bathing suits, were snug and safe below.

Another time, in the changing room, she said almost rapturously, "There's nothing like swimming, is there? Your mind just dissolves."

She asked my name, and when I told her, she stared at me and said, "*Sylvie*—I had a close friend once named Sylvie, a long time ago. I loved that name, and I loved her."

I was embarrassed, but pleased. It astonished me that an adult woman, a woman my mother's age, might be so certain of her feelings and so direct in expressing them to a stranger. I fantasized that Joan Lunt came from a part of the world where people knew what they thought and announced their thoughts importantly to others. This struck me with the force of a radically new idea.

I watched Joan Lunt covertly, and I didn't even envy her in the pool—she was so far beyond me. Her face that seemed to me strong and rare and beautiful and her body that was a fully developed woman's body—prominent breasts, shapely hips, long firm legs—all beyond me. I saw how the swiftness and skill with which Joan Lunt swam made other swimmers, especially the adults, appear slow by contrast; clumsy, ill-coordinated, without style.

One day, Joan Lunt was waiting for me in the lobby, hair damp at the ends, face carefully made up, her lipstick seemingly brighter than usual. "Sylvie," she said, smiling, "let's walk out together."

So we walked outside into the snow-glaring, windy sunshine, and she said, "Are you going in this direction? Good, let's walk together." She addressed me as if I were much younger than I was, and her manner was nervous, quick, alert. As we walked up Main Street, she asked questions of me of a kind she'd never asked before, about my family, about my "interests," about school, not listening to the answers and offering no information about herself. At the corner of Chambers and Main, she asked eagerly if I would like to come back to her apartment to visit for a few minutes, and although out of shyness I wanted to say "No, thank you," I said "Yes" instead, because it was clear that Joan Lunt was frightened about something, and I didn't want to leave her.

Her apartment building was shabby and weather-worn, as modest a place as even the poorest of my relatives lived in, but it had about it a sort of makeshift glamour, up the street from the White Owl Tavern and the Shamrock Diner, where motorcyclists hung out, close by the railroad yards on the river. I felt excited and pleased to enter the building and to climb with Joan Lunt—who was chatting briskly all the while—to the fourth floor. On each floor, Joan would pause, breathless, glancing around, listening, and I wanted to ask if someone might be following her, waiting for her. But, of course, I didn't say a thing. When she unlocked the door to her apartment, stepped inside and whispered, "Come in, Sylvie," I seemed to understand that no one else had ever been invited in.

The apartment was really just one room with a tiny kitchen alcove, a tiny bathroom, a doorless closet and a curtainless window with stained, injured-looking Venetian blinds. Joan Lunt said with an apologetic little laugh, "Those blinds—I tried to wash them, but the dirt turned to a sort of paste." I was standing at the window peering down into a weedy backyard of tilting clotheslines and wind-blown trash, curious to see what the view was from Joan Lunt's window, and she came over and drew the blinds, saying, "The sunshine is too bright, it hurts my eyes."

She hung up our coats and asked if I would like some coffee or fresh-squeezed orange juice. "It's my half day off from Kress's," she said. "I don't have to be there until one." It was shortly after 11 o'clock.

We sat at a worn dinette table, and Joan Lunt chatted animatedly and plied me with questions, as I drank orange juice in a tall glass, and she drank black coffee, and an alarm clock on the windowsill ticked the minutes briskly by. Few rooms in which I've lived even for considerable periods of time are as vividly imprinted in my memory as that room of

410

Joan Lunt's, with its spare, battered-looking furniture (including a sofa bed and a chest of drawers), its wanly wallpapered walls bare of any hangings, even a mirror, and its badly faded shag rug laid upon painted floorboards. There was a mixture of smells—talcum powder, perfume, cooking odors, insect spray, general mustiness. Two opened suitcases were on the floor beside the sofa bed, apparently unpacked, containing underwear, toiletries, neatly folded sweaters and blouses, several pairs of shoes. A single dress hung in the closet, and a shiny black raincoat, and our two coats Joan had hung on wire hangers. I stared at the suitcases thinking how strange, she'd been living here for weeks but hadn't had time yet to unpack.

So this was where the mysterious Joan Lunt lived! The woman of whom people in Yewville spoke with such suspicion and disapproval! She was far more interesting to me, and in a way more real, than I was to myself; shortly, the story of the lovers Clyde Farrell and Joan Lunt, as I imagined it, would be infinitely more interesting, and infinitely more real, than any story with Sylvie Farrell at its core. (I was a fiercely introspective child, in some ways perhaps a strange child, and the solace of my life would be to grow not away from but ever more deeply and fruitfully into my strangeness, the way a child with an idiosyncratic, homely face often grows into that face and emerges, in adulthood, as "striking," "distinctive," sometimes even "beautiful.") It turned out that Joan liked poetry, and so we talked about poetry, and about love, and Joan asked me in that searching way of hers if I were "happy in my life," if I were "loved and prized" by my family, and I said, "Yes—I guess so," though these were not issues I had ever considered before, and would not have known to consider if she hadn't asked. For some reason, my eyes filled with tears.

Joan said, "The crucial thing, Sylvie, is to have precious memories." She spoke almost vehemently, laying her hand on mine. "That's even more important than Jesus Christ in your heart, do you know why? Because Jesus Christ can fade out of your heart, but precious memories never do."

We talked like that. Like I'd never talked with anyone before.

I was nervy enough to ask Joan how she'd gotten the little scar beside her mouth, and she touched it, quickly, and said, "In a way I'm not proud of, Sylvie." I sat staring, stupid. The scar wasn't disfiguring in my eyes but enhancing. "A man hit me once," Joan said. "Don't ever let a man hit you, Sylvie."

Weakly, I said, "No, I won't."

No man in our family had ever struck any woman that I knew of, but it happened sometimes in families we knew. I recalled how a ninth-grade girl had come to school that winter with a blackened eye, and she'd seemed proud of it, in a way, and everyone had stared—and the boys just drifted to her, staring. Like they couldn't wait to get their hands on her themselves. And she knew precisely what they were thinking.

I told Joan Lunt that I wished I lived in a place like hers, by myself, and she said, laughing, "No you don't, Sylvie, you're too young." I asked where she was from and she shrugged, "Oh—nowhere," and I persisted, "But is it north of here, or south? Is it the country? Or a city?" and she said, running her fingers nervously through her hair, fingering the damp ends, "My only home is *here, now*, in this room, and, sweetie, that's more than enough for me to think about."

It was time to leave. The danger had passed, or Joan had passed out of thinking there was danger. She walked with me to the stairs, smiling, cheerful, and squeezed my hand when we said goodbye. She called down after me, "See you next Saturday at the pool, maybe——" but it would be weeks before I saw Joan Lunt again. She was to meet my uncle Clyde the following week and her life in Yewville that seemed to me so orderly and wonderful would be altered forever.

● ● ●

Clyde had a bachelor's place (that was how the women in our family spoke of it) to which he brought his women friends. It was a row house made of brick and cheap stucco, on the west side of town, near the old, now defunct tanning factories on the river. With the money he made working for a small Yewville construction company, and his occasional gambling wins, Clyde could have afforded to live in a better place, but he hadn't much mind for his surroundings and spent most of his spare time out. He brought Joan Lunt home with him because, for all the slapdash clutter of his house, it was more private than her apartment on Chambers Street, and they wanted privacy, badly.

The first time they were alone together, Clyde laid his hands on Joan's shoulders and kissed her, and she held herself steady, rising to the kiss, putting pressure against the mouth of this man who was virtually a stranger to her so that it was like an exchange, a handshake, between equals. Then, stepping back from the kiss, they both laughed—they were breathless, like people caught short, taken by surprise. Joan Lunt said faintly, "I—I do things sometimes without meaning them," and Clyde said, "Good. So do I."

● ● ●

412

Through the spring, they were often seen together in Yewville; and when, weekends, they weren't seen, it was supposed they were at Clyde's cabin at Wolf's Head Lake (where he was teaching Joan Lunt to fish) or at the Scholharie Downs racetrack (where Clyde gambled on the standardbreds). They were an attractive, eye-catching couple. They were frequent patrons of local bars and restaurants, and they turned up regularly at parties given by friends of Clyde's, and at all-night poker parties in the upstairs, rear, of the Iroquois Hotel—Joan Lunt didn't play cards, but she took an interest in Clyde's playing, and, as Clyde told my father, admiringly, she never criticized a move of his, never chided or teased or second-guessed him. "But the woman has me figured out completely," Clyde said. "Almost from the first, when she saw the way I was winning, and the way I kept on, she said, 'Clyde, you're the kind of gambler who won't quit, because, when he's losing, he has to get back to winning, and when he's winning, he has to give his friends a chance to catch up.'"

In May, Clyde brought Joan to a Sunday gathering at our house, a large, noisy affair, and we saw how when Clyde and Joan were separated, in different rooms, they'd drift back together until they were touching, literally touching, without seeming to know what they did, still less that they were being observed. So that was what love was! Always a quickness of a kind was passing between them, a glance, a hand squeeze, a light pinch, a caress, Clyde's lazy fingers on Joan's neck beneath her hair, Joan's arm slipped around Clyde's waist, fingers hooked through his belt loop. I wasn't jealous, but I watched them covertly. My heart yearned for them, though I didn't know what I wanted of them, or for them.

At 13, I was more of a child still than an adolescent girl: thin, long-limbed, eyes too large and naked-seeming for my face and an imagination that rarely flew off into unknown territory but turned, and turned, and turned, upon what was close at hand and known, but not altogether known. Imagination, says Aristotle, begins in desire: But what *is* desire? I could not, nor did I want to, possess my uncle Clyde and Joan Lunt. I wasn't jealous of them, I loved them both. I wanted them to *be*. For this, too, was a radically new idea to me, that a man and a woman might be nearly strangers to each other, yet lovers; lovers, yet nearly strangers; and the love passing between them, charged like electricity, might be visible, without their knowing. Could they know how I dreamt of them!

After Clyde and Joan left our house, my mother complained irritably that she couldn't get to know Joan Lunt. "She's sweet-seeming,

413

and friendly enough, but you know her mind isn't there for you," my mother said. "She's just plain *not there*."

My father said, "As long as the woman's there for Clyde."

He didn't like anyone speaking critically of his younger brother apart from himself.

• • •

But sometimes, in fact, Joan Lunt wasn't there for Clyde: He wouldn't speak of it but she'd disappear in her car for a day or two or three, without explaining very satisfactorily where she'd gone, or why. Clyde could see by her manner that wherever Joan had gone had, perhaps, not been a choice of hers, and that her disappearances, or flights, left her tired and depressed; but still he was annoyed, he felt betrayed. Clyde Farrell wasn't the kind of man to disguise his feelings. Once, on a Friday afternoon in June before a weekend they'd planned at Wolf's Head Lake, Clyde returned to the construction office at 5:31 P.M. to be handed a message hastily telephoned in by Joan Lunt an hour before: CAN'T MAKE IT THIS WEEKEND. SORRY. LOVE, JOAN. Clyde believed himself humiliated in front of others, vowed he'd never forgive Joan Lunt and that very night, drunk and mean-spirited, he took up again with a former girlfriend...and so it went.

But in time they made up, as naturally they would, and Clyde said, "I'm thinking maybe we should get married, to stop this sort of thing," and Joan, surprised, said, "Oh, that isn't necessary, darling—I mean, for you to offer that."

Clyde believed, as others did, that Joan Lunt was having difficulties with a former man friend or husband, but Joan refused to speak of it; just acknowledged that, yes, there was a man, yes, of course he was an *ex* in her life, but she resented so much as speaking of him; she refused to allow him re-entry into her life. Clyde asked, "What's his name?" and Joan shook her head, mutely, just no; no, she would not say, would not utter that name. Clyde asked, "Is he threatening you? Now? Has he ever shown up in Yewville?" and Joan, as agitated as he'd ever seen her, said, "He does what he does, and I do what I do. And I don't talk about it."

• • •

But later that summer, at Wolf's Head Lake, in Clyde's bed in Clyde's hand-hewn log cabin on the bluff above the lake, overlooking wooded land that was Clyde Farrell's property for a mile in either direction, Joan Lunt wept bitterly, weakened in the aftermath of love, and said,

"If I tell you, Clyde, it will make you feel too bound to me. It will seem to be begging a favor of a kind, and I'm not begging."

Clyde said, "I know you're not."

"I don't beg favors from anyone."

"I know you don't."

"I went through a long spell in my life when I did beg favors, because I believed that was how women made their way, and I was hurt because of it, but not more hurt than I deserved. I'm older now. I know better. The meek don't inherit the earth and they surely don't deserve to."

Clyde laughed sadly and said, "Nobody's likely to take you for meek, Joan honey."

● ● ●

Making love, they were like two swimmers deep in each other, plunging hard. Wherever they were when they made love, it wasn't the place they found themselves in when they returned, and whatever the time, it wasn't the same time.

● ● ●

The trouble came in September: A cousin of mine, another niece of Clyde's, was married, and the wedding party was held in the Nautauga Inn, on Lake Nautauga, about ten miles east of Yewville. Clyde knew the inn's owner, and it happened that he and Joan Lunt, handsomely dressed, were in the large public cocktail lounge adjacent to the banquet room reserved for our party, talking with the owner-bartender, when Clyde saw an expression on Joan's face of a kind he'd never seen on her face before—fear, and more than fear, a sudden sick terror—and he turned to see a stranger approaching them, not slowly, exactly, but with a restrained sort of haste: a man of about 40, unshaven, in a blue seersucker sports jacket now badly rumpled, tieless, a muscled but soft-looking man with a blunt, rough, ruined-handsome face, complexion like an emery board, and this man's eyes were too bleached a color for his skin, unless there was a strange light rising in them. And this same light rose in Clyde Farrell's eyes, in that instant.

Joan Lunt was whispering, "Oh, no—no," pulling at Clyde's arm to turn him away, but naturally, Clyde Farrell wasn't going to step away from a confrontation, and the stranger, who would turn out to be named Robert Waxman, Rob Waxman, Joan Lunt's former husband, divorced from her 15 months before, co-owner of a failing meat-supplying company in Kingston, advanced upon Clyde and Joan, smiling as if he knew them both, saying loudly, in a slurred but vibrating voice. "Hello, hello, hello!" and when Joan tried to escape, Waxman leapt after her, cursing, and Clyde naturally intervened, and suddenly, the two men were scuffling, and voices were raised, and before anyone could separate them, there was the astonishing sight of Waxman, with his gravelly face and hot eyes, crouched, holding a pistol in his hand, striking Clyde clumsily about the head and shoulders with the butt and crying, enraged, "Didn't ask to be born! Goddamn you! I didn't ask to be born!" And "I'm no different from you! Any of you! *You*! In my heart!" There were screams as Waxman fired the pistol point-blank at Clyde, a popping sound like a firecracker, and Waxman stepped back to get a better aim—he'd hit his man in the fleshy part of a shoulder—and Clyde Farrell, desperate, infuriated, scrambled forward in his wedding-party finery, baboon style, not on his hands and knees but on his hands and feet, bent double, face contorted, teeth bared, and managed to throw himself on Waxman, who outweighed him by perhaps 40 pounds, and the men fell heavily to the floor, and there was Clyde Farrell straddling his man, striking him blow after blow in the face, even with his weakened left hand, until Waxman's nose was broken and his nostrils streamed blood, and his mouth, too, was broken and bloody, and someone risked being struck by Clyde's wild fists and pulled him away.

And there on the floor of the breezy screened-in barroom of the Nautauga Inn lay a man, unconscious, breathing erratically, bleeding from his face, whom no one except Joan Lunt knew was Joan Lunt's former husband; and there, panting, hot-eyed, stood Clyde Farrell over him, bleeding, too, from a shoulder wound he was to claim he'd never felt.

● ● ●

Said Joan Lunt repeatedly, "Clyde, I'm sorry. I'm so sorry."

Said Joan Lunt carefully, "I just don't know if I can keep on seeing you. Or keep on living here in Yewville."

And my uncle Clyde was trying very hard to understand.

"You don't love me, then?" he asked several times.

He was baffled, he wasn't angry. It was the following week and by this time he wasn't angry, nor was he proud of what he'd done, though everyone was speaking of it, and would speak of it, in awe, for years. He wasn't proud because, in fact, he couldn't remember clearly what he'd done, what sort of lightning-swift action he'd performed; no conscious decision had been made that he could recall. Just the light dancing up in a stranger's eyes, and its immediate reflection in his own.

Now Joan Lunt was saying this strange, unexpected thing, this thing he couldn't comprehend. Wiping her eyes, and, yes, her voice was shaky; but he recognized the steely stubbornness in it, the resolute will.

She said, "I do love you. I've told you that. But I can't live like that any longer."

"You're still in love with *him*."

"Of course I'm not in love with him. But I can't live like that any longer."

"Like what? What I did? I'm not *like* that."

"I'm 36 years old. I can't take it any longer."

"Joan, I was only protecting you."

"Men fighting each other, men trying to kill each other—I can't take it any longer."

"I was only protecting you. He might have killed you."

"I know. I know you were protecting me. I know you'd do it again if you had to."

Clyde said, suddenly furious, "You're damned right I would. If that son of a bitch ever————"

Waxman was out on bail and returned to Kingston. Like Clyde Farrell, he'd been treated in the emergency room at Yewville General Hospital; then he'd been taken to the county sheriff's headquarters and booked on charges of assault with a deadly weapon and reckless endangerment of life. In time, Waxman would be sentenced to a year's probation: He had no prior record except for traffic violations; he was to impress the judge with his air of sincere remorse and repentance. Clyde Farrell, after giving testimony and hearing the sentencing, would never see the man again.

Joan Lunt was saying, "I know I should thank you, Clyde. But I can't."

Clyde splashed more bourbon into Joan's glass and into his own. They were sitting at Joan's dinette table beside a window whose grimy and cracked Venetian blinds were tightly closed. Clyde smiled and said, "Never mind thanking me, honey: Just let's forget it."

Joan said softly, "Yes, but I can't forget it."

"It's just something you're saying. Telling yourself. Maybe you'd better stop."

"I want to thank you, Clyde, and I can't. You risked your life for me. I know that. And I can't thank you."

So they discussed it, like this. For hours. For much of a night. Sharing a bottle of bourbon Clyde had brought over. And eventually, they made love, in Joan Lunt's narrow sofa bed that smelled of talcum powder, perfume and the ingrained dust of years, and their lovemaking was tentative and cautious but as sweet as ever, and driving back to his place early in the morning, at dawn, Clyde thought surely things were changed; yes, he was convinced that things were changed. Hadn't he Joan's promise that she would think it all over, not make any decision, they'd see each other that evening and talk it over then? She'd kissed his lips in goodbye, and walked him to the stairs, and watched him descend to the street.

But Clyde never saw Joan Lunt again.

• • •

That evening, she was gone, moved out of the apartment, like that, no warning, not even a telephone call, and she'd left only a brief letter behind with CLYDE FARRELL written on the envelope. Which Clyde never showed to anyone and probably, in fact, ripped up immediately.

It was believed that Clyde spent some time, days, then weeks, into the early winter of that year, looking for Joan Lunt; but no one, not even my father, knew exactly what he did, where he drove, whom he questioned, the depth of his desperation or his yearning or his rage, for Clyde wasn't, of course, the kind of man to speak of such things.

Joan Lunt's young friend Sylvie never saw her again, either, nor heard of her. And this hurt me, too, more than I might have anticipated.

And over the years, once I left Yewville to go to college in another state, then to begin my own adult life, I saw less of my uncle Clyde. He never married; for a few years, he continued the life he'd been leading before meeting Joan Lunt—a typical "bachelor" life, of its place and time; then he began to spend more time at Wolf's Head Lake, developing his property, building small cottages and renting them out to vacationers, and acting as caretaker for them, an increasingly solitary life no one would have predicted for Clyde Farrell.

He stopped gambling, too, abruptly. His luck had turned, he said.

I saw my uncle Clyde only at family occasions, primarily weddings and funerals. The last time we spoke together in a way that might be called forthright was in 1971, at my grandmother's funeral: I looked up and saw through a haze of tears a man of youthful middle age moving in my general direction. Clyde, who seemed shorter than I recalled, not stocky but compact, with a look of furious compression, in a dark suit that fitted him tightly about the shoulders. His hair had turned not silver but an eerie metallic blond, with faint tarnished streaks, and it was combed down flat and damp on his head, a look here, too, of furious constraint. Clyde's face was familiar to me as my own, yet altered: The skin had a grainy texture, roughened from outdoor living, like dried earth, and the creases and dents in it resembled animal tracks; his eyes were narrow, restless; the eyelids looked swollen. He was walking with a slight limp that he tried, in his vanity, to disguise; I learned later that he'd had knee surgery. And the gunshot wound to his shoulder he'd insisted at the time had not given him much, or any, pain gave him pain now, an arthritic sort of pain, agonizing in cold weather. I stared at my uncle thinking, *Oh, why? Why?* I didn't know if I were seeing the man Joan Lunt had fled from or the man her flight had made.

But Clyde sighted me and hurried over to embrace me, his favorite niece, still. If he associated me with Joan Lunt—and I had the idea he did—he'd forgiven me long ago.

Death gives to life, to the survivors' shared life, that is, an insubstantial quality. It's like an image of absolute clarity reflected in water—then disturbed, shattered into ripples, revealed as mere surface. Its clarity, even its beauty, can resume but you can't any longer trust in its reality.

So my uncle Clyde and I regarded each other, stricken in that instant with grief. But, being a man, *he* didn't cry.

We drifted off to one side, away from the other mourners, and I saw it was all right between us, it was all right to ask, so I asked if he had ever heard from Joan Lunt after that day. Had he ever heard of her? He said, "I never go where I'm not welcome, honey," as if this were the answer to my question. Then added, seeing my look of distress, "I stopped thinking of her years ago. We don't need each other the way we think we do when we're younger."

I couldn't bear to look at my uncle. *Oh why? Why?* Somehow, I must have believed all along that there was a story, a story unknown to me, that had worked itself out without my knowing, like a stream tunneling its way underground. I would not have minded not knowing this story could I only know that it *was*.

Clyde said, roughly, "*You* didn't hear from her, did you? The two of you were so close."

He wants me to lie, I thought. But I said only, sadly, "No, I never hear from her. And we weren't close."

Said Clyde, "Sure you were."

The last I saw of Clyde that day, it was after dark and he and my father were having a disagreement outside the back of our house. My father insisted that Clyde, who'd been drinking, wasn't in condition to drive his pickup back to the lake, and Clyde was insisting he was, and my father said, "Maybe yes, Clyde, and maybe no," but he didn't want to take a chance, why didn't *he* drive Clyde home and Clyde pointed out truculently that, if my father drove him home, how in hell would he get back here except by taking Clyde's only means of transportation? So the brothers discussed their predicament, as dark came on.

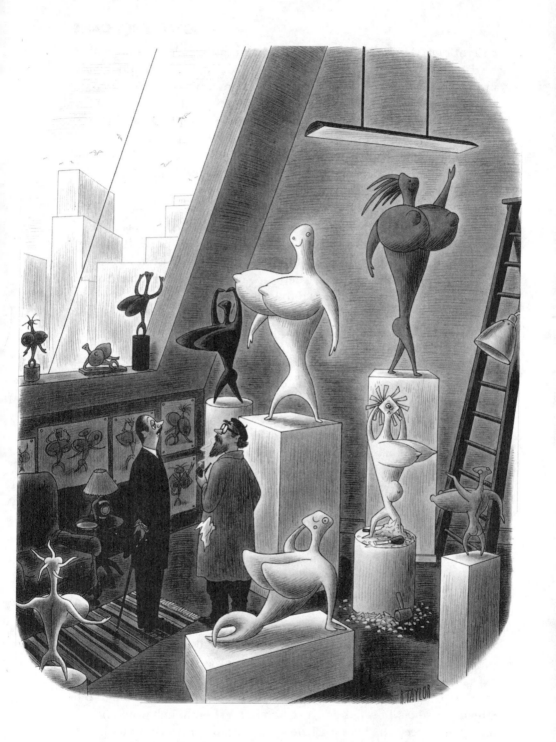

"I wouldn't know—I'm a leg man myself."

The Hildebrand Rarity

fiction by IAN FLEMING

T he stingray was about six feet from wing tip to wing tip and perhaps ten feet long from the blunt wedge of its nose to the end of
its deadly tail. It was dark gray with that violet tinge that is so often a
danger signal in the underwater world. When it rose up from the pale,
golden sand and swam a little distance, it was as if a black towel were
being waved through the water.

James Bond, his hands along his flanks and swimming with only a
soft trudge of his fins, followed the black shadow across the wide, palm-
fringed lagoon, waiting for a shot. He rarely killed fish except to eat,
but there were exceptions: big moray eels and all the members of the
scorpion fish family. Now he proposed to kill the stingray because it
looked so extraordinarily evil.

It was ten o'clock in the morning of a day in April and the lagoon,
Belle Anse near the southernmost tip of Mahé, the largest island in
the Seychelles group, was glassy calm. The northwest monsoon had
blown itself out months before and it would be May before the south-
east monsoon brought refreshment. Now the temperature was 80 in
the shade and the humidity 90, and the enclosed water of the lagoon
was near blood heat. Even the fish seemed to be sluggish. A ten-pound
green parrot fish, nibbling algae from a lump of coral, paused only to
roll its eyes as Bond passed overhead, and then went back to its meal.
A school of fat gray chub, swimming busily, broke courteously in half to
let Bond's shadow by, and then joined up and continued on their opposite course. A chorus line of six small squids, normally as shy as birds,
did not even bother to change their camouflage at his passage.

Bond trudged lazily on, keeping the stingray just in sight. Soon it
would get tired or else be reassured when Bond, the big fish on the
surface, did not attack. Then it would settle onto a patch of flat sand,
change its camouflage down to the palest, almost translucent gray and,
with soft undulations of its wing tips, bury itself in the sand.

The reef was coming nearer and now there were outcrops of coral niggerheads and meadows of sea grass. It was like arriving in a town from open country. Everywhere the jeweled reef fish twinkled and glowed and the giant anemones of the Indian Ocean burned like flames in the shadows. Colonies of spined sea eggs made sepia splashes as if someone had thrown ink against the rock, and the brilliant blue and yellow feelers of langoustes quested and waved from their crevices like small dragons. Now and then, among the seaweed on the brilliant floor, there was the speckled glitter of a cowrie bigger than a golf ball—the leopard cowrie—and once Bond saw the beautiful splayed fingers of a Venus' harp. But all these things were now commonplace to him and he drove steadily on, interested in the reef only as cover through which he could get to seaward of the ray and then pursue it back toward the shore. The tactic worked and soon the black shadow and its pursuing brown torpedo were moving back across the great blue mirror. In about 12 feet of water the ray stopped for the hundredth time. Bond stopped also, treading water softly. Cautiously he lifted his head and emptied water out of his goggles. By the time he looked again the ray had disappeared.

Bond had a Champion harpoon gun with double rubbers. The harpoon was tipped with a needle-sharp trident—a short-range weapon but the best for reef work. Bond pushed up the safety and moved slowly forward, his fins pulsing softly just below the surface so as to make no sound. He looked around him, trying to pierce the misty horizons of the great hall of the lagoon. He was looking for any big lurking shape. It would not do to have a shark or a large barracuda as witness to the kill. Fish sometimes scream when they are hurt, and even when they do not the turbulence and blood caused by a sharp struggle bring the scavengers. But there was not a living thing in sight and the sand stretched away into the smoky wings like the bare boards of a stage. Now Bond could see the faint outline on the bottom. He swam directly over it and lay motionless on the surface looking down. There was a tiny movement in the sand. Two minute fountains of sand were dancing above the nostril-like holes of the spiracles. Behind the holes was the slight swelling of the thing's body. That was the target. An inch behind the holes. Bond estimated the possible upward lash of the tail and slowly reached his gun down and pulled the trigger.

Below him the sand erupted and for an anxious moment Bond could see nothing. Then the harpoon line came taut and the ray showed, pulling away from him while its tail, in reflex aggression, lashed again and again over the body. At the base of the tail Bond could see the jagged poison spines standing up from the trunk. These were the spines that were supposed to have killed Ulysses, that Pliny said would destroy a tree. In the Indian Ocean, where the sea poisons are at their most virulent, one scratch from the ray's sting would mean certain death. Cautiously, keeping the ray on a taut line, Bond trudged after the furiously wrestling fish. He swam to one side to keep the line away from the lashing tail which could easily sever it. This tail was the old slave-drivers' whip of the Indian Ocean. Today it is illegal even to possess one in the Seychelles, but they are handed down in the families for use on faithless wives and if the word goes round that this or that woman "*a cu la crapule*," the Provençal name for the stingray, it is as good as saying that that woman will not be about again for at least a week. Now the lashes of the tail were getting weaker and Bond swam round and ahead of the ray, pulling it after him toward the shore. In the shallows the ray went limp and Bond pulled it out of the water and well up on the beach. But he still kept away from it. It was as well he did so. Suddenly, at some move from Bond and perhaps in the hope of catching its enemy unawares, the giant ray leaped clean into the air. Bond sprang aside and the ray fell on its back and lay with its white underbelly to the sun and the great ugly sickle of the mouth sucking and panting.

Bond stood and looked at the stingray and wondered what to do next.

A short, fat white man in khaki shirt and trousers came out from under the palm trees and walked toward Bond through the scattering of sea grape and sun-dried wrack above high-water mark. When he was near enough he called out in a laughing voice, "The old man and the sea! Who caught who?"

Bond turned. "It *would* be the only man on the island who doesn't carry a machete. Fidele, be a good chap and call one of your men. This animal won't die and he's got my spear stuck in him."

Fidele Barbey, the youngest of the innumerable Barbeys who own nearly everything in the Seychelles, came up and stood looking down at the ray. "That's a good one. Lucky you hit the right spot or he'd have towed you over the reef and you'd have had to let go your gun. They take a hell of a time to die. But come on. I've got to get you back to Victoria. Something's come up. Something good. I'll send one of my men for the gun. Do you want the tail?"

Bond smiled. "No. But what about some *raie au beurre noir* tonight?"

"Not tonight, my friend. Come. Where are your clothes?"

On their way down the coast road in the station wagon Fidele said, "Ever hear of an American called Milton Krest? Well, apparently he owns the Krest hotels and a thing called the Krest Foundation. One thing I can tell you for sure. He owns the finest damned yacht in the Indian Ocean. Put in yesterday. The Wavekrest. Nearly 200 tons. Hundred feet long. Everything in her from a beautiful wife down to a big transistor gramophone on gimbals so the waves won't jerk the needle. Wall-to-wall carpeting an inch deep. Air conditioned throughout. The only dry cigarettes this side of the African continent and the best after-breakfast bottle of champagne since the last time I saw Paris." Fidele Barbey laughed delightedly. "My friend, that is one hell of a bloody fine ship and if Mr. Krest is a grand slam doubled in bastards, who the hell cares?"

"Who cares anyway? What's it got to do with you—or me for that matter?"

"Just this, my friend. We are going to spend a few days sailing with Mr. Krest—and Mrs. Krest, the beautiful Mrs. Krest. I have agreed to take the ship to Chagrin—the island I have spoken to you about. It is bloody miles from here—off the African Banks, and my family have never found any use for it except for collecting boobies' egg. It's only about three feet above sea level. I haven't been to the damned place for five years. Anyway, this man Krest wants to go there. He's collecting marine specimens, something to do with his Foundation, and there's some blasted little fish that's supposed to exist only around Chagrin island. At least Krest says the only specimen in the world came from there."

"Sounds rather fun. Where do I come in?"

"I knew you were bored and that you'd got a week before you sail, so I said that you were the local underwater ace and that you'd soon find the fish if it was there and anyway that I wouldn't go without you. Mr. Krest was willing. And that's that. I knew you'd be fooling around somewhere down the coast so I just drove along until one of the fishermen told me there was a crazy white man trying to commit suicide alone at Belle Anse and I knew that would be you."

Bond laughed. "Extraordinary the way these island people are afraid of the sea. You'd think they'd have got on terms with it by now. Damned few of the Seychellois can even swim."

"Missionaries. Don't like them taking their clothes off. And as for being afraid, don't forget you've only been here for a month. Shark, barracuda—you just haven't met a hungry one. And stonefish. Ever see a man that's stepped on a stonefish? His body bends backwards like a bow with the pain. Sometimes it's so frightful his eyes literally fall out of their sockets. They very seldom live."

Bond said unsympathetically, "They ought to wear shoes or bind their feet up when they go on the reef. They've got these fish in the Pacific and the giant clam in the bargain. It's damned silly. Everybody moans about how poor they are here although the sea's absolutely paved with fish. And there are fifty varieties of cowrie under those rocks. They could make another good living selling those round the world."

Fidele Barbey laughed boisterously. "Bond for Governor! That's the ticket. Next meeting of LegCo I'll put the idea up. You're just the man for the job—far-sighted, full of ideas, plenty of drive. Cowries! That's splendid. They'll balance the budget for the first time since the patchouli boom after the war. 'We sell sea shells from the Seychelles.' That'll be our slogan. I'll see you get the credit. You'll be Sir James in no time."

"Make more money that way than trying to grow vanilla at a loss." They continued to wrangle with lighthearted violence until the palm groves gave way to the giant sangdragon trees on the outskirts of the ramshackle capital of Mahé.

It had been nearly a month before when M. had told Bond he was sending him to the Seychelles. "Admiralty are having trouble with their new fleet base in the Maldives. Communists creeping in from Ceylon. Strikes, sabotage—the usual picture. May have to cut their losses and fall back on the Seychelles. A thousand miles farther south, but at least they look pretty secure. But they don't want to be caught again. Colonial Office says it's safe as houses. All the same I've agreed to send someone to give an independent view. When Makarios was locked up there a few years ago there were quite a few security scares. Japanese fishing boats hanging about, one or two refugee crooks from England, strong ties with France. Just go and have a good look." M. glanced out of the window at the driving March sleet. "Don't get sunstroke."

Bond's report, which concluded that the only conceivable security hazard in the Seychelles lay in the beauty and ready availability of the Seychellois, had been finished a week before and then he had nothing to do but wait for the S.S. Kampala to take him to Mombasa. He was thoroughly sick of the heat and the drooping palm trees and the plaintive crying of the terns and the interminable conversations about copra. The prospect of a change delighted him.

Bond was spending his last week in the Barbey house and after calling there to pick up their bags they drove out to the end of Long Pier and left the car in the Customs shed. The gleaming white yacht lay half a mile out in the roadstead. They took a pirogue with an outboard motor across the glassy bay and through the opening in the reef. The

Wavekrest was not beautiful—the breadth of beam and cluttered super-structure stunted her lines—but Bond could see at once that she was a real ship, built to cruise the world and not just the Florida Keys. She seemed deserted, but as they came alongside, two smart-looking sailors in white shorts and singlets appeared and stood by the ladder with boathooks ready to fend the shabby pirogue off the yacht's gleaming paint. They took the two bags and one of them slid back an aluminum hatch and gestured for them to go down. A breath of what seemed to Bond to be almost freezing air struck him as he went down the few steps into the lounge.

The lounge was empty. It was not a cabin. It was a room of solid richness and comfort with nothing to associate it with the interior of a ship. The windows behind the half-closed Venetian blinds were full size as were the deep armchairs round the low central table. The carpet was the deepest pile in pale blue. The walls were paneled in a silvery wood and the ceiling was off-white. There was a desk with the usual writing materials and a telephone. Next to the big gramophone was a sideboard laden with drinks. Above the sideboard was what looked like an extremely good Renoir—the head and shoulders of a pretty, dark-haired girl in a black-and-white-striped blouse. The impression of a luxurious living room in a town house was completed by a large bowl of white and blue hyacinths on the central table and by the tidy range of magazines to one side of the desk.

"What did I tell you, James?"

Bond shook his head admiringly. "This is certainly the way to treat the sea—as if it damned well didn't exist." He breathed in deeply. "What a relief to get a mouthful of fresh air. I'd almost forgotten what it tastes like."

"It's the stuff outside that's fresh, feller. This is canned." Mr. Milton Krest had come quietly into the room and was standing looking at them. He was a tough, leathery man in his early 50s. He looked hard and fit and the faded blue jeans, military-cut shirt and wide leather belt suggested that he made a fetish of doing so—looking tough. The pale brown eyes in the weather-beaten face were slightly hooded and their gaze was sleepy and contemptuous. The mouth had a downward twist that might be humorous or disdainful, probably the latter, and the words he had tossed into the room, innocuous in themselves except for the patronizing "feller," had been tossed like small change to a couple of coolies. To Bond the oddest thing about Mr. Krest was his voice. It was a soft, most attractive lisping through the teeth. It was exactly the voice of the late Humphrey Bogart. Bond ran his eyes down the man from the sparse close-cropped black and gray hair, like iron filings sprinkled over the bullet head, to the tattooed eagle above a fouled anchor on the right forearm and then down to the naked leathery feet that stood nautically square on the carpet. He thought: This man likes to be thought a Hemingway hero. I'm not going to like him.

Mr. Krest came across the carpet and held out his hand. "You Bond? Glad to have you aboard, sir."

Bond was expecting the bone-crushing grip and parried it with stiffened muscles.

"Free-diving or aqualung?"

"Free, and I don't go deep. It's only a hobby."

"Whaddaya do the rest of the time?"

"Civil servant."

Mr. Krest gave a short, barking laugh, "Civility and servitude. You English make the best goddamn butlers and valets in the world. Civil servant you say? I reckon we're likely to get along fine. Civil servants are just what I like to have around me."

The click of the deck hatch sliding back saved Bond's temper. Mr. Krest was swept from his mind as a naked, sunburned girl came down the steps into the saloon. No, she wasn't quite naked after all, but the pale brown satin scraps of bikini were designed to make one think that she was.

"'Lo, treasure. Where have you been hiding? Long time no see. Meet Mr. Barbey and Mr. Bond, the fellers who are coming along." Mr. Krest raised a hand in the direction of the girl. "Fellers, this is Mrs. Krest. The fifth Mrs. Krest. And just in case anybody should get any ideas, she loves Mr. Krest. Don't you, treasure?"

"Oh don't be silly, Milt, you know I do," Mrs. Krest smiled prettily. "How do you do, Mr. Barbey. And Mr. Bond. It's nice to have you with us. What about a drink?"

"Now just a minute, treas. Suppose you let me fix things aboard my own ship, eh?" Mr. Krest's voice was soft and pleasant.

The woman blushed. "Oh yes, Milt, of course."

"OK then, just so we know who's skipper aboard the good ship *Wavekrest*." The amused smile embraced them all. "Now then, Mr. Barbey. What's your first name, by the way? Fidele, eh? That's quite a name. Old Faithful," Mr. Krest chuckled bonhomously. "Well now Fido, how's about you and me go up on the bridge and get this little old skiff moving, eh? Mebbe you better take her out into the open sea and then you can set a course and hand her over to Fritz. I'm the captain. He's the mate, and there are two for the engine room and pantry. All three Germans. Only darned sailors left in Europe. And Mr. Bond. First name? James, eh. Well Jim, what say you practice a bit of that civility and servitude on Mrs. Krest. Call her Liz, by the way. Help her fix the canapes and so on for drinks before lunch. She was once a Limey too. You can swap yarns about Piccadilly Circus. OK? Move, Fido." He sprang boyishly up the steps. "Let's get the hell outta here."

When the hatch closed, Bond let out a deep breath. Mrs. Krest said apologetically, "Please don't mind his jokes. It's just his sense of humor. And he's a bit contrary. He likes to see if he can rile people. It's very naughty of him. But it's really all in fun."

Bond smiled reassuringly. How often did she have to make this speech to people, try and calm the tempers of the people Mr. Krest had practiced his "sense of humor" on? He said, "I expect your husband needs a bit of knowing. Does he go on the same way back in America?"

She said without bitterness, "Only with me. He loves Americans. It's when he's abroad. You see his father was a German, a Prussian really. He's got that silly German thing of thinking Europeans and so on are decadent, that they aren't any good anymore. It's no use arguing with him. It's just a thing he's got."

So that was it! The old Hun again. Always at your feet or at your throat. Sense of humor indeed! And what must this woman have to put up with, this beautiful girl he had got hold of to be his slave—his English slave? Bond said, "How long have you been married?"

"Two years. I was working as a receptionist in one of his hotels. He owns the Krest group, you know. It was wonderful. Like a fairy story. I still have to pinch myself sometimes to make sure I'm not dreaming. This, for instance," she waved a hand at the luxurious room, "and he's terribly good to me. Always giving me presents. He's a very important man in America, you know. It's fun being treated like royalty wherever you go."

"It must be. He likes that sort of thing, I suppose?"

"Oh yes," there was resignation in the laugh. "There's a lot of the sultan in him. He gets quite impatient if he doesn't get proper service. He says that when one's worked very hard to get to the top of the tree one has a right to the best fruit that grows there." Mrs. Krest found she was talking too freely. She said quickly, "But really, what am I saying? Anyone would think we had known each other for years." She smiled shyly. "I suppose it's meeting someone from England. But I really must go and get some more clothes on. I was sunbathing on deck." There came a deep rumble from below deck amidships. "There. We're off. Why don't you watch us leave harbor from the afterdeck and I'll come and join you in a minute. There's so much I want to hear about London. This way." She moved past him and slid open a door. "As a matter of fact, if you're sensible, you'll stake a claim to this for the nights. There are plenty of cushions and the cabins are apt to get a bit stuffy in spite of the air conditioning."

Bond thanked her and walked out and shut the door behind him. It was a big well deck with hemp flooring and a cream-colored semicircular foam-rubber settee in the stern. Rattan chairs were scattered about and there was a serving bar in one corner. It crossed Bond's mind that Mr. Krest might be a heavy drinker. Was it his imagination, or was Mrs. Krest terrified of him? There was something painfully slavish in her attitude toward him. No doubt she had to pay heavily for her "fairy story." Bond watched the green flanks of Mahé slowly slip away astern. He guessed that their speed was about ten knots. They would soon be at North Point and heading for the open sea. Bond listened to the glutinous bubble of the exhaust and idly thought about the beautiful Mrs. Elizabeth Krest.

She could have been a model—probably had been before she became a hotel receptionist, that respectable female calling that yet has a whiff of the high demimonde about it—and she still moved her beautiful body with the unself-consciousness of someone who is used to going about with nothing, or practically nothing, on. But there was none of the chill of the model about her—it was a warm body and a friendly, confiding face. She might be 30, certainly not more, and her prettiness, for it was not more than that, was still immature. Her best feature was the ash-blonde hair that hung heavily to the base of her neck, but she seemed pleasantly lacking in vanity about it. She didn't toss it about or fiddle with it and it occurred to Bond that she didn't in fact show any signs of coquetry. She had stood quietly, almost docilely, with her large, clear blue eyes fixed almost the whole time on her husband. There was no lipstick on her mouth and no lacquer on her fingernails or toenails and her eyebrows were natural. Did Mr. Krest perhaps order that it should be so—that she should be a Germanic child of nature? Probably. Bond shrugged his shoulders. They were certainly a curiously assorted couple—the middle-aged Hemingway character with the Bogart voice and the pretty, artless girl. And there was tension in the air—in the way she had cringed as he brought her to heel when she had offered them drinks, in the forced maleness of the man. Bond toyed idly with the notion that the man was impotent and that all the tough, rude act was nothing more than exaggerated virility-play. It certainly wasn't going to be easy to live with for four or five days. Bond watched the beautiful

Silhouette Island slip away to starboard and made a vow not to lose his temper. What was that American expression? "Eating crow." It would be an interesting mental exercise for him. He would eat crow for five days and not let this damnable man interfere with what should be a good trip.

"Well, feller. Taking it easy?" Mr. Krest was standing on the boat deck looking down into the well. "What have you done with that woman I live with? Left her to do all the work, I guess. Well, and why not? That's what they're for, ain't it? Care to look over the ship? Fido's doin' a spell at the wheel and I've got time on my hands." Without waiting for an answer, Mr. Krest bent and lowered himself down into the well deck, dropping the last four feet.

"Mrs. Krest's putting on some clothes. Yes, I'd like to look over the ship."

Mr. Krest fixed Bond with his hard, disdainful stare. "'K. Well now, facts first. It's built by the Bronson Shipbuilding Corporation. I happen to own 90 percent of the stock so I got what I wanted. Designed by Rosenblatts—the top naval architects. Hundred feet long, 21 broad, and draws six. Two 500-horsepower Superior diesels. Top speed, 14 knots. Cruises 2500 miles at eight. Air conditioned throughout. Carrier Corporation designed two special five-ton units. Carries enough frozen food and liquor for a month. All we need is fresh water for the baths and showers. Right? Now let's go up front and you can see the crew's quarters and we'll work back. And one thing, Jim," Mr. Krest stamped on the deck, "this is the floor, see? And the head's the can. And if I want someone to stop doing whatever they're doing I don't shout 'belay,' I shout 'hold it.' Get me, Jim?"

Bond nodded amiably. "I've got no objection. She's your ship."

"It's my ship," corrected Mr. Krest. "That's another bit of damned nonsense, making a hunk of steel and wood a female. Anyway, let's go. You don't need to mind your head. Everything's built to a six-foot-two clearance."

Bond followed Mr. Krest down the narrow passage that ran the length of the ship and for half an hour made appropriate comments on what was certainly the finest and most luxuriously designed yacht he had ever seen. In every detail, the margin was for extra comfort. Even the crew's bath and shower was full size and the stainless-steel galley, or kitchen as Mr. Krest called it, was as big as the Krest stateroom. Mr. Krest opened the door of the latter without knocking. Liz Krest was at the dressing table. "Why, treasure," said Mr. Krest in his soft voice, "I reckoned you'd be out there fixing up the drink tray. You've sure been one heck of a time dressing up. Puttin' on a little extra ritz for Jim, eh?"

"I'm sorry, Milt. I was just coming. A zipper got stuck." The girl hurriedly picked up a compact and made for the door. She gave them both a nervous half-smile and went out.

"Vermont birch paneling, Corning glass lamps, Mexican tuft rugs. That sailing ship picture's a genuine Montague Dawson, by the way...." Mr. Krest's catalog ran smoothly on. But Bond was looking at something that hung down almost out of sight by the bedside table on what was obviously Mr. Krest's side of the huge double bed. It was a thin whip about three feet long with a leather-thonged handle. It was the tail of a stingray.

Casually Bond walked over to the side of the bed and picked it up. He ran a finger down its spiny gristle. It hurt his fingers even to do that. He said, "Where did you pick that up? I was hunting one of these animals this morning."

"Bahrain. The Arabs use them on their wives." Mr. Krest chuckled easily, "Haven't had to use more than one stroke at a time on Liz so far. Wonderful results. We call it my 'Corrector.'"

Bond put the thing back. He looked hard at Mr. Krest and said, "Is that so? In the Seychelles where the Creoles are pretty tough it's illegal even to own one of those, let alone use it."

Mr. Krest moved toward the door. He said indifferently, "Feller, this happens to be United States territory. Let's go get ourselves something to drink."

Mr. Krest drank three double bullshots before luncheon and beer with the meal. The pale eyes darkened a little and acquired a watery glitter, but the sibilant voice remained soft and unemphatic as, with a complete monopoly of the conversation, he explained the object of the voyage. "Ya see, fellers, it's like this. In the States we have this Foundation system for the lucky guys that got plenty of dough and don't happen to want to pay it into Uncle Sam's Treasury. You make a Foundation—like this one, the Krest Foundation—for charitable purposes—charitable to anyone, to kids, sick folk, the cause of science—you just give the money away to anyone or anything except yourself or your dependents and you escape tax on it. So I put a matter of $10 million into the Krest Foundation and since I happen to like yachting and seeing the world I built this yacht with $2 million of the money and told the Smithsonian, that's our big natural history institution, that I would go to any part of the world and collect specimens for them. So that makes me a scientific expedition, see? For three months of every year I have a fine holiday that costs me next to nothing!" Mr. Krest looked to his guests for applause. "Get me?"

Fidele Barbey shook his head doubtfully. "That sounds fine, Mr. Krest. But these rare specimens. They are easy to find? The Smithsonian it wants a giant panda, a sea shell. You can get hold of these things where they have failed?" Mr. Krest slowly shook his head. He said sorrowfully, "Feller, you sure were born yesterday. Money, that's all it takes. You want a panda? You buy it from some goddamn zoo that can't afford central heating for its reptile house or wants to build a new block for its tigers or something. The sea shell? You find a man that's got one and you offer him so much goddamn money that even if he cries for a week he sells it to you. Sometimes you have a little trouble with governments. Some goddamn animal is protected or something. All right. Give you an example. I arrive at your island yesterday. I want a black parrot from Praslin Island. I want a giant tortoise from Aldabra. I want the complete range of your local cowries and I want this fish we're after. The first two are protected by law. Last evening I pay a call on your Governor after making certain inquiries in the town. Excellency, I says, I understand you want to build a public swimming pool to teach the local kids to swim. OK. The Krest Foundation will put up the money. How much? Five thousand? Ten thousand? OK so it's $10,000. Here's my check. And I write it out there and then. Just one little thing, Excellency, I says, holding onto the check. It happens I want a specimen of this black parrot you have here and one of these Aldabra tortoises. I understand they're protected by law. Mind if I take one of each back to America for the Smithsonian? Well there's a bit of a palaver, but seeing it's the Smithsonian and seeing I've still got hold of the check, in the end we shake hands on the deal and everyone's happy. Right? Well on the way back I stop in the town to arrange with your nice Mr. Abendana, the merchant feller, to have the parrot and tortoise collected and held for me and I get to talking about the cowries. Well it so happens that this Mr. Abendana has been collecting the damn things since he was a child. He shows them to me. Beautifully kept—each one in its bit of cotton wool. Fine condition and several of those Isabella and Mappa ones I was asked particularly to watch out for. Sorry, he couldn't think of selling. They meant so much to him and so on. Crap! I just look at Mr. Abendana and I say, how much? No, no. He couldn't think of it. Crap again! I take out my checkbook and write out a check for $5,000 and push it under his nose. He looks at it. Five thousand dollars! He can't stand it. He folds the check and puts it in his pocket and then the damn sissy breaks down and weeps! Would you believe it?" Mr. Krest opened his palms in disbelief. "Over a few goddam sea shells. So I just tell him to take it easy and I pick up the trays of sea shells and get the hell out of there before the crazy so-and-so shoots himself from remorse."

Mr. Krest sat back, well pleased with himself. "Well, whaddaya say to that, fellers? Twenty-four hours in the island and I've already knocked off three-quarters of my list. Pretty smart, eh Jim?"

Bond said, "You'll probably get a medal when you get home. What about this fish?"

Mr. Krest got up from the table and rummaged in a drawer of his desk. He brought back a typewritten sheet. "Here you are." He read out: "'Hildebrand Rarity. Caught by Professor Hildebrand of the University of the Witwatersrand in a net off Chagrin Island in the Seychelles group, April 1925.'" Mr. Krest looked up. "And then there's a lot of scientific crap. I got them to put it into plain English and here's the translation." He turned back to the paper. "'This appears to be a unique member of the squirrelfish family. The only specimen known, named the "Hildebrand Rarity" after its discoverer, is six inches long. The color is a bright pink with black transverse stripes. The anal, ventral and dorsal fins are pink. The tail fin is black. Eyes, large and dark blue. If found, care should be taken in handling this fish because all fins are even more sharply spiked than is usual with the rest of this family. Professor Hildebrand records that he found the specimen in three feet of water on the edge of the southwestern reef.'" Mr. Krest threw the paper down on the table. "Well, there you are, fellers. We're traveling about a thousand miles at a cost of several thousand dollars to try and find a goddam six-inch fish. And two years ago the Revenue people had the gall to suggest that my Foundation was a phony!"

Liz Krest broke in eagerly, "But that's just it, Milt, isn't it? It's really rather important to bring back plenty of specimens and things this time. Weren't those horrible tax people talking about disallowing the yacht and the expenses and so on for the last five years if we didn't show an outstanding scientific achievement? Wasn't that the way they put it?"

"Treasure," Mr. Krest's voice was soft as velvet. "Just supposin' you keep that flippin' trap shut about my personal affairs. Yes?" The voice was amiable, nonchalant. "You know what you just done, treas? You just earned yourself a little meeting with the Corrector this evening. That's what you've gone and done." The girl's hand flew to her mouth. Her eyes widened. She said in a whisper, "Oh no, Milt. Oh no, please."

● ● ●

On the second day out, at dawn, they came up with Chagrin Island.

HILDEBRAND RARITY

It was first picked up by the radar—a small hump in the dead-level line on the scanner—and then a minute blur on the great curved horizon grew with infinite slowness into half a mile of green fringed with white. It was extraordinary to come upon land after two days in which the yacht had seemed to be the only moving, the only living thing in an empty world. Bond had never seen or even clearly imagined the doldrums before. Now he realized what a terrible hazard they must have been in the days of sail—the sea of glass under a brazen sun, the foul, heavy air, the trail of small clouds along the rim of the world that never came closer, never brought wind or blessed rain. How must centuries of mariners have blessed this tiny dot in the Indian Ocean as they bent to the oars that moved the heavy ship perhaps a mile a day! Bond stood in the bows and watched the flying fish squirt from beneath the hull as the blue-black of the sea slowly mottled into the brown and white and green of deep shoal. How wonderful that he would soon be walking and swimming again instead of just sitting and lying down. How wonderful to have a few hours' solitude—a few hours away from Mr. Milton Krest!

They anchored outside the reef in ten fathoms and Fidele Barbey took them through the opening in the speedboat. In every detail Chagrin was the prototype coral island. It was about 20 acres of sand and dead coral and low scrub surrounded, after 50 yards of shallow lagoon, by a necklace of reef on which the quiet, long swell broke with a soft hiss. Clouds of birds rose when they landed—terns, boobies, men-of-war, frigates—but quickly settled again. There was a strong ammoniac smell of guano, and the scrub was white with it. The only other living things were the land crabs that scuttled and scraped among the *liane sans fin* and the fiddler crabs that lived in the sand.

The glare from the white sand was dazzling and there was no shade. Mr. Krest ordered a tent to be erected and sat in it smoking a cigar while gear of various kinds was ferried ashore. Mrs. Krest swam and picked up sea shells while Bond and Fidele Barbey put on masks and, swimming in opposing directions, began systematically to comb the reef all the way round the island.

When you are looking for one particular species underwater—shell or fish or seaweed or coral formation—you have to keep your brain and your eyes focused for that one individual pattern. The riot of color and movement and the endless variety of light and shadow fight your concentration all the time. Bond trudged slowly along through the wonderland with only one picture in his mind—a six-inch pink fish with black stripes and big eyes—the second such fish man had ever seen.

"If you see it," Mr. Krest had enjoined, "just you let out a yell and stay with it. I'll do the rest. I got a little something in the tent that's just the dandiest thing for catching fish you ever saw."

Bond paused to rest his eyes. The water was so buoyant that he could lie face downward on the surface without moving. Idly he broke up a sea egg with the tip of his spear and watched the horde of glittering reef fish darting for the shreds of yellow flesh among the needle-sharp black spines. How infernal that if he did find the Rarity it would benefit only Mr. Krest! Should he say nothing if he found it? Rather childish, and anyway he was under contract, so to speak. Bond moved slowly on, his eyes automatically taking up the search again while his mind turned to considering the girl. She had spent the previous day in bed. Mr. Krest had said it was a headache. Would she one day turn on him? Would she get herself a knife or a gun and one night, when he reached for that damnable whip, would she kill him? No. She was too soft, too malleable. Mr. Krest had chosen well. She was the stuff of slaves. And the trappings of her "fairy tale" were too precious. Didn't she realize that a jury would certainly acquit her if the stingray whip were produced in court? She could have the trappings without this dreadful, damnable man. Should Bond tell her that? Don't be ridiculous! How would he put it? "Oh Liz, if you want to murder your husband, it'll be quite all right." Bond smiled inside his mask. To hell with it! Don't interfere with other people's lives. She probably likes it—masochist. But Bond knew that that was too easy an answer. This was a girl who lived in fear. Perhaps she also lived in loathing. One couldn't read much in those soft blue eyes, but the windows had opened once or twice and a flash of something like a childish hate had shown through. Had it been hate? It had probably been indigestion. Bond put the Krests out of his mind and looked up to see how far round the island he had got. Fidele Barbey's snorkel was only a hundred yards away. They had nearly completed the circuit.

They came up with each other and swam to the shore and lay on the hot sand. Fidele Barbey said, "Nothing on my side of the property except every fish in the world bar one. But I've had a stroke of luck. Ran into a big colony of green snail. That's the pearl shell as big as a small football. Worth quite a lot of money. I'll send one of my boats after them one of these days. Saw a blue parrot fish that must have been a good 30 pounds. Tame as a dog like all the fish round here. Hadn't got the heart to kill it. And if I had, there might have been trouble. Saw two or three leopard sharks cruising around over the reef. Blood in the water might have brought them through. Now I'm ready for a drink and something to eat. After that we can swap sides and have another go."

They got up and walked along the beach to the tent. Mr. Krest heard their voices and came out to meet them. "No dice, eh?" He scratched angrily at an armpit. "Goddamn sand fly bit me. This is one hell of a godawful island. Liz couldn't stand the smell. Gone back to the ship. Guess we'd better give it one more going-over and then get the hell out of here. Help yourselves to some chow and you'll find cold beer in the icepack. Here, gimme one of those masks. How do you use the damn things? I guess I might as well take a peek at the sea's bottom while I'm about it."

They sat in the hot tent and ate the chicken salad and drank beer and moodily watched Mr. Krest poking and peering about in the shallows. Fidele Barbey said, "He's right, of course. These little islands are bloody awful places. Nothing but crabs and bird dung surrounded by too damn much sea. It's only the poor bloody frozen Europeans that dream of coral islands. East of Suez you won't find any sane man who gives a damn for them. My family owns about ten of them, decent-sized ones too, with small villages on them and a good income from copra and turtle. Well, you can have the whole bloody lot in exchange for a flat in London or Paris."

Bond laughed. He began, "Put an advertisement in the *Times* and you'd get sackloads——" when, 50 yards away, Mr. Krest began to make frantic signals. Bond said, "Either the bastard's found it or he's trodden on a guitarfish," and picked up his mask and ran down the beach to the sea.

Mr. Krest was standing up to his waist among the shallow beginnings of the reef. He jabbed his finger excitedly at the surface. Bond swam softly forward. A carpet of sea grass ended in broken coral and an occasional niggerhead. A dozen varieties of butterfly and other reef fish flirted among the rocks and a small langouste quested toward Bond with its feelers. The head of a large green moray protruded from a hole, its half-open jaws showing the rows of needle teeth. Its golden eyes watched Bond carefully. Bond was amused to note that Mr. Krest's hairy legs, magnified into pale tree trunks by the glass, were not more than a foot away from the moray's jaws. He gave an encouraging poke at the moray with his spear, but the eel only snapped at the metal points and slid back out of sight. Bond stopped and floated, his eyes scanning the brilliant jungle. A red blur materialized through the far mist and came toward him. It circled closely beneath him as if showing itself off. The dark-blue eyes examined him without fear. The small fish busied itself rather self-consciously with some algae on the underside of a niggerhead, made a dart at a speck of something suspended in the water and then, as if leaving the stage after showing its paces, swam languidly off back into the mist.

Bond backed away from the moray's hole and put his feet to the ground. He took off his mask. He said to Mr. Krest, who was standing gazing impatiently at him through his goggles, "Yes, that's it all right. Better move quietly away from here. He won't go away unless he's frightened. These reef fish stick pretty well to the same pastures."

Mr. Krest pulled off his mask. "Goddamn, I found it!" he said reverently. "Well, goddamn I did." He slowly followed Bond to the shore.

Fidele Barbey was waiting for them. Mr. Krest said boisterously, "Fido, I found that goddamn fish. Me—Milton Krest. Whaddaya know about that? After you two goddamn experts had been at it all morning. I just took that mask of yours—first time I ever put one on, mark you—and I walked out and found the goddamn fish in 15 minutes flat. Whaddaya say to that eh, Fido?"

"That's good, Mr. Krest. That's fine. Now how do we catch it?"

"Aha," Mr. Krest winked slowly. "I got just the ticket for that. Got it from a chemist friend of mine. Stuff called rotenone. Made from derris root. What the natives fish with in Brazil. Just pour it in the water where it'll float over what you're after and it'll get him as sure as eggs is eggs. Sort of poison. Constricts the blood vessels in their gills. Suffocates them. No effect on humans because no gills, see?" Mr. Krest turned to Bond. "Here Jim. You go on out and keep watch. See the darned fish don't vamoose. Fido and I'll bring the stuff out there," he pointed up-current from the vital area. "I'll let go the rotenone when you say the word. It'll drift down toward you. Right? But for land's sakes get the timing right. I've only got a five-gallon tin of this stuff. 'K?"

Bond said "All right," and walked slowly down and into the water. He swam lazily out to where he had stood before. Yes, everyone was still there, going about his business. The moray's pointed head was back again at the edge of its hole, the langouste again queried him. In a minute, as if it had a rendezvous with Bond, the Hildebrand Rarity appeared. This time it swam up quite close to his face. It looked through the glass at his eyes and then, as if disturbed by what it had seen there, darted out of range. It played around among the rocks for a while and then went off into the mist.

Slowly the little underwater world within Bond's vision began to take him for granted. A small octopus that had been camouflaged as a piece of coral revealed its presence and groped carefully down toward the sand. The blue and yellow langouste came a few steps out from under the rock, wondering about him. Some very small fish like minnows nibbled at his legs and toes, tickling. Bond broke a sea egg for them and they darted to the better meal. Bond lifted his head. Mr. Krest, holding the flat can, was 20 yards away to Bond's right. He would soon begin pouring, when Bond gave the sign, so that the liquid would get a good wide spread over the surface.

"OK?" called Mr. Krest.

Bond shook his head. "I'll raise my thumb when he's back here. Then you'll have to pour fast."

"OK, Jim. You're at the bombsight."

Bond put his head down. There was the little community, everyone busied with his affairs. Soon, to get one fish that someone vaguely wanted in a museum 5,000 miles away, 100, perhaps 1,000 small people were going to die. When Bond gave the signal, the shadow of death would come down on the stream. How long would the poison last? How far would it travel on down the reef? Perhaps it would not be thousands but tens of thousands that would die.

A small trunkfish appeared, its tiny fins whirring like propellers. A rock beauty, gorgeous in gold and red and black, pecked at the sand, and a pair of the inevitable black-and-yellow-striped sergeant majors materialized from nowhere, attracted by the scent of the broken sea egg.

Inside the reef, who was the predator in the world of small fishes? Who did they fear? Small barracuda? An occasional billfish? Now, a big, a fully grown predator, a man called Krest, was standing in the wings, waiting. And this one wasn't even hungry. He was just going to kill—almost for fun.

Two brown legs appeared in Bond's vision. He looked up. It was Fidele Barbey with a long-handled landing net and a big creel strapped to his chest.

Bond lifted his mask. "I feel like the bomb-aimer at Nagasaki."

"Fish are cold-blooded. They don't feel anything."

"How do you know? I've heard them scream when they're hurt."

Barbey said indifferently, "They won't be able to scream with this stuff. It strangles them. What's eating you? They're only fish."

"I know, I know." Fidele Barbey had spent his life killing animals and fish. While he, Bond, had sometimes not hesitated to kill men. What was he fussing about? He hadn't minded killing the stingray. Yes, but that was an enemy fish. These down here were friendly people. People? The pathetic fallacy!

"Hey," came the voice of Mr. Krest. "What's goin' on over there? This ain't no time for chewing the fat. Get that head down, Jim."

Bond pulled down his mask and lay again on the surface. At once he saw the beautiful red shadow coming out of the far mists. The fish swam fast up to him as if it now took him for granted. It lay below him, looking up. Bond said into his mask, "Get away from here, damn you." He gave a sharp jab at the fish with his harpoon. The fish fled back into the mist. Bond lifted his head and angrily raised his thumb. It was a ridiculous and petty act of sabotage of which he was already ashamed. The dark-brown oily liquid was pouring out onto the surface of the lagoon. There was time to stop Mr. Krest before it was all gone—time to give him another chance at the Hildebrand Rarity. Bond stood and watched until the last drop was tilted out. To hell with Mr. Krest!

Now the stuff was creeping slowly down on the current—a shiny, spreading stain which reflected the blue sky with a metallic glint. Mr. Krest, the giant reaper, was wading down with it. "Get set, fellers," he called cheerfully. "It's right up with you now."

Bond put his head back under the surface. Everything was as before in the little community. And then, with stupefying suddenness, everyone went mad. It was as if they had all been seized with St. Vitus' dance. Several fish looped the loop crazily and then fell like heavy leaves to the sand. The moray eel came slowly out of the hole in the coral, its jaws wide. It stood carefully upright on its tail and gently toppled sideways. The small langouste gave three kicks of its tail and turned over on its back, and the octopus let go its hold of the coral and drifted to the bottom upside down. And then, into the arena drifted the corpses from upstream—white-bellied fish, shrimps, worms, hermit crabs, spotted and green morays, langoustes of all sizes. As if blown by some light breeze of death, the clumsy bodies, their colors already fading, swept slowly past. A five-pound billfish struggled by with snapping beak, fighting death. Down-reef there were splashes on the surface as still bigger fish tried to make for safety. One by one, before Bond's eyes, the sea urchins dropped off the rocks to make black ink-blots on the sand.

Bond felt a touch on his shoulder. Mr. Krest's eyes were bloodshot with the sun and glare. He had put white sunburn paste on his lips. He shouted impatiently at Bond's mask, "Where in hell's our goddamn fish?"

Bond lifted his mask. "Looks as if it managed to get away just before the stuff came down. I'm still watching for it."

He didn't wait to hear Mr. Krest's reply but got his head quickly underwater again. Still more carnage, still more dead bodies. But surely the stuff had passed by now. Surely the area was safe just in case the fish, his fish because he had saved it, came back again! He stiffened. In the far mists there was a pink flash. It had gone. Now it was back again. Idly the Hildebrand Rarity swam toward him through the maze of channels between the broken outposts of the reef.

Not caring about Mr. Krest, Bond raised his free hand out of the water and brought it down with a sharp slap. Still the fish came. Bond shifted the safe on his harpoon gun and fired it in the direction of the fish. No effect. Bond put his feet down and began to walk toward the fish through the scattering of corpses. The beautiful red and black fish seemed to pause and quiver. Then it shot straight through the water toward Bond and dived down to the sand at his feet and lay still. Bond only had to bend to pick it up. There was not even a last flap from the tail. It just filled Bond's hand, lightly pricking the palm with the spiny black dorsal fin. Bond carried it back underwater so as to preserve its colors. When he got to Mr. Krest he said, "Here," and handed him the small fish. Then he swam away toward the shore.

● ● ●

That evening, with the *Wavekrest* heading for home down the path of a huge yellow moon, Mr. Krest gave orders for what he called a "wing-ding." "Gotta celebrate, Liz. This is terrific, a terrific day. Cleaned up the last target and we can get the hell out of these goddamn Seychelles and get on back to civilization. What say we make it to Mombasa when we've taken on board the tortoise and that goddamn parrot? Fly to Nairobi and pick up a big plane for Rome, Venice, Paris—anywheres you care for. What say, treasure?" He squeezed her chin and cheeks in his big hand and made the pale lips pout. He kissed them wetly. Bond watched the girl's eyes. They had shut tight. Mr. Krest let go. The girl massaged her face. It was still white with his finger marks.

"Gee, Milt," she said half-laughing, "you nearly squashed me. You don't know your strength. But do let's celebrate. I think that would be lots of fun. And that Paris idea sounds grand. Let's do that, shall we? What shall I order for dinner?"

"Hell, caviar of course." Mr. Krest held his hands apart. "One of those two-pound tins—the grade-ten shot size, and all the trimmings. And that pink champagne." He turned to Bond. "That suit you, feller?"

"Sounds like a square meal." Bond changed the subject. "What have you done with the prize?"

"Formalin. Up on the boat deck with some other jars of stuff we've picked up here and there—fish, shells. All safe in our home morgue. That's how we were told to keep the specimens. We'll airmail that damned fish when we get back to civilization. Give a press conference first. Should make a big play in the papers back home. I've already radioed the Smithsonian and the news agencies. My accountants'll sure be glad of some press cuttings to show those darned Revenue boys."

Mr. Krest got very drunk that night. It did not show greatly. The soft, Bogart voice became softer and slower. The round, hard head turned more deliberately on the shoulders. The lighter's flame took increasingly long to relight the cigar and one glass was swept off the table. But it showed in the things Mr. Krest said. There was a violent cruelty, a pathological desire to wound quite near the surface in the man. That night, after dinner, the first target was James Bond. He was treated to a soft-spoken explanation as to why Europe, with England and France in the vanguard, was a rapidly diminishing asset to the world. Nowadays, said Mr. Krest, there were only three powers—America, Russia and China. That was the big poker game and no other country had either the money or the cards to come into it. Occasionally some pleasant little country—and he admitted they'd been pretty big league in the past—like England would be lent some money so that they could take a hand with the grown-ups. But that was just being polite like one sometimes had to be—to a chum in one's club who'd gone broke. No. England—nice people, mind you, good sports—was a place to see the old buildings and the Queen and so on. France? They only counted for good food and easy women. Italy? Sunshine and spaghetti. Sanatorium, sort of. Germany? Well they still had some spunk, but two lost wars had knocked the heart out of them. Mr. Krest dismissed the rest of the world with a few similar tags and then asked Bond for his comments.

Bond was thoroughly tired of Mr. Krest. He said he found Mr. Krest's point of view oversimplified—he might even say naive. He said, "Your argument reminds me of a rather sharp aphorism I once heard about America. Care to hear it?"

"Sure, sure."

"It's to the effect that America has progressed from infancy to senility without having passed through a period of maturity."

Mr. Krest looked thoughtfully at Bond. Finally he said, "Why, say, Jim, that's pretty neat." His eyes hooded slightly as they turned toward his wife. "Guess you'd kinda go along with that remark of Jim's, eh treasure? I recall you saying once you reckoned there was something pretty childish about the Americans. Remember?"

"Oh, Milt," Liz Krest's eyes were anxious. She had read the signs. "How can you bring that up? You know it was only something casual I said about the comic sections of the papers. Of course I don't agree with what James says. Anyway it was only a joke, wasn't it, James?"

"That's right," said Bond. "Like when Mr. Krest said England had nothing but ruins and a queen."

Mr. Krest's eyes were still on the girl. He said softly, "Shucks, treasure. Why are you looking so nervous? Course it was a joke." He paused. "And one I'll remember, treasure. One I'll sure remember."

Bond estimated that by now Mr. Krest had just about one whole bottle of various alcohols, mostly whiskey, inside him. It looked to Bond as if, unless Mr. Krest passed out, the time was not far off when Bond would have to hit Mr. Krest just once, very hard on the jaw. Fidele Barbey was now being given the treatment. "These islands of yours, Fido. When I first looked them up on the map, I thought it was just some specks of fly dirt on the page." Mr. Krest chuckled. "Even tried to brush them off with the back of my hand. Then I read a bit about them and it seemed to me my first thoughts had just about hit the nail on the head. Not much good for anything, are they, Fido? I wonder an intelligent guy like you doesn't get the hell out of there. Beachcombing ain't any kind of a life. Though I did hear one of your family had logged over 100 illegitimate children. Mebbe that's the attraction, eh feller?" Mr. Krest grinned knowingly.

Fidele Barbey said equably, "That's my uncle, Gaston. The rest of the family doesn't approve. It's made quite a hole in the family fortune."

"Family fortune, eh?" Mr. Krest winked at Bond. "What's it in? Cowrie shells?"

"Not exactly." Fidele Barbey was not used to Mr. Krest's brand of rudeness. He looked mildly embarrassed. "Though we made quite a lot out of tortoise shell and mother-of-pearl about a 100 years ago when there was a rage for these things. Copra has always been our main business."

"Using the family bastards as labor I guess. Good idea. Wish I could fix something like that in my home circle." He looked across at his wife. The rubbery lips turned still further down. Before the next jibe could be uttered, Bond had pushed his chair back and had gone out into the well deck and pulled the door shut behind him.

Ten minutes later Bond heard feet coming softly down the ladder from the boat deck. He turned. It was Liz Krest. She came over to where he was standing in the stern. She said in a strained voice, "I said I'd go to bed. But then I thought I'd come back here and see if you'd got everything you want. I'm not a very good hostess, I'm afraid. Are you sure you don't mind sleeping out here?"

"I like it. I like this kind of air better than the canned stuff inside. And it's rather wonderful to have all those stars to look at. I've never seen so many before."

She said eagerly, grasping at a friendly topic, "I like Orion's Belt and the Southern Cross the best. You know, when I was young, I used to think the stars were really holes in the sky. I thought the world was surrounded by a great big black sort of envelope and that outside it the universe was full of bright light. The stars were just holes in the envelope that let little sparks of light through. One gets terribly silly ideas when one's young." She looked up at him, wanting him not to snub her.

Bond said, "You're probably quite right. One shouldn't believe all the scientists say. They want to make everything dull. Where did you live then?"

"At Ringwood in the New Forest. It was a good place to be brought up. A good place for children. I'd like to go there again one day."

Bond said, "You've certainly come a long way since then. You'd probably find it pretty dull."

She reached out and touched his sleeve. "Please don't say that. You don't understand." There was an edge of desperation in the soft voice. "I can't bear to go on missing what other people have—ordinary people. I mean," she laughed nervously, "you won't believe me, but just to talk like this for a few minutes, to have someone like you to talk to, is something I'd almost forgotten." She suddenly reached for his hand and held it hard. "I'm sorry. I just wanted to do that. Now I'll go to bed."

The soft voice came from behind them. The sibilants had slurred, but each word was carefully separated from the next. "Well, well. Whaddaya know? Necking with the underwater help!"

Mr. Krest stood framed in the hatch to the saloon. He stood with his legs apart and his arms upstretched to the lintel above his head. With the light behind him he had the silhouette of a baboon. The cold, imprisoned breath of the saloon rushed out past him and for a moment chilled the warm night air in the well deck. Mr. Krest stepped out and softly pulled the door to behind him.

Bond took a step toward him, his hands held loosely at his sides. He measured the distance to Mr. Krest's solar plexus. He said, "Don't jump to conclusions, Mr. Krest. And watch your tongue. You're lucky not to have got hurt so far tonight. Don't press your luck. You're drunk. Go to bed."

"Oho! Listen to the little feller." Mr. Krest's moon-burned face turned slowly from Bond to his wife. He made a contemptuous, Hapsburg lip grimace. He took a silver whistle out of his pocket and whirled it round on its string. "He sure don't get the picture, does he, treasure? You ain't told him that those Heinies up front ain't just for ornament?" He turned back to Bond, "Feller, you move any closer and I blow this—just once. And you know what? It'll be the old heave-ho for Mr. Goddamn Bond," he made a gesture toward the sea, "over the side. Man overboard. Too bad. We back up to make a search and you know what, feller? Just by chance we back up into you with those twin screws. Would you believe it! What lousy bad luck for that nice feller Jim we were all getting so fond of!" Mr. Krest swayed on his feet. "D'ya get the photo, Jim? OK, so let's all be friends again and get some shut-eye." He reached for the lintel of the hatch and turned to his wife. He lifted his free hand and slowly crooked a finger, "Move, treasure. Time for bed."

"Yes, Milt." The wide, frightened eyes turned sideways. "Good night, James." Without waiting for an answer she ducked under Mr. Krest's arm and almost ran through the saloon.

Mr. Krest lifted a hand. "Take it easy, feller. No hard feelings, eh?"

Bond said nothing. He went on looking hard at Mr. Krest. Mr. Krest laughed uncertainly. He said, "OK then." He stepped into the saloon and slid the door shut. Through the window, Bond watched him walk unsteadily across the saloon and turn out the lights. He went into the corridor and there was a momentary gleam from the stateroom door and then that too went dark.

Bond shrugged his shoulders. God, what a man! He leaned against the stern rail and watched the stars and the flashes of phosphorescence in the creaming wake and set about washing his mind clear and relaxing the coiled tensions in his body.

Half an hour later, after taking a shower in the crew's bathroom forward, Bond was making a bed for himself among the piled foam-rubber cushions when he heard a single, heart-rending scream. It tore briefly into the night and was smothered. It was the girl. Bond ran through the saloon and down the passage. With his hand on the stateroom door, he stopped. He could hear her sobs and, above them, the soft, even drone of Mr. Krest's voice. He took his hand away from the latch. Hell! What was it to do with him? They were man and wife. If she was prepared to stand this sort of thing and not kill her husband or leave him it was no good Bond playing Sir Galahad. Bond walked slowly back down the passage. As he crossed the saloon, the scream, this time less piercing, rang out again. Bond cursed fluently and went out and lay down on his bed and tried to focus his mind on the soft thud of the diesels. How could a girl have so little guts? Or was it that women could take most anything from a man? Anything except indifference? Bond's mind refused to unwind. Sleep got further and further away.

An hour later Bond had reached the edge of unconsciousness when, up above him on the boat deck, Mr. Krest began to snore. On the second night out from Port Victoria Mr. Krest had left his cabin in the middle of the night and had gone up to the hammock that was kept slung for him between the speedboat and the dinghy, but that night he had not snored. Now he was snoring with those deep, rattling, utterly lost snores that come from big blue sleeping pills on top of too much alcohol.

This was too damned much. Bond looked at his watch. One-thirty. If the snoring didn't stop in ten minutes Bond would go down to Fidele Barbey's cabin and sleep on the floor even if he did wake up stiff and frozen in the morning.

Bond watched the gleaming minute hand slowly creep round the dial. Now! He had got to his feet and was gathering up his shirt and shorts when, from up on the boat deck, there came a heavy crash. The crash was immediately followed by scrabbling sounds and a dreadful choking and gurgling. Had Mr. Krest fallen out of his hammock? Reluctantly Bond dropped his things back on the deck and walked over and climbed the ladder. As his eyes came level with the boat deck, the choking stopped. Instead there was another, a more dreadful sound— the quick drumming of heels. Bond knew that sound. He leaped up the last steps and ran toward the figure lying spread-eagled on its back in the bright moonlight. He stopped and knelt slowly down, aghast. The horror of the strangled face was bad enough, but it was not Mr. Krest's tongue that protruded from his gaping mouth. It was the tail of a fish. The colors were pink and black. It was the Hildebrand Rarity!

The man was dead—horribly dead. When the fish had been crammed into his mouth he must have reached up and desperately tried to tug it out. But the spines of the dorsal and anal fins had caught inside the cheeks and some of the spiny tips now protruded through the blood-flecked skin round the obscene mouth. Bond shuddered. Death must have come inside a minute. But what a minute!

Bond slowly got to his feet. He walked over to the racks of glass specimen jars and peered under the protective awning. The plastic cover of the end jar lay on the deck beside it. Bond wiped it carefully on the tarpaulin and then, holding it by the tips of his fingernails, laid it loosely back over the mouth of the jar.

He went back and stood over the corpse. Which of the two had done this? There was a touch of fiendish spite in using the treasured prize as a weapon. That suggested the woman. She certainly had her reasons. But Fidele Barbey, with his Creole blood, would have had the cruelty and at the same time the macabre humor. "*Je lui ai foutu sou sacré poisson dans la gueule.*" Bond could hear him say the words. If, after Bond had left the saloon, Mr. Krest had needled the Seychellois just a little bit further—particularly about his family or his beloved islands—Fidele Barbey would not have hit him then and there, or used a knife, he would have waited and plotted. On the other hand, it could even have been one of the German helots....

Bond looked round the deck. The snoring of the man could have been a signal for any potential murderer. There were ladders to the boat deck from both sides of the cabin deck amidships. The man at the wheel in the pilot house forward would have heard nothing above the noise from the engine room. To pick the small fish out of its formalin bath and slip it into Mr. Krest's gaping mouth would have needed only seconds. Bond shrugged. Whoever had done it had not thought of the consequences—of the inevitable inquest, perhaps of a trial in which he, Bond, would be an additional suspect. They were certainly all going to be in one hell of a mess unless he could tidy things up.

Bond glanced over the edge of the boat deck. Below was the three-foot-wide strip of deck that ran the length of the ship. Between this and the sea there was a two-foot-high rail. Supposing the hammock had broken and Mr. Krest had fallen and rolled under the speedboat and over the edge of the upper deck, could he have reached the sea? Hardly, in this dead calm, but that was what he was going to have done.

Bond got moving. With a table knife from the saloon he carefully frayed and then broke one of the main cords of the hammock so that the hammock trailed realistically on the deck. Next, with a lamp cloth, he cleaned up the specks of blood on the woodwork and the drops of formalin that led from the specimen jar. Then came the hardest part— handling the corpse. Carefully Bond lulled it to the very edge of the deck and himself went down the ladder and, bracing himself, reached up. The corpse came down on top of him in a heavy, drunken embrace. Bond staggered under the low rail and eased it over. There was a last hideous glimpse of the obscenely bulging face and the protruding fish tail, a sickening fume of stale whiskey, a heavy splash and it was gone and rolling sluggishly away in the small waves of the wake. Bond flattened himself back against the saloon hatchway, ready to slip through if the helmsman came aft to investigate. But there was no movement forward and the iron tramp of the diesels held steady.

Bond sighed deeply. It would be a very troublesome coroner who brought in anything but misadventure. He went back to the boat deck, gave it a final look over, disposed of the knife and the wet cloth, and went down the ladder to his bed in the well. It was 2:15. Bond was asleep inside ten minutes.

• • •

By pushing the speed up to 12 knots they made North Point by six o'clock that evening. Behind them the sky was ablaze with red and gold streaked across aquamarine. The two men, with the woman between them, stood at the rail of the well deck and watched the brilliant shore slip by across the mother-of-pearl mirror of the sea. Liz Krest was wearing a white linen frock with a black belt and a black-and-white handkerchief round her neck. The mourning colors went well with the golden skin. The three people stood stiffly and rather self-consciously, each one nursing his own piece of secret knowledge, each one anxious to convey to the other two that their particular secrets were safe with him.

That morning there had seemed to be a conspiracy among the three to sleep late. Even Bond had not been awakened by the sun until ten o'clock. He showered in the crew's quarters and chatted with the helmsman before going below to see what had happened to Fidele Barbey. He was still in bed. He said he had a hangover. Had he been very rude to Mr Krest? He couldn't remember much about it except that he seemed to recall Mr. Krest being very rude to him. "You remember what I said about him from the beginning, James? A grand slam redoubled in bastards. Now do you agree with me? One of these days, someone's going to shut that soft ugly mouth of his forever."

Inconclusive. Bond had fixed himself some breakfast in the galley and was eating it there when Liz Krest had come in to do the same. She was dressed in a pale blue shantung kimono to her knees. There were dark rings under her eyes and she ate her breakfast standing. But she seemed perfectly calm and at ease. She whispered conspiratorially, "I do apologize about last night. I suppose I'd had a bit too much to drink too. But do forgive Milt. He's really awfully nice. It's only when he's had a bit too much that he gets sort of difficult. He's always sorry the next morning. You'll see."

When eleven o'clock came and neither of the other two showed any signs of, so to speak, blowing the gaff, Bond decided to force the pace.

He looked very hard at Liz Krest, who was curled up in the well deck reading a magazine. He said, "By the way, where's your husband? Still sleeping it off?"

She frowned. "I suppose so. He went up to his hammock on the boat deck. I've no idea what time. I took a sleeping pill and went straight off."

Fidele Barbey had a line out for amberjack. Without looking round he said, "He's probably in the pilot house."

Bond said, "If he's still asleep on the boat deck he'll be getting a hell of a sunburn."

Liz Krest said, "Oh, poor Milt! I hadn't thought of that. I'll go up and see."

She climbed the ladder. When her head was above the level of the boat deck she stopped. She tailed down, anxiously, "James. He's not here. And the hammock's broken."

Bond said, "Fidele's probably right. I'll have a look forward."

He went to the pilot house. Fritz, the mate, and the engineer were there. Bond said, "Anyone seen Mr. Krest?"

Fritz looked puzzled. "No, sir. Why? Is anything wrong?"

Bond flooded his face with anxiety. "He's not aft. Here, come on! Look round everywhere. He was sleeping on the boat deck. He's not there and his hammock's broken. He was rather the worse for wear last night. Come on! Get cracking!"

When the inevitable conclusion had been reached, Liz Krest had a short but credible fit of hysterics. Bond took her to her cabin and left her there in tears. "It's all right, Liz," he said. "You stay out of this. I'll look after everything. We'll have to radio Port Victoria and so on. I'll tell Fritz to put on speed. I'm afraid it's hopeless turning back to look. There've been six hours of daylight when he couldn't have fallen overboard without being heard or seen. It must have been in the night. I'm afraid anything like six hours in these seas is just not on."

She stared at him, her eyes wide. "You mean—you mean sharks and things?"

Bond nodded.

"Oh Milt! Poor darling Milt! Oh, why did this have to happen?"

Bond went out and softly shut the door.

● ● ●

The yacht rounded Cannon Point and reduced speed. Keeping well away from the broken reef it slid quietly across the broad bay, now lemon and gun metal in the last light, toward the anchorage. The small township beneath the mountains was already dark with indigo shadow in which a sprinkling of yellow lights showed. Bond saw the Customs and Immigration launch move off from Long Pier to meet them. The little community would already be buzzing with news that would have quickly leaked from the radio station to the Seychelles Club and then, through the members' chauffeurs and staffs, into the town.

Liz Krest turned to him. "I'm beginning to get nervous. Will you help me through the rest of this—these awful formalities and things?"

"Of course."

Fidele Barbey said. "Don't worry too much. All these people are my friends. And the Chief Justice is my uncle. We shall all have to make a statement. They'll probably have the inquest tomorrow. You'll be able to leave the day after."

"You really think so?" A dew of sweat had sprung below her eyes. "The trouble is I don't really know where to leave for or what to do next. I suppose," she hesitated, not looking at Bond. "I suppose, James, you wouldn't like to come on to Mombasa? I mean, you're going there anyway and I'd be able to get you there a day earlier than this ship of yours, this Camp-something."

"Kampala." Bond lit a cigarette to cover his hesitation. Four days in a beautiful yacht with this girl! But the tail of that fish sticking out of the mouth! Had she done it? Or had Fidele, who would know that his uncles and cousins on Mahé would somehow see that he came to no harm? If only one of them would make a slip. Bond said easily. "That's terribly nice of you, Liz. Of course I'd love to come."

Fidele Barbey chuckled. "Bravo, my friend. And I would love to be in your shoes, but for one thing. That damned fish. It is a great responsibility. I like to think of you both being deluged with cables from the Smithsonian about it. Don't forget that you are now both trustees of a scientific Koh-i-noor. And you know what these Americans are. They'll worry the life out of you until they've got their hands on it."

Bond's eyes were hard as flint as he watched the girl. Did that put the finger on *her*?

But the beautiful, candid blue eyes did not flicker. She looked up into Fidele Barbey's face and said, easily, charmingly, "That won't be a problem. I've decided to give it to the British Museum."

James Bond noticed that the sweat dew had now gathered at her temples but, after all, it was a desperately hot evening....

The thud of the engines stopped and the anchor chain roared down into the quiet bay.

"Hello, Mom? I got the job in the TV commercial!"

How It Ended

fiction by JAY McINERNEY

I like to ask married couples how they met. It's always interesting to hear how two lives become intertwined, how of the nearly infinite number of possible conjunctions this one or that one comes into being, to hear the beginning of a story in progress. As a matrimonial lawyer I deal in endings, and it's a relief, a sort of holiday, to visit the realm of beginnings. And I ask because I have always liked to tell my own story—our story, I should say—which I had always felt was unique.

My name is Donald Prout, which rhymes with trout. My wife, Cameron, and I were in the Caribbean on vacation when we met Johnny and Jean Van Heusen. We were staying at a tiny, expensive resort in the Virgin Islands, and we would see them in the dining room and later on the beach. Etiquette dictated respect for privacy, but there was a countervailing, quiet camaraderie born of the feeling that one's fellow guests shared a level of good taste and financial standing. And they stood out as the only other young couple.

I had just triumphed in a difficult case, sticking it to a rich husband and coming out with a nice settlement despite considerable evidence that my client had been cheating on him for years with everything in pants. Of course, I sympathized with the guy, but he had his own counsel, he still had inherited millions left over and it's my job to give my client the best counsel possible. Now I was enjoying what I thought of as, for lack of a better cliche, a well-earned rest. I hadn't done much resting in 12 years, going from public high school to Amherst—where I'd worked part-time for my tuition—to Columbia Law to a big midtown firm where I'd knocked myself out as an associate for six years.

It is a sad fact that the ability to savor long hours of leisure is a gift some of us have lost, or never acquired. Within an hour of waking the first morning in paradise, I was restless, watching stalk-eyed land crabs skitter sideways across the sand, unwilling or unable to concentrate on the Updike I had started on the plane. Lying on the beach in front of

HOW IT ENDED

our cabana, I noticed the attractive young couple emerging from the water, splashing each other. She was a tall and elegant brunette. Sandy-haired and lanky, he looked like a prep-school boy who had taken a semester off to go sailing. Over the next few days I couldn't help seeing them frequently. They were very affectionate, which seemed to indicate a relatively new marriage (both wore wedding bands). And they had an aura of entitlement, of being very much at home and at ease on this pricey patch of white sand and turquoise water, so I assumed they came from money. Also, they seemed gloriously indifferent, unlike those couples who, after a few days of sun and sand and the company of the loved one, begin to invite their neighbors for a daiquiri on the balcony to grope for mutual acquaintances and interests, anything to be spared the frightening monotony of each other, without distraction or relief.

• • •

The example of the Van Heusens was invigorating. Seeing them together revived the concept of matrimony for me. After all, I reasoned, we were also an attractive young couple—an extra pound or two notwithstanding. I thought more of us for our ostensible resemblance to them, and when I overheard him tell an old gent that he had recently graduated from law school and passed the bar, I felt a rush of kinship and self-esteem, since I had recently made partner at one of the most distinguished firms in New York.

On the evening of our fifth day we struck up a conversation at the poolside bar. I heard them speculating about a yacht out in the bay and I told them who it belonged to, having been told myself when I'd seen it in Tortola a few days earlier. I almost expected him to recognize the name, to claim friendship with the yacht owner, but he only said, "Oh, really? Nice boat."

The sun was melting into the ocean, dyeing the water red and pink and gold. We all sat, hushed, watching the spectacle. I reluctantly broke the silence to remind the waiter that I had specified a piña colada on the rocks, not frozen, my teeth being sensitive to crushed ice. Within minutes the sun had slipped out of sight, sending up a last flare, and then we began to chat. Eventually, they told us they lived in one of those eminently respectable communities on the north shore of Boston.

They asked if we had kids and we said no, not yet. When I said, "You?" Jean blushed and referred the question to her husband.

After a silent exchange he turned and said, "Jeannie's pregnant."

"We haven't really told anyone yet," she added.

Cameron beamed at Jean and smiled encouragingly in my direction.

452

We had been discussing this very topic lately. I was ready; for some reason she didn't feel quite so certain. But I think we were both pleased to be the recipients of this confidence, though it was a function of our lack of real intimacy, and of the place and time (we learned, somewhat sadly, that this was their last night).

When I mentioned my profession, Johnny solicited my advice about firms; he was going to start job-hunting when they returned. I was curious, of course, about how he had come to law so relatively late and what he had done with his 20s, but I thought it would be indiscreet to ask.

We ordered a second round of drinks and talked until it was dark. "Why don't you join us for dinner?" he proposed as we all stood on the veranda, reluctant to end the moment. And so we did. I was grateful for the company and Cameron seemed to be enlivened by the break in routine. I found Jean increasingly attractive—confident and funny—while her husband was wry and self-deprecating in a manner that suited a young man who was probably a little too rich and happy for anyone else's good. He seemed like someone who was consciously keeping his lights on dim.

As the dinner plates were being cleared away I said, "So tell me, how did you two meet?"

Cameron laughed; it was my favorite parlor game. Telling the story of meeting and courting Cameron gave me a romantic charge that I had ceased to feel in the actual day-to-day conduct of our marriage.

Johnny and Jean exchanged a meaningful look, seeming to consult about whether to reveal a great secret. He laughed through his nose and then she began to laugh. Within moments they were both in a state of high hilarity. Of course, we'd had several planter's punches and two bottles of wine with dinner and none of us except for Jean was legally sober. Cameron in particular seemed to me to be getting a little sloppy, especially in contrast to the abstinent Jean, and when she reached again for the wine bottle, I tried to catch her eye, but she was bestowing her bright, blurred attention on the other couple. Finally Johnny said to his wife, "How we met. God. You want to tackle this one?"

She shook her head. "You try, babe."

"Do you smoke a cigar, Don?" He produced two metal tubes from his pocket. Although I am not a big fan of cigars, I occasionally smoke one with a client or a partner, and I took one now. He handed me a cutter and lit us up, then leaned back and stroked his sandy bangs away from his eyes and released a plume of smoke.

"Maybe it's not such an unusual story," he proposed.

Jean laughed skeptically.

"You sure you don't mind, honey?" he asked her.

She considered, shrugged her shoulders and then shook her head. "It's up to you."

"I think this story begins when I got thrown out of Bowdoin," Johnny said. "Not to put too fine a point on it, I was dealing pot. Well, pot and a little coke, actually." He stopped to check our reaction.

I, for one, tried to keep an open, inviting demeanor, eager to encourage him. I wouldn't say I was shocked, but I certainly was surprised.

"I got caught," he continued. "By agreeing to pack my old kit bag and go away forever, I escaped prosecution. My parents weren't too pleased about the whole thing, but unfortunately for them, virtually that same week I had come into a little bit of gramp's filthy lucre and there wasn't much they could do about it. I was tired of school anyway. It's funny, I enjoyed it when I finally went back a few years ago to get my B.A. and then do law school, but at the time it was wasted on me. Or I was wasted on it. Wasted in general. I'd wake up in the morning and fire up the old bong and then huff up a few lines to get through a geology seminar."

He inhaled on his stogie and shook his head ruefully at the memory of this youthful excess. He did not seem particularly ashamed but rather bemused, as if he were describing the behavior of an incorrigible cousin.

"I went sailing for about a year—spent some time in these waters, actually, some of the best sailing waters in the world—and then I drifted back to Boston. I'd run through most of my capital and I didn't feel ready to hit the books again and somehow I just kind of naturally got back in touch with the people who had been supplying me when I was dealing at Bowdoin. I still had a boat, a 36-footer. And I got back in the trade. It was different then—this was more than ten years ago, before the Colombians really moved in and took over Stateside distribution. Everything was a lot more relaxed. We were gentleman outlaws, adrenaline junkies, sail bums, freaks with an entrepreneurial jones."

He frowned slightly, as if hearing the faint note of self-justification, of self-delusion, of sheer datedness. I had largely avoided the drug culture of the Seventies, but even I could remember when drugs were viewed as the sacraments of a vague, joyous liberation theology or, later, as a slightly risky form of recreation. But in this decade the romance of drug dealing had become a hard sell, and Johnny seemed to realize it.

"Well, that's how we saw it back then," Johnny amended. "Let's just say that we were less ruthless and less financially motivated than the people who eventually took over the business."

454

Wanting to discourage his sudden attack of scruples, I waved to the waiter for another bottle of wine.

"Make sure the wine's not too chilled," Cameron shouted at the retreating waiter. "My husband has sensitive teeth." I suppose that she thought this was funny.

"Anyway, I did quite well," Johnny continued. "Initially, I was very hands-on, rendezvousing with mother ships out in the water off Nantucket, bringing in small loads in a hollow keel. Eventually, my partner Derek and I moved up the food chain. We were making money so fast we had a hard time thinking of ways to make it legit. I mean, you can't just keep hiding it under your mattress. First we were buying cars and boats with cash and then we bought a bar in Cambridge to run some of our earnings through. We were actually paying taxes on drug money just so we could have some legitimate income. We always used to say we'd get out before it got too crazy, once we'd put aside a really big stash. But there was so much more cash to be made, and craziness is like anything else, you get into it one step at a time and no single step really feels like it's taking you over the cliff. Until you go right over the edge and down and then it's too late. You're smoking reefer in high school and then you're doing lines and then you're selling a little and then you're buying an AK-47 and then you're bringing a hundred kilos into Boston harbor."

I wasn't about to interrupt to question this logic, to say that some of us never even thought of dealing drugs, let alone buying firearms. I filled his wineglass, nicely concealing my skepticism, secretly pleased to hear this golden boy revealing his baser metal. But I have to say I was intrigued.

"This goes on for two, three years. I wish I could say it wasn't fun, but it was. The danger, the secrecy, the money." He puffed on his cigar and looked out over the water. "So anyway, we set up one of the bigger deals of our lives, and our buyer's been turned. He's facing 15 to life on his own so he delivers us up on a platter. An exciting moment. We're in a warehouse in the Back Bay and suddenly there are 20 narcs pointing .38s at us."

"And one of them was Jean," Cameron proposed.

I shot her a look but she didn't turn to catch it.

"For the sake of our new friends here I wish I had been," Jean said. She looked at her husband and touched his wrist and at that moment I found her extraordinarily attractive. "I think you're boring these nice people."

"Not at all," I protested, directing my reassurance at the storyteller's wife. I was genuinely sorry for her sake that she was a part of this sordid tale. She turned and smiled at me, as I had hoped she would, and for a moment I forgot about the story altogether as I conjured up a sudden vision of the future—slipping from the cabana for a walk that night, unable to sleep, and encountering her out at the edge of the long beach, talking, claiming insomnia, and then confessing that we had been thinking of each other, a long kiss and a slow recline to the soft sand.

"You must think——" She smiled helplessly. "I don't know what you must think. John's never really told anyone about all of this before. You're probably shocked."

"Please, go on," said Cameron. "We're dying to hear the rest. Aren't we, Don?"

I nodded, a little annoyed at this aggressive use of the marital pronoun. Her voice seemed loud and grating and she was wearing a gaudy print top that I hated, which seemed all the gaudier beside Jeannie's elegant but sexy navy halter.

Johnny said, "Long story short—I hire Carson Baxter to defend me. And piece by piece he gets virtually every shred of evidence thrown out. Makes it disappear right before the jury's very eyes. Then he sneers at the rest. I mean, the man is the greatest performer I've ever seen."

"He's brilliant," I murmured. Carson Baxter was one of the finest defense attorneys in the country. Although I did not always share his political views—he specialized in left-wing causes—I admired his adherence to his principles and his legal scholarship. He was actually a hero of mine. I don't know why, but I was surprised to hear his name in this context.

"So I walked," Johnny concluded.

"You were acquitted?" I asked.

"Absolutely." He puffed contentedly on his cigar. "Of course, you'd think that would be the end of the story and the end of my illicit but highly profitable career. Unfortunately not. I told myself and everyone else I would go straight. But after six months the memory of prison and the bust had faded and a golden opportunity practically fell into my lap—a chance for one last big score. The retirement run. That's the one you should never make—the last one. Always a mistake. Remember, never do a farewell gig. Always stop one run before the final one." He laughed.

"That waiter is asleep on his feet," Jean said soberly. "Like the waiter in that Hemingway story. He's silently poxing you, Johnny Van Heusen, with a special voodoo curse for long-winded white boys, because he wants to reset the table and go back to the cute little turquoise-and-pink staff quarters and make love to his wife, the chubby laundress waiting for him all naked on her fresh white linen."

"I wonder how the waiter and the laundress met," said Johnny cheerfully, standing up and stretching. "That's probably the best story."

Cameron, my beloved wife, said, "Probably they met when the waiter comforted her after Don yelled at her about a stain on his shirt."

Johnny looked at his watch. "My goodness, 10:30 already, way past official Virgin Islands bedtime."

"But you can't go to bed yet," Cameron said. "You haven't even met your wife."

"Oh, right. So anyway, later I met Jean and we fell in love and got married and lived happily ever after."

"No fair," Cameron shrieked.

"I'd be curious to hear your observations about Baxter," I said.

"The hell with Carson Baxter," Cameron said. When she was drinking her voice took on a more pronounced nasal quality as it rose in volume. "I want to hear the love story."

"Let's at least take a walk on the beach," Jean said, standing up.

So we rolled out to the beach and dawdled along the water's edge as Johnny resumed the tale.

"Well, Derek and I went down to the Keys and picked up a boat, a Hatteras 62 with a false bottom. Had a kid in the Coast Guard on our payroll and another in Customs. They were going to talk us through the coastal net on our return. For show, we loaded up the boat with a lot of big-game fishing gear, big rods and reels. And we stowed the real payload—the automatic weapons with night scopes and the cash. The guns were part of the deal, 30 of them, enough for a small army. The Colombians were always looking for armament, and we picked these up cheap from an Israeli in Miami who had to leave town quickly. It was a night like this, a warm, starry, Caribbean winter night, when the rudder broke about a hundred miles off Cuba. We started to drift and by morning we were picked up by a Cuban naval vessel. Well, you can imagine how they reacted when they found the guns and the cash. I mean, think about it, an American boat loaded with guns and cash and high-grade electronics. We tried to explain that we were just drug dealers, but they weren't buying it."

We had come to the edge of the sandy beach; farther on, a rocky ledge rose up from the gently lapping water of the cove. Johnny knelt down and scooped up a handful of fine silvery sand. Cameron sat down beside him. I remained standing, looking up at the powdery spray of stars above us, feeling in my intoxicated state that I exercised some important measure of autonomy by refusing to sit just because Johnny was sitting. By this time I simply did not approve of him. I did not approve of the fact that this self-confessed drug runner had just passed the bar and was about to enter the practice of law. And I suppose I did not approve of his happiness, of the fact that he was obviously rich and had a beautiful and charming wife.

"That was the worst time of my life," he said softly, the jauntiness receding. Jean, who had been standing beside him, knelt down and put a hand on his shoulder. Suddenly he smiled and patted her arm. "But hey—at least I learned Spanish, right?"

Cameron chuckled appreciatively at this statement.

"After six months in a Cuban prison, me and Derek and the captain were sentenced to death as American spies. I hadn't even seen either of them the whole time. They kept us apart hoping to break us. And they would have broken us, except that we couldn't tell them what they wanted to hear because we were just dumb drug runners and not CIA. Jesus, God," he muttered.

I sat down on the sand, finally, drawing my knees up against my chest, watching Jean's sympathetic face as if the sordid ordeal of the husband would be more real reflected there. I didn't feel sorry for him—he'd gotten himself into this mess. But I could see she knew at least some of the story that he was editing for us and that it pained her. I felt sorry for her.

"Anyway, we were treated better than some of the Cuban dissidents because they always had to consider the possibility of using us for barter or propaganda. A few weeks before we're supposed to be shot, I manage to get a message to Baxter, who uses his left-wing contacts to fly down to Cuba and get an audience with fucking Castro. This is when it's illegal to even go to Cuba. And Baxter has his files with him, and—here's the beauty of it—he uses the same evidence he discredited in Boston to convince Castro and his defense ministry that we are honest-to-God drug dealers as opposed to dirty Yankee spies. And they finally release us into Baxter's custody. Well, we fly back to Miami and——" He paused, looked around at his audience, "the feds are waiting for us on the tarmac. A welcoming committee of sweating G-men in cheap suits. They arrest all of us for coming from Cuba. But of course the feds are aware of our story—they've been monitoring this for the better part of a year. Out of the fucking frittata pan——"

"The *sartén*, actually," Jean corrected impishly.

"Yeah, yeah." He stuck his tongue out at her and resumed. "I mean, I thought I was going to lose it right there on the runway, after almost seven months in a cell without a window, thinking I was free and then——"

Cameron blurted, "God, you must have been...I mean——"

"I was. So now the federal boys contact Havana and ask for the evidence that led to our acquittal as spies so that they can use it for a smuggling rap."

I heard the sounds of a thousand insects and the lapping of water on the beach a few feet away as he paused and smiled.

"And the Cubans say, basically—Fuck you, Yankee pigs. And we all walk. Lord, it was sweet."

To my amazement, Cameron began to applaud. I realized that she was drunk.

"We still haven't heard about Jean," I noted, wanting to challenge him in some way. As if I suspected, and was about to prove, your honor, that they had in point of fact never actually met at all.

Jean shared with her husband a conspiratorial smile that deflated and saddened me, reminding me that they were indeed together. Turning to me, she said, "My name is Jean Carson Baxter."

I'm not a complete idiot. "Baxter's daughter?" I asked.

She nodded.

Cameron broke out laughing. "That's great," she said. "I love it."

"How did your father feel about it?" I asked, sensing a weak point.

Jean's smile disappeared. She picked up a handful of sand and threw it out over the water. "Not too good. Apparently, it's one thing to defend a drug dealer, prove his innocence and take his money. But it's quite another thing when he falls in love with your precious daughter."

"Jeannie used to come to my trial to watch her father perform," Johnny explained. "And that, to answer your question finally, is how we met. In court. Exchanging steamy looks, then steamy notes, across a stuffy courtroom." Pulling Jean close against his shoulder, he said, "God, you looked good."

"Right," she said. "Anything without a Y chromosome would have looked good to you after three months in custody."

"We started seeing each other secretly after I was acquitted. Carson didn't know when he flew to Cuba. He didn't have any idea until we walked out of the courthouse in Miami and Jean threw her arms around me, and except for a few scream-and-threat fests, he hasn't really spoken to us since that day." He paused. "He did send me a bill, though."

Jean said, "The really funny thing is that Johnny was so impressed with my dad that he decided to go to law school."

Cameron laughed. At least one of us found this funny. My response was more complicated and, in fact, it took me a long time to sort it out.

"What a great story," Cameron said.

I wanted to slap her, tell her to shut the hell up.

"So what about you guys?" said Jean, sitting on the moonlit sand with her arm around her husband. "What's your wildly romantic story? Tell us about how you two met."

Cameron turned to me eagerly, smiling with anticipation. "Tell them, Don."

I stared out into the bay at a light on the yacht we had all admired earlier, and I thought about the boy who'd been polishing brass when Cameron and I had walked up the deck in Tortola, a shirtless teenager with limp white hair and a tiny gold ring through his nostril who'd told us the name of his employer, the owner, before he turned back to his task, bobbing his head and humming, looking forward, I imagined, to a night on the town.

I turned back to my wife, sitting beside me on the cold sand.

"You tell them," I said.

SILVERSTEIN'S ZOO

PROLOGUE

Now the Bears and the Bees and the Chimpanzees
Are creatures with which we're familiar.
But what do we know of the Humplebacked Mo,
Or the ring-tailed breckspeckled Hillyar?
Or the tongue-twisted rubber-necked Bylliar?
Or the Gorp-eating Kallikozilliar?

satire **By SHEL SILVERSTEIN**

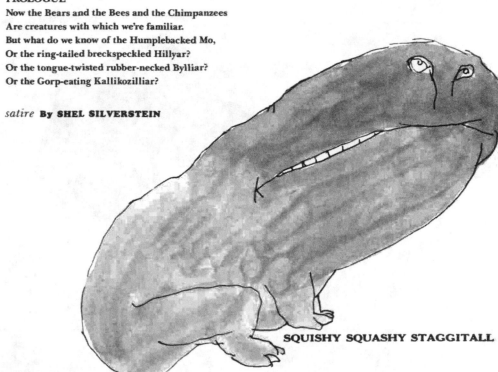

SQUISHY SQUASHY STAGGITALL

THE WORST

When
Singing songs of
Scaryness,
Of bloodyness
And hairyness,
I-feel-obligated-at-this-moment-to-remind-you
Of-the-most-ferocious-beast-of-all,
Six thousand tons
And nine miles tall,
The Squishy Squashy Staggitall . . .
That's standing right behind you.

ZIPPITY

THE SKINNY ZIPPITY

O, pity the poor, poor Zippity,
For he can eat nothing but Greli —
A plant that grows only in New Caledoni,
While the Zippity lives in New Dehli.

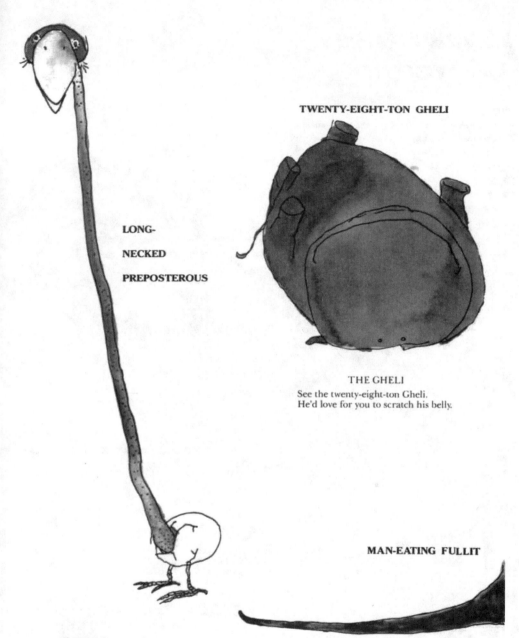

TWENTY-EIGHT-TON GHELI

LONG-

NECKED

PREPOSTEROUS

THE GHELI
See the twenty-eight-ton Gheli.
He'd love for you to scratch his belly.

MAN-EATING FULLIT

DONALD
This is Donald,
A Long-Necked Preposterous,
Looking around for a female
Long-Necked Preposterous.
But there aren't any.

THE TAIL OF THE FULLIT
This is the tail of the
Man-Eating Fullit.
Let's not pull it.

How to Date a Girl Smarter Than You

commentary by WILL LEE

You are the Great 21st Century Man, reared in the information age, butch with the knowledge that all those axons, dendrites and neurons do their jobs with sturdy, vitamin-packed reliability.

You know who Tiger Woods is, and you know he makes more money than you do by playing golf. You know what the 33 signifies on a bottle of Rolling Rock, and how to open that bottle with a cigarette lighter. You know to split eights and double down on 11, when to lift on the throttle through a hairpin, where to go for a swell time when you're in Montreal and why double-vented suit jackets fit you better than single-vented ones. You know pi to three decimal places (or at least that it's somewhere around five), and that it was Barzini all along. You are the Great 21st Century Man, hear your knowledge roar.

You know what? Forget it all: WOMEN ARE SMARTER THAN YOU ARE. You're becoming an intellectual artifact, more Cro-Mag than sapiens, comprehensively outmatched, outpaced and outwitted by the fairer sex. The distaff team isn't just gaining on you; they're past you, looking at you disdainfully in the rearview mirror.

Here's the reality: Fifty-seven percent of straight-A students are girls. Fifty-seven percent of high school dropouts are boys. In 2000, for the first time, more women than men applied to law school. As recently as 1970, more than 90 percent of law school students were male. The percentage of female MBA candidates at Harvard Business School has more than doubled in less than 20 years, and now it's at 30 percent and growing.

Across the land, colleges scramble to get men into the ivory tower. Women outnumbered men in Berkeley's 2000 freshman class. Two years ago, at Dickinson College, a well-regarded liberal-arts school in

463

Pennsylvania, only 37 percent of the freshman class was male. Robert Massa, vice president for enrollment at Dickinson, is trying to close the gender gap, though he admits that some people "might say it's preposterous for me to say white males add diversity." As *USA Today* recently observed, some schools (such as Fisk University in Nashville and Merrimack College in North Andover, Massachusetts) recruit male applicants to compensate for student populations that—as in Fisk's case—run more than 70 percent female.

And men are flailing in areas other than academics. In a Rutgers Marriage Project study of sex and relationships among noncollege men and women under 30 conducted in 1999, women were found to be more confident and responsible, with, as the study put it, "clear and generally realistic plans for moving up the career ladder." Men, on the other hand, seemed less focused: When they talked about getting ahead, their goals included such lofty ambitions as winning the lottery.

There's a fair probability your girlfriend—that lithe, ponytailed blonde with the long neck and perfect upper lip who has a master's in linguistic anthropology from Brown and a J.D. from Columbia, started her own hedge fund and was gathering specimens in the park for her monograph on South American *polyommatinae lycaenids* when you, trying vainly to walk while unscrewing the cap from a Powerade, swung your elbow into her face—is also smarter than you are. It's not idly or flippantly that she says she loves you for your "reassuring impassivity" (and your meaty thighs). If too many repeats of *The Man Show* and that constant flow of Old Milwaukee have addled your brain, let Paul Theroux, the novelist and travel writer, summarize it for you: "I have always disliked being a man," he writes in an essay called "Being a Man." "The whole idea of manhood in America is pitiful, in my opinion." And not just pitiful, according to Theroux, but "unfeeling," "primitive," "crippling," "hideous" and, naturally, "stupid" as well.

Your only hope, then, is more knowledge. Herewith, we present a guide to smart girls, and how to keep them happy.

SMART GIRL PHYLA

Obviously, smart girls come in all shapes and sizes. Not all of them fall under the following four classifications. But the taxonomy goes roughly like this:

MISS GOLDMAN-SKADDEN-SCALIA

WORKS AS: Investment banker, corporate law partner, Supreme Court clerk, TV business reporter. LOOKING FOR A GUY WHO: Will either provide necessary leverage to get further ahead or, occasionally, a slacker type who gives her hip credibility. WILL ONE DAY: Be managing partner of the firm, owner of several small islands. PERSONALITY PROFILE: A frightening but often alluring mix of native intelligence, drive, power and ambition. Can be extremely temperamental. BETWEEN THE SHEETS: "I went out with one girl—a mutual fund manager—who was so intense and was always the best in everything," says Adam, 28, also an investment banker. "So when she gave me head, which was often, she absolutely had to make me come, even if I had other things in mind. Which led to a lot of soreness, frankly."

MISS MENSA

WORKS AS: Doctor, engineer, professor, think-tank researcher. LOOKING FOR A GUY WHO: Spends as much time as she does in the lab, hospital or reading room and doesn't care that she doesn't have time to spend an hour every morning putting herself together. WILL ONE DAY: Accept a Nobel Prize from the king of Sweden. PERSONALITY PROFILE: The least communicative of the bunch, and weighted toward painful shyness brought about when teased by classmates after she won the Physics Olympiad championship as a teenager. BETWEEN THE SHEETS: The sleeper, so to speak, of the smart girls. Pure intellectual prowess and generally reserved manner may mask intense need for excitement and action—i.e., dirty, unrestrained sex—outside work or school. "When my girlfriend first told me that she had been a math and accounting major in college," remembers Todd, 24, "and was working as an actuary, I thought, Wow, she sounds astoundingly dull. But she's as close to a nymphomaniac as I think a woman can come without being self-destructive."

MISS SEMIOTICS ON FIRE

WORKS AS: Novelist, playwright, activist, editor of left-wing political journal, grad-student stripper. LOOKING FOR A GUY WHO: Can sit across from her at a coffee bar (perhaps somewhere more socially conscious than Starbucks) and talk for 18 hours straight without flagging about the function of ekphrasis in the description of cities as portrayed in the *Iliad* and Hesiod's *Shield of Heracles*. WILL ONE DAY: Live in a small New England town writing a treatise. PERSONALITY PROFILE: Often wide-eyed, gregarious and emotionally unlocked. Will often explain why the switch her parents made from cotton to disposable diapers has altered her thinking about poststructuralism. BETWEEN THE SHEETS: Open, experimental, wild. "We'd been dating for all of six days," says Russell, 29, of his writer–grad student fiancée, "when completely naked, spread-eagled pictures of her—like 70 of them—suddenly went up in my college art gallery."

MISS GUM-SNAPPING PHILOSOPHER

WORKS AS: Supermarket checkout girl, Denny's waitress, nurse's assistant. LOOKING FOR A GUY WHO: Won't sneer and pat her behind as she walks by, and who loves spending Friday nights chilling out with a little Velvet Underground, smoking butts and rapping about Borges. Actually, is a little embittered toward men in general, since the guy she married at the age of 17 ditched her and her two-year-old last Christmas Eve. WILL ONE DAY: Be doing exactly what she's doing now. PERSONALITY PROFILE: Sullen, even churlish, she's the proverbial smart-girl iceberg. It's all under the surface. BETWEEN THE SHEETS: A toss-up: could be something of a jewel or could be tired of men and sex and all that.

WAYS TO FUMIGATE YOUR APARTMENT OF THAT PREVAILING DUMB-GUY STENCH

(1) Ditch the PlayStation, at least for one night. No matter how good you are at Final Fantasy VI, you do not want to conjure the image of you in your briefs at two in the morning, control pad dangling between your legs, as you tap away mindlessly with a droopy jaw.

(2) Bury your dog-eared copies of *Car and Driver*, the Victoria's Secret catalog and *Circumaural Stereo Headphone Monthly*. Stack your PLAYBOYS and leave the top one open to the interview. (When she finds it, let her walk you through the pictorials and *The Playboy Advisor*—you will be well rewarded.) Throw out *Maxim*. Get the latest issues of *Granta*, *Harvard Business Review*, *Lingua Franca* and *Scientific American*, and preemptively bend the spines.

(3) Rethink the refrigerator: Shove those cans of Schlitz to the back, get rid of the eight moldy jars of salsa, and find a bottle of Riesling (maybe a 1998 Trimbach) and some interesting vegetables—like white asparagus and haricots verts—to brighten the landscape. And another thing: Lose the Cindy Margolis calendar magnet.

(4) As beloved as your Chris Farley DVD and Slayer boxed sets are to you, smart girls will sneer at lowbrow taste, so better to prominently display a complete set of Bruckner symphonies and a well-worn Kurosawa collection on DVD.

(5) Trash the beer bong. It'll be better for you in the long run.

YOU MAY BE IN OVER YOUR PUNY HEAD WHEN...

(1) She figures out 10, 15 and 20 percent of the tip, both pretax and posttax, before you've found the bottom line.

466

(2) She answers every question correctly on a master's edition of *Jeopardy*.

(3) She and your dad have an intense conversation about economics that you can't begin to understand.

HOW TO SEEM SMARTER THAN YOU ARE

(1) Use props. For instance, arrange to meet her at a cafe and get there 15 minutes early. Look deep in concentration as you attempt to comprehend the preposterous milieu of Bulgakov's *Master and Margarita*. And when she strolls up, ever so rakishly slip off those horn-rimmed spectacles and fold them into your breast pocket.

(2) Know obscure facts about obscure subjects. Mention casually that you've been trying to work out how Proust's living in a room with cork walls influenced his prose stylings or whether maple or pearwood purling gave better resonance to 19th century Italian cellos. But when she follows up, for instance, by asking, "That's fascinating. Why did Proust live in a room with cork walls?" the skill is all in the swift dodge. ("Because he liked to keep his emotions all bottled up.")

(3) Read the daily paper—and not just *USA Today*, and not just the box scores.

(4) Be prepared. Before you go to that trendy Austrian-Cantonese fusion joint for dinner, read a few reviews so when you sit down, you can make an informed suggestion. Better yet, stop by the place before and find out where the bathroom is, so when she asks, you appear to have been a frequent guest.

(5) Make yourself useful. Even smart girls aren't especially mechanically inclined, so fixing her computer printer with a nail clipper and a pen cap would be a good thing. Assemble her Ikea couch with your bare hands. Or tell her when she's getting shafted by the local auto mechanic.

(6) Wear good shoes. For one night at least, pair your Levi's with some cordovan tassel-free and metal-free loafers, rather than those ancient Chuck Taylors.

(7) Be decisive. It's more important to her than what's on your bookshelf (though you should have a bookshelf). When a girl asks what you want to do and you say, "I don't know," or "Whatever you want," you come across dumb as dirt. If a credit card doesn't work at a restaurant, have another way to pay instead of sitting there astonished. If you seem to know what you're doing and act confident, you'll look smart and she'll be impressed.

HOW TO DATE A GIRL SMARTER THAN YOU

FROM THE MOUTHS OF HIGH-IQ BABES

"The whole not-going-to-the-doctor, not-asking-for-directions thing is a dumb-guy problem," says Nicole, 34, an orthopedic surgeon. "Men think being all macho-stoic and refusing to get help is a sign of intelligence. It makes their lives unnecessarily difficult and it lessens their longevity. What confounds me is all the extra aggravation guys go through spending hours and gallons of gas looking for someplace or suffering with some unspeakable illness for days when all it would take is three minutes to pull over to a gas station or pick up the phone and make an appointment with a doctor.

"One of the smartest things about smart people, men or women, is knowing—and admitting—what they don't know. So ask for directions when you're lost, and go to the doctor when you're sick. Oh, and buckle your seat belt. Guys who don't buckle their seat belts are dumb."

Marika, 31, who has a doctorate in Asian languages from Oxford and who now runs her own consulting firm, says that guys "who try too hard to make me feel smart or interesting by making a big show of asking all these ridiculous questions about consulting and my work in Asia—when they don't know the first thing about it and don't care—are in trouble from the start."

MAKING IT A BRAIN-BUSTER NIGHT

Eventually you're going to find yourself browsing with the smart girl in the video store. Much as you want to see *Point Break* for the 14th time, the following will have her going home happier.

The Unbearable Lightness of Being (1988): Directed by Philip Kaufman. Starring Daniel Day-Lewis, Juliette Binoche and Lena Olin. Adapted from the Milan Kundera novel—a smart girl favorite, by the way—in which a young Czech doctor (Day-Lewis) gets caught up in Sixties Czech political turmoil and caught between the two women in his life.

Why she likes it: The emotional conundrum raised by the characters of Olin and Binoche, and for Day-Lewis' convincingly hollow-cheeked intellectualism.

What to say: "I love how Kaufman's camera was observant and detached, not voyeuristic."

How to seize the moment: Ask if you can photograph her slinking around on a full-length mirror wearing only a bowler. Failing that, say that you're so madly in love with her that you'll leave your wife to be with her.

Discreet Charm of the Bourgeoisie (1972): Directed by Luis Buñuel. Starring no one in particular. A dinner party for six upper-class friends provides the backdrop and starting point for a lot of surreal shit.

Why she likes it: Stinging satire on the worthlessness of cultivated society.

What to say: "Was it A.O. Scott or Pauline Kael who said this belongs to Buñuel's old age and his second childhood? Either way, I completely agree."

How to seize the moment: Suggest a romp in the woods before you grab your postflick dinner.

Rear Window (1954): Directed by Alfred Hitchcock. Starring James Stewart and Grace Kelly. A photographer (Stewart) gets laid up with a broken leg and plays peeping tom. Lots of commentary on "being a viewer" and "cameras" and "seeing," if you must know.

Why she likes it: The reflexive allegory on cinema and the viewer.

What to say: "Doesn't it say everything about being isolated yet over-stimulated in the big city?"

How to seize the moment: Right as you're about to make your move, fling open the curtains and turn on all the lights.

Nights of Cabiria (1957): Directed by Federico Fellini. Starring Giulietta Masina. A troubled prostitute roams the streets looking for love and nearly gets drowned in the process.

Why she likes it: The heartbreaking struggle of the heroine.

What to say about it: "You know, after this it was all downhill for Fellini."

How to seize the moment: Tough call. Whatever you do, don't suggest putting her under hypnosis for kinks.

Howards End (1992): Directed by James Ivory. Starring Anthony Hopkins, Emma Thompson, Helena Bonham Carter. English period drama (asleep yet?) involving a country house and two sisters with differing views about how to treat the unwashed.

Why she likes it: Bonham Carter is fiery and ill-tempered, while Thompson is steely and even-tempered. The smart girl likes to be a convincing amalgam.

What to say about it: "Forster knew how to write an ending, didn't he?"

How to seize the moment: Tell her you like her irrational, wild-haired side, too.

SMART GIRL SMACKDOWN

A cautionary tale from Jack, 30, a dot-com executive: "I dated this woman who was incredibly pretty—sort of Natalie Portman plus 10 years, six inches and 12 pounds—and ridiculously bright. She had an Ivy League degree in French literature, was an editor at a university press, decided to get her MBA and became a hotshot venture capitalist.

"We went out for about two months. I don't think a day went by that she didn't tell me how hard it had been for her to maintain relationships because her boyfriends were intimidated by her intelligence, and that she was glad that finally she'd found someone who was comfortable with her intellect. She claimed she'd never dated anyone for more than three weeks. I thought she was being dramatic. But then I found out about her dishwasher dogma.

"One night she made dinner for me at her place. Now, everybody who has a dishwasher has a dishwasher protocol, whether consciously or not. Some people like to run it after every meal, and some people think you should wait until it's completely full. There are people who rinse before loading, others who don't.

"Liza, on the other hand, had developed what she called the dishwasher dogma. She was a chess player, so she designed her dishwasher-loading approach after some Queen's Gambit or Indian Defense— some sequence of chess moves. So if the dessert plates were arrayed in the bottom shelf on the left side and the juice glasses were lined up on the top shelf on the right side and the earth was 34 degrees distant of perihelion, then you put the knives in the middle left quadrant of the silverware basket. Or something like that. She explained the basics to me, and I really thought she was being at least half funny, so I stuck a glass or something in a weird spot for fun, like underneath a colander. She took one look at that, and all in the space of about three seconds looked like she was going to weep, holler and laugh out loud. Instead, she just narrowed her eyes and said, 'You're really just not capable of getting this, are you?'"

DENIAL ISN'T A RIVER IN SINGAPORE

There will always be some men, of course, who refuse to acknowledge their growing obsolescence. Says Louis, 28, a hedge fund analyst: "I'm genuinely fascinated by women, and have been in love several times. But they will not—ever—be more intelligent than men. Maybe more cunning, more verbal, more interesting. Just not more intelligent."

Frankly, that kind of attitude is going to get us all into trouble. If the pattern holds, we may find ourselves addressing the same problems currently faced by Singapore. In that enlightened nation, older men and high-achieving women are being left unmarried in equal numbers. Singapore's 2000 census showed that 21 percent of men 40 to 44 years old with below secondary-level education were single, compared with 12 percent a decade ago. One Chinese man, quoted by the *Straits Times* newspaper, blamed it on the rise of materialistic women: "Singapore women are pragmatic. The men they want must have more money and status in society." The census showed that academic qualifications were a hindrance to marriage: About 30 percent of older women who went to college stayed single. And the hordes of educated single women are apparently a source of concern for the government, which has been trying to cajole them into marrying and reproducing for the greater social benefit. So get out there, and be all you can be—the rest is up to her.

"I guess you ladies are kind of wondering why I asked you to be here this morning in your garter belts and high heels."

The Hustler

fiction by WALTER S. TEVIS

They took Sam out of the office, through the long passageway, and up to the big metal doors. The doors opened, slowly, and they stepped out. The sunlight was exquisite; warm on Sam's face. The air was clear and still. A few birds were circling in the sky. There was a gravel path, a road, and then, grass. Sam drew a deep breath. He could see as far as the horizon.

A guard drove up in a gray station wagon. He opened the door and Sam got in, whistling softly to himself. They drove off, down the gravel path. Sam did not turn around to look at the prison walls; he kept his eyes on the grass that stretched ahead of them, and on the road through the grass.

When the guard stopped to let him off in Richmond he said, "A word of advice, Willis."

"Advice?" Sam smiled at the guard.

"That's right. You got a habit of trouble, Willis. That's why they didn't parole you, made you serve full time, because of that habit."

"That's what the man told me," Sam said. "So?"

"So stay out of pool rooms. You're smart. You can earn a living."

Sam started climbing out of the station wagon. "Sure," he said. He got out, slammed the door, and the guard drove away.

It was still early and the town was nearly empty. Sam walked around, up and down different streets, for about an hour, looking at houses and stores, smiling at the people he saw, whistling or humming little tunes to himself.

In his right hand he was carrying his little round tubular leather case, carrying it by the brass handle on the side. It was about 30 inches long, the case, and about as big around as a man's forearm.

At ten o'clock he went to the bank and drew out the $600 he had deposited there under the name of George Graves. Only it was $680; it had gathered that much interest.

Then he went to a clothing store and bought a sporty tan coat, a pair of brown slacks, brown suede shoes and a bright green sport shirt. In the store's dressing room he put the new outfit on, leaving the prison-issued suit and shoes on the floor. Then he bought two extra sets of underwear and socks, paid, and left.

About a block up the street there was a clean-looking beauty parlor. He walked in and told the lady who seemed to be in charge, "I'm an actor. I have to play a part in Chicago tonight that requires red hair." He smiled at her. "Can you fix me up?"

The lady was all efficiency. "Certainly," she said. "If you'll just step back to a booth we'll pick out a shade."

A half hour later he was a redhead. In two hours he was on board a plane for Chicago, with a little less than $600 dollars in his pocket and one piece of luggage. He still had the underwear and socks in a paper sack.

In Chicago he took a $14-a-night room in the best hotel he could find. The room was big, and pleasant. It looked and smelled clean.

He sat down on the side of the bed and opened his little leather case at the top. The two-piece billiard cue inside was intact. He took it out and screwed the brass joint together, pleased that it still fit perfectly. Then he checked the butt for tightness. The weight was still firm and solid. The tip was good, its shape had held up; and the cue's balance and stroke seemed easy, familiar; almost as though he still played with it every day.

He checked himself in the mirror. They had done a perfect job on his hair; and its brightness against the green and brown of his new clothes gave him the sporty, racetrack sort of look he had always avoided before. His once ruddy complexion was pale. Not a pool player in town should be able to recognize him: he could hardly recognize himself.

If all went well he would be out of Chicago for good in a few days; and no one would know for a long time that Big Sam Willis had even played there. Six years on a manslaughter charge could have its advantages.

In the morning he had to walk around town for a little while before he found a pool room of the kind he wanted. It was a few blocks off the Loop, small; and from the outside it seemed to be fairly clean and quiet.

Inside, there was a short-order and beer counter up front. In back there were four tables; Sam could see them through the door in the partition that separated the lunch room from the pool room proper. There was no one in the place except for the tall, blond boy behind the counter.

Sam asked the boy if he could practice.

"Sure." The boy's voice was friendly. "But it'll cost you $1 an hour."

"Fair enough." He gave the boy a $5 bill. "Let me know when this is used up."

The boy raised his eyebrows and took the money.

In the back room Sam selected the best 20-ounce cue he could find in the wall rack, one with an ivory point and a tight butt, chalked the tip, and broke the rack of balls on what seemed to be the best of the four tables.

He tried to break safe, a straight pool break, where you drive the two bottom corner balls to the cushions and back into the stack where they came from, making the cue ball go two rails and return to the top of the table, killing itself on the cushion. The break didn't work, however: the rack of balls spread wide, five of them came out into the table, and the cue ball stopped in the middle. It would have left an opponent wide open for a big run. Sam shuddered.

He pocketed the 15 balls, missing only once—a long shot that had to be cut thin into a far corner—and he felt better, making balls. He had little confidence on the hard ones, he was awkward; but he still knew the game, he knew how to break up little clusters of balls on one shot so that he could pocket them on the next. He knew how to play position with very little English on the cue, by shooting "natural" shots, and letting the speed of the cue ball do the work. He could still figure the spread, plan out his shots in advance from the positions of the balls on the table, and he knew what to shoot at first.

He kept shooting for about three hours. Several times other players came in and played for a while, but none of them paid any attention to him, and none of them stayed long.

The place was empty again and Sam was practicing cutting balls down the rail, working on his cue ball and on his speed, when he looked up and saw the boy who ran the place coming back. He was carrying a plate with a hamburger in one hand and two bottles of beer in the other.

"Hungry?" He set the sandwich down on the arm of a chair. "Or thirsty, maybe?"

Sam looked at his watch. It was 1:30. "Come to think of it," he said, "I am." He went to the chair, picked up the hamburger, and sat down.

"Have a beer," the boy said, affably. Sam took it and drank from the bottle. It tasted delicious.

"What do I owe you?" he said, and took a bite out of the hamburger.

"The burger's 30 cents," the boy said. "The beer's on the house."

"Thanks," Sam said, chewing. "How do I rate?"

"You're a good customer," the boy said. "Easy on the equipment, cash in advance, and I don't even have to rack the balls for you."

"Thanks." Sam was silent for a minute, eating.

The boy was drinking the other beer. Abruptly, he set the bottle down. "You on the hustle?" he said.

"Do I look like a hustler?"

"You practice like one."

Sam sipped his beer quietly for a minute, looking over the top of the bottle, once, at the boy. Then he said, "I might be looking around." He set the empty bottle down on the wooden chair arm. "I'll be back tomorrow; we can talk about it then. There might be something in it for you, if you help me out."

"Sure, mister," the boy said. "You pretty good?"

"I think so," Sam said. Then when the boy got up to leave he added, "Don't try to finger me for anybody. It won't do you any good."

"I won't." The boy went back up front.

Sam practiced, working mainly on his stroke and his position, for three more hours. When he finished his arm was sore and his feet were tired; but he felt better. His stroke was beginning to work for him, he was getting smooth, making balls regularly, playing good position. Once, when he was running balls continuously, racking 14 and 1, he ran 47 without missing.

The next morning, after a long night's rest, he was even better. He ran more than 90 balls one time, missing, finally, on a difficult rail shot.

The boy came back at 1:00, bringing a ham sandwich this time and two beers. "Here you go," he said. "Time to make a break."

Sam thanked him, laid his cue stick on the table, and sat down.

"My name's Barney," the boy said.

"George Graves." Sam held out his hand, and the boy shook it. "Just," he smiled inwardly at the thought, "call me Red."

"You *are* good," Barney said. "I watched you a couple of times."

"I know." Sam took a drink from the beer bottle. "I'm looking for a straight pool game."

"I figured that, Mr. Graves. You won't find one here, though. Up at Bennington's they play straight pool."

Sam had heard of Bennington's. They said it was a hustler's room, a big money place.

"You know who plays pool there, Barney?" he said.

"Sure. Bill Peyton, he plays there. And Shufala Kid, Louisville Fats, Johnny Vargas, Henry Keller, a little guy they call the Policeman…"

Henry Keller was the only familiar name; Sam had played him once, in Atlantic City, maybe 14 years ago. But that had been even before the big days of Sam's reputation, before he had got so good that he had to trick hustlers into playing him. That was a long time ago. And then there was the red hair; he ought to be able to get by.

"Which one's got money," he asked, "and plays straight pool?"

"Well," Barney looked doubtful, "I think Louisville Fats carries a big roll. He's one of the old Prohibition boys; they say he keeps an army of hoods working for him. He plays straights. But he's good. And he doesn't like being hustled."

It looked good; but dangerous. Hustlers didn't take it very well to find out a man was using a phony name so he could get a game. Sam remembered the time someone had told Bernie James who he had been playing and Bernie had got pretty rough about it. But this time it was different; he had been out of circulation six years, and he had never played in Chicago before.

"This Fats. Does he bet big?"

"Yep, he bets big. Big as you want." Barney smiled. "But I tell you he's mighty good."

"Rack the balls," Sam said, and smiled back. "I'll show you something."

Barney racked. Sam broke them wide open and started running. He went through the rack, then another, another, and another. Barney was counting the balls, racking them for him each time. When he got to 80 Sam said, "Now I'll bank a few." He banked 7, knocking them off the rails, across, and into the pockets. When he missed the 8 he said, "What do you think?"

"You'll do," Barney said. He laughed. "Fats is good; but you might take him."

"I'll take him," Sam said. "You lead me to him. Tomorrow night you get somebody to work for you. We're going up to Bennington's."

"Fair enough, Mr. Graves," Barney said. He was grinning. "We'll have a beer on that."

At Bennington's you took an elevator to the floor you wanted: billiards on the first, pocket pool on the second, snooker and private games on the third. It was an old-fashioned set-up, high ceilings, big, shaded incandescent lights, overstuffed leather chairs.

Sam spent the morning on the second floor, trying to get the feel of the tables. They were different from Barney's, with softer cushions and tighter cloths, and it was a little hard to get used to them; but after about two hours he felt as though he had them pretty well, and he left. No one had paid any attention to him.

After lunch he inspected his hair in the restaurant's bathroom mirror; it was still as red as ever and hadn't yet begun to grow out. He felt good. Just a little nervous, but good.

Barney was waiting for him at the little pool room. They took a cab up to Bennington's.

Louisville Fats must have weighed 300 pounds. His face seemed to be bloated around the eyes, like the face of an Eskimo, so that he was always squinting. His arms, hanging from the short sleeves of his white silk shirt, were pink and dough-like. Sam noticed his hands; they were soft looking, white and delicate. He wore three rings, one with a diamond. He had on dark green wide suspenders.

When Barney introduced him, Fats said, "How are you, George?" but didn't offer his hand. Sam noticed that his eyes, almost buried beneath the face, seemed to shift from side to side, so that he seemed not really to be looking at anything.

"I'm fine," Sam said. Then, after a pause, "I've heard a lot about you."

"I got a reputation?" Fats' voice was flat, disinterested. "Then I must be pretty good maybe?"

"I suppose so," Sam said, trying to watch the eyes.

"You a good pool player, George?" The eyes flickered, scanning Sam's face.

"Fair. I like playing. Straight pool."

"Oh." Fats grinned, abruptly, coldly. "That's my game too, George." He slapped Barney on the back. The boy pulled away, slightly, from him. "You pick good, Barney. He plays my game. You can finger for me, sometime, if you want."

"Sure," Barney said. He looked nervous.

"One thing." Fats was still grinning. "You play for money, George? I mean, you gamble?"

"When the bet's right."

"What you think is a right bet, George?"

"Fifty dollars."

Fats grinned even more broadly; but his eyes still kept shifting. "Now that's close, George," he said. "You play for a hundred and we play a few."

"Fair enough," Sam said, as calmly as he could.

"Let's go upstairs. It's quieter."

"Fine. I'll take my boy if you don't mind. He can rack the balls."

Fats looked at Barney. "You level with that rack, Barney? I mean, you rack the balls tight for Fats?"

"Sure," Barney said, "I wouldn't try to cross you up."

"You know better than that, Barney. OK."

They walked up the back stairs to the third floor. There was a small, bare-walled room, well lighted, with chairs lined up against the walls. The chairs were high ones, the type used for watching pool games. There was no one else in the room.

They uncovered the table, and Barney racked the balls. Sam lost the toss and broke, making it safe, but not too safe. He undershot, purposely, and left the cue ball almost a foot away from the end rail.

They played around, shooting safe, for a while. Then Fats pulled a hard one off the edge of the rack, ran 35, and played him safe. Sam jockeyed with him, figuring to lose for a while, only wanting the money to hold out until he had the table down pat, until he had the other man's game figured, until he was ready to raise the bet.

He lost three in a row before he won one. He wasn't playing his best game; but that meant little, since Fats was probably pulling his punches too, trying to take him for as much as possible. After he won his first game he let himself go a little and made a few tricky ones. Once he knifed a ball thin into the side pocket and went two cushions for a break up; but Fats didn't even seem to notice.

Neither of them tried to run more than 40 at a turn. It would have looked like a game between only fair players, except that neither of them missed very often. In a tight spot they didn't try anything fancy, just shot a safe and let the other man figure it out. Sam played safe on some shots that he was sure he could make; he didn't want to show his hand. Not yet. They kept playing and, after a while, Sam started winning more often.

After about three hours he was five games ahead, and shooting better all the time. Then, when he won still another game, Sam said, "You're losing money, Fats. Maybe we should quit." He looked at Barney and winked. Barney gave him a puzzled, worried look.

"Quit? You think we should quit?" Fats took a big silk handkerchief from his side pocket and wiped his face. "How much money you won, George?" he said.

"That last makes $600." He felt, suddenly, a little tense. It was coming. The big push.

"Suppose we play for $600, George." He put the handkerchief back in his pocket. "Then we see who quits."

"Fine." He felt really nervous now, but he knew he would get over it. Nervousness didn't count. At $600 a game he would be in clover and in San Francisco in two days. If he didn't lose.

479

THE HUSTLER

Barney racked the balls and Sam broke. He took the break slowly, putting to use his practice of three days, and his experience of 27 years. The balls broke perfectly, reracking the original triangle, and the cue ball skidded to a stop right on the end cushion.

"You shoot pretty good," Fats said, looking at the safe table that Sam had left him. But he played safe, barely tipping the cue ball off one of the balls down at the foot of the table and returning back to the end rail.

Sam tried to return the safe by repeating the same thing; but the cue ball caught the object ball too thick and he brought out a shot, a long one, for Fats. Fats stepped up, shot the ball in, played position, and ran out the rest of the rack. Then he ran out another rack and Sam sat down to watch; there was nothing he could do now. Fats ran 78 points and then, seeing a difficult shot, played him safe.

He had been afraid that something like that might happen. He tried to fight his way out of the game, but couldn't seem to get into the clear long enough for a good run. Fats beat him badly—125 to 30—and he had to give back the $600 from his pocket. It hurt.

What hurt even worse was that he knew he had less than $600 left of his own money.

"Now we see who quits." Fats stuffed the money in his hip pocket. "You want to play for another $600?"

"I'm still holding my stick," Sam said. He tried not to think about that "army of hoods" that Barney had told him about.

He stepped up to the table and broke. His hand shook a little; but the break was a perfect one.

In the middle of the game Fats missed an easy shot, leaving Sam a dead setup. Sam ran 53 and out. He won. It was as easy as that. He was $600 ahead again, and feeling better.

Then something unlucky happened. Downstairs they must have closed up because six men came up during the next game and sat around the table. Five of them Sam had never seen, but one of them was Henry Keller. Henry was drunk now, evidently, and he didn't seem to be paying much attention to what was going on; but Sam didn't like it. He didn't like Keller, and he didn't like having a man who knew who he was around him. It was too much like that other time. That time in Richmond when Bernie James had come after him with a bottle. That fight had cost him six years. He didn't like it. It was getting time to wind things up here, time to be cutting out. If he could win two more games quick, he would have enough to set him up hustling on the West Coast.

480

And on the West Coast there weren't any Henry Kellers who knew that Big Sam Willis was once the best straight-pool shot in the game.

After Sam had won the game by a close score Fats looked at his fingernails and said, "George, you're a hustler. You shoot better straights than anybody in Chicago shoots. Except me."

This was the time, the time to make it quick and neat, the time to push as hard as he could. He caught his breath, held steady, and said, "You've got it wrong, Fats. I'm better than you are. I'll play you for all of it. The whole $1,200."

It was very quiet in the room. Then Fats said, "George, I like that kind of talk." He started chalking his cue. "We play $1,200."

Barney racked the balls and Fats broke them. They both played safe, very safe, back and forth, keeping the cue ball on the rail, not leaving a shot for the other man. It was nerve-wracking. Over and over.

Then he missed. Missed the edge of the rack, coming at it from an outside angle. His cue ball bounced off the rail and into the rack of balls, spreading them wide, leaving Fats at least five shots. Sam didn't sit down. He just stood and watched Fats come up and start his run. He ran the balls, broke on the 15th, and ran another rack. 28 points. And he was just getting started. He had his rack break set up perfectly for the next shot.

Then, as Fats began chalking up, preparing to shoot, Henry Keller stood up from his seat and pointed his finger at Sam.

He was drunk; but he spoke clearly, and loudly. "You're Big Sam Willis," he said. "You're the World's Champion." He sat back in his chair, heavily. "You got red hair, but you're Big Sam." He sat silent, half slumped in the big chair, for a moment, his eyes glassy, and red at the corners. Then he closed his eyes and said, "There's nobody beats Big Sam, Fats. Nobody *never*."

The room was quiet for what seemed to be a very long while. Sam noticed how thick the tobacco smoke had become in the air; motionless, it was like a heavy brown mist, and over the table it was like a cloud. The faces of the men in the chairs were impassive; all of them, except Henry, watching him.

Fats turned to him. For once his eyes were not shifting from side to side. He looked Sam in the face and said, in a voice that was flat and almost a whisper, "You Big Sam Willis, George?"

"That's right, Fats."

"You must be pretty smart, Sam," Fats said, "to play a trick like that. To make a sucker out of me."

"Maybe." His chest and stomach felt very tight. It was like when Bernie James had caught him at the same game, except without the hair. Bernie hadn't said anything, though; he had just picked up a bottle.

But, then, Bernie James was dead now. Sam wondered, momentarily, if Fats had ever heard about that.

Suddenly Fats split the silence, laughing. The sound of his laughing filled the room, he threw his head back and laughed; and the men in the chairs looked at him, astonished, hearing the laughter. "Big Sam," he said, "you're a hustler. You put on a great act and fooled me good. A great act." He slapped Sam on the back. "I think the joke's on me."

It was hard to believe. But Fats could afford the money, and Sam knew that Fats knew who would be the best if it came to muscle. And there was no certainty whose side the other men were on.

Fats shot, ran a few more balls, and then missed.

When Sam stepped up to shoot he said, "Go ahead, Big Sam, and shoot your best. You don't have to act now. I'm quitting you anyway after this one."

The funny thing was that Sam had been shooting his best for the past five or six games—or thought he had—but when he stepped up to the table this time he was different. Maybe it was Fats or Keller, something made him feel as he hadn't felt for a long time. It was like being the old Big Sam, back before he had quit playing the tournaments and exhibitions, the Big Sam who could run 125 when he was hot and the money was up. His stroke was smooth, steady, accurate, like a balanced, precision instrument moving on well-oiled bearings. He shot easily, calmly, clicking the shots off in his mind and then pocketing them on the table, watching everything on the green, forgetting himself, forgetting even the money, just dropping the balls into the pockets, one after another.

He did it. He ran the game. 125 points, 125 shots without missing. When he finished Fats took $1200 from his still-big roll and counted it out, slowly, to him. He said, "You're the best I've ever seen, Big Sam." Then he covered the table with the oilcloth cover.

After Sam had dropped Barney off he had the cab take him by his hotel and let him off at a little all-night lunch room. He ordered bacon and eggs, over light, and talked with the waitress while she fried them. The place seemed strange, gay almost; his nerves felt electric, and there was a pleasant fuzziness in his head, a dim, insistent ringing sound coming from far off. He tried to think for a moment; tried to think whether he should go to the airport now without even going back to the hotel, now that he had made out so well, had made out better, even, than he had planned to be able to do in a week. But there was the waitress and then the food; and when he put a quarter in the juke box he couldn't hear the ringing in his ears any more. This was no time for plane trips; it was a time for talk and music, time for the sense of triumph, the sense of being alive and having money again, and then time for sleep. He was in a chromium and plastic booth in the lunch room and he leaned back against the padded plastic backrest and felt an abrupt, deep, gratifying sense of fatigue, loosening his muscles and killing, finally, the tension that had ridden him like a fury for the past three days. There would be plane flights enough tomorrow. Now, he needed rest. It was a long way to San Francisco.

The bed at his hotel was impeccably made; the pale blue spread seemed drum-tight, but soft and round at the edges and corners. He didn't even take off his shoes.

When he awoke, he awoke suddenly. The skin at the back of his neck was itching, sticky with sweat from where the collar of his shirt had been pressed, tight, against it. His mouth was dry and his feet felt swollen, stuffed, in his shoes. The room was as quiet as death. Outside the window a car's tires groaned gently, rounding a corner, then were still.

He pulled the chain on the lamp by the bed and the light came on. Squinting, he stood up, and realized that his legs were aching. The room seemed too big, too bright. He stumbled into the bathroom and threw handfuls of cold water on his face and neck. Then he dried off with a towel and looked in the mirror. Startled, he let go the towel momentarily; the red hair had caught him off guard; and with the eyes now swollen, the lips pale, it was not his face at all. He finished drying quickly, ran his comb through his hair, straightened out his shirt and slacks hurriedly. The startling strangeness of his own face had crystallized the dim, half-conscious feeling that had awakened him, the feeling that something was wrong. The hotel room, himself, Chicago; they were all wrong. He should not be here, not now; he should be on the West Coast, in San Francisco.

He looked at his watch. Four o'clock. He had slept three hours. He did not feel tired, not now, although his bones ached and there was sand under his eyelids. He could sleep, if he had to, on the plane. But the important thing, now, was getting on the plane, clearing out, moving West. He had slept with his cue, in its case, on the bed. He took it and left the room.

The lobby, too, seemed too bright and too empty. But when he had paid his bill and gone out to the street the relative darkness seemed worse. He began to walk down the street hastily, looking for a cab stand. His own footsteps echoed around him as he walked. There seemed to be no cabs anywhere on the street. He began walking faster. The back of his neck was sweating again. It was a very hot night; the air felt heavy against his skin. There were no cabs.

And then, when he heard the slow, dense hum of a heavy car moving down the street in his direction, heard it from several blocks away and turned his head to see it and to see that there was no cablight on it, he knew—abruptly and lucidly, as some men at some certain times know these things—what was happening.

He began to run; but he did not know where to run. He turned a corner while he was still two blocks ahead of the car and when he could feel its lights, palpably, on the back of his neck, and tried to hide in a doorway, flattening himself out against the door. Then, when he saw the lights of the car as it began its turn around the corner he realized that the doorway was too shallow, that the lights would pick him out. Something in him wanted to scream. He pushed himself from his place, stumbled down the street, visualising in his mind a place, some sort of a place between buildings where he could hide completely and where the car could never follow him. But the buildings were all together, with no space at all between them; and when he saw that this was so he also saw at the same instant that the carlights were flooding him. And then he heard the car stop. There was nothing more to do. He turned around and looked at the car, blinking.

Two men had got out of the backseat; there were two more in front. He could see none of their faces; but was relieved that he could not, could not see the one face that would be bloated like an Eskimo's and with eyes like slits.

The men were holding the door open for him.

"Well," he said. "Hello, boys," and climbed into the backseat. His little leather case was still in his right hand. He gripped it tightly. It was all he had.